AF181000

PROPHET OF THE JUBILEE

RELIGIOUS STUDIES CENTER PUBLICATIONS

BOOK OF MORMON SYMPOSIUM SERIES

The Book of Mormon: The Keystone Scripture
The Book of Mormon: First Nephi, the Doctrinal Foundation
The Book of Mormon: Second Nephi, the Doctrinal Structure
The Book of Mormon: Jacob Through Words of Mormon, To Learn with Joy
The Book of Mormon: Mosiah, Salvation Only Through Christ
The Book of Mormon: Alma, The Testimony of the Word
The Book of Mormon: Helaman Through 3 Nephi 8, According to Thy Word
The Book of Mormon: 3 Nephi 9–30, This Is My Gospel
The Book of Mormon: Fourth Nephi Through Moroni, From Zion to Destruction

MONOGRAPH SERIES

Nibley on the Timely and the Timeless
Deity and Death
The Glory of God Is Intelligence
Reflections on Mormonism
Literature of Belief
The Words of Joseph Smith
Book of Mormon Authorship
Mormons and Muslims
The Temple in Antiquity
Isaiah and the Prophets
Scriptures for the Modern World
The Joseph Smith Translation: The Restoration of Plain and Precious Things
Apocryphal Writings and the Latter-day Saints
The Pearl of Great Price: Revelations From God
The Lectures on Faith in Historical Perspective
Mormon Redress Petitions: Documents of the 1833–1838 Missouri Conflict
Joseph Smith: The Prophet, the Man

SPECIALIZED MONOGRAPH SERIES

Supporting Saints: Life Stories of Nineteenth-Century Mormons
The Call of Zion: The Story of the First Welsh Mormon Emigration
The Religion and Family Connection: Social Science Perspectives
Welsh Mormon Writings from 1844 to 1862: A Historical Bibliography
Peter and the Popes
John Lyon: The Life of a Pioneer Poet
Latter-day Prophets and the United States Constitution
View of the Hebrews: 1825 2nd Edition
Book of Mormon Authors: Their Words and Messages
Prophet of the Jubilee
Manuscript Found: The Complete Original "Spaulding Manuscript"

OCCASIONAL PAPERS SERIES

Excavations at Seila, Egypt

OTHER

Christopher Columbus: A Latter-day Saint Perspective
Church History in Black and White: George Edward Anderson's Photographic Mission to Latter-day Saint Historical Sites
California Saints: A 150-Year Legacy in the Golden State

PROPHET OF THE JUBILEE

Translated and Edited by
RONALD D. DENNIS

Volume Ten
in the Religious Studies Center
Specialized Monograph Series

Religious Studies Center
Brigham Young University
Provo, Utah

Copyright © 1997 by
Religious Studies Center
Brigham Young University

All rights reserved

Library of Congress Catalog Card Number: 96-71245
ISBN 1-57008-296-0

First Printing, 1997

Distributed by
BOOKCRAFT, INC.
Salt Lake City, Utah

Printed in the United States of America

To Captain Dan Jones

HE IS a regular Welshman; having waged war once, nothing but a thorough victory will do for him. And you know of the war he has waged with the kingdom of darkness in Wales. No one, as yet, can describe to you the wonderful success of his courage and wisdom. The gates of hell, throughout Wales, have made him the object of their arrows, but the little champion of the cross of Christ, with the armour of the gospel, clothed with the salvation of God, returns heaven's ammunition to meet the arrows of hell with such power that the very gates of darkness begin to shake.

William Howells to Orson Spencer, 11 May 1848
Millennial Star, 1 June 1848, p. 175

Prophwyd y Jubili, courtesy Harold B. Lee Library,
Brigham Young University

CONTENTS

TRANSLATIONS

BLAEN-DAL, 3c.] [OL-DAL, 3½c.

ATOCH deuaf etto,—a gwir wedaf,
Cewch gredu neu beidio;
Er pob daint, nad faint a fo,
Ni pheidiaf a phrophwydo.

PROPHWYD Y JUBILI,

NEU

SEREN Y SAINT.

"YR ARGLWYDD IOR A LEFARODD, PWY NI PHROPHWYDA? CANYS NI WNA YR ARGLWYDD DDIM, A'R NA DDANGOSO EI GYFRINACH I'W WEISION Y PROPHWYDI."

RHIF. 1.] GORPHENAF, 1846. [CYF. I.

CYNNWYSIAD.

MERTHYR-TYDFIL:
CYHOEDDWYD AC AR WERTH GAN D. JONES;
AC AR WERTH HEFYD
GAN Y SAINT YN GYFFREDINOL, A LLAWER
O LYFRWERTHWYR.
1846.

July 1846 wrapper, page 1, courtesy Harold B. Lee Library, Brigham Young University

List of Illustrations

Foreword

The church of the Latter-day Saints launched its English mission in 1837. Three years later the missionaries James Burham and Henry Royle were active in Cheshire and on the Welsh border and succeeded in establishing a branch at Overton in Flintshire, east of the river Dee, on the 8th of October. The earliest Welsh-language newspaper, *Seren Gomer*, reported in 1841 the simple fact that a "new sect of American missionaries" were active in Cheshire. The editor refrained from further comment, omitting any reference to their success at Overton which by that time was a fairly anglicised village. He expressed no unease, knowing that these non-Welsh-speaking missionaries had no chance of gaining converts further west in the Welsh-speaking towns and villages and in the countryside of the northern counties of Wales. Indeed, the American missionaries themselves soon discovered that further penetration into Wales would not result in converts without the aid of Welsh-speaking missionaries. The Mormon newspaper, *Millennial Star*, founded by Brigham Young and Parley P. Pratt in 1840, was an effective medium for the English and the anglicised communities in the border areas, but of little use further west.

The missionaries William Henshaw and John Needham, both non-Welsh speaking, had by 1843 succeeded in gaining a few converts in the linguistically mixed industrial community of Merthyr Tydfil in South Wales and had established a Mormon branch at Penydarren. This success did cause some alarm among

Nonconformists, and *Seren Gomer* in 1844 issued a warning to its readers describing the Mormons as a "plaid gyfeiliornus" (heretical sect). The editor of *Seren Gomer* was the Reverend Joseph Harris, a Baptist minister. His priorities were the propagation of Welsh Nonconformity and its defence when challenged, though loyalty to local chapels was not always based on Biblical belief and morality but frequently on the fact that they provided a venue for social and cultural activity. Denominational differences had resulted from the right of individuals to pick and choose from Biblical teaching. There was throughout Wales, both in agricultural and new industrialised areas, a high proportion of the population who remained uncommitted—not having embraced any religious belief—a fact frequently ignored in most history books.

In the new industrial areas at the heads of the Glamorgan and Gwent valleys the old established parish churches failed to catch up with the increasing population, and there was an upsurge in the variety of Nonconformist chapels following the inflow of newcomers who had earlier established a relation with the different denominations in the rural areas. In the mid-nineteenth century seven out of every ten of the churches of Wales were Nonconformist, the Baptists being the third strongest denomination, and eight out of every ten of its population were members or supporters of Nonconformist chapels. A new missionary campaign by a strange sect was regarded as a challenge to the Nonconformist establishment.

It was in these Welsh Nonconformist chapels and their Sunday schools that the Welsh people had learned to read their own language. It was through the medium of that language that they had been made familiar not only with the Bible and its imagery but also with emotional congregational hymn singing and passionate preaching.

The increase of literacy had led to an increase in the demand for Welsh reading material. Another newspaper, *Yr Amserau*, also a staunch supporter of Welsh Nonconformity and radicalism, was established in 1843, serving mainly the tastes and needs of Independents, Baptists, Wesleyans, Unitarians, radicals and social reformers. Undoubtedly other newspapers would have been established were it not for the cost of distribution and the fact that all newspapers had to pay stamp duty, which greatly increased the cost of production. When the stamp duty was abolished between 1853 and 1861 the Welsh people witnessed an increase in the number of Welsh newspapers and magazines, denominational, literary and political, such as *Udgorn Cymru*, *Y Gwladgarwr* and *Yr Adolygydd.*

The late thirties and early forties was a period of great depression in Wales when hundreds of workmen in the industrial south were reduced almost to starvation, and in 1842 the workers in the Merthyr Iron Works, the leaders of the Welsh industrial economy, went on strike. Their wages in 1848, during the trade depression, were reduced by a fifth. A third of the Welsh population were employed on the land and the wages of agricultural laborers employed by the landed gentry were as low as seven pence to one shilling a day.

The Welsh people (who had for centuries learnt to live with denial), having lost their national independence, and having no political means to bring economic and political changes since only property owners could vote and stand for Parliament, resorted to other means of addressing the situation. Merthyr became the centre of the militant Chartist movement in Wales and it was its Merthyr leader, Morgan Williams, together with David John, both Unitarians, who published the Welsh magazine *Udgorn Cymru* which appeared in 1840 to gain support for their less militant campaign for reform after the initial failure of the Chartists.

The Chartist movement had in 1839 submitted a petition to Parliament signed by a million-and-a-quarter demanding the abolition of the need for parliamentary candidates to have private property, calling for universal suffrage, secret ballot, constituencies of equal size and salaries to Members of Parliament.

The Westminster Parliament refused the Petition. This refusal led to the Chartist Riot in Newport on the 4th of November 1839, the banishing of its South Wales leaders, John Frost of Newport and Zephaniah Williams of Nant-y-glo, the death of twenty-two campaigners and the wounding of fifty. Zephaniah Williams was earlier responsible for establishing a Welsh society called "Y Dynolwyr" (The Humanists) which sought, amongst other things, to have Welsh taught in schools and to give Welsh speakers the right to hold managerial posts in the iron and coal industries, as there was a tendency for new English entrepreneurs in most cases to introduce Englishmen to manage their industries.

In its pages *Udgorn Cymru* condemned, amongst other injustices, church tithes, the Poor Law, the financial upkeep of royalty, advocated the disestablishment of the Anglican Church and campaigned for temperance. With the failure of the second petition submitted in April 1842, *Udgorn Cymru* ceased publication in July 1842.

The campaign for the disestablishment of the Church was continued by The Liberation Society, which was launched in 1844 and which published *The Eclectic Review* with the support of *Seren Gomer* and *Y Diwygiwr*.

Political frustration, social injustices, landlord oppression, church tithes, unemployment and poverty led some Welshmen to believe more than previously that their only hope of justice was to emigrate to the New World. After all, America, they had been made to believe, was discovered by a Welshman, Madog ab Owain Gwynedd, in 1169, and according to another Welshman John Dee (1527-1608), Queen Elizabeth's astrologist, it followed that the New World was the property of Britain. The myth grew that descendants of the Madog crew had settled in the New World, and that there was an Indian tribe in the upper Missouri who spoke Welsh. This myth was given wide publicity and general credibility with the publication of the tale by the historian John Williams in 1790. One of the conditions of membership of The Gwyneddigion, a London Welsh Society founded in 1770, was the belief that Madog did discover America, and a collection was made to finance John Evans of Waun-fawr on an expedition in 1792 to discover the Welsh-speaking Indians. Having failed in his quest, he settled in New Orleans as cartographer in the service of the Spanish authorities.

Thomas Stephens, a Unitarian, antiquarian and critic, living in Merthyr Tydfil, competed in the Llangollen Eisteddfod of 1858 for the essay prize on "Madoc: an Essay on the Discovery of America by Madoc ap Owen Gwynedd." According to the adjudicators, his essay was by far the best entry, but as he had convincingly proved the falsehood of the whole tale, the prize was withheld. By this time Captain Dan Jones, equally taken in by this tale, had already completed his vain adventure in Southern Utah in search of the Welsh-speaking Indians, and had published a full report of his journey.

Some individuals with industrial experience had begun to emigrate to North America to work in the new iron mills there as early as 1817. From 1830 the discovery of coal in the eastern states attracted hundreds of Welsh coalminers. Samuel Roberts, an Independent Minister in Llanbryn-mair and the editor of *Y Cronicl*, sought from 1850 to encourage impoverished farmers and agricultural workers in mid-Wales to emigrate to Eastern Tennessee, and a group of them emigrated in 1856. Similarly a company of Welshmen emigrated to Brazil in 1851.

Other popular myths provided the downtrodden Welsh *gwerin* (commoners) of the period with a national and social uplift. Jeffrey of Monmouth, author of *Historia Regum Britanniae*, in his attempt to explain the name Cymru (Wales), had stated that it was derived from the name Camber, the son of Brutus, the Trojan hero, who had after the fall of Troy settled in Britain, a name, so he claimed, derived from Brutus. This link with the classical world was a real boost to the Welsh identity. Later Latin writers coined the noun Cambria for Wales, together with the adjective Cambrian. William Vaughan sought to establish a Welsh colony as early as 1616 in what was later named

Newfoundland and called it Cambriol. Similarly, Morgan John Rhys, a Baptist minister and editor of the short-lived monthly, *Cylchgrawn Cymraeg*, spurred on by prospects of religious and political freedom in the new independent America, founded a Welsh colony in the Allegheny Mountains of Pennsylvania in 1794 and called it Cambria. Captain Dan Jones, in his introduction to his Welsh translation of Brigham Young's *Proclamation of the Twelve Apostles* published in 1845, refers to the Welsh people as "Cambria's sons" and the Welsh Mormon provisional settlement in Kanesfield was proudly called the "Cambrian Camp."

Other similar fabrications found a way into Welsh magazines and history books and into the minds of the Welsh. John Bale, the author of *Index Britanniae Scriptorum* (1557), started a myth that the Welsh were the descendants of Gomer, the son of Japheth, the son of Noah, and that the Welsh language, "Gomeraeg," as he called it, was the language spoken by Gomer. This alleged ethnical connection with the patriarchs was welcomed by all Welsh church and chapelgoers including the Welsh Mormon missionaries, who were more than happy with the Biblical connection and ready on all occasions to address themselves as the "the sons of Gomer'. The first Welsh newspaper, mentioned earlier, had been given the name *Seren Gomer* (Star of Gomer).

The early nineteenth century witnessed an upsurge in cultural activities, the publication of a large body of early Welsh literature and the spread of interest in the traditional Welsh poetic art. This can be attributed to the multiplicity of literary and philanthropic societies and the spread of the *eisteddfod* (literary competition) movement throughout Wales. The London Gwyneddigion Society published the works of the famous medieval Welsh poet Dafydd ap Gwilym and *The Myfyrian Archaeology*, hoping to draw the attention of scholars to some of the most important Welsh literary treasures. They also became patrons of the *eisteddfodau* held in the taverns of North Wales, where the Methodist, Dafydd Ddu Eryri, Bardd Cadeiriog Gwynedd, ruled the poetic roost and was mentor to a number of Gwendotian poets. Edward Williams (Iolo Morgannwg), another Unitarian, founded the Gorsedd of Bards, claiming that it had an unbroken record dating back to the Brythonic period. This movement and the Provincial Eisteddfod Society, established in 1818 by Bishop Burgess of St. Davids and other Established Church adherents to give the Church body a less anglicising image in the eyes of the Welsh, had a profound influence on the development of Welsh literature. Only one Nonconformist was allowed on the central committee of this Provincial Society, namely Iolo Morgannwg who was regarded by his contemporaries as a trustworthy authority on Welsh history and literature. Later generations found this opinion to have been grossly misconceived. Iolo had once stated that the rules of the Welsh poetic art were set forth by the poets Taliesin, Aneirin and Myrddin at a meeting of the Round Table in King Arthur's Court at Caerleon in Gwent. This claim, a stroke of fantasy, led to the establishment in the seventies of the literary society called Urdd y Ford Gron (Order of the Round Table), founded by the popular and romantic poets Ceiriog and Mynyddog.

In Merthyr Tydfil and district in the opening decades of the century there were numerous Welsh literary and philanthropic societies which met in the only nonreligious places of assembly available at the time, namely public houses. These were numerous and included The Vulcan, The Lamb, The Bush, Y Gwladwr, The Swan, The King's Head, The Plough, The Boar, The White Horse, and The Boot. The most famous of these literary societies were Cymdeithas y Cymreigyddion, Cymdeithas Llenyddion Merthyr, Cymmrodorion Merthyr, and Cymdeithas Cadair Merthyr. The aim of Cymdeithas Cadair Merthyr, which was founded in 1823, was to instruct young poets and harpists in the traditional poetic art. Frequent *eisteddfodau* were arranged, and in 1825 a *gorsedd* of bards was held in Twynyrodyn (a suburb of Merthyr), conducted by Taliesin ab Iolo, the headmaster of a local school and contributor to the *Merthyr Guardian*. The poetic works of the Merthyr poets were published in such anthologies as *Blwch y Cantorion* (1816) which contains the works of eighteen local poets, *Awenyddion Morganwg*, *Awen Merthyr Tydfil* (1822) and *Awen Gwent a Morganwg* (1824).

Myfyr Morganwg, watchmaker, Independent lay preacher, poet, exponent of eastern religions and self-named Archdruid of the Isle of Britain, formed in 1850 a Welsh druidical fellowship to hold *eisteddfodau* and practice rituals within a circle of stones arranged on the lines of the serpent temples of the Middle East. At the outset he had a good following, but criticism from local Nonconformist ministers led to its decline. Nevertheless, Myfyr Morganwg continued to practice these rituals on the Rocking Stone in Pontypridd four times a year for almost twenty years, ending we are told with associates who were mainly non-churchgoers.

In the Aberdare valley, at Trecynon, a Cymreigyddion Society was regularly held in The Red Stag, a tavern owned by William Williams, under the leadership of David Williams (Alaw Goch), a coal mine owner who in 1860 was appointed first treasurer of the new Council of the National Eisteddfod of Wales. He, together with William Williams and Abraham Mason, was also responsible for publishing *Y Gwladgarwr* to fight for the rights of workers and to defend the Nonconformist cause. In 1854 an anthology of verses composed by members of the society appeared under the title *Gardd Aberdâr*.

Abergavenny in Gwent had also by the thirties become an important centre of Welsh cultural activity. Under the patronage of Lady Llanover (Gwenynen Gwent), wife of Benjamin Hall, M. P., a Cymreigyddion Society was established in 1833 which aimed at holding Welsh Sunday schools, teaching Welsh in the local schools and holding *eisteddfodau* for poets, authors and harpists. The first *eisteddfod* was held in the Angel Hotel, Abergavenny, in 1834. Earlier in the same year Gwenynen Gwent had been made a member of the Gorsedd of Bards at a meeting held in Pontypridd having been awarded a prize for literature at the Cardiff National Eisteddfod held earlier the same year.

The philanthropic societies of the region were similarly functioning in Welsh and acting as patrons of the Welsh language and culture. The Druid Order, for example, was a keen supporter of the Abergavenny *eisteddfodau*, and in Swansea the local branch was solely responsible for holding an *eisteddfod* in 1841. The Oddfellows published a Welsh magazine known as *Y Gwron Odyddol*. Its editor, the chaired bard Cawrdaf, served on the staff of the radical *Merthyr and Cardiff Chronicle*, which was printed in Merthyr. Both Cawrdaf, a Wesleyan, and Josiah T. Jones, the owner of the paper and press, on account of their radicalism, were ousted from the town by Sir Josiah John Guest, also a Wesleyan, husband of Lady Charlotte Guest, the translator of the Mabinogion, a collection of famous Welsh medieval tales. Sir John was not only Conservative member of Parliament for Merthyr but also manager and part owner of the Merthyr Iron Works where he employed as many as 12,000 workers. Cawrdaf moved to Cowbridge and continued to publish *Y Gwron Odyddol*. There he was instrumental in holding an *eisteddfod* and *gorsedd* under the auspices of the Cymreigyddion Cadair Morganwg.

Captain Dan Jones reached the radical cultural cauldron of Merthyr Tydfil and its neighbouring towns in 1845, apparently after a short mission in North Wales, determined that "Cambria's sons" would get Brigham Young's "timely warning in their national tongue." He realised that unless he did so his mission would be a failure and the Welsh people would lend a deaf ear to the Mormon message. Dan Jones undoubtedly had the charisma, the conviction, the genius, the loyalty to the Mormon vision, and the understanding of the Welsh mentality and national ethos, and most important of all, a mastery of the Welsh language to ensure the success of the mission amongst the Cambrian Hills. After a short while he was in a position to assure his leaders in England that the missionaries were preaching in almost every county in

Wales, that he himself had travelled round every county in Wales but one, preaching every night in the largest towns, and that he had already published twelve Welsh-language treatises explaining and defending Mormon principles.

According to a report on the Manchester Annual Conference held in May 1846 published in *Prophwyd y Jubili* (August 1846) Dan Jones had been sent from America by the highest authority in the church to preside over all the districts throughout Wales, and his duties were to organise all matters within them and to take the best measures to further the work.

Earlier non-Welsh-speaking missionaries belonging to other denominations had experienced failure in Wales and had learnt the lesson. In 1800 Thomas Coke, a non-Welsh-speaking native of Brecon and leader of the Wesleyan mission, after experiencing such failure, persuaded the British Congress to send two Welsh preachers to North Wales. This resulted in the establishment of the first Welsh Wesleyan cause, that of Ruthin in Denbighshire. In 1809 the Welsh magazine, *Yr Eurgrawn Wesleyaidd* appeared, followed in 1825 by *Trysorfa'r Plant*, a religious monthly for children.

Richard Wright, the Unitarian missioner who visited Wales in 1816 and 1819, discovered to his dismay that his Unitarian mission had made little progress in Wales not only because he had not been allowed to publicise his meetings, as was his experience in Tenby, but also because he had no knowledge of the Welsh language. He wrote:

> I recommend the publication of a small periodical written in the Welsh language which might produce important effects; a missioner should be constantly employed which can preach to the Welsh people in their own language and tracts liberally circulated.

The Unitarian Society of Wales had earlier published sermons and treatises, original and translations, and a number of hymn books, but it was not until 1847 that their periodical *Yr Ymofynnydd* appeared.

The Calvinistic Methodist or Presbyterian Church of Wales, established in 1811, was from the outset a Welsh movement. Its missionary problem was, contrary to that of the other denominations, that of providing English churches in the partly anglicised towns of Wales. Attempts to meet the demand, known as the "English causes," resulted in much controversy within the denomination. This movement, the largest of all the Welsh denominations, had been enriched by the contribution of the Welsh revivalists Daniel Rowlands and Thomas Charles and that of the hymn writers William Williams Pantycelyn and Ann Griffiths. The greatest benefactor of the Calvinistic cause at the time of the Mormon mission was Lewis Edwards, who in 1845 launched *Y Traethodydd*, a high-standard quarterly magazine dealing with theological, philosophical and educational matters.

Such was the situation in Wales when Captain Dan Jones was preparing the first number of his Welsh magazine, *Prophwyd y Jubili, Seren y Saint* (The Prophet of the Jubilee, Star of the Saints), dealing, as he stated, in a letter to Wilford Woodruff concerning his first publication, with "the order of the Kingdom set up in the days of the Apostles & illustrating the first principles, the immutability of the Gospel... in the Welsh language of course." In the "Greeting of the publisher to his compatriots," printed in the opening pages of the first number (July 1846) of *Prophwyd* we find sentences such as these:

> Let the inhabitants of the earth rejoice, and let every Welshman give a hearkening ear to the good news of great joy that is sounded through this last trumpet... No prophet has ever striven on behalf of truth more than this one shall strive, according to his ability and his advantages, and he takes pride somewhat in the latter also, because of his link with the source from whence his elder brothers drew the sweet streams which made their vineyards fruitful and green, and which shall yet adorn the tops of the mountains of Wales until they blossom down to the bottom of the vales like the garden of paradise and drip honeycombs from each flower to all who accept him for their use.

In the section "Greeting of the *Prophet*" (p. 3) we read:

> My mission—oh, wonder of wonders—is good news. It is a mission of peace that I offer to every Welshman who will hear me. Something new and strange

has been wrought on the earth in these latter days! – something very few of you have understood yet, because it has not been put before you.

The dual title, *Prophwyd y Jubili, Seren y Saint*, was undoubtedly an attempt to convey the meaning suggested by the title *Millennial Star*, the English mission's periodical which was launched earlier by Brigham Young.

Prophwyd y Jubili served as expositor of Mormonism and its apocalyptic expectations and was a platform for defending the Saints against onslaughts on their Biblical teachings by denominational ministers. Later more space was given to the foundation of the New Jerusalem in California and to emigration matters, prospects and plans. As in all Welsh magazines of the period, poetry in the free and traditional strict meters found place in nearly all numbers.

Even in the first number (p. 22) Captain Dan Jones refers to what he calls the unfair attitude of the Welsh denominational press towards the Mormon mission, another reason why a Welsh organ was so essential, especially as these papers would not allow opportunity for the Mormons to defend their cause in their columns. He mentions some of these by name:

Amongst others, not the least are the *Star of Gomer*, the *Times*, the *Baptist*, the *Educator*, etc.... It is sad to say, indeed, that such people have polluted even the Welsh press, staining its fine vestment.

In the December 1846 number (p. 148) of *Prophwyd*, specific reference is made to the editor of *The Baptist*:

We implored earnestly and humbly for the opportunity to clear ourselves from the villainous filth with which we were plastered without provocation; but, as usual, the answer we received from him was a shameless refusal.

Little by little the idea of emigration was given a more prominent place in *Prophwyd* and more details were given in each issue. In the June 1847 number (p. 87) we find the statement:

It is on the American continent that God commanded his people to build a city of refuge [the New Jerusalem] for those of his children who gathered there.

The following January the Welsh converts were told:

> Now, you dear Saints throughout Wales, here is the news that you have waited long to hear. Behold the place, yes the refuge for deliverance has been found, the one which from now on will be the counterpoint for all the children of Zion from every nation, tongue and people to gather to—who is ready to get under way? (P. 8)

And in the February 1848 number (p. 29) further details are given:

> The center point of the gathering is the valley of the mountains near the "*Salt Lake*" in *California*. The recommended way is through New Orleans, up the *Mississippi* river and the *Missouri* to *Council Bluffs*, and from there overland in wagons to the end of the journey.

In the September number (p. 141) we read in the "Proclamation" written by Dan Jones:

> Our intention is to emigrate to California next January or February.

And in the October number (p. 153):

> We wish to inform the Welsh Saints, that president Pratt has entrusted to our care the preparation for the emigration of the Saints from Wales, and we intend to obtain a shipload of Welsh to go with each other, if there are about three hundred ready by January.

As the emphasis on emigration to Zion increased it was thought appropriate to change the name of the periodical from *Prophwyd y Jubili* to *Udgorn Seion* (The Trumpet of Zion), a name reminiscent of the Chartist magazine *Udgorn Cymru* (The Trumpet of Wales) which ceased circulation in 1842. If the call of the Chartists' trumpet had fallen on deaf ears, there had been already promising signs that the Mormon trumpet would be heard and thousands would answer its call. Captain Dan Jones, the president of the Welsh mission, preacher, editor of its monthly, and publisher of twenty Welsh pamphlets and a hymn book, made known his intention to lead the Welsh emigration party. He appointed John Davis, an experienced printer, to take over the editorship of *Udgorn Seion*. After five years of editing, writing and publishing numerous Welsh pamphlets and hymn books, and translating such works as The Book of Mormon,

Davis himself, on the return of Dan Jones on his second visit to lead the Welsh mission and embark on another series of publications, also emigrated to Zion, where he served on the staff of the Mormon newspaper *Deseret News*.

In many Welsh history books dealing with the religious movements of this period one finds no reference to the religious works of either of these prolific authors. One hopes that this additional contribution by Dr. Ronald Dennis to Welsh Mormon writings will go far to remedy this omission.

Geraint Bowen
Former Archdruid of Wales

INTRODUCTION

THE first meeting between Captain Dan Jones and the Prophet Joseph Smith on 12 April 1843 at Nauvoo, Illinois, was a positive experience for both men. Joseph Smith took an immediate liking to Jones and his steamboat, the *Maid of Iowa*. And as a recent convert to Mormonism, Dan Jones became an ardent admirer of the Prophet Joseph. Exactly one month later the two became business partners when Joseph Smith purchased a half interest in the *Maid of Iowa* from Levi Moffat, Jones's original partner.

In May 1844 Joseph Smith negotiated with Dan Jones to buy the other half of the steamboat and thus allow Jones to be off to his native Wales on the mission he had been called to serve a year earlier. The following month he said to Jones: "I have a check in the house for $1200 as soon as I can get it cashed you shall have $1100 of it, and the start for Wales, not with your fingers in your mouth but prepared to buy a press, and do business aright" (Jones to T. Bullock, 20 January 1855, LDS Church Archives). Because of the Martyrdom of Joseph Smith a short time later, Jones did not ever receive the aforementioned check; however, Brigham Young, the Prophet Joseph's successor, sent an order for $500 to the Liverpool office of the Church of Jesus Christ of Latter-day Saints on which Jones was allowed to draw for his living expenses and his publishing activities as a missionary in Wales.

Dan Jones arrived in Great Britain in January 1845 and was assigned to North Wales where his family lived. Within three months he published his first pamphlet to assist him in propagating Mormonism to his compatriots. (For particulars of this forty-eight-page publication see my *Welsh Mormon Writings from 1844 to 1862: a historical bibliography* [Provo, Utah: Brigham Young University Religious Studies Center, 1988], pp. 13–16.) But neither this pamphlet nor any others of Jones's first mission to Wales were published on a press owned by Jones. Lacking sufficient money to purchase his own, Dan Jones was forced to rely on the presses of others.

Coincidentally, Jones's brother John owned and operated a press in the little village of Rhydybont, near Llanybydder in Carmarthenshire. And although the Reverend John Jones was an ordained Congregational minister, he permitted the use of his press for his younger brother Dan to promote the cause of Mormonism. His press was soon labeled "the prostitute press" by other ministers because its services were sold to the "enemy" of all other Christian religions in Wales – the Mormon Church. The Reverend Jones made money not only by printing the materials of the Latter-day Saints, but also by preaching against their doctrines from his pulpit. Ironically, the Reverend's wife and daughters later converted to Mormonism.

The first item printed on the press at Rhydybont was Dan Jones's translation of *Proclamation of the Twelve Apostles* in early December 1845 (see *Welsh Mormon Writings*, pp. 16–19). Later that same month Elder Dan Jones received the assignment to move to Merthyr Tydfil and preside over the LDS missionary effort in all of Wales. Elder William Henshaw had been in Merthyr Tydfil for nearly three years and had established in the midst of considerable opposition a few branches of the Church with a total of nearly five hundred members. The opposition from the press and over the pulpit increased in proportion to the growth of the Latter-day Saint movement.

To answer the criticism of Mormonism's adversaries Dan Jones published in early February 1846 a twenty-four-page pamphlet entitled *Reply to the objections which are most commonly brought throughout the country against the Latter-day Saints* (see *Welsh Mormon Writings*, pp. 20–23). The wrapper of this publication contains the prospectus for a monthly periodical that Dan Jones intended to begin in June 1846 and one that he intended to call *Prophwyd y Jubili* (Prophet of the Jubilee).

This curious publication made its debut in July 1846, just one month after Jones's predicted date. On the second page of the July 1846 wrapper, Jones's enthusiasm about this momentous occasion for all Welsh Latter-day Saints is clear: "Is everyone allowed to put out his *magazine* but us? Is the press locked against us? Is that the freedom of Wales in the nineteenth century? Have the monthlies been locked? We shall open our own monthly, then. Has the press been polluted by libeling us? We shall cleanse it by defending ourselves, then." Several religious periodicals had published anti-Mormon articles but then refused to publish the rebuttals sent them. With his own publication the feisty Captain Jones believed that he was now on even ground with his numerous opponents. In each issue he could answer the charges made against Mormonism, as well as defend, expound, and clarify the doctrines of the faith he had adopted just three years earlier. He proceeded to do all of these things with great relish and enthusiasm.

The typesetting and printing of all but the final two issues of *Prophwyd y Jubili* were done on the press at Rhydybont. Its basic layout, size, and appearance are virtually identical to those of *Y Golygydd* (The Editor), a periodical begun by Dan Jones's brother John in January 1846.

The title that Dan Jones gave to his periodical was probably inspired by Orson Pratt's *The Prophet*, a publication that Jones came to know as he passed through New York en route to Wales in late 1844. Because the title of *Prophwyd y Jubili* was changed after the December 1848 issue, the series is complete with the thirty issues that were published during the preceding two-and-a-half years. The final two issues of *Prophwyd* were printed on the press of John Davis in the town of Carmarthen, and the same

John Davis assumed the editorship of *Udgorn Seion* (Zion's Trumpet), the successor to *Prophwyd.* (For details on *Udgorn Seion* see *Welsh Mormon Writings*, pp. 72–79.)

Each of the six issues of *Prophwyd* for 1846 came with a four-page printed wrapper. When the wrappers were bound with the issues of *Prophwyd y Jubili* they were placed all together in sequence following the final page of the December 1846 issue, and the same procedure has been followed for this translation.

The six issues of 1846 and the twelve for 1848 have their own title pages, forewords, and tables of contents. The twelve issues for 1847, however, do not. Because the January 1847 issue begins with page 5, it is evident that the editor intended to produce a title page, a foreword, and a table of contents for that year, but none of the extant volumes of *Prophwyd y Jubili* has these items for 1847.

My own fascination with *Prophwyd y Jubili* began nearly twenty-five years ago when I obtained a copy of all thirty issues from a friend who knew of my interest in my great-great grandfather, Captain Dan Jones. At about this same time I read in the *Millennial Star* concerning the conversion of William Howells, a lay Baptist minister in Aberdare. After reading a publication of Dan Jones in late 1847, Howells walked the four miles from Aberdare to Merthyr Tydfil to seek out the author and request baptism at his hands. On the evening of 2 November 1847 following his conversation with Dan Jones, his first with any LDS missionary, Howells was baptized. During the following eighteen months he was instrumental in bringing into the Church nearly one hundred of his family, friends, and former parishioners. In July 1849 he became the first LDS missionary to France. (See my "William Howells: First Missionary to France," in *Supporting Saints: Stories of Nineteenth-Century Mormons*, edited by Donald Q. Cannon and David J. Whittaker [Salt Lake City, Utah: Bookcraft, 1985], pp. 43-81.)

If the writings of Dan Jones could have such an impact on a person like William Howells, I wanted to know their contents.

Consequently, I set about to learn the Welsh language, a process that was greatly enhanced by living in Wales during the first half of 1976. Although it has been laborious and time consuming, I have greatly enjoyed the discovery of every page of *Prophwyd y Jubili* and the challenge of translating its fascinating contents into English so that others may follow the fortunes of the Latter-day Saints in Wales during the two-and-a-half-year period from July 1846 to December 1848.

Since July 1996 represents the sesquicentennial of the appearance of Volume I, Number 1, of *Prophwyd y Jubili*, a facsimile edition seemed appropriate. But since Welsh is an unknown tongue among virtually all LDS historians, a facsimile edition would serve little purpose. And a mere translation would lack the appearance and flavor of the original. Thus I decided to prepare this "facsimile translation" to provide the non-Welsh-speaking reader with the contents of this little-known periodical while preserving the look and feel of the Welsh original. I am indebted to many people for their help in preparing the translation; however, the ultimate responsibility for its accuracy rests with me.

Ronald D. Dennis
Provo, Utah
June 1996

Bwriedir Cyhoeddi, yn Mis Mehefin, 1846, ac i ddyfod allan yn Fisol,

DAN OLYGIAD CAPT. D. JONES,

PROPHWYD Y JUBILI,

YR HWN A GYNNWYSA, YN—

I. TRAETHODAU Byrion ar Byncian Athrawiaethol SAINT Y DYDDIAU DIWEDDAF; megys Ffydd—Edifeirwch—Bedydd er Maddeuant—Arddodiad Dwylaw, er derbyn yr Ysbryd Glan—y Doniau Ysbrydol—Adferiad yr Iuddewon i'w Gwlad—yr Adgyfodiad Cyntaf—Teyrnasiad Crist ar y Ddaear—y Farn Gyffredinol—y Nef a'r Ddaear Newydd—a Thynghedfen Dragwyddol y Bydyssawd a'i Drigolion.

II. DYFYNIADAU O LYFR MORMON, a Phrofion o'i Eirwiredd, ynghyd ag Helyntion yr Eglwys, a'i Chynnydd—Merthyrdod llawer o'r Saint, a'u blaenoriaid, yn yr Amerig, gan Lygad-dyst; a'r pethau hynotaf a fu yn eu plith, yn Nghymru a Gwledydd Tramor.

III. AMDDIFFYNIAD O GYMMERIADAU Y SAINT, yn ngwyneb ymosodiadau eu gelynion, drwy yr ystoriau disail a daenir drwy y wlad.

IV. AMRYWIAETHAU, yn cynnwys hanes helyntion, rhyfeloedd, heintiau, chwyldroadau, a barnedigaethau Duw yn ngoruchwyliaeth y dyddiau diweddaf hyn,

Ymdrechir gwneyd y Cyhoeddiad yn deilwng o'i enw, drwy gyflawni ei swydd, a dwyn gwirioneddau newydd a hen i'r amlwg, er cysur a lles i bawb a'i darlleno.

Ei Bris fydd Tair Ceiniog y Rhifyn i'r sawl a'i derbynio am Chwe Mis, ac a dalant 2s. 6c. yn mlaen llaw. Y neb a gasglo Ddeg o Enwau, ac a anfono yr arian, a gaiff un Rhifyn am ei drafferth.

*** Cyfeirier pob llythyron (wedi eu rhagdalu) at *Capt. D. Jones, 45, Cyfarthfa Row, George Town, Merthyr-Tydvil.*

Prophwyd y Jubili prospectus, courtesy The National Library of Wales

To be Published, in June, 1846, and to come out Monthly,

UNDER THE EDITORSHIP OF CAPT. D. JONES,

PROPHET OF THE JUBILEE,

WHICH WILL CONTAIN—

I. BRIEF Treatises on Doctrinal Subjects of the LATTER-DAY SAINTS; such as Faith—Repentance—Baptism for Forgiveness—Laying on of Hands, to receive the Holy Ghost—the Spiritual Gifts—the Restoration of the Jews to their Land—the First Resurrection—the Reign of Christ on the Earth—the Final Judgment—the Heaven and the Renewed Earth—and the Eternal Destiny of the Universe and its Inhabitants.

II. QUOTATIONS FROM THE BOOK OF MORMON, and Proofs of its Truthfulness, together with the Affairs of the Church, and its Progress—the Martyrdom of many of the Saints, and their leaders, in America, by an eyewitness; and the most remarkable things that have happened among them, in Wales and in Overseas Countries.

III. DEFENSE OF THE CHARACTER OF THE SAINTS, in the face of attacks by their enemies, through the baseless stories that are being spread throughout the country.

IV. MISCELLANIES, containing the story of their affairs, wars, afflictions, revolutions, and the judgments of God in the dispensation of these latter days.

Every effort will be made to make the Publication worthy of its name, by fulfilling its office, and bringing new and old truths into the open, for the comfort and benefit of all who may read it.

Its Price will be Three Pence per Issue for those who subscribe to it for Six Months, and who pay 2 shillings 6 pence in advance. Whoever gathers Ten Names, and sends the money, will receive one Issue for his trouble.

*** All letters (prepaid) are to be addressed to *Capt. D. Jones, 45, Cyfarthfa Row, Georgetown, Merthyr Tydfil.*

Facsimile Translation Considerations

1. **Size**. The size of the page and the print of the original has been enlarged by about thirty percent to facilitate reading.

2. **Leading and point size**. Whatever variations occur in space between lines and print size in the original are imitated in the translation.

3. **Pagination**. All major and minor headings are on the same page as the original, although the content of each page may vary by as much as four or five lines. No additional pagination to distinguish among the three volumes has been added; however, the part pages that precede each volume will distinguish between the years and ease the finding of specific items.

4. **Paragraphs and sentences**. The tendency of nineteenth-century writers was to use fewer paragraph breaks and much longer sentences than might seem appropriate today. However, for the sake of flavor the inordinate paragraph size and the seemingly interminable sentence length are imitated in the translation.

5. **Brackets and parentheses**. The only editorial comments in the translation are those of Dan Jones from the original; consequently, all brackets and parentheses are his.

6. **Italicized words**. Italics in the original are retained in the translation. Besides the normal practice of italicizing the names of periodicals, books, ships, etc., the editor used italics either to provide emphasis or to indicate the use of a borrowed word or phrase from English.

7. **Punctuation**. Some changes in punctuation and capitalization have been made to facilitate reading. Double quotations within double quotations are imitated, as are the occasional extra spaces around exclamation points and question marks.

8. **Quotations**. Even when placed between the appropriate marks, quoted material in *Prophwyd* often does not contain the exact wording used in the source. This is true also when the scriptures are quoted. This lack of precision is imitated, as is the method used for citing scriptural chapter and verse.

9. **Typesetting errors**. The typesetters of the original sometimes inverted letters, cited verses that did not match the accompanying scriptural quotation, left incomplete sentences, misspelled words, or committed other typesetting errors. Lacking an unobtrusive method of indicating such aspects of the original in the translation and fearing that confusion would result for today's reader if such flaws were duplicated, I decided to "correct" these kinds of imperfections in the translation. Considering the painstaking procedure required of nineteenth-century typesetters, the wonder is that more such miscues did not occur.

10. **Typesetting oddities**. Ending a page with only the first line of a new paragraph or with a hyphenated word is a frequent occurrence in the Welsh original. Also, the section headings are often near the end of a page. These practices are imitated in the translation.

11. **Poetry**. The primary focus in translating the poetry of *Prophwyd y Jubili* has been its content. However, D. L. Davies, Cwmaman, South Wales, has rendered poetic translations for several poems in the 1846 and 1847 issues.

12. **Titles of foreign-language publications**. To facilitate reading, I have used the English translations for all titles in the text and in the Annotated Contents. Titles in Welsh of all items published by Dan Jones are found in *Welsh Mormon Writings*. The following is a list of other publications mentioned in the Foreword and in the text and their corresponding titles in English and in Welsh:

The Apostolic Witness	*Y Tyst Apostolaidd*
The Baptist	*Y Bedyddiwr*
Trumpet of Chartism	*Udgorn Chartiaeth*
The Chronicle	*Y Cronicl*
The Congregational Treasury	*Y Drysorfa Gynnulleidfaol*
The Deceit of the Latter Saints Exposed	*Twyll y Seintiau Diweddaf yn Cael ei Ddynoethi*
The Educator	*Y Dysgedydd*
The Essayist	*Y Traethodydd*
The Inquirer	*Yr Ymofynnydd*
The Latter-day Saints and Miraculous Gifts	*Saint y Dyddiau Diweddaf a Doniau Gwyrthiol*
The Latter Saints. Substance of a Sermon on the Miracles.	*Y Seintiau Diweddaf. Sylwedd Pregeth a Draddodwyd ar y Gwyrthiau.*
The Oddfellow Hero	*Y Gwron Odyddol*
The Patriot	*Y Gwladgarwr*
The Reviewer	*Yr Adolygydd*
The Revivalist	*Y Diwygiwr*
Star of the Saints	*Seren y Saint*
Star of Gomer	*Seren Gomer*
The Times	*Yr Amserau*
The True Mirror	*Y Drych Cywir*
Trumpet of Wales	*Udgorn Cymru*
Welsh Magazine	*Cylchgrawn Cymraeg*
Zion's Trumpet	*Udgorn Seion*

13. **Place names**. The modern spelling is used for all place names. The name in English is used for places that have both an English name and a Welsh name (e.g., Swansea for Abertawe, Cardiff for Caerdydd, and Blackwood for Coed-duon). Places mentioned in the text that are now known by a different name are Llwyni (now Maesteg), Newmarket (now Trelawnyd), and Penycae (now Ebbw Vale).

14. **Proper names**. I have corrected the spelling of Biblical and historical names; however, I have preserved the spelling used for all other proper names, even when the same individual's

name has two spellings (e.g., Harries and Harris, M. Comb and Macomb, Morgans and Morgan).

15. **Annotated contents**. Instead of inserting numbers and notes and detracting from the facsimile appearance of the translation, I have prepared an article-by-article commentary of the entire thirty issues. In many instances I give simply a brief statement of the article's contents, together with an indication of a source if the article is borrowed. I provide more detailed observations for those articles that contain historical information pertinent to the nineteenth-century movement of the Latter-day Saints in Wales.

Acknowledgments

I am indebted to a number of people for making this "facsimile translation" possible. Five of the six issues for 1846 were translated in their entirety by Marilyn Davies of Prestatyn, North Wales. Tecwyn Evans of Ellesmere Port, Cheshire, and Rozelle James Kania of Newcastle-under-Lyme, Staffordshire, provided assistance with the 1847 and 1848 volumes. Dr. Geraint Bowen and his wife Zonia of Caernarfon, North Wales, were kind enough to furnish translations for dozens of "problem areas" throughout the entire periodical. D. L. Davies of Cwmaman, South Wales, offered invaluable help in reviewing and improving the translations for the poetry throughout. My special thanks to David R. Coughanour of Provo, Utah, for his careful and creative typesetting. Thanks also to Arle Lommel of Anchorage, Alaska, for preparing the index and helping with the typesetting. For proofreading I express appreciation to Linda Hunter Adams of the Brigham Young University College of Humanities Publications Center and her very able students: Jane Clayson, Allison Clinger, Chandelle Crane, Paula Messer Hiatt, Kristen Jafek, Janette Jeffress, Karen Lusby, Emily Manwaring, Kristina McGuire, Suzanne Schurig, and Teresa Silfies. Lisa Kurki and Jason Roberts of the Brigham Young University Religious Studies Center spent many hours proofreading. And Ana Nelson Shaw, also of the Religious Studies Center, read the entire manuscript and offered many helpful suggestions. To all I express my heartfelt gratitude.

Annotated Contents

JULY 1846

Most of the doctrinal segments sprinkled through the thirty issues of *Prophet of the Jubilee* were borrowed from other authors such as Elders Orson and Parley P. Pratt. Rarely are the source articles simply translated, however, without also being embellished. Even the items from the *Millennial Star* that Dan Jones presents as translations are not word-for-word renditions of their English versions. Jones's inspiration for these four articles on angels appears to have been the *Millennial Star*, April 1845, pp. 180–82, and 15 January 1846, pp. 29–32.

Loose translations of segments of the Orson Pratt pamphlet entitled *Interesting account of several remarkable visions*, issued in Edinburgh in 1840. Dan Jones does not quote his source, nor does he present these writings as being anyone's work but his own. In doing so he was certainly not out of line with other nineteenth-century writers.

Begins as a discussion of the prophetic warning given to Joseph Smith by the angel Moroni that he and his followers would suffer much persecution because of their beliefs. Jones explains that the unjustified persecution heaped on him and other Latter-day Saints in Wales constituted a fulfillment of this dire prophecy. He then focuses on the following specific example of persecution, an unsigned article published in the March 1846 issue of *The Baptist*.

The title of this article is not the same as the one listed in the table of contents on the wrapper for this issue ("Reply to the article of the Rev. W. R. Davies, of Dowlais, in the *Baptist* for March"). It is actually the title used for the article written by Jones's antagonist, whom he identifies as the Reverend W. R. Davies, minister of the Baptist congregation of the Caersalem chapel in Dowlais, a town about two miles from Merthyr Tydfil. The Reverend W. R. Davies was the archenemy of the Saints from the time of his first published criticisms of Mormonism in 1844 until his death from cholera in September 1849. (For more information about the battle between him and Dan Jones, see "The Reverend W. R. Davies vs. Captain Dan Jones," *Brigham Young University Studies*, 27 [Spring 1987]: 53–65.)

AUGUST 1846

SEPTEMBER 1846

have had was nullified by this comment from the editor: "Whether the letter referred to is false or authentic, the writing is very much like the writing of this letter. They are so similar that everyone who saw them decided at once that it was the same hand that wrote the two letters." Dan Jones defends Henshaw and Evans in the columns of *Prophet of the Jubilee* and answers the charges made by W. R. Davies. In the opening lines of the article Jones makes two erroneous statements: (1) that the letter of defense by Henshaw and Evans had been published in the July *Prophet of the Jubilee*, and (2) that the letter had been refused publication in *The Baptist*. He corrects the first error on page 2 of the wrapper for the September 1846 issue of *Prophet of the Jubilee* by printing the full text of the letter, and the second in a one-page follow-up article on page 2 of the October 1846 issue. (A discussion of this incident is in my *Indefatigable Veteran: History and Biography of Abel Evans, a Welsh Mormon Elder* [Provo, Utah: Rhydybont Press, 1994], pp. 32–39). Curiously, it was the Reverend John Jones, Dan Jones's brother, who in 1841 began a publication called *The Baptist* to ridicule the practice of baptism by immersion. The following year the Baptists responded with a periodical entitled *The True Baptist* (the title used in this article in *Prophet of the Jubilee*), removing the "true" from the title a year later when John Jones's publication ended.

OCTOBER 1846

A series of quotations from several biblical scholars in an effort to show that their views concerning baptism and the spiritual gifts coincided with the doctrine of the Latter-day Saints. Albert Barnes from Philadelphia and Matthew Henry from Caerleon are quoted most.

A statement of LDS doctrine concerning death and resurrection.

Dan Jones's aggressive way of bearing his testimony and persuading others to read it. Certainly he was aware that his claim for three hundred thousand eyewitnesses was a tenfold exaggeration of the actual count of LDS converts; part of his reason for using this kind

NOVEMBER 1846

DECEMBER 1846

JULY 1846 WRAPPER

AUGUST 1846 WRAPPER

SEPTEMBER 1846 WRAPPER

OCTOBER 1846 WRAPPER

NOVEMBER 1846 WRAPPER

DECEMBER 1846 WRAPPER

JANUARY 1847

FEBRUARY 1847

APRIL 1847

JULY 1847

AUGUST 1847

SEPTEMBER 1847

NOVEMBER 1847

A former distributor of *The Baptist* and persecutor of the Saints writes to Dan Jones to tell him that he had converted to Mormonism and been baptized a week before. He mentions that he had never suffered so much persecution during his eight years with the Baptists as he received from them during the previous week since becoming LDS.

At the end of this article Dan Jones states that this doctrinal discussion is from his *Scriptural Treasury*, a book that he published in five segments between September 1847 and July 1848. *Scriptural Treasury* is essentially a reworking of Benjamin Winchester's 1842 *Synopsis of the holy scriptures and concordance*; nevertheless, putting together this 288-page publication in the midst of all else Jones was involved in at the time was no small feat.

Dan Jones's response to a review of the 2 and 3 September 1847 lectures on Mormonism that appeared in *Star of Gomer*, a Baptist periodical, for October 1847, p. 318. The writer, who signs himself simply "A listener," claims that the Reverends E. Roberts and D. Jones had delivered the "homestroke" to the Saints in that area and that two of their leading elders and others had left as a result of the lectures. Dan Jones sarcastically refutes such claims in his article; furthermore, he states not a week had passed since then without new converts from Dowlais.

A glowing portrayal of the Sacramento valley quoted from the *New York Herald.*

Jones encourages all the Latter-day Saints throughout Wales to remain faithful to their beliefs and not to listen to those who would have them turn their backs on Mormonism.

An eyewitness report of two persons who, as they traveled from California to St. Louis, had met with the first and second companies of Saints heading to the Great Salt Lake. They reported in the *St. Louis Republican*, 24 August 1847, that these companies were moving along "very successfully."

DECEMBER 1847

Jones is obviously very pleased to make this year-end report of the tremendous growth in the strength of Mormonism throughout Wales. He focuses on nineteen different areas with comments that range from two or three lines for some to over thirty lines for others. The Merthyr Tydfil branch was continuing with steady growth and had grown to be over six hundred strong. The branch at Llanelli had experienced an astounding increase lately: forty-one baptisms since the last conference, despite the persecution of the Reverend James Spencer, a Baptist minister.

An appeal for all to settle up their accounts by the end of the year.

Scheduled for December 26th and 27th at the White Lion Inn in Merthyr. Visitors from America are expected.

JANUARY 1848

Designed to be the title page for the twelve issues of 1848. Along with the foreword and contents, it was distributed with the December 1848 issue.

Dated 15 December 1848 this foreword sends *Prophet of the Jubilee* to his "resting place" and announces the forthcoming publication of *Zion's Trumpet.*

Four articles are not included in this otherwise complete list of the articles of the 1848 *Prophet* ("Letter of W. Woodruff, one of the Apostles," p. 101; "To our subscribers," p. 111; "The means to have a perfect government and to sustain it," p. 154; "Sorrow and bliss," p. 191). Four incorrect page references have been corrected in the translation.

Jones's optimistic forecast for the fortune of Mormonism during 1848. He commits to produce the *Prophet of the Jubilee* each month with many things that will benefit all its readers.

In the December 1847 *Revivalist*, p. 391, was an account taken from the *Ottoway Free Trader* of "the prophet Strang" and his miracle with phosphorus. The heading in the *Revivalist*, "Mormon miracle," was obviously to link Strang with Mormonism even though he had been excommunicated some time before. In Jones's righteous indignation he puts the editor of the *Revivalist* through a wringer of rhetoric for knowingly casting Mormonism in a light that it did not deserve. Then he reports some bona fide miracles in the *Prophet* for his adversary to read. A translated letter of William Atholl McMaster to Orson Spencer follows. (See *Millennial Star*, 1 December 1847, pp. 364–65).

The opening paragraph is quoted from the *New York Herald* and is a description of the generosity of the wife of President Polk and others who wished to help the Saints, who had been driven from their homes. The second paragraph, an enthusiastic reaction to such kindness, is from the *Millennial Star* as indicated by Dan Jones at the end of the article. However, a comparison of the *Millennial Star* version and what appears in *Prophet of the Jubilee* reveals that it is far from being a translation. Although Jones uses the basic ideas from the English original, he frequently omits phrases and injects his own personal touches, certainly not an unusual procedure for that time. (See *Millennial Star*, 1 December 1847, pp. 360–61.)

Orson Hyde reports on 7 October 1847 that Brigham Young was on his way back to Council Bluffs after being with the first company of Saints to reach the Great Salt Lake. Dan Jones rejoices at the determination of a place of settlement, for now he can tell the Welsh Saints where they are going when they leave "Babylon."

Taken from the *St. Louis Republican* this article reports a more exact location for the primary gathering place of the Saints in the Rocky Mountains—"half way between the *Salt Lake* and *Lake Eutah*, in California."

Held on 26 and 27 December 1847 in Merthyr Tydfil, this conference had President Orson Spencer in attendance. The minutes

APRIL 1848

MAY 1848

JULY 1848

AUGUST 1848

A rather lengthy description of Jones's latest publication, *Scriptural Treasury*, and a fervent appeal for all the Saints to obtain a copy of this 288-page volume. (See *Welsh Mormon Writings*, p. 65.)

Soon after twenty-nine Saints were dismissed from their jobs by the chief steward, the chief steward was fired by the company. The unemployed men sent a petition of complaint to John Bidelph, the new steward, along with a book which contained "the main tenets of our religion." This book could have been the newly published *Scriptural Treasury*, but since Bidelph probably did not speak or read Welsh it may have been a book in English. Dan Jones includes a copy of the petition in this month's *Prophet* along with other evidence that the lost jobs resulted from religious persecution.

Poem of four stanzas of four lines each.

John Davis's responses to "erroneous" statements by the Rev. Thomas Williams, a Baptist minister, in his 2 July 1848 sermon about Saints in Llangynog Parish near Carmarthen. Davis sent copies to Williams and to Dan Jones, who printed it in this issue of the *Prophet*. A short time later the letter was printed as a four-page pamphlet. (See *Welsh Mormon Writings*, pp. 68 – 71.)

Poem of four stanzas of eight lines each.

Detailed account of the 16 and 17 July 1848 gathering in the White Lion Inn at Merthyr Tydfil. The total number of baptisms—938—combined with the total number of members in Wales reported at the December 1847 conference—1,933—should give a total of 2,871 instead of the reported 2,747. The discrepancy of 124 is probably because of the number of excommunications or disfellowshipments, statistics that were not reported at this time.

Following the Monday morning session of the conference a banquet was held for the purpose of socializing and raising money for the Missionary Society, an organization established two years earlier to offer financial support to those who volunteered to serve as missionaries. The banquet lasted from 2:30 p. m. until 8:00 p. m. Afterwards several lectures were presented.

On 25 July 1848 a meeting of the "Council" was held. This body apparently consisted of officers of various kinds, about sixty of whom were present. It was resolved that each branch in Wales would collect money toward book debts each week with the goal of getting completely caught up before the next conference in December.

SEPTEMBER 1848

More information on the glories of California, this time from John Bartleson.

The conversion of Rees Price was probably one of the greatest triumphs of the Saints over the Reverend W. R. Davies of Dowlais, since Price had been a Baptist for nine years and Davies's "right hand man" during part of that time. Dan Jones announced Price's baptism in the March 1848 *Prophet*, p. 45. Price gives credit to the anti-Mormon lectures of the Reverend Edward Roberts for convincing him to have a closer look at the teachings of the Saints. Rees Price, his wife Jane, and their five children sailed on the *Buena Vista* with 242 other Saints. Jane and one of the children died on the Missouri River in May 1849. There is no evidence that Rees Price ever arrived in the Salt Lake Valley.

This letter to the editor of the *Prophet* is signed "A friend of the Bible." He declares himself an unbeliever because of all the confusion he has encountered in the various religions in his community. He is more inclined toward Mormonism than any of the others, but he expresses concern as to why the Saints do not perform public miracles as did the Apostles in the time of Christ. Dan Jones

DECEMBER 1848

The Reverend David Evans from Carmarthen gave a sermon about the Saints on 27 August 1848, and a short time later he printed the contents of his sermon in a twenty-page pamphlet entitled *The Latter-day Saints and miraculous gifts*. John Davis wrote this response at the request of Dan Jones since the latter was extremely busy. A short time later Davis's response was published as an eight-page pamphlet. (See *Welsh Mormon Writings*, pp. 71–72.)

After hearing some anti-Mormon preaching, a member of the LDS church who calls himself "Iolyn Mai" writes his reaction to the editor of the *Prophet*. Most of the writing consists of a song of six stanzas of eight lines each with an eight-line chorus. The writer calls on his opponents to awake from their sleep and recognize that the true church has been restored.

This article is signed "Omega" and is taken from the *Millennial Star*. The writer tells of recent discussions in the United States about constructing a railway that would extend across the nation and one that would therefore make a tremendous difference in the Saints' journey from Council Bluffs to the Rocky Mountains. Most of the Welsh converts who eventually made that journey would not benefit from this railway since it would not be completed for another twenty years. (See *Millennial Star*, 1 August 1848, p. 235–37.)

Three stanzas of twelve lines each written by John Davis for the departing Saints to sing on the ship as it leaves the harbor. Dan Jones later reported that this was, in fact, the song that was sung on the occasion of the departure of the *Buena Vista* group on 26 February 1849. (See *Call of Zion*, p. 14.)

The editor reports that the Baptists, the Methodists, and several other denominations in the United States were owners of hundreds of thousands of slaves. He is proud to point out that the Saints do not believe in slavery and that they held no slaves at all.

1846

PROPHWYD Y JUBILI,

NEU,

SEREN Y SAINT;

YN CYNNWYS

HANES SEFYDLIAD "GORUCHWYLIAETH CYFLAWNDER YR AMSEROEDD,"

YNGHYD AG

ERLIDIGAETHAU, MERTHYRDOD, AC ALLTUDIAETH EI HUFYDDION, A'U LLWYDDIANT,
&c., &c.

"YR ARGLWYDD IOR A LEFARODD, PWY NI PHROPHWYDA? CANYS NI WNA YR ARGLWYDD DDIM, A'R NA DDANGOSO EI GYFRINACH I'W WEISION Y PROPHWYDI."

CYFROL I.

MERTHYR-TYDFIL:
CYHOEDDWYD AC AR WERTH GAN D. JONES;
AC AR WERTH HEFYD
GAN Y SAINT YN GYFFREDINOL, A LLAWER O LYFRWERTHWYR.
1846.

1846 title page, courtesy Harold B. Lee Library, Brigham Young University

PROPHET OF THE JUBILEE,

OR,

STAR OF THE SAINTS;

CONTAINING AN

ACCOUNT OF THE ESTABLISHMENT OF THE "DISPENSATION OF THE FULNESS OF TIMES,"

TOGETHER WITH THE

PERSECUTIONS, MARTYRDOM, AND EXILE OF ITS FOLLOWERS, AND THEIR SUCCESSES,
&c., &c.

"THE LORD GOD HATH SPOKEN, WHO CAN BUT PROPHESY? SURELY THE LORD GOD WILL DO NOTHING, BUT HE REVEALETH HIS SECRET UNTO HIS SERVANTS THE PROPHETS."

VOLUME I.

MERTHYR TYDFIL

PUBLISHED AND FOR SALE BY D. JONES;

AND FOR SALE ALSO

BY THE SAINTS IN GENERAL, AND MANY BOOKSELLERS.

1846.

FOREWORD.

EVERY sect must have its oracle—its monthly, its defense publication, in this inquisitive age and in this inquisitive country; so must we also have. We have now published six issues of the PROPHET. In it one may have a clarification of a variety of our principles, our defense in face of the lying and unfair accusations of our opponents, stories of our success and the strivings of our preachers and our members in various parts of the country, together with proofs from doctrinal segments and prophecies of the Holy Scriptures of our divine establishment, authority, and support.

We begin to prove, clarify, and defend ourselves and our principles; but we expect a continuation of age and opportunity, and support in order to go forward, until we convince our compatriots in general of our Christianity and our heavenly and important stewardship.

Regardless of what is said about *us*, and about our *principles*, and about our *practices*, it is for certain that everyone, although doubting our professions in this, must recognize that in our vessel are found all the apostolic proofs that were promised about persecutions for the faith. They also must recognize that many of the important truths hidden under the mantle of darkness, are shining through the pages of the PROPHET; and thus they will continue to gaze in the eyes of all who read them, until they fill our country with the light of the Jubilee.

CONTENTS.

PROPHET OF THE JUBILEE.

"THE KINGDOM HAS COME."

No. 1.] JULY, 1846 [Vol. I.

GREETING OF THE PUBLISHER TO HIS COMPATRIOTS.

Dear Reader,—Behold the beginning of a new era of our age, yea, the most remarkable which has ever been, the most wondrous in its preparations, the most goodly in its deeds, and the most glorious in its effects of every previous age. Once more the golden keys of heaven have been entrusted to men for them to open all treasures, to unlock all mysteries and for the clarification of all errors in the midst of mankind. Already the doors of eternity can be seen opening on their rusty hinges, its hidden pearls and the treasures old and new are once again starting to shine before the eyes of men as in the days of the Lord! Let the inhabitants of the earth rejoice, and let every Welshman give a hearkening ear to the good news of great joy that is sounded through this last trumpet.

My excuse for bringing this new and strange "Prophet" into your midst is that I know that he has much true, glorious and beneficial news to set before your eyes; news that is worthy of every man's consideration; things that bring light, knowledge and joy to everyone who accepts them and a pure benefit to all. There is in him no inclination to harm anyone, rather his heart is a bright flame of love to every man, especially to the benefitting of his brothers and sisters of the same blood.

He can deceive no one, for he carries guileless scales always—*logic* in one hand, and the divine, infallible standard of the holy book itself in the other—as a sure rule to weigh each statement that he brings before you; and whosoever writes "*Mene, Mene, Tekel,*" on his forehead without being found "wanting" in these true scales, does an injustice to himself, refuses the good things of heaven, angelic manna and tasty morsels from the table above—which he offers to bring as tasty dishes from the best markets of heaven and earth and place them on your table every new moon for as little as three pence each!

Even though it is strange, it is true enough that every prophet who has ever been from the least unto the great Prophet himself, had hosts of enemies; but we are confident that nobody, even those who hate the name of every one of the prophetic family, will pour out his ire before a paper prophet; and since the anger of the world refuses to allow anyone of this name to live, it is better to have a paper one than to be without one. One need only look into their history to see that the more truth they prophesied, the more frequent and cruel were their enemies while they were alive; but upon dying at their hands, each one of the prophets in his turn, killed off all his enemies—not as Samson, rather in that their children and their children's children became more acquainted with the work of godly martyrs after their fathers had killed them; yes, out of respect for them they adorned their graves and martyred anyone who said a word scornfully about their memory; and at the same instant, they "fulfilled the measure of their fathers" by martyring the more godly of their own contemporaries. Oh, strange traditional blindness of every previous age; yet it would surprise me if this age is any better than the others. But do not shut your doors on this last one who comes to defend the character and teachings of his forefathers; for the most truthful Prophet who ever was, said that he who accepts a prophet in the name of a prophet shall receive the reward of a prophet.

No prophet has ever striven on behalf of truth more than this one shall strive, according to his ability and his advantages, and he takes pride somewhat in the latter also, because of his link with the source from whence his elder brothers drew the sweet streams which made their vineyards fruitful and green, and which shall yet adorn the tops of the mountains of Wales until they blossom down to the bottom of the vales like the garden of paradise and drip honeycombs from each flower to all who accept him for their use.

His testimony is not to be refused as heresy just because Tradition and all her servants, Prejudice and her thousand tongues declare that it is to be so; for this is exactly what they said concerning his brothers before, yea, concerning every one of this godly family, as it is written, "Blessed are ye when men shall say all manner of evil against you and persecute you, for so persecuted they the prophets before you."

Nothing has to be true just because the majority says it is; if that were the case, it was not true that the earth was turning in the time of Galileo, the philosopher, for he was the only one in his day who believed that it was turning. And despite all his greatness and wisdom, Prejudice threw him into prison for saying that. The truthfulness of your PROPHET shall depend not upon the witness of Prejudice, but shall venture forth amongst you as an enemy to her and all her seed, and on the authority of his mission and the strength of his great bow and his own godly shield shall attack her castles, and pursue all her giants into the land of oblivion, setting the prisoners free.

GREETING OF THE *PROPHET*.

I AM written about in the roll call of the books, and in the fulness of times I visit you. My mission—oh, wonder of wonders—is good news. It is a mission of peace that I offer to every Welshman who will hear me. Something new and strange has been wrought on the earth in these latter days!—something very few of you have understood yet, because it has not been put before you, although it is the greatest wonder of the age; it is an object that will cause astonishment to the world and will be a subject of rejoicing to the family of heaven and all the inhabitants of the earth; yea, temporal and spiritual happiness and the eternal glory of all members of the human race which are now, or are yet to be born, are inextricably connected with finding knowledge of its teachings, believing them and obeying them. My mission is more valuable than the pearls of Ceylon or the gold of India and all the treasures of the earth. In a word, the Universe and all its fulness are but foolishness in comparison to it. It is not to be had from princes or kings of the earth; it does not exist in the palaces for the great people; it is useless to penetrate into the depths of the libraries of the theologians to search for it, for it is not there. The ignorant wisdom of the philosophers, soothsayers and wise men of the world can understand nothing concerning it, nor discover its pedigree or its abode. Its ways, to all human wisdom, how untraceable they are! Thanks be to its Author for hiding from the wise and great men and revealing once again to the poor things of the world, the art of arts and the generating cause of every good effect. The Almighty has revealed to our earth the great axis upon which turn all the moral wheels of heaven and earth that have ever been, that are now, and that shall come.

It is true that many of the wise, gifted and perceptive men have brought out many good inventions, fine artifices and almost miraculous machines in this enlightened age so that the world today quickly enjoys the effects of their penetrating minds, their profound achievements, their untiring study; but when the greater effects of the object to which I refer are enjoyed, all the philosophers of Greece and Rome, the theologians of the age, and the wise men of the world should throw away all their excellencies as useless things at its feet, so great shall they prize it.

Great are the commotion, the stir and the agitation which our world is thrown into at times, when the astronomers say that they have seen through their great telescopes now and then some planet jumping from darkness to be hurtled through the starry worlds in their high orbits until one might think that they could see the family of the firmament dancing with joy, keeping holiday with the harp and dance, in welcoming the coming of their sister to add to their innumerable host. But the light of all the planets shall hide in the planetary depths under the eternal *eclipse*, like things of the past, before the divine fervor of the glorious, shining world which I intend to show as it shines in its resplendence and essential glory. By now I think I can prophesy that there is a desire in the mind of the reader to ask, "What is this new and remarkable light?" I answer that it is a pearl, yea, the pearl of pearls, the pearl that raised those who possessed it from the depths of poverty and greatest distress to the fulness and the greatest wealth. It is a noble lady who took some of the darkest prisons and placed them in the finest palaces that the world possessed; she saved some from the flooding streams of the drowning element as thousands sank around them into the depths of eternity! She embraced others in the flames, carrying them lovingly at her breast without singeing the hair of their heads. In a word, she does every good deed to all who receive her, and those who love her need lack for no heavenly or earthly goodness. And is this pearl not above price? Who would not wish to have it, yea, even if it cost all they possess? I should like to hear of everyone earnestly seeking after it; that would show a brave and inquiring spirit. But I sense that the formal beliefs of Tradition are so strong and the bonds of Prejudice so firm about the souls of hosts of people, even in Wales, that they lock up their minds like a kernel in a shell; they do not believe that it is possible for them to have such things in this age. There is an old saying that it is easy to get a man to believe what he wants to, but it does not hold true in this matter. This news is too good to be true in the views of some, and that is because their teachers have no knowledge of it, because they know not the way to reach it. Since it is your benefit, readers, that is in view, would it not be better sooner rather than later for you to enjoy the things of which you have been deprived? But although this news is so beneficial and reasonable, I do not doubt that there will be varied opinions of it, as of every other new and good thing. It will appear incredible and erroneous to some, true and constant to others; unnecessary in the view of one, essential in the view of another. One will say, "It is all evil deceit," and another will say, "It is the best news we have ever heard." There is nothing about which there are more different opinions at first sight than these things; nor is there anything, I dare say, that will give greater contentment to all who come to a knowledge of their authenticity. They will be sought after at the cost of every other thing when their value is understood; and after once possessing them properly, one's life would be given as a voluntary sacrifice for them, so greatly would they be loved; and if I could describe one thousandth part of their worth, it would not be too much for kings to give their crowns, nor emperors their thrones for them. Oh, dear reader, are you now ready to hear what they are and to be fair with yourself by searching into them as for hidden treasures? If so, gather your wandering thoughts, quiet every traditional passion, and I shall say what they are. After that gather together your strongest reasons to gainsay them, if you can, on grounds of reason or scripture. Do not wonder at her. She is a regal lady from above, wondrously beautiful and of royal blood and divine pedigree—this is she; and MORMONISM she is called, in disrespect, by all her ignorant enemies. And there is no one who maligns her except those who know her not. MORMONISM, as she is called, even though she is so badly spoken of, brings in her hand the keys of heaven, the ladder of old father Jacob, the staff of God (that which was given to Moses), the foresight of prophets, the shield of Paul, the sword of Peter, the helm of salvation, the eternal gospel from the bosom of God to our earth, by his sending some of the heavenly family to us. Fear not, reader; it is true enough that pure angels from the third heaven landed on our earth in the nineteenth century; and this is their mission—to restore this valuable mission to us. This is the good news to which we refer, and who shall not rejoice in it? Now I have said it, and you know what it is; do not reject my testimony, for it is true, and time shall bear it out. Now let this important testimony be weighed in the proper scales, that is *logic* and *scripture*; for I am certain that it will hold the weight according to my promise. I admit that to say that such messengers visit our earth in this age is an unpopular statement—that it is contrary to the beliefs of the country and considered unscriptural by the general commentaries; but that of necessity does not prove it so; and only to hold it up in the face of the proper and scriptural mirror, all the brass doors of tradition are opened, the iron-like chains of prejudice are broken like threads of wool; it shall disperse the thick, black darkness until it shines supreme in the midst of his firmament; it shall break the rock-like hardness of the Pharisaic hearts of this age until streams of joy and knowledge flow into those who are honest in heart. Only to have a fair chance, it will drive away before it the opposing mountains like chaff before the hurricane; yea, it shall march in an abundance of divine strength, trampling down everything that stands in opposition like the fine dust of the scales. And concerning this subject, here in the book of books appears its pedigree, here shine its small pearls, speckling the pages like *diamonds* amidst the stones of the seashore. If one does not believe, after scrutinizing the divine words in the book of God, that angels are to visit our earth as late as these days, it is vain for such a person to spend words in maintaining his belief in anything it says; on the other hand, if the truthfulness of the holy book is acknowledged, I am certain to prove this statement through more than two or three, yea, through more than ten witnesses.

ANGELIC MINISTRY IS LOGICAL.

It is completely illogical to deny angelic ministry nowadays, while admitting that it was reasonable for angels to come to men in former times, such as to the patriarchs and the prophets—to eat and drink with Abraham, Lot, the wife of Manoah, &c., without proving that a gulf has been formed, so that they cannot come, or some other proofs in this matter. I have yet to see one of those who deny this truth offer any proof or justification, except that they are not necessary; and since they do not come to them, they cannot come to anyone else; and they cry, "Deceivers," "false prophets," "poo poo!" This is the only voice of Tradition, like the hunter's horn—always the same *tune*, until all the hunting dogs have learned it; or like the story of the parrot—what he hears everyone saying, he says too. It is admitted also that an angel came to Zacharias, Mary, and many other servants of God, in former times. Who but an angel gave John the message to go out and baptize? and why can an angel not do the same thing in this age? They admit that those who professed this at that time were truthful and godly people, and their profession of this quite reasonable, with no case for anyone to say otherwise; but this is the question, why can it not be as reasonable for the same thing to occur in our day? Does time change the logical truth of one age into blasphemous heresy in another age? Oh no, logic is the same in every age; but there are some who prefer practical tradition to human logic. How unreasonable to condemn and kill the Latter-day Saints because they receive heavenly visitors; and in the same instant to adorn the graves of saints of former days, who were killed for the same thing! but, they say, they were telling the truth, but you do not receive visitations as they did. Well, how can this be proven? the assertion is not sufficient to withstand the reasonable testimony of hundreds. Besides, did not the contemporaries of the early saints say the same thing? They were the deceivers at that time, each in his lifetime; and the others who had died ages ago were the truthful ones, although they professed the same thing! And who condemns us more for professing angelic ministry, than those who a few years ago believed and professed the same thing, yes, and even prayed publicly for it? It is only a few years since hundreds said they heard heavenly choirs singing hallelujah in the sky, above their meetings, from Beddgelert to the ends of the principality; and I do not doubt that the same story would be believed if it were told on Bala *Green*; but let no one *else* dare profess such a thing. I have heard preachers asserting from the pulpits to hundreds, that angels bring blessings from heaven now, and associate with the occasional old lady in her cottage, &c.; but, if others profess the same thing, woe betide them: "all deceit," they say, And when they are asked how profession of the thing can be deceit in the one case, without being so in the other, "Oh, we do not think (they say) that we see angels with our physical eyes, rather it is some mysterious apparition," like the "still, small voice:" and is this not folly of the most foolish kind, indeed, a contradiction? Who ever saw an angel, and yet did not see it? And how could anyone see an angel except with his eyes? This is how saints saw them in former times; they would look into their eyes, speak to them, eat at the same table, walk hand-in-hand with them, and sometimes struggle with them until they had proof of their strength. There is a race now living which testifies to the truth of this, since they will not eat "the thigh joint" in memory of the injury sustained by their father in his struggle with an angel; and although others did not see them at the time, that does not prove that they were not there, but rather that angelic ministry is a gift of God; and if they were not there, how could they see them? If they did not see them, they were deceivers for asserting that! Oh no, it was not some *witchcraft* that the early saints practiced, any more than we do; it was angels they saw when they said they did, that is persons from other worlds, of various degrees; and the reason others did not see them was that the veil had not been lifted from their eyes through receiving that gift; and that, perhaps, because they were not as godly as the others, or because the particular angel's message was not for them personally. It is questionable whether any angel would dare reveal himself to anyone without permission; and even then, it is doubtful whether he would be allowed to appear to anyone except the one he is sent to, because "they are dutiful *servants*." They are subject to laws in their circles, and they do not come on paltry, unnecessary errands, to satisfy the eyes or the whims of men. It is seen that it is a contradiction for one to see an angel, and yet not see him, but to see him mysteriously without his physical eyes.

It is illogical to deny angelic ministry in this age; and those who deny it show themselves to be evil men, for they admit that those who were guilty of the same denial were evil men in every previous age. I do not suppose that the Saints ever professed to have seen an angel without receiving the same condemnation; and the greater the zeal for the religion of the fathers, the longer the faces, the more frequent the synagogue meetings, the longer the false prayers, and the harsher the verdict always. What gave rise to greater wrath among the false prophets and the false teachers against the patriarchs, the prophets, and the saints in every age, than this? The enemies regard this as a blasphemy against their God, and an insult to the religion of their fathers; it is easier for them to swallow a camel than to believe this, and there was nothing to be done but kill them if they would not be silent about their angels, their revelations, and indeed everything they themselves did not possess. If they would join with them in "denying its power," they would happily walk hand-in-hand with them; but, "we cannot but speak the things we have seen, and heard and felt" is the defense of God's missionaries in every age, even if speaking them should cost them their lives. So it was with Zacharias; he was killed in the temple. It was the angels' message to the shepherds which aroused Herod's jealousy, prompting the cruel killing of hundreds of innocent babies. When Stephen said that he had seen Jesus Christ sitting on his Father's right hand, stones were showered on his head. The religious men of the time listened to Paul tell his story quite happily, until he said he had seen an angel, and that was enough; that was the end of his life as far as they were concerned; they swore they would eat no food until he was killed. The multitudes listened quite happily to Christ until he performed a miracle, or referred to his being sent from another world; and as soon as the words came from his pure lips, everyone had a stone in his hand. Had they been asked if they believed the prophets, they would have said they were willing to die in defense of their godly fathers; and when this generation is asked, were they not evil men, despite their great profession of faith? Oh yes, they say, worse than their fathers. For what? Was it not for disbelieving their godly contemporaries, and persecuting them? Well, dear reader, beware lest "thou be the man" who "fills the measure of thy fathers" in this age; if it be so, "how shalt thou escape the judgment of hell?" Although there are so many examples in the scriptures that prove how unreasonable it is to persecute for this thing, yet so do the children after their fathers, and their children's children after them. "Oh that they were wise, that they understood this!"

It is illogical for those who profess to be children of God in one age, to deny the ministering of God's angels to his children in another age, and to profess that he is unchanging! He is no respecter of persons, but in every age the righteous are acceptable to him; for logic tells us that such an assertion is a contradiction, and as impossible as it would be for an earthly father who had a number of sons serving him here and there throughout the world, to visit or send messengers to the one and never to send word or message to the others who served him just the same. Such a father would be a respecter of persons in everyone's view; so then must be the other, if he does not send his angels with the message to the younger brothers in this age, as he did to their older brothers in former times. This is the language of reason. But, they say, by now, if we were as godly as our older brothers, we too would have the company of angels as did they. And indeed, we must admit this now or get into worse confusion: if this is admitted, it would be the end of the argument, by recognizing that angelic ministry is logical in this age; for it was the logic of the matter that was in question, not the fact.

Enough has been said for now to prove that it is not the *logic*, but the *tradition* of the age which denies the coming of angels in our time: and logic in every way, if given a fair chance, proves the consistency of the statement; and every logical thinker will believe consistent testimony about the coming of an angel to our earth, now as before, and will act accordingly.

Next, we shall weigh this statement on the scriptural scales: if it is found wanting there, beware—we do not wish anyone to believe it; but, on the other hand, if the weight bears up in this correct scales, I am confident that everyone will be pleased to believe and accept it.

PRESENT-DAY MINISTERING OF ANGELS IS SCRIPTURAL.

THE FIRST witness to prove that an angel was to come to our earth, as late as this age, was John. When he was on the isle of Patmos, "on the Lord's day," and "in the Spirit," about the year A.D. 96, "the Lord showed unto him the things that should be *thereafter*." And the most notable thing was the strange "beast" which was to rise up, and "war against the saints, until he *overcame* them," by killing them. Then the kingdom of God, namely the apostolic church, would go to the wilderness for a time, and times, and half a time, in which season God would not authorize servants to do work for him. Even though there might be in the world a certain number of good, gifted, moral, God-fearing men who would worship him the best they could, and acceptably in his eyes according to the light they had received, this does not prove that even the best of them would be servants sent from God, which they could not be unless they were sent by God; "for no man taketh this honor unto himself, but he that is called of God, as was Aaron," namely, through some kind of revelation. Paul agrees with this—"How shall they preach, except they be sent?"—that is, by God, of course. And since God did not send a message to our ancestors before they died, they are not under condemnation as if they had refused a message from God through his messengers.

And after the whole world has been in the confused and divided situation described by John, for that space of time, it is shown to him (in Rev. xiv, 6) that God would send an angel to restore that which had been lost, namely the right or effective authority to preach the eternal gospel—not a new gospel, but a new dispensation to preach the old gospel, which is the laws of the kingdom of God. In this way would they receive the authority, not only to restore and to administer the ordinances of his house, but to authorize others to do likewise. The necessity for this must be recognized, in order for the great work of the latter days to be fulfilled. It must also be recognized that it is impossible even for the Almighty himself, and I say this with the greatest respect, ever to send a servant to do anything for him, without revealing this to him in one way or another. He had several ways of sending servants, from the beginning of the world; through his own voice, by sending his Son, or through his angels. He has the right to choose his own way, and his own time; and although his ways do not always please men, he will act according to his own counsel and purpose though all the people of the world oppose him. It was through sending an angel that John says this great work would start; and since all the theologians and wise men of earlier times, for centuries, from what we hear of them, deny that an angel came on such a mission to them, it is useless for us, or any of their successors, to claim otherwise. Let us await, then, the fulfillment of this valuable prophecy, and let us be prepared to receive it. We know that there are many different opinions among men about this remarkable prophecy, as about almost every other one. Some say it refers to the Bible Society; others, as appropriately, that it is to the Missionary Society, or the *air balloons*, &c. It would take too long to trace men's fertile imaginations on this subject; and since everyone follows his own commentator, I shall follow John himself. An *angel* is what John says; and to say anything different is, according to my interpretation, "to add to the words of the book of this prophecy." There is solid evidence of the state of deterioration the world would be in up until this time, in the fact of an angel coming from heaven on such a mission; and either the necessity for it must be recognized or else the angel comes on an unnecessary errand. If the ones who dwelt on the earth had either the pure gospel, or the right to minister it, then it would be unnecessary for an angel to bring them from heaven something they already possessed. Each is free to choose the explanation he wishes.

Something else that is obvious in this prophecy is the time this angel would come. The same message informs us—"For the hour of his judgment is come," that is, after the eternal gospel this angel presented to men was preached "unto them that dwell on the earth; and to every nation, and kindred, and tongue, and people:" not after some other doctrines were preached to the whole world, but *this gospel* brought by this angel at this time. Ver. 8 also proves that it would be accomplished as late as our time, since the next angel says, "Babylon is fallen, is fallen, that great city." Every Protestant we have seen agrees that this is the "mother whore of all the earth," as she is called; and everyone knows that she has not yet fallen, but is gathering strength as if she were going to live for eternity; but there was not much time between the coming of the angel mentioned with the eternal gospel and the fall of Babylon—only enough time for the inhabitants of the earth to hear, to understand, to believe, and to obey the message, not from the mouth of the angel, but from the mouths of men; for it has been God's custom to "put this treasure (the gospel) in earthen vessels," in every previous age. This is John's testimony about the coming of an angel in the latter times. If no other witness were available, this statement weighs fully on the scriptural scales, as well as the logical one. But in order to give a clearer explanation of the matter, see Matt. xxiv, 31, "And he shall send his angels with a great sound of a trumpet, and they [the angels] shall gather together his elect, from the four winds." "His elect," I venture to say, are the wandering Jews; and I shall prove this later.

"To gather them together." To which place, I wonder, except to the land that God vowed through an oath to give to their fathers. Not to the sky—not to another planet—not to any earth other than this one; for it is here that the "Son of Man," their Messiah, will come to be King over them forever. He will come on the clouds of heaven, and all his saints with him. Neither he nor they will remain on the clouds of heaven, but those will be their chariots to come "to reign with him on the EARTH," "for a thousand years." This is the testimony of the Son of God himself on the subject, and it is stated more clearly in verse 14—"And THIS gospel of the kingdom SHALL BE PREACHED [this could not be done without divine authority, which could not be obtained without revelation through an angel, or in some manner] in all the whole world, FOR A WITNESS, and then shall the *end* come." This is further proof that he does not refer here to the dispensation he gave to the apostles, for it was not *for a witness at the end* that they preached it, and there could be no consistency in that for some 1800 years, since the end has not come yet; for it is of the end of this deformed and sinful world that he speaks, and that in response to a question from his disciples seen in ver. 3. Nor is ver. 34 any obstacle to this; if it is thought to be, ver. 33 removes it instantly, with one word, "when ye shall see these things," that is, you who will be living in that age in which they take place—when *ye shall see* them, your age shall not pass until all these things be fulfilled. But, to be brief, let us compare these two reliable witnesses with each other. "And this gospel," says Christ; "the eternal gospel," says John. "Shall be preached," says Christ, i.e., I shall give the right through revelation to do that; "And I saw an angel," says John. "To preach," "*for a witness*, and then shall the end come," says the one; "the hour of his judgment is come," says the other. It can be seen that the two agree word for word, to prove that there are promises in the book of God about the coming of angels as late as our time. If anyone has any further objection to that, let it be between him and the Bible; I have proved it there, as I promised; and if it were not for fear of being too lengthy, I would bring several other witnesses to prove the same thing. But for the time being, let us proceed to look into the same accurate mirror in order to see what kind of persons the angels are. Since so much mention is made of them, if we can only get to know them better, and understand their nature, their composition, and their work, perhaps that will be a means of eliminating some of the opposition created by prejudice against them, and making men willing for angels to come into our midst from time to time, to deliver their message, and return in peace. Or else, let us take warning from what happened in the days of Lot; for "the same way also that it was in the days of Lot, so shall it be in the day when the Son of man is revealed." No doubt poor Lot committed unpardonable sin in the eyes of the Sodomites, by mentioning that angels were coming to the earth; but if the profession of such a thing made them act cruelly towards him, they became even worse when their eyes forced them to believe in angelic ministry. They tried to destroy them! Strange, is it not, that they did not believe after seeing? Not so strange, either, when we consider that the eyes are not the best guides to find God; rather faith, from reliable testimony, is the means which He provided. "PREACHING Christ crucified" was the apostolic way, and not proclaiming themselves great miraculous doctors to the world.

ANGELIC BEINGS AND THEIR INFLUENCES.

FROM what we understand from the Scriptures, there are three, if not more, types of angels. 1. The archangels Paul and Judas speak of, namely the highest in authority and the strongest in power. 2. The angels, or those early saints who were resurrected, and consequently are corporeal beings, or like Enoch or Elijah, were translated. There is mention in Gen. xviii of angels eating and drinking with Abraham and Lot; and they did not just pretend to eat, otherwise where did the calf, the cakes, and the milk go? 3. The angels which are called "ministering spirits;" and if one were to search carefully, perhaps it could be proven that this third category of spiritual beings comprises two groups in the heavenly realms. The Psalmist says that God created man "a little lower than the angels:" let this be linked with what Paul says in the proper translation—"Who maketh [or sendeth] his ministering spirits, his angels [messengers], *a* flame, or *in* flames of fire." Such would make up the fourth class of angels. There is further proof that one class of angels eats, from what Paul says—"Be not forgetful to entertain strangers, for thereby have some entertained angels unawares." It is said also in the Psalms, that man eats the bread of *angels*. The risen Christ ate bread, and fish roasted on a fire he himself had lit on the seashore. If he had not flesh and bones, why did he say to Thomas, "Reach hither thy hand, and thrust it into my side, and thy finger into the print of the nails," &c.? What is clearer in the Bible, than that the angelic beings have flesh and bones, eat and drink like men, and with men; and if *here*, then why not at home?—although we cannot describe their food there. The saying "Flesh and blood cannot inherit the kingdom of God," does not contradict this; for there is a big difference between saying "flesh and *blood*," and saying "flesh and *bones*:" and it is this difference that confuses the minds of many. And however small one thinks the difference between them is, it is as great as between Christ resurrected and Christ before he died, yes, as much as there will be between "this mortal" and "immortality." And since such persons exist, why would it be illogical for them to associate with men now as before?

From these examples, and others that could be noted, it is seen that there are resurrected angelic beings—that it is they who come on errands from God to man, and spirits ministering to spirits. John fell at the feet of one angel, about to worship him, but the angel told him, "See thou do it not; I am thy FELLOW-SERVANT, and of thy brethren that have the testimony of Jesus. Worship God; for the testimony of Jesus is the spirit of prophecy." One might think from these words, especially the English version of them—"*One of thy brethren the prophets*," that this angel could be godly old Daniel, or one of the prophets who was resurrected with Christ.

Satan says that the angels are the guardians of the saints; and even he would not dare lie to the Son of God. He says—"He shall give his angels charge over thee, lest at any time thou dash thy foot against a stone." It seems to me, from detailed searches of the Scriptures, that the angels, when God has saints on earth who are worthy of it, stay on earth with them, to protect them from harm, if they recognize and listen to their voice. There are several witnesses that prove this, such as Isaiah, Abraham, &c., as well as the enemies of the Lord, such as Hagar, Balaam, and others, who bear witness to this. We can see that they recognize the authority and the offices of angels on the earth to a great extent. But, of all the mysteries pertaining to angels, I think that their influence on men, without their seeing them or hearing them, is the most incomprehensible mystery in the opinion of this age. Some deny this, because they cannot comprehend it; and there is another group of men who go to the opposite extreme of inconsistency, saying that some things are "mysteries to be believed, but not to be comprehended"—that it is presumptuous of men to look into them, or to express their opinion on them; and it is too great a task for me to show which of the two groups is the more illogical. But I know of nothing that God has ever revealed, that he does not wish men to understand. What other purpose did he have in revealing it? No heavenly or earthly creature can arrive at more knowledge on the right path than God, who is the source of light and knowledge, wishes him to have; "Who will have all men come unto the knowledge of the truth;" yes, step by step, "until (man) be filled with all the fulness of God."

But to return. How do angels have such a mysterious influence on the minds of men? This is the question of many who already understand the profound mysteries of the philosophy, *astrology*, and *philology* of this age, to a large extent. Their ignorance of this proves that proper research is unknown to them.

To shed light on this I refer first to the ladder that Jacob saw, with one end placed on the earth, the other end reaching to the heavens, and the angels of God descending and ascending along it. Also the dream of Pharaoh, and Joseph's interpretation of it. How could he be sure of his interpretation unless there was some association between Pharaoh's angel and Joseph's angel? Also, the dream of Nebuchadnezzar about the great idol gone from his mind by the time he awoke. Through that mysterious association between their angels, Daniel was able to bring to light not only the idol, but also its interpretation. Daniel says—"There is a God in heaven that revealeth secrets," not by coming from heaven to reveal the dream and its interpretation, but by sending his angels, "his ministering spirits," to explain the mystery to them. We find that the wise men from the east "were warned of God in a dream that they should not return to Herod." And after they had gone away, "behold, the angel of the Lord appeared to Joseph in a dream." These examples are sufficient to prove that spirit ministers to spirit, and so we dream revelations because good or bad angels reveal to our spirits what to dream; and this is one way which heaven and its hosts have to mingle with the inhabitants of the earth!

"Some men's sins are open beforehand," before they themselves go before the Judge, "going before to judgment:" because they did not receive forgiveness for them before they died; "and some men they follow after." "Likewise also the good works of some are manifest beforehand; and they that are otherwise cannot be hid." It is obvious that this is done because spirits from God report all we do. "There are three that bear record in heaven, the Father, the Word and the Holy Ghost; and these three are one." "And there are three that bear record in earth, the Spirit, and the water, and the blood; and these three agree in one." No wonder, then, that the sins of some go before them to judgment—that we must give an account in the judgment "for every act which we do in the flesh, whether it be good or bad;" for it all amounts to this:—Our blood, which is our life—our spirit, which is immortal—and the water, in which we are baptized "for the remission of sins," all testify to God of our acts in the flesh, and "the angels of our presence" are the messengers who testify that to him; and we are rewarded, or punished, accordingly. The sins of the ungodly follow after them before the judgment; and since their "summer is ended, and the harvest of their souls is past," they receive "for every transgression full payment."

The angels come in and through the authority of God, as is obvious in the account of Jacob wrestling with God. "And when Jacob was left alone, there wrestled a *man* with him until the breaking of the day;" but when he prevailed not, he inquired "the name of the *man*;" so he called "the name of the place Peniel, the face of God." This is also confirmed by the coming of "the Captain of the Lord's host" to Joshua, and his revealing to him precisely the way to take Jericho, its fate, and everything it was essential for him to know in order to fulfill the work of the Lord. To prove this even more clearly, read the testimony of John on the isle of Patmos—"The revelation of Jesus Christ, which God gave unto HIM [Jesus Christ], to shew unto his servants things which must shortly come to pass; and he *sent* and signified it by HIS ANGEL, unto his servant John." This has now been clearly enough proven; but perhaps it will be said that there are some who do not dream at all, and others who have bad dreams. We can acknowledge that also as being consistent with what has been said. There are some men who do not believe in God, angels or spirits. Others believe the one thing and the other, but do not behave according to their belief. There are evil and good spirits that deal with man's spirit asleep and awake, and that influence him to the extent that he allows them; but they have no power over him, except through persuasion. They are completely opposite to each other in their effects, with the exception of times when the evil one assumes the form of an "angel of light." With regard to man's ability to withstand them, before they get too strong of hold on him, the Apostle says, "Try the spirits whether they are of *God*." "Resist the devil and he will flee from you." Let everyone do thus, so as not to sadden the spirit of God.

PRESENT-DAY MINISTERING OF ANGELS.

HAVING proved in such detail, in the previous treatise, the existence, offices, and influences of angels and spirits on men, let us proceed to refer the reader to some promises given to us by God, through his servants, that such ministerings would be received, through such beings, yes, even "in these latter days." Read Acts ii, 17, 18. Even though it is so clearly stated here, nearly everyone explains that this refers to the day of Pentecost; yes, even though Peter says the opposite—even though God says that it is "*in the last days*;" and so says Joel ii, 28—"and it shall come to pass *after* THAT." Read the previous verses, and it will be seen that the prophet is referring to the great work that would be done on earth (ver. 21), when the children of Zion would rejoice (ver. 23). After restoring to the Jews the possession of their country (ver. 27)—when Christ would reign in the midst of Israel temporally and spiritually, *after their* LAST *restoration* from their *last* dispersal, which would be because they "refused to listen to the voice of the Holy One of Israel," which is proved in these words—"And my people shall NEVER be ashamed." After that, Joel says, the above prophecy will be fulfilled; and if only he will look at the words, no logical person can think that they were fulfilled at that time; "for in mount Zion and in Jerusalem shall be DELIVERANCE, as the Lord hath said" (ver. 32). What DELIVERANCE was there at that time? Was it not the complete opposite of *deliverance* that there was then, and up to now? "Behold, I leave your house desolate," says Christ. It was a scattering at that time; it will be a *deliverance* at that time to which Joel, Peter, and God refer; namely, "In the last days"—"Before the great and the terrible day of the Lord come" (ver. 31)—"I will pour out my Spirit upon all flesh, and your sons and your daughters shall prophesy, your old men shall dream dreams, your young men shall see visions," &c.

The angels are the instruments God uses to *gather* his elect to those places which he has prepared for them for their deliverance, when the "vials" of his wrath shall be poured onto the ungodly, before he comes to reign on the earth with his saints for a thousand years. The angels are the soldiers of heaven, to report the things which men do, and which God chooses for them to do; it is they who will *gather* his wheat into his storehouse, before he burns "the chaff with unquenchable fire." And this will be done by influencing them in the manner stated, namely through giving to them revelations, the spirit of prophecy, &c. It is these who bottle "the prayers of the saints" in "golden vials" and take them before the throne! By now, it can be seen that angelic ministry is not only as logical and scriptural in this age as in any previous age, but is more necessary, because of the greater work God will do on earth. Oh, how useful they are! How merciful is gracious God to send them "in this dispensation of the fulness of times," in which "HE WILL GATHER TOGETHER in one all things in Jesus Christ." Let us thank him for such heavenly blessings. Let no one be found in this age "filling up the measure of their fathers," yes, those fathers whom they condemned for refusing these things in earlier times. And should not the testimony of those who are alive now, yes, hundreds of the elect of the earth, who know in fact that pure angels have come to our earth in this age, have some effect in persuading men to believe this? They cannot all have been deceived in what their eyes saw, their ears heard, their hands felt, and which they know for themselves. If we have been deceived in *this*, our reason, our ears and our eyes have been deceived. And if this is deception now, it would be the same as claiming that the whole story about such strange things as happened in the earlier times was deception; and I am prepared to be deceived to believe the scriptures, as were the saints in former times; and the more the better of such deceit. Thus shall we be deceived into their company in the end, and that is my wish. We cannot deceive others in this; for if they obey the same heavenly order, it will prove itself to be true to all who are honest in their principles, in every corner of the earth; indeed, it has already, and is doing so to hundreds now in Wales, by conferring heavenly blessings and spiritual gifts on them; not so that they might believe, but, as before, *after* they have believed and obeyed, to strengthen, sanctify, and perfect them. And whoever experiences the principles of "Mormonism," as it is called, "shall know of the doctrine, whether it be of God, or whether I speak of myself." It will prove itself to be divine truth, "eternal gospel," "the power of God unto salvation;" and this is why I said that it cannot deceive anybody. Do not fear it, reader; prove it; and I guarantee that, if your purpose is honest, you will never regret it. Having prepared the way, by removing the previous obstacles, I think you are anxious to ask, To whom did that angel appear? I in turn ask, does the truth of the story depend on the character of the person to whom he appeared? If so, if I said he appeared to Mohammed, the whole Christian world would reject him. If it were to the Pope of Rome, would the Protestants believe that? Or, if the angel had come with this message to one of the most prominent, godly men of the highest character, who leads some sect now, perhaps that party would believe; but I have no doubt that all the others would reject him and his testimony as deception, and they would say all manner of evil about his character and that of his followers. That would cause such animosity and jealousy towards them that they would kill them, if they could. If they were asked why they do that, their answer would be, "They deserve to die; they deceive the minds of the weak, and they as good as say that no one is right but they; we cannot bear for anyone to insult in any way the religions given to us by our godly fathers, who died in godliness believing them!" Could not the children of all fathers in every age and country defend their religions as appropriately as this? We have heard as good a reason as that from the Hindus for worshipping Juggernaut! "Oh no," they say, "it is the religion of the Bible that we have; not idolatry." But there is a great difference between *professing* and *believing* the religion of the Bible, for the religion of the Bible is *angelic ministry* in every age of the world. In fact, neither the accuracy nor the usefulness of this phenomenon depends very much on the character given by popular opinion to the person who had the great honor of witnessing it; for it is God who chooses his instruments, and it was the lowliest of the earth that he chose in former times, "that the excellency of the power may be of God, and not of men." The glory of his name and the good of mankind are his purpose.

Since I have been acquainted for years with that person who had the sublime honor of being an instrument in God's hand, to establish his kingdom on earth in these latter days; having heard the story from his own lips; having seen his conduct and his behavior; having associated with him in private and in public, and with his family members on their peaceful hearth; having been at his side in the midst of riotous mobs of cruel enemies who sought his life, because of this testimony; having been with him in jail for the forty-seventh time he was imprisoned for his beliefs; having heard his testimony in the depths of the prison, behind the strong doors, where he was thrown on the accusation of treason against the government for preaching from Dan. ii, 44. Since, as I say, I know that he, without *judge* or *jury*, sealed with his blood the testimony about an angel bringing this message to him: since I heard this from his lips in his last hour, how can I doubt it? Hundreds of cruel men, most of them drunk, came having blackened their faces before rushing on him, and killed him and his brother there, without one examination of his case according to the law of the land. Hundreds of bullets were shot at them through the windows and the door. Four went through him, and the same number through his brother; and I know that they died as martyrs, completely innocent of all the accusations against them that are spread the length and breadth of the world. If persecution, killing, and spinning lies in every age are the work of the devil and his instruments, against what sort of men will they fight? "If a kingdom be divided against itself, it cannot stand." So says every reasonable man. Since I have had all these advantages, and understand the importance of this thing to a great extent, is it not a sin for me not to open the eyes of my compatriots to these new, strange, divine, and beneficial truths? I shall give, then, a brief summary this time, and at greater length next time, of the manner, the way and the time Joseph Smith received this great honor. Do not wonder, reader; for that is his name: or, "old Joe Smith, the false prophet, the evil, presumptuous, foolish, crafty cheat," &c., &c., as he is called by the enemies of truth and the numerous family of prejudice. The less well they know him, the greater their animosity toward him; and indeed, I was much the same, until I was forced to believe, through careful research and association with him, that he was not the evil man I had imagined him to be. And I am answerable for the truth of the following story, even if all the theologians and wise men of Wales should speak against it. I challenge the whole age to gainsay my witness, according to the scriptures and the laws of common testimony.

EARLY HISTORY OF JOSEPH SMITH.

JOSEPH SMITH was born in the town of Sharon, Windsor County, state of Vermont, in the United States of America, on the 23rd of December, 1805. When he was ten years old, his parents with their family moved to Palmyra, in the state of New York. They resided in this county about eleven years; the latter part of the time in the town of Manchester. They were farmers by occupation. Joseph's advantages, and consequently his knowledge of the different branches of learning, were exceedingly small, amounting only to being able to read, write, and do a little arithmetic. Between the ages of fourteen and fifteen, he began to seriously reflect upon the necessity of preparing for his future state of existence; but how to do so was a question as yet undetermined to his satisfaction in his own mind. It seemed to him to be a question of infinite importance, insofar as the salvation of his soul depended upon a correct understanding of it. If he could not find the right way to it, then he saw that it would be impossible for him to walk in it, except by chance—venturing toward the just Judge, and resting all he had on chance. This was something that he was unwilling to do. If he inquired with the various religious denominations, each would refer him to their own particular tenets, saying, "This is the way, walk in it." He discovered they had many things which were in direct opposition to one another. It seemed reasonable to him that God would organize only one way to be saved; and consequently, he could not believe that of all the different churches in the world any but *one* was the true church of God, and that one would have to be built on the same foundation, believe the same doctrine, practice the same ordinances, be bound in the same Spirit, and bring forth the same fruit as the early church, before God would approve it in this age. And since he could not rely on such changing and different foundations for eternal life, he determined to search the scriptures carefully and without bias. He continued in this manner for a period of time, believing what he read. In the midst of the various wonderful truths which studded its pages, and delighted his heart, hardly one caught his attention more than the following:—"If any of you lack wisdom, let him ask God who giveth to all men liberally and upbraideth not, and it shall be given to him." It is difficult to describe what joy this valuable promise caused him, when he saw that it was the privilege of all men to ask, yes, and with the certainty of receiving from God the knowledge that was so essential in order to walk uprightly in the way of truth, and put an end to the difficult argument which was in his thoughts. This was like a light shining forth in a dark place, to guide him to the path he wished to tread; and consequently, he decided to retire to a secret place in the woods, a little way from his father's house, to pray to God to fulfill this valuable promise, and show him which of all the denominations was the church of Jesus Christ. After kneeling there, and beginning the important task of calling on the Lord with all his heart, he was tempted (apparently) by the powers of darkness, in many ways, to think that his prayer was not being heard, and that such a thing is not to be had now; but he continued more and more fervently to seek for deliverance, until the darkness began to disperse from his mind, and he was able to pray as if in the strength of the Spirit, and in unwavering faith. While continuing to pour out his soul to God in this way for an answer to his prayer, he soon saw a light shining wondrously in the sky above him; he strove even more to pray, and the light was descending gradually towards him, and as it drew near, it increased in brilliance and magnitude so that, by the time it reached the tops of the trees, the wood seemed to be illuminated in a brilliant and glorious manner around him. At first he expected to see the boughs and the leaves being scorched around him. But since it did not have that effect on them, he was encouraged to be able to withstand the brilliance. It continued thus to descend slowly, until it reached the earth, and he was enveloped in the midst of it. When it first came upon him, it produced strange sensations throughout his whole system, and immediately his mind was caught away from the objects with which he was surrounded, as in a heavenly vision. He saw two glorious personages, who resembled each other in their features or likeness. They told him his sins were forgiven. He was informed upon the matters about which he was inquiring, and which had caused him such mental anguish—that all the religious denominations in the country believed imperfect doctrines, to a greater or a lesser degree, and that consequently God did not acknowledge any of them as his church; even though many of them were zealous, conscientious, God-fearing men, fleeing evil, and worshipping him according to the light which they had. He was commanded not to join any of them. He received a promise that the true doctrine—the fulness of the gospel, should, at some future time, be restored to him; and after these things, the vision disappeared, leaving his mind overflowing with indescribable peace and joy. Some time after having received these divine manifestations, his mind was overtaken somewhat by the desires of youth, of which he afterwards sincerely repented before God.

REVELATION OF THE GOLD PLATES.

On the 21st of September, 1823, it pleased the merciful and gracious God not only to hear, but also to answer the prayers of Joseph Smith. Having retired to rest, as usual, his mind was set in fervent prayer, and the earnest desire of his soul was to have the fellowship of some divine messenger who would announce to him his acceptance with God, and unfold to him the principles of the religion of Christ, according to the promise he had received in the former vision. While he persisted thus before the throne of God, endeavoring to exercise faith in the promises which were so sweet to his soul, on a sudden a light like that of day, only of a purer and far more glorious appearance and brightness, burst into the room. The first sight was as if the house were filled with consuming fire! Such a sudden appearance of a light so bright occasioned a shock to his whole body; but it was soon followed by such joy and rapture that he desired with all his heart to associate with the cause of it. Thereupon, a glorious personage appeared before him. And notwithstanding the brightness of the light which filled the room, some divine rays of an even more intense and glorious light again surrounded this personage! Though his countenance was as lightning, yet love and innocence were so clearly marked on it that every fear was banished from the mind, and the soul was pervaded by its image. His stature was a little above the common size of men in this age: his garment was as white as snow, and had the appearance of being without any manner of seam. This luminous being spoke to him, saying he was an angel of God, sent forth by commandment to communicate to him that his sins were forgiven, that his prayers were heard, and also to bring him the good tidings of great joy; namely, that the time was at hand for the Lord to fulfill the covenant which he had made with ancient Israel, concerning their posterity;—that the great, wondrous, and strange work God had promised to fulfill on the earth, as a preparation for the second coming of the Messiah, was about to commence; and also, that the time was at hand for the gospel to be preached in its fulness to all the nations, that a people might be prepared in holiness and faith to be worthy of enjoying his glorious resting place, in his victorious reign on the new and restored earth.

He was also informed that he was chosen and called, to be an instrument in God's hand to bring forth the wondrous work of this glorious dispensation. It was made manifest to him that the "American Indians" were a remnant of Israel; that when they first came to the continent they were a people of beautiful and pleasant aspect, possessing a knowledge of the only true God, enjoying his favor, and receiving peculiar blessings from his hand; that the prophets and inspired writers among them had written an account of the most remarkable of God's dispensations to them, from age to age, for many generations, until they were overcome by the judgments of God for their wickedness, and the greatest part of them were destroyed; but that the records which contained their history (through the commandment of God to one of their last prophets) had been hidden, to protect them from the wicked men who sought to destroy them. He said these records contained many divine revelations, pertaining to the gospel of the kingdom; as well as prophecies about the remarkable, glorious and dreadful things which would be fulfilled in the last days. And it was so that God could fulfill his promises to his ancients who wrote the records, and accomplish his purpose in their restitution, &c., that these records were to be brought forth. If he were faithful, he would have the privilege of being an instrument in bringing these holy mysteries to the light. He gave him a solemn warning to remember always to do everything for the glory of God. These records would not be entrusted to anyone who sought his own aggrandizement, glory and benefit through them. After advising him to live righteously, to be of upright principle in the service of God, and showing him many things past and to come, too numerous to mention here, the angel departed, and the light and glory of God withdrew with him, leaving Joseph's mind calm and joyous, to ponder the things he had heard and seen. But before morning, the vision was twice repeated, instructing him further and in greater detail concerning the great and wondrous work God was about to perform on earth.

In the morning, he went out to his work as usual; but soon the vision was repeated once again, and the angel appeared before him; and having been informed by the previous visions concerning the place where the records were hidden, he was commanded to go there forthwith to view them. Immediately, leaving his tasks, he went to the place where he was instructed.

I shall give a brief description of that place where the records lay, in the words of a gentleman by the name of Oliver Cowdery, who subsequently visited the spot. "On the east side of the common road which leads from the town of Palmyra, Wayne County, to Candandaigua, Ontario County, in the state of New York (U.S.A.), about four miles before reaching the little town of Manchester, there is a large hill—I say large, because it is as large as, if not larger than, any in those environs." After giving a detailed description of the hill, he adds—"It was near the top of it, on the east side, that the [aforementioned] records were found. When I visited the spot in 1830, there were several trees growing there, enough to provide shade from the heat of summer, but not so numerous as to prevent grass from growing. How deep in the earth the records were hidden it is difficult to say; but from the fact that they had been some fourteen hundred years lying there, on the side of a hill so steep, it could be imagined that they were several feet below the surface when they were put there, since it is natural for the surface to wear away, more or less, in that length of time; although it would not wear as much near the summit as lower down, perhaps. In this place a hole had been dug. A stone with a smooth upper surface filled the bottom; around its edges was a sort of *cement* in which were placed erect four thin stones along the outer edges of the lower stone. All of them when placed like this formed a box, and the corners were filled carefully with *cement* so that the moisture from without was prevented from entering. The inner surfaces of the other stones were also smooth. This box was sufficiently large to admit a breastplate, such as was used by the ancients to protect the chest from the arrows of the enemies. From the bottom of the box, resting on the breastplate, arose three pillars composed of the same *cement* as was in the sides. Upon these three pillars lay the records. This box was covered with another stone, the bottom surface being flat and the upper crowning. When Mr. Smith visited the place on the morning of the 22nd of September, 1823, the upper surface of the stone was visible, but its sides were concealed by soil and grass; so it is evident that, although it is not known how deep they were hidden in the first place, the time had been sufficient for the earth to be worn away from them and bring them into view. When once directed, it was easy for him to find them, although they were not so remarkable as to draw the attention of anyone passing by. After reaching the spot with some effort, he lifted the uppermost stone and, to his great surprise, his eyes beheld the wondrous contents of the box. As he gazed upon this sacred treasure, marveling and pondering upon what he had previously heard from the angel, behold, the angel of the Lord, who had appeared to him before, stood before him, and his soul was filled with rejoicing as it was the evening before, and he was filled with the Holy Spirit, and the glory of the Lord shone around him, and rested upon him. When he was in this blessed state, gazing at the glorious scene before him, the angel said to him, "Look!" and as the angel spoke, he beheld the prince of darkness surrounded by his innumerable host. After these had passed from his sight, the angel spoke further, saying, "All this was shown to you—the good and the evil, the holy and the impure, the glory of God and the power of darkness—that you may know the two powers, and not be overcome by evil. Behold, whatsoever enticeth and leadeth to good and to do good is of God, and whatsoever doth not is of that wicked one: it is he that filleth the hearts of men with evil, to walk in darkness and blaspheme God; you see from henceforth that his ways are to destruction, but the ways of holiness are peace and rest. You cannot at this time obtain these records, for the commandment of God is strict concerning them. Thou must see them before obtaining them, through sincere prayer and faithfulness in keeping the commandments of the Lord. They are not deposited here for the sake of profiting from them, nor for self-glory; but they were sealed by the prayer of faith, because of the knowledge they contain; and they are of no worth to anyone, except for the knowledge they contain. They will reveal the fulness of the gospel of Jesus Christ, as it was given to his people who formerly lived on this land."

[*To be continued.*]

FULFILLMENT OF A PROPHECY.

SINCE there has been so much shouting for a *sign* in these days, although we no more than our elder brothers profess to give a sign of ourselves to anyone, we hope that everyone will be satisfied with the remarkable sign that was given by the angel; and here it is—"When they begin to hear that God has shown you these things, the workers of iniquity will seek your overthrow; they will proclaim and publish stories and lying accusations about you to destroy your reputation, and also will seek to take your life without cause, and as a result they will persecute those who believe in the same organization. The discovery of the records shall cause those pure of heart to rejoice and the wicked and jealous to rage; with the one it shall be had in honor and respect, and with the other in reproach and contempt." A clear enough sign for anyone, is it not? It shows the character of every man according to his actions. What man with his eyes open can doubt the truth of this clear prophecy, published to the world before its fulfillment? If there is such a one to be had, let him believe his own ears testifying the literal fulfillment of it, when they are filled to overflowing with the lying, foolish and unfounded stories that he may hear, not only from the pulpits, but from there to the ends of the country. And if he does not believe his ears, he may believe his own eyes, we hope, when he reads the false accusations, contrary assertions, and concocted lies that were published, and that are now published from time to time, in the publications of those who "profess the truth." Amongst others, not the least are the *Star of Gomer*, the *Times*, the *Baptist*, the *Educator*, &c. Due to the multifarious testimony of these enemies, one must admit the divinity of the above prophecy. If this plan were not from God, I do not think that wicked men would take so much trouble to distort it and to make so many men of straw so different from one another, calling them all *Mormonism*, for the sake of the pleasure that they have in plaguing and mocking their own work. It is sad to say, indeed, that such people have polluted even the Welsh press, staining its fine vestment, and that through it they have filled high positions in the hosts of hell in order to fulfill the above prophecy, and to place obstructions in the way of their compatriots who are searching for the truth, so that they can bind them, poor things, tighter to their prejudiced beliefs and keep them in darkness. But lest there be any disbeliever in the country who still doubts the fulfillment of this clear prophecy, we refer him to issues of the *True Baptist* for the last two or three years, and I venture to say if he is satisfied with *facts*, he shall there have a sufficiency in order to remove every jot of doubt concerning the truth of that which the angel prophesied. But lest anyone think that we are without feeling and ungrateful for the least good deed that may be done for us, we thank those people very greatly; yea, they are worthy of the consideration of all lovers of the truth, for their hard work and their faithfulness, for spending so much money and taking so much trouble in such good work as to set the people straight, for showing publicly, and admitting so sincerely who they are; "for by their fruits shall ye know them." And it is pleasant to say that their diligence has already been crowned with success until complete satisfaction, I think, is given to everyone who is satisfied with facts concerning the divinity of the above prophecy and of our religion, as well as of many of the prophecies of Christ such as, "Blessed are ye when men shall say all manner of evil against you;" "Ye are not of the world, therefore the world hateth you," &c. And have they not labored hard to fulfill the scripture that says, "All who live justly in Christ shall suffer persecution." And anyone who is not satisfied with their former efforts to fulfill the above prophecy, shall have to be dissatisfied; for it is sad that these "workers of iniquity" shall destroy their characters, and trouble their minds any longer; and in thinking that success in their work costs them their immortal souls, it would be tragic to try to get them to kick against the divine pricks and the work of God; for, though Christ has said, "It must needs be that offenses come," he says also, "woe unto those through whom they come." And who would not pity these persecutors in the face of what follows—"It were better for him that a millstone were hanged about his neck, and that he were drowned in the depth of the sea, than he should offend one of these little ones." They are poor wretches, the children of darkness; it is sad that they have chosen the ways of Balaam, the son of Bosor, who preferred the reward of injustice. "O that they were wise, that they understood this, that they would consider their latter end." The many proofs which they have already given of the divinity of Mormonism (since the word of people like these about it is praise for it) are too good to be lost; and since one cannot expect their bitter source to continue spewing out such floods any longer, we shall give to the readers through the mouth of the PROPHET a taste of them now and again, arranged so that they might understand their composition and their effects on the intellect. And the first one to be brought before the judgment seat is the professed general of the army. Since his bravery and diligence in this army are far beyond that of many of his friends, he should be first. When he fought on the other side of the fence, he changed his name as often as the *chameleon* changes its color. But by now his face is like flint. Since judgment concerning bad deeds is not effected soon, his heart has grown bold in doing evil. But the old saying is true that "Murder will out;" so he at last signs himself "W. R. Davies" from Dowlais, in the March issue of the *Baptist*, substantiating the stories of which we now have testimonies in our possession; these shall come out in their time in order to prove those of Davies completely false, although he has published them before under various pen names. He fears that someone has forgotten them by now and brings them out a second time in sweet tidbits. I suppose that he could not *manufacture* new lies that were as terrible, but he had to have something to say. But thanks to him, he has come into the trap now; he shall be placed under the *spectacles* of the PROPHET from time to time. It will not be so easy to shut the mouth of a Prophet as it was to shut the mouth of the press from defending us. It will be seen now who has the truth.

We do not wish to squabble with corrupt men like these, since preaching Christ crucified is our work, although that to these men is a stumbling block and foolishness. Like their brothers formerly, they seek a sign and human wisdom. But after being silent for years, we owe it to the public to defend the truth now, so that their evil may be exposed to everyone who loves the truth. We did not intend the following things to be published to the world any more than the hundreds of other blessings that are enjoyed in our midst; for we do not expect those who deny the scriptures so arrogantly to believe such things. But the foolishness and enmity of Satan and his tools become obvious in their work, in their publishing, and in their so terrible distortion. The defense of the truth shows forth their lies and the great deeds of God. Men find it difficult to believe, of those who profess to be children of God, without mentioning their claim to be shepherds of the flock of gentle Jesus, that anyone in Wales could be so wicked, so cruel, so unprincipled and lying as to weave such a web of false accusations about others, so foolish as what follows because of a difference of opinion concerning religion. It is important to accuse such people of being guilty of fabricating known lies with the purpose of deceiving, and of satisfying their evil passions; but they have published them in the face of light, knowledge, judgment and Judge, and every other thing that should fill them with horror and fright in thinking about such work. Their consciences must have been seared with a hot iron when they published such things in the face of scores and hundreds of witnesses who know that they are lies. And anyone who doubts the corrupt depths of humanity may have sufficient proof of that to his sorrow and surprise by reading the *Baptist* for the month of March, page 111, as follows:—

A MIRACLE! A MIRACLE! AT LAST!

I confess that we have never before seen a treatise half as large as this published, especially in a periodical that professes to be religious, but not more than one statement of it was truth, in some corner or another. If anyone else has seen such a thing, we would like to know about it; but from our part we think, no matter how much "*Quick in Water,*" its author, mocks the miracles of God, this treatise is a miracle of his own! His wrath must have been full and overflowing before he started, because not even the first word is true. "The SATANISTS professed," says he. And who are these "Satanists" in his opinion? Do not be angry with him, dear reader, for those whom he calls "Satanists" are none other than the Saints of the Almighty God. And worse still, it is a man who professes to be a minister of the gospel with the Baptists who has called us by this name! Let even Dowlais be ashamed in seeing a man who professes to be a servant of God climbing into their pulpits, and in a foolish and blasphemous "fair," teaching his fellow travelers towards wise judgment "not to call" those who worship the God of heaven and believe in Christ according to the scriptures "Saints, rather call them (says he) Latter-day

Satanists." Oh, humanity, what shame on you! His name—no need to ask; who does not know that it is the Rev. W. R. Davies who is the father of this name? Does not his "speech condemn him?" Let him deny it if he can; or then let him be ashamed. "*Satanists*," is it, sir? He kills two birds, besides himself, with this one stone. He fulfills the prophecy of the angel fully, and he proves true the old saying, "A thief calls thief first." Satan shouts Satanists first; and the most impudent servants of Beelzebub shout Beelzebub first, even at the Son of God himself. We do not place that name on him, but "his own mouth condemneth him." "The SATANISTS professed many of their miracles," says this "Quick in Water." Well, count, reader, here is the first lie in this terrible heap. The Saints have never professed that they have done miracles up to now. "And they *deceived* a lot of people." This is the second lie, without offering any proof of it. "Oh, unlearned little men, without any religion, without anything good," says he. This is the third already. "They sought to charm a nasty little group of the dregs of Merthyr to follow them." If this is true, we take pride in it, for it proves our similarity to our brothers, saints of the former days. The hypocrites and deists of that age said about them also that they were the "filth of the world and the offscouring of all things." Yet again he says, "They carried on their deceit quite well until the praiseworthy apostle came." This is the fourth lie, because up to now not one *apostle* has come into their midst, and there is not and never has been anyone claiming to have the office of this name in their midst in Wales. This also is one of the bugaboos of Mr. Davies of Dowlais; and it is a surprise how he mocks it after making it! It is a pity that this man did not know now that principled and reasonable men ignore him and despise him and his lies; and so then, be quiet, for shame! "Here to be strengthened in the faith and to sell a sort of *pamphlet*, the most foolish that has ever been seen, beneath the notice of every man in his senses," says he. His work in taking so much notice of it proves him out of his senses then, according to his own admission. But hear more of his wisdom,—"This was published by some little creature." Who would not be proud of being reviled by Mr. Davies? "This treatise asserts the ability of the Satanists to work miracles." This is at least the fifth lie. I wonder whether he knows the difference between God and man. "To speak with the fairies, &c." That is the sixth. Are there not thousands of our treatises throughout Wales now showing to everyone who reads them the presumption of this reverend gentleman asserting such things? What will he not say? Who can believe such a man as this? No one who loves the truth, I believe! It is futile to attempt to notice all his foolish and erroneous assertions now. But let us compare his story of the misfortune that befell a man by the name of William Hughes, Collier's Row, with a testimony of the man himself, and others who saw what happened.

QUICK IN WATER says: "He is one of the Satanists. He broke a LITTLE bone in his leg at work. Dr. Davies was sent to him, and he put it back in its place and bound it up, &c. Then he was followed in a visit by the praiseworthy apostle and a large group of the Satanists with him, and they pulled the *bandage* free, and the apostle set his hand on the place pretending to pray." This is not only the seventh and the eighth, but quite a blasphemy also. "And the Satanists assert, in the strongest way possible, that they saw the swelling die down and disappear under his hand, &c." His is a confession as strong as the testimony of eyewitnesses that the swelling died down, is it not!! Who knew better than they whether what they said was true or not when their eyes testified to that? What reason would they have to assert that, had it not been so? Who would believe them when they saw differently, were it not the truth? Behold the prejudice and illogic of this slanderer, denying without any foundation, while he admits that the testimony of a "group" of eyewitnesses proves the healing a fact. Oh, foolishness! "These things [says he] were proclaimed throughout the whole area." Yes, by a host of our enemies, and hardly any two of them gave the same account. Would they have done all this if there were not something to it? And who was distorting and condemning but those who professed to believe the Bible, a book that is full of such happenings. But here is the strongest admission of the truth of the matter by the storyteller himself:—"He said in leaving the man that he should come to the prayer meeting the following day to show himself, that he had been completely healed." I do not claim that all this is true, but the teller of the tale proves too much against himself, to the point of showing that the man had been completely healed; otherwise, no one with his eyes open would tell him to come to the prayer meeting the following day over a mile away!! We thank him for this. And did the injured person himself and his brothers at his side not know better than a disbeliever from somewhere over in Dowlais? "The following day [says he] Dr. Davies called with the intention of seeing the man, and to his great surprise he found him far worse than expected with his leg swollen; and he was in great pain, &c." Now reader, count the lies if you can, for there is the same number of them as there are words in the assertion. There is not so much as one syllable of it true! But let us see even further—"The doctor failed to understand how things could be like this; but to his surprise in looking at the leg, he saw that some fool had opened the bandage that he had placed about it the previous day, and this had caused everything that was noted; and after questioning, the sufferer admitted everything, and the silly wretch is not healed to this day." Here is more counting work, and every word of his assertions adds one more lie to the shameful list, as is seen through reading the testimonies of unbiased and truthful eyewitnesses. Let us compare the one with the other, and then let the reader form his own opinion concerning this slander as he wishes. And if he does not admit the wondrous fulfillment of the prophecy of the angel previously noted, the divinity of Mormonism, he shall have more proofs of that in the next issue.

Behold a copy of the letter that was sent to the Editors of the *Baptist*, but which they refused to print:—

"*To the Editors of the* BAPTIST.

"Sirs:—Since you have published in the March issue of the *Baptist* the correspondence of some man who calls himself 'Quick in Water,' concerning the misfortune that befell a man by the name of William Hughes, Collier's Row, when, as your writer says, 'he broke a *little* bone in his leg,' and since he has deceived you and the public for giving a distortion of that circumstance, we would beg you to be fair with your publication and its readers by also providing space in one of your next issues for the following testimonies given by eyewitnesses of the happening.

"Here first is the *testimony of William Hughes himself* :—

"'On Saturday, January the 18th, a great weight fell on me in the Cyfarthfa coal mine; and after I was freed from underneath it by others, it was found that two bones of my left leg had been broken in the fall. I was taken to my house, and Dr. Allday (who works for the mine), came and put them in their place with splints, &c., around it, and went away leaving me in very great pain. In the evening one of the elders of the Church of which I am a member, came and anointed my leg with holy oil, and placed hands on me and prayed for the Lord to take away the pain, &c. And I testify, in words of soberness, that I had complete relief from my pain immediately and continued without pain. The afternoon of the following Tuesday, another Elder, Capt. Jones, came by himself to visit me; then various of my neighbors, who disbelieved our faith, came in. At my wish he administered this ordinance to me according to the scriptures, i.e.,—" Is any sick among you? Let him call for the elders of the Church; and let them anoint him with oil in the name of the Lord: And the prayer of faith shall save the sick," &c. And I testify sincerely before God and men, that I immediately, yes, when his hands were still on me, received great healing from the Lord, and not from man; I pulled away the splints and everything, and within five minutes I jumped from the bed to the floor in the sight of all, praising God for his goodness. Some of our enemies were listening in the next room, and when they heard our joy, they came in and believed that I was healed through the power of God. And no matter how strange it may seem, it is true enough that the other leg is painful when I walk, and the broken leg without pain. I walked about within three days. The following Thursday Capt. Jones came to visit me again, since he was starting out to the north. The following day (Friday) I saw Dr. Davies coming to the house, and in great haste I bound the splints in their place and lay on the bed lest he should find fault with me. After looking at my leg he said that he was greatly surprised that the swelling had gone down and that it was getting better so well. He said also that it had been broken on the ankle in addition to two bones in the shin; and if it continued to improve so well, I could get up soon. After he went away, I threw the splint away and got up from bed. On the fifth day the doctor came again, but he did not see me because I had gone away from home. I used a stick for some days in going about, not because of the weakness of my leg, but because of the weakness of my faith, which was clearly proved by my leaving it at home without any inconvenience. I failed to find work; and since we are poor people, my wife went against my will to the *relieving officer* for help. In the meantime there was no small commotion throughout the neighborhood, and many unfounded stories were spread concerning the matter on the wings of the wind; some asserting that the bones had not been broken; others testifying that they had seen them and felt them broken; some asserted that I had not gotten better, but worse, and that the doctors wanted to cut my leg off, &c.: and perhaps it was on some of these bases that your reporter wrote his account. As an example of the lies that were told concerning me, the following shall suffice:—A man came to a neighbor's house within forty yards of my house, and started his story concerning this matter; that what had been said about the healing of the injured person was a lie, that he had seen the injured person himself today—that he was on his back in his bed worse by far, and that the doctors were about to amputate his leg, &c. My wife was there at the time listening, although he did not know; and since she had seen me return to my house from work already, she came to fetch me to confront him; but that man understood immediately and went away as quickly as he could, and I after him.—I would not seek this favor from you if it were not that you have provided space to that distorted correspondence; and I can have dozens of true witnesses to prove the above story true.

William X Hughes, Hannah X Hughes.
Hugh X Jones,

"'We testify that the above story is true, to the utmost of our knowledge. We know that William Hughes's leg was broken; we also heard the doctor say on the spot that the two bones were broken completely; and although we do not profess or believe in the faith of the Latter-day Saints, yet what we felt with our hands and saw with our eyes, we testify to it to give truth a fair chance.

Thomas X Dafydd, Richard X Hugh,
James X Harris, William X Davies.

"'I also testify that William Hughes broke his leg, because of what I felt and saw I testify unto my friends.

Edw. T. Edwards, David X Jenkins,
David X Vaughan, Catherine X Thomas.

VERSES OF GREETING.

There is a race of rascals——passionate
For disputations;
Others like witches, far worse thing,
Pre-judge us in their pleading.
They glory in being arid——in harrying,
In obstructing the valid!
It's their disgrace they cannot win
Their war against our doctrine.
Let all their stalwarts come with plans——bitterly,
To beat the Mormons:
To injure, yet to no effect,
Our faith stands firm and perfect.
Their failure strives in fury——but flounders;
In a feeble hurry!
We raise the cross in our age
And win——we have the advantage!

RHYDYBONT : PRINTED BY JOHN JONES.

PROPHET OF THE JUBILEE.

"THE KINGDOM HAS COME."

No. 2.] AUGUST, 1846. [Vol. I.

WHAT IS "MORMONISM?"

This question is so oft repeated that we do not have time to answer everyone who asks it; and yet, we desire for everyone throughout the world, but especially in Wales, to know *what Mormonism is*; and since the purpose of this publication is to explain the excellence of this glorious plan, this Prophet can answer for himself, and set the following things before his readers:—

"My descent is from the tribe of Joseph, who was sold to the Egyptians. My fathers came out of Jerusalem in the time of king Zedekiah, about six hundred years before its destruction, and the enslavement of its inhabitants by Shalmaneser: they brought the five books of Moses, and Elijah's prophecy with them. After traveling in the wilderness for a year-and-a-half, as they were led by the Lord their God, they landed on a continent [now called America]; and as it was a fine and excellent land in which to dwell, they began to work it, and settle in it, according to the commandment of the Lord their God; and while they were faithful, keeping the Lord's commandments, and listening to the voice of his prophets who were in their midst, they prospered, increasing greatly; and when they transgressed against his commandments, he sent judgments upon them. At some times they rose against each other, killing throngs of each other; at other times God raised up prophets to teach them, and they thrived. They lived thus for hundreds of years, keeping from age to age the history of the most ancient things of God's dispensation to them, until they went into great decline, about four hundred years after the birth of Christ. And I, Mormon, was the last prophet who was in their midst, and they sought to take my life too; but I hid from them, and made an abridgement of the history of my ancestors from the plates I received from my father, and inscribed it on gold plates, according to God's instruction to my fathers; and after finishing I gave them to my son Moroni to hide at the top of a high mountain, until the prophecies about my brethren were fulfilled, as God revealed that they would go into complete decline, until they lost all knowledge of their ancestors, and receive twofold from the Lord's hand for their sins; and God revealed that he would visit them again in mercy in his own good time, and he made a promise to me, and to my fathers, that he would reveal this book to the Gentiles, and from them to the rest of my people in the latter days, and this when he was about to restore them to possession of the country, in order to civilize and settle them in this land which God had promised to my fathers; and let my brethren know for certain that when God reveals these oracles to men, he is extending his hand a second time to gather the remnant of his people from the four corners of the earth, the Jews to the land of Canaan, and the remnant of Israel on this continent. That he is at that time, by revealing these things, beginning to fulfill his promise to our father Abraham. This is the banner which he will raise to the Gentiles from afar; at this time will he begin to build Zion in the latter days, by restoring the fulness of the eternal gospel to men. Therefore, let those who will be living on earth when these things are made known, know that the Lord began it, and he will finish it; yes, even though all the kings of the earth rise against him. The Lord swore in an oath to our fathers that he would not turn away his hand until it was finished. And to Moses he says of Israel, Though you be pushed to the ends of heaven, the Lord your God will gather you from there; he will make with the house of Jacob a new covenant in the latter days, and will set his fear in their hearts, that they may not retreat from him ever more and for eternity; and he will be their king for ever, and his sanctuary shall be among them for ever. Blessed will be those who are alive when the Lord begins this work, if they obey him, but woe unto those who rebel against him."

This is a little of the history of the prophet Mormon, and his testimony; and thousands of men alive now, testify that he speaks the truth, that God has revealed the said oracles in this age, that he has begun this great work by giving the dispensation of the fulness of times to men, in which he gathers all things in Christ Jesus; that he has established his kingdom through divine power once again, according to the plan of his Son; and sent servants to invite all who will come to the wedding feast of the Lamb, for he is now preparing his bride for his coming, through her obedience first to the following conditions:

I. That there is but one true gospel or plan revealed under heaven among men, whereby a sinner may be reconciled with God, sanctified, and prepared to have a part in the "adoption, that is the redemption of the body," to enjoy the company of the firstborn, and all the saints perfected; when they will reign with their Lord for a thousand years, and thereafter may dwell eternally in the presence of Him who is a consuming fire, and eternal burning of all imperfections. That this plan is perfect, like its Author, conceived in the divine council before the world existed, that it is like its Author unchangeable, functioning according to that design in all its parts, and its movements bearing the same fruits, or answering such purposes in every age in the world, in which it has been, is, or will be. That Jesus Christ, who is the true Son of God, was born of woman, and satisfied divine justice by offering himself on the cross as a blameless offering acceptable to God, and rose from the grave, according to the scriptures, in the fulness of the times preordained in the early council, and thereby arranged or opened the way, and established that perfect plan, that he could not have established any other, without making one or the other superfluous, and therefore imperfect, and that this plan is to be believed and obeyed in all things, according to his design; that not one iota, not one assertion can be changed or rejected, nor anything eliminated from it, without its being imperfect, and thereby ineffective in bringing "life and immortality to light."

II. That this same perfect plan was revealed by the good Creator and Father of mankind, to his children in the beginning, by himself, by angels sent from him, through visions, the spirit of prophecy, and revelations in all manner of ways.

III. That this same perfect plan has been corrupted and perverted by men, in many ages of the world to such an extent that it became necessary for its author, the Creator and Sustainer of the world and its inhabitants, to restore it, through such means, and in the same manner as it was first established. Hence the necessity for the several dispensations given to the world, in different ages, as is proved in the holy book.

IV. That Jesus Christ, the Messiah, did after his resurrection appear, and minister to the Jews in Palestine, to the tribe of Joseph in America, to the remnant of Israel in the north country, to the spirits in prison, who had died previously without being offered this plan, 1 Peter iii, 19, 20; iv, 6. "Other sheep I have, which are not of this fold, which must hear my voice." Not the Gentiles, for they did not hear his voice; they did not call anyone but the seed of Abraham *sheep*; the others were *dogs*. And that he established this perfect and glorious plan in those parts of the world.

V. That the Gentiles were partakers of this plan, some years after Christ rose on high, not by his personal ministry, but through his servants, and by the Holy Ghost, which revealed to them his truth, his resurrection, and his elevation to the right hand of the Almighty as Prince and Savior.

VI. That that perfect plan has been changed and corrupted by men to such an extent, for hundreds of years, that it is no longer to be found in its power, its purity, and its essential glory among Jews, Gentiles, or Israelites; and this is the cause of all the different divisions and sects that overwhelm the world because men are seeking to rediscover that plan; and, having failed, they make ones of their own as similar to it as they can, and give it that name, denying its essential power, according to the prophecies about the latter days.

VII. That this same perfect plan has again been restored to the earth, and established in this age, in the same manner, and by the same means, as in every previous dispensation; viz, by the voice of God in heaven, by angelic ministry, visions, and revelations from the Lord. This is a new dispensation, not a new plan, but a complete restoration of the original plan, namely the one which was purchased in the eternal council, which was established by the patriarchs, the prophets, by Christ, and the apostles, and this last time, that is the eleventh hour, to bring in "the latter-day glory," "the fulness of the Gentiles," "the restoration of Judah," and "the remnant of Israel," yes, that "the times of the restoration of all things" that God spoke through the lips of all his holy prophets ever might come, to prepare the way for the second coming of the Messiah to reign triumphantly over all his enemies in glory, for a thousand years. If this is the true religion, what important consequences follow its acceptance and its rejection!

FIRST PRINCIPLES OF CHRISTIANITY.

THE first principles in the fulness of the eternal gospel in this age, as in every previous age, are:—

Firstly,—To believe in Jesus Christ, as Savior and the atoning one, crucified and resurrected.

Secondly,—To repent of all their sins, and leave them, walking a new life, doing justice to all men, and serving God.

Thirdly (but not first or second),—To be buried in water and resurrected, by one of God's chosen servants, in the name of Jesus Christ, for the remission of sins. See Acts xi, 38, and xxii, 16; 1 Peter iii, 21, &c.

Fourthly,—To receive the Holy Ghost, through the laying on of hands by the elders of The Church of Jesus Christ of *Latter-day Saints.* See Acts viii, 17, 18, 20, and xix, 6; 1 Tim. iv, 14; 2 Tim. i, 6; Heb. vi, 1, 2.

Fifthly,—To believe in, and pray to enjoy the spiritual gifts, and the good blessings, that were enjoyed by those who obeyed this heavenly plan in former ages; such as, speaking wisdom—speaking knowledge—miraculous faith—the gift of healing, and being healed, through anointing with holy oil in the name of the Lord, the prayer of faith, and the laying on of hands. See James v, 14, 15; Mark xvi, 18. Also, to endeavor to gain the gift of prophecy, discerning of spirits, speaking with strange tongues, interpreting the same, receiving revelations from God, angelic ministry, the company of good spirits from the eternal world in visions, &c., and all other blessings that are promised in the scriptures to the children of God. See 1 Cor. xii, and xiv, 1, 5, 18, 39; Acts ii, 39, and xix, 6; Mark xvi, 17, 18; Eph. iv, 11—14, &c.

Sixthly,—All who profess this plan, should live in holiness and righteousness, praying with every prayer, as the Spirit lends them expression; do good to all, especially to the family of faith; pray for those who do them harm and persecute them; dissociate themselves from all the Babel-forms, and every form of unsound doctrine, remembering that such things corrupt good morals; come out of Babylon, do not partake of its sins, lest you receive its plagues.

And lastly,—Those who come into the bond of this new covenant, and the fulness of the gospel, should watch and pray, lest they fall into temptation, but be ready, waiting for the coming of the Son of Man; for he will come suddenly and immediately on the children of darkness, when they say, Peace, peace; when they, after all the warning, as in the days of Noah, are eating and drinking, marrying and giving in marriage, and casting the evil day far away from them; therefore, the Son of Man will come in such an hour as they think not.

This is the correct depiction of the evangelical plan according to the scriptures, and as the Latter-day Saints have it, and all that is contrary to this comes from evil; and if anyone should come to you, professing to be servants of God, without bringing this doctrine—yes, "though an angel from heaven preach any other gospel unto you than these things, let him be accursed." As John says, so say we—"If there come any unto you, and bring not this doctrine, receive him not into your house, neither bid him God speed: For he that biddeth him God speed is partaker of his evil deeds." We are frequently accused of preaching a new gospel, throwing these scriptures in our faces, yes, by some as conscientious as David was, when he gave the verdict on himself; and it was not more appropriate for Nathan to say to him, "Thou art the man," than it would be for us to say the same thing to these our accusers. And whosoever takes the trouble to compare our profession with the scriptures will see clearly that it is a completely false accusation, and that it is the eternal plan we have—that it is our accusers who are preaching new gospels, if in fact they are gospels. Dear Welshman, do not believe them, without looking for yourself; for some of these prefer to see you lose your life, than see the hope of their profit fading; and then they shout loudly, Away with these people, they speak against our "great goddess," whom our fathers have worshipped.

REVELATION OF THE GOLD PLATES.

[CONTINUED FROM PAGE 22.]

WHEN it shall be brought forth by the power of God, it shall be carried to the Gentiles, of whom many will receive it, and afterwards will the seed of Israel be brought into the fold of their Redeemer, by obeying it also. Those who kept the commandments of the Lord on this land desired this at his hand, and through the prayer of faith they obtained the promise that if their descendants should transgress and fall away, these records would be restored to their children. These things are sacred and must be kept so; for the promise of the Lord concerning them must be fulfilled. No man can obtain them if his heart is impure, because they contain that which is sacred. By them will the Lord work a great and marvelous work. The wisdom of the wise shall become as naught, and the understanding of the prudent shall be hid, because the power of God shall be displayed. Those who profess to know the truth, but walk in deceit, shall tremble with anger against him; but with signs and with wonders, with gifts of healing—the manifestations of the power of God, and with the Holy Ghost, shall the hearts of the faithful be comforted. You have now beheld the power of God manifested, and the power of Satan; you see that there is nothing desirable in the works of darkness; that they cannot bring happiness, that those who are overcome therewith are miserable; while, on the other hand, the righteous are blessed with a place in the kingdom of God, where joy unspeakable surrounds them. There they rest, beyond the power of the enemies of truth, and where no evil can disturb them. They are continually crowned with the glory of God, and they feast upon his goodness, and enjoy his smiles. Behold! notwithstanding you have seen this great manifestation of power, by which you may ever be able to detect the evil one, yet I give unto you another sign, and when it comes to pass then know that the Lord is God, and reigneth, and that he will fulfill his purposes, and that the knowledge which this record contains will go to every nation, kindred, tongue, and people under the whole heaven. This is the sign: when they begin to hear that God has revealed these things to you, the workers of iniquity will seek your overthrow. They will proclaim and circulate stories, and false accusations to destroy your reputation, and also will seek to take your life without cause; but remember this, if you are faithful, continuing to keep the commandments of the Lord hereafter, he will preserve you from their hands, and he will enable you to bring knowledge of these records to men; for in due time God will give you a commandment to come and receive them. When they are interpreted, the Lord will give the holy priesthood to some, and they shall begin to proclaim this gospel, baptizing by water for remission of sins, and after that they shall have the power to give the Holy Ghost by the laying on of hands. Then will persecution rage more and more; for the iniquities of evil men shall be revealed, and those who are not built upon the rock will seek to overthrow the church; but it will increase the more opposed, and spread farther and farther, increasing in knowledge till it shall be sanctified, and receive its inheritance when the glory of God will rest upon it. And when this takes place, and all things are prepared, the ten tribes of Israel will be revealed in the north country, whither they have been for a long season; and when this is fulfilled the saying of the prophet will be brought to pass,—'And the Redeemer shall come to Zion, and unto them that turn from transgression in Jacob, saith the Lord.' But, notwithstanding the workers of iniquity shall seek your destruction, the arm of the Lord will defend you, and will make you victorious over them all, to bring these things forth, if you keep all his commandments. Your name shall be known among the nations, for the work which the Lord will perform by your hands shall cause the righteous to rejoice, and the jealous to rage; with the one it shall be had in respect and honor, and with the other in reproach and contempt; yet with these it shall cause fear and terror, because of the great and marvelous work which shall follow the coming forth of this fulness of the gospel. Now, go thy way rejoicing; remember the great things the Lord hath done for thee. Be diligent in keeping his commandments, and he will deliver thee from temptations, the arts and devices of the wicked, until thy work is complete. Forget not to pray, that thy mind may become strong, that when he shall manifest unto thee thou mayest have power to escape the evil, and to obtain these precious records."

Many more instructions and pieces of information were given by the mouth of the angel to Mr. Smith, which are too lengthy to publish here. During the period of the four following years, he frequently received revelations from the mouths of heavenly messengers; and on the morning of the 22nd of September, 1827, the angel of the Lord delivered the records into his hands. And now, reader, what really makes these truths seem more unreasonable or incredible in our times, than it was for those heavenly messengers to do similar things to others in former times? I venture to say that no one who believes the one can produce an answer, nor offer an objection to the other, only the unfounded tales of tradition and prejudice. Yet, we do not ask anyone to depend entirely on the testimony of Joseph Smith for the truth of this, any more than we do; but hundreds of thousands are alive now in every corner of the earth, and hundreds now in Wales, who have received sufficient testimonies from God according to his promise, that it is true; and not only that, but every man of honest heart who obeys this eternal gospel, will receive testimonies also from the same source for himself. Is this not a valuable promise? Then prove it, and see that it is true.

DESCRIPTION OF THE PLATES.

HAVING proved in the previous issue of the PROPHET that angelic ministry, in these latter days, is logical, scriptural, and a genuine fact, we gave a little of the history of the visit of holy messengers to Mr. Joseph Smith in America, their message, the wonderful discovery of precious old records, and the way they were delivered into his hands; and as we promised we will give a description of them, how they were translated, the testimonies of those who saw them with their eyes, and felt them with their hands, and so knew the things of which they testified. We will also give a brief summary of the contents of these old, profitable, and glorious records. Our knowledge and experience of prejudice and its harmful effects, are sufficient to excuse us for warning the gentle reader not to judge the following story, according to the unfounded stories that have already filled the country almost to overflowing. And, for his own and the truth's sake, let him not weigh it either in the religious scales of the age. If angels had nothing to do with the discovery of the aforementioned records, no doubt the wise and great historians of the country would approve it as the most precious thing that has taken place on the continent since its original settlement; it would have a place next to the highest shelf in the libraries of the theologians, and it would be seen gilded, and in its proper place on the tables of the leaders of the world; yes, it would create a new era in the history of the world! What a great objection the family of man has to angels associating with them in our days! Where is the essential principle that was created in man to fit him to associate with his brothers above? Has it completely disappeared from the human race by now? Where is reason? Has tradition swallowed it entirely? Many other things were brought forth on the continent, and in other places, more incredible than the things under consideration; but the one is generally believed, and the others are denied in the face of incontrovertible and divine facts! We remember one remarkable occasion that came to our attention while we were there, as an example, to prove what has been said, and to show the irrationality and power of prejudice. On the 16th of April, 1843, a man by the name of Robert Wiley, a merchant in Kinderhook, Pike County, state of Illinois, dreamt that there were some treasures hidden in a hillock known to him in the neighborhood; and after digging for about thirteen feet from the surface, he found six brass plates, four inches long, an inch-and-three-quarters wide at one end, and two-and-three-quarter inches wide at the other end; four lists of letters *(hieroglyphics)* on each side of them. On one of the plates is the picture of three skulls, the largest in the middle, surrounded by rays similar to those one sees surrounding the head of our Savior in the pictures that are made of him now. Underneath the two smaller ones is the picture of two trees, and their branches; on one of the plates is the picture of a large head, and the picture of two hands pointing to it. We saw those plates, and the case was publicized through the newspapers, and I did not hear that anyone disbelieved it; but if the one who found them were to utter a word that angels had anything to do with the matter, we do not think that he would be believed about this, any more than Joseph Smith is believed that he received gold plates. Thus the prejudice is so strong against angels, that people would rather believe the testimony of this professed deist, than the other godly man. There is every sign that these plates had been hidden there for many an age, for trees two-and-a-half feet thick were growing on top of those artificial mounds. The wise men of the world have imagined a great deal about the origin of these mounds, and many other remains of the buildings of the ancients; but their history and their makers, and everything else that pertains to them, are entirely unknown to the world; only what is shown on the plates is revealed from time to time. And is not the discovery of the one that is generally accepted (and if anyone should doubt, he can see the picture of them here), an admission of the other? And is not the fact that this uneducated Joseph Smith has translated the one set of plates, while knowledge of the *hieroglyphics* has been lost to the world, almost since time immemorial, apart from a few letters, proof that he also translated correctly the others that were given to him through angelic ministry? No doubt these, in addition to the many others that could be noted, are incontrovertible facts in the eyes of every reasonable man.

But to return to the story about the gold plates, for such they appear to be. The *hieroglyphics* were engraved upon them, on each side. The size of the plates was seven to eight inches in length and width, and thinner than common *tin*, bound into a volume, with three rings running through holes at one edge of the whole. The volume was something near six inches in thickness, a part of which was sealed. The letters on the unsealed part were small and beautifully engraved. The whole book exhibited many marks of antiquity in its construction, as well as much skill in the art of engraving. With these records was found a curious instrument, called by the ancients the Urim and Thummim, which consisted of two transparent stones, clear as crystal, set in the two rims of a bow. This instrument was in use in ancient times by persons called "seers," and through it things past and future, far and near, were revealed to them.

PERSECUTION CONCERNING THE PLATES.

WHEN the inhabitants of that vicinity heard that Mr. Smith had seen heavenly visions, and that he had discovered those sacred records, they began to ridicule him and persecute him; even when he was taking the plates home, he was waylaid by two men who had secreted themselves for the purpose of robbing him of the records on his return; for there had been great excitement in those areas since the time he was informed that he would receive them, and everyone was in a state of anticipation or fear; one of the two struck Mr. Smith with a club before he perceived them; but being a very strong man and large in stature, with great exertion he cleared himself from them and ran towards home, being closely pursued until he came near his father's house, and having failed to get hold of him again, they fled, and for fear of being caught, they withdrew from the country licking their wounds, and no more was heard of them; but the wife of one of them, fifteen years later, happened to be in a company in England where everyone was doing his worst in telling stories about the saints, and she admitted that her husband was one of the two above, that he was never well after that, but died because of the thing, and that that was the reason she had left the country. But before these two men fled they spread the word that Mr. Smith had obtained the gold plates, and soon the news was broadcast through those parts, and they started inventing misrepresentations, and false accusations to slander his character, in accordance with what the angel had told him previously; and not only were all manner of tales about him flying as if upon the wings of the wind, but frequently a riotous mob of evil men attacked the house at night. Several times he was shot at and very narrowly escaped. Every device and evil plan they could invent was tried to get the plates away from him. And being continually in danger of his life from such a gang of cruel and abandoned wretches, he decided to leave the place and go to Pennsylvania; and accordingly he packed up the few goods he intended to take with him in a wagon, hiding the plates in a barrel of beans. He had not gone far before he was overtaken by a man who told him to stop, that he had a *warrant* to search his wagon, although he did not say for what; but Mr. Smith knew that his purpose was to obtain the plates; and after searching everywhere except where they were, he went away sadly disappointed. After he had driven on, another came in the same manner and with the same purpose, and after ransacking almost everything, he too went away equally chagrined because of his disappointment. After that Mr. Smith pursued his journey without any further molestation until he came into the northern part of Pennsylvania, near the Susquehanna river, where he had intended to go when he set off.

STORY OF THE TRANSLATION OF THE PLATES.

HAVING provided himself with a home, Joseph Smith commenced translating the records, with the help of God, and through the means of the Urim and Thummim.

Being a poor writer, he employed a scribe to write the translation as it came out of his mouth. In the meantime, a few of the original characters of the plates were accurately transcribed by Mr. Smith, which, with the translation, were taken by a gentleman by the name of Martin Harris to the city of New York, and which he presented to a learned linguist by the name of Dr. Anthon, who professed to be extensively acquainted with many languages, both ancient and modern. After examining them carefully for a while, he said he was unable to decipher them correctly, but he translated a few here and there, writing them down on paper; then he said that if the book were brought to him, he could assist in translating them. He questioned Mr. Harris about them, by whom and where they were found; he said they were very old *Egyptian hieroglyphics*, and that he knew of no one who could translate them more accurately than himself. He listened very intently to Mr. Harris telling the story, until he said that it was an angel who had given them to a young man of his acquaintance. The doctor leapt to his feet in rage when he heard about the angel. "Trickery, all trickery," he said; "talking about an angel now, indeed!—all lies—be off with you," he said; and shouting "Poo, poo!" he threw what he had translated into the back part of the fire; but Mr. Harris was agile enough to snatch them from there before they were destroyed; and despite all his prejudice, the whole thing was published in the newspapers there, together with the conversation the two of them had, and the doctor later admitted the truth of it. And whosoever believes the Bible will be completely satisfied by comparing these things with what is seen in Isaiah xxix, 11—"And the vision of all is become to you as the WORDS of a book that is sealed, which men deliver to one that is learned, saying, Read this, I pray thee; and he saith, I cannot, for it is sealed." Ver. 12—"And the BOOK is delivered to him that is not learned, saying, Read this, I pray thee: and he saith, I am not learned." Behold the literal fulfillment of a remarkable prophecy, over two thousand years after its proclamation, and three times as many miles away from the place where it was made! Is this not solid proof? It will be noticed that it was the WORDS of the book that were to be given to the learned one, yes, the words of that "sealed" book. But the BOOK itself would be given "to him that was not learned," namely Joseph Smith; and so it was done. Perhaps some of the "terrible ones" and the "scornful ones" of this age will wonder that we venture to prove the truth of the Book of Mormon through the scriptures, but they need to do so no longer; for if the Bible did not prove it true, it would not be believed by us any more than by them. Oh, yes; the prophets have spoken clearly about it in many an age, as well as the great and marvelous work God would do on the earth when he revealed the Book of Mormon to the world: see ver. 14 of the same chapter—"Therefore, behold, I will proceed to do a marvellous work among *this people*, even a *marvellous work* and a *wonder*: for the wisdom of their wise men shall perish, and the understanding of their prudent men shall be hid." In order to see when these things were to take place, follow that phrase "*this people*." See the previous verse—"Forasmuch as *this people* draw near me with their mouth, and with their lips do honor me, but have removed their heart far from me, and their fear toward me is taught by the precept of men." "*This people*" will be contemporary with the bringing forth of the "sealed book."

If the prophet were living in the nineteenth century, I wonder if he could have given a more detailed and skillful description of it than he gave here?

Some say that these things were accomplished in ancient times; but let them read it again, in order to better understand it, especially ver. 17—"Is it not yet a very little while [that is after beginning the great work, when the "sealed book" is revealed] and Lebanon [an expanse of wilderness in Palestine] shall be turned into a fruitful field, and the fruitful field shall be esteemed as a forest?" Ver. 18—"And in THAT day shall the deaf hear the *words of the* BOOK and the eyes of the blind shall see out of obscurity, and out of darkness." Are those not great miracles? And yet, no greater than have already been accomplished since this sealed book was revealed; i.e., if these eyes of mine testify the truth. It is evident, throughout this chapter, but especially in ver. 22, that this work is as recent as our times, when the Lord will fulfill his covenant with Abraham, namely—"And I will give unto thee, and to thy seed after thee, the land wherein thou art a stranger for an everlasting possession;" and here he says, "Jacob shall not now be ashamed [his seed amidst the gentiles], neither shall his face now wax pale." Why so? Ver. 23 gives the answer—"But when he seeth his children, the work of mine hands, in the midst of him [possessing the "land wherein they are strangers," after their last dispersal], they shall sanctify my name; and sanctify the *Holy One* of Jacob [Jesus Christ, their Messiah], and shall fear the God of Israel." For refusing "the Holy One of Israel," they were scattered to the four corners of the earth. Since Jacob and Israel are one and the same, the Holy One of each name is the same; and everyone knows that all Israel does not yet sanctify the name of the Son of Man, but rejects him as a fraud; but when the above prophecy is fulfilled, they will believe in him, although not before they are gathered back to their country either, but after that. So, it is clear enough that Isaiah, apart from many other prophets, proves the divinity of the Book of Mormon, and these others will be brought forward in their time; but for the time being, let us proceed with the story.

Mr. Smith continued the work of translation, as diligently as his circumstances would permit, until he finished the unsealed part of the records, which is called the "BOOK OF MORMON," and which contains nearly as much reading as the Old Testament.

THE BOOK OF MORMON—ITS DESCRIPTION.

WE have given a brief history, in the previous chapter, of the origin of this book, which has given rise to such excitement, joy, lies, and truths, and has caused such an indescribable revolution in the four corners of the earth, that almost all the people are already taking up arms in its favor, or against it. Ever since its first appearance to the world, the pastors and the leaders of the people have attacked it at the tops of their voices; writers seized upon their invented tales, too, until the ears of the people are made numb by the sound of their bells ringing, "Deceivers, false teachers, false prophets, fools, cunning frauds, liars," &c., &c.; and that is echoed from the tongues of religious people, drunkards, learned and unlearned heretics. They have by now sounded and resounded until they have almost stunned the world, and have been instrumental, although unwillingly, in bringing it to the attention of the people; and in the midst of all the noise, there are some of honest principle, who are searching for the truth, and who ask them, what is the cause of all this strange agitation? Why does everyone unite, from every party and no party, great and small, noble and plebeian, in every country, to oppose these people? The only answer that could be had from them would be:—"Oh, we do not really know what the matter is, except that some deceitful and uneducated wretches have come to our midst, as the apostles once did, testifying that angels have appeared to some men in these days; they profess to have revelations, miracles, &c., as though it were necessary to restore in our midst in this enlightened age the religion of the ancient times, and that faith which once was given to the saints; and through that they endanger all the religions and the numerous sects which our godly fathers gave to us, and which have been constructed on the basis of the wisdom of the theologians and the great men of the whole world, independent of the Spirit of God, and all its facts; this is the cause" (they say); and then they raise their voice in unison, shouting, "Great is human wisdom, great and excellent are the new forms of theological beliefs of this age; great is the ability of our uninspired pastors, who do not want to know anything but their own imaginings and opinions, and how strange it is the way they satisfy us with enticing words of human wisdom which are not the explanation of the Spirit and the power, for there is no need for that now; otherwise our faith would rest on the power of God rather than on the wisdom of the wise men." It is not surprising, then, that it is so difficult to obtain from the populace, in the midst of such noise and stupor, a hearing or credence for even the best, sweetest, and most remarkable news that was ever offered to them.

I suppose that no book ever had so much said against it by those who knew so little about it, as the Book of Mormon. Wherever it goes in every country, the ears of the populace are filled to the brim with stories and tales as numerous and varied as their authors, which consequently contradict each other; many of them published and preached by those who have never seen the book; others by those who have dipped into it here and there, purposely to pick faults, and not infrequently one sees quotations from it greatly distorted and twisted. Some describe it as an invented tale; others say it is a new Bible, to supersede the old. Some condemn it for being the most worthless tissue of foolishness they ever saw; others say that it is the most skillful fraud possible. Some find fault with it because it is too similar to the Bible, that its testimony coincides with it, and is therefore unnecessary; but others assert that it is a fraud because it is not similar enough to the Bible. Some condemn the principles it contains because they are immoral, totally evil, and blasphemous; but others of their brothers proclaim to their faces that the principles teach morality, chastity, and holiness, as though it had been purposely composed to trick in that way. Amongst others, one learned minister went to the trouble of publishing a 60-page treatise, against the Book of Mormon, &c., accusing it unsparingly of comprising a strangely foolish mixture, "*of faith and acts, of God's mercies, and of asking obedience of his creatures.*" Some of the great men of the age have proclaimed that its idiom, its language, and its contents prove its antiquity; and others of the same class, that it bears every mark of a recent forgery. Some cannot make out what use it could be, or how to prove its truth, unless there were some prophecies in it to be fulfilled, from which they could prove its divinity; others quote extensively from the prophecies that are about to be fulfilled, and they condemn it for being too clear: the old prophets did not do thus, they say.

Now, in the face of such a variety of conflicting claims about something that is so essential to understand properly, it would be not only very beneficial, but in the common interest to present a summary of the contents of the Book of Mormon, until we can print it in Welsh; although it is not, as we are accused, *instead of* or to *replace* the holy Bible, in any manner or means. There is not a word in it that contradicts the Bible, but it proves the divinity of the Bible undeniably, so that one need only read it to remove not only that false accusation, but every other one, and believe its truth and the Bible's too.

EARLY INHABITANTS OF AMERICA.

IN this valuable book can be found the ancient history of the American continent, from its early settlement by a colony who came there from the great separation which occurred at the tower of Babel, to the beginning of the fifth century of the Christian era. By these records we are informed that America in ancient times was inhabited by two distinct races of people; the first came directly from the tower of Babel, being called Jaredites; the second came from the city of Jerusalem, about six hundred years before Christ, being Israelites, principally the descendants of Joseph. The first nation, or Jaredites, were destroyed about the time that the Israelites came from Jerusalem, who succeeded them in the inheritance of the country. The majority of the second race fell in battle towards the close of the fourth century, and the remaining remnant gradually dwindled into an uncivilized state, until they divided into a multitude of nations, who are now called by Europeans, the "American Indians."

We also learn from this ancient book that the Jaredites were a righteous people, that they obtained favor in the sight of the Lord, so that, at the confusion of languages, they were not confounded; but because of their righteousness, the Lord miraculously led them from the tower to the great ocean, where they were commanded to build vessels, in which they sailed across the great deep and landed on the shores of North America. The Lord swore unto them in his wrath, that whosoever should possess this land of promise should serve him, the true and only God, or they should be swept off when the fulness of his wrath should come upon them, and they were fully ripened in iniquity. But he promised that if they kept his commandments he would make them the greatest and most powerful nation of all the nations of the earth.

In the process of time they increased greatly, becoming a very numerous and powerful people, occupying a large part of the country, building many large cities and being a civilized and comfortable nation. They were well versed in agriculture and machinery to a great extent. Trade and commerce flourished on every hand; yet, in consequence of wickedness they were often visited by the Lord with terrible judgments. Many prophets were raised up among them from generation to generation, who warned the people to forsake their evil ways, and prophesied of judgments and calamities which would overtake them if they did not repent. Sometimes they were visited by pestilence and plagues; at other times by famine and war, until at length (having occupied the land for some sixteen hundred years) their wickedness became so great that the Lord threatened, by the mouth of his prophets, to utterly destroy them from the face of the land. Even so they gave no heed to these warnings until the word of the Lord was fulfilled, and they were entirely destroyed, leaving their houses, their cities, and their possessions desolate. Their sacred records, which were kept on gold plates, were hidden by one of their last prophets, until they were discovered by the remnant of Joseph, which soon afterwards was brought there from Jerusalem to inherit the land.

JEWISH INHABITANTS OF AMERICA.

THIS remnant of Joseph was also led in a miraculous way from Jerusalem, in the first year of the reign of Zedekiah, king of Judah. They were first led to the eastern borders of the Red Sea; then they journeyed along the borders thereof in a southeastern direction; after which they went eastward, until they came to the great ocean. There, by the command of God, they built a vessel in which they were safely brought across the ocean, landing upon the western coast of the American continent. In the eleventh year of the reign of Zedekiah, at the time the Jews were carried away captive into Babylon, more people came from Jerusalem, some of whom were descendants of Judah; they landed in the north part of America, and emigrated into the northern parts of South America, where they lived until they were discovered by the remnant of Joseph, about four hundred years later.

From these records we learn that this remnant of Joseph, soon after they landed, separated themselves into two distinct nations. This division was caused by a certain portion, in their wickedness, persecuting and pursuing the remainder who were more righteous than they, until they came to the northern parts of South America, leaving the wicked nation in possession of the middle and southern parts of the same. The first nation was called Nephites, being led by a prophet whose name was Nephi. The other nation was called Lamanites, being led by a wicked man whose name was Laman. The Nephites had in their possession a copy of the five books of Moses, together with the writings of the holy prophets down to Jeremiah, in whose days they left Jerusalem; these were engraved on plates in Egyptian characters. They themselves also made plates soon after their landing, on which they engraved their history, as well as many of the prophecies, visions, and revelations they received. These sacred records were kept by holy and inspired men, who handed them down from generation to generation. The Lord gave unto them the whole continent for a land of promise, and he promised that they and their children after them should inherit it, on condition of their obedience to his commandments; or, if they were disobedient, they should be cut off from his presence. And the Nephites prospered in the land according to their righteousness, and they multiplied greatly and spread forth to the east, and west, and north: they built cities, synagogues, and temples, together with towers, castles, fortifications, and strong fortresses, to defend themselves against their enemies. They cultivated the earth, and raised various kinds of crops in abundance; they also possessed large flocks, and many domestic animals; they became a contented people, and were made wealthy by the abundance of their gold, silver, copper, tin, and iron. They were very skillful in the arts; they made various accurate and useful kinds of machinery; cloths of various kinds were manufactured, &c. Swords, scimitars, and various implements of war were made, together with shields and bucklers, to defend themselves in battle with their enemies. And in the days of their righteousness they were a civilized, able, and happy people.

But, on the other hand, the Lamanites, because of the hardness of their hearts and their disobedience, brought down the judgments of God on their own heads in many ways; nevertheless they were not destroyed as a nation, but the Lord God sent forth a curse upon them and they declined into a people no longer fair of appearance, color, or habits; yes, into a loathsome, uncivilized, cruel, and bloodthirsty people; being great enemies to the Nephites, whom they sought to overcome and destroy. Many times they came against them with their numerous hosts to battle; but they were repulsed by the Nephites almost always, not, however, without great loss on both sides; and thousands were frequently slain in their battles, and were piled together in slaughtered heaps, and covered with earth, which is proved to be true by the numerous mounds found in North and South America, filled with human bones, &c.

The second colony left Jerusalem eleven years after the remnant of Joseph, lived in the North, and after that emigrated to the South, until they were found by the Nephites; these were called the people of Zarahemla. They too had gone into a sad decline, and there had been civil war among them for many years, and they had brought no records with them; so their language too had been greatly corrupted and altered. They denied the existence of God; and at the time they were visited by the Nephites, although numerous, they were only in a partial state of civilization. But in time, after the Nephites united with them, they taught them the scriptures which were in their possession; they restored them to civilization and became one nation with them. And in the process of time, the Nephites built ships near the Isthmus of Darien, in which great numbers of them sailed northward, and colonized that part. Other colonies emigrated by land to the same place; and so, in a few centuries, nearly the whole continent became peopled. The north, at that time, was almost entirely destitute of timber, it having been destroyed by the more ancient race; that is those who came there first from the tower of Babel, as was mentioned; and because of that, the Nephites were obliged to build their houses, for the most part, of *cement*: also they carried much timber there from the south, and planted many types of trees there too, which they brought from the south, so that they would grow and in time their wants would be supplied. So, large cities were built in time, not only by the Nephites, but also by the Lamanites. The law of Moses was observed by the former, and God raised up prophets among them from time to time throughout their generations. Many records, both historical and prophetical, which were of great size, were kept among them; some on plates of gold, brass, and many other materials. The records of the more ancient race who had been destroyed before they came here were also found by them; these were engraved on plates of gold; they translated them into their own language by the power of God and through the means of the Urim and Thummim. They contained a historical account from the creation down to the tower of Babel, and from that time down until they were destroyed, comprising a period of fourteen or fifteen hundred years. They also contained many prophecies, great and marvelous, reaching forward in time to the end of the era of the new heaven and the new earth, and the final consummation of all things.

The prophets also among the Nephites prophesied of great things and opened the secrets of futurity; they foresaw the coming of the Messiah in the flesh, the strange and great things which would take place in ages to come; the blessings and the unutterable glory that God intends for their descendants in the latter days, according to his eternal design in the morning council. They would break out in floods of joy and song, as they gazed through their divine binoculars, at the establishment of the kingdom of peace, the peaceful reign of righteousness, when the world would be restored to purity. We are reminded how the public was recently amazed because some wealthy astronomer had built a telescope of enormous size in order to see further into the starry depths and understand their numbers, their orbits, and their order. But he and one Herschel would be consigned to oblivion if one had a mere glimpse through that wonderful telescope, through which those ancient godly prophets saw not only the orbits and the magnificence of the lunar bodies and those close by, but also the composition and establishment of the worlds before the morning stars did sing, and the sons of God did leap with joy,—the incomprehensible blessedness, and the unsearchable glory of those eternal abodes, which eyes have not seen, ears have not heard, and which it has never come into man's heart to imagine. Also, when they looked through the other end of it, they saw a detailed and correct description of the tumult of nations, wars, diseases, plagues, and pestilences—the judgments of God on empires, earthquakes, and revolutions; they saw kings rolling in the dust, and emperors on the dungheaps. And, further still, they saw the saints of the Most High taking possession of the kingdom, and the greatness of the kingdom, beneath all the heavens—the coming of the Ancient of Days, with his head like fleece, and the restoration of the keys of all dispensations to his hand—the greatness, glory and excellence of the Second Adam, coming triumphantly, with his crown on his head, his imperial scepter in his hand, and all his saints with him, in their beautiful aerial chariots;—yes, this would be shown to them now and again in their turn, until they saw the King of kings riding on his white stallion, as on a sea of glass, an innumerable multitude with him in glory, and a thousand myriads throwing their crowns at his feet, serving him and praising him who loved them, and bought them, and washed them in his blood, of every tribe and tongue, people and nation under heaven, and made them kings and priests for him, to reign *with Him* on the perfect and undefiled EARTH. Through this excellent telescope, the Nephites saw the birth, crucifixion, and resurrection of the Son of God in the land of their forefathers, and together the celestial and terrestrial phenomena at the time bore out the truth of the prophecies of their fathers. Notwithstanding all this, they fell into great wickedness, and cast out the saints of God, and the prophets, and stoned and killed those that God sent to them. Therefore, at about the time of the crucifixion of the Son of God, they were visited in great judgment. Thick darkness covered the continent for a time, the earth groaned terribly in anguish and sorrow at their transgressions, leaping like a boat before the furious waves of the ocean; the limestone was rent in fear into broken fragments, and shot in pieces far away; mighty mountains were sunk into valleys, to hide their heads in shame, and in their indignant rage they boiled up and raised the bottom of their fertile meadows to shroud their heads in a blanket of cloud, to remain as a monument to testify to future generations how the elements felt excruciating agony and grief when the nails were driven into the pure hands of him who made us; yes, they sympathized as though the stab of the long, sharp lance were penetrating to the depths of their very bowels, when it pierced the heart of the Creator of heaven and earth. Many large cities at the time ceased to be; their synagogues and fine temples were torn to shreds; their foundations, together with their cities and their citizens by the thousands in places were massacred and swallowed up into the depths of oblivion—there to recall and promise a literal fulfillment of the divine prophecies of their fathers, according to the Book of Mormon; and in Yucatan, Guatemala, Mexico, and many other places on the continent, there are brimstone and salt lakes—the ruins of their castles, their fortified cities, and a host of other facts which remain today and are truthful witnesses to the fulfillment of the prophecies of the ancestors of the American Indians, and consequently of the Book of Mormon. Through dreadful judgments the Lord destroyed most of the Nephites and the Lamanites, that the blood of the saints and the prophets they had killed might no longer cry to him for vengeance.

MANCHESTER ANNUAL CONFERENCE,

WHIT SUNDAY, May 31, 1846. This Conference was held this year in the *Hall of Science*, Manchester. The first meeting was opened at ten o'clock in the morning, with singing and prayer. R. Hedlock, Esq., was called to preside; and Thomas Ward and John Banks as vice-presidents. The officials present were counted as follows: Elders, 107; priests, 63; teachers, 24; deacons, 7; and about 5000 listeners. The President announced in a simple and clear manner the purpose of the meeting, the importance and glory of the great work before us, and he expressed an earnest desire to have a part in the Saints' prayers, that the Spirit of Light might lead us to all truth, so that everything might be done for the edification of the church, and the glory of Him to whom it belongs. Then he called on the Representatives of all the Conferences throughout Britain to report the number of their officials, their members, and how many were baptized since the last Conference; and 29 Conferences were present, comprising 10,345 members, 224 elders, 637 priests, 323 teachers, 178 deacons, 2,268 baptized since the last Conference.

N.B. There are five large Districts that were not represented in the Conference, and consequently are not included in the above reckoning; but sufficient proofs can be seen here that all those who say we are "dying of consumption, vertigo, cholera and every disease" they can imagine, are false prophets thus far. Not only England, but Wales too, are troubled by them, yes when we are more successful than any other denomination; but they prophesy their own will, and we will succeed until we fill the world.

In the afternoon meeting the Lord's Supper was served to some three thousand Saints, all in unity and love. They were addressed by several of the officials on numerous important matters; and doubtless the Comforter filled everyone's hearts with joy throughout the place. Several of the Representatives rose to make known the general quality of their Conferences, and the great works of God in their midst: there was never a time of greater unity and success in general than this.

In the evening meeting, the meeting was addressed by president Hedlock. He gave beneficial teachings on several matters, but particularly about the gathering together according to God's command, the necessity for it, the salvation and great blessings to be gained from it, together with the most convenient and advantageous way of doing so. He showed clearly that the "*British and American Commercial Joint Stock Company*," would be prepared to bring about this great aim, and that it would allow the poor from every country, those who cannot join with the Saints in any other way, to enjoy this great privilege. And he revealed that the above Company is now in operation, having been established by the *Act of Parliament*, and urged everyone to cooperate for its success. The vice-presidents enlarged warmly and eloquently on the same matters, and they were followed by Elders C. Kimball, Samuel Downe, and D. Jones; then the meeting was closed with prayer and singing, and, to judge from the congregation's good cheer, they went away in complete satisfaction and great joy.

Monday at 10, the meeting was begun by John Banks; then the Presidents of the various Districts were appointed and arranged for the future. Some new ones were established; among others, it was proposed by D. Jones, and seconded by the President, that eleven of the churches in Monmouthshire be a Conference belonging to Wales, and that John Morris preside over it, which was passed unanimously. Then the President made it known that D. Jones had been sent from America by the highest authority in the church to preside over all the Districts throughout Wales, and that his duty is to organize all matters in them, and arrange the best measures in order to spread the work throughout Wales, &c. Then the meeting ended.

At half past two, the afternoon meeting was begun as in the usual manner. Some matters were decided relating to the Scotland, and Isle of Man Districts, and several preachers were sent to assist the presidents who were there, and in some places in England. It was proposed by J. Johnson that the Garway District be linked with Wales, under the presidency of D. Jones; the President greatly supported that, and he requested that D. Jones send a president for Garway. In reply he indicated his willingness to comply with their counsel, although he had so much to supervise already; but he said that the present religious restoration reminded us of the national decline many years ago, when it was agreed to give to the foreign oppressors one county of Wales every century and that he almost thought that these latter days are the "times of the restitution of all things," since a District in the year was being restored to the principality; and he promised to do what he could for the welfare and comfort of those under his care. Before the end of the meeting the president announced his intention of setting the *Commercial Joint Stock Co.* before them in the next meeting, so that they could arrange together the best measures to be brought forward.

Tuesday, the meeting was opened at ten o'clock by D. Jones. Then, according to his promise, the President put the matters of the *Joint Stock Co.* before the Conference, and showed that this company was founded on the laws of Britain, fully registered in *Chancery*, and that every measure was to be carried out by twelve deputies elected by a majority of the members, and that these were bound in surety to behave according to the *Act of Parliament*, and for the greatest good of the members, independently of the church, because hundreds of members, yes, some of them having taken hundreds of shares, were not in the church; yet, he demonstrated that the Company in many ways tended to the advantage of the church, especially with regard to the settlement of the Saints in California, to trade with them, since our own ships take loads of all sorts of goods and merchandise from England and other places, which is not only essential, but advantageous, in order to go to such a new land so far from the markets of the commercial world. The Company intends to send one of its ships there towards the end of this year, with a load of merchandise, and those emigrants who choose to go there. They also intend to take several machines to establish *manufactories* to make clothes, &c., and establish various branches of the arts, and all that they will need for their sustenance, their comfort, and their success in that western paradise, together with some others who wish to go there, where they will find peace to worship God according to their conscience, without mobs of those who call themselves Christians martyring them, imprisoning them, oppressing them, and robbing them of their possessions, burning their houses over their heads by the score, and exiling them from place to place, as they have continued to do without any cause, for the last sixteen years. The President showed that the Saints in every settlement they made had enriched their enemies, who, having taken their money, often turned traitor against them, and after leaving, greatly misrepresented them, in order to incite persecution against them; but through this company the Saints are enabled to meet their own needs on the way of righteousness, and to bring profit to the company too, independent of their enemies. He showed the varied and beneficent aims of this excellent company, and he was followed by Messers. Ward, Jones, Wiley, and others, who enlarged on the aims and powers of the company to benefit not only its members, but the Saints too, for unity is strength; and the Saints had not begun one work so far which they had not through the help of God succeeded in finishing; yes, even though the whole world and the devil set every obstacle they could in their way. Our opponents say that we have been prevented from building the temple in Nauvoo; that is not true, for it has been finished despite everything, and thousands have received their endowment in it, and several of them have reached England afterwards.

Others say that we have been exiled from "*the promised land*," because we were exiled from Nauvoo, and from the United States; that is not true either, for we never thought that the City of Nauvoo was the "Promised Land." Do our accusers not know the difference between a *city* and a "*land?*" Those are their words; and their work of exiling the Saints from one end of that country to the other does not prove that the Saints are disappointed in their expectation, and they will not be disappointed in that, any more than in their obedience to the other commandments of their Lord and God.

They also showed that this company would be an instrument under God's blessing, to bring about those aims with great success and diligence, to the undoubted amazement of our opponents.

After that, the meeting was adjourned until the afternoon.

At two o'clock, the meeting was opened, and the matters of the *Joint Stock Company* were pursued. On the 17th of April last, the dealings of this company were endorsed in *Chancery*; there is permission to sell ten thousand shares, for a pound each, with a right to increase them, and already over eight thousand have been distributed, and over four thousand more are on the register of applicants; and the presidents of the various districts and churches are requested to sell as many shares as they can, so that a new ship the *Directors* have in mind can be bought, and sent out this year to California.

It was proposed by D. Jones, for the *Directors*, that they not only approve what was done by the President in their absence, but that he was deserving of their gratitude for his diligence and ability, and that they should join with the company in saluting his unusual success in establishing the company under many disadvantages, without falling into one error, or illegality which might cause legal penalty. This was approved unanimously.

It was also proposed by D. Jones, and was warmly approved by everyone,—That the Conference approve the previous conduct of President Hedlock, and his counselors, for the churches in Britain, and that we continue to assist them through our faith and our prayers.

The Presidents returned their thanks with great affection, and with a fervent prayer that the Lord lead us with his spirit always, so that we may continue in the unity of that faith once given to the saints; and thus ended the largest, pleasantest, and most beneficial conference, I should think, held by us in Britain.

We will give more information about the *Joint Stock Company* to our readers, together with its rules, its actions, and its success, through the PROPHET from time to time; but it would be too long in this issue.

So we had a rewarding conference, and every sign, through our unity, zeal, and determination, that the work is in the hand of our God, to go on to universal success.

ACCOUNT OF THE MERTHYR TYDFIL CONFERENCE.

ON SUNDAY, the 12th of July, a conference was held in the Cymreigyddion Hall, in the above town. The morning meeting began at ten o'clock, and Capt. D. Jones was called to be president, and William Davies of Rhymni, and Edward Edwards, as scribes.

After singing and praying, the president called on the presidents of the various branches throughout Wales, to report on their present situation, the number of their officials, members, and their progress in the last three months; and these were the results:—Number of branches, 34; members, 670; elders, 22; priests, 42; teachers, 25; deacons, 15. Baptized during the last three months 110. N.B. There are three preachers and several Saints in Pembrokeshire, apart from the above number.

The audience was warmly addressed by several of the elders, on the magnitude of this work, the glory of the "dispensation of the fulness of times," the necessity for unity and faithfulness, and the help of the Spirit of God under all persecutions, in order to continue faithful to the end. They showed the general situation of the branches to be quite comfortable and successful. Then the Monmouthshire branches were established as a district, and brother John Morris, Victoria, to preside over it. The assembled Saints in Llanybydder, Machynlleth, Harlech, Ffestiniog, Hirwaun, and Cefncoedycymer were recognized as branches of this district for the present time. Then the meeting was adjourned until two o'clock.

At two, the Saints' meeting was held. The meeting was begun with singing and prayer, by the president. Afterwards he indicated our duty to comply with the sacrament of the Lord's Supper; and its purposes, namely to remember the Lord's death: the continuance of the sacrament, that is "until he comes" in his kingdom, in power and glory; and the blessed state of those who continue to do this worthily, that they shall enter into the joy of their Lord, "to the wedding feast of the Lamb;" that it will be said to them, "Come, ye blessed of my Father, inherit the kingdom," &c. When the King is among them, having prepared for them "a feast of rich delicacies, and of pure clear wine," or as he says himself, "until I drink it new *with you* in my father's kingdom," &c. He showed the necessity for everyone to be reconciled, if there was any disagreement between them, before they could be worthy to eat or drink. After that the sacrament was administered to about five or six hundred Saints, all rejoicing in the unity of the Spirit and the bond of peace. Afterwards several testified, especially the missionaries who had returned from preaching the gospel throughout Gwynedd, about the certainty they have, and their determination to carry on with the work, depending on their heavenly Father for strength according to the day, and success in their labor, for the glory of his name, the establishment of his kingdom, and the saving of the souls of their fellow-countrymen. In about three months Abel Evans baptized over twenty in the counties of the North, several of whom had never heard the gospel before; four new churches were established there, all enjoying the gifts and blessings of the Holy Ghost, more or less, and in several places the sick were receiving health through God's power. Brother Robert Evans of Arfon said he had been preaching the gospel to mostly numerous congregations, from Conway to Rhuddlan, Newmarket, and as far as Rhosllanerchrugog; and that in every place those of honest heart searched the scriptures, and found the things that are preached "so," believed them, and in some places obeyed them; that the harvest was indeed great, and ripe, but the workers scarce. Eliezer Edwards also, from Carmarthenshire, informed us that many places are anxious to hear our principles preached, because they were tired of reading and believing the stories that are preached and published against us; that reasonable men could see that we must have more religion than our persecutors, for us to be persecuted or to suffer persecution so cruelly and without cause; thus the false accusations and counter-claims are controlled from above, to be for the success of the gospel, and to bring shame to their inventors. Brother Ebenezer Morris said that several preachers with him were getting on successfully in Pontypridd, Dihewyd, Llantrisant, &c., and several had been baptized since the last conference, and that they had hopes of many more soon. All agreed that it was from the preachers and professors of the sects that they had the cruelest persecution; and in some places, that it was men without religion who prevented them from being stoned by the believers. The meeting was closed with a prayer for the Lord of the harvest to remove the obstacles from their way, and send workers to his harvest.

At half past six, after opening the meeting in the usual manner, the president showed briefly and comprehensively the glory of the eternal gospel, that it is through it that "life and purity" will be brought "to the light," its unchangeableness, &c., and afterwards he testified that a dispensation has been given to men, in these latter days, to preach the gospel through God's power, and that He works with and confirms the word through the powers and the marvels of those who follow. He was followed by brother John Morris, in English, on the same important matter. Afterwards Robert Evans showed clearly the impossibility of a BOOK authorizing anyone to preach, to administer the sacraments of God's house, or to send out servants for God, unless they were called by God in some way, and ordained by his servants. He also proved the necessity for all the offices and sacraments, together with all the spiritual gifts, in order to make the body or church of Christ perfect, from the similar necessity for all the members (according to the comparison used by Paul in 1 Cor. xii) to make the human body perfect; then he testified solemnly and fearlessly that he had found such a church now, possessing all the members, that is the gifts; and he earnestly urged all his listeners to come into it quickly, before the door was closed, so that they too might enjoy these blessings, and inherit eternal life. After closing the meeting two were baptized, and the large crowd left, to all appearances having found great satisfaction.

Monday at ten, the meeting was begun with singing and prayer. The president announced that the main aim of the meeting was to elect and ordain officials, demonstrating the difference between the two priesthoods, the necessity for the one and the other in the church, along with all the offices that belong to them, before one can minister lawfully in any office. He made clear the careful account that must be given for these precious talents, from the example of the "unprofitable" servant, who was cast into the uttermost darkness, Meroz, &c. He demonstrated the danger of, and the punishment for, misusing their talent, or not using it at every opportunity, that it is a priceless pearl, which with faithfulness will ensure for its owner eternal life, and an enduring crown to wear; and on the other hand, if it was misused, it would be the odor of death until death. He showed the great need there is for workers in the vineyard, and earnestly urged his fellow officials to take courage in the work, to seize every opportunity to do good, taking care to be "clean vessels" when dealing with things as sacred as the ordinances of the house of God, and rely on him whose work it is, to strengthen us from day to day, in order to build his kingdom, magnify the name of his Son Jesus, and save our fellow-countrymen. He urged all the Saints, but especially the officials, to be patient and forebearing when opposed by the religious people of the country; not to be annoyed, but to take pity on them, and pray for them, since that was how some of us were until we were enlightened; and not to "dote about questions and strifes of words," but out of love for them, endeavor through testimony and good examples to win them to the kingdom of God; for they are poor creatures, they know not what they do, nor what things they oppose; that hundreds and thousands of honest-hearted people desire to grasp the substance of the gospel, but even so, in their ignorance, are misled by their pastors onto the ways they tend to, often without looking into the matter; eager to believe the shameful stories about us which they would want to be true, until the mark of the persecuting shepherd is seen on his flock much too often; but even so let us follow the example of our great Shepherd, who when he was reviled did not revile in turn, for a soft word turns away wrath; therefore, dear brethren, "in your patience possess your souls," "in due season we shall reap, if we faint not." Let us remember that we are blessed when everyone speaks ill of us for the sake of Christ and the gospel, for so did they say of our brethren before us. And with many other counsels the president urged his brethren to carry on with courage and warmth, as we know that our labor is not in vain in the Lord. After that, apt explanatory comments were made on the matters under consideration, by brother Thomas Pugh, Cwmbach. He demonstrated the superiority of this plan over the human doctrines he had preached in his ignorance, for years. He was determined to go on, since he had got hold of a religion with "power" in it, which brought him more light, knowledge, and happiness, in a few hours than what he had before brought him in many years. Then ten of the priests were called and ordained as elders. Twenty-three other priests, eleven teachers, and four deacons, belonging to the various branches throughout Wales, were called. Those who were called testified to their knowledge of the truth, and their determination to endeavor to fulfill their various duties, relying on God for the help of his Spirit to lead them to all truth, for the glory of his name and the benefit of mankind.

After that the meeting was concluded, to make way for the many kind sisters who were already waiting to prepare the magnificent feast in the Hall, in accordance with the previous announcement; and by two o'clock the scene had changed remarkably from the previous meetings—tables were to be seen all over the Hall laden with delicacies of many colors, shapes, and flavors. The dishes were exquisitely beautiful and well arranged, the tea tasty and good, and the company remarkably cheerful and happy. In the course of the afternoon, about seven hundred, who had obtained tickets, sat at the tables, and some hundreds more came, paying without tickets, as not enough had been prepared. To judge by all appearances, we would say from the unity, the happiness, and the love, that everyone was delighted. Hundreds of respected friends from the world came to join in our feast, and we greatly enjoyed their company. Throughout it all, our minds ran back and forth, from the blessed time when the first parents of all of us feasted in unity and happiness, with no enemy, with no trouble, pain, or error, but all content. But what of the blessed day that is to come, of which feasts such as these are but drops in the ocean. Hail to the "times of the restitution of all things which God hath spoken by the mouth of all his holy prophets;" then—

"The wolf in contentment and innocence will be
In loving affection caressing the lamb;
The stag and the lion will lick in true love,
And rest as friends in a meadow of flowers.

"The mute and the deaf will harmoniously sing,
The lame and the wounded will dance roundabout;
The eyes of the blind will see light again,
And they too will join in rejoicing and praise.

"The earth will be covered in worshipping,
And Jesus's name will be hailed above all;
And all faithful nations will be seen on that day,
Coming in myriads to join in the throng;
Steam-driven trains and full-laden ships
Of sons and of daughters for Zion all bound.

"From the ends of the earth come Ephraim and Judah,
To greet Jesus joyfully as the Messiah:
And if their rejection of him was once bitter,
They'll feel their repentance as life after death.

"All malice and envy will be there assembled,
With the spirit of war, and complaint, and contention;
Self-interest and pride and all hateful greed—
There to be cast to oblivion, like dross.

"The church will be cleansed in the light of her laws,
Till seraphim also will yearn to enroll;
And her bridegroom her company so often will seek,
Thousands of angels will herald his path.

"Joy and much praise and increasing affection,
Will fill every heart in that happy assembly:
Praise be and glory, amen, hallelujah,
From saints and from angels to the name of Jehovah."

At half past seven, the tables were moved and the remains of the feast, and the President took the chair; and after singing, rhymes were made up on the occasion of the conference, the feast, the success of the cause, and the Saints were urged to continue in brotherly love, and to live peacefully with all men as far as possible.

The President revealed the necessity of sending missionaries to preach the gospel throughout the principality, the great and numerous difficulties that lie on the way, especially considering that not many of the wise and the great of the world have yet been called in Wales—that God now, as before, had revealed these great things to the lowliest of the Welsh, so that the magnificence of the power would be of God, and not of us. And although we preach the gospel free to the world, it cannot be done without food and clothes any more than before, especially in the midst of this perverse and unbelieving generation. God does not expect that, for the worker deserves his food and clothes; and who expects that more than those who have tasted forgiveness, known the sweetness of the feast, become children of the light, and received of the Spirit of Christ, who is a burning flame of love for the salvation of every man.

Then the following were proposed by the President, seconded, and unanimously approved by the large crowd:—

"That the Missionary Society be established tonight, with the sole purpose of assisting the missionaries who are sent from here throughout the country, to places where there are no Saints to supply their needs.

"That a committee be formed, comprising the presidents of all the different branches throughout Wales, and that they choose their president, treasurer, and secretary; and that the majority be entitled to change any officer or member of the committee, when they deem it necessary.

"That the treasurer give surety for the money in his possession, and that he not pay any of the society's money to anyone, without obtaining a ticket signed by the president on the instructions of the majority of the committee; and that he take a receipt for what he pays, signed by the recipient.

"That the president be empowered to summon the committee when he deems it necessary, giving each member ten days' notice.

"That the secretary keep a record of the actions and accounts of the society, to show his accounts at every festival of the society in public, as well as whenever the majority of the committee requests it.

"That the remainder of the money produced by this *tea party*, after paying all costs, be used for the sole benefit of the society.

"That the president of every branch hold a meeting every first Monday evening of the month, to pray to God to prosper the efforts of the society, then to announce the progress of the missionaries, and urge everyone to contribute what they can at the time, in order to help the society; and that he send what is collected to the chief treasurer, at the first opportunity after every meeting, and obtain a receipt from him for it."

The President was chosen to be president of the society; William Phillips, Merthyr, treasurer; and William Davies, Rhymni, secretary, and Edward Edwards, Abercanaid, to assist them.

Robert Evans and Abel Evans gave a comprehensive and entertaining report on their travels through the North, earnestly desiring their brethren in Merthyr to come out to the fight, to help them in the army of the God of Israel against the strong giants who are building the walls of great Babylon.

Then the President called on those preachers present who could arrange their affairs so that they could go into the vineyard for a while, to indicate this by standing up; and behold, fifteen stood up, indicating, "Here we are, send us;" these indicated their willingness and determination to go out into the vineyard, some for three months, some for five, and others on whom no one depended for sustenance, devoted their whole time to preaching the gospel. The committee decided to assist them as far as possible out of the fund, according to their needs.

Then William Phillips gave a detailed account of what had been received, and the costs of this feast, and there was found to be a profit of £22 10s.

Thanks were given by the Saints to their friends from the world for their company, their good cheer, and their courtesy, throughout the conference and the feast.

The congregation's thanks were given to Mr. Hopkins, the owner of the Hall, for his kindness and his amiability in providing every facility asked of him. And then the President closed the most highly attended, successful, and well mannered conference and *tea party* we have ever seen in Wales, with a prayer for God to bless our work, and keep us all faithful until we end our race in eternal happiness. Amen.

COUNTER-EXHORTATION.

To WHAT end are we driven out hither and thither?
To what end are we slandered by the tongues of one and all?
Why do they disperse our meetings, try to silence us entirely?
If there is some aim beneath it all, what is it? who can tell?

What! to halt the ocean's tide? what! to turn back the sea? What!
Are your sights on halting the flow of a *volcano*, feeble folk?
Try to halt the cloud's course, try to halt the waves of the sea;
They are more easily halted than the Lord's Saints are silenced.

If Christ saved our life, if he gave us his Holy Spirit—
If this spirit fills our soul, and burns like fire—
If a wealth of promises yonder awaits faithful saints—
Oh! how can we be silent, with our honor, and our privilege?

Who attempted, but your brothers, to silence in days of yore
The saints and the apostles—first stalwarts who had the faith?
If they failed then, in the heat of the great battle,—
If their fate was giving up, you too should give up now.

RHYDYBONT: PRINTED BY JOHN JONES.

PROPHET OF THE JUBILEE.

"THE KINGDOM HAS COME."

No. 3.] SEPTEMBER, 1846. [Vol. I.

TESTIMONY OF CHURCH HISTORIANS REGARDING MIRACLES.

Our opponents say that the miracles ended with, or soon after, the apostolic age; but their own church historians contradict them. Here is an example from the "History of the Church of Jesus Christ," by the Rev. Dr. Barth, that was published by the Religious Treatises Society in London. Now, if miracles continued like this until the middle and end of the third century, what else but Constantine's corruption in linking religion and politics, &c., distanced the Spirit of God in his gifts from them?

"Although these several church positions led to the separation between clergy and laity, it could not occur in full while the miraculous gifts of the Spirit continued; for these gifts were not confined to one class. There are several credible proofs that those particular gifts did not end with the apostolic age. Justin Martyr writes to the emperor of Rome, at the beginning of the second century, like this:—'There is a host, throughout the world in general, and in this city (Rome), who have been cleansed of unclean spirits, when they could not be cured by your sorcerers and diviners, only through us, the Christians, using the name of Jesus who was crucified under Pontius Pilate; and the same thing is being done to this day; for unclean spirits are truly being cast out of men.' In the last part of this century (the second) Irenaeus, the bishop of Lyons, writes:—'Some, in fact, cast out devils in the name of Jesus: and often, those who are saved from unclean spirits become believers, and are received as members of the church. Others have the gift of foreseeing things; and of prophetic dreams and predictions. Others heal all sorts of sickness through the laying on of hands. Yes, even the dead have been brought to life, and have been among them for years afterwards. Who can count the merciful gifts God imparts to his church in every part of the world, which are daily freely given, in the name of Jesus, for the salvation of the nations!' At the end of this century (the second) Tertulian challenges all the Roman governors of the provinces, saying, 'Let any devilish person be brought before your court, and you shall see with your own eyes, that, by a Christian saying only a word, the spirit that previously pretended to be a god, is bound to recognize that it is only a demon.' Indeed all the Christian writers almost till the time of Eusebius, at the beginning of the fourth century, say they themselves bear witness to seeing and hearing the fact that it is a common practice among Christians to see evil spirits being cast out in the name of Jesus; that others of their brethren have supernatural knowledge of things to come, through visions and divine revelations; and that others heal miraculously through the laying on of hands."

APPEARANCE OF CHRIST TO THE AMERICAN INDIANS—THEIR WARS—AND THE STORY OF MORMON.

AFTER Christ arose from the dead, finished his ministry at Jerusalem, and ascended to the right hand of Majesty in the heavens, he appeared to the most righteous of the Nephites, when they were assembled round their temple in the northern parts of South America. He exhibited to them the marks of the nails in his hands, feet and wounded side; he abolished the law of Moses, establishing his gospel in its stead; he chose twelve disciples from among them to preach it, and administer its ordinances, together with the sacrament. He prayed for and blessed their children; he healed their sick, blind, deaf, injured, and those who were afflicted in any way. He showed forth his power in their midst, through raising the dead; he expounded the scriptures which had been given from the beginning down to that time, and he made known unto them the most remarkable and glorious things he would fulfill among them, and their children after them, until he should come in the fulness of time in glory; and from that time down to the end, when everyone, of every kindred, tongue, people, and nation, should be gathered before the throne of God to be judged according to the actions they accomplished in the flesh, whether good or evil, until the heaven and the earth should pass away, and there should be a new heaven and a new earth. All these revelations of Christ were engraved on plates; and the Book of Mormon contains quotations from some of them, but much the greater part are hidden to this day and are to be made manifest to the Saints in God's good time, in order to fulfill his intentions. We have no doubt that it will be considered a strange thing, and perhaps doubtful by some, that Jesus Christ appeared in person on the continent; and yet, I cannot comprehend what counter-argument, even Prejudice itself, could bring to disprove it. If such as these were asked to whom Christ was referring when he said, "And other sheep I have, which are not of this fold: them also I must bring, and they shall hear my voice; and there shall be one fold" (John x, 16). He does not mean the Gentiles, because he did not call them *sheep* or anyone else but "the lost sheep of the house of Israel." He said that he came only to the "*sheep*," yes, sheep too of some other "fold" [country], than Palestine. Why, then, can it not be admitted that it is to this "remnant of Joseph" that it refers? It cannot here refer to the Gentiles either because he says, "and they shall hear *my voice*." Not the voice of his servants, but *his* voice, as those sheep heard his voice in Judea. When it is proved that it is not to them that Christ refers in this strange saying, we will bring other resources which will give clear, positive proof; but until then, it must be admitted that Jesus Christ himself, yes, in our Bible, proves the truth of the Book of Mormon!

After Jesus Christ had finished his ministry among the Nephites, he ascended into heaven in their presence; and the twelve disciples whom he had sent, went forth upon all the face of the land, preaching his gospel, and baptizing those who repented for the remission of sins; and after that, they received the Holy Spirit through the laying on of hands of the disciples. Many great miracles were wrought by them and by others in the church, until almost all the remaining Nephites and Lamanites throughout the north and the south became obedient; and they dwelt in righteousness for nearly three hundred years: but towards the beginning of the fourth century of the Christian era, they so far apostatized from God that he again suffered destructive judgments to fall upon them. The Nephites at that time dwelt in the north, and the Lamanites in the southern part of America. There were cruel wars between them which lasted for many years and resulted in the complete overthrow of the Nephites and their destruction as a nation. These wars commenced near the Isthmus of Darien, and at length the Nephites were driven before their enemies to the north and the east of it, where they were still pursued until they gathered their whole remaining nation together, men, women, and children, and encamped around the hill Cumorah, where the records were found by Joseph Smith, as previously noted. Here too they were pursued by the Lamanites; and having gathered together their numerous hosts, they attacked them, and laid them low with hard slaughter for many days, hewing down mercilessly the aged, the young and the middle-aged, indiscriminately. Hundreds of thousands were slain on both sides, and the entire nation of the Nephites was destroyed from off the face of the earth, excepting a few who had deserted over to the Lamanites, a few who escaped into the south country, and a few who fell wounded and were left on the field of battle for dead. Among these last were Mormon and his son Moroni, who were righteous men.

Mormon had made an abridgement from the records of his forefathers upon plates, which he entitled the "*Book of Mormon;*" and, being commanded of God, he hid in the hill Cumorah all the sacred records of his forefathers that were in his possession; and he gave only the Book of Mormon to his son Moroni to finish.

Moroni survived a few years after this destruction of his nation, and continued the writings, in which he informs us that the Lamanites hunted those few Nephites who escaped the tremendous slaughter on the hill Cumorah, and killed them, excepting those who had fled to the Lamanites, and that he alone was left, and kept himself hid, for they destroyed every Nephite who would not deny the Christ, even after the war. He furthermore states that the Lamanites were at war one with another, and over the whole face of the land they were plundering and killing each other. He continues the history until the four hundred and twentieth year of the Christian era, when, by the commandment of God, Moroni hid up the records in the hill Cumorah, where they remained concealed until by the ministry of an angel they were discovered to Mr. Smith, who, by the power of God, translated them into English by means of the Urim and Thummim, as is known.

TESTIMONIES ABOUT THE BOOK OF MORMON.

HAVING given from time to time a summary of the contents of the

Book of Mormon, it is natural to ask now, is it not a valuable book? Many say that if they were to see the plates on which it is engraved, they would believe it to be true: but it is the same as saying that they will believe that God exists when they see him; or, that they would believe that Christ had risen if they had seen him. Some claim that they should see those plates, before they should believe it. With a little reflection, one would realize that it is well-nigh impossible for everyone in every part of the world to see them. How long would it take, and at what cost, for the same ones to go and show the plates to every one of the six hundred million of the human race, for they could not show them in more than one place at once! Any reasonable man would say that that was impossible. Well, then, how unreasonable it is for certain persons to ask to see them, any more than all the others. If it is reasonable for anyone to believe testimony about this, without seeing them, then so should it be for everyone. What better is one man in the sight of God than the other? He is no respecter of persons. Had he not the same right to choose his witnesses to this, as the Son of God had to choose his witnesses to his resurrection? Those who reject the testimony about this are imitating those unbelieving Pharisees who rejected testimony about the resurrection of Christ, because they did not see him. We do not expect anyone to believe the Book of Mormon, or any other revelation that professes to come from God, without abundant testimonies; for we do not do so ourselves. But, perhaps some think it presumptuous of us, to say that we offer them as much as they have to prove the truthfulness of the scriptures; however, I venture to say that, although there are plenty of incontrovertible testimonies to prove the divinity of this sacred volume, which we believe completely, yet we have more proofs of the truth of the Book of Mormon than that! But, they say, are they not all biased witnesses that you have; and what value is the testimony of the Saints themselves about the matter under debate? I ask, What witnesses have we to prove the truth of the New Testament? I know of no witness apart from totally biased ones, and only six of those, namely Matthew, Mark, Luke, John, Peter, and Paul. Were they not biased in all that they wrote? and is their testimony any less forceful because they are biased in the matter? If it is not, why is the testimony of those witnesses who testify so strongly to the truth of the Book of Mormon, invalid, then? For my part, I admit that I cannot comprehend how a single unbiased witness to the one or the other can be had; unless some people were to say that they know the Book of Mormon to be true, but even so, they are willing to lose their souls rather than accept it, in order to be unbiased witnesses, so that others might believe it! Who would say that he disbelieved the New Testament, although witnessing to others of its truth, thereby depriving himself of eternal life? How foolish this would be; and yet no more foolish than expecting to find an unbiased witness to the Book of Mormon; for at the moment of believing, he would necessarily become biased; and would not such a biased witness be rejected because his assertion contradicted his *example*, which is the truest witness of all? "Do not the miracles prove the truth of the New Testament?" some say; "and are there not hosts of those who were inside and outside the church who bear witness to their truth?" I answer that, of all those hosts, not even one has given us his testimony about this, except those six biased ones. There is a difference between having the testimony of the people themselves, and having testimony of others about them! If the reader answers the following questions, then I think we shall come to the same conclusion about this:—Did your eyes see the miracles being performed? Did your ears hear them speaking in tongues? Have you seen any witness who saw them healing as much as one sick person? Have you read the testimony of as much as one unbiased witness outside the church who says he saw them performing one miracle? If the New Testament is believed without as much as one unbiased witness, why can the same not be done with the Book of Mormon? We accept that the testimony of those partial witnesses is sufficient to prove the truth of the New Testament, and it should be sufficient for everybody. But it is seen that those who refuse the Book of Mormon because the witnesses are biased, refuse the New Testament according to the same reasoning!

From what has been under consideration previously, it is evident to every unbiased mind that more testimonies exist to the truthfulness of the aforementioned book than for the New Testament, insofar as there are hundreds now living who have come to know the truth of the Book of Mormon and testify to it, when there is no one alive today who can testify to the truth of the New Testament. We have further proofs and testimonies to bring before our readers, but we shall leave them aside for now, while promising to give them in the next issue, the testimonies of those who saw and felt the gold plates of the book, those to whom it was explained through the power of God, and who know with certainty that they are true, and derive from the ancients previously mentioned.

"All things together go to shew,
That the Book of Mormon is all true."

PROOFS OF THE TRUTHFULNESS OF THE BOOK OF MORMON.

PERHAPS some will be surprised when I venture to prove from the Scriptures, that such a book as "THE BOOK OF MORMON" has long been promised to be revealed to the world; but in any case, it is obvious to me, that that was to take place; and we shall now endeavor to prove scripturally that it was in this age that it was to be revealed, and that America was the place.

1. We shall prove that the American continent was promised by God to the seed of Joseph, namely the two halves of the tribes of Ephraim and Manasseh; that is, that God would reveal his mind and his will to them there, as he had given the revelations of our Bible to the Jews, and also that the books which contained those things would be joined together in the latter days.

Firstly, note the blessing given by Jacob to the two sons of Joseph, in Gen. xlviii, 16. "Let them grow into a multitude in the midst of the earth." In the same blessing he says of Ephraim, "And his seed shall become a multitude of nations." If this is connected, it will be seen that Ephraim would be a multitude of nations in the midst of the earth. On Joseph's head, Jacob said (Gen xlix), "Joseph is a fruitful bough—even a fruitful bough by a well; whose branches run over the wall. The archers have sorely grieved him, and shot at him, and hated him. But his bow abode in strength," &c. He says again, "The blessings of thy father have prevailed above the blessings of my progenitors, unto the utmost bound of the everlasting hills; they shall be on the head of Joseph, and on the crown of the head of him that was separate from his brethren."

I ask, who were the fathers of Jacob, and what blessings were promised to them? Abraham and Isaac were his fathers, and the blessing they promised to Jacob was the land of Canaan; no more and no less than God promised to Abraham, namely, "I will give to thee and to thy seed, the land of thy journey [Canaan] as an inheritance forever." But Joseph's blessing "*prevailed*" above the blessing of his fathers; yes, it prevailed as much as the "utmost bound of the everlasting hills" over the land of Canaan. Jacob was in Egypt at this time, and where could one look for the "utmost bound of the everlasting hills" more reasonably than to the *Andes*, or the rocky mountains of the Continent? The Prophet also says that they would be in the west, "for when the Lord shall roar, then the children of Ephraim shall tremble from the west." It is obvious from what has been said, that Ephraim was to be a multitude of nations in the midst of the earth, and that Joseph was to inherit the widest and most fertile country under the sun, in the west; yes, as far as America. And if one searches the earth from pole to pole, one will not find a multitude of nations, who could possibly have descended from Ephraim, except in America. Although there are different nations in some other countries, yet, they are so mixed, and so different in their origins, that they cannot fulfill the above prophecy; whereas, on the other hand, one can see in America scores of nations, dwelling in a wide country, which contains the abundance of the world, and "bears the blessings of the earth below." And every historian who has traveled among them, admits that they are of one common origin. One must admit that the American Indians are the remnant of Joseph, or deny this prophecy, as it cannot refer to anyone else.

The next thing we shall prove is that the prophets demonstrated that God would give revelations to Ephraim and Manasseh in America. See Hosea viii, 12. When speaking in the spirit of prophecy, he says, "I have written to him the great things of my law, but they were counted as a strange thing." Ezekiel also says in chap. 37, not only that Ephraim, as well as Judah, would have a book containing the revelations of God to his prophets, but that these two books would be joined together, when God was about to restore them to possession of their promised rights (ver. 16). "Moreover, thou son of man, take thee one stick, and write upon it, For Judah, and for the children of Israel his companions: then take another stick, and write upon it, For Joseph, the stick of Ephraim, and for all the house of Israel his companions: and join them one to another into one stick; and they shall become one in thine hand. And when the children of thy people shall speak unto thee, saying, Wilt thou not shew us what thou meanest by these? Say unto them, thus saith the Lord God; Behold, I will take the stick of Joseph, which is in the hand of Ephraim, and the tribes of Israel his fellows; and will put them with him, even with the stick of Judah, and make them one stick, and they shall be one in mine hand. And the sticks whereon thou writest shall be in thine hand before their eyes; and say unto them, Thus saith the Lord God, Behold, I will take the children of Israel from among the heathen, whither they be gone, and will gather them on every side, and bring them into their own land: And I will make them one nation in the land upon the mountains of Israel, and one king shall be king to them all: and they shall be no more two nations, neither shall they be divided into two kingdoms any more at all."

It is known to every historian that the children of Israel were never one nation or kingdom on the mountains of Israel, nor anywhere else, from the time they were divided into two kingdoms under Rehoboam, son of Solomon, and Jeroboam, son of Nebat. Yet, the prophet informs us that God will make them one kingdom; yes, in their own country, that is among the mountains of Israel. This will be accomplished by God's gathering them from all the nations they went to.

This gathering will begin directly after the Lord takes the stick of Joseph, which is in the hand of Ephraim, and puts it with the stick of Judah, and in his hand they become one stick. Note, on one of these sticks would be written by God's commandment certain things for Judah, and on the other for Ephraim (for it is called the stick of Ephraim as well as the stick of Joseph), and I ask what things God commanded to be written on them, except those things Hosea said, "I have written to him [Ephraim] the great things of my law," that is, in order to govern the two branches of the house of Israel, and consequently, they contained prophecies about the things which would befall them in the future, for all the writings which God commanded to be written to every kindred, tongue, and nation, contain that; and so it is reasonable for us to expect that the stick of Joseph or Ephraim would contain "the great things of God's law," in order to teach them, govern them and indicate their destiny to them, as to their companions. The stick of Judah contained the great things of his law for Judah (that is the tribe of Judah). But why are they called *sticks*, says the reader? I answer that the art of making paper was not known in the days of Ezekiel; consequently, they would have to prepare something else for that purpose. Sometimes they wrote on skins tanned smooth, which they called parchment. Sometimes they used tree bark for that purpose, which they called *papyrus*; and sometimes they hewed sticks smooth for this purpose. These last were the easiest to prepare; and because of that, God commanded the prophet to prepare two sticks immediately, to show them to the people, to be an example or sign to them that God would join the tribes of Israel, as, and at the time those two books are joined together. This is the reason, I imagine, they are called sticks instead of books.

The most natural question to an eager enquirer is, Where are these oracles to be found? The prophet says the stick of Joseph is already in the possession of the sons of Ephraim, and that God would take it from there, and move it to the stick of Judah, so that they became one in his hand. Although it is not stated where the stick of Judah is, it is mentioned that it is not to be moved like the other, from the place where it is; so I understand that the stick of Judah is already in the possession of the inhabitants of the earth; and since the stick of Ephraim is hidden, God will take it from the place where it is, will bring it into the open, and put it with the stick of Judah. It is not news now to the reader that the Bible is the stick of Judah; for it does not contain the story of any other tribe or people but they, since the said dispersal, except for the history of others in relation to them.

It contains the great things of God written to the tribe of Judah, by prophets and apostles of the house of Judah. It also contains prophecies about future things, which are already in the possession of the world. Now, as we have identified the stick of Judah, let us go on to search out the stick of Joseph, remembering when we find it, that it also must contain great things of the law of God for Ephraim; give the story of this branch of the house of Joseph, written by prophets and apostles descended from Joseph's loins, as the stick of Judah is from his. Also, it implies that this book would be hidden in the region of the country where the sons of Ephraim dwelt at the time God brought it into the open, for it is taken *from the hand of* Ephraim; and as the word Ephraim here signifies his descendants who issued from his loins, so "*from the hand of*" signifies from the possession of, or from the country where the Ephraimites dwell. As we have already proved that "Ephraim would be a multitude of nations in the midst of the earth," to the "west" of Jerusalem, "to the utmost bound of the eternal hills," that is, the continent of America; for if one journeyed to the west of Jerusalem until one found a multitude of nations of the same origin, nothing of the sort would be found until one crossed the Atlantic Ocean, towards the latitude of Charleston, South Carolina, United States of America. One would think that the traveler would consider his task at an end when he reached here, and found such a multitude of nations on a continent stretching almost from the northern circle to the southern; and he would say, here are the Ephraimites as the most detailed fulfillment of the prophecies about them; and then the *stick* [book of law] of Ephraim must be found here in their midst, and no book found anywhere else can answer this detailed description. Well, has such a book as is described been seen, in their possession, by anyone? says the reader. And one would think that if such a book were found in their midst giving the story of their origin and their experiences, that would be incontrovertible proof, and that even the most hardened unbelievers would admit the truth of the one book and the other, for two witnesses are better than one. Then, let us search more carefully in their midst for such a book, for the prophets spoke the truth; and since these are the Ephraimites, such a thing must be revealed from their midst; and all those who wish to defend the truthfulness of the Bible [which bears witness about the book of Ephraim] should not only rejoice, believing the same when it is found, but endeavor to inform everyone of it. Whosoever despises or rejects [this book] rejects the witness to it [namely the Bible], as lies.

As none of these Indians, from what has been seen, can read, it could hardly be expected that there would be many books in their midst now, but that does not prove that they did not possess books at one time, and were able to read them and write them, any more than the complete fall of Babylon, and the great cities of Egypt and other places, together with the utter decline of their inhabitants, prove that they were not in their time the main academies or *Thebes* of the world. And like many of those, the American Indian now can only refer the traveler for an answer to his questions to the most magnificent ruins of the largest, most exquisitely crafted, and strongly defended cities ever seen in the world. These remains speak clearly and perpetually, in many ways, of the skill of their fathers, and show the complete decline which has overtaken their children. Recent travelers admit that the old cities, the great and numerous temples, the enormous columns, the high walls, the strong defenses, and the fortified cities, prove that they are not only as old, but of similar arts as those of the Egyptians, when in the height of their pomp and power. As to who made them, when, and what is their history, none of the travelers among them has found a satisfactory answer to these questions, and the answers one gets from the uncivilized inhabitants themselves is the tradition taught from father to son, and they are remarkable for imprinting the strangest things which were in their midst on the memories of the young children. I found it interesting to see the old grey-haired men sitting by their *Wigwam*, and the little boys of the fourth generation sitting on their knees, to be taught their history, especially their wars, the story of the braves of their own family, and the traditional tales of their prophets, whom they call their *Medicine man*. This instills in the children love for their own tribe, causing them to imitate them in bravery; and not infrequently jealousy is fostered toward another tribe through such teaching, from their boyhood. The task of the elders is to teach the young ones the traditions taught to them by their forefathers, while the active men hunt, the heroes fight, and the young lads and lasses are at their games, and learning to shoot with a bow, wield the *war club* and the *tomahawk* the fastest, which they do with great skill from the sound of their musical instruments, their cymbals, and a number of pipes. They have a kind of dance before going to war, and another kind after returning, if they are victorious, as well as several methods for their domestic entertainment. When they are about to attack their enemies, they have a habit of shouting in unison as loudly and as terribly as they can, in order to embolden each other, and terrify their enemies; and it is not unlikely that they have followed this practice for ages, for it is "similar to the roar of the children of Israel when they were victorious." But not to be too long, let us pass over the numerous facts which throughout the country prove their antiquity, and we shall give a description of the cities and mounds, &c., in another issue.

TESTIMONY OF INDIAN TRADITIONS.

ONLY in order to have the story of the Record, namely *"the stick of Ephraim"* in their midst, I ask the reader's unbiased attention to the following stories, which were made known to the world a few years ago, by impartial men, and of high character, and which prove that a quite similar tradition exists among the various tribes throughout the continent, regarding the remarkable book in question.

Mr. Boudinot gives the following story about the Indians he was among:—"There is a tradition among their chiefs that their forefathers had a book very similar to the book the white people have now [the Bible], that they were a contented, civilized, and successful people. They say also that their fathers possessed wisdom and supernatural powers from 'the Great Spirit,' whereby they were empowered to foretell future events, and to oversee the fate of nations; which knowledge they transmitted to their children, on condition that they obey the holy laws contained in *that book*; and that they thereby received many blessings and great salvations, until they were a blessed people; but, that those powers had since been lost from their midst a long time ago."

Col. James Smith writes the account of his journey, when he was taken in their midst,—"They have a tradition that the angels, or 'those who dwell in heaven,' as they call them, visited their forefathers frequently when they first settled in the continent, that they spoke to them, teaching them how to pray to the Great Spirit; and there are many more things which they are not now allowed to know anything of."

Mr. Boudinot, in his remarks on their language, says,—"Their language, in its origins, the idiom of its sentences, and its particular construction, shows all the properties of Hebrew; and what is very remarkable, and merits particular attention, is that it contains most of the particular features of that language, especially those things which distinguish it from other languages. I heard a tradition from an old man of the *Stockbridge* tribe, that his forefathers possessed a *Sacred Book*, which was passed down from generation to generation, and was eventually hidden in the earth, and ever since then they have been downtrodden by their enemies; but that those records were to be restored to them, and that they would then have supremacy over their enemies, possession of their country, and would enjoy their original rights and privileges." After relating many traditions similar to the above, Mr. Boudinot notes, "Can any man, having read the account of these Indian traditions, which are found among the tribes of these various nations, from the west to the east, and from the south to the north, completely apart from each other, written by different historians of high learning and character, having the best advantages, in different places, and at different times, without their being able to associate with each other; can anyone, I say again, disbelieve their testimony, thinking all this stems from accident, or a deliberate intention to deceive, when no one would gain by it?"

From these traditions, it can be seen that these people in early times had a holy or "Sacred Book," containing sacred laws [or the great things of God's law], written for them by their forefathers, through the supernatural influence of God's Spirit, through which they prophesied. They inform us that this book was passed from father to son, until it was hidden in the earth, but not to remain there forever either, rather to be revealed in the fulness of time which God saw fit, as a great blessing, and to be a means to gather them all back to possession of their country. And is this not totally in keeping with what Ezekiel prophesied with regard to the "stick of Joseph?" namely that God would take it from the place it was hidden in the midst of the Ephraimites, and that he would put it with the stick of Judah, that is the Bible, and then would take the sons of Israel from the midst of all the nations they went to, and would gather them to their own country.

The prophet Jeremiah speaks clearly about this last gathering to their country, chap. xxxi, 8, —"Behold, I will bring them [his people Israel] from the north country, and gather them from the coasts of the earth, and with them the blind and the lame; the woman with child and her that travaileth with child together: a great company shall return thither; for I am a father to Israel, and Ephraim is my firstborn," namely in the last gathering or restoration to their country which God had promised their fathers. So it is reasonable to expect that God would start the work in their midst. In ver. 18, he says—"I have surely heard Ephraim bemoaning himself thus: Thou hast chastised me, and I was chastised, as a bullock unaccustomed to the yoke; turn thou me, and I shall be turned; for thou art the Lord my God." How similar this is to the lamenting of the Ephraimites at present, according to the previous traditions, is it not? and the next verse shows that the missionaries of the sects are working in vain, trying to make the American Indians repent and comply with their forms, and their human creeds; for, "Surely *after* that I was turned, I repented [and not before that]; and *after* that I was *instructed* [that that book had been revealed], I smote upon my thigh, I was ashamed, yea, even confounded, because I did bear the reproach of my youth;" namely the decline because of their disobedience to that "sacred book" which had been hidden from them in the earth. Yet, it will be restored to them, for the next verse shows that,—"Is Ephraim my dear son? is he a pleasant child? for since I spake against him, I do earnestly remember him still; therefore my bowels are troubled for him; I will surely have mercy on him, saith the Lord." We see that the mercy is to begin from the Lord's side—not by sending missionaries to preach the "stick of Judah" to them, but by restoring to them their own *stick*, the "sacred book" which was hidden from them, according to their own expectation. It is not strange then that thousands, if not millions, in money that was wasted on missionaries to preach to them is only loss, and worse than loss, by hardening them, and binding the few who might believe them [although I have not yet seen one of the thousands who listened to them who believed them] tighter with doctrinal ropes, so that they will not be so ready to accept their "sacred book," when God reveals it to them.

By now we have doubtless found Ephraim in "multitudes of nations in the midst of the earth," "to the west of Jerusalem," with many traditions among themselves, that the stick of Joseph, "the sacred book" which their forefathers had, was hidden in some corner of the country; and not only that, but they also testify that they expect it to be restored to their possession, and that it will be instrumental in giving to them a knowledge of God's dispensations to their fathers, and that they will return to their proper course and privileges. And now, reader, is the *Book of Mormon* this stick of Ephraim perhaps? Why can it not be? Indeed, it is very similar to the description. It was found in the land of Ephraim; it contains the great things of the law of God to Ephraim, written under the supernatural influence of the Spirit of God to the prophets and apostles who issued from his loins. It has been hidden in the earth for hundreds of years, and in these latter days it has been brought forth by the power of God. It has been put with the stick of Judah, that is the Bible; and behold, the two have become one stick in his hand. They are one in their Author and their origin—one in purpose—one in doctrine—composed under the influence, and by the instructions of the same Spirit—and they are one in the hand of God's chosen servants, preached throughout the world, and it is strange how they agree in everything! And he who professes to believe the Bible, and at the same time denies the truth of the Book of Mormon, must do so without scriptural or logical grounds. No thoughtful man will think less of it because it was found in America, for it can be seen that that is a proof of its truthfulness. It would not be possible for it to answer the prophecies had it been found anywhere else. Neither should it be judged without being read, or by the erroneous stories that are told about it by its enemies; because that is how such people spoke of the Bible in turn, and that is how the majority speak of it now. That does not prove it to be fraudulent, any more than similar testimony proves the Book of Mormon to be fraudulent.

REVIEW.

SUBSTANCE OF A SERMON ON THE MIRACLES, *in order to enlighten the Public, and show the Deceit of the Creatures who call themselves "Latter-day Saints."* By W. R. DAVIES, Dowlais.

HERE we find Mr. Davies, at last, after boring the public by delivering from the pulpits his stories about the Saints, has published a little treatise, and called it "Substance of a Sermon," thinking it will sell better, and that it will be more profitable than the other way. We would like to see Mr. Davies, or someone else, attacking our doctrines, in order to show our errors, or else leaving us alone. But, let the reader not suppose that what he calls a "sermon" is any cleaner than usual of the ink of libel, and the stains of calumny. But our eyes will run first over this essay, in order to collect a few proofs of Mr. Davies's feelings when composing it; for the success of a theologian depends greatly on the moods which govern him in his task. And Mr. Davies gives us this rule by which to judge him too when he says:—"The tendency of every act demonstrates its source; if the spring is bad, its streams must also be bad." The following are the pious sentences of the pen and soul of the reverend minster of Caersalem, Dowlais:—"The creatures," "something below men," and yet able to deceive the public, yes, his own sensible listeners and members! "Such transparent trickery," "the false Christs," "an ignorant, characterless Englishman, who has been in Cardiff jail for his wickedness," "this scoundrel," "fool-headed followers," "braggart preaching," "ignorant fools," "a mockery of administering sacraments," "deceitful leaders," "an abyss of presumption," "foul fiends," "let them be given the name of Satanists of the nineteenth century." We have already read about forty-seven lines, that is a large part of a book of 20 pages, which is called "*Substance of a Sermon* of the Rev. W. R Davies," and have had quite a fine gleaning of the *Davisism* it contains! Dear brethren, pray for this Mr. Davies, for his soul too is precious despite everything! We and he are known by our fruits. And also, we would like the reader to bear in mind that we are not attacking Mr. Davies, but we are merely men who have finally been forced to defend that way in which we worship the God of our fathers in all conscience, and we shall endeavor to be as gentle as his needless attacks on us allow us to be; but it is a duty to our God and to our religion to defend our characters from false accusations, even though we expose the character of our libeler; for we have already given sufficient examples to show that he deserves that name, and is a liberal reviler and gossip-monger. But let us take note of his assertions, in order to see the great difference that exists between *Davisism* and *Apostolicism.*

"Paul mentions several gifts, &c., all effects of the same Spirit, and the aims were *one*, namely the edifying of the church." *Well done*, Mr. Davies! That is how it was; and that is what we say too. But why do you deny it in the same breath? If you admit that the miraculous gifts were for the edifying of the church, you must admit the necessity for them, or you must be accusing Christ of arranging vain and unnecessary means of edifying. If you admit that the church of Christ is the same now, does it not need edifying now? What sort of edifying is needed now but the apostolic kind? And how is that to be had except through the same divine Spirit? And how, Mr. Davies, can that divine Spirit do its work now, except by imparting the same miraculous gifts that it imparted to that end in the apostolic age? What, sir! Are there two types of edifying? The one apostolic and the other Davisistic? The one for sinners of that age, and the other for sinners of this age? But, carry on; edify yourself in your Caersalem with the Davisistic one, at the cost of those who shall be so foolish as to listen to you; and we shall take and proclaim to everyone, that edifice which you yourself admitted to be apostolic. Revile and persecute until you grate on the ears of the rest of your listeners, concerning us. "We raise the cross of the age; we run and succeed," before your eyes.

"II. Our text speaks of officials of the apostolic church together with the various gifts that were given them, to make them fit and proper to fill and fulfill their important posts," says Mr. Davies. This is another very good admission; and do you not assert that you fill some of these church posts? Are you so much better than they, that you can fill them whilst denying and mocking those gifts? You can fill the offices of the Davisistic order fully, with nothing of the Spirit of God. But not even Timothy could fill the post you claim, without the gifts of the Holy Spirit, which he received "through the laying on of hands, and prophecy" (1 Tim. iv, 14). But you possess enough authority to boast that you have wiped out the "Papist tradition, *alias* that holy ordinance," from Caersalem, when you had the "bridle in your hand!" When we heard you arguing with the established priests, we thought you were a very fervent supporter of the apostolic plan. Very good, then; keep on so. But, why do you turn from the apostolic one, mocking and abolishing its ordinances as Papism, in persecuting us? "All Apostolic" is your cry to them; "apostolicism has died out," with Davisism on its ruins, is your cry in our faces in the same breath. Where is James? Behold, we have found out the spring that gives forth sweet and bitter waters! He did not know where it was. Yes, certainly; Timothy in Ephesus failing to fulfill his office without a *gift*, together with the laying on of hands and the spirit of prophecy; and the Timothy of Dowlais claiming that he fills the same post easily without one of the gifts of the Spirit! You see that you paid nothing to fill your post in Ephesus; and how, say you, shall you pay to fill it in Caersalem? You have many men there, doubtless honest of purpose, trying to worship God as best they may. How can you deprive them of the heavenly gifts and blessings which you admitted God placed in the Church for its "edifying, for the perfecting of the saints, for the work of the ministry?" Are you not Timothy by office, but a Timothy who is devoid of the gift for that office?

"III. The object of the false prophets of the prophecy of Moses was to lead their followers to worship false gods, by promising great things to them. The object of the elders of the Satanists is to defraud unlearned and weak-headed men; not to urge them to be godly, but by promising them heaven and paradise in America, and feeding them some rubbish beneath common sense."

Now, Mr. Davies, we think you know better than this. Here is an example of comparative reasoning:—"Because men had bad purposes in the days of Moses, these must have bad purposes now," he says: because he has not shown, and cannot show, any similarity in us to the deceit of those men. And could one not as appropriately say, "Thou art the man" who is guilty of deceit? According to his reasoning, one could condemn any denomination or persons in Dowlais as deceivers, because he himself is such. If our sermons are "rubbish beneath common sense," how do we have more numerous congregations than you! Why do we baptize so many more than you? Is every one of the scores who turned to us from your sect "beneath common sense?" Do you think to keep your members in their darkness, by reviling us, as "Martha of the two baptisms," &c., and saying that we are weak in the head, &c? If so, you will not succeed in upholding your "goddess," any more than your fellow-craftsman Demetrius formerly succeeded. Men see better now. "Money," you say: we have shown in this issue of the PROPHET that that is your craft; and we shall show it more clearly yet. Is it amongst us, or in Caersalem, that many pounds are *demanded* each month, and a fair, or auction every time someone is baptized? Answer true, for the common people have known this for a long time. "A *fund* to help the Apostle to go to Jerusalem" you say, also. We deny every syllable of that, and we find it difficult to think that you yourself believe it. You know full well, or should know, that there neither is, nor has been anyone in our midst claiming to be an apostle. We say to you also that none of us has any intention of going to Jerusalem and that none of us said any such thing; and so we have no *fund* to that end, nor any other end, except what is according to the *Act of Parliament*. If you have any proofs of your assertions, out with them; if not, do not sell yourself to form harmful false accusations about your neighbors. How do you know that we do not urge people to live a godly life? Have you ever been in our meetings? No! This, like every other accusation of yours, is to be taken to mean the opposite, and our fruits testify publicly to that. But about "going to America," everyone has free agency,—they may go or not; and do not you also give the same freedom to your followers? If you are willing to judge us by our fruits, come closer, and we invite you to publish to the world every bad thing we have done, if you will permit in return publishing one of a hundred of your faults so that the world may judge; otherwise, leave characters in peace, and come now to reason or scripture. Answer, who has sects, hatred, various opinions, and splits; yes, who, Mr. D.? we, or the *Baptists No.* 1, *No.* 2, *No.* 3, *No.* 4,—or who then? Come closer and judge without bias for once. Who persecutes you, calling you "rubbish," &c.? On what tree and in what vineyard grew the golden apples of calling men who are in the name of Christ, "*Satanists*"? From what holy mouth were honest neighbors heard being called a "vile mob?" If the Pharisees formerly were known by their fruits, and we too now, why is Mr. Davies from Dowlais not also known by his fruits?

"IV. There were never miracles in the church, but out in the world," says Mr. D. To assert such a thing is no more than to proclaim deceit. I wish the reader to look closely, yes, to note minutely, whether it was in rooms, or in the church, or in the world, that miracles were performed.

Ha! Mr. Davies, you admitted that the greatest miracle that was performed was the resurrection of Christ; but who, from the world, saw that? Who, from the world, saw Dorcas, or that young man being raised to life by the apostles? and that girl, or the mother of Peter, by Christ, and a host of other miracles? and yet, you assert that miracles were performed publicly, in the world. A pity that you had not researched somewhat into your subject and your assertion. Who was the Mr. Davies who said a few pages back, that the gifts under observation were "for the edifying of the church?" Strange how short his memory is, is it not? If the miracles of Christ and the apostles were to benefit the world, why did they not immediately heal all the sick people of the world? And if it was according to their own minds, without feeling the exhortation of the Spirit to that, that they healed the sick, why would they not drive the devil out of that man? Why did they all leave poor Timothy, in his "frequent weakness?" And since Paul said that it was "for the edifying of the church" that God set up all the offices and that the duty of one of the offices, i.e., the presbytery, as you admitted, is to anoint the sick saints with oil, who are you, and from whom did you receive authority, Mr. Davies, in all seriousness, to abolish and deny all this, persecuting those who use them, whilst also calling yourself a minister of the gospel of Christ? Answer, Sir, for people fail to understand how these things can be so. You should profess miracles, or cease forming assertions and setting them to hang one another like this.

"V. If the men who claim their miracles can fulfill them," he says, "why do they not do that in the markets of Merthyr, on the mountaintops," &c. Here is the trumpet voice of his brother, the giant from Abercanaid; the same tune like the hunter's horn, and this horn has been in the family from the day when our Master was tempted to turn that stone into bread in the wilderness. But for more of the history of this voice, and its owners, see "*The Scales*." Had Mr. Davies been with Jesus Christ, he would have mocked him for a deceiver, because he said, "that he could not do many miracles in Nazareth, because of their disbelief." If Christ did his miracles in order to prove his mission and gospel, and if Mr. Davies admits that he did enough for that, what drives him to ask more of us, to prove what he admits. And, is it reasonable for you to seek from us, or for us to seek from you, a sign to prove the truth of the New Testament? Christ's were signs going *before* belief, it is true, in order to prove that he was the Only Begotten from the Father. We do not claim to be such as he; and why do you seek of us to prove that we are what we do not profess? Signs "*following* them that believe," are what we have. You will place us on the mountain top *before* believing, you say. "Which shall *follow* them that believe," says Christ. Whom shall we obey, you or Christ? If you want more signs to affirm the faith, go to its great Founder; but if you are satisfied with the signs which *follow* obedience to it, we have them according to the promise; and they are so greatly needed, they are so sweet, so precious, for the edifying of our church, that we would not wish to lose them for the world and its fulness, yes, even giving our lives for them. No more proof is needed that Mr. Davies is completely ignorant of them, than his admission that they are not needed in this age. And if we did not have them, you ought to search them out, and be ready to accept them instead of refusing and denying them after they have come, even though that might burst the fetters of prejudice; we say that they pay better in this world, by perfecting you, even though the hope of your profit may fade. What power have we over the fact that they *follow* belief? If you reject them because they are not in Merthyr market, take up the argument with their Author himself, for we do not claim to be able to accomplish the least of them of ourselves. Many a one who, like you, has been mocking, doubting, has come closer, listened, and understood that you tell lies about us; they have believed, obeyed, and had divine and clear proofs of the truth of our faith, by enjoying the gifts full of grace from God's Spirit. What carries these men on under every scorn and persecution, then? You, who profess to be a philosopher, and know the human heart, when were a half million, in such an enlightened age as this, seen embracing any religion, which promised powerful gifts to them; and then, although finding it lacking in the gifts that it promised, persevering through all persecutions? We dare say that such a thing has never been in our world; yet, we must have it, if we are deceiving the world concerning the spiritual gifts that are in the church. Here is a subject for you, Mr. Davies, that would repay you better for discussing it, than all the *business* of reviling.

Mr. Davies shows his complete ignorance of the gifts of the Spirit, especially the "gifts of healings" in the following—"A miracle was not contained in the faith of the man, but in the powerful name of Jesus of Nazareth—remember the lame man at the door of the temple; that poor wretch expected nothing but money; and if faith is necessary, there must be, according to their own reasons and admission, few of the men of least faith under God's heavens, for they lay hands upon themselves." We have quoted this sentence in order to show how many lines this talented man wastes to say *nothing at all!* "A few of the men of *least* faith,"—what does he mean? "According to their own reasons," who, and what? "and their own admission." What are they, I wonder? Who "lay hands upon themselves," I wonder? He forgot to tell us that; and if he himself understands what he means, we must admit to being beaten in this! As for that lame man to whom he refers, he has brought a witness against himself; and if he had read his Bible, he would have seen that he was healed through his faith. Acts iii, 12. Peter denies that he healed the lame man—"Why marvel ye at this? or why look ye so earnestly on us, as though by our own power or holiness we had made this man to walk [it is not we who have done this], rather the God of our fathers has glorified his son Jesus." Yes, there is the mystery of the matter, Mr. Davies; and God shall glorify the name of his son Jesus again when, where, and in whatever manner he wishes, yes, through healing *Little Maggie* when he so wills, whether that pleases you or not. Although the miracle was not contained in the faith of the man, he did not receive healing without faith. Shall we believe you or Peter? Ver. 16:—"And his name [that is, Jesus] through faith [of the lame man] in his name [Jesus] hath made this man strong, whom ye see and know; yea, the faith [which the lame man had] which is by him [Jesus], hath given him [the lame man] this perfect soundness in the presence of you all." If Mr. Davies will not admit his mistake, let the argument be between him and Peter, from now on. Although at first the lame man expected to receive money, yet it is obvious that he changed his expectation as soon as Peter started to speak. We ask Mr. Davies, What did Peter give the lame man? He will admit that it was neither silver, nor gold, nor anything of the things of the world, and yet it is said in ver. 6 that Peter gave something to him,—"But *such* as I have, *that* [what was that?] give I thee." He could not present him with anything but what he had, namely a testimony of a crucified and resurrected Healer, who could heal him if he took the medicine—"this treasure (that is the gospel) in earthenware vessels. And the lame man believed *that*, which is proved in that he immediately received the blessing. And his name, that is Jesus, through the faith of the lame man in him, according to the testimony which he heard from Peter concerning him, healed him. Why does Mr. Davies bring examples like *this* to try to prove his belief, when they are completely contrary to it? Why would you not remember the example of that other lame man in Lystra? Here is an *analogous case*, or similar situation, Mr. Davies. The two men were lame from their mother's womb—the one at the gate of the one temple, and the other at the gate of the other temple. Peter and Paul offered the same cure to the sick men, on the same conditions, for they were fellow-workers for the same powerful Healer. Read the story in Acts xiv, 9, as follows,—"The same [that is the lame man] heard Paul speak [as the other heard Peter], who [that is Paul] steadfastly beholding him [that is the lame man] and perceiving that he [the lame man] had FAITH TO BE HEALED, said with a loud voice, Stand upright on thy feet." One wonders whether Mr. Davies wishes us to believe that Paul ordered this one, or Peter the other, to stand on their feet against their will? Could they have done that without an effort, or would they be striving without faith? Is faith not the cause of every effort? Let this philosopher search the laws of *philosophy*, before showing his foolishness to the world. Paul would not have ordered him to stand until *he saw that he had* FAITH, despite testifying strongly to him, which is the basis of faith, and continuing to do so, and steadfastly beholding the lame man, for what but to see whether he had *faith?* It would have been presumption for Paul to order him to stand without seeing his faith, for the disappointment would have been a shame to the name of Jesus. And, one wonders whether Peter would have caused the other to stand up, without seeing that he too had that faith that Paul judges so essential to receive such a blessing from the same God? Oh, no; no one but Mr. Davies thinks so, I suppose. You insist on our healing whomever you will, without faith or any necessary qualification. Is this not like that madman who found fault with the doctor for not curing him, when he refused to take any of his medicine. "If you are a doctor," he said, "you should cure me by looking at me." "By only saying the word," says Mr. Davies. If faith is not necessary to receive temporal blessings, why is it so essential in order to receive spiritual blessings, which are imparted by the One? If faith is not necessary to receive healing, why does James say "the prayer of *faith* shall heal the sick?" and why does Christ say, "Thy faith hath made thee whole," "All things are possible to him that believeth," "If thou believest, it is possible," &c.? Where is our preacher's memory? He mocks us for demanding faith! He would have mocked Jesus Christ for the same thing. If he admitted the New Testament as a yardstick, we would soon show that he knows little of the plan of its miracles or its faith.

After showing us two definite commands to anoint the sick with oil, and the laying on of hands, on page 6, Mr. Davies denies all this on page 14. "Not using medicine, the hands of the apostles and the prayers of the saints, but only saying the word," he says. Which of the two shall be believed? His object in asserting this is so that he might ask some "presumptuous creatures" whom he calls "Satanists" to heal the sick in the markets of Merthyr against their will. The reason that he gives for their abolishing ordinances, and the practice of the ways laid down, according to their duties, are the unpromised exceptions that the shadows of the apostles, their clothes, &c., have healed the sick. Does he not know the difference between custom and exception? Would it not be the same thing for him to ask us to forgive the sins of the worst unconditionally, because Christ said to one, "Thy sins are forgiven;" and ask our shadow to heal the sick, because God has done that through some of his servants! Is there any *promise* that someone would be healed thus, as there is the promise that the sick saints would be healed through practice of the ordinance through faith?

"He claims that some presumptuous man, whom he calls a praiseworthy Apostle, is here, now," and he asks whether the "presumptuous man," "the praiseworthy Apostle," the "Satanist," has done any of God's miracles? Here is an example of his terrible calumny. We, and the public, we believe, press him only to name one presumptuous man who calls himself an Apostle, or even people who are called Satanists. Then you shall hear William asking, Did his shadow heal anyone in Merthyr; and Davies answering, "No," without offering any proof of his assertions, any more than usual. Then, we shall hear Richard, I suppose, as judge before his friends. "Then we shall see," he says. See, indeed! What shall you see, judge? We see not one witness, only the unfounded assertions of your own two elbows, namely W. asking, and Davies swearing to him, let him say what he might. We see some strange trail between the two of you, say his friends. Well, no one dares say a word against us, says the judge; on with his sentence. Yes, say his two witnesses. "His assertions are not—" But wait, Mr. Judge; what are the assertions? They are not proved yet, say his friends. Bah, that doesn't *matter*; are not the assertions of W. and D. enough? And on with it! "And his followers also, just a heap of lies." Take it slowly, say his friends again; we cannot follow you Mr. Judge. Followers of whom? What proves them mad; and how do we know that they are lying, unless we hear their claims. Oh, says he, "do not listen to anything they say for themselves; otherwise, you will not believe my witnesses, and you dare not doubt a judge like me, who has had his own way every time, and preaches every Sunday, administering the holy ordinances to you, and to be sure you should believe me in everything, since you maintain me with your money, like a gentleman, to rule over you, take care not to doubt me, nor to listen to that "presumptuous man," for fear of my rod; know you not that I shall excommunicate you from the synagogue also!" Thereupon, I think I hear someone, more reasonable and brave than the others, having partly opened his eye to see the oppressor's tyranny, shouting out, "Turn you away; the sooner the better you break our bonds, and turn us out of such a prison, so that we might dare to think for ourselves; this is a worse prison than the bondage of the blackest Negro; the greatest blessing you can do for us is to excommunicate us from this Davisism, so that we might receive apostleship." When the judge heard that, his face paled, and the legs of his two witnesses shook like Belshazzar of old, for he would lose their pennies if he lost them. And, alas! what shall I do? If they listen to apostleship they will leave me. If I prevent them from listening to it, away they will go on that road. Say what shall I do; say you, Davies." "Oh," says Davies, with a victorious smile, "I know what we shall do! Since they must have witnesses, do you not remember that we three wrote a splendid epistle about the "Satanists" which was so highly recommended that it was printed in our denominational publication!" "Very good, Davies," says the judge. "Yes, friends, see the *Baptist* for March, and you shall find enough proofs that we three are truthful enough." "Well," say his friends, "if those are the best proofs you have of your truthfulness, it's all up with you. What, to offer us the *Baptist* as true! He has himself been carrying the word "TRUE" on his forehead for years, but has failed to convince us despite that; and now his guilty conscience has come to believe that an unfinished task, and more honestly than you has rubbed the word clean off his forehead for shame,—is it he whom you offer us as true? Is this not the *sinkhole* into which you have spewed the contents of your foul insides for years, and would you wish us to sully our noses again in your stinking liquid? Oh, no, thanks be to the truth, the issues of the PROPHET have opened our eyes at last to see that it was you two who originated that *hermaphrodite*, under the influence of *delirium tremens*, or some other *hydrophobia*! No, no, Mr. Judge, we cannot believe your witnesses there, nor here either, for they contradict one another; for example, William says in the *Baptist*, "Were hands laid on T——s, J——s, to be healed? *No*, men know better." But listen, Mr. Judge, what your other dear witness says, namely Davies. On page 16, of his essay,—"Hands were laid on T——s J——s," says he; how shall we believe witnesses like these? No wonder you would not want to cross-examine them; they say too much to be true; and indeed, sir, the two make a liar of you often. On page 6, William asserts that no one has been healed through those he calls Satanists, so says Davies, on page 9, that no sign has ever been seen with them.

[*To be continued.*]

THE EDITOR OF THE *TRUE BAPTIST*.

OUR readers will remember the letter sent to this man, in response to the libelous accusations of his brother from Dowlais, a copy of which is to be found in the July PROPHET; and that the editor decided that the best way to demonstrate his fairness to all sides was not to publish it—that the most gentlemanly approach to us was to open his monthly periodical for our enemies to accuse us of every folly and evil under pseudonyms, but to close it immediately against any word of self-defense we might offer, in the face of such accusations. Mr. Davies of Dowlais accused William Henshaw and another brother of issuing a challenge to him to come out to debate, which was a complete lie, worded and devised in such a way as to give the said Mr. Davies a reason to laugh at them. The two brethren tried to defend themselves through the same press that had condemned them, but they were not allowed to do so. That was too much justice for the Editor to permit. If he had given them space, he would be praised, but he did not do so. He thinks he has got the keys into his own hands, and that he would scarcely take the trouble to go from Cardiff to see if he is telling the truth or not. And then, after all the two men did, poor things, to assert their innocence—after testifying so soberly that it was not they who issued the challenge, the Editor would have everyone believe that it was; and the proof he offers of this is, "that the writing is very similar to the writing of that letter." How similar, I wonder? Similar enough to contradict the testimony of two witnesses? It was not his fault that he could not get more weight than this feather to put in the scales in the face of the testimony of the two men. Is it reasonable to suppose that they would give such an opportunity to a man they know has been for years with all his might accepting every evil about them eagerly, and searching for libel material, as the tiger for prey? If not, no one but his *partner* dares think like that, I suppose. Let everyone notice the outpouring of his heart through five lines which he calls his five "*reasons*."

His *first* "reason" is,—"The people who address me are beneath my notice." Yes, reader, this is the "reason" he offers for his lengthy essay, which takes a large part of four pages of the *Baptist*, to answer those "who are beneath his notice." Let the reader judge if he believes himself. He is a strange man, taking such notice of something "beneath his notice!" His proof that they are beneath his notice is, because of their names: "Abel and Henshaw; Oh excellent names! Oh shining characters!" There is a *specimen* of new-fashioned *logic*, or old-fashioned from the days of *Bajazett*. Who has heard that Mr. Davies has ever discussed one subject? His subject is persons; assertion is his reason; and libeling is his trade! And so here, because a man's parents named him "Abel," he and every other Abel, from the oldest down, are "beneath the notice" of this famous man! Let those parents who desire his *notice*, take care to ask him what names they can give their children. "Henshaw;" what a pity his ancestors did not foresee that his name would lower him "beneath the notice" of the sages of this age! "Oh shining characters!" he says; yes, so shining that even he was not able to find a blemish on them since they have been in the church of Christ, even though he tried hard; and if there were some blemishes on them, would that condemn the principles they profess? He is a strange reasoner; he would reason not only himself and his brethren to be deceivers, but even Christ's religion to be a fraud, because Peter, and Judas, &c., betrayed him. We do not profess to be perfect, and it would be useless for him to profess that to his acquaintances. It is not long since Mr. Davies considered William Henshaw's character to be shining enough for him to bring him to his house, and extend an offer for him to join with him, and be a preaching assistant to him. And the next thing this gentle man offered him after he had refused his services, and shown abhorrence for his company, was to ask him if he would drink a glass of poison, to prove that Christ had spoken the truth—"If they drink any deadly thing, it will do them no harm." But Henshaw refused to satisfy his desire, as his teacher refused the invitation of the other's master to cast himself from the pinnacle of the temple. Henshaw took his leave from him, and from that time Mr. Davies has been trying to blacken his character with every story he can find, until Henshaw is not only unworthy to be a servile preacher for him, but is "beneath his notice." He is "fool-headed Henshaw." Let "this scoundrel" go, not as a preacher under Mr. Davies of Dowlais, but to "Cornwall" now, "and let him make fools of the Cornishmen," instead of the Dowlaisites, as Mr. Davies wanted him to do a short time ago; "and he can live there on *their* backs." It would be an unending task to talk about grammatical errors where so many moral errors are deliberate ones. "At last [Henshaw] came, and laid his unclean and sinful hands on her," that is those hands he thought a few months before, were clean and holy enough to break the sacrament for his flock! It is strange the sudden change that has happened to his hands, as well as every other part of his body and his name! Yes, poor thing, he has turned into sour grapes, every joint and bone, from his head to his toes, like those did in the wolf's eyes, in the old *fable*. Then, his "character," he says; that must be reviled too after he has refused my service, so that he does not do good to anyone else. Characters, is it? he should be silent until the latest ditch in Dowlais has defended its character. Pity the poor *Cornishmen* if they relied on such a shepherd as this to feed them; and if the character he gives to Henshaw is true, the Dowlaisites would be to be pitied too if Henshaw had acceded to his request, i.e., according to his own reasoning; and yet, if all he says is true, their hunger for wholesome food would not be greater than it is now. Perhaps he justifies himself by saying that he did not know at that time that Henshaw was so *unclean*, *sinful*, *Satanic*, *devilish*, *&c*. Worse still then, to have offered a man such a position over immortal souls, without knowing who and what he was. May his flock forgive him for this, if they can. But why does he still continue to persecute such people? Was it not the same one who made us all? If they had drunk *brandy* until they turned their noses blue, and disfigured their faces like turkey heads, and if they had stayed in the school of Bacchus until Sunday morning, he would not have cause to publish it in the *Baptist*. If they had appropriated to themselves three or four undeserved names and titles, as well as a list of pseudonyms, they would still be no worse than those who profess to be in the list of theologians. But having failed to devise one blemish on their persons, he closes his first *reason* by saying in borrowed words—"O my soul, come not into their secret." We are very pleased to hear this, and more of an Amen is said to this than to anything he says. We cannot stay with that pipe any longer. Hurry, the gas is lighting in the second, and is pouring out blue.

He says—"The names you give yourselves are beneath contempt." What! what name is beneath contempt? The name of a listener to this wise man who calls himself a preacher of the gospel, and a servant of God, answering for himself. "Like the only true church of Christ." Is it a man who professes to be a shepherd of the flock of Jesus Christ who says that being "the only true church of Jesus Christ" is "beneath contempt?" Yes, reader, and without offering so much as one proof of his assertion either. The *gas* is high in this pipe—"praiseworthy apostle, Capt. D. Jones," he says. He does not love me much either, evidently; it is strange how he hates a man with whom he has never exchanged a word, has never been in his company, nor wished to be! It is foolish to hate and persecute the whole lineage of him who flogs him with his own stick. If he were to be silent, people would forget the shame he suffered in time; but his old wounds are festering and gathering again, and there is nothing to be done but change the plaster, in order to get to the bottom of it, or let them take his life. As for the first title, it is more honorable than any we ever claimed. The father is the same as that of the "Satanists," "little creature," "sinful creature," "apostolic Capt.," "lying, deceiving, devilish tribe," "living in idleness at the expense of deceit, lies, and presumption," &c. Every reasonable man believes we have cause to be proud of these titles, considering from whence they come; and, indeed, it must be admitted that we sometimes take some pride in being worthy of the evil words of professed persecutors; yet not ourselves, but because of our religion. We do not expect as many titles as our brethren in early times, or our holy Teacher except insofar as we are like them. As for the last title, it is one that was honestly earned, through many years of hard efforts, diligence, and morality, and is respected in the four corners of the earth; and he is the first one in the world found to be hardfaced enough to publish one insult or scorn of it; but he cannot scorn it either, for it is out of reach of his unhealthy odor, and if it does not satisfy him, he should not take it in vain so needlessly. But listen how intense this pipe is by now—"Names that the most presumptuous man would fear to adopt [so we are more so than the majority can be], unless he is a perfect atheist." There, now the pipe has burst, and in its destruction can be seen how it fulfills the old proverb that "it is the thief who shouts thief first;" and the atheist is the first to shout atheist. Listen, all Christians of the world! According to Mr. Davies's logic, those who profess to be "the only true church of Jesus Christ," are atheists! Here is a hard judge. What will become of us if the rod of iron is in his hand, and if he gets a foot on the bench? You must be "as ignorant as the pagan [he says] concerning the things that constitute a church and an apostle," before you would claim to be "the only true church of Jesus Christ!" And does he not claim to be in the only true church of Jesus Christ himself? If so, according to his reasoning, he proves himself to be an atheist like us! Did not Paul truly say that *God* set some in the church—"First APOSTLES [that is as the head of the church, or the body of Christ on the earth, after Christ's ascension into heaven. Who has seen a living body without a head on it? Those who see the body of Christ, with Mr. Davies as a borrowed head of it in Dowlais, having cut off the apostolic head which Christ set on it for the head of an *atheist!* This is one of Mr. Davies's miracles, like the "swallowing his meeting house"], secondarily prophets, gifts of miracles, gifts of healings," &c., 1 Cor. xii, 28. And does Mr. Davies not assert so fearlessly that that is atheism? and that it would be "the same to claim to be Jesus Christ as to claim to be an apostle?" Which of the two is to be believed? They are completely contrary to each other. Is it not the same thing to claim that the apostles whom God set in his "only true church" are atheists in one age or country as in the other? Paul says to the Ephesians (chap. 4,) that they are essential "for the perfecting of the saints, for the work of the ministry, for the edifying of the body of Christ," in that age. Are they not essential for "the perfecting of the saints" in this age too? If the work of the ministry could be carried on in that age without apostles, was it not unnecessary for God to set them for that? If they could not edify the body of Christ without apostles, &c., how can even Mr. Davies, or anyone else now, do more than they could then? If he can answer this without being an atheist, or at least a deist, he can do more than anyone else we have seen yet. But I fancy I can see him starting to look for his interpreters, and then he will shout victory, and "Oh! they were only to continue through the apostolic age; they are not needed afterwards." Yes, but it is Mr. Davies of Dowlais who says that, and is it a speck closer to the truth because of that? No, it is not, even if all the people of the world said it. Paul knows better than they all, and he says that it is all to continue in the church "till we all come in the unity of the faith," &c., that is, in his only true church, "and the knowledge of the Son of God, unto a perfect man." If Mr. Davies claims to be perfect enough without them, he should leave in peace those who choose to enjoy them, in order that they too may be perfected. I wonder if the Son of God was so specific as to set down the plan of his "only true church" in the New Testament, putting in it *apostles*, *prophets*, and the *spiritual gifts* promised to *those who believe*, in every age and country, and then authorized Mr. Davies to establish a church for him in Dowlais on some different plan? He claims that it is atheism to profess His original and divine plan!

But although the second pipe burst, there is yet more and hotter metal in the third. Here he rushes out like a furnace ember, without fear of God or man; and says—"The mad and presumptuous doctrines you proclaim are beneath the notice of every man of common sense," i.e., admitting his first epistle about them testifies that he himself does not possess "common sense;" and as he admits it so fearlessly, let us proceed to see one of his wonders. Here at last Mr. Davies offers *one* proof or example of his claims, and even stranger is the example he quotes—"Such as the gift of healing the sick, and receiving health through the laying on of hands in the name of Jesus." This is an example, says Mr. Davies, of "the doctrine of men and *devils*!" Well, what does Christ say? This is what he said, and says to his saints in every age, "They shall lay hands on the sick, and they shall recover;" yes, that is the doctrine this reverend calls "presumption," "madness," and "devilishness." This is fulfilling the proverb to its limits. Let the reader choose which of the two authors he believes; he cannot believe both. But we shall see how Mr. Davies fares in the face of Paul on these "devilish doctrines" in 1 Cor. xii, 9,—"To another faith; to another the gifts of healing by the same Spirit." Well, Paul, there you are, as devilish as we, according to Mr. Davies. Ver. 28,—"After that miracles, then *gifts of healings*." 30,—"Have all the gifts of healing?" No; but God "gives to each one [in his "only true church"] separately, as it pleases him." 31,—"But covet earnestly the best gifts," says Paul. Oh no; do not covet earnestly any such thing, says Mr. Davies, otherwise you will be as bad as the "Satanists:" that is "the doctrine of devils." There are two strong witnesses, namely the Son of God and Paul, at loggerheads with him already. But we offer one more apostle to prove the "presumption and madness" we profess, so that from the lips of three such witnesses, can be seen if it is we or Mr. Davies who deserves the above accusations. Come, James, what do you say? Is it "the doctrine of devils" to accept health in the name of Jesus? James answers that he says the same thing now as he said before (chap. v, 14),—"Is any sick among you [you saints]? let him call for the elders of the church; and let them pray over him, anointing him with oil in the name of the Lord: and the prayer of faith shall save the sick, and the Lord shall raise him up." It can be seen, by now, whether Mr. Davies for denying, or we for believing, who Jesus Christ, Paul, James, and others say, are the most like atheists. Another outpouring from this third fiery pipe is "an example of the doctrine of devils," namely "casting out devils," he says. This is not so devilish either, according to what our Lord says, when he was similarly accused—"A kingdom divided against itself will not stand." How does Mr. Davies make professing the casting out of devils in the name of Jesus a doctrine of devils, without making what Christ says—"In my name shall they cast out devils," the same thing too. He puts a twist in this pipe now, and says that no one but the apostles were to do that. He must twist it until he makes the Son of God a liar, when he says in Mark xiv, 17—"And these signs shall follow THEM THAT BELIEVE," in every country, and Wales too, at all times, yes, even now. When he proves that no one but the apostles were to enjoy these signs, he will have proved also at the same time, by the same reasoning, that no one but they was to preach, to believe, or to be saved, for the one and the other are commanded, and promised in the same commission. When Mr. Davies finishes this task, he will have an atheist crown on his head; but until then he should leave in peace anyone who chooses to profess them. But the furnace is seething hotter and hotter, until it blows this pipe to shreds again— "And even to see visions, and speak with spirits from the invisible world." Is one to hear the view of a preacher of the gospel in this enlightened age about the above doctrine? "One would think [he says] that no man, even in Merthyr, would lower his ear to listen to such *madness*, *presumption*, and *lies*" as the gifts of the Holy Ghost, which the Son of God promised to the believers, while there was still one imperfect one in their midst! I do not think that Paine or Voltaire ever claimed such dreadful blasphemies as this on the church of God.

But, reader, listen to his fourth pipe roaring. He says "he thinks [on what basis he did not see fit to inform us, if not a guilty conscience rankling] that the aim was to run a fair in order to gather fools, but mainly in an effort to collect money." In this, too, he verifies the old proverb. Who but he has for years now been idling at the expense of the poor Welsh, who work hard in order to contribute many pounds to him every month for standing over their heads to prove that the gospel of the Son of God is "doctrine of devils, deceit, presumption, madness, atheism," &c., &c., and call his children "Satanists," &c. Who but he shouted on the river bank, as soon as he got his feet on *terra firma*, with the water pouring from his clothes, "for the money—bring forth that money, people!" and if one followed him to his pulpit, one would think that it was as easy for angels to fly without wings as for him to carry on without the *money*. When he was lucky enough, some time ago, to baptize three at once, it is strange how he shouted for the money; and he taunted a congregation of white people that they had contributed such and such before, when there was only one baptized, but "now for three times as many!" It is not known what would become of Dowlais if he baptized often. Despite all this, it is not very long since he accused us, although quite falsely, of charging half a crown for baptizing; but we challenge anyone to prove that we have ever charged a halfpenny; and we do not care how much he gets either. But the wonder is that such a man as this can sear his conscience so completely as to be able to accuse the innocent so unsparingly. A man who makes a business of the souls of hundreds between his shop and his three chapels! It is he who accuses us of trying to make a fair out of him in order to obtain money! I wonder if he thinks so much of himself, that we would come to make an offer for him?

But anyone who wants to hear an example of shameless hypocrisy, to hear Satan assuming the form of an angel of light, his face as long, and his tone as howling as if the "hope of his profit" was all about to fade. Listen to him, in all seriousness! "Oh my fellow countrymen, the dear Welsh." "Dear," indeed! dear enough to fill the ears of one part with invented fables about the other part?

But listen, reader, how he turns the fifth pipe against himself. It is so much against his grain that it crosses his own grain, and in his great desire to do evil to others, he says too much to be true—"And it gives me great happiness to announce that only a *few* of my fellow countrymen have been ensnared by these evil creatures." Well, poor wretch! he has enjoyed the "great happiness," as can be seen from issues of the *Baptist*, for a long time. "Few, very few, the dregs of Merthyr, foolish, senseless people," &c., is his refrain always. But listen to him in the next line—"And of those who have been tricked by them, *many* have seen the deceit." Everyone will thank him for this. *A few* have joined, and *many* have turned back. It is beyond common scholarship to say, when one takes *many* out of *a few*, how many will be left? Only Mr. Davies's arithmetic can answer that. This reverend goes so far as to contradict his own brethren. Mr. Editor says in his introductory "fiends" to the above letters—"and the fact that they [the saints] beguile *many*." Here are two old contemporaries who are at loggerheads with each other. They have been at other people's heads for long enough. But listen to this prophet prophesying about himself; for it is by the *rule of contradiction* that he continues on. "But it is true that these presumptuous people will not continue much farther; their foolishness is apparent to all," he says. He has prophesied this amazing prophecy in almost every chapel, where he has proclaimed his names for the saints, and it has been published as a tail to almost every accursed story of his; and although he sees that it is being fulfilled on his own head, he will not admit that it is about himself; yes, although his foolishness is apparent to all.

RHYDYBONT : PRINTED BY JOHN JONES.

PROPHET OF THE JUBILEE.

"THE KINGDOM HAS COME."

No. 4.] OCTOBER, 1846. [VOL. I.

THE COMMENTATORS ARE WITH US!!!

WHO really, would expect it? But it is true enough, nevertheless. All the commentators we have seen, Sprinklers and Immersionists, Episcopal and Nonconformist, Protestant and Catholic—all, we say, are with us! "Barnes is not with you," says someone, "nor Lewis, nor Phillips, nor Jenkins from Hengoed, nor Henry, nor Scott, these notables." Yes they are; Oh, they are!

Barnes, what do you say, then, about our subject, of BAPTIZING FOR THE FORGIVENESS OF SINS? Our opponents maintain now that it is not in order to *receive* forgiveness that is meant by Peter's phrase in Acts ii, 38; what do you say? You are valued by the measure of the "two-and-a-half thousand" among the Independents of South Wales. *Your* word is important, for us to be able to present it to them on behalf of our doctrine. Come, dear Barnes, bring the truth out to your disciples.

BARNES: "*For the forgiveness of sins*. Not only the sin of crucifying the Messiah, but *every* sin. [So say we also.] There is nothing in *baptism itself* that can wash away sin. [True every word. There is nothing in *baptism itself*. You know that the words italicized for emphasis are yours.] That was done [namely washing away sin] by the forgiving mercy of God through Christ's atonement. [Very good again. By that mercy, and through that Atonement, we say also.] But baptism is indicative of willingness to receive forgiveness in that way [True again! For no one willing to receive forgiveness "in that way"—God's way, comes out of the water without it], and is a solemn proclamation of our conviction that there is no other way to forgiveness. He who comes to be baptized, comes with a professed conviction that he is a sinner, that there is no form of mercy except in the gospel, and with a professed willingness to fall in with the conditions of salvation, and to accept it as it is offered through Jesus Christ. [Thank you very much, reverend sir! You proclaim here that he who is baptized professes all this; that is what we proclaim too. You proclaim that no one ever truly fulfills all this, without receiving forgiveness too: so do we. Others from Wales say on this subject that it is a remission of sins as a dispensation that is meant in the text; you say the same thing as we do, that receiving personal forgiveness of sins, namely "all sins" is the meaning. Baptism by immersion (remember your commentary on Rom. vi, 4) is what you have corresponding with forgiveness of all sins, by God's mercy through Christ's atonement. That is the baptism of the gospel, namely this gospel which is preached by us, and us alone. We are *in this*, as are, of course, your 2500 Welsh receivers, true Barnesians; and you, along with them, on the other hand, true Mormons, in principle.] My commentary on Matt. iii, 6, is that John's baptism "is a solemn ordinance, signifying their cleansing from their former sins, and their purification for the particular service of Jehovah." [Yes, it was a solemn ordinance. If it signified a fact, and that fact was a cleansing from their sins; it signified forgiveness, unless you, Albert Barnes, maintain that sins are clean without forgiveness. Now, if their baptism signified "their cleansing" through forgiveness, when, pray, did they receive the forgiveness? You will not say, I know, that it was before the baptism; and if you say after the baptism, I would ask, How long after it? For it was their *own* "cleansing" that was signified, which would be pure deceit, if they did not receive forgiveness. You can see that you are a pure Mormon here too on this clear subject.]

You say again on the same page—"He administered this rite of baptism, or washing, to signify the cleansing from their sins." [All of the same drift, proving that your considered opinion is Mormonism, or forgiveness corresponding with, or through, baptism.]

Matthew Henry, you say a word about this too.

HENRY: "By thus professing their faith in Him, they received forgiveness of their sins, and they partook of the gifts and graces of the Holy Ghost." [Yes, yes; "let each of you be baptized for forgiveness:" which you and we interpret as "*they received* forgiveness," is the word. All one again! Who can deny this subject any more? Over fifteen hundred of yours have been published, received, presumably, and revered as the best gospel. They will accept *your* teaching, no doubt, from *us too* now. It is of no importance *from whom* they receive it; receiving it pure with its heavenly authority is the main thing.]

Now, both of you, Barnes from Philadelphia, and Henry from Caerleon, listen to one thing now. One Evan Griffiths, a respectable man from Swansea, has had a mission and strong support from the Welsh, to proclaim this doctrine under your name, Matthew Henry; and one Thomas Rees, another respectable man from Llanelli, has had a mission and support from the Welsh, to proclaim this doctrine under your name, Albert Barnes; but we receive neither a mission nor strong support from the same Welsh people, to proclaim the same doctrine under the name of one Simon Peter, a great preacher, greater than you two, you know, from Jerusalem, in Palestine. If it were possible to get you two to the next conference meeting of this respectable denomination, we would set this knotty problem before you; namely, why is "baptism for the forgiveness of sins" proclaimed to be *sweet truths* under your names by two of their own preachers, while the same truth precisely is *bitter heresy* under the name of Simon Peter by our preachers.

Here is the state of the parties now on the important subject of *forgiveness of sins through baptism*:— Simon Peter, Matthew Henry, Albert Barnes, Evan Griffiths, Thomas Rees, all the Mormons and the Campbellites—*against* all Independents, Baptists, Methodists, Episcopalians, apart from the supporters of the said Henry and Barnes.

All the *Baptists* are with us!! We have the great commission according to Mark, beginning with—"Go ye into all the world, and preach the gospel to every creature;" and according to Matthew—"Go ye therefore and teach all nations, baptizing them in the name of the Father, and of the Son, and of the Holy Ghost," &c. According to Mark—"He that believeth and is baptized shall be saved." It is the same commission that is given, we say, by the two of them, in different words. "They are the same," say all of the Immersionists too. "They are the same," said the Sprinklers, too, recently. "They are the same," says Dr. Edward Williams, and Evans from Trewen, and Dr. Wardlaw, and Mr. Ewing, and Mr. Munro, and all the others, as we mentioned, who have written on this commission, until recently. All the old sprinklers are with us on the subject.

THE SPIRITUAL GIFTS.—"The two commissions are the same," says Dr. Gale, the Immersionist, and his brethren, Mr. Dore, Dr. Gill, Mr. Gibbs, Mr. Stennett, Mr. Robinson, Mr. Ivimy, Mr. Booth, Mr. A. Fuller, Dr. Ryland, and Mr. Jenkins of Hengoed, and Mr. Evans of Rhuddlan. Yes, "They are the same," says the famous Dr. Carson.

But what of that? says someone. This is what, gentle reader, that Christ set all these things in the commission:—

1. Go ye into all the world, and teach all nations, and preach the gospel to every creature;

2. Baptizing them in the name of the Father, and of the Son, and of the Holy Ghost; and he that believeth and is baptized will be saved;

3. These signs shall follow them that believe; In my name shall they cast out devils; they shall speak with new tongues; they shall take up serpents; and if they drink any deadly thing, it shall not hurt them; they shall lay hands on the sick, and they shall recover;

4. Teaching them to observe all things whatsoever I have commanded you; and lo I am with you alway, even unto the end of the world.

Is the commission to "Go and preach" to stand until the end of the world? Is the commission to "Baptize them," to stand until the end of the world? Is the commission "He that believeth and is baptized," to stand until the end of the world? And is not the other part that is in the middle of the same commission to stand until the end of the world? If the first clause, namely the "Go and preach," and the last clause, namely "I am with you," are to stand until the end of the world, are not the parts which are in the middle of the commission to stand until the end of the world? And are those parts not "these signs that shall follow?" Is that not a commission? And are you all, the learned men named, by saying first that the commission of the two evangelists is the same commission, and by saying secondly that the "unto the end of the world" that is in the commission, is until the end of this dispensation, that is until judgment, are you not, in effect, *Mormons in principle?* You say true that the commission is still in force; consequently, you are thus bound to admit, by your own definition, that the signs that are mentioned in it also remain in force. But what have you done with these signs? Where did you lose them? Yes, why do you not preach the middle of the commission, as well as the first clause, and the last clause? It does not pay to shy away from an answer; the country makes its own interpretation.

Now have you heard the message? No news matches this before!
Caerleon's mighty HENRY, and BARNES of U. S. shore —
They were true Presbyterians, that is the story told;
But now as is recounted both men are Mormons bold.

And Evan Griffiths also as Mormon is half-won,
He Griffiths was of Swansea, the Independents' son:
If not, why are we praising, though pained by deed and din,
A creature who was Mormon, a Saint, beneath his skin?

FATE OF THE HUMAN BODY.

WE believe that the whole human race is subject to suffer punishment because of the transgression of our first parents, i.e., death, or the separation of body and spirit eternally and unconditionally. "From the dust thou camest, and unto dust shalt thou return." But, their seed, apart from those who have sinned, is not under the other punishment which belongs to the transgression, namely the exile of its spirit for eternity from the presence of God, without ever being able to restore itself; for God is the great covenantor (the covenant of multiplication) for the spiritual side, as Adam is for the earthly side, which was the only covenant transgressed in the garden. "For the soul that sins, shall die" for eternity. We do not believe that a just God, who is Father of the spirits, sends sinful spirits into contact with the earthly temples, neither that he exiles those spirits from his presence, when they suffer the punishment for Adam's transgression, namely the separation of spirit and body, in their infancy, or before they actively sin. But we do believe that those spirits "return to God, who gave them" to the bodies in the beginning.

We believe that it is only through the sufferings, death, resurrection, and intercession of Jesus Christ, that each one of the human race will be restored completely and without exception, from the exile or separation of body and spirit because of Adam's transgression, and that every one will have that restoration or resurrection, the worst who was ever on our earth, as well as the best, and that entirely unconditionally. No one's resurrection depends in any way on anything he may do for good or ill.

The best man who ever was, as well as the worst, came under this punishment, in the same completely unconditional manner, without will or power in the matter; and, consequently, the one comes as unconditionally as the other, completely free of it, as Paul says in Rom. v, 18—"Therefore as by the offense of one judgment came upon all men to condemnation; even so by the righteousness of one the free gift came upon all men unto justification of *life*," which is reconnecting the body and the spirit. "For as in Adam all die [that is the separation of body and spirit], even so in Christ shall all be made alive [or the body and spirit shall be restored]." In this sense, we believe in "universal atonement," unconditional and without one exception. Through this atonement will be resurrected every body that was ever made of the soil of this earthly valley, and it will be possessed by its own spirit. It was as proof of this that Jesus Christ said, in John xii, 32—"And I, if I be lifted up from the earth, will draw all men unto me." "For the hour is coming, in the which *all* that are in the graves shall hear his voice, and shall come forth." After this complete, unconditional, and universal salvation, from all of the effects and consequences of Adam's transgression, through Christ's atonement, the human race will enjoy perfect happiness, and an endless eternity in which to enjoy it, unless they are guilty of actual sins; for they will have suffered the punishment for Adam's transgression by dying, and had salvation or restoration, because Jesus Christ destroyed him who had the power of death, despoiled death and the grave, by "becoming death to death, and an end to the grave"—rising as conqueror of everything, with the keys of hell and death at his belt. Everyone will be able to enjoy the presence of his Father in glory and neverending elevation, i.e., *if*—yes, note, if they themselves are not found to be personal transgressors against some law that was given to them.

We believe that babies are incapable of knowing the difference between good and evil, of obeying or disobeying any law; consequently, that God gave them no law; and where there is no law, there is no sin, "for lawlessness is sin;" so they are without sin, and if they die in their infancy, they shall inherit eternal life.

ADDITIONAL TESTIMONIES TO THE TRUTHFULNESS OF THE BOOK OF MORMON.

WE said in the previous chapter that there are more witnesses to prove the Book of Mormon than there are to prove the New Testament. No reasonable person will think, because there are greater proofs of the one, that that diminishes the other at all.

Witnesses to the New Testament.	*Witnesses to the truthfulness of the Book of Mormon.*
Six eyewitnesses, who wrote in their time, eighteen hundred years ago, that they and their brethren had performed miracles.	Three hundred thousand eyewitnesses to the fact that miracles are being performed in the present time.
Not so much as one living witness who was healed in the days of the apostles;—it all rests on the testimony of the six.	There are thousands who testify in our day, that they themselves have received health, without relying at all on hearsay evidence.
The six witnesses of the New Testament are dead, so we cannot cross-examine their testimony.	Tens of thousands of witnesses to the Book of Mormon who are alive today, are reasonable beings, yes, are Welsh, some hundreds of them, so that they can be cross-examined.
Not so much as one impartial witness outside the church, to the fact that miracles were performed in the days of the apostles.	Hundreds of thousands of reliable witnesses who testify that God performs miracles in these days through his servants.

Now, is it not obvious that there are more witnesses to the truth of the Book of Mormon, than remain now to the New Testament? Although there are sufficient to prove the one true, at present there exist more for the other. And does not reason teach us to judge according to witnesses about the matter? So, if one of them is believed, both must be believed. There are several, even among those who profess to be impartial scholars in our time, who assert that no one saw the gold plates, &c., except Joseph Smith; indeed, in Merthyr recently, some people preached from chapel to chapel against this book, when they had never seen it; and when an offer was made to put them straight on the subject, they confessed that they were not telling the stories as truth, but as local legends. The following testimonies are printed in the Book of Mormon; and yet, a man recently published a little anonymous essay, full of unfounded tales, and amongst other lies he announced that no one saw the plates, except Joseph Smith—yes, he asserts this when the Book of Mormon had been in his hands, and contradicts him completely.

We give the testimony of the following people in addition, because they are as impartial and incontestable as it is possible to be; for they were considered truthful, honest men of high character by their acquaintances until the time they saw these things and testified about them to the world—yes, several of them at the time were good enough to hold high positions in the sectarian churches: and yet, their actions in viewing and testifying about the gold plates in question, caused them to be cast out as wrongdoers, as Christ says—"They shall put you out of the synagogues." Even so, no one has been able, nor will be able either, to disprove their testimony: none of them has ever denied it, as Peter and others did, even under duress: but some of them sealed the truth of it with their blood, when they were martyred because of it; they were offered their lives to deny it, but they did not accept deliverance, "that they might obtain a better resurrection."

WITNESSES TO THE GOLD PLATES.

"Be it known unto all nations, kindreds, tongues, and people, unto whom this work shall come, that Joseph Smith, the translator of this work, has shown unto us the plates of which hath been spoken, which had the appearance of gold: as many of the leaves as Mr. Smith has translated we did handle with our hands, and we saw the engravings thereon, which had the appearance of ancient and curious workmanship. This we bear record with words of soberness, that the said Smith has shown unto us those plates, that we have seen and hefted them, and know of a surety that he has got them. We give our names unto the world, to witness unto the world that which we have seen; and we lie not, God bearing witness of it.

"CHRISTIAN WHITMER,	JOSEPH SMITH, Sen.,
"HIRAM PAGE,	JOHN WHITMER,
"PETER WHITMER Jr.,	HYRUM SMITH,
"JACOB WHITMER,	SAMUEL H. SMITH."

What reasonable man will continue to doubt the truth of the Book of Mormon? What book in the world produces more witnesses of its truthfulness? And would not such testimony be admissible in every court, in every land? And yet, these are not the only ones who are in its favor; out of many, we put before you for the time being the testimony of three other acceptable men of that country, who could not possibly have been deceived, or deceived others either.

"We make it known, with words of soberness, unto all nations, kindreds, tongues and people, who shall see this work, that we, through the grace of God the Father and our Lord Jesus Christ, have seen the plates which contain this record [the Book of Mormon], which is a record of the people of Nephi, and also of the Lamanites, their brethren, and also of the people of

Jared, who came from the tower of Babel. We know that they have been translated by the gift and power of God, for his voice hath declared it unto us; wherefore we know of a certain surety that these things are true. We also testify that we have seen the engravings which are upon the plates; for they have been shown to us by the power of God, and not of man. And we also declare, with words of soberness, that an angel of God came down from heaven, and laid the plates before our eyes, that we beheld and saw them and the engravings thereon; and we know that it is by the grace of God the father, and our Lord Jesus Christ, that we beheld them. We therefore bear record that these things are true, and they are marvelous in our eyes. Nevertheless, the voice of the Lord commanded us that we should bear record of them; wherefore, to be obedient unto the commandments of God, we bear testimony of these things, knowing that if we are faithful in Christ, we shall be rid of the blood of all men, and be found spotless before the judgment seat of Christ, to dwell with him eternally. And the glory be to the Father, and to the Son, and to the Holy Ghost, who are one God. Amen.

"OLIVER COWDERY, MARTIN HARRIS."
"DAVID WHITMER,

JOSEPH SMITH'S AUTHORITY TO BAPTIZE, PREACH, &c., TOGETHER WITH THE ESTABLISHMENT OF THE CHURCH.

IN the year 1829, Mr. Smith and Mr. Cowdery, having learned the correct *mode* of baptism from the teachings of Christ to the Nephites, as recorded in the Book of Mormon, had a great desire to be baptized; but knowing of no one who had the necessary authority to administer that sacred and important ordinance, they prayed fervently to the Lord to show them how the necessary authority to administer the ordinances of the gospel was to be restored; and behold an angel of the Lord stood before them! and, laying his hands upon their heads, he ordained them, and commanded them to baptize each other, which they did. This strange circumstance may seem incredible in the eyes of present-day prejudice. But this is not the first time that the Lord has made exceptions to the established laws of the gospel. If one believes the scriptures, it was in a not dissimilar fashion that John the Baptist was sent out to baptize; neither he nor any other of God's servants ever went forth to baptize, nor to do anything else in his name, without being sent by him, through some means or other. John says, "*He* that *sent* me to baptize with water, *he* said unto me." This is his testimony; not only that *someone* sent him, but proof too that it was some real prophet who sent him, because he foretold to him,—"Upon whom thou shalt see the Spirit descending, and remaining on him, the same is he which baptizeth with the Holy Ghost." John, together with the fulfillment of this prophecy about Christ, testifies that it was some prophet of God who sent him. And since there was no prophet of God on earth at that time, nor had been, as far as we know, for some one hundred and fifty years at least, was it not perhaps some angel from God, "who had been of his brethren the prophets," who ordained him also to baptize? If so, what is unreasonable about sending an angel in the same manner again? It is obvious, from what follows, that the Levites did not possess the authority to baptize, nor did the priests. John i, 25—"And they [the priests and the Levites, for the Jews in general] asked him, and said unto him, Why *baptizest* thou then, if thou be not that Christ, nor Elias, neither that prophet?" There is an admission here that Elias baptized with authority, and that Christ would do so, as well as that other prophet, whoever he was. They also confessed that they themselves had no authority to baptize; and so they could not have sent John, even though he was of their lineage, the son of a prophet. Who sent him, then? Ver. 6 gives a satisfactory answer—"There was a man sent from *God*, whose name was John." And since God had no servant on earth who had the right to ordain John, he doubtless sent an angel to ordain him, as he did in these latter days to Joseph Smith, and for all we know, the angel may have baptized John, yes, with his own hands; for it is not likely that he would send him to baptize, without first being baptized himself. God alone has the right to make exceptions, and to do as he wishes; and thus did he do of necessity at the establishment of every previous dispensation, as well as this latest one; and did not the religious leaders of those ages oppose such exceptions, just as these things are now opposed?

But, to continue with the story, after the restoration of divine authority to men in this manner, in the year 1830, a large edition of the Book of Mormon first appeared to the world in print. And, as some began to peruse it carefully, the Spirit of the Lord bore witness to their spirits that it was true, and, being obedient to its requirements, they repented before God, with a broken heart and a contrite spirit; and they were immersed in water, for the remission of their sins; after which, by the commandment of God, hands were laid upon them, that they might receive the gift of the Holy Spirit. On the sixth day of April, 1830, in the town of Manchester, Ontario County, state of New York, United States of America, the Church of Jesus Christ of "*Latter-day Saints*" was established. Some were called through revelation and the spirit of prophecy; and, having been ordained, they went about preaching and bearing testimony of these things, as the Spirit gave them utterance. And, although they themselves were the weak things of the earth, yet they were strengthened by the Holy Ghost, becoming the means whereby many were brought to repent and forsake their evil ways, and were baptized in water confessing their sins, and were filled with the Holy Ghost by the laying on of hands, and they saw visions and prophesied; devils were cast out, and the sick were healed through the prayer of faith and the laying on of hands. Thus the preaching of the gospel increased greatly, and the Lord worked with them as before, by *confirming* the *preaching* of the *word*, through the signs *following* those who had already believed the *word*. Miracles do not *precede* the word, but *follow* after it. Thus God raised up witnesses to bear testimony of his name, and lay the foundation of his kingdom in these last days; and he does not leave himself without a witness now, but pours out his Spirit abundantly on those who obey him. And, although there were only six in this church at that time, they went about to preach as they were commanded, testifying to the things they had seen and heard, and the people believed them, obeyed the gospel, and received the Holy Ghost, in every place they went. Some of those who were ordained went to the states of Michigan, Ohio, Pennsylvania, &c.; and Joseph Smith went to Upper Canada, and had great success, so much so that the numbers of the Saints were over a thousand before the end of that year. In some places the leaders, the wise men, and the preachers obeyed the call, and entire congregations were converted and baptized. By now, harsh persecution arose against them, for jealous pastors were losing their sheep: they started to preach against them, plan and publish untrue stories about their characters, such as saying that Joseph Smith professed to be able to perform miracles, &c. The cause of this was that he placed his hands on the head of, and prayed over, sick people who were almost dying, and they were soon restored to health; although Joseph Smith did not claim any power of his own to perform miracles, any more than do any others of the Saints, merely that God found us worthy of being *instruments* in His hand.

FURTHER PROOFS OF THE BOOK OF MORMON.

It is evident that our Bible, and every one of the prophets almost, show that a book like the Book of Mormon would appear, and that as recently as our age; and if it is not this one, let it be searched for until it is found, or let the book that testifies about it be denied; but I prefer to believe them both.

Again, listen to the testimony of the Psalmist about this gathering, and the way it would begin, in Psalm lxxxv,—"Mercy and truth are met together; righteousness and peace have kissed each other." What causes this is—"*Truth* shall spring out of the earth; and righteousness shall look down from heaven. Yea, the Lord shall give [to Israel] that which is good; and our land shall yield her increase. Righteousness shall go before him; and shall set us in the way of his steps." David has foreseen that God's wrath would turn away from Jacob, that they would be restored, and that the glory of God would shine upon them; and this is how the work will start—"Truth shall spring out of the earth," &c. In another place, David says that God's law is what he means by truth—"Thy law is the truth." It is even clearer in Psalm cli—"Thou art near, O Lord, and all thy commandments are truth." Christ confirms this too—"Sanctify them through thy truth: thy word is truth." The law, word, and commandments of God are *truth*. Then David says—"Truth shall spring out of the earth; and righteousness [knowledge and power to administer the law] shall look down from heaven," and shall go before the face of Israel, to set its feet on the way of righteousness.

I think every man will admit the consistency there is among all these witnesses, proving that the stick of Ephraim [The Book of Mormon] is to be taken from the earth. Let us hear the testimony of Isaiah on this too, chap. xlv—"Drop down, ye heavens, from above, and let the skies pour down righteousness: let the *earth* open, and let them bring forth salvation, and let righteousness spring up together; I the Lord have created it." It is seen in chap. xxix, that the book is to come from the earth, ver. 1—"Woe," and at the side of the page more reasonably also, "O Ariel, Ariel!" Ver. 4—"And thou [Ariel, which signifies light, or the lion of God] shalt be brought down, and shalt speak out of the *ground*, and thy speech shall be low out of the dust, and thy voice shall be, as of one that hath a familiar spirit, out of the *ground*, and thy speech shall whisper out of the dust." "Ariel, the city where David dwelt," signifies that the people from there will possess the light of the Spirit of God, and will be brought down low into the dust. "And thy voice shall be out of the ground," which is not possible, unless their words have been written and hidden in the earth, and revealed afterwards; then it could be, because people could read and understand them, as it is said—"And thy voice shall be out of the ground, and thy speech shall whisper out of the dust." By now I think we have plenty of proofs that the stick of Joseph is to be taken from the earth, in the country where Ephraim dwells; that the American Indians are the seed of Ephraim; and that God would put the stick of Joseph and the stick of Judah together.

Next, we shall prove that this is the ensign he will set up for the nations [as Isaiah says], when God sends out his servants, because heaven drops down justice, that is it gives the right and the power to administer the laws of righteousness. See Isaiah, chap. xi, 12—"And he shall set up an ensign for the nations, and shall assemble the outcasts of Israel, and gather together the dispersed of Judah from the four corners of the earth." Some commentators tell us that this prophecy refers to the time of Christ's first coming, and the proof they offer is ver. 1—"And there shall come forth a rod out of the stem of Jesse, and a branch shall grow out of its roots." One need only read the chapter without bias to see that the prophet was not referring to the *first* coming, but to the *second* coming of Christ, otherwise what can be understood by ver. 4—"And he shall smite the earth with the rod of his mouth, and with the breath of his lips shall he slay the wicked"? It is said that it is in his second coming that he will do this, namely "When he comes on the clouds of heaven, with all his holy angels, in flaming fire taking vengeance on them that know not God, and that obey not the gospel of our Lord Jesus Christ." If his first coming is meant, how can this be reconciled with ver. 6—"The wolf also shall dwell with the Lamb, and the leopard shall lie down with the kid;" &c., when the enmity of all the beasts of the forest, birds of the air, and fish of the sea shall depart? That has not yet been accomplished, by a long way. But they say that that is not to be understood literally; it must be inspired, to show *men* of those tendencies. Well, that only leads to even worse difficulties; for men have not become so either. Ver. 9 shows when this prophecy will be fulfilled—"They shall not hurt nor destroy in all my holy mountain: for the earth shall be full of the knowledge of the Lord, as the waters cover the sea." What is to be made of this, I wonder, if this is a reference to his first coming? It is strange how stubborn some men are about their crooked paths, and their own beliefs; for they prefer to distort the words of God than to change their view on an old subject. But it is obvious that the prophet was referring, yes, was saying in clear words, that it was in the latter days that this would be fulfilled—"When the Lord shall set his hand again the second time to recover the remnant of his people," then "he shall set up an ensign for the nations, and shall assemble the outcasts of Israel [were they not dispersed at his first coming?] and gather together [at this time] the dispersed of Judah from the four corners of the earth." Ver. 13—"The envy also of Ephraim shall depart, and the adversaries of Judah shall be cut off." But at that time Judah was cut off by his adversaries, namely the Romans. "Ephraim shall not envy Judah, and Judah shall not vex Ephraim," at this time, "but they shall fly upon the shoulders of the Philistines toward the west." Read also chap. xlix, to prove this thorough restoration, and the way it will be begun, more clearly. Here the prophet shows the glory of the work of the latter days, and its unusual success. Ver. 22—"Thus saith the Lord God, Behold I will lift up my hand to the Gentiles, and set up my standard to the people: and they shall bring their sons in their arms, and thy daughters shall be carried upon their shoulders." Chap. lxvi, 18,—"For it shall come, that I will gather all nations and tongues; and they shall come, and see my glory. And I will set a SIGN among them, and I will send those that escape of them unto the nations [to show this sign], to Tarshish, Pul, and Lud, that draw the bow, to Tubal, and Javan, to the isles afar off, that have not heard my fame, neither have they seen my glory; and they shall declare my glory among the Gentiles. And they shall bring all your brethren for an offering unto the Lord out of all nations to my holy mountain Jerusalem, saith the Lord. For as the new heavens and the new earth, which I will make, shall remain before me, saith the Lord, so shall your seed and your name remain."

The statement in question, that is that God will set up a standard to the people when this wondrous restoration begins, is now beyond any question. It is also evident that the sign he will give is when the stick of Judah is joined to the stick of Ephraim, namely the Bible and the Book of Mormon, and they "would become one in his hand." And how shall this be a sign to the people, unless they see them, and understand what they are? or as Paul says, "And how shall they believe in him of whom they have not heard? and how shall they hear without a preacher? And how shall they preach, except they be sent?" And I ask, who shall send them but God? And how he shall send them without revealing that to them, I cannot imagine; and it is not possible for any man to answer either, for that is impossible. Then it is seen who are not servants of God, according to their own admission; for "their own mouth condemneth them, and their own lips testify against them;" and so we leave the deniers of revelation to plead their mission in the face of impossibility. But the scriptures show that God would send servants to show this sign, to the Gentiles first, and then to the Jews, and "declare his glory among them," and after the fulness of the Gentiles be come in, "then all Israel shall be saved," as Paul says.

Jeremiah proves this even more clearly in chap. xvi, 14—"Therefore, behold, the days come, saith the Lord, that it shall no more be said, The

Lord liveth, that brought up the children of Israel out of the land of Egypt; but, the Lord liveth, that brought up the children of Israel from the land of the north, and from all the lands whither he had driven them: and I will bring them again into their land that I gave unto their fathers. Behold, I will send for many fishers, saith the Lord, and they shall fish them; and after will I send for many hunters, and they shall hunt them from every mountain, and from every hill, and out of the holes of the rocks." One more witness to prove that God would send servants to carry his ensign unto all the people, so that no one may be left in doubt, and that is Isaiah xviii, 3—"All ye inhabitants of the world, and dwellers on the earth, see ye, when he lifteth up an ensign on the mountains; and when he bloweth a trumpet, hear ye." An ensign is the banner of an army, ship, or nation, by which it is recognized from afar. It is essential that there be officers in every government, authorized to act in their various functions under this ensign. The officers who carry the ensign are called by various names; sometimes *cornets*, sometimes *ensigns*, and *standard bearers*. When Isaiah says that "God will set up his ensign to the nations, and will set a sign to the people," it is evident that it refers to his work in going to make some *thing* other than what existed before, and that there would be inscribed on that *thing* certain symbols, through the seeing and understanding of which the people would know that those who bore and defended this ensign were officers in the kingdom of God. This ensign would be a sign to the people that those soldiers who bore it had been sent from God, to declare his glory in their midst, to fish and hunt the children of Israel from the mountains, the hills, and the holes of the rocks, and gather them back to their country. Through these fishers and hunters will he assemble the outcasts of Israel [that is, the ten tribes], and gather together the dispersed of Judah from the four corners of the earth.

We could bring more testimonies similar to the previous ones, but we have brought enough already to prove the following statements incontrovertible:—

1. We have proved that the "stick of Ephraim" contained great things of God's law to Ephraim.

2. That the seed of Ephraim is in America. We have also proved from the scriptures, not only that that "sacred book" was hidden in the earth, but that it would be revealed again through the power of God in America, when God would make "their seed known among the nations." And who of all the historians of the world could say that the American Indians are the seed of Ephraim, unless God had revealed it?

3. That the work which would be done as recently as our age would be this, "for in the latter days you shall understand this." Also, that it would be the beginning of the restoration of the tribes of Israel to their country.

4. That it was by joining these two sticks or books together, that God would set up his ensign to the nations, and that this is the sign he gives to the people that the great and glorious work of the latter days is about to begin.

5. That God will use men to carry this ensign, by preaching the contents of the books, and by men believing and obeying them.

I ask, What unbiased man can believe, in the face of such a host of truthful witnesses, and of indisputable proofs, that the BOOK OF MORMON is not the "stick of Ephraim," and "this sacred book?"—that this is not the "ensign," and the "sign" which were referred to? And what man who believes the prophets, and allows reason, and admits facts as sufficient proofs, can deny that the *Latter-day Saints*, who have been sent by a dispensation from God, and bear this ensign to the people, through every affliction, scorn, and persecution, are these "fishers and hunters," who "declare his glory among the Gentiles," and who will be instruments in the hand of God to gather the dispersed of Judah, and assemble the outcasts of Israel from the four corners of the earth?

Whoever doubts these remarkable facts any longer, would doubt if someone arose from the dead to relate them to him! And it is probably to this work that the prophet is referring when he says—"Behold I work a work among this people, saith the Lord; and although men declare the thing to them, even so they will not believe." Referring to this Isaiah says—"Behold, I will proceed to do a marvellous work among this people, even a marvellous work and a wonder: for the wisdom of their wise men shall perish, and the understanding of their prudent men shall be hid." Therefore, dear reader, beware lest you be carried away with the current to oppose it before you know what you are doing. But of what use is the Book of Mormon if it were true? say the opposers. I answer, that it is a great task to describe all its usefulness; but I shall note some of its virtues:—

1. It contains historical information about a large part of the world, which was previously hidden from the other part.

2. It reveals the origin of the American Indians, something unknown to the world for ages.

3. It contains important prophecies, which will be fulfilled in this age, and are consequently relevant to everyone who dwells on the earth.

4. It sheds a great deal of light and clarity on those doctrines about

which there is so much difference of opinion among religious believers.

5. It deals a mortal blow to atheism, because it is in many ways incontrovertible evidence of the divinity of the holy scriptures, as the scriptures also bear witness to its truth. And for the testimony of living witnesses to its truthfulness, I refer the reader to the testimony of the eleven already published, who testify that it was translated through the power of God: we also refer to the thousands who have obeyed the teaching it contains, who have received knowledge from the truthful God. May the great works of God in our midst bear witness to its truthfulness; and if that is not satisfactory, there are abundant proofs in itself; or else, if you are not satisfied after that, gentle reader, "come and see" if it is true, obey the teaching it contains, and thus you like others shall end the argument forever, to your endless benefit and joy, by receiving the fulfillment of its valuable promises.

EPISTLE OF DEMETRIUS, THE SILVERSMITH,

To all of his fellow-craftsmen, showing the best way to defend their craft, and to silence the "Latter-day Saints."

GENTLEMEN,—You are nearly all well aware, by now, of those men who turn the world upside down, namely the *Latter-day Saints*, having come into our midst, and that they teach things that are not appropriate for us *Sectarians* to receive. They have come not only to Merthyr and its environs, but thence to the frontiers of Wales; and, I regret to say, there is not one county or scarcely a parish throughout the south and the north, without some of them preaching there, and the people running to listen to them in their hundreds and thousands, so that there is talk of hardly anything else throughout the country but the Saints and the potato blight. Is it not high time for us all to unite, dear fellow-craftsmen, to call a committee to organize some measures to silence them? If we allow them to continue like this, they will disgrace our great goddess, who sits upon her scarlet stallion, with her golden cup in her hand; her magnificence will be despised, her worshipers will leave her temples to the mole and the bats, they will go after these people, and alas! the hope of our profit will fade. Now, dear brethren, since such a harmful medium is at our door, awake, and arm yourselves for the battle. I shall tell you some of the tricks of these old Saints, so that you may see their deceit, and take up arms against them. They cunningly plot to entice, not only our listeners, but our most faithful members, and several of our gifted preachers, leading them astray off the old smooth, popular, and comfortable road, on which our godly fathers walked many years ago.

In the first place, in their great ignorance, they are foolish enough to teach people to believe the scriptures as they are written, to believe the prophets' interpretation of their prophecies, and the parable-teller's explanation of his parable, &c. So they greatly insult the spirituality of our theologians and our learned rabbis; and worse still, they despise that glorious title which is so notable on the forehead of our great goddess, namely "*Mystery*." They teach the people, having torn the veil of mystery from their eyes, that they should listen to their reason when reading the scriptures. They keep to that commandment that says—"Be not ye called Rabbi, for one is your Master, and all ye are brethren." They say that all the glorious names, and the many titles, which are the foundation of our honor and wealth, are blasphemies, and that our goddess is "full of names of blasphemy." They say as Paul did, that "Not many wise men after the flesh, not many mighty, not many noble are called: but, that God hath chosen the foolish things of the world to confound the wise, and base things of the world, and things which are despised, to bring to naught things that are; that no flesh should glory in his presence." Those Saints know no better than to believe these scriptures literally, rejecting our pastors, and claiming that our sheep are not a true flock, and leading them astray from our folds. Who has heard of such obvious deceit as this since the days of the apostles? If we left them alone, our honor and respect would very soon end, and our comfortable living, and all our profits too; yes, his grace the archbishop would be on a level with his grace the laborer! Was that not the endeavor of the old apostles many years ago, when my father and his fellow-craftsmen made such a bold stand against them at Ephesus? These dullards say, as they did, that there is only "one Lord, one faith, one baptism," and one Spirit leading them all to the unity of the faith. By taking these words literally, they prove that there is only one true, perfect plan, or church to God, all agreeing, holding to that form of doctrine to which the apostles of old held, and that they all must unite under the name of "SAINTS." Here again they undermine our many plans, endangering our craft. And what man is there among you, but what knows that among the titles and venerable names which belong to our goddess are, Catholicism, Episcopalianism, Calvinism, Methodism, Wesleyanism, Waldensism, Baptistism, Puseyism, and hundreds of other sects, about which no one else has dared say anything scornful? It is admitted that all of these have their different lords, faiths, baptisms, and different spirits, all contributing to improving our craft, and decorating the magnificent temples of our great goddess, whom almost all the world worships. But neither are those all the heresies of these Saints. They go on deeper and deeper in their deception, teaching the people to believe that the same ordinances are needed in the church now as previously, and persuading them to pray for that Holy Spirit which imparted the spiritual gifts, and temporal blessings, urging them to strive for "that faith which was once given to the saints," and that it is the privilege of everyone who complies with the one plan to receive knowledge of the truth, and certainty of his acceptance by God, as Christ promised them. They promise that God will give them the Spirit of prophecy, revelations, visions, and gifts of healing, &c., as he himself wills it, for the benefit and edifying of their church, and to perfect them for the fulfillment of their duties, &c. We could overlook every other folly on their part, if it were not for this last; but this is a greater danger to our craft than anything, yes, absolutely intolerable; for once the people come to obey their plan, and obtain the blessings, it is a fruitless task to try to attract them back to us, and through those things are clearly shown the great difference among all the branches of our craft and the original principles that were taught to the saints. The veil is rent by these people, exposing all our mysteries. It is strange that the people do not see how much we excel over them in brotherly love! Our goddess, and all her worshipers, allow freedom for everyone to go his own way, and we can greet with *hail, fellows well met*, all our various forms, yes, we go hand in hand with all who are satisfied with a pretence of godliness, or some form of it, if they deny its strength, that is the spiritual gifts, and God's power. You know well, brethren, that those were the greatest enemies and the worst poison ever given to our goddess. The examples of our brave fathers in days gone by should stir us to emulate them in bravery against this common enemy. We remember that they cast that Daniel into the lions' den, for believing in visions and ministering of angels. Our general, Herod, killed hundreds of little children, because God announced that a king of the Jews would come there. Did they not stone Stephen too as soon as he spoke such blasphemy as saying that he saw heaven opening, and Jesus seated there? Paul (my father's old enemy) was imprisoned and martyred, along with all his brethren, for testifying that they had had visions, and the gifts. In short, my fellow-craftsmen, you see that our fathers, in any age on earth, have never tolerated anyone having spiritual gifts and revelations from God. And who among you cannot see that this would tear the veil off all our mysteries, and would show our trickery and our *schemes*, yes, would completely undermine in time all our babel-forms, and would fill the earth, not with sects and opinions, but with light and a *knowledge* of the TRUTH. Woe betide us, brethren, consider! I could tell you much more of the folly of these Saints, and their dreadful delusions, but I trust you all see by now how dangerous they are to the whole plan, and, consequently, to our craft. You also know the cost, the trouble, and the great pain our godly and learned fathers had, after they martyred those old deceivers, Paul, Peter, and their followers, and what dedication there was among all the Demetrius family, and all their friends, to improve and change, mold and adorn the Christian religion, until at length they made it suit the taste of the world, so that the world in its present state loves it greatly. The kings and the queens glory in it; the nobles and the priests fatten and enrich themselves from it; the sons and daughters of our church are adorned with gold and silver, decked with fine linen, purple, and scarlet; and are their silky, satiny, costly robes not a credit to our religion, an adornment to our temples, apart from bringing great profit to our craft? Our worshipers too, from among the great of the world, come in their chariots, and tread on *tapestry*, and trade in gold, silver, and pearls, yes have grown rich, not in animals alone, but at the cost of the bodies and souls of the poor who are dying of need before their eyes, until all the world has drunk from the golden cup which is in the hand of our great goddess. And now, fellow-craftsmen, will you stand by while these old Saints disrespect us, and speak against all this greatness and magnificence? Shall they be allowed to annihilate all this glory, after all the trouble and cost of bringing religion to its present perfection? Shall uneducated men such as these go around the country to say that all this is not the Christian religion, saying that if our religion were genuine, the world would hate it, and that we would be hated by everyone because of it, as they are hated by all for their religion? They say that the words spoken by Christ—"Blessed are ye when all shall say all manner of evil against you, and persecute you for the sake of my gospel, for in the like manner did they to the prophets which were before you; but woe unto you, when the world shall speak well of you"—they say that is in force now. Who does not know that a complete change has taken place in that? There you are, gentlemen, you see that if the founders of the Christian religion had been wise enough to do as we have done, that is to smooth and modify gradually in order to adorn the religion, what a great benefit it would have been, what painful sufferings it would have saved them, and what tremendous success they would have had; for, if they had done thus, the world would not hate the religion, but everyone would unite in sending the gospel throughout the whole world. But now, after almost all the world has come to walk hand in hand with the gospel for many ages, in unity and brotherly love, here come these mischievous men to disturb us, endeavoring to bring back the old apostolic faith, which the world in every age hated so much, and I hope they will hate it again! And I am not without hope, if we, gentlemen, are all faithful to each other and to our craft, that the world will hate them and their religion *now* too; and as encouragement to you, and praise to the brave ones among you who have fought against them, I will say that we have already succeeded in getting many of our old followers to hate them and their religion; but even so, they are succeeding, so that we are all in great danger! This is the reason, Sirs, for my writing this Epistle to you, in order to stir your faithful minds into devising some *scheme* to silence them, for I must now admit that I do not know what to do to them; every device of mine has failed; they carry on through all obstacles; and if I admit the truth to you, our craft has been severely hit by them in places. None of the measures we have arranged up until now, even though we have carried them out bravely too, has been any more effective than those ropes were in binding Samson. This little, insignificant, young church has been persecuted from its infancy, with every sort of lies, slander, false accusations, and stories of every shape and form our American fellow-craftsmen could invent, but all to no avail; it still rose steadily upward through it all. They drove them from one state to the next, burning their houses over their heads, flogging them, and robbing them of their possessions, their lands, and their animals, yes, of everything they owned. They tied some of them to stakes, promising them every reward and respect if they would renounce this false religion; but they raised their hands toward heaven, as they died under their hands, and testified that their religion was the truth; yes, scores of them, men, women, and children, have sealed its truth with their blood! The roar of our most frightful cannons and guns have failed to frighten them. The edge of our swords cannot separate them from it. They prefer to endure prisons, and every scorn, and pain, than to leave it! The more you oppose them, the more they succeed still! Were over two hundred of their homes not burned last year by fellow-craftsmen in America, even though they had exiled them four times before? We thought we would put an end to them when we killed their fraudulent leaders in jail, but we were disappointed in that too, since their assassination brought more success to the deceit than anything we had done before. Our American brethren, after failing to disperse them in one way, have exiled them by the thousands, the old and the young, men and women, noble and common indiscriminately, at the cost of all they owned, beyond the Rocky Mountains; but they prefer that to leaving their deceit, and it is impossible for us to win anyone back from the deceit. Plan, dear brethren, some device that will prevent them from enticing more of our worshipers. We said from the start that it was so poor and so small that it was not worthy of our notice; and yet we could not smother it. Again, it was declared to be such a large, dreadful, dangerous deceit; even so the people ran after it in droves. The writers of England did their best, by publishing everything that was heard against it, as well as inventing many a skillful story of their own, but despite everything these people succeed by the thousands there every year; and we fear greatly that that is how they will succeed in Wales, if you cannot invent some new device, better than anything we have so far. It is pointless for us to publish the lies and those old stories about that Joseph Smith, for they have caused the people to look into his story more; and these Saints have published the other side of it in Welsh. Have not the *Baptist*, the *Star of Gomer*, the *Times*, the *Revivalist*, the *Educator*, and the *Treasury* from Carmarthen, yes, almost every publication throughout Wales, been publishing with all their might every story about them, and yet the people are not satisfied without hearing them; and some of them, alas, in their great zeal for our craft, have said too much bad about them, so that the unbiased people are coming to understand our trickery as soon as they hear some of them preaching.

It is folly for us to expect to defeat them either by preaching from the pulpits against them, for the most hot-headed among us have given that a fair trial in every place the tricksters have been. We follow on their heels to every new community, and warn the people against them, and say that they will trick them out of their possessions, remembering to tell those stories about the *walking on the water in America*, *raising the dead*, *moving mountains*, and the like; but it is all to no avail, because the people believe them in almost every place they preach.

Does not the failure of our praiseworthy brother from Dowlais, despite his hard work and his diligence for years, speaking throughout the south against them, with many of his faithful brethren, giving them every bad name they could invent, such as "Satanists," "devilish men," "sorcerers," "Deists,"

"Atheists," "Chartists," &c., prove to us that we cannot succeed in that way? Was one of our most skillful craftsmen with the Methodists not in the Pwllheli quarterly meeting, in front of some ten thousand people, accusing them unsparingly of every sort of deception, in their absence? But it made no difference, the people in droves despised him for his unfairness and his false reasoning in being capable of condemning men in their absence, because of the false accusations he brought against them. We must change our weapons, now, friends; the people are too wise for those old worn-out ones to have any effect in a free country, and especially in a country where there is so much enlightenment.

The best device we had was warning the people not to listen to them, but to take our word, and condemn them before hearing them. We thought we would surely succeed in that way, but we have been disappointed in this too; although we warned them not to, the people still went to listen to them. Have we not excommunicated several from our churches, as an example to others, because they listened to them? but that does not frighten the people any more. The Calvinists excluded one innocent lad from Liverpool for listening to them, and that was enough at the time. But, the *trick* is old by now; our listeners will not be enslaved by us in this enlightened age, as in the old days, for they still want old Paul's advice, namely, "Prove all things; hold fast that which is good."

We have tried my father's old plan, of shouting, "Great is the City of the Ephesians! Great is the mystery of the great Goddess who sits upon the scarlet stallion, with her golden cup in her hand;" but to no avail. We have also shouted from the pulpits that it is the filth of the world, and the offscouring of all things, that become Saints, and even so they go to them. We announced that they were dying out here, and dying out there, but they are flourishing. We have often preached their funeral sermon, and have prophesied on the graves where we thought they still lay, but they rose up under our hands, and to our surprise and dismay they are more alive than ever! And now, idle and cheerless fellow-craftsmen, we begin to fear that they will live, after we have died, and gone to the land of oblivion, if you cannot devise some new way to hamper their progress. What shall we do? Do not despair; but let us rally against them again. I wish every one of you who is ardent for the craft, to give this important matter your consideration, and meet us all in *Caersalem Hall* at the first opportunity, in order to devise some other new way to persecute the Saints; and until then keep all the religious publications full of every sort of libelous stories about them, without allowing them space to defend themselves properly; and persuade the people not to read their books for anything! Be faithful, and we shall succeed yet. Oh, if only I could achieve my aim, so that I could sleep peacefully!

I am, your dissatisfied fellow-craftsman,

DEMETRIUS JUNIOR.

Diana's Square, Silver-smith Street,
Ephesus.

REVIEW.

SUBSTANCE OF A SERMON ON THE MIRACLES, *in order to enlighten the Public, and show the Deceit of the Creatures who call themselves "Latter-day Saints."* By W. R. DAVIES, Dowlais.

[CONTINUED FROM PAGE 78.]

ON page 6, William asserts that no one has been healed through those he calls Satanists; and Davies says also, on page 9, that no sign was seen among them. And do the two of them not admit, Mr. Judge, on page 20 of the same essay, that "men testify that they have received health THROUGH THEM?" How shall we believe any one of you? You must be contradicting one another. "Oh," says the judge, "it is only a few who testify thus." But how few? Are there not two or three, if so, is it not in the mouths of two or three witnesses that every word shall be established? And so, Sir, you admit that those whom you call *Satanists* are servants of God! You admit yourself false in the same sentence, by accusing these men of "taking it upon themselves to heal the sick," and in the next line you admit that someone else received health *through them*; and from whom would they receive it but from God? Why do you contradict yourself like this in the same breath, Sir? Do you not know the difference between accusing men of taking it upon themselves to do miracles, and their being instruments in the hand of God for that? You show up worse and worse the more you are cross-examined. "Wait," says the Judge, frightened by now, "those witnesses must be destroyed, and how shall I do it? It were best for me to admit that." "Shout out that they are evil men" says Davies in his ear. "Yes, that's it." "Harlot shouts harlot first," says the proverb; but no matter what, in a tight spot. "They are but a few and evil," says the judge, at the top of his voice. "But what proves them evil?" say his friends; "a witness of this, again." Is it their testimony that proves this? Worse still; we almost believe that those who said that the apostles were "few and evil" for the same testimony, were brothers of yours; and if you were to admit the truth, the few would rise to hundreds of witnesses at least, yes in Merthyr, in Wales.

But do you, Sir, have as many proofs that you are a servant of God, as you have admitted that these Satanists, as you call them, have, and those proofs miraculous ones, like theirs? How can you have someone who testifies to receiving health from God through you, when you deny and mock the ways laid down for that, saying that they are not needed, and calling those who profess them "a foul mob?" We must abhor the *anti*-apostolic assertions of you three, and search, for ourselves, according to Paul's command. "Prove all things," he said; so we have proved the *Baptist* and your false accusations in it, in the face of the truth, in the face of reason, in your own faces, and found them (borrowing your own words to describe them) "a pack of the most terrible and fearsome lies that any evil man, or the sons or daughters of perdition, have claimed in any age of this world."

Behold more of your preacher's deceit; for after claiming that we do not lay hands on the sick, and saying afterwards that we do, he says—"With the object of attempting to hide their shame over this matter, they place the blame on the faith of whoever is under their hands." And with the object of hiding what, does he assert that to profess apostleship is deceit and "devilish presumption" and that the conditions of the most wanton harlots, and the most villainous thieves in the *cellars* of *Pont-y-storehouse* are innocent, yes, even the foul deeds of *Dic Tamar* and his like, when they are compared with those of the Satanists, pale from sight, and that they are not a thousandth part as purple and scarlet as those of the "praiseworthy apostle," and his brother, namely "the prophet of perdition." Here is another example of Davisism *versus* Apostleship. The one justifies its *devotees*, that is harlots and thieves; and the other, through their faith, receives gifts of God, the one *ransacks* the *vocabulary* of Dic Tamar, and from the cellars of Pont-y-storehouse as far as Billingsgate, and for bad enough names to give to the character of men who defend the apostolic truth,—while they are praying and exhorting others to pray for him, and exerting themselves to save souls from his deadly claws. Ought this not to be testimony enough to the world that "the apostle and his brother" to whom he refers, are good men, before they be condemned in front of the *judge* who justifies harlots and thieves? We remember that a thief and murderer was chosen ahead of the innocent before now. "Birds of a feather flock together." One expects to see Davisism flourishing in the cellars of Pont-y-storehouse from now on. Their speech accuses them now; and it is quite likely that their bullies will defend their hall when a candle is brought in to search their *pack*. But let us leave those dear friends with one another, and let us show what Apostleship says about faith being necessary to be healed. "Has Little Maggie no faith? Did she receive a strong hip in place of the withered one? I expect to see her next time without her crutch; but in the same way, if I meet her, do not talk of a miracle, for shame's sake, &c.," says this reverend. Come with us, reader, to one of the streets of Phillippi to see the unchristianity of this man in a reflection. There comes Paul on one side; there is Mr. Davies crossing the road to him, with a mocking smile on his face. "Well, you great old deceiver," says he, "you, claiming to heal the sick! Why would you not heal your own dear disciples? When you are asked to heal the disbelievers, you start to preach that Carpenter's Son to them, excusing yourself, as you did with that lame man, that you could not heal him until you had looked closely, and seen that he had *faith* to be healed. Has Timothy no faith? Did he receive a strong body instead of the "frequent weakness" he had? I expect to see him next time without his weakness, a strong and active lad: but in the same way, if I meet him on one of the streets of Ephesus (for I shall go there in haste to sell my mocking sermon against you), do not talk of a miracle, for shame's sake." Don't run away, at that, Mr. Davies. Who but an apostle of Davisism is seen (according to this own logic), persecuting and reviling Paul on the beach in Miletum, and reproaching him for going away on the ship, leaving Trophimus, his dear brother and fellow-official, sick in the midst of pagans, though he was needed so much in the ministry. "There, you're caught, Paul, in your deceit," say you. "Do you not profess to heal all the sick where you walk? But now we see that your claims are nothing but a pack of lies." But away with Paul to the ship, despite their mockery; and after reaching Rome, he writes to Timothy, "I left Trophimus sick in Miletum." There, sir, you have placed your fist on Paul's mouth; and it is in vain for you to pretend hypocritically that you preach his gospel any longer! And hear the sentence on you—"Though we, (though Mr. Davies of Dowlais), or an angel from heaven preach any other gospel unto you than that which we have preached to you, let him be accursed."

[*To be continued.*]

EXILE OF THREE HUNDRED THOUSAND AMERICANS FROM THEIR COUNTRY, FOR THEIR RELIGION!!

THE signs of the times, and the strange and incredible things that are taking place on the western continent these days, demonstrate that the last ray of the blazing star of American liberty is about to be extinguished, under a jet-black veil, on the western horizon.

The *official documents* from Illinois announce that the General of the President's Army, Justice Douglas, members of the Senate, and many other officials who hold high positions in the state, as well as the citizens of Hancock County, have given the choice to over three hundred thousand subjects of the American government, the citizens of Nauvoo, of being either martyred unmercifully in their homes, or robbed of their houses, their lands, their possessions, and exiled at their own cost, beyond the Rocky Mountains; yes, they force them to go this year, ready or not! Instead of defending innocent and peaceful citizens in the enjoyment of their possessions, their liberty, and their rights, we see a nation becoming a mob, the judges, the governors, and the leaders consulting together, against the Lord, against the church of his Christ, and his assembled people, encouraging inhuman *banditti* to rob them, and eventually to exile them, through a public admission that the government has neither the power nor the will to defend the *Mormons*, as they call them, from the violence and oppression of their enemies. Of the two evils here, the Saints chose exile instead of being killed. Despite it all the persecution of their enemies did not cease; but while their hands are still dripping with the blood of godly prophets and saints, whom they killed without cause, without defense, and without inquiry, they thirst again for the blood of the other leaders; they plan false accusations against innocent men, yes, even when they were preparing for their exile, with the aim of dragging them, like their brethren before them, to the Carthage slaughter-house. Their decision was that they could not live in their midst, or depart from their midst alive. And there has been great commotion throughout the country to try to mobilize a sufficiently numerous mob, to attack the Saints, and kill them when they began their journey to the desert! But they were disappointed in this. Thanks to Him who has his eternal arms under them! We are pleased to announce that the leaders left Nauvoo before the mob expected, and so they have escaped from the lions' mouths, and from the clutches of those bears, and hundreds of their brethren with them, for the last time, we hope, after many years of persecution, prison, and the wrath of their enemies. The remainder of the Saints intend to leave from Nauvoo this summer, and may their God be with them, to comfort and defend them.

This remarkable and general exile brings about the strangest and most peculiar, most glorious and terrible period that has been, not only in the history of the church, but probably in the world, since God's people came out of Egypt in the days of Moses. This appears to be a literal and direct fulfillment of old and recent prophecies. The Book of Mormon says—"At that day when the Gentiles shall reject the fulness of my gospel, behold I will bring the fulness of my gospel from among them, saith the Father." Now, what more could that nation do, to prove that they rejected the "fulness of the gospel," namely the Book of Mormon, than they have done? Can one crime be named of which they are not guilty as a nation? Have they not robbed the Saints of tens of thousands of acres of land, which they had bought from them, and for which they had paid them their money, by letting a mob persecute and torment them, until many were killed, and others were exiled three times, at the cost of almost all they owned, and letting their enemies take possession of their lands and property in Missouri after that; yes, to this day, without trying to restore them to them! Are they not guilty of shedding innocent blood, since they let thousands of murderers and plunderers of the Saints go completely free and unrebuked in their midst? And do they not still continue to chase and drive them out with unending persecution? Are they not exiling them now, the old grey-haired man and the active one alike, the defenseless mother as well as her innocent children, yes, all unsparingly, beyond the Rocky Mountains? Is it not the nation, the government, and not some individuals, who are doing all this, yes, in the land of the free, in this "enlightened age!" while boasting of being a *republic*, the kingdom of freedom, a refuge and an *asylum* to the oppressed, inviting the exiles of Poland, the slaves of the European tyrants, and all the oppressed of the world to them, promising protection to all, and professing, bringing contempt and scorn on Christianity, in the eyes of the world's pagan kingdoms, that they are CHRISTIANS ! ! And are they not, as a nation, guilty of all this, and much more, since they have the ability to defend, and yet refuse to do so? If the committing of all these cruelties does not prove their rejection of the "fulness of the gospel," we do not know what more they can do to "fulfill the measure of their iniquity," and fit them for judgment! Does their cup not run over? And then, is the time not at hand for the Lord to take the "fulness of his gospel" from among that perverse nation? Is not the exile of the Saints to the western desert, among the remnant of Joseph, for the purpose of fitting the wicked to judgment, and saving the righteous? Are they not thus commanded to "go to their chambers, and hide for a little moment, until the persecution and indignation be past,"so that God may fulfill his threats to their persecutors? How could the gospel be taken from among the nation, while the priesthood and the Saints remained in their midst? After the exile of the gospel from among the nations, "then," says the Book of Mormon, "will I remember my covenant which I have made unto my people; O house of Israel, I will bring my gospel unto you, and ye shall come unto knowledge of the fulness of my gospel." Has perhaps the awaited time already come to take the gospel to the remnant of Israel? The signs of the times, and the fulfillment of clear prophecies, demonstrate that the happy day is about to dawn. Then raise your heads, you Saints, and rejoice, for the time of your deliverance is nigh. The thing that you have been praying a great deal for, and waiting patiently for, is already at the door; be ready to meet it. Yet, it will take some considerable time for all of the Saints to emigrate from all the states of that cruel nation. The Saints who are in the eastern states are emigrating by sea, past Cape Horn, to California. S. Brannan has already left in a ship, from New York, and over two hundred of the Saints with him, loaded with all the provisions essential to settle in that western paradise; and many other shiploads of the Saints are preparing to leave shortly from there, and from the ports of the other states. All this bears witness to everyone that the religion of the Saints is such that they prefer to lose their possessions, their country, and their lives, than to lose it! Are they not evil people who are so Pharoah-like in their persecution? Do they persecute people better, or worse, than themselves? Are they not fulfilling notable prophecies in this, which were made among them many years ago? And do these not stare them in the face now when they fulfill them? Who can deny them, then, or save these people when what has already been declared to them comes upon them? Now the trumpet sounds loud and long—"Come out of her, my people, that ye be not partakers of her sins," for it is the blood of *saints* and *prophets* that *they* have spilt. "Great and marvellous are thy works, Lord God Almighty; just and true are thy ways, thou King of *saints*."

LETTER FROM THE " CAMP OF ISRAEL."

OUR subscribers will be pleased to read the following letter from John Taylor, one of the twelve apostles, which was received from him recently, and which shows how they are getting on in their exile from their country. The following is an extract from the letter:—

"We started from Sugar Creek Bottom, and we continued traveling slowly, in consequence of bad roads and cold and inclement weather until the 25th of April, when we arrived at the west fork of the Grand River, about 160 miles from Nauvoo, and about 15 miles from the state of Missouri. At this place we made an encampment, and commenced ploughing the earth, and building some log-houses for the accommodation of our brethren who should come after us. We left men to take care of the farm, and we went on to this place which is called Mount Pisgah, and we established another farm on the same principle as we had the first. This place is situated about 40 miles to the north of the first farm; it is beautifully situated, abundance of wood and water being convenient. We calculate to start from here in a few days, for Council Bluffs, and from there to the Rocky Mountains, i.e., the twelve, their families, and such men as they shall select. I have been at Nauvoo on *business* lately; the place has altered very much. *'Civilization and its consequences are making rapid strides, and the people have become much better Christians.'* They have made a *ten-pin alley* opposite the temple; groggeries are already plentiful, and at night one can hear unruly drunkards yelling and cursing through the streets, things of which there was no sign when we were there. Our brethren are trying to sell their possessions, though at very low prices. The Saints are moving to the west as rapidly as they can, with everyone desirous to be first. On my journey back from Nauvoo I passed over eight hundred wagons, besides large droves of cattle, and numerous herds of sheep, moving slowly and happily away from their captivity, much like Israel from Egypt centuries ago; and in the midst of all their difficulties, the Saints are rejoicing, looking forward, and lifting up their heads, for the time of their deliverance is nigh. All are united and working together to carry forward this great work, through the help of God, come whatever obstacles may come. The two lower floors of the temple are finished, and they look beautiful and very elegant. While standing in the baptismal font, gazing at all the fine work that surrounded me, and the excellence of this great edifice; as I walked through the rooms one by one, to take one last look perhaps at the structure whose completion was the desire of my soul for several years, so as to worship God therein; when I recall the great efforts of the Saints, under every disadvantage, to build it, and now being forced without cause to leave it, as well as their homes, their lands, and their possessions, in the hands of their enemies;—some feelings too peculiar to describe, were I permitted, filled my breast. But off I went, under the burden of my cares, for our oppressors have no place in their breast for compassion.—Brothers Hyde and Woodruff are on their way to this place from Nauvoo.—Remember me affectionately to all the Saints and our friends.

"Yours in the everlasting covenant,

"JOHN TAYLOR."

SUCCESS OF TRUTH.

HOWEVER harsh the brashness——of the sects,
Daily and relentless,
Doing their worst, remorseless
Truth beats those who slander us.

Truth's name will be long-famed;——let all foes
Of this be well-minded:
It sees them, when life's ended,
Earth-bound and sound 'midst the dead.

RHYDYBONT : PRINTED BY JOHN JONES.

PROPHET OF THE JUBILEE.

"THE KINGDOM HAS COME."

No. 5.] NOVEMBER, 1846. [VOL. I.

THE SPIRIT OF ACCUSATION.

WHEN observing human nature, we find many things in it to glorify, and many virtues made clear, which shine like a rainbow in a storm, and bring a delightful respite, from the sight of the dark picture of human life. It is a great blessing, for whoever possesses it, to be able to perceive and bring out the various virtues that belong to our fellow-creatures; and to be able through love, which comes only from heaven, to hide the faults and imperfections of our common fraternity, and pick out the virtues of a man's character, and describe them with delight. How like God, and how blessed is such a spirit, and what happiness emanates from him, and how contrary is he to the spirit that tries only to accuse, reveling in the defects and faults of the human race. We have made these general remarks by way of a warning to the Saints, lest they partake of the same spirit. We have learned one great principle, which is that we are to be savers of mankind. But what is he who constantly labors to find out defects and weaknesses in his brethren, but a destroyer? It is doubtless the work of Satan, and those who serve him in that way are his servants. We would wish to reason gently with those who partake of such a spirit, and ask them to question themselves carefully, and look into what motivates them to act in such a way. Does the fact that some brother has defects bring them pleasure? It may do, if it satisfies them when they look at their own; but let us be spared from such satisfaction. Banish it far from us, Oh God, and give us that love that covers a multitude of sins.

But we know very well that there is scarcely any fault that men are as apt to slip into as this; and once it has started, it sticks in their nature, until their whole mind and life are used to show the faults of their fellowman. Oh, what a dreadful situation this is! Indeed, to those who perceive it correctly, it is a demonstration of hell on earth! But the main point of trickery of the tempter is—that he makes those who act so, think that their behavior is entirely righteous, and arises from their greater purity, and their hatred of everything sinful; and thus the chief deceiver leads them to be accusers of their brethren, when by so doing, they themselves are his most faithful and most direct servants.

But yet, let us inquire what is the aim in view when embarking on such a practice, and particularly in the kingdom of God. Does he intend to enjoy the faith of the Saints, by noting the defects of a brother? Does he mean to create trust in the church authorities, by showing that they are imperfect beings, and open to weaknesses, like other men? This cannot be what drives him, because the aims could never be effected, and only a madman would take such a course. But we can account for a few reasons for such conduct. Bad temper, disappointed expectations, and jealousy or malice, are the only motives from which such a hellish principle stems. Its beginning was in hell, and its end will be in the same place. Therefore, beware, you Saints of God, of this devilish principle.

With regard to the truth of the above statements, let us take a look for a minute at the general conduct of the enemies of God, and the Saints. What was the behavior of all the apostates, by whom the church was troubled and tried in America? Men, who were overtaken by evil, and who had been kept out of the church, have come out in a garment of professed purity, and have justified themselves in their apostasy, because of the imperfection and faults of the Saints. The history of times past confirms this statement; and it is not confined to apostates alone, but applies to the persecuting common folk who glory in the destruction of life and property, and try to justify themselves by bringing charges of evil against those they persecute. Let us endeavor to reconcile principles and behavior in their correct light, restore a brother from his faults through love and tenderness; and if we fail to succeed with him, let our testimony be against his faults, and not his person, and that before the appropriate court for the same, in order to save him, and not in order to blacken or anger him. If he does not reform, let the "accuser of the brethren" be put in the same category as his secret friends, the apostate, the murderer, and the devil, so that peace may dwell perpetually in our churches.

COMFORT UNDER PERSECUTION.

THERE is scarcely a principle that proves itself more true to the Saints of the Most High, and is more often commensurable with their experience, than "that we must through much tribulation enter into the kingdom of God." This was the inheritance promised to the Saints in early times. These are the best promises that are given to us now. "In the world ye shall have tribulation; and ye shall be hated of all men for my name's sake," says our King. Let us be of good cheer, then, since they met with the same obstacles, and were more than conquerors, through Jesus Christ, who delivered them, why should we fear the same obstacles, as we tread the same path? And since God saw fit to perfect the Prince of our salvation through suffering, and made him a man of sorrows, and acquainted with grief—and since all our brethren went through the fiery forge, before they could be purified, we too will be disappointed if we expect a good life and daily abundance, and expect to live on the world's delicacies, soft pillows, the popularity of the age, rather than troubles, trials, persecutions, and much opposition from the world, the flesh, and the devil. "If we be without chastisement, then we are bastards, and not children." Our father scourges every son and daughter he receives, and all because of his love for us, so that the tin is taken away, and we are purified of the poor trinkets of the earth, so that we may be worthy and suitable to appear in the presence of God's angels, and wear permanent crowns. Who would not boast of being under such a teacher, to such glorious purpose! This is the only way prepared by God to perfect and bring many sons to glory; so he allows Satan to incite our persecutors to tempt us, and say and do all they can against us, in order to purify us, so that proof of our faith may be obtained; for without faith we can endure nothing, without suffering we cannot be purified, and without being purified we shall not be worthy to inherit the glorious kingdom, or to fill the circles on high with which our father intends to endow us. Let us expect, then, greater and greater obstacles and troubles every day from the prince of this world, and all his armies, while building the kingdom of Emmanuel in the middle of their treacherous territories; for the more we manage to win their subjects from their clutches, the more the foundations of their government will shake, and the more, in consequence, their anger and jealousy will increase, and not surprisingly either. But there is one heavenly principle, which we note to encourage the Saints to continue bravely, patiently, and faithfully till the end, despite everything, and that is—Our God is stronger than the strong and the armed, and he will not allow us to be tempted beyond our capacity. If we ask for strength according to the occasion, he is more ready to give than we are to ask of him, and he uses even our persecutors for our benefit, yes, all things work together for our good, if we keep the confidence of our faith sure until the end.

THE LAW AND THE GOSPEL.

We believe the human race, when they reach the age of reason, to be capable of differentiating between good and bad, capable of obeying or disobeying a law, that a law has been given to them, and that the punishment for transgressing it is exile from the presence of God, in their body and spirit, after their restoration and their deliverance under the verdict of the first man's transgression.

We believe that no one is punished according to this second law, unless they have had the advantage of understanding it in this life; for although the light they all have teaches them good and bad, yet that light does not teach them all of this law, or the consequences of breaking it. And although the pagan portion of them may give rise to many lashings, yet, it is not just to judge them by, or punish them according to, the rule of this law, because they can excuse themselves under the mantle of complete ignorance of it; consequently, they are punished, not according to the revealed law of which they are totally ignorant, but according to their conscience, which punishment is commensurate with the light and the opportunities they had to get a more perfect light, for willing negligence is no excuse. "As many as have sinned without law shall also perish without law."

We believe that knowing transgressors of this law, or those who gain knowledge of it in this life, are to be judged and punished according to this law, whose sentence will be carried out, not in this life, but in the life to come; consequently, such people are condemned prisoners in this life, waiting in fear and trembling for the time of the eternal exile!

I think the poor sinner is ready to shout out in fright—What! Is there no longer a way of salvation for me? Is my situation hopeless? Can I not devise some way of escaping this second law, and deliver myself from the second death? I answer, if you can hide from the piercing stare of the almighty God—if you can take arms against him, and prevent him from fulfilling the sentence of his broken law, then you can escape. If you can ensure that your faith, your repentance, and the best of your deeds, are sufficient atonement for your sins, then you can deliver yourself from the dreadful sentence that is hanging over your head. But let this be a warning to you, O sinner, that impossibility is imprinted on every one of your attempts to deliver yourself; and that you can do nothing that can make atonement for your sins, yes, though you were to weep bottles full of tears, and give your body to be burned to ash. Your situation is completely hopeless, unless the sentencer against whose law you transgressed has arranged deliverance for you. Then know that your salvation depends entirely upon getting hold of, and obeying that order thoroughly, whatever it may be; and no less, and no more, and nothing other than what he said, can save you. But do not lose heart, poor sinner; for although you cannot save yourself, yet there is hope for the worst. Oh good tidings of great joy! Oh incomparable grace! The glorious Person who gave that law has arranged a way of salvation, although it cost him dearly, yes, to suffer great scorn and pain—it cost him dying by the accursed death of the cross, and becoming death to death, and an end to the grave. The same dear Jesus who delivered the whole human race from the punishment for the sin of our first parents, has arranged a way of deliverance for every man from second death for his own sins; and he offers that deliverance now, and calls upon the worst sinner to be reconciled with him, so that he may be saved for eternal life. We believe that this can be achieved only through obedience to the conditions he himself set; for it was free mercy for him to offer any conditions: no one else could do that; consequently, no one should change one jot, or one tittle of his conditions, or say why they would not be like this, or why they are like that, but obey them as they are, and be thankful for them.

THE *REVIVALIST* A MORMON !

In the October issue of this monthly, we have Mr. Rees's interpretation of 1 Cor. xiii, 10—"When that which is perfect is come, then that which is in part shall be done away." In answer to someone, the Editor says that it is to the state of the saints in heaven that the text refers. Now, if it is so (and it is like that too), Mr. Rees is found to be making a plea for Mormonism. "We prophesy in part," the previous verse says; "but when that which is perfect is come, then that which is in part shall be done away," and no sooner. And since that which is in part is this "prophesying," and since Mr. Rees interprets so unhestitantly, that that which is in part is to continue until the day of judgment, the prophecy and the tongues, according to verses 8 and 9, are to continue until then. The Rev. David Rees, of Als Chapel, Llanelli, and in its "only publication" the respectable denomination of Welsh Independents, particularly the great Conference in Solfach and Neath, believe, print, and profess that that which is in part, namely the tongues and the prophecy, has been put in the church to stay until the perfection of heaven comes. How difficult it is for the people of a country to accept a subject from a new sect, and Oh how easily the same people, at the same time, swallow the same subject, when it is offered to them by the right hand of their own oracle! Let us take comfort, Saints of God, this large denomination will come to us before long. May the Lord make speed to facilitate their coming.

But the Editor of the *Revivalist* is not unique among his brethren. That is how nearly all of them interpret this phrase. Thus Matthew Henry, Barnes, Gill, Scott, and Burkitt. And in the name of all fairness, why can we not interpret in the same way? When one of the Mormons says—"That which is in part, namely the tongues and the prophecy, is to continue until the whole church goes to heaven," behold every Independent, and the great Conference too, shouting, "false prophets," "deceivers," &c.; but let Mr. Rees say—"That which is in part is to continue until the whole church goes to heaven," and behold every Independent on his feet, and particularly the great Conference, shouting, "The *Revivalist* has it," "The only publication of the Denomination is right."

SIGNS OF THE TIMES.

READER, RESPOND !

WHY was the potato crop spoiled throughout the whole of Ireland, Scotland, and a large part of England, in one night? What is the cause of such a destructive and unprecedented disease killing so many thousands of our animals so suddenly? Why have the crops rotted in Scotland? Why have the oats and the turnips rotted in Ireland, and the barley too in many places? What are all the dreadful storms that are over the seas, which sweep thousands of our fellow creatures into the eternal world completely without warning? Why did all the fish of the sea die along the coasts of America, for over five hundred miles? Why does the earth shake like a drunkard? Why are its bowels churning with trouble? Why is it seen in its fury casting its brimstone and its flames over almost whole towns and cities, swallowing their inhabitants by the thousands, and sending them in a completely unprepared state, most likely, to the spirit world? Why do the seas and the rivers surge and swell over their limits, and in the severity of their rage bury thousands in a second? Why do we hear of fires here, and incomparable conflagrations there, yes, of almost entire towns and cities, blazing at once? Why are the hearts of kings and rulers, together with their subjects, believers, and unbelievers, weary, fearful, and frightened, waiting for the dreadful things that are coming on earth? Why does black famine stare us so severely in the face? Why all this so unexpectedly, and yet so inevitably? Is this not a fulfillment of notable prophecies? Are not these and similar things, signs, and forerunners of the strange time, and the great day that is fast approaching? What is the answer? Here it is —Because an angel flew in the midst of heaven, with the eternal gospel, to preach to every kindred, tongue, people, and nation, that dwell on the earth, saying with a loud voice, "Fear God, and give glory to him, FOR THE HOUR OF HIS JUDGMENT IS COME ! !"

VIRTUE'S VENGEANCE.

ALWAYS vex your foe with justice,
Not with witch's curse, or malice;
Pay him back his ill with goodness–
Best revenge is loving kindness.

ESTABLISHMENT OF THE SAINTS IN KIRTLAND, AND THE PERSECUTION IN MISSOURI.

About the year 1831, the Saints from every state started to gather in Kirtland, a small town in the State of Ohio, a few miles south of Lake Erie. Several of them bought land, and worked it diligently; others of them built houses; and the craftsmen among them went into business, according to their various crafts; and thus they carried on for a while successfully and comfortably. Great success crowned the efforts of those who were preaching in the other states. As soon as men complied with the gospel in the midst of the world, they would despise and persecute them, fashioning all manner of false accusations against them, which caused those who could, to move near their brethren in Kirtland. Having increased their numbers to some thousands, they set to building a house of worship, or large temple, in Kirtland, and they persisted diligently, under all sorts of disadvantages, until they completed a convenient and beautiful building.

Soon afterwards, their neighbors were jealous of their success, and they feared that the "Mormons," as they called them, would be so numerous in time as to have an influence against them in the elections; as though their fellowmen would forfeit their freedom and their civil rights when they believed the gospel; and the only plan they could devise, in order to keep the reins of power in their own hands, was to bring false accusations against peaceful and innocent people. Here was begun that devious old trick that was practiced so much after that in other places, of setting some of their own old cottages on fire, and then accusing some of the Saints of doing it. Then it was reported in the newspapers far afield that the Mormons killed, and burnt the houses of their neighbors. Not unlike old Nero's trick of setting Rome on fire, and accusing the Christians, so as to stir up the populace against them. It was about this time that the foolish story about Joseph Smith, that he "walked on the water," was invented. But it was said beforehand that it was a woman called Anne Lee, in the eastern states, who did that; and we remember hearing that story being brought against Johannah Southcott, when we were schoolchildren; but most recently it was attributed to Joseph Smith: and however foolish and offensive the story is, yes, without ever so much as one word of truth, or any substance to it, about Joseph Smith, yet it has been proclaimed in the newspapers and across the pulpits of America. It is also a surprising thing that this story, like thousands of others that are just as groundless, has gained a *passage* across the Atlantic Ocean, has gone around England and Scotland, and is now traveling rapidly through Wales; it is being helped on its way from chapel to chapel—riding swiftly on the saddles of preachers, from one county to another—mounting the pulpits of one denomination that is just as welcoming as the next; and it is strange how it satisfies the taste of those who have given themselves up to solid error, so that they believe lies, those who do not accept truth's love. This is such a tasty morsel that the respectable editor of the *Revivalist* embraced it with the right hand of society, writing *holiness* on its forehead, and giving it a *passport*, and as free a passage as he could, in its ungodly task of deceiving his fellow countrymen, so that it might prepare the way for his own carriage. We do not think that it would be necessary for anyone to say that every word of this story is false, if it were not for the fact that some reverend gentlemen like these were trying to sanctify it with their corrupt lips, and thus give it an appearance of truth. But the people have had enough proof by now that the reverends are no more remarkable than their neighbors at telling the truth.

But to return to the story. The persecution against the Saints grew as much as their success. Joseph Smith was brought many times before the courts, and he was accused of almost everything that evil men could devise, in order to bring him down. In their great eagerness, the witnesses swore too much to be true; and since they swore opposite things to each other, yes, although he was judged by his professed enemies, he escaped from their grasp each time greater than a conqueror. Since they could not prove him guilty of transgression against civil law, a mob would often attack his house at night, threatening him with death, unless he took the Saints away from there. Once in particular they attacked his house in the middle of a cold night, when there was considerable snow and ice; they dragged him from his house by his feet, and they beat him cruelly, until they thought they had killed him; even so, there was life left in him, and he could hear them discussing amongst themselves what to do with him. Some advocated digging a grave there, and burying him. They went to fetch spades to that end, but since the earth was too hard for them to do that, some of them went back to Mr. Smith's house and took a pillow off his bed. After tearing off his clothes, they plastered his body with pitch; then they rubbed the feathers in the pitch, and left him there for dead. Soon after they went away, he got up, and went to his house. His wife had gone to tell people about it, and to beg her neighbors for help. Mr. Smith took care of himself, and it was found that his bones were in one piece, but that his front teeth were broken. The next morning (the Sabbath), he preached to a large crowd, keeping his engagement. The story of the persecutions and the oppression suffered by the Saints after this would be too long to describe here; but since there was no justice or peace for them to enjoy in Kirtland, nor any hope of such, in the year 1834, some of them went towards the west in search of a place where they could live together in peace. They settled in Jackson County, State of Missouri; they bought lands from the government, which they continued to pioneer and to work, and the Saints from Kirtland would emigrate there from time to time, as their circumstances permitted. They soon began to preach there; and the inhabitants had nothing in particular against them or their doctrine for a while, apart from some of the sectarians who shouted after them, "deceivers, and false prophets."

In the following July, several thousand of the Saints came to settle in Jackson County, and they very soon turned the wilderness into meadow land. They built a town called Far West, in a salubrious and attractive location. The surrounding country was owned by the Saints. They built cottages, mills, and villages; and they put seeds in the ground, expecting to have that peace and freedom to worship God according to their conscience, which the laws of the republic promised each and every one of its subjects. The Saints took care, as much as they could, not to give their neighbors any reason to persecute them, so that some of them had denied themselves to the extent of promising not to interfere in anything pertaining to the state; but others claimed their right to that. Because the Saints had voted in the election of state officials, some of the old settlers immediately agitated against them, and there was disturbance and fighting between some of them. From thenceforth, those who misrepresented the quarrel accused the Saints of refusing to allow others to cast their vote. They falsely accused the Saints of many tales, of being traitors to the government, &c. Some of them forged the names of the leaders, announcing in one of the newspapers that the Saints were inviting Negro slaves to escape from their owners, and come to them, and they would have their freedom. They could not invent anything that would excite the state more than this, because Missouri is a state where slave-trading is very common. Although the Saints did not interfere with their slaves, it is true that they did not support keeping their fellow creatures captive like animals; but they knew that they would be endangering their lives, and breaking state law, if they said anything against them. The inhabitants who settled in this part of the state had mostly moved from Kentucky, Tennessee, and the other slave and semi-barbaric states. It had for years been a haven to which debtors would flee, and those who were escaping punishment for their crimes against the law of their own country. They were quite like their Indian neighbors, but much more cruel. In order to fan the flames even more, the missionaries who were among the Indians accused the Saints of scheming with the Indians to come and kill the citizens, and possess the land. The only reason they had was that the Saints preached to the Indians who came into their midst, and two or three preachers returned to the woods with the Indians to teach them, and that at their own request. This so incensed the missionaries that they came to the slave-traders, who were only too pleased to have some case against the Saints. This accusation was an excellent basis on which to carry on their invention, especially since their riotous mob was presided over by such godly preachers; and, strange though it is to tell, yet it is true enough that these missionaries of peace did not rest until they had eighteen of them to preach throughout the country against the Saints, until they incited them in their hundreds to attack and kill them, if they did not leave the country forthwith. They burned their own property so as to send word to the Governor of the State that the Saints did it; they destroyed many of the Saints' houses, they burned their crops, they stole their animals, and they frequently gathered in armies against them, having blackened their faces, dressed in skins, with feathers on their heads, shouting frightfully like Indians; and wherever the hatred of these uncivilized preachers fell, would fall the vengeance of their inhuman and merciless followers. In vain the Saints would call on the government for protection, for the state officials had believed the false accusations that were brought against the Saints. More than once the Governor of the State, with the magistrates, instructed them to defend themselves, which they had not yet ventured to do; and as soon as they defended their houses and their families in the face of attack from the evil men, stories flew through the country that the Mormons had killed some large number of people, adding and misrepresenting until others were even more incensed against them, without inquiring if what they heard was true. In the end, the Governor called out the militia to help the rioters to exile the Saints from the country, at the cost of everything they owned, without permitting them an inquiry or any other justice, as will be clearly seen from the following testimony of an eyewitness and fellow sufferer, given under oath before one of the courts of the state of Illinois in the year 1838, endorsed also by many others, proclaimed to the world to their faces, and one which stands today as incontrovertible testimony against them, and will continue to shout in the ears of the Lord of Sabaoth until he judges his people in justice.

Read and wonder, reader, and then remember that you have not been told half the cruelties and persecution suffered by the innocent and defenseless Saints, because of their religion, in Missouri!

TESTIMONY OF HYRUM SMITH, PATRIARCH, BEFORE THE COURT IN NAUVOO, STATE OF ILLINOIS.

This testimony was given by Hyrum Smith on behalf of his brother Joseph Smith, who was brought before the courts at Nauvoo, on the instruction of the Governor of the State of Missouri, and who was accused of treachery in that state. It is right to note here that the witness was a brother to Joseph Smith, the prophet, who was the founder of Mormonism. The size of our publication does not allow us to give more than just a short abridgement of this important testimony, which contains the whole story of the persecution in Missouri.

After clearing his brother's character, Hyrum Smith goes on to say that when his brother was in the State of Missouri, the people who were commonly called Mormons were being threatened most dreadfully; and about the first Monday in August, 1838, at the election in Gallatin, Davies County, Mormons were forbidden to exercise their rights of franchise; and because of that circumstance, agitation and fighting began among the citizens of that place, which caused a mob to rise up in that county thenceforth, threatening the extermination of the Mormons. After our witness and his brother heard that rioters were rising up, and that they had murdered two of the citizens of the place, and would not suffer them to be buried, they went over to learn the particulars of the situation, but they learned that none were killed, rather several were wounded. On their return, they called on the authorities, and pleaded with them to attempt to calm the rioters, which, in writing, they promised to do; and soon afterwards, there was peace.

Things did not continue in this way for long; for very soon the mob began to collect again, so that several hundred of them attacked the Mormons in Millport, a few miles from Diahman, taking away their animals, and threatening them with extermination. They frequently took men, women and children prisoners, whipping them and treating them in the most cruel manner, tying them to trees and depriving them of food until they were compelled to gnaw the bark from the trees in order to sustain life. In short, they did everything to them that they thought would most excite the indignation of the other Mormons, and get them to put up a defense, so that they could accuse them of breaking the law, and thus excite the populace to assist them in exterminating those innocent people. Messengers were dispatched immediately to the authorities, and military assistance was procured to defend the town; but after things quieted down, and the soldiers left, the animosity of the persecutors rekindled, and they rose up in several other places where the Mormons lived, dispossessing them of their property, and treating them brutally. The soldiers in most places were refusing to do their duty. It was thought best now to send a petition to the Governor, and another to Judge King. The Mormons were still in a dreadful state; they saw themselves completely surrounded by armed enemies, some of whom would be under the leadership of ministers of the gospel. They made the Mormons give up everything in their possession, under threat of death, and forced them to promise to leave their country, and go to Far West, otherwise they would drive them there, and then to hell.

While this situation persisted, the answer came back from the Governor and others, informing them that the Mormons could have no assistance, and because they had fought for themselves, that they had no intention of worrying about them.

All the scattered families of these people in all the counties except Davies County, were forced to go to Far West, but not before many of them starved to death on the way. This only increased their hardship, for many thousands were driven to a place where there were no habitations to shelter them, rather they had to huddle together, some in sorts of tents, others under blankets, and many with no shelter from the inclemency of the weather. For two months they were in this state, many of them being killed, while others were so badly whipped that they had to swathe up their bowels to prevent them from falling out. About this time, one General Parks came from Richmond, Ray County, who was one of the commissioned officers sent out to Diahman, and Hyrum Smith and his brother went from there at the same time. After they had all arrived at Diahman, and gone to the house of one Colonel Wight, about eleven o'clock at night, a Mormon woman came in, bringing her two children along with her, one about two-and-a-half years old, the other a babe in her arms. She came in on foot, a distance of about three miles, through the snow, and waded across the Grand River when the water was waist deep. She stated that some of the rioters had turned her out of doors, had taken all her household goods, and had burnt her house, and she had barely managed to save herself and her children. Her husband at that time was in Virginia, and she was living alone.—This cruel transaction excited the feelings of Colonel Wight, and he asked General Parks, in the hearing of the others, how long they had to suffer like this? This caused the mob to be dispersed, and their arms to be taken away. But they soon devised a new trick; instead of burning the Mormons' houses now, they set fire to their own houses (having first emptied them), and sent all over the country to say that it was the work of the Mormons. Thereafter, it was impossible to persuade anyone that it was not the Mormons who were guilty, and the prejudice of the country against them was excited even further. Noticing the suffering of the people in Diahman, our witness and his brother returned to the city of Far West, and dispatched a messenger to Governor Atchinson, stating the facts as they did then exist, and praying for assistance if possible. In the meantime, the Judge of the County Court issued orders to the county militia to stand in constant readiness, day and night, to prevent the citizens from being massacred, which fearful situation they were exposed to every minute. Everything continued to be very alarming. Notwithstanding all this, the people still hoped that the Governor would render them assistance; and while they were waiting for deliverance, praying and weeping, they beheld a large army approaching the town, brandishing their glittering arms in the bright sunshine; and the inhabitants could not but feel joyful for a moment, thinking that the Governor had sent relief. But, to their surprise, when the army arrived there, they formed up into a double file, and dispatched three messengers bearing white flags to the town to ask for three persons to be brought out of the town, before they should massacre the rest and set the town ablaze. The three said to them, "If the people must be destroyed, and the city burned, we are prepared to accept the same fate." After this, the army retreated about a mile-and-a-half back from the town; and soon a messenger was sent to talk to the two generals, but before he reached their camp, he was shot by one of the Methodist preachers, by the name of Bogard; however, he managed to see one of them, who told him that the other was not there, and that he had sent him back because he was too merciful to the Mormons. The messenger begged him to spare the town until the next morning, which he coolly agreed to do, as he had not yet received the Governor's order, which he expected at any hour. A second messenger was dispatched to the same general, imploring him to use his best endeavors to preserve the lives of the people, and he returned with the news that many had been wretchedly killed by some of the soldiers of another general called Lucas. These crimes were committed previous to having received the Governor's order. A little before sundown, another army came in, under the leadership of one Cornelius Gillum, who had been committing dreadful depredations previously in another place. This army had painted their faces like Indians. They would whoop and roar like Indians all night. Early in the morning, a messenger was sent to have another interview with General Doniphan; and on his return, he informed them that the Governor's order had arrived; and that General Doniphan had said that the Governor's order was to exterminate the Mormons, but that he would be damned if he would obey it, and that General Lucas might do what he pleased. But it was learned that this order was only a copy of the original, which was in the hands of Major General Clark, who was on his way to Far West, with an additional army of six thousand men. Soon after this, there came into the town a messenger, bringing the intelligence that an awful massacre of the people of Haun's Mill had taken place, as a result of the Governor's order to exterminate the Mormons.

The army which went to Far West, during all the while they were encamped there, continued to lay waste the arable fields, steal the animals, and kill them for sport. They held the city under siege, and no one was permitted to come in or go out under penalty of death. Many of the citizens were shot when they ventured out to obtain sustenance. There was one field of twelve hundred acres, which was mostly covered with arable crops; and it was entirely laid waste by the horses of the army. The day after the arrival of the army there, in the evening, Colonel Hinkle went to the city, requesting to see Joseph Smith (Sen.), Parley P. Pratt, Sidney Rigdon, Lyman Wight, and George W. Robinson, and stating that the officers of the army wanted a consultation with them, and that they assured them they would not be harmed. They agreed, and went with the colonel towards the camp, when soon they were surrounded by soldiers. They supposed their purpose was to guard them into the camp in safety; but to their surprise, when they were brought to General Lucas, Hinkle went up to him and said, "These are the prisoners I agreed to deliver up to you." Lucas drew his sword, and said, "You are now my prisoners;" and at that time, the main army came to meet them. They opened to the right and left, and Smith and his friends were led between them, amidst the shouting and whooping of the soldiers. After being thus betrayed, they were placed under guard, and they were compelled to lie on the cold ground all night, and were told that they dare not ever expect their liberty again. The next morning, the soldiers were permitted to go to the town to disturb the people at their leisure, to enter into their houses and pillage them, ravish the women, and take away every weapon they could find. About twelve o'clock, Colonel Hinkle came to the house of our witness (Hyrum Smith), and he was taken prisoner with the others, despite his sickness and that of his family at the time. Within half an hour, one Amasa Lyman was held and placed under the same guard. They were out again that night; and Hinkle came to H. Smith, and said he would plead their case in the court martial, but he was afraid he should not succeed. He said also that there was another court then in session, in which there were about twenty different preachers. In the morning, General Doniphan came to them and said that the verdict of the court was that they were to be shot that morning, but that he wanted no hand in the work, and that he and his brigade were leaving the place, considering that they would be spilling innocent blood. This movement of Doniphan's made considerable excitement in the army, and much talk amongst the officers; and the prisoners heard that "the damned Mormons would not be shot that morning, because General Doniphan had frustrated the plan, and that another court had ordered them to be taken to Jackson County, to be executed there." In a few moments, two wagons came to fetch them, and while they were getting into them, the prisoners were shot at by four or five men, but without effect. The men were secured, and they drove off. After much pleading, they were permitted to go to the city under guard, to bid their relatives farewell, and get some clothing, but they were not allowed to say a word. Then they went on towards Jackson County, and after traveling 12 miles, they stopped for the night, and the prisoners were permitted to sleep out in the snow, from which they suffered severely. In the morning at the dawn of day, they were made to continue on their journey, and were exhibited to everyone along the road, as though they were elephants or camels. They were stared at and examined from head to foot by men, women, and children, only they did not look at their teeth. This treatment of them was continued, until they arrived at Independence, in Jackson County, when they were exhibited once again all over town. After that, they were placed in an old log house under guard, where they were compelled to stay all that night and the next day. After being in the town about four days, a messenger came from General Clark to order them back to Richmond, Ray County, where he and his army had arrived to await them there; but on the morning they were to depart, the prisoners were informed by General Wilson that it was expected by the soldiers that they would be hanged on the road, except that the other general wanted to have the pleasure. They arrived at Richmond on the 9th of November, where they were again secured in an old log house. In half an hour, a man came in with chains and padlocks, saying he was authorized to put them in chains. The soldiers were aiming their guns at them while the man fastened the chains about them. In a few minutes, General Clark came in, and the prisoners asked him what was the cause of this treatment; but he gave no reply, saying that they would be told in a few days. Whilst they were still in this situation, a young man of the name of Grant came to see them, and told them that he had seen General Clark make his choice of men to shoot them on Monday morning; he also saw them loading their rifles with two balls in each, and after they had finished, the general addressed them thus:—"Gentlemen, you shall have the honor of shooting the Mormon leaders on Monday morning at eight o'clock!" But because of something or other, the general durst not carry out his intentions; and so he sent to Fort Leavenworth for the military code of laws, to find out if preachers, who never did military duty, came under his jurisdiction; and he spent a week searching: so the Monday passed away without their being shot. It was strange that a man such as the general knew no better. However, when he had discovered that they were not in his power to punish, he came to the prisoners in the log house, and said he had concluded to deliver them over to the civil authorities, as persons guilty of treason, murder, and quite a number of things. Accordingly, they were handed over to those pretended authorities; and the next morning, they were released from their chains, and were led to the court. Austin A. King was the judge, and one Mr. Birch the district attorney, namely the two gentlemen who sat previously on the court martial when the prisoners were sentenced to be shot. This court continued to sit over fourteen days, in some manner, and the portrayal given by our witness of its proceedings is a disgrace to a country which boasts so much of its freedom and its Christianity.—*(To be continued.)*

REVIEW.

SUBSTANCE OF A SERMON ON THE MIRACLES, *in order to enlighten Everyman, and show the Deceit of the Creatures who call themselves "Latter-day Saints."* By W. R. DAVIES, Dowlais.

[CONTINUED FROM PAGE 109.]

IF the fact that we have not healed anybody whom you wished us to, to please your mocking assertions, proves that signs do not follow those who believe the gospel that we preach, Paul's leaving Trophimus sick, and Timothy under his frequent weakness must prove that signs did not follow him either. Strange, Sir, that you would not understand the apostolic plan better than that, before ever daring to climb into a pulpit to offer it to others! No; it is God who imparts out the blessings as he himself wishes; and your text says that in your face, if you wished to hear it. Read again, Sir, the eleventh verse of the chapter which you distort, namely 1 Cor. xii—"And all these things (that is the gifts), the one and the same Spirit works them, sharing to everyone individually [of the saints], as he (God's Spirit), wills." Not as you will. Then read ver. 30, and cease asking for signs, for shame. "Does everyone have gifts of healing? Does everyone speak with tongues? Does everyone interpret?" I wonder if you, in all seriousness, Mr. Davies, are so foolish as to believe that anyone claims the power to do one of these things except in the way, and at the time, and as God would do it through them? If you are not, why do you show yourself more foolish still by challenging us to do them when you wish? No, Sir! The signs follow believers, and do not go in front of their deniers, as their giver says in Mark xvi, 17, 18. You have them not, for you admit that, and you deny their existence, and yet you claim that you are a believer. How can that be, without your making the Son of God a liar? Remember that they were promised to "them that believe;" and not to the apostles alone. All your scorn and reviling at the cost of the lameness of the poor person under observation is naught but scorn adapted to Paul, yea, to the Son of God himself. And after God imparts healing blessings to these saints, who but you is the first and loudest of voice, shouting, "deceit, deceit," completely distorting it all in the *Baptist* and in the same breath shouting, "A miracle, do a miracle." Remember the use made of that obvious miracle, namely the healing of the broken bones of William Hughes's leg, so that he walked immediately when hands were laid upon him; yes, remember many things that were done in our midst, Sir, and remember to give the glory to God, for he alone is worthy of that. Not one of the servants of God could practice one of the gifts except as they were moved by the Holy Ghost. Their duty is to administer the established ordinance, that is anointing with oil, and laying on of hands, and that at the wish of the afflicted. "Let [the afflicted] call to him elders of the church." I wonder whether they would call them unless they had faith that they would be healed? Why then does the preacher mock us for requiring faith? He cannot show one promise in the word of God that anyone was to be healed through these ways except the saints. The examples of some being excepted from the rule, in that the Spirit of God urged them on for his glory, do not contain any command for anyone else to do likewise, until they have the same exhortation, for God alone has the right to make exceptions; but, for his servants, they must walk according to the rules laid down. Mr. Davies admits that healing men's bodies is a miracle, and is it not more of a miracle to heal men's souls, Sir? A miracle, you say, is everything that is "above the order of nature." Do you ever pray for anything, Mr. Davies? Well then, if you are answered in anything, that is a miracle, according to your own reasoning. Do you pray for the Spirit of God? You must be praying for a miracle, or confess that you are answered in accordance with the order of nature. But is it not you who shouts, at the top of your voice, for God to save your listeners and confessing that that would be a miracle; but in the same cry, from the same pulpit, and above the same people, shouts that "miracles have died out and that there is no need of them," reviling those who profess them as "Satanists," &c.

Do devils not need to be cast out now? Let the groans of the thousands which echo through the walls of all the *Lunatic Asylums* throughout the country answer. Do not the sick need to be healed now? Let all the doctors of the country be witnesses against you. Do the saints throughout the world not need to be perfected now? How can you say that there is no need of the means laid down for that now, nor faith in the practice of them? What is your basis for such assertions?

After wasting a number of pages trying to prove what a miracle is, by contradicting himself, and quoting the works of others that contradict one another, Mr. Davies makes his own imaginings a rule to prove a miracle. How can one thing, which is the effect of a cause, be a miracle, and the effect of some other cause not be a miracle? Is it a miracle to see a man being healed by practicing the means appointed for that? And is it not a miracle to see fruits growing on trees? Does not the one through his faith expect the blessing, because of the connection of the promise to their obedience, as the other expects to have his wheat back in the harvest, which he sowed through his faith? And is it not God who gives the increase to the one and the other, according to his promise? Oh, no, the Physicist himself does not go against his established laws, Mr. Davies. Had he not promised that they should be healed in that way? Then, it is like unto a miracle to see you mocking those ways, and yet seeking the blessing through your Davisistic system, with neither the means nor faith. Have you not admitted that a miracle is an act? If so, it is not above the understanding of the performer, or it would be an accident; for the miracle disappears after the understanding of such a person increases. *Well done*, Mr. Davies. But after seeing that that goes against his Davisism, he jumps into the breach to defend that too, by referring us to Joshua commanding the sun to stop. I wonder whether Joshua said that haphazardly, without knowing anything about the connection, or the effect that would be brought about? Was is not for that that Joshua prayed? Well, here it is completely the wrong way about again; for, according to Mr. Davies's reasoning, everyone who performs a miracle must be completely without faith in the act, as he calls it, because it is not possible that there should be faith in what they would be completely ignorant of! Paul says in Heb. xi, 1—

"Now faith is the substance of things hoped for, the evidence of things not seen." If you were to read ver. 30, you would see that "through faith the walls of Jericho fell." And was it not through faith that he ordered the sun to stop, Mr. Davies? Did he therefore have faith in what he did not understand? Strange how you knock yourself down with every blow! Read this chapter, Mr. Davies, together with many other places in your Bible, and you will see that it was through faith that miracles were done. "Through faith they overcame kingdoms, shut the jaws of lions, suffered the heat of the fire, and through faith the women received their dead," &c. And yet you insist on having the dead alive, the lame to walk, and the blind to see, against their will, faith or not!! Is it not "the prayer of faith that will heal the afflicted?" Is it not "without faith it is impossible to please God?" And shall he work a miracle for them, unwillingly? "The Lord shall raise him up," says the Bible. No, says Mr. Davies, we must do that against their will, otherwise we are proved deceivers. Well, we ask the fool a question according to his foolishness, lest he be proud in his own sight. Why would you not force all the disbelievers of Dowlais to believe in Davisism, Sir? "Oh, the means God arranged to bring men to belief is preaching," he says. Why so? "Because faith comes through hearing," he says. Yes indeed; faith is required in order to become children of God, then, and that through hearing. Very well, that is what we say too; but we ask again, Is not faith necessary to receive blessings, or the "bread of the children," then? If so, why do you say that to say so is but "hiding deceit?" And is your deceit not quite obvious, since you claim to be a minister of the gospel, and deny it like this? You say, "that to claim the continuance of miracles proves disbelief, hardness of heart, and the faithlessness of evil men." And yet, you prove us such, yes, "Satanists" because not even our shadow, our clothes, &c., do miracles in the markets of Merthyr, and every time you wish, and all that to prove to yourself that we are what you already say we are! Have you not assured the world for years that we are devilish men, &c.? You must be doubting yourself, Sir! Would you believe that we are servants of God after seeing a miracle? If you would, that would prove that you are not a servant of God now. Who has seen a servant of God requesting a sign from those whom he calls servants of the devil? Admitting that they do miracles too, and in the same admission saying that these are "the extremes of presumption, that the devil cannot make a man more devilish and hellish" than that? Are you not like unto old Saul in this? And we fear that your answer and your end would be like unto his.

On page 18, Mr. Davies asserts that previously miracles were done to strengthen Christianity, and that to claim their continuation throws scorn at those early ones. One knows not whether it is William, or Richard, or Davies, who claims this; for one of them, a while back, claimed they were "for the edifying of the church;" and as a result, the recipients of the miracles had believed and obeyed the gospel, before they could be in the church. After that, we hear someone claiming that the object of a miracle was to prove the mission of the people. All right, Mr. Davies, there you are in your own trap again, for no reasonable person will believe that you have a mission, unless you prove that through your miracles! Is that not fair enough for you, Sir?

And are you not willing to be weighed in your own scales? Well, do not profess to be sent from God then until you do some small miracle on the streets of Dowlais, or Merthyr's markets; yes, if it were only to drink a glass of poison, as you sought for W. Henshaw to do. If you were a servant of God, according to your own reasoning, you should have healed "Little Maggie" as you call her: you had plenty of time, and she followed your sect for about forty years, and you a servant of God, never having administered a blessing of health to her, nor even prayed for her to be healed; since that would be to pray for a miracle, to be sure. You try to get people to believe that you are sent to preach, whilst mocking and abolishing the ordinances that those sent by God administered in the early ages, do you; and not as much as one miracle to prove that either! You should retract your assertions, or the missionary speech that you made, recently; for how can your missionaries strengthen your gospel amongst the pagans, without showing miraculous proofs of their mission, any more than the apostles could? Do you expect the pagans to leave the religions of their forefathers, for which they gave their lives, through nothing but the assertions of some stranger from a far land? How shall you offer them the New Testament as a rule, when it testifies against you, promising the gifts of the Holy Ghost to those who believe it, while you deny them? Are things like this not vain work? But, for the Saints, they do not need to prove their mission, for they preach the gospel that Christ and his apostles preached, according to the scriptures; and so our God proves our mission indisputable by imparting the spiritual gifts, &c., according to his promise, for the edifying of the saints. But yet, I would wish to know who sent you to preach some other gospel, not founded on the Bible.

Next, he says—"To claim the continuation of miracles wrecks and destroys miraculous proof forever, by making them common things." There's the end of it, now! If so, Elias's miracles destroyed the former ones of Moses; the later miracles belittled those others that had been done. By following this reasoning, we gather that the greatest miracle was the first ever done! And that the first miracle of Christ was the greatest he did, and the others continually becoming lesser, according to their abundance! Who admitted that the last miracle that he did, namely the resurrection of Jesus Christ, was the greatest? According to Mr. Davies, Christ would have proved his mission by not doing any miracles, lest he belittle the miracles of former ages, which had been common for four thousand years, more or less. It is a pity that the apostles did so many powerful miracles in the name of Jesus when, according to Mr. Davies, there is a tendency in each one of them to belittle those which he himself did, by making them common things. What a strange way God had—*belittling* instead of *glorifying* the name of his Son Jesus! Let the world and your friends judge whether you are in your senses! Would it not be the same for you to assert that the fruit which grew on such a tree was an apple in ages gone-by, but that since it is common by now, it is not an apple? Behold an example of Mr. Davies's syntactical *logic*, and we leave the reader to ponder it. "To ask why miracles do not occur daily, is to ask, Why do miracles not cease to be miracles ! !"

[*To be continued.*]

THE JOINT STOCK COMPANY.

WE are very happy to inform the well-wishers of this excellent Company of its remarkable success already. All the shares that may be sold (that is, ten thousand) have been taken up, and there is demand for several thousand more. The board of directors intends, when Parliament next convenes, to increase the number of shares to twenty thousand, at a pound apiece, as before. The rules allow the members a reasonable time to pay for their shares, but everyone is requested to endeavor to pay the total as soon as they can, and the sooner the better for their own sakes.

Perhaps a few remarks on the nature and aims of this Company would not come amiss with our readers, insofar as some have mistaken its aims. It is true that our critics are ready to find fault when we say a word about anything relating to money. There is no cause for surprise here either, when they are so eager to prophesy evil for everything we do. They have been talking a lot in America about our sharing our possessions in general, and that those who join our church are expected to give their possessions to the Company, &c. But we solemnly testify that these are complete lies. Our church does not demand or condone anything of the sort, and not one example can be found of any of us having done that in any part of the world; rather, on the contrary, everyone retains every right over his own property, under every circumstance, as before, in this country, and in America too; and everyone has greater free will to contribute to the poor, and every other good cause, with us, than is allowed with any denomination we know. Our leaders in America were so far from taking the property of others, that they received nothing for their sustenance from the church, but each one worked with his own hands, or did business, like other men, for his living; even Joseph Smith was like this too. That business of holding all things in common belongs to the *Owenites*, and the *Shaking Quakers*, but never to us.

Some think that this Joint Stock Company is linked to our church. But that is a mistake too; for it has no links of any sort with the church, as can be seen when one considers that the Company has been regulated according to the laws of Britain, officially registered in *Chancery* according to an *Act of Parliament*, like other mercantile societies, and has established for itself officials, and a board of directors, who are bound in surety to do justice to every member, according to the law of the land; and each one can be protected by that law, so that they cannot do an injustice to any of the members. And apart from that, some thousands of shares have been bought by gentlemen who are not in our church.

This is not an emigration Company either, as others suppose, to help them to cross the sea when they wish. But one of the aims of this Company is to do business with the *capital*, so that the members may have the gains as interest for their money. Through unity we are enabled to do this much more profitably than in any other way; yet, the presidents of the Company are men tried and tested in the church for years. Another aim the Company has in mind is, while bringing profit to the members, to assist in providing the means of transporting the Saints who wish to go across. Another aim is to do business with those who have already gone across to California. It is intended to send the new and excellent ship, "*Zion's Hope*," at the Company's expense, with a cargo of all sorts of commercial and artistic goods, from Liverpool to California, in November, to meet our exiled brethren, so that they may till the soil in that wonderful land, and raise food for themselves, and for those who come there to join them. It is intended to carry on all sorts of industry there, which are thought profitable to the Company; and the ships will bring the produce back to England, and other places.

Perhaps the poor man is ready to ask, What advantages can such a Company bring him? We reply, many, in many ways. First, by enabling him to gather with the children of God at the place where God promised them deliverance, when he pours down his plagues and his judgments on the ungodly who live in great Babylon. How then, says the member again, at the cost of our Company? No, friend; not at anyone's expense but his own, and that by paying the cost of his transport to the Company, perhaps, after arriving over there, which a man with a large family cannot easily do in this country, where the wages are low, and food costs are high. I do not think any of the Saints would wish to leave a brother or sister behind under God's vengeance in the midst of their enemies, because of their poverty; yet, what will they do, unless God arranges some means of deliverance? Well, God has already opened up the way before them through this beneficent Company, if only they do what they can, and that will be to the Company's advantage too.

If some of the poor Saints were to go to some of those merchants who have grown rich on the Saints' money, and ask them to help them to go across on their ships, what would they be told, I wonder? I should expect to hear them either laughing at them, or saying they were deranged. From this, then, can be seen the usefulness of this Company in this matter; and let even the poor make efforts in its favor, for their temporal deliverance depends on its success.

This Company also appears very useful to the Saints too, considering it enables them, through their cooperation, to have shops, *manufactories*, and everything they will need in their own midst there, rather than continuing, as they have through the years, to give wealth to strangers, who brought their expensive goods into their midst, and after getting their money turned into cruel, persecuting betrayers of them. The Saints in Missouri, and in Illinois, have been under great disadvantages because of such things, and it is time now for them to enjoy the fruits of their hard labor among themselves, and help each other in that country, since there are in their midst men able in every business, and eager to benefit everyone, especially the family of faith.

The Saints see their duty and their privilege to pay for their shares as soon as possible, considering the great cost of buying a new ship, preparing it and its cargo of the merchandise most suitable and most profitable in those parts of South America they will call at on the way, so that they need only be told that it is intended to pay for this ship between now and next Christmas.

The presidents of the various areas in Wales should hold their meetings to that effect as regularly as they can, and send what is paid to the Treasurer, W. Phillips, Merthyr, as soon as possible after each meeting, so that he can send it all together to the chief treasurer in Liverpool without delay.

Every member should take care to get a *ticket* from the secretary, showing what he pays to the treasurer, and they should be kept carefully until they have finished paying their contribution, and receive a *deed* of their share or shares, in accordance with the law of the country, as when land, or some other property, is bought, which they can sell to someone else if they wish. It would be very desirable for everyone to endeavor to pay for his shares before emigrating to America, and obtain his deeds too, and afterwards their place of residence does not affect their association with the Company in any way, except to know where they will be.

The secretaries and all the treasurers, as well as the members, are expected to keep their accounts carefully and clearly; because the presidents and the committee must take a copy of all their accounts, how much money they have received, have paid, and in what manner, together with an accurate description of the Company's situation, to every annual meeting at the *Chancery*, where no accounts are accepted except those which agree with the *tickets*, signed by the various officials: and although we do not receive, pay, or *handle* one penny of the Company's money in any shape or form, yet we would wish to see the officials doing everything correctly, so that there be no misunderstanding in relation to the Company, but that it may succeed in winning the trust and the support it deserves from everyone.

N.B. There are more of the *printed receipts* available from William Phillips, Merthyr. Copies of the *Deed of Settlement* can be obtained too, in English, for 4c. each.

AMERICAN MISSION TO BRITAIN.

THE Saints will be happy to hear of the coming of three of the twelve Apostles, namely Orson Hyde, Parley P. Pratt, and John Taylor, to England once more. They are in full health, and enveloped in the fiery spirit of their high office. It will be a greater joy, I should think, especially to the Welsh, to hear that the last two have promised to pay a visit to their brothers and sisters in Wales before long; perhaps they will come to Merthyr before next Christmas, but information will be given later. These faithful brethren left their wives and their children, and all they possessed, in the Saints' main encampment in the desert, and they have returned through many dangers and difficulties on land and sea, to serve the church in Britain; and to publicize and organize important matters, on which the success, unity, perfection, and salvation of all the Saints depend, to a great extent. Their self-denial, their faithfulness, and their incomparable diligence, are clear witnesses to their love for the Saints, and their great desire to benefit them. There is no need to indicate that the costs of these brethren have been, and continue to be, very high, for that can be clearly seen. We should also like the Saints to understand that these are men who live, and come from the depths of the far west at their own expense. There is no toll, or tax, or any other way to pay the expenses, except what the Saints contribute of their free will. We have witnessed that these people over the years work with their hands to support themselves and their families, sacrificing what they could of their time to the work of the ministry, and they have most recently been deprived of all they possessed because of their religion; but, despite everything, it can be seen that they are determined, like good shepherds, to feed the flock with the honest milk of the word—yes, to lay down their lives for the flock of their Great Shepherd, rather than leave them as prey for the wolves. We hope, then, that the Saints in Wales will show they are worthy of the service of such men, by preparing to contribute from their means, as much as they can, according to how God has prospered them, to pay the costs and provide for the needs of these brethren, when they come into our midst. We believe that we need only remind the Saints of this, that their eyes will immediately be opened, to see the necessity for it—our duty to do what we can for them, and the great privilege of being able to contribute to those whom we very well know to be servants of the living God, missionaries of peace, emissaries of the King to gather his children to "the wedding feast of the Lamb," in order to inherit blessedness, elevation, and eternal glory, when the kingdom of God comes in its essential might and magnificence. Let no one think it too much, then, to contribute from his worldly goods to those who bring him the fulness of the blessings of the gospel of peace. These brethren left the Saints' encampment amid the Indians, near Council Bluffs, beyond the frontiers of the white people, by some hundreds of miles. They are camping there for the winter. They live in tents, collect hay for their animals, and hunt food for themselves for the winter, such as the meat of wild oxen, deer (*elk*), &c. They have in the camp over fifty thousand horned animals, apart from horses, mules, sheep, &c. We are pleased to hear that all the Indians are very hospitable to them—the chiefs of every tribe they have seen have allowed them complete freedom to possess and live peacefully in the place they choose of their territories, without any money or payment at all. What a lesson! What an example of the humanity and the tenderness of feeling of the pagans of the woods, to those inhuman Christians who robbed the Saints of their land, from one state to the next, for almost twenty years, yes, after they had bought it and paid their money to the government for it!! No wonder that the Indians refuse those religions that cause such unjust effects as this. Oh, Sectarianism, when will you be satisfied with bleeding prey? But my soul rises from the scene; a sweeter tale is that of the children of the desolate woods, who have not heard the voice of the turtle dove of Heaven, but only the voice of the eagle and the owl, who have not crossed the path of a missionary, apart from the steps of the bear and the fox. The Indians provide the Saints with free wood, and wish them to stay in their midst to instruct them in art, agriculture, &c. The Saints are putting crops in the ground in readiness for the coming of the second encampment there who will benefit from them. They intended to take up their tents and journey on at the beginning of the summer, when grass grew for the animals, and these three brethren intend to return there to start with them at that time. We hope everyone will make every effort to make contributions to the above brethren, in order to assist those poor creatures who are hunting their daily food in the woods, depending on Providence for their daily ration, as they go on. Their expectations lie with us who are in plenty at present, and their pitiful situation deserves our help; there is an opportunity now, and it may be the last opportunity, to send to them, as they will be beyond the Rocky Mountains the next summer. Donating to them is lending to Him who owns the earth and its fulness, and he will repay an hundredfold: he says too, "Inasmuch as ye have given to these my brethren, verily ye have done it unto me." We intend to hold a conference in Merthyr, when the aforementioned brethren come over, and there will be an opportunity then to make contributions to them. But P. P. Pratt and J. Taylor have asked us to receive for them that which is donated beforehand, and as their stay will only be short, and many important matters will take time then, it is better for everyone to send what they can to us in advance, and they will have a receipt for it. Dear brothers and sisters, there has not been such a call as this upon you before, and it is not likely there will be again; so strive for once to help them now, and they will pay it back, by preparing places to receive us to their eternal dwelling places there, when no other city of refuge will be available to shelter from the enemy's wrath, plagues, diseases, wars, the tumult of nations, and all the dreadful judgments which the Lord of the whole earth intends to pour down in his wrath on all the unrepentant and persecuting inhabitants of Babylon the great, "the Mother of harlots of the earth," together with all her family. Great and sudden will be her destruction. "The destroyer of the Gentiles" will brandish his shaken sword, great and strong, in his own hand, until all those of honest principle have escaped from the midst of her, so that they do not receive her plagues. Verily, I say unto you, this age and this generation shall not pass, until he completes his work, his strange and wondrous work; he will cut it short and make it short in righteousness. Let the Saints remember this, then, that here we have no continuing city; for on mount Zion, and in Jerusalem only, will there be temporal and eternal deliverance.

MANCHESTER CONFERENCE.

On Saturday, Sunday, and Monday, the 17th, 18th, and 19th of October, a general Conference was held in this town, on which occasion we had the great pleasure of meeting many of our dear brethren from America, having had the company of some for years, and the honor of working with several of them in our Lord's vineyard in the far west, under much opposition. Great joy filled our bosoms at meeting again, to do battle in this country under the banner of the same King. These brethren have received their endowment in the temple of God in Nauvoo before leaving, and are now on a mission to Britain. In their midst are three of the apostles, Orson Hyde, P. P. Pratt, and John Taylor.

On Saturday, at ten, O. Hyde was approved as president for the entire conference, and with his usual warmth and eloquence he began by setting down the important matters of the conference, and showing the importance of the wonderful work in hand, and rejoicing greatly at his return to the vineyard he had been instrumental in beginning to plant. When he, and two or three of his brethren, had come here from America, about six years ago, no one here had heard a word of this gospel; but now, to his surprise, he saw himself surrounded by loving Saints in their thousands, who know now that their testimony was true in the beginning—namely, that God had sent them there to preach his eternal gospel. This faithful brother thanked God, that he had been able to come once again into our midst, and wished God to bless each of us according to his need, and keep us faithful to the end.

He was followed by P. P. Pratt, who said that the beautiful scene before him took his mind back to the establishment of the church here—the opposition he had had here: the smiling faces reminded him of remarkable scenes he had seen in this country, in America, and on his journey to the western desert; and when he found himself in their midst, despite everything, his joy was greater than his feelings permitted him to express, but he testified soberly and solemnly to the truth of this great work, and urged all to renew themselves more and more to carry it on. He felt a greater desire to sit down, to gaze into the dear faces of his old brethren, than to address them now, and he finished by blessing everyone of every degree and station, from her gracious Majesty on her throne to the lowest of the human race. His heart was full of blessings, and nothing but blessings. Then he called on D. Jones to address the meeting, saying it would be a pleasure for him to hear once again the beloved voice that sounded in his ears years ago. He enlarged upon his faithfulness, and the affection he had for him a long time ago, when he fought alongside him in America.

Then D. Jones stood up, and described the scene and the present company as unexpected to him at the time, and almost too good to be true. He told of the first time he met Mr. Pratt, when he had the honor of conveying him together with his family, and nearly three hundred Saints who had come with him from England, up the Mississippi river, from St. Louis to Nauvoo, in his steamboat. He remembered well enough the teaching he had heard at the time; that that was the time his eyes were opened to see the disadvantageous situation of his brothers and sisters in Wales, and the first spark of zeal and desire was kindled in his bosom to visit his country, to offer them the divine light that had shone so brightly on his own eyes, and that he was never satisfied while he stayed there, but his zeal grew greater and greater, and his desire and his love for his country, until it became a passionate and inextinguishable flame. He was very grateful for the high honor of having such a mission, and offering this gospel which brings blessings to all, and nothing but blessings to all who believe it. He regretted nothing more than that he had not come sooner. He knew that it was God's work he has in hand, and he was determined with God's strength to go on to benefit his fellow-countrymen, by giving them the light of the gospel until the chains of prejudice were shattered, and they were made free, yes, sons and daughters of God. He was happy to announce that the gospel was having gradual and constant success everywhere it was preached in Wales; that they had baptized over a hundred and fifty in the last three months; that their present number in Wales was about nine hundred, and that there were hosts of others besides who believed. He announced that missionaries were preaching in almost every county in Wales, that he himself had traveled round every county in Wales but one, preaching every night, in the largest towns, last summer; and that crowds came to listen, and most of them amiable too, apart from the occasional old sectarian Pharisee, or pastor who was afraid of losing the fleece. He said he himself had published twelve treatises, explaining the principles, defending them, &c., in the past year-and-a-half, including over a million 12-fold pages, and that they had almost all been distributed throughout the country. He said he had high hopes for the conversion of many of his brothers and sisters of the same blood—that throngs were still coming into the vineyard of the Lord of hosts, and that he is determined to go on, come what may, even though it should cost him his life.—Then the morning meeting was closed with a prayer.

At two in the afternoon, brothers John Taylor and P. P. Pratt fervently addressed the large congregation on the resurrection, its manner and its order, and the way to ensure a part in it.

In the evening, the meeting was taken up mainly with matters pertaining to the Joint Stock Company. The president and others greatly supported, on several counts, the advisability of postponing its activities for the present time; it was impossible for it, under present circumstances, to succeed in answering the beneficial purposes of its establishment. Much was said for and against the proposal; but at the end of the meeting, it was decided unanimously not to proceed with it at present.

On Sunday, meetings were held in the *Hall of Science*, because the other was too small to hold the congregation.

The morning meeting, and much of the afternoon, were spent in arranging the affairs of the various conferences throughout Britain, appointing presidents for them, and in instruction on how to carry on the work more successfully; and the president greatly urged all of these presidents to branch out right and left, to widen their borders, by preaching only those things that start some in Christ, and he hoped they would have more of the spirit of their offices than ever, until the impressions of their counsels in this Conference, like showers of timely rain on a bed of flowers, spread their fragrance throughout Britain like the herbs of paradise, for the glory of God.

In the evening, brother John Taylor addressed the crowd in his warm and eloquent manner. He proved that it is through many obstacles that one must enter into the kingdom of God. He gave a comprehensive account of the main persecutions suffered by the church in America since he had joined it, and especially in Nauvoo, the martyrdom of Joseph and Hyrum Smith in the prison, together with the subsequent exile of the Saints to the wilderness. He described their journey to the wilderness, full of difficulties, except that all the Saints were hopeful and determined, all united, and caring for, and helping each other, so that they did not feel, or have the time to think much about their own tribulations. They enjoyed excellent health, considering how many women and children were in their midst, who had never before been used to living and being in the woods, sleeping out in their tents at night, or being unable to have their food on time; but they had a comfort which the world knows not, to keep their minds above the raging waves of persecution and adversity. He noticed that the greater their distress, the greater their faith, their dedication, and their comfort. In the midst of it all they raised up their heads, knowing that the time of their deliverance was nigh. He had left his wife and children joyfully in the camp, in Council Bluffs, in Indian country, to come on this mission. He considered it a greater honor to have the office and the work he had, than anything the world could present to him; and he urged the Saints to be joyful and patient under all tribulations; saying that "after much waiting comes the blessing," and that "in due season we shall reap, if we faint not." And we should think he had such an influence on the congregation that everyone there was willing to suffer everything for Christ and the gospel, yes, even if it cost them everything they had, and their lives too, relying on Christ's promise—"Verily I say unto you, Every one that hath forsaken houses, or lands, or father, or mother, or any other thing, for my name's sake and for the gospel, shall receive an hundredfold in this life, and shall inherit everlasting life in the world to come." Mr. Taylor, like many of the Saints, could not only preach this doctrine, but also rejoice because he had given many examples of it, by renouncing all he owned, rather than the gospel. In four parts of America, there are houses and possessions that belonged to him, which were stolen from him without any sort of compensation for them ever. He said he considered his sacrifices still very small, considering to whom they were made. The Saints will remember that Mr. Taylor was with Mr. Smith in jail, when he and his brother were killed. He was hit by four bullets at the time, and yet all this does not dishearten him one bit, but rather encourages him to go on. The last time we had the honor of standing next to Mr. Taylor in front of a crowd was in Carthage jail, and we remember very well the subjects of our sermons, through the iron bars, to the mob that was seeking to take the life of J. and H. Smith. Yes, we continued to preach the conditions of peace to them there, until within a few hours of the time they were killed, and with God's strength we shall continue to preach the same message until our own last hour, leaving the consequences in the hands of our Master. Mr. Taylor was followed by the president, with an important counsel to the preachers about how to fulfill their task, and to the members about how to live to the glory of God, and the meeting ended with prayer and singing. Then the pleasant crowd left with every appearance of great satisfaction.

Monday was again spent mainly on the *business* of the Joint Stock Company, and various matters of the presidents of the conference branches.

And so ended this successful and beneficial conference, with the president giving his *farewell address* emotionally and very effectively, and praying to God for his blessing and his divine seal on our efforts, in order to build the kingdom of Emmanuel, and bring life and purity to light, until the world is filled with the light and knowledge of God, as the waters cover the sea—when there will be only one King reigning, and his name will be one, and everyone will worship him in joy and eternal glory.

THE CITY OF NAUVOO.

THE *American Sun* announces that the City of Nauvoo continues to be disturbed. It appears that the most recent residents, namely those who immigrated here from the other states, and bought the possessions of the exiled Saints, have decided to defend themselves and their possessions from the inhuman attacks of the host of villains who continue to destroy and threaten to kill in those parts. The general public takes pity on the present inhabitants of Nauvoo, but the Saints were not treated so. But it can be seen now who was to blame before, since these rioters continue the same in their evil behavior. We hope the residents will defend the city, until the remainder of the Saints who are there have time to escape to the desert. The newspapers brought over by the ship the *St. George*, inform us that the anti-Mormons are a thousand fully-armed men, on their way to Nauvoo, on the 26th of last month, and that there is likely to be a battle. It was easy for authors to publish "Mormon War," "Disturbance among the Mormons," and ascribe every blame and trouble in that country to the Mormons, as they call them, throughout the years, as though they were the cause of it all. But now, when the characters of the one faction and the other appear in their true colors, it is not known under what glorious name they will publish the battles, the disturbance, the killing, and the burning, which continue there, after nearly all the Mormons have gone hundreds of miles from there.

A CALL TO SINNERS.

OH, SINNERS, turn! repent in time!
With sinning do not dwell nor chime;
Forgiveness seek—God will impart
To humble soul and sorry heart.

The price full-paid upon the tree,
Was paid by Heaven's Anointed, see!
To clear transgressions small or dire,
To save you from impending fire.

If you obey, you'll win God's grace,
Eternal life by his Son's face:
His blessing's free, He's keen that all
Mankind should hearken to his call.

RHYDYBONT : PRINTED BY JOHN JONES.

PROPHET OF THE JUBILEE.

"THE KINGDOM HAS COME."

No. 6.] DECEMBER, 1846. [Vol. I.

THE BODY OR CHURCH OF CHRIST.

"THERE is one body, and one Spirit," says the scripture; and there belong to this body, as to the human body, various members, all set in it and joined together as the Spirit wills it. As there is need in the human body for all the members, so there is need in the body or church of Christ for all the different members which belong to it. The human body cannot do without the eyes; it needs those to lead and guide it. The ears are just as useful in their function: the feet, the arms, and all the members, are essential and useful in their place. The ear does not say to the eye, I have no need of you. The foot does not say that the arm is not necessary; nor does the arm say that the foot is not necessary. All compose and serve the same body. They all need to continue in their appropriate work; the eye to watch, the ears to hear, the arms to defend, and the feet to make their way. The eyes dare not leave the body when young, and say that they have fulfilled enough in its youth to satisfy it in its old age. The same can be said of the other members. They are all to be in unity, and to continue in unity.

The body of Christ is composed in this way. "And God hath set some in the church, first apostles, secondarily prophets, thirdly teachers, after that miracles, then gifts of healings, helps, governments, diversities of tongues." All these things are "for the perfecting of the saints, for the work of the ministry, for the edifying of the body of Christ;" and all these things are to serve in their various capacities while the need of the body remains—yes, "till we all come in the unity of faith, and of the knowledge of the Son of God, unto a perfect man, unto the measure of the stature of the fulness of Christ."

Dear reader, have you been baptized through the Spirit into this glorious body, and your thirst quenched by it? It is essential that you know. You have seen that the aims of the body of Christ are very clear. All the members are regulated in it, for it is God who has joined them together. Let no man say that some of the members can be dispensed with; the Lord arranged them, and therefore let man be silent. The will of God, reader, is for you to come into unity with this body, if you are not, and have the knowledge that you are in it. But, if you do belong to it, your privilege is great!

ELIAS.

THERE is scarcely any person who is mentioned in the scriptures, as well known as this one. After all the interpretation and talk of him, we too are often asked, Who is that Elias! As we have not been satisfied with any answer we have seen yet, we shall venture to offer the following as an answer to the question; and if we can only show clearly the difference that exists between the person and the office or the character that belongs to him, that will provide a key to the mystery of understanding that strange office the Elias was to sustain, according to the prophecy of Malachi, in chap. iv, 5, 6:—"Behold I will send you Elijah the prophet, before the great and dreadful day of the Lord: and he shall turn the heart of the fathers to the children, and the heart of the children to their fathers, lest I come and smite the earth with a curse."

The great point at issue is, Is John the Baptist meant by this Elias? We admit that there is some difficulty in understanding the scriptures that refer to these persons, that they seem to be contradictory, and that they are, like some other places, used by atheists as sweet morsels to disprove the divinity of the prophecies, when, in fact, the facts are completely the opposite, as we shall endeavor to explain. The angel Gabriel said to Zacharias, Luke i, 13-17:—"Fear not Zacharias; for thy prayer is heard; and thy wife shall bear thee a son; and thou shalt call his name John, and thou shalt have joy and gladness; and many shall rejoice at his birth, for he shall be great in the sight of the Lord, and shall drink neither wine nor strong drink; and he shall be filled with the Holy Ghost, even from his mother's womb. And many of the children of Israel shall he turn to the Lord their God. And he shall go before him in the *spirit* and *power* of Elias, to turn the hearts of the fathers to the children, and the disobedient to the wisdom of the just; to make ready a people prepared for the Lord."

It was thought that this angel showed, beyond any doubt, that it is to this John that Malachi refers above. But, says the arguer, If so, why does John deny that so fearlessly to the priests and the Levites, in John i, 21?—"And they asked him, what then? Art thou Elias? and he [John] answered, *No.*" Which of the two do I believe? I reply that I believe both completely, and I believe Jesus Christ too, when he says in Matt. xi, 13,14,—"For all the prophets and the law prophesied until John. *And if ye will receive it,* this [John] is Elias, which was for to come." Well, says the reader, you are making the subject more complex now than before, through some strange co-mixture of prophecies and assertions at complete variance with each other; and, to judge by the number of witnesses, John must be lying about the truthfulness of Gabriel and the Son of God, for they say yes, and he denies it, and says "*No.*" What will you do? Explain his meaning differently from what he says? No, never. Will you admit that John is lying, or blame the translation? Oh no, that is not necessary either; and if we cannot reconcile the scriptures without that, we shall freely admit our ignorance, and say as Paul once did—"Let God be true and every man a liar." We do not here admit the infallibility of lawyers either. And before we evade this dilemma, we shall venture an assertion about it, however anomalous it may appear, and we give the freedom and the encouragement to anyone who wishes to improve it; i.e., *That John was the Elias.* We say also, *That John was not the Elias*! Bear with us, reader, for by making counter-claims like this, we are only repeating the previous scriptures. And now to the task of proving this to be reasonable, scriptural, and, of course, divine truths.

The scriptures speak of *the Elias*, that is the *spirit*, *power*, or *office* of the Elias, frequently, rather than of a person by this name. They refer to the success of that great work to which the first person by that name received the keys, namely *restoration*, which Christ proves in Mark ix, 12, when he says—"Elias verily cometh and *restoreth* all things," &c. So John the Baptist must have been the Elias Christ refers to in what follows, ver. 13, "But I say unto you that *Elias is indeed come*, and they have done unto him whatsoever they listed, as it is written of him."

But although one can see more clearly the distinction made between the various persons, and the connection seen between the same offices in the complete and wondrous *restoration* which the wise God planned in the early council, to be fulfilled by degrees, from age to age, until it is completed, stand back to take a look at the magnificent and skillful picture that was planned before it was needed, to bring forth the restoration of all things, yes, before the deterioration of one thing. When this earth was *chaos*, formless and empty, covered with water, and the elements not regulated in their proportionate correspondence, to work together for the glory of its Architect, and for the benefit and enjoyment of its descendants; and before God said "Let there be light;" yes, before the morning stars sang, or the sons of God leapt for joy, the piteous fate, and complete corruption of all the elements *which* made up this little football, and all its inhabitants, were foreseen. And not only was all this foreseen, but a perfect plan was arranged to bring not only men, but everything that was corrupted, back to perfection. Yes, the plan was arranged, or the machinery if you wish, that is the manner in which all this would be done, in that marvellous council which the Gods held on the morning of the day they began the work of setting their garden in order, and creating servants to keep it so. The *main spring* of this machine, or the self-motivating axis on which turned all of its wheels is *that Lamb slain from the foundation of the world*. The plan of Jehovah was as perfect, and the outlines and axes of the picture appeared to them as clearly as they do now; and the interstices are being filled up, from age to age, with the skill of a master craftsman; and he will go on until this world and its fulness is a *facsimile* of the picture drawn of it that strange morning. Nothing in it can be different from the pattern, without the patternmaker being disappointed. The restoration cannot be an improvement on the pattern, without proving the imperfection of the pattern, and consequently, without proving the imperfection of him who made it. But it will soon be seen that everything is going on according to the rule, and that nothing is an accident to the omniscient God. He sets a bridle in the mouth of the usurper, and sets a limit to the chain of the prince of this world. The same finger guides this globe in its orbits, and overrules the scepters of its emperors, as started it on its icy poles in the beginning; yes, one day in the future the only imperial scepter will be seen in the hand where it belongs; and it will turn into a rod of iron to one part, and a golden scepter to the other part, when it is held out above our world, and comes to possess the world, to bind the devilish traitor, to restore the earth and its fulness, and to make the kingdoms of the world the property of our Lord and his Christ.

This complete *restoration* of the earth and its fulness will be brought about through the power of God, through the agency of that divine staff given by God to all his servants, namely the priesthood which is according to the strength of everlasting life, which binds in heaven that which is done by its possessors on earth. And since the days of the first transgressors, through the ages, those men who have been clothed with the authority of the priesthood, and with the spirit of prophecy, to the extent that the curtain was torn, and the doors of the eternal world opened before their eyes, have been rejoicing in the hope for, and showing in their turn this strange and glorious restoration. The pious muse struck sweet songs of praise to this day. This was the favorite subject of the prophets. The pencil of the portaitist hastened to capture it, the tongue of the learned took pleasure in its praise, and the writer's pen kept to this godly loadstone almost without wavering. The Spirit of God did not fill the souls of the prophets and the godly saints with more joy when dealing with hardly any subject than when he showed them the glorious restoration,—when the mountains should drop down sweet wine, and the wilderness should blossom as the rose; when the lion cub and the lamb should lie down together; when there should be nothing to do damage or harm in all the mountain of his holiness, that is the earth; when the earth should be filled with the knowledge of the Lord, as the waters cover the sea; when Zion should be established in glory, and all nations flock to her standard; when the temple of God should be reared, and rivers of the waters of life flow from it; when the inhabitants of Zion should dwell in peace; when none should say, I am sick, but each should sit under his own fig tree, and Jerusalem be the throne of the Lord forever.

In the hope of fulfilling this restoration, the prophets and saints of God agreed and endeavored, through their faith and their acts, to fulfill the office and task of Elias, namely *restoring*. Enoch did what he could in his day to restore the earth. He walked with God for three hundred years. He had great faith. He established an excellent church, and taught his people the principles of righteousness; but nevertheless, the earth was too corrupt, unbelieving, and disobedient, for him to be able to restore it; therefore, God took him and his church to himself; hence the saying, "Zion is fled." Once the salt was removed, there was not enough goodness left to save the earth; but its face was overthrown by God with the flood.

Moses also strove greatly to accomplish some part of this revolution. He drew nigh unto God by faith, and obtained great promises from God on behalf of his people, such as—"Ye shall be a peculiar treasure unto me above all people: for all the earth is mine: And ye shall be unto me a kingdom of priests, and an holy nation," &c. Through this he shows that they could be a peculiar treasure, or instruments, as a nation, in establishing the government of peace in general, and that knowledge of God, and the principles of peace, would flow through these channels from the source, bringing about restoration; but all this, like every other promise, depended on their obeying the conditions, namely, "If they keep my laws." Instead of that, they broke his laws, and continued as a troubled and obstinate nation; then he took the greatest honor, the most powerful scepter, for bringing this about, namely the *Melchizedek priesthood*, away from them; and instead of being a kingdom of priests together as a nation, they had only one high priest who could go into the holy of holies into the presence of God, and that only once a year, instead of the whole nation being able to withstand the presence of the one who is a searing fire, and eternal flames to the imperfect. Then, because of their imperfection, they could not bear such blazing glory, and that because of disobeying the law which was given in order to perfect them. And so they were justly deprived of the promised blessing, namely that of being a kingdom of priests. Thus Moses failed to achieve his aim in the restoration, and God took him away too, to wait until someone else accomplished what he had failed to do, and then he too would have his part according to what he did. That perverse nation was placed under a schoolmaster to bring them to Christ.

That Elijah of whom John was a shadow, was a great and wonderful prophet. The Spirit of Heaven rested upon him in a most marvellous manner. But what did he bring about, poor thing? What could he do with such a perverse and rebellious nation? God did not send his servants to force men to keep his laws, but to persuade them; and if they did not obey willingly out of principle, they left them in the hand of a just God, warning them that they were clean of everyone's blood. Thus godly Elijah, having failed to bring it about, because of the disobedience of the age to his message, we hear him wailing from the depths of his hiding-place in the rock—"They have killed thy prophets, and digged down thine altars; and I am left alone and they seek my life." He knew no different, but he was quite unlikely to accomplish that complete restoration at that time, was he not? God knew that well enough. But that attempt would be testimony against them; and he sent the chariot of Israel and his riders to fetch the godly old prophet from their midst, because they did not know his worth, and kept him until the time he would be sent with a loan of some of his keys to another to fill his circle as he did, and to bear witness to incriminate some future generation.

John the Baptist also came in his day as an *Elias*, or a *restorer*. The angel Gabriel said he would come in the "spirit and power of Elias;" and if the people had submitted to his teaching, and to what Jesus commanded them, the prohecies about him would have been fulfilled then, and their children would have been gathered together as the hen gathers her chicks under her wing; but, says the Savior, you were not willing; thus did he see their refusal of the Elias, or this restorer, namely John, too. "If ye will receive it, this is the Elias which was for to come," says Christ. Yes, *if* they would receive it; but at the same time he clearly tells them that they would not receive it, and that he would not fill this character, or succeed in fulfilling the office of Elias, by restoring them. He compares this generation to children sitting in the marketplace—neither his speech and teaching nor those of John were to their taste, and they did not wish them as teachers. "John came neither eating nor drinking, and they say, He hath a devil. The Son of man came eating and drinking, and they say, Behold a man gluttonous, and a wine bibber, a friend of publicans and sinners." Thus they rejected John the Baptist completely, "and did with him what they listed," namely cutting off his head. And although he was indeed the Elias, yet, because of their rejection of him, he could not be so to them; and this is why, when they asked him, "Art thou the Elias?" he answered, "I am not." But if their conduct towards him had been as it should have been, they would have received a completely different reply to their question. This is the mystery which appears contradictory, namely that he was referring to the fact of his office, and they to the man. John knew they were forfeiting their right to the restoration, and refusing to become "a kingdom of priests, and a nation or peculiar treasure unto the Lord," this time again as before, by scorning his message, together with him who sent him, and the kingdom of God was taken away from them, as Jesus Christ foretold.

We do not hereby attach blame to the old prophets, as they did the best they could; even so they failed to bring about this complete restoration, because of the unbelief and the rebelliousness of their contemporaries, although each had made some contribution towards bringing it about in its own time. And as the time appointed by Jehovah had not come, they could not be made perfect without us also, or us without them as well. And as has been noted previously, the eternal priesthood, in heaven and on earth, must work together to achieve this restoration. And insofar as the Latter-day Saints have had the great honor of receiving the fulness of the gospel at the "dispensation of the fulness of times" which Paul talks about, when "he might gather together in one all things in Christ, both which are in heaven, and which are on earth; even in him." Inasmuch as they have been presented with all the previous provisions of the *restorers* of former times, with the faith and deeds of those and these latter servants, as well as the keys to this restored dispensation, we can say to this nation as they said to their contemporaries, "If they wish to receive them, and submit to their message, that the Latter-day Saints are the Elias which was to come before the coming of the Lord's great and dreadful day." Yes, they, if the teaching they preach is obeyed, are the Elias of this age, and they will "turn the heart of the fathers to the children, and the heart of the children to the fathers." If they do not receive them, then they cannot be an Elias or a restorer for them; but the Lord will come, and will strike the whole earth with judgment, because they refused to be restored. But although different from the previous dispensations in this, yet, if only the Saints are faithful, and make proper use of their valuable talents, by warning their contemporaries, they will be found innocent of the blood of all; they shall enjoy their portion and their inheritance which they won among all the restorers of the past, when they will be rewarded according to the deeds they performed in the flesh; they shall inherit the resting-place which still remains for God's people, to be restored to them; for we too are seeking, as Paul once did, an eternal city, whose architect and builder is God. Blessed are those who seek a better country than this, where they can all unite in singing the song of Moses, and the song of the Lamb, when everyone therein will be an Elias, filled with the spirit and power of the God of Elijah. The times of the restoration of all things are a fine time, are they not? Who will not say, Hail to it, let it hasten to its completion!

DEFENSE OF THE SAINTS *VERSUS* THE ACCUSATIONS OF THOMAS JONES, MERTHYR, AND OTHERS.

Dear Reader,—The following defense was written with the expectation that it would be allowed to appear in the *Baptist*. We took it to the office in Cardiff for that purpose and offered it to that same Editor who was sufficiently liberal to publish the terrible false accusations and every other scornful thing about us as a denomination, that is, he who boasts that his *Baptist* is a publication free to all to defend their character. We implored earnestly and humbly for the opportunity to clear ourselves from the villainous filth with which we were plastered without provocation; but, as usual, the answer we received from him was a *shameless refusal!* Yes, poor thing, he was terrified; he turned blue, red, black and pale; he fumed and raged without a single cause except the malicious agitations of a guilty conscience until his knees and his whole body trembled worse than those of Belshazzar of long ago. And in the face of all earnestness, logic and justice—it was no use no matter how much he gnashed his teeth and foamed at the mouth, and made additional, baseless accusations and called us bad names, yes, even to our face! He accused the Saints of having said that the William Hughes who broke his leg did not receive assistance from the parish of Merthyr, and that through that they had lost their credibility; and, as a result, they could not defend themselves in the *Baptist*. We said that even the most godly men who ever lived on the earth could be proved liars according to that reasoning, that is, to believe the false accusations of professed enemies who refused to listen to the other side. We challenged him to prove those shameful accusations against us as a denomination, or even to prove that as much as one Saint has ever said such a thing as that. Oh, the fact that one Edward Lewis from Blackwood had written that to the *Baptist* was sufficient proof to him, he said. We said that that man had not proven his credibility sufficient for us to believe him. And if that man can prove that W. Hughes did not receive assistance from the parish of Merthyr, let him proclaim their names to the world as witnesses of that; then we shall call such to give an accounting, for we have questioned many and have failed to find one who said that. And what if one, two or three were to say this in their ignorance? Would this prove nearly a thousand people to be liars? Do we, by proving your persecuting correspondent a liar so clearly, prove through this that all Welsh Baptists are liars? We do, according to your own reasoning!

We said that the testimony of Wm. Hughes about that matter has been written, and that his credibility has been attested by many eyewitnesses, that he himself sent his testimony to the *Baptist* with receipt acknowledged, and it has been refused publication until this very day!—that his testimony was published to the world at that time, a testimony in which Wm. Hughes himself claimed to have received assistance from the parish of Merthyr, all of which proves clearly that the Saints did not ever say that he did not receive assistance from the parish.

The treachery and guile of this crooked invention can be seen clearly. The aim of the enemies of the truth in forming that accusation is to try to prove the Saints liars in one thing, so that it will not be believed that Wm. Hughes even broke his leg or was healed! It is a wonder how they succeed in their slanderous invention. Notice their proof and their constructed *sophistry*! Some Edward Lewis says [some one, two, or three, I suppose, did not see fit to say, but] that the Saints in Blackwood said that Wm. Hughes did not receive assistance from the parish of Merthyr, and that lying "Quick in Water" got the *relieving officer* to say that Hughes had received assistance. And here is proof, says the editor of the *Baptist*, that the man did not break his leg and that he was not healed! What proof is that? How does that *relieving officer* know whether the man broke his leg? Which one was it—he or "Quick in Water" who wrote that? The two are of the same speech, taste and purpose. The mad tricksters ought to be ashamed of such malicious deceptive reasoning! But this is the best they can come up with against the Saints; and they prefer this to admitting the truth and acknowledging the power of God in this thing. If one of the Saints said that he had not received anything from the parish, how in the name of reason would this prove the entire denomination of people liars? And why would this prejudiced editor refuse them space to defend their mistake? I answer that it is because he foresaw himself in his proper color through that, that is, as a cruel persecutor and a constant slanderer. He meant to keep his readers under his paws, and keep the Saints in the dirt which he daubed on them. What else could he do? What else could we ourselves do? We offered him plenty of proofs of their innocence, and in face of it all he pranced around like a wild man, shouting, "Poo! poo! poo!—deceit, all deceit." He did not wish to hear anything from us, nor to look at our writing. "*I shall have nothing to do with you*," said he; and away he went to his hole in a bad temper, *slamming* the door after him! Yes, Welshmen, this is the behavior of the editor of this religious *Baptist*, in spite of all his boasting of "freedom." This is very one-sided freedom—yes, freedom for him to make false accusations as he wishes, and freedom for us to suffer it all, defenseless, as far as he was concerned. We are thankful for the freedom of the press and the truth to defend us, and we shall make the proper use of them also, in spite of him and his slanderous party. We are sorry that we have nothing to do with him; that is his fault. But so much like this has been done by him—that it is too late for him now to shout, "I shall have nothing to do with you" after slandering us and publishing every kind of calumny about us for years. As soon as we begin to cleanse ourselves he throws the basin down and full of envy shouts, "I shall have nothing to do with you." And as soon as some of his sycophants have fashioned some story sufficiently bad and lying to suit his taste, out it comes in the *Baptist* like a shooting star, and perhaps the name of some respected person is attached to it, so that it will be more easily believed by the people; and immediately upon our beginning to defend ourselves, he escapes like the fox to his hole, his posterior first, gnashing his teeth from there, shouting, "I shall have nothing to do with you!" What is that except to say he will continue with our head under his armpit as long as he can, and that he will invite every Rev. Mr. Davies from Dowlais, Rev. Mr. Tobit by the Bridge, Rev. T. ab Ieuan, Rev. D. Williams from Abercanaid, Thomas Jones from Merthyr, lying Quick in Water, illogical Meiria*dog*, and every other barking *mad dog* and *coward* throughout the principality, to hit us on the forehead and to help himself to his rush arrows every opportunity that he gets. It is loathsome to us to have to soil our hands to treat such a stinking fox, nor would we bother except that his readers ought to get to see him by his tail in front of their faces, so that they can see what kind he is, and understand how to believe him and his slanderous *Baptist* from now on. Let them read the following to start with, and they will have even more odors from his lair so that everyone can form his own opinion of the color and shape of his heart.

WILLIAM PHILLIPS,
WILLIAM HENSHAW,
THOMAS PUGH.

[*Copy of the letter to the Editor of the* BAPTIST.]

MR. EDITOR,—We owe it to you, to the public, to our own characters, and especially to the religion which we rely on for eternal life, to defend ourselves against the shameful false accusations which are brought against us by a man by the name of Thomas Jones, Merthyr, and which appear in the October issue of the *Baptist*.

1. He accuses us of using the names of some "Ahiram and Joseph Smith upon blessing," which is totally baseless, in fact.

2. "They can own their places in Nauvoo," &c. This is not so either; but that which we believe with respect to the "emigration to America," is that which is in the holy scriptures; and the above man knows that no ownership was promised to us, nor to him, in Nauvoo, nor in any other *specified place* on the continent.

3. "We claim (says he) to have seen Jesus Christ in *red whiskers*," &c. This accusation is not true in any way, shape, or form, in fact, as far as the Saints have anything to do with it. What he could be after by asserting such a thing, we do not know, and we are not answering for him.

4. With respect to the frightful invention which he accuses us of, that is, our pretending to receive revelation, accusing the first president of misconduct with another man's wife, so that the other man could have his office, &c. His own lips condemn him, as follows—"We judged that the latter would do better," says he. And in the next breath he says, "The latter was considered the first president" already! Needless to elaborate, because this lie is sufficiently obvious. But we state soberly that this accusation, yes, every word of it, has been proved entirely false in a detailed inquiry which was held here on the matter in front of hundreds, to which they will testify also. It was proved that such a presumptuous and ungodly invention never existed except in his own jealous heart. He asserts that *others* agreed with him in this. Never before did he say that there was but *one*; and in spite of getting every exhortation from us to prove this in the same thorough inquiry which was held about it, he failed to prove that even one of us knew anything about such an atrocious calumny. And strange, if the accusation were true, that Thomas Jones uttered not a word about such a thing for many months after the time he says it took place!

Such an invention was not necessary, nor any other invention to meet the purpose which he mentions, because the coming of the latter president to this country had no effect in any way on the one who was residing here before. And—"*No object in view, no design.*" If this man were to tell the truth, he knows full well that he did not see an accusation received against any of us except by eyewitnesses. As for his work of asserting that he heard one of us claiming to have received revelations, which decency does not allow him to put before the public—may you, Sir, or anyone else, not believe it. And we suppose that if you were to know this man, as he is known here in his home, that not one of his claims would be allowed to appear in your columns, that is, if you have any respect for your publication. We do not wish to blacken the character of this man in any way, but we would very much like to leave it in the hand of a just God. To remain silent about them in the face of such accusations would be to suffer like a murderer or a thief. But it is he who has obliged us to come out like this, to show him in his proper color, so that you and your readers can understand the character of the only witness who stands up against the testimony of hundreds of Welshmen, to degrade them beneath humanity and all which is worth living for (if his assertions were true). But in fact, Sir, his accusations against us are no different from the poisonous effects of his own vindictive heart, accusations which were made *after he was excommunicated from our church* and after he was proven guilty of many sins more atrocious than we wish to name. He tried to come back several times; yes, even after his first letter appeared in the *Baptist*, he said that he would be glad to come back to our church. There are hundreds who testify that they heard him say, after being cut off, that "no one else has the true religion except our church." Despite that, his immoral and unrepentant behavior continued as such, so that when he stood up before our church to request his place in our midst, not so much as one of nearly three hundred members raised his hand in his favor! He asserted at that time that he had not made the above accusations to the Baptists, when we knew that he had already done so. When he saw that he would not be accepted, he had such an emotional outburst that he made public threats, saying that he wished revenge against us somehow, and that he would publish everything he could against us in the *Baptist*, &c., which proved to everyone that he was not truly repentant for his previous sins; and as a result, our church rules did not allow him, or anyone else like him, membership in our midst. This man became so unruly that the officers were obliged to turn him out of one meeting before the end. After being refused by us, he offered himself to the Baptists again; but we heard that they themselves refused him in more than one church, and that their members threatened to leave rather than associate with such a man. And last of all, he was sanctified with the holy water of the Papists. He baptized his children with them, and he claims now that only they have the true religion! Why does your correspondent consider the contradictions of a professed and excommunicated enemy like this as being worthy of space in a religious publication, rather than the more accurate testimony of hundreds of neighbors, the direct opposite of him? He knew perfectly well that this vindictive witness was considered by his brethren as being too bad to be allowed to come into their midst; and yet, he considered him sufficiently righteous to condemn the denomination of other men. Would not such a witness be sufficient against his denomination or against some other church besides the Saints, perhaps? Most certainly not, any more than the testimony of Judas Iscariot was sufficient against the denomination to which he belonged. What reasonable man would expect to hear much truth from an excommunicated man, sufficiently bad to admit that he had battled voluntarily for over three years against God and conscience?

If the assertions of this man or any like him were true about our religion, would over half a million reasonable people of this enlightened age cling to it under every scorn and persecution, the greater part of them having been with other denominations previously? If deception were what we have, do you seriously suppose that these deceivers would persecute us so severely? Once again we testify, in truth, that the great profession which this man makes about his *conscientiousness* to "expose deceit," &c., is nothing more than shameless hypocrisy, to get others to believe him; and his only purpose is revenge against those who can no longer put up with his evils. From the first time he came to us we had a lot of trouble trying to get him to walk in the paths of righteousness; but at last we had to cut him off, and here he has shown who he is, and that "an accuser of brothers" has turned into "an angel of light." True is the maxim that says: "A bad man with a bad treasure in his heart will bring forth bad things."

Since your publication is sufficiently free for these shameful accusations, we are very confident that it will be sufficiently free to likewise receive this letter in our defense. We could give to you many additional names of reputable men, but we hope these which follow will suffice for now in the face of ONE witness:—Samuel Morris, John Phillips, David John, William Morgan, Daniel Williams, David Rees, Thomas Rees, Thomas Smith, Morgan Morgans, Howell Williams, David Jones, Jenkin Hughes, Joseph Davies, Edward Edwards, William Hughes, Hugh Jones, Jenkyn Thomas, John Griffiths, Timothy Wosley.

In addition to that which has been said, here is the testimony of William Henshaw, himself:—"Since I myself am that first president to whom Thomas Jones refers, I must state that what he says is entirely untrue. Never did Capt. D. Jones seek my office. His office has no effect whatsoever on my duties; and furthermore, there was not one of the Saints guilty of inventing the terrible calumny that Thomas Jones mentions, except he himself. Even to think of such presumption fills us with fear and terror."

Yours, &c., WILLIAM PHILLIPS,
WILLIAM HENSHAW,
THOMAS PUGH.

The reader will see further that the testimony of this excommunicated Thomas Jones is not worthy of his trust, because he states too much to be true and contradicts himself. In the previous issue of the *Baptist*, this man calls the Saints deceivers, &c. He claims that the spiritual gifts that they profess are fake, and gives an example of speaking in strange tongues, and the interpretation, &c., "to prove the deceit of the Saints." And after all, does he not prove our truthfulness irrefutably to every reasonable man? Certainly; for this our professed enemy admits that we speak in tongues, interpret, &c., and as a result, that we imitate the apostolic church in our profession at least. They said, "Desire spiritual gifts;" here is the admission that we do so. "Covet to prophesy, and forbid not to speak with tongues," says Paul; Thomas Jones admits that we do that. Furthermore—"Let him that speaketh in an unknown tongue pray that he may interpret," was the apostolic commandment; and behold our chief enemy testifying that the Saints do so. Is this perhaps not a sufficiently unbiased witness for even the Editor of the *Baptist* to believe? We preach to the world, and profess ourselves that we enjoy these gifts of the spirit in our churches. The world doubts, our enemies deny; but at last here is a strong enough witness for them, we would suppose, that we believe that we enjoy the gifts; and who knows better than those who profess the heavenly gifts by the hundreds? Had Thomas Jones been so clever as to deny that we claim to enjoy the gifts in the church, then, as far as his word can be believed, he would have succeeded in his ungodly purpose. But it is too late for that now, for he has already admitted that we practice them. It is true that Thomas Jones asserts that the gifts are fake, but it is also as true that he does not offer any kind of proof of that; no indeed, in any way, except his own word alone: and what is his assertion in the face of hundreds who know better? Can anyone reasonable believe that hundreds of those who were gifted preachers, faithful deacons, and respected members with the various other sects, would continue to pretend to have spiritual gifts for years, in unity and love, without getting one bit of benefit, pay or profit by so doing? Oh no, such a thing is impossible; and anyone who asserts this, asserts in the same breath that the practice of the same gifts in the same kind of causes by the saints of the early days was fake. Professed deism is the one denial as well as the other.

A GLANCE AT THAT DAVID WILLIAMS FROM ABERCANAID, WHO HAS PUT HIS FINGER SO DEEP IN THIS SALTY POTTAGE.

Here is that man who published the fruit of his mixed-up brain and his dirty slander against the Saints in a small treatise lately. And here is the man who was weighed so fairly in his own scales and found wanting with respect to logic, scripture and truth; and he was proven a libelous deist through his little booklet. And after that, instead of proceeding in a fair battle through the press after beginning, he got revenge in every way he could from behind the bush. We do not claim that it was he who persuaded one of his members to turn all the Saints from their work and from their homes, on the assertion that only because of their religion was that done. But this we shall say, If he was not the instigator of this shameless persecution and incomparable cruelty, this David Williams did not prevent one of his flock from doing it. Does he not profess to be a pastor over a flock of gentle Jesus? But this is more like the madness of a wolf. The Bible tells us that "by their fruits ye shall know them." Also, he who proclaims God freely to anyone who does such a thing is an associate in his evil doings. It is said also, "Do not seek vengeance;" but revenge is sweet to this one. And after all that, he is heard in the pubs on Saturday nights scolding the Saints, among drunks, swearers and profaners. We are reminded of the saying "birds of a feather flock together." We heard of some persecuting preacher who failed to keep his feet under him, and where do you suppose he found himself, rather, where he was found by others, upon returning from preaching on Sunday night, but in a duck pond! We shall not give the identity of that unfortunate wretch. But we do know that David Williams, from Abercanaid, is the correspondent who fashioned, who inquired, who wrote, and who sent the answers of that Thomas Jones to the *Baptist*, and who wished for its readers to believe his individual testimony against all the Saints and their religion. But hear the opinion of David Williams himself about the truthfulness and character of that Thomas Jones. There are witnesses who happened to hear him say that that witness was a bad and lying man and that his word was worth nothing in his sight, and that all his members refused to accept Thomas Jones as a member of their church; and yet, he expects the country to believe his testimony against the Saints. Readers of the *Baptist*, what do you think of this? Let it be between you and him. Next, we shall show the false perplexity which these two *partners* have woven and how they hang themselves with the same rope. In the preface to his catechism in the October issue of the *Baptist*, David Williams says to the editor: "The conversation [with T. Jones] did not end with that [namely that which had come out in an earlier issue], rather we continued on." Did they "continue on" with the account that is in the October issue?

What else could it refer to? And if so, why does the same D. Williams ask T. Jones in that conversation: "Are you staying with the same decision at the present time [notice, with what tense?] as you were when we were conversing about this matter before?" What! Did he not say the minute before that the conversation had not ended at that time? Does he not say that he has four religious witnesses, that the whole conversation, i.e., that which was in the previous issue, and the one being considered, had taken place on the same "work afternoon" in the same Chapel of the Baptists? Yes, that is what David Williams says. But let it be noticed how Thomas Jones affirms the complete opposite of that! He says that it was some other time that this last conversation took place, and that he continued in the same brave decision, namely to malign the children of God, that he had stated the previous time. Which of the two is to be believed? It is impossible to believe both of them. No reasonable person can believe either of them, say I. It is better for him to have so few witnesses like this, is it not, because they turn out to be witnesses against him. Who would be so foolish as to expect to hear the truth from such genial friends as these? The lie is a lame man. Once again, as for this David Williams, he says that he did not think the Saints were worth any further notice, until that "Meiriadog" asked Thomas Jones, by way of the *Baptist*, if he had admitted to Robert Evans that what he had written about the Saints was lies and if he was repentant. And then, who do we see jump into the gap, because he could not get Thomas Jones to deny this now, but David Williams, like a tiger seeing his chance to get his prey in his claws; and the way that he arranged the previous answers of Thomas Jones to do the trick now, and to prove Robert Evans a liar, and to keep the first impressions in the mind of the country, is to change his first question to make it appear that he had asked it after Meiriadog had come to the field, and so the answer would seem to answer Meiriadog also. That's a bit of clumsy work, is it not? We have already proved that he hanged himself in his own net by admitting in his preface that the later answers were given before T. Jones reneged. It is obvious that his preface was intended to be *private* to his dear *partner*, namely the editor, and that he, either in his haste or by some other unfortunate mix-up, allowed it to slip out.

It is a pity, for the benefit of their cause that the two traitors did not understand each other better. Let the Goliath of the rail workers take care next time to send his poisonous *secrets* separately, for shame. But how could his correspondence be the answer of Thomas Jones to Meiriadog, except that he be a prophet, and answer questions before they are asked? But in order to see more of the shameful *business* which this preacher carried on with his salaried Judas, as *sly*, so they supposed, as sheep-killing dogs, read the following, and the *new member* of this sanhedrin, namely Meiriadog, will be pulled through the mill again on his own, and he will see that he has begun a worse *job* than that treachery of stealing the body of Christ from the tomb, and that he is in worse company than those liars.

ROBERT EVANS VERSUS MEIRIADOG.

"We testify to having heard Thomas Jones say to Robert Evans these statements which Meiriadog sent to the *Baptist*, and we heard Thomas Jones say a lot more at the time, and for the same purpose. Robert Evans asked Thomas Jones three times over, in the presence of over twenty men, of the world, for the most part, these questions and others, and he received these answers. Thomas Jones admitted that those accusations that were published in the *Baptist* against the Saints are untrue. Question by Robert Evans—'Do you, Thomas Jones, admit in the presence of this crowd that you are repentant for causing those things to go to the *Baptist*?' Answer from Thomas Jones—'I am repentant, and I did not think that they would appear there.' Question by Robert Evans—'Do you give me permission to use your name to retract them?' Answer by Thomas Jones—'I do, and say that I state that they are untrue.' We saw Robert Evans write some of Thomas Jones's answers in his journal on the spot in the presence of us all; and so we know to be true that which Robert Evans said to Meiriadog about this matter."

HOWEL PHILIPS, JOHN ROBERTS,
EDWARD OWENS, HOPKIN MATHEWS,
BENJAMIN JONES DANIEL WILLIAMS,
THOMAS JOHN, JENKYN THOMAS.

REVIEW.

SUBSTANCE OF A SERMON ON THE MIRACLES, *in order to enlighten Everyman, and show the Deceit of the Creatures who call themselves "Latter-day Saints."* By W. R. DAVIES, Dowlais.

[CONTINUED FROM PAGE 131.]

MR. DAVIES says again—"To claim the continuation of miracles deposes faith, since it is the will of God that we live by faith." When shall the idiocy of this man cease? not before the end of his essay, at least. The cart is before the horse again, for he gives the cause to kill the effect. "If one needs miracles, one does not need faith," says he. But the Bible teaches us, yes, the Son of God teaches everyone, that if they want miracles, they must have faith: "If you had faith as great as a grain of mustard seed, you would tell this mountain, Remove hence." "If you believe, it is possible," said he, "everything is possible to him who believes." Enough has been shown to prove that it was not possible for them to receive one blessing except according to their faith. And does not Paul, yes, in the chapter which Mr. Davies takes as a text, urge the saints—"But seek the best gifts." Oh, no, says Davisism, do nothing of the sort, lest you depose faith! But let us hear Paul, despite that, sticking to his subject, opposing Davies to his face—"Seek spiritual gifts, but rather that you might prophesy." Oh, no, says Mr. Davies, I bid you not to seek any of the spiritual gifts for there is scarcely anyone who professes them but Satanists; and it is the will of God for you to live by faith, that is, the cause; but deny its effects lest you imitate apostleship. However, says another witness, do you not know, Mr. D., "that faith without works is dead." It matters not what you say, says he; I do not wish to hear of God's power; I prefer the illusion of piety, and deny its *power*. And then, says Paul to him, Go and remember the sentence which is upon you. Gal. i, 7, 8. And turning to others, he puts an end to the discussion, 1 Cor. xiv, 39: "Therefore, brothers, be anxious to prophesy [despite Mr. Davies], and do not forbid speaking in strange tongues," as he does. If miracles depose faith in this age, why did they not do so in that age, I wonder? But it is vain to ask him anything further about this.

"To claim the continuation of miracles is the chief mark of an anti-Christ, and evil men," says he again. But *vice-versa* says the Bible. *To deny* miracles is the chief mark of unbelievers. Miracles were the chief mark of God's people in every age of the world. This is the *sign* or mark by which they shall be known, says Christ himself, as has already been proved and as Mr. Davies admitted once. Is not your object, in asserting that to claim miracles is the chief mark of an anti-Christ, to keep man in the darkness by hiding your deceit; and, to use your own language, "to defraud ignorant and weak-headed men of their money?" Not urging them to live piously, but teaching them to revile and persecute people better than you; promising to your beguiled people some imaginary and Davisistic heaven, about which you say that they can have no certainty here, only live on your imaginings until death, and then they may do what they will for all you care; and you shall remain behind to lead others to that place, feeding them, for their money, with rubbish, below common sense." But men, poor things, shall not be kept in darkness much longer, by vehemently shouting your old lying stories against those who preach the gospel freely, yes, not seeking a penny from anyone, but out of love for men's souls; and that is why you too have the disease of Demetrius, because the hope of profit of the great goddess of Dowlais Davisism is in danger.

Next, after challenging us about miracles continuously and condemning us as "a foul, devilish, hellish mob," &c., &c., because we do no miracles for him, he says—"God never performs miracles where there be sufficient reasons for belief without them." That is what we too say; and do we not offer you enough reasons for our religion? We prove it scriptural in every proposition. Do you not admit the apostolic plan to be reasonable? Well, that is what we preach. But as for Davisism, you should do many miracles, according to your own admission, to prove it, and show its origin; for a bad spring cannot give good streams. But in order to see the mixed-up streams of your brain, read the sentence next to the one that was quoted. Do you, I wonder, think so poorly of the Son of God, that he would make himself a servant to servants of the devil, by coming down off the cross at their request? Did he not come to do the will of his Father? There is not one example of Christ giving a sign to any evil man who asked him; and Mr. Davies knows this, for behold him jumping into the breach to try to shut himself up, lest anyone bring Christ's words against him. Oh no, it is useless for anyone to say that it is an evil generation, &c., that seeks a sign; but that is not true, says he, in fact now. Does he not remember that Jesus

Christ refused to obey the devil every time he requested that of him? And where is the difference between throwing himself off the pinnacle of the temple at Satan's request, and throwing himself from the cross at the request of Satan's servants?

Dear reader, think not as poorly as that of the Son of God, until some example is found of him or his apostles giving signs at the request of evil men. He did not raise the dead, nor blacken the sun, nor did he do anything else at the request of his enemies. But on the next page Mr. Davies comes to his senses for a moment again, destroying the whole web which he wove through his essay. He says,—"If the godly dead arose, and were sent from heaven to address you and had permission to inform you of the wonderful scenes of the country up above—and if the spirits of evil men came from the flames and told of the horrors of the worm that does not die, &c., it would all be too little and feeble to convince one sinner." We thank him for admitting that. If so, why does he claim that the purpose of the miracles was to convince sinners of someone's mission, and ask for miracles to convince the inhabitants of the truth of our religion? Not only is that their purpose but "they have answered their purpose in every place," he says. If so, why did Christ himself in the middle of a shower of stones, shout: "For which of the great works that I have done do you stone me?" Did they answer that purpose somewhere, Mr. Davies? If so, why did they not believe that Jesus Christ was sent by God, instead of persecuting him and crucifying him and scourging his servants when they did miracles in his name? Were they not scourged and imprisoned, the more miracles they did? Do not miracles in every age of the world, mostly harden and stir up evil men? So it is in this age also, as you well know through experience. You admit that in Christ's words—"if they believe not Moses and the prophets [concerning Christ], neither will they be persuaded, though one rose from the dead." That is our belief also. Now follow your own reasoning, and you must admit that you would not believe now that those whom you call "Satanists" are servants of God, nor that what you call a "heap of lies," &c., is the gospel of Christ, if one, yes, a thousand, rose from the dead, if they drank poison, if "the hip of Little Maggie were healed," yes, you confess yourself beyond convincing, if you are not convinced through the scriptures and the incontrovertible reasons we preach. And then, see and admit your folly and blasphemy in the previous lines, yes, which you wrote with the same pen, dipped in the same ink, and in the same breath; for before the one dried, you condemn us for not giving eyes to the blind, hips to the crippled, ears to the deaf, and raising up the dead, &c., in your presence. Would you believe even then? No, you would not, says Christ; no, you would not, say we too: no, you would not, you say yourself! How, then, can miracles be to convince men? And since you have already admitted that God does not perform miracles without worthy purposes, what is your purpose in begging for them all the time? What is your purpose in all these contrary assertions? How shall you be made consistent with yourself, never mind making you consistent with the scriptures? This is too much of a task for you or us, or anyone else either.

From what sort of spring do these waters come forth? You judge—and let your friends and the world judge you. We are not concerned with judging you; but we are concerned with defending our religion, and our characters against your terrible false accusations; and the world expects this of us. You show an incomparable impudence, telling such obvious and incredible lies about us; such as asserting that the "Address of the Twelve Apostles" maintains our ability to do miracles. There are thousands of those essays in the hands of the public now, throughout Wales, and we challenge you to show that there is in it such a thing as maintaining our ability to accomplish one miracle; if there is, note it in public, the page and the sentence if you can, and we shall immediately recant it as an error; if not, your sins shall be printed like the *mene*, *tekel*, *upharsim*, on your forehead from now on. You also accuse us of saying that Jesus Christ appears to us personally, in the rooms and our special meetings, &c. We deny that also and do not believe that you have heard any one of us saying such a thing. Prove this again, if you can, and we shall be answerable for the result. For the third time, you refer to the story which you published about some "woman in Penydarren." How did you not know at the time that that story was a lie? Had you not come next door to her when you formed the foul tissue of lies? But you and the country shall see an example of yourself in that story also, from eyewitnesses, to your shame. But as if you had sold yourself to evil, you accuse some "Little Maggie" and others, of saying that we can do miracles. You know better than this too by reading our books, &c., and the people of Dowlais know better than to believe your shameless false accusations from now on. Yes, Mr. Davies, we have many old scores to settle with you. We are ready to start that now; you knew that we could not at that time; and we wish you to prepare to defend your accusations against us. You have had too much rope by far, and you shall be seen from now on in the scales of truth. Enough, yes, far too many years have gone past for you to persecute us so cruelly and without cause. Do not be too ungodly lest the great God against whom you fight, cut you down, before you have time to repent, like Herod of old who "was eaten of worms, and gave up the ghost."

But having searched carefully through what you see fit to call "The Substance of a Sermon," we have failed to find any substance in it; and if this is an example of your sermons one need not ask who sent you to preach them, for by your sermons shall ye be recognized. Did you not promise to "enlighten the common folk, and show the deceit of the creatures who call themselves Latter-day Saints?" But have you done that? No! You gave no shaft of light. You grope in the darkness and darken counsel with words, with neither reason nor scripture. You fight against yourself continuously, making bogeys and tearing them to shreds, such as are found nowhere but in the mind which is agitated by the *horrors*. You have surely forgotten your promise, and you had better try again, or everyone will think that you have no reason or scripture to enlighten them concerning our deceit. Alas, Mr. Davies, not to offer as much as one proof against us, in an essay for that purpose, containing twenty pages. Only to condemn us continuously for presumption, because we venture to profess the apostolic faith, which, you yourself say sometimes, was the only rule. Making up false stories about us, with neither shape nor form to them in truth and then pouring out your anathemas on us. This is a strange way of showing our deceit, is it not? You show your own deceit, Sir! We do not claim perfection; but we claim, and also prove ourselves to be, guiltless of the presumption and villainous faults of which you accuse us, to the satisfaction of every man who is satisfied by facts. But would it be fair to your brothers if their doctrine were condemned because of and according to the number and wickedness of your sins, and the wretchedness of your character? If not, why do you take so much trouble to try to kill off our doctrine, by trying to blacken our characters? If you have as much as one reason or scripture against our principles, bring it forward now, because we have waited long to hear you proclaiming some of your proofs, and we, and the public shall thank you for the good deed, for thus would you do us good; but do not expect to blind reasonable people with a heap of contrary assertions and by giving us bad names, &c. Thus, you pile up fiery brands on your own head, and praise us and our doctrine. The country has long since had a surfeit of your assertions; and they ask you proofs of them now; and it is high time for you, as much as any other fallible man, to give them proofs, or recant; otherwise, they shall blacken your face in time to come. We shall yet note his "speaking with tongues," his "prophesying," and his conversation with "Wm. Henshaw," with witnesses of them.

MONMOUTHSHIRE CONFERENCE.

On Sunday, the 15th of November, the first Conference was held by the Saints in Nantyglo. Ten branches were represented, including 157 members; 7 elders; 12 priests; 8 teachers; and 3 deacons. 21 had been baptized in the last three months. Two elders, three priests, four teachers, and two deacons were ordained. It was decided that Nantyglo was a branch of this conference, and that Thomas Giles was to preside over it; also, Blaenafon, and brother Henish to preside; and Newport, and brother White to preside.

There was a large crowd of well-disposed listeners all day, and throngs of the Saints gathered from the Merthyr conference. The whole thing was listened to attentively, despite the previous threats to disrupt and prevent our worship, apart from some Pharisee who was shouting for a miracle. Between four and five hundred Saints were communing in the afternoon meeting, all in unity and brotherly love. Several testified strongly to the hope they have, and to their determination to go on with this excellent work. Brother Morris described the whole conference, almost, as being in a beautiful and successful condition, and the hope that multitudes would obey the gospel soon. President D. Jones proposed that brother William Henshaw should take charge of the Garway conference, which is under his supervision, and joined to Wales, and that Abergavenny and Newport be part of that conference. This was unanimously approved; brother Henshaw indicated his willingness, and his determination to do what he could in order to build the kingdom of Emmanuel. Brother Henish's child was blessed; and there was no doubt but what the Spirit of the Lord God of Elijah was in our midst, the spirit of love and joy. In the evening meeting at six o'clock, the hall was overflowing, although it was so full in the morning that *props* had to be put under the floor, in case it broke under them. The crowd was given a fervent and gifted address by elders William Pugh, Merthyr, Thomas Pugh, Cwmbach, and Capt D. Jones, Merthyr; and one could have thought that the eternal gospel they preached under the guidance of the divine Spirit, was being engraved, as though with an iron pen, on the hearts of the listeners; that it existed, not in word alone, but in great power and certainty in the Holy Ghost; and our fervent prayer is, that everyone who heard it may experience it as the power of God for salvation. Fifteen of the pure in heart were baptized, from among the various denominations, despite their opposition; and thanks be to God that they are enjoying great happiness in the Holy Ghost. Nine more were baptized there the following week, and there are many more at the door. The gratitude of the conference was expressed to Mr. Evans of the Cokers Arms for the hall, and for his kindness throughout the day to the Saints, at the cost of Nero's frequent favor. May the great God repay him an hundredfold.

MISSIONARY WORK IN THE COUNTIES OF WALES.

Pembrokeshire.—Brothers G. Davies and J. Price have baptized three recently, and have a numerous and attentive audience usually, and several promising to submit to the gospel soon.

Carmarthenshire.—Brother T. Jeremy writes an encouraging letter about the Llanybydder branch, saying that all the Saints are determined and united in the faith, and that they are enjoying the gifts of the Holy Ghost in their midst. He baptized two women in Pencarreg, and he and brothers Harris and Evans are preaching in nine or ten places in their area. There are some Saints in Brechfa, and several at the door. Elder Thos. Harris baptized three more in the town of Carmarthen, on the 15th of November, who received testimony through the Spirit of God of their acceptance with him. This branch is strong and flourishing, despite their disadvantages and their lack of the privileges of a house of God. Elder J. Morris was sent to visit them on his way to Pembrokeshire, and we hope they will soon have a good pastor. Brother Abel Evans baptized three more there soon after this.

Cardiganshire.—Elder Alfred Clark has returned from his journey through this county, and he has high hopes of an abundant harvest of the pure in heart. There is a great call for preaching, and the people are surprised how different our principles are from what they had heard about the Saints, and they are searching the scriptures themselves.

Montgomeryshire.—Several were baptized in Machynlleth recently. The number of Saints here now is about forty, all in just a few months! The gifts of the Holy Ghost are enjoyed in their midst too, according to the promise of Christ to those who believe his gospel, and who live in a godly manner. The unity of Spirit and love reigns here too in the bond of peace, as in all the churches of the Saints.

Merionethshire. —Brother Wm. Jones writes that the Saints in Harlech, Ffestiniog, &c., continue fervently in that faith which was once given to the Saints, and that their heavenly Father blesses them with heavenly blessings through his Holy Ghost, and the sick receive health through the exercise of the means set down through faith. Some were baptized there recently by Abel Evans, and some in Maentwrog. More are expected daily.

Caernarvonshire.—Elder Eleazer Edwards has preached the gospel almost every night, from Nefyn to Lleyn; from Pwllheli, Cricieth, to Portmadoc, with throngs believing the gospel. He has baptized some in Cricieth, and he was given an attentive hearing generally, and people liked him and the gospel he preaches. In Pwllheli, in the Calvinists' Quarterly Meeting, one of their preachers, by the name of Evan Harris, tried as hard as he could to arouse persecution against the Saints, and numb the ears of his listeners, by misrepresenting their principles, &c. The mayor of this town (under the influence of the Calvinist temperament which burned Servetus and others) refused to allow Brother Edwards to preach on the street, although the meeting houses were closed to him. The *police* drove him from one corner to the next, yes, he could not borrow the seashore which was lent so easily to the Calvinists to hold their Meeting. Thanks be to God for keeping the bridle of the "red stallion" in his own hand, otherwise its rush would be terrible. But through the kindness of a gentleman by the name of Mr. Evans, the brother and the large crowd were given permission to go into his lumber *yard*, to hear that divine gospel which closed the other *zealots* out of their bounds. Elder Jonah Richards has baptized some (we are not sure of the number) in Caernarvon, and the gospel is prospering in other parts of the County, despite its enemies.

Anglesey.—Elders Jonah Richards, Abel Evans, and others, have been preaching throughout the main towns of this county after us, to large crowds, and have received every kindness, and an invitation to continue to preach in their midst. There is here a general demand for the truth as it is in Jesus. We heard some were baptized there recently by J. Richards.

Denbighshire.—Abel Evans baptized two in addition to those who were already in Llandudno, and one in Dwygyfylchi. Elders William Evans, Richard Griffiths, and others, have been working successfully in Rhosllanerchrugog, and have baptized several there. They preached in Cefnmawr and Llangollen until the Rev. Mr. Prichard, the Baptist minister, endangered the people who opened their houses to them, and excluded them. I wonder if this gentle man will ask God to bless his behavior towards the servants he sent, towards his gospel, and towards the souls of his fellow-travelers in the day of judgment?

Flintshire.—Elder R. Evans is laboring in the main towns of this county, and has baptized some in several places, such as Newmarket, Rhuddlan, &c. Elder A. Evans also baptized two at Newmarket about the middle of this month, and three others promised to submit to the gospel the next time he came there, or someone else who had the necessary authority from God to baptize "for the forgiveness of sins."

It gives us great pleasure to announce also that the divine gospel is having great success with our fellow-countrymen in Cheshire and Liverpool. No doubt it will cause the Saints great happiness to hear that Mr. John Parry (formerly of Newmarket), his three sons, and his wife, like the family of that Lydia of old, have become subjects of the kingdom of the living God. Mr. Parry's name is respected, and is quite well known throughout the principality, especially in Gwynedd, as a fervent revivalist, as a lover of the truth wherever he might find it, regardless of prejudice and party. God loves honesty and courage in every man, and he arranges some way for such ones to be offered the truth; and it is pleasing to see these people prepared to examine it when it is offered to them, as Mr. Parry did, and without prejudice. There is no doubt that there are hundreds still who, as he did, believe they are closer to the truth than others. But by now Mr. Parry sees (as everyone sees who comes through the same door into the same divine kingdom) the difference between doing the best they can and *believing* they are right, and the *certainty* he receives from God through the Spirit of adoption of his acceptance in his sight. Mr. Parry was one of the main founders and a pillar of Campbellism in Wales, and many of the churches he planted accepted his advice as a father, and followed him from darkness to degrees of light through frowns and scorn; we hope they will follow him again into the middle of the blazing light of the eternal gospel. Mr. Parry and his eldest son have been ordained elders, and we hope their former brethren will have the honor of hearing them, and complying with their heavenly call, before next summer. Several have been baptized in Liverpool recently.

THE GOSPEL IN ENGLAND, SCOTLAND, &c.

ALL the news we receive constantly from these places proves that God has awakened as it were from the slumber of ages to do his great and wondrous work in these latter days. The kingdom of Emmanuel is succeeding and spreading strangely, and people of every station and denomination are flooding into it, and are able to feast on its heavenly delicacies as in the days of the Lord. The missionaries who came over from America recently are turning the counties of England on their heads, we should think, almost, and are baptizing more than ever. In some areas gentlemen who own large estates, justices, and some who hold high offices under the government, as well as the common people, are complying. In Scotland and the Isle of Man they are baptizing daily in some parts. Soon this kingdom will become like the prophet Daniel foresaw it, as a "stone cut out of the mountain without hands, and changed until it filled the whole earth" with light and knowledge of God, as the waters cover the sea.

AUSTRALIA.

IT is scarcely more than two years since an elder took the mustard seed to these remote parts of the world; and how wonderfully that climate agrees with it, so that it is already quite a tree with numerous strong branches, and the delightful breezes of Paradise breathing sweetly on its magnificent flowers. In a letter the brother there sent recently, he said that he was often called from his bed at night to baptize, and that they came some scores of miles purposely to fetch him to baptize those who believed the gospel there!

THE SOUTH SEA ISLANDS.

ELDERS Pratt, Richards, and others, continue to be very successful in these islands, and have baptized hundreds recently, especially since God in his providence, through the French, caused the sectarian missionaries (who persecuted the Saints so mercilessly, told the old unfounded stories about Joseph Smith, &c., and strived to incite jealousy against them in the natives) to have to withdraw from there for the most part. Those poor pagans, after being adopted as children of God through this gospel, receive the "bread of the children," the promised inheritance of his people, in abundance, and receive sufficient proofs that he is no respecter of persons, but that he and his word are unchanging, and that he who said, "And these signs shall follow them that believe," &c., also said, "Heaven and earth shall pass away, but my words shall not pass away." Let us thank him for his valuable promises.

THE FIRST RESURRECTION.

WELL blessed are those that slumber in Jesus in the grave,
For they will be yet risen as those in glory saved;
When the archangel trumpets his resurrecting chord,
These dear ones will all gather to meet their mighty Lord.

A bounteous host of firstfruits our God has gleaned of earth—
Those who were not corrupted ascend to share new birth;
And those on earth remaining that Jesus know and love,
Will be transformed one moment and join the throng above.

But woe betide those others who linger long below,
Such sorrow'll come upon them, such grief within them grow;
The Lord above with escort they'll see approach so fleet,
With flames about his person for those who chose deceit.

J. D.

RHYDYBONT : PRINTED BY JOHN JONES.

WRAPPERS

PRE-PAYMENT, 3c.] [POST-PAYMENT, $3^{1}/_{2}$c.

I COME to you again,— and tell the truth,
You can believe or not;
Despite each grudge, however great,
I shall not cease to prophesy.

PROPHET OF THE JUBILEE,

OR

STAR OF THE SAINTS.

"THE LORD GOD HATH SPOKEN, WHO CAN BUT PROPHESY? SURELY THE LORD GOD WILL DO NOTHING, BUT HE REVEALETH HIS SECRET UNTO HIS SERVANTS THE PROPHETS."

NO. 1.] JULY, 1846. [VOL. I.

CONTENTS.

MERTHYR TYDFIL:
PUBLISHED AND FOR SALE BY D. JONES;
AND FOR SALE ALSO
BY THE SAINTS IN GENERAL, AND MANY BOOKSELLERS.

TO THE SUBSCRIBERS.

DEAR FELLOW–COUNTRYMEN,—Your attention has not previously been drawn to a Publication with such new contents as this. It is not thereby certain to be truly worthy, any more than unworthy of your acceptance. Our motto is, "Prove all things; hold fast that which is good." He who greets you with such words cannot harm you. We know that our religion is from God, and know from irrefutable proofs, and those proofs are none other than the proofs of the apostolic faith of your Bible and ours. What advantage, you say, have we had to pay for deceiving our fellow-countrymen? Consider seriously, what can be exciting us? We must believe our own doctrine. Let our sufferings bear witness to that. We had no way of keeping our characters above all invention, libel, and lies, except, like you, through the medium of the printing press. You know how we have been accused of every evil, trickery, yes, and of every foolishness. We sent, in the mildest manner, to the monthlies which accused us, letters asserting our innocence. But, were they allowed to appear? No! Were we accused in the *Times, Star of Gomer, Educator, Baptist,* etc.? Yes, yes. Was space provided for us to clear ourselves? No, no! rather every poor excuse was sought. What shall we do? Do we claim more than every other sect claims? Does not each one of them claim to be right? Is that not a condemnation of the peculiarity of every other sect? We do not damn anyone; and if we did, we could scrape plenty of examples out of books already in the language, of how to phrase our condemnations. Is everyone allowed to put out his *magazine* but us? Is the press locked against us? Is that the freedom of Wales in the nineteenth century? Have the monthlies been locked? We shall open our own monthly, then. Has the press been polluted by libeling us? We shall cleanse it by defending ourselves, then. And in the name of all reason and history, what danger can happen to anybody? If our message is untrue, the message of all the Christians of our country is untrue, for Christianity is our burden, and our privilege, and our reward.

TO THE SAINTS.

DEAR BRETHREN,—We know you will do your best to circulate our Publication. You will find in it from time to time an account of the establishment of your stewardship, the troubles and successes of your brethren, in every corner of the earth. You will also find articles supportive of your beliefs, your discipleship, and your whole system. Everyone who reads without prejudice will benefit from it in seeing what we are—that we are not some unprincipled liars, and who we are—that we are not some dozen or two here and there in Wales. They

(See page 3 of the Wrapper.)

can all see, that the religion, which is slandered by those who do not know it, is not one of the common sects of the earth—that the one which has gained, in a dozen years, over half a million followers, is not something to be laughed at. Urge your PROPHET upon them, brethren, so that they may not wait any longer in the darkness for us.

TO OUR LIBELERS.

PRECIOUS SOULS,—The PROPHET does not intend to *settle* the account with you. Another has taken that solemn task upon Himself! You will receive from us only bare testimonies to the world on behalf of our characters, and fervent prayers to heaven on your behalf. Forgiveness and brotherly love once conquered the world in the apostolic age. Forgiveness and brotherly love are fast conquering it in your age too. This will conquer you also. It will turn your hatred into love, and your slander into prayers. Draw near, brethren, and look at us. Make sure you know us before you turn away. You are slandering what you do not know. We are not *perfect*. It is our plan that possesses that quality. Attack it, and we shall assist you as soon as you prove it to be trickery, or our knowledge of it unworthy.

CONDITIONS.

I. THE PROPHET contains Essays on the Teachings and Doctrine of the Saints, an Account of their troubles in every part of the world, as well as every other story which relates to their message, or hopes.

II. It will appear monthly, and towards the end of the month, so that it may contain everything essential which pertains to the month named on that number.

III. The Price will be Three Pence to the Pre-payers, and Threepence Halfpenny to the Post-payers.

IV. An Introduction and an Index will be provided annually, so that it can be bound as a compact book for continual use.

TO THE READERS.

The Annual Conference.—Was held this year in the *Hall of Science*, Manchester. We were unable to find space for a report on it in this Number, but it will be found in the next.

A review of the Sermon of Mr. Davies from Dowlais, on *The Miracles*, in

PUBLICATIONS OF THE LATTER-DAY SAINTS.

I.

Published recently, Price Sixpence,

THE DEAD RAISED TO LIFE !

OR

THE OLD RELIGION ANEW.

TREATISE

SHOWING

THE IMMUTABILITY OF THE KINGDOM OF GOD.

BY CAPT. D. JONES.

*** There are only a few copies of the treatise left unsold. It can be obtained with the PROPHET.

II.

Just published, by the same, Price only Three Pence,

REPLY

TO THE OBJECTIONS WHICH ARE BROUGHT MOST COMMONLY THROUGHOUT THE COUNTRY

AGAINST

THE LATTER-DAY SAINTS,

And the Doctrine they profess ;

IN THE FORM OF A DIALOGUE BETWEEN THE MASTERS OF TRADITION, A SECTARIAN, AND A SAINT.

III.

Published recently, by the same, Price a Penny Halfpenny.

ADDRESS

OF

THE TWELVE APOSTLES TO ALL KINGS, COUNSELORS, JUDGES, AND PEOPLE OF THE WORLD.

IV.

Just Published, by the same, Price Two Pence

THE SCALES,

IN WHICH ARE SEEN

DAVID WEIGHING WILLIAMS, AND WILLIAMS WEIGHING DAVID;

OR

David Williams, of Abercanaid, contradicting himself, caught in his deceit, and proved guilty of Deism.

PRE-PAYMENT, 3c.] [POST-PAYMENT, 3½c.

I COME to you again,— and tell the truth,
You can believe or nay;
Despite each grudge, however great,
I shall not cease to prophesy.

PROPHET OF THE JUBILEE,

OR

STAR OF THE SAINTS.

"THE LORD GOD HATH SPOKEN, WHO CAN BUT PROPHESY? SURELY THE LORD GOD WILL DO NOTHING, BUT HE REVEALETH HIS SECRET UNTO HIS SERVANTS THE PROPHETS."

No. 2.] AUGUST, 1846. [VOL. I.

CONTENTS.

MERTHYR TYDFIL:
PUBLISHED AND FOR SALE BY D. JONES;
AND FOR SALE ALSO
BY THE SAINTS IN GENERAL, AND MANY BOOKSELLERS.
1846.

CONDITIONS.

I. The Prophet contains Essays on the Teachings and Doctrine of the Saints, an Account of their troubles in every part of the world, as well as every other story which relates to their message, or hopes.

II. It will appear monthly, and towards the end of the month, so that it may contain everything essential which pertains to the month named on that number.

III. The Price will be Three Pence to the Pre-payers, and Threepence Halfpenny to the Post-payers.

IV. An Introduction and an Index will be provided annually, so that it can be bound as a compact book for continual use.

TO OUR SUBSCRIBERS.

We promised an account about California, but since other things are pressing, we have had to delay that again for a month or two.

A review of a sermon from Dowlais will appear *in the next* without fail, and the proud mocker will be seen unveiled. All in all each of our mockers will come to understand, little by little, that it is better to leave us alone. While a free press exists, lies will be revealed.

Let our enemies look over the accounts of our success in this number. They will read reports on our conferences, and they will compare them with reports on the conferences of the Baptists and the Congregationalists; yes, each with that of the apostles, and afterwards they will testify on whom is the image of the Lamb and his followers, and on whom is the image of the beast with the turbulent horns. Let the country judge everyone, yes a Mormon, by his fruits! Or, do what he will, a Mormon can appeal to a Judge who will do that later on.

PUBLICATIONS OF THE LATTER-DAY SAINTS.

I.

Published recently, Price Sixpence,

THE DEAD RAISED TO LIFE !

OR

THE OLD RELIGION ANEW.

TREATISE

SHOWING

THE IMMUTABILITY OF THE KINGDOM OF GOD.

BY CAPT. D. JONES.

*** There are only a few copies of the treatise left unsold. It can be obtained with the PROPHET.

II.

Just published, by the same, Price only Three Pence,

REPLY

TO THE OBJECTIONS WHICH ARE BROUGHT MOST COMMONLY THROUGHOUT THE COUNTRY

AGAINST

THE LATTER-DAY SAINTS,

And the Doctrine they profess ;

IN THE FORM OF A DIALOGUE BETWEEN THE MASTERS OF TRADITION, A SECTARIAN, AND A SAINT.

III.

Published recently, by the same, Price a Penny Halfpenny.

ADDRESS

OF

THE TWELVE APOSTLES TO ALL KINGS, COUNSELORS, JUDGES, AND PEOPLE OF THE WORLD.

IV.

Just Published, by the same, Price Two Pence

THE SCALES,

IN WHICH ARE SEEN

DAVID WEIGHING WILLIAMS, AND WILLIAMS WEIGHING DAVID;

OR

David Williams, of Abercanaid, contradicting himself, caught in his deceit, and proved guilty of Deism.

REUBEN HEDLOCK,

AMERICAN EMIGRATION, COMMISSION, FORWARDING,

AND

GENERAL SHIPPING AGENT,

STANLEY BUILDINGS, BATH-STREET, PRINCE'S DOCK,

LIVERPOOL.

THE man named here is an official of the Emigration Society which is recommended by us from time to time in the PROPHET.

Goods of all sorts are transported by him, to everywhere in the United States, Canada, South America, the East and West Indies, China, Bombay, Calcutta, Australia, New Zealand, &c., &c.

Emigrants are transported in the biggest and safest ships to New York, Boston, Philadelphia, Baltimore, Charleston, New Orleans, Mobile, Quebec, Montreal, &c., on the lowest terms; and every provision is made for the comfort and convenience of emigrants, as much as can be in the main, highest priced ships on the route.

A one pound deposit is requested for each emigrant of age, towards the emigration, in order to secure them a place on the ship.

All letters, after paying the toll, should be addressed to *Reuben Hedlock, Licensed Emigration Agent, Stanley Buildings, Bath Street, Prince's Dock, Liverpool*, and a straightforward answer will be received immediately.

*** *We know through bitter experience, that there are men in our ports, fair of face and gentle of tongue, inveigling strangers into emigrating in dangerous ships, as well as sucking twice as much money as necessary out of their pockets. There are, at this moment, hundreds of innocent Welshmen, feeding the fish of the Atlantic, because of negligence at the beginning of their voyage. Mr. Hedlock is not one of these. His terms will be found to be lower, his food, convenience and safety to be equal to the best ships out of Liverpool.*

MERTHYR TYDFIL.

THE WELSH are invited to the CYMREIGYDDION HALL *(White Lion)*, in this town, to hear the APOSTOLIC FAITH, as it has been restored through Angelic Ministry.—Lectures will be delivered every Sunday at 11 o'clock, and at 6 in the evening, to prove the following Doctrinal Subjects scriptural and reasonable:—Faith in the Son of God as a sufficient Savior—Repentance—Baptism for remission of sins—Laying on of hands to receive the Holy Ghost—Restoration of the Spiritual Gifts—Restoration of the Jews to Palestine—The first Resurrection—Christ's personal reign on the Earth for a Thousand Years—The General Judgment—The new Heaven and earth, and the eternal fate of the Universe and its Inhabitants!!!

N.B. Everyone is welcome to come in without charge.

PRE-PAYMENT, 3c.] [POST-PAYMENT, 3½c.

I COME to you again,— and tell the truth,
You can believe or nay;
Despite each grudge, however great,
I shall not cease to prophesy.

PROPHET OF THE JUBILEE,

OR

STAR OF THE SAINTS.

"THE LORD GOD HATH SPOKEN, WHO CAN BUT PROPHESY? SURELY THE LORD GOD WILL DO NOTHING, BUT HE REVEALETH HIS SECRET UNTO HIS SERVANTS THE PROPHETS."

NO. 3.] SEPTEMBER, 1846. [VOL. I.

CONTENTS.

MERTHYR TYDFIL:
PUBLISHED AND FOR SALE BY D. JONES;
AND FOR SALE ALSO
BY THE SAINTS IN GENERAL, AND MANY BOOKSELLERS.
1846.

TO OUR READERS.

WE WISH to draw the attention of our readers to an error which we made on page 78 of this number. In the third line of the piece entitled "The Editor of the *True Baptist*," it is said that a copy of a letter mentioned there, is to be found in the July PROPHET, which is incorrect, since it is in the above piece that the said letter should appear; but since that escaped our notice, we now give a copy of it here:—

"DEFENSE OF THE SAINTS.

"MR. EDITOR,—Recently the March issue of the "Baptist" came into our hands, and we saw, to our great surprise and dismay, our names signed under some letter, which the Rev. W. R. Davies, Dowlais, says we wrote to him, calling upon him to debate with our "praise-worthy apostle, Capt. D. Jones," &c. But we testify in sobriety and truth, in the presence of God and men, that we never wrote, or caused to be written, the aforementioned letter, or any other piece of writing to this man; and if someone else wrote this letter to him, we are completely unaware of it. All we know of anything like it is, that we heard that the Rev W. R. Davies was showing some letter rather similar to the above one to his neighbors in scorn, with Capt. D. Jones's name attached to it, about three months ago, and he threatened to publish it, &c., which caused Mr. Jones to announce publicly at the time, if the said letter appeared, that the public should not believe it, and that every word of it was a *forgery*. Notice of this was also sent to Mr. Davies, and it was expected that the matter had gone to the land of oblivion until we saw the aforementioned letter in the "Baptist," with our names on it. It is easy for every man who knows anything about us to see that that letter is a fake. We do not, and neither does Capt. D. Jones claim to be an "apostle," and no one in Britain, as far as we know, claims, or is given the title of apostle in our midst.

"We expect you will give space to this defense in one of your next issues. It is fair for everyone to have the truth, whatever his opinion may be. We should like to make use of your columns to comment on Mr. Davies's reply to the said letter, and we hope that neither you, nor the Editor of any other religious publication in Wales, would publish such things about any of your fellow-countrymen, unless you were willing to publish the defense too. At the very least, we are doing no more than our duty by giving you this information, so that you can, if you wish, take back the libels, so that we are not obliged finally to employ other means to obtain the justice and the freedom accorded to our characters by the laws of our land. Yours respectfully,

"ABEL EVANS,
"WILLIAM HENSHAW."

CONDITIONS.

I. THE PROPHET contains Essays on the Teachings and Doctrine of the Saints, an Account of their troubles in every part of the world, as well as every other story which relates to their message, or hopes.

II. It will appear monthly, and towards the end of the month, so that it may contain everything essential which pertains to the month named on that number.

III. The Price will be Three Pence to the Pre-payers, and Threepence Halfpenny to the Post-payers.

IV. An Introduction and an Index will be provided annually, so that it can be bound as a compact book for continual use.

THOMAS WARD,

AMERICAN EMIGRATION, COMMISSION, FORWARDING,

AND

GENERAL SHIPPING AGENT,

STANLEY BUILDINGS, BATH-STREET, PRINCE'S DOCK,

LIVERPOOL.

THE man named here is an official of the Emigration Society which is recommended by us from time to time in the PROPHET.

Goods of all sorts are transported by him, to everywhere in the United States, Canada, South America, the East and West Indies, China, Bombay, Calcutta, Australia, New Zealand, &c., &c.

Emigrants are transported in the biggest and safest ships to New York, Boston, Philadelphia, Baltimore, Charleston, New Orleans, Mobile, Quebec, Montreal, &c., on the lowest terms; and every provision is made for the comfort and convenience of emigrants, as much as can be in the main, highest priced ships on the route.

A one pound deposit is requested for each emigrant of age, towards the emigration, in order to secure them a place on the ship.

All letters, after paying the toll, should be addressed to *Thomas Ward, Licensed Emigration Agent, Stanley Buildings, Bath Street, Prince's Dock, Liverpool*, and a straightforward answer will be received immediately.

*** *We know through bitter experience, that there are men in our ports, fair of face and gentle of tongue, inveigling strangers into emigrating in dangerous ships, as well as sucking twice as much money as necessary out of their pockets. There are, at this moment, hundreds of innocent Welshmen, feeding the fish of the Atlantic, because of negligence at the beginning of their voyage. Mr. Ward is not one of these. His terms will be found to be lower, his food, convenience and safety to be equal to the best ships out of Liverpool.*

MERTHYR TYDFIL.

THE WELSH are invited to the CYMREIGYDDION HALL *(White Lion)*, in this town, to hear the APOSTOLIC FAITH, as it has been restored through Angelic Ministry.—Lectures will be delivered every Sunday at 11 o'clock, and at 6 in the evening, to prove the following Doctrinal Subjects scriptural and reasonable:—Faith in the Son of God as a sufficient Savior—Repentance—Baptism for remission of sins—Laying on of hands to receive the Holy Ghost—Restoration of the Spiritual Gifts—Restoration of the Jews to Palestine—The first Resurrection—Christ's personal reign on the Earth for a Thousand Years—The General Judgment—The new Heaven and earth, and the eternal fate of the Universe and its Inhabitants!!!

N.B. Everyone is welcome to come in without charge.

PUBLICATIONS OF THE LATTER-DAY SAINTS.

I.

Published recently, Price Sixpence,

THE DEAD RAISED TO LIFE!

OR

THE OLD RELIGION ANEW.

TREATISE

SHOWING

THE IMMUTABILITY OF THE KINGDOM OF GOD.

BY CAPT. D. JONES.

*** There are only a few copies of the treatise left unsold. It can be obtained with the PROPHET.

II.

Just published, by the same, Price only Three Pence,

REPLY

TO THE OBJECTIONS WHICH ARE BROUGHT MOST COMMONLY THROUGHOUT THE COUNTRY

AGAINST

THE LATTER-DAY SAINTS,

And the Doctrine they profess;

IN THE FORM OF A DIALOGUE BETWEEN THE MASTERS OF TRADITION, A SECTARIAN, AND A SAINT.

III.

Published recently, by the same, Price a Penny Halfpenny.

ADDRESS

OF

THE TWELVE APOSTLES TO ALL KINGS, COUNSELORS, JUDGES, AND PEOPLE OF THE WORLD.

IV.

Just Published, by the same, Price Two Pence

THE SCALES,

IN WHICH ARE SEEN

DAVID WEIGHING WILLIAMS, AND WILLIAMS WEIGHING DAVID;

OR

David Williams, of Abercanaid, contradicting himself, caught in his deceit, and proved guilty of Deism.

PRE-PAYMENT, 3c.] [POST-PAYMENT, 3½c.

I COME to you again,— and tell the truth,
You can believe or nay;
Despite each grudge, however great,
I shall not cease to prophesy.

PROPHET OF THE JUBILEE,

OR

STAR OF THE SAINTS.

"THE LORD GOD HATH SPOKEN, WHO CAN BUT PROPHESY? SURELY THE LORD GOD WILL DO NOTHING, BUT HE REVEALETH HIS SECRET UNTO HIS SERVANTS THE PROPHETS."

NO. 4.] OCTOBER, 1846. [VOL. I.

CONTENTS.

MERTHYR TYDFIL:
PUBLISHED AND FOR SALE BY D. JONES;
AND FOR SALE ALSO
BY THE SAINTS IN GENERAL, AND MANY BOOKSELLERS.
1846.

TO OUR READERS.

THE TRUTH requires that we inform our readers, that the previous number slipped from the press without our seeing it, because we were traveling through the North and England, for almost a quarter of a year; and we take the first opportunity to announce that the Editor of the *Baptist* gave space to W. Henshaw and A. Evans's letter of defense; and the mistake regarding the matter in the PROPHET (see page 78), occurred because the Printer lost the beginning of the copy. Yes, the *Baptist* did worse than refuse to publish it; for he insisted that those who cannot come to Cardiff to see for themselves, believe him, that the similarity of the two pieces of writing was sufficient to prove that the same persons wrote the two letters in question. We went to the office soon after that, we showed him the great wrong we had suffered, but we did not see those two writings either. Since Mr. Davies claims that it was some man who brought that letter to his house, and the Editor of the *Baptist* was an eyewitness to that, why do they not say who gave him that letter? They admit that the key to the mystery of that fictitious letter is in their hand; and if they do not bring it out into the open, who will not attribute the false letter to them? But more of this later. We continue to defend ouselves, while these two partners continue to accuse us falsely. Once again we say—It was not our brothers who wrote this challenge to Mr. Davies to come out to debate; its creators are obviously enemies of ours. Was it not Mr. Davies, and his brother from Cardiff, who lends his name to be a witness for him, who composed the false challenge in order to disgrace us? The *Baptist's* action in claiming that it was the same hand that wrote the challenge as wrote the defense to be put in his monthly, and his action in failing to show the two pieces of writing before our eyes, and his action also in standing so conveniently as a witness for his brother, although there are twenty miles between the homes of the two, and every other plan and scheme of theirs, lead us to suspect them strongly, despite ourselves. This is a serious accusation against Mr. D.; but let it be remembered that it would then be against the man who has employed all his inventiveness, for years, to falsely accuse us, and who has traveled a great deal throughout the country to disgrace us—against the polite man who has dubbed us with two or three dozen nicknames through the press and the pulpit. And we do not accuse anyone of eating dirt except the one who usually has dirt on his plate. That is all. If Mr. D. writhes (and who would not writhe from such a suspicion?); *let him name the bearer of that evil old letter*, then, and then he will be free, and not before. It is a pity that we, who have so many important tasks relating to the salvation of the age on our hands, should have to waste time with these things; but any other behavior on our part would be to suffer like a murderer or a thief.

THOMAS WARD,

AMERICAN EMIGRATION, COMMISSION, FORWARDING,

AND

GENERAL SHIPPING AGENT,

STANLEY BUILDINGS, BATH-STREET, PRINCE'S DOCK,

LIVERPOOL.

THE man named here is an official of the Emigration Society which is recommended by us from time to time in the PROPHET.

Goods of all sorts are transported by him, to everywhere in the United States, Canada, South America, the East and West Indies, China, Bombay, Calcutta, Australia, New Zealand, &c., &c.

Emigrants are transported in the biggest and safest ships to New York, Boston, Philadelphia, Baltimore, Charleston, New Orleans, Mobile, Quebec, Montreal, &c., on the lowest terms; and every provision is made for the comfort and convenience of emigrants, as much as can be in the main, highest priced ships on the route.

A one pound deposit is requested for each emigrant of age, towards the emigration, in order to secure them a place on the ship.

All letters, after paying the toll, should be addressed to *Thomas Ward, Licensed Emigration Agent, Stanley Buildings, Bath Street, Prince's Dock, Liverpool*, and a straightforward answer will be received immediately.

*** *We know through bitter experience, that there are men in our ports, fair of face and gentle of tongue, inveigling strangers into emigrating in dangerous ships, as well as sucking twice as much money as necessary out of their pockets. There are, at this moment, hundreds of innocent Welshmen, feeding the fish of the Atlantic, because of negligence at the beginning of their voyage. Mr. Ward is not one of these. His terms will be found to be lower, his food, convenience and safety to be equal to the best ships out of Liverpool.*

MERTHYR TYDFIL.

THE WELSH are invited to the CYMREIGYDDION HALL *(White Lion)*, in this town, to hear the APOSTOLIC FAITH, as it has been restored through Angelic Ministry.—Lectures will be delivered every Sunday at 11 o'clock, and at 6 in the evening, to prove the following Doctrinal Subjects scriptural and reasonable:—Faith in the Son of God as a sufficient Savior—Repentance—Baptism for remission of sins—Laying on of hands to receive the Holy Ghost—Restoration of the Spiritual Gifts—Restoration of the Jews to Palestine—The first Resurrection—Christ's personal reign on the Earth for a Thousand Years—The General Judgment—The new Heaven and earth, and the eternal fate of the Universe and its Inhabitants!!!

N.B. Everyone is welcome to come in without charge.

PUBLICATIONS OF THE LATTER-DAY SAINTS.

I.

Published recently, Price Sixpence,

THE DEAD RAISED TO LIFE!

OR

THE OLD RELIGION ANEW.

TREATISE

SHOWING

THE IMMUTABILITY OF THE KINGDOM OF GOD.

BY CAPT. D. JONES.

*** There are only a few copies of the treatise left unsold. It can be obtained with the PROPHET.

II.

Just published, by the same, Price only Three Pence,

REPLY

TO THE OBJECTIONS WHICH ARE BROUGHT MOST COMMONLY THROUGHOUT THE COUNTRY

AGAINST

THE LATTER-DAY SAINTS,

And the Doctrine they profess;

IN THE FORM OF A DIALOGUE BETWEEN THE MASTERS OF TRADITION, A SECTARIAN, AND A SAINT.

III.

Published recently, by the same, Price a Penny Halfpenny.

ADDRESS

OF

THE TWELVE APOSTLES TO ALL KINGS, COUNSELORS, JUDGES, AND PEOPLE OF THE WORLD.

IV.

Just Published, by the same, Price Two Pence

THE SCALES,

IN WHICH ARE SEEN

DAVID WEIGHING WILLIAMS, AND WILLIAMS WEIGHING DAVID;

OR

David Williams, of Abercanaid, contradicting himself, caught in his deceit, and proved guilty of Deism.

PRE-PAYMENT, 3c.] [POST-PAYMENT, 3½c.

I COME to you again,— and tell the truth,
You can believe or nay;
Despite each grudge, however great,
I shall not cease to prophesy.

PROPHET OF THE JUBILEE,

OR

STAR OF THE SAINTS.

"THE LORD GOD HATH SPOKEN, WHO CAN BUT PROPHESY? SURELY THE LORD GOD WILL DO NOTHING, BUT HE REVEALETH HIS SECRET UNTO HIS SERVANTS THE PROPHETS."

NO. 5.] NOVEMBER, 1846. [VOL. I.

CONTENTS.

MERTHYR TYDFIL:
PUBLISHED AND FOR SALE BY D. JONES;
AND FOR SALE ALSO
BY THE SAINTS IN GENERAL, AND MANY BOOKSELLERS.
1846.

ADDRESS.

Dear Reader, —

Before we appear again, it will be time for you to decide about receiving us next year. You know us well by now, and are consequently well fitted to judge us. You receive from us an explanation of the nature of our principles, so that you need not listen to our enemies' misrepresentation of them. You are able to read the truth in our pages about the stories which are spread about the country about our behavior. You are, by receiving it, doing a little toward spreading the truth about us throughout the country. You do, perhaps, consider that a duty, a pleasure, and a privilege. We are very grateful for your attention to us, and confidently hope that that you will go forward with us for the coming year.

We know of you, dear brothers and sisters, that you will not go back on your usual practice. And we shall do our best to teach you and instruct you in our principles and practices, according to the New Testament.

Published recently, price Four Pence,

HYMNS, composed and collected most particularly, for the use of the Latter-day Saints. Merthyr Tydfil: published and for sale by Capt. D. Jones.

MERTHYR TYDFIL.

THE WELSH are invited to the CYMREIGYDDION HALL *(White Lion)*, in this town, to hear the APOSTOLIC FAITH, as it has been restored through Angelic Ministry.—Lectures will be delivered every Sunday at 11 o'clock, and at 6 in the evening, to prove the following Doctrinal Subjects scriptural and reasonable:—Faith in the Son of God as a sufficient Savior—Repentance—Baptism for remission of sins—Laying on of hands to receive the Holy Ghost—Restoration of the Spiritual Gifts—Restoration of the Jews to Palestine—The first Resurrection—Christ's personal reign on the Earth for a Thousand Years—The General Judgment—The new Heaven and earth, and the eternal fate of the Universe and its Inhabitants!!!

N.B. Everyone is welcome to come in without charge.

CONDITIONS.

I. THE PROPHET contains Essays on the Teachings and Doctrine of the Saints, an Account of their troubles in every part of the world, as well as every other story which relates to their message, or hopes.

II. It will appear monthly, and towards the end of the month, so that it may contain everything essential which pertains to the month named on that number.

III. The Price will be Three Pence to the Pre-payers, and Threepence Halfpenny to the Post-payers.

IV. An Introduction and an Index will be provided annually, so that it can be bound as a compact book for continual use.

PUBLICATIONS OF THE LATTER-DAY SAINTS.

I.

Published recently, Price Sixpence,

THE DEAD RAISED TO LIFE!

OR

THE OLD RELIGION ANEW.

TREATISE

SHOWING

THE IMMUTABILITY OF THE KINGDOM OF GOD.

BY CAPT. D. JONES.

*** There are only a few copies of the treatise left unsold. It can be obtained with the PROPHET.

II.

Just published, by the same, Price only Three Pence,

REPLY

TO THE OBJECTIONS WHICH ARE BROUGHT MOST COMMONLY THROUGHOUT THE COUNTRY

AGAINST

THE LATTER-DAY SAINTS,

And the Doctrine they profess;

IN THE FORM OF A DIALOGUE BETWEEN THE MASTERS OF TRADITION, A SECTARIAN, AND A SAINT.

III.

Published recently, by the same, Price a Penny Halfpenny.

ADDRESS

OF

THE TWELVE APOSTLES TO ALL KINGS, COUNSELORS, JUDGES, AND PEOPLE OF THE WORLD.

IV.

Just Published, by the same, Price Two Pence

THE SCALES,

IN WHICH ARE SEEN

DAVID WEIGHING WILLIAMS, AND WILLIAMS WEIGHING DAVID;

OR

David Williams, of Abercanaid, contradicting himself, caught in his deceit, and proved guilty of Deism.

PRE-PAYMENT, 3c.] [POST-PAYMENT, $3\frac{1}{2}$c.

I COME to you again,— and tell the truth,
You can believe or nay;
Despite each grudge, however great,
I shall not cease to prophesy.

PROPHET OF THE JUBILEE,

OR

STAR OF THE SAINTS.

"THE LORD GOD HATH SPOKEN, WHO CAN BUT PROPHESY? SURELY THE LORD GOD WILL DO NOTHING, BUT HE REVEALETH HIS SECRET UNTO HIS SERVANTS THE PROPHETS."

NO. 6.] DECEMBER, 1846. [VOL. I.

CONTENTS.

MERTHYR TYDFIL:
PUBLISHED AND FOR SALE BY D. JONES;
AND FOR SALE ALSO
BY THE SAINTS IN GENERAL, AND MANY BOOKSELLERS.
1846.

CHANGE IN SIZE OF THE PROPHET.

THE *Prophet* will appear next year as sixteen pages, of the same folding as before; its price will be twopence per issue.

THE causes of this change are, so that we shall able to publish several essays on doctrinal subjects, which are too long for the *Prophet,* without dividing them; yet if they were divided, they would not be as useful to those who are not regular subscribers to the *Prophet.* By lowering its price it will be possible for many more to receive it than at its present price. Apart from the fact that the amazing success of the Saints in Wales, and other countries, requires and deserves more of our attention than can be devoted to it in the *Prophet*, in its present form, there is also a demand for more advice, disciplinary rules, and matters relating to the proper order and structure of the Saints throughout the principality in its holiest faith, and their perfecting in unity and brotherly love. And we trust that the change will bring about, not only its spread, but its usefulness to the Saints.

The *Prophet* contains—I. Brief and comprehensive comments on those subjects of ours which are most opposed by our fellow-countrymen.

II. Church stories, such as, conferences, baptisms, persecutions, as well as the great works of God among the Saints in Wales.

III. Stories of the American Saints in the wilderness, their journey and their progress in California, as well as the nature of that beautiful land. Also, the most interesting things that happen in the church in Europe, the islands of the sea, and throughout the world.

IV. Signs of the times from time to time—the effects of the great strong sword of the God of war, which is shaken now over the whole earth.

V. Replies to the questions of the officials and the Saints, in order to explain our doctrine, our discipinary rules, &c., and bring them all into the unity of the faith.

VI. Defenses in the face of false accusations against the Saints, and misrepresentations of their doctrine.

Published recently, price Four Pence,

HYMNS, composed and collected most particularly, for the use of the Latter-day Saints. Merthyr Tydfil: published and for sale by Capt. D. Jones.

MERTHYR TYDFIL.

THE WELSH are invited to the CYMREIGYDDION HALL *(White Lion)*, in this town, to hear the APOSTOLIC FAITH, as it has been restored through Angelic Ministry.—Lectures will be delivered every Sunday at 11 o'clock, and at 6 in the evening, to prove the following Doctrinal Subjects scriptural and reasonable:—Faith in the Son of God as a sufficient Savior—Repentance—Baptism for remission of sins—Laying on of hands to receive the Holy Ghost—Restoration of the Spiritual Gifts—Restoration of the Jews to Palestine—The first Resurrection—Christ's personal reign on the Earth for a Thousand Years—The General Judgment—The new Heaven and earth, and the eternal fate of the Universe and its Inhabitants ! ! !

This doctrine will be preached in the HALL OF THE DOWLAIS INN, DOWLAIS, every Sabbath at the above time.

N.B. Everyone is welcome to come in without charge.

PUBLICATIONS OF THE LATTER-DAY SAINTS.

I.

Published recently, Price Sixpence,

THE DEAD RAISED TO LIFE!

OR

THE OLD RELIGION ANEW.

TREATISE

SHOWING

THE IMMUTABILITY OF THE KINGDOM OF GOD.

BY CAPT. D. JONES.

*** There are only a few copies of the treatise left unsold. It can be obtained with the PROPHET.

II.

Just published, by the same, Price only Three Pence,

REPLY

TO THE OBJECTIONS WHICH ARE BROUGHT MOST COMMONLY THROUGHOUT THE COUNTRY

AGAINST

THE LATTER-DAY SAINTS,

And the Doctrine they profess;

IN THE FORM OF A DIALOGUE BETWEEN THE MASTERS OF TRADITION, A SECTARIAN, AND A SAINT.

III.

Published recently, by the same, Price a Penny Halfpenny.

ADDRESS

OF

THE TWELVE APOSTLES TO ALL KINGS, COUNSELORS, JUDGES, AND PEOPLE OF THE WORLD.

IV.

Just Published, by the same, Price Two Pence

THE SCALES,

IN WHICH ARE SEEN

DAVID WEIGHING WILLIAMS, AND WILLIAMS WEIGHING DAVID;

OR

David Williams, of Abercanaid, contradicting himself, caught in his deceit, and proved guilty of Deism.

1847

PROPHWYD Y JUBILI,

NEU

SEREN Y SAINT.

RHIF. 7.] IONAWR, 1847. [PRIS 2*g*.

ANERCHIAD AT Y CYMRY.

ANWYL GYDWLADWYR,—Wrth anfon yr ail gyfrol o'r PROPHWYD i'ch plith, taer erfyniwn eich sylw difrifolaf arno. Gwnewch degwch â'ch eneidiau eich hunain a'r gwirionedd wrth ei ddarllen, fel y derbynioch y lles a amcanwn i chwi wrth ei gyhoeddi. Gwyddom y cynnwysa lawer o faterion pwysig, sy'n dwyn perthynas agos â phob un o honoch; ac er y dichon amryw o honynt ymddangos yn newydd ac yn anmhoblogaidd ar yr olwg gyntaf, etto byddwch bwyllog, canys yr un yw eich Bibl chwi a minnau. Yn y glorian gywir hon y pwyswn bob egwyddor, ynte.

Gwyddom ein bod (trwy drugaredd ein Duw) yn feddiannol ar drysorau dwyfol a gwerthfawr, pa rai a'ch cyfoethogant chwithau yn dragywyddol. Yr ydym wedi ein hanrhegu â'r *perl* nefol hwnw yr ymchwiliwch chwi am dano, o gapel bwy gilydd, o'r naill enwad i'r llall ar hyd y blynyddoedd—sef *crefydd bur*—egwyddorion y nef—yr efengyl dragywyddol; yr hon sy'n dwyn bywyd ac allygredigaeth i oleuni. Yr ydym yn gwneyd a allom i gyflwyno gwybodaeth o honi i chwithau yn mhob dull a modd a allwn; ac er mor ddaionus yw, y mae miloedd o honoch yn diystyru cynghor Duw yn eich herbyn eich hunain, heb ufyddhau i, na gwrando ar, yr alwedigaeth nefol a phwysig a gynnygir i chwi.

Y mae ugeiniau o honom yn cyhoeddi y newyddion da hyn yn eich plith ers rhai blynyddau bellach, ar ein cost ein hunain, a pha dderbyniad geir? Gallesid dysgwyl yn rhesymol i'r rhai hyny a addefant wirionedd y grefydd gristionogol yn ei sefydliad cyntefig a phur, ac a broffesant y fath fawr sel drosti, ei chofleidio fel trysor y trysorau pan y clywent hi etto yn cael ei phregethu genym ninnau yn ei chyflawnder, wedi ei hail-sefydlu fel cynt, a'i phregethwyr wedi eu hanfon drwy awdurdod dwyfol fel y rhai a ganmolwch gymmaint.

Ond gwyddoch chwi mai hollol groes i hyny y mae. Pa well der-

January 1847, page 5, courtesy Harold B. Lee Library,
Brigham Young University

PROPHET OF THE JUBILEE,

OR

STAR OF THE SAINTS.

No. 7.] JANUARY, 1847. [PRICE 2c.

PROCLAMATION TO THE WELSH.

DEAR COMPATRIOTS,—As we send this second volume of the PROPHET into your midst, we fervently beseech your most serious attention to it. Do justice to your own souls and to the truth as you read it, so that you may receive the benefit we intend in publishing it. We know it contains many important matters, which closely relate to each one of you; and although several things in it may appear new and unpopular at first glance, yet be patient, for your Bible is the same as ours. It is therefore in these accurate scales that we weigh every principle.

We know that we are (through the grace of our God) in possession of divine and precious treasures, which will enrich you also for eternity. We have received the gift of that heavenly *pearl* for which you search, from one chapel to the next, and from one denomination to the other, over the years—namely *pure religion*—the principles of heaven—the eternal gospel; that which brings life and purity to light. We are doing our best to present knowledge of it to you in every manner and way we can; and although it is so beneficial, thousands of you are disregarding God's counsel against you, not obeying or listening to, the heavenly and important call that is presented to you.

Scores of us have been proclaiming this good news in your midst for some time now, at our own cost; and what reception have we had? One could reasonably expect those who admit the truth of the Christian religion in its original and pure establishment, and who profess such great zeal for it, to embrace it as the treasure of treasures when they hear it again being preached by us in its fulness, re-established as before, and with its preachers sent by divine authority as were sent those whom you hold in high regard.

But you know that it is the complete opposite of that. What better reception do God's emissaries get from you now, especially from those who are zealous for the traditions of the fathers, than similar emissaries with the same sort of message got from their contemporaries? *Rabbis*, teachers, and the most zealous religious believers of the land were their chief enemies; these were the ones who preached most from the pulpits against them, who most often told unfounded tales about their characters, and who proclaimed that what they had was deceit, and that their leader was a deceiver, and all that without offering one proof of anything, except their assertions. Is that not exactly how such people behave towards us? The best welcome they received from the beguiled of such people was the shouting of false prophets, false teachers, deceivers, &c., after them in the streets. So it is with us. Were not the authors of their age spreading every unfounded false accusation about them, without taking the trouble to search out what they were? So do they with us. Did they not turn them and those who listened to them out of their synagogues? Is not the same done to us, and to the honest of heart who are searching for the truth? Did Christ not say that they would do so; and so it is.

It was said of them, "Those who disturb the world, such have come here also." This is what we hear everywhere we go. "What does this speaker say," says one; "These people are disturbing the city," says another about them. We too are thus accused. They bring a new doctrine into our midst, which it is not fitting for us to receive, they said about them. These people are preaching a new gospel, which it is not fitting for us, sectarians, to receive, they say now about us. Did not our Teacher say that that was how false believers would deal with the truth? Yes; and our contemporaries prove his words and our religion, as true in this age as in that one. "Whosoever will live godly in Christ Jesus shall suffer persecution," was the case then; that is how we also feel, quite truly; and if we and they were scrutinized in every particular, and our contemporaries' behavior towards us and our religion, it would be seen that it is true that the same cause brings about the same effect in this age as in that. Why is all this not evidence to you, gentle friends, of our similarity to them? Why do you take measures, and follow the steps of the persecutors of old, with your eyes open? Was their religion not unpopular then? What wonder that the same religion is as unpopular in its second beginning now? "Has any of the leaders believed?" says one. Oh no, they are the "filth of the world and the offscouring of all things," say the others of that time. So is it now. They preached free to the poor. So do we. The preachers of that age were persuading people not to listen to them, that they were beneath their notice. So is it now, exactly. It was fear that their profit would fail that motivated those people. You judge whether that is the reason that the religious merchants and craftsmen of this age attack us! The salvation of their contemporaries was bound up in obeying their message. So now, gentle reader, it is equally as certain that the forgiveness, resurrection, ascension, and glory of our contemporaries depend on their obedience to the message of the *Latter-day Saints*; yes, even if all the people of the world were to speak ill of them, we know that the God of heaven has sent them. We know, dear Welshmen, despite our weakness. We bear solemn and sober witness in the fear of God, that we may be clean from the blood of all. We have received the keys to the dispensation of the fulness of times —the ministry of the covenant, that is the dispensation of the eleventh hour! The Lord of the harvest has sent us with a mission to gather his wheat into his barn, before he comes to burn the chaff with inextinguishable fire. Again, we testify quite fearlessly that your age and generation shall not pass away before the God of Israel proves beyond any argument, that the Latter-day Saints have been sent by him to prepare the way for his second coming, and he proves every jot and tittle of their message to be abiding truth. Is this testimony not important to you, and a sign of life to life, or of death to death, to everyone who has the advantage of hearing it? Willful neglect is no excuse for anyone. It is its importance that compels us, yes, that obliges us to be so plain with you, and woe betide us if we do not do this; a necessity has been laid upon us. Answer, is testimony such as this not worthy of your attention, and your detailed investigation? It is true, dear Welsh people; search and test us fairly, and show our errors if you can; and we shall be grateful to you. We are answerable to God for what we say; we know that too, and yet we love and entreat an examination of our religion before the court of the unchanging word of that just Judge. Has anyone in the country proved one of our principles to be erroneous according to the Bible? No, not one! It is true that many have proved the false accusations of our enemies against us to be very offensive. And what have we to do with that until they attack what we believe, and not what we and they deny. Until they do this, what reason is there to persecute us, to revile us, and refuse to listen to us? Yet, for our part, persecute as you will, and we shall give thanks for the honor and the strength to suffer unfairly for those divine truths for which our elder brethren and our Lord also gave their lives as willing sacrifices for them; and despite all this, in order to convince you who seek a religion with strength in it, and make you heirs of substance, we testify, and we continue to explain the message that has been entrusted to our care; and we know that while we continue thus we can render our account joyfully when our Master comes to be glorified in all those who believe and obey our testimony. We are not without a feeling of our unworthiness to such a task as this, but we know that the eternal arms are beneath us. We also know that he who proclaims great and numerous truths to his contemporaries, thereby wins for himself numerous and mighty enemies. The popularity of the age is the strongest enemy of the truth, if it breaks over its banks: and under the present circumstance, if we possessed an angelic clarion—the apostolic zeal—and hearts as wide as eternity—and the wisdom of heaven—and the love of God burning as a fiery flame in our bosom, and if we were sent to proclaim the best message ever brought from the third heaven by the archangel Michael; yet, it would be as impossible for us to present knowledge of it to the people now as it was for Paul to prove the divinity of their crucified Messiah in Ephesus, when his voice was drowned in the middle of that great shout, "Great is Diana of the Ephesians." If you want to prove the strength of traditional ties, teach some great and divine truth; and we would be surprised if it was not like unto trying to reason amid a battle, amid the roar of the cannons and guns with slaughter of war, while you are up to your ankles in blood. Speak to the rushing whirlwind as it rips the forest from its roots—preach to a sleeping man or teach a drunkard in his drunkenness; then you will see how difficult it is for the arrows of truth to penetrate the ears and lodge in the mind of a man that has made up his mind without searching—a man who believes the one side and refuses to listen to the other side;—then you will believe how great and difficult the task of the Latter-day Saints is to get the people to listen to their message.

Welsh people, how long will you take pleasure in mocking? how long will you turn a deaf ear to this important message from heaven? It is the voice of your Judge, offering you temporal salvation from plagues, diseases, famine and terrible judgments that are to come; yes, offering you also eternal salvation, without money and not for sale. Remember that God never sent a message into the world unless the temporal and spiritual salvation of that age depended on obedience to it! Remember how Noah was received! What was the result of rejecting his message! Remember Sodom and Gomorrah—the destruction of the Jews in spite of their faithfulness to the traditions of their fathers. Remember also the saying of our Lord clearly in your Bible and ours that, "as it was in the days of Noah, thus it will be in the coming of the Son of man." Remember also his saying to you, that God has sent the Latter-day Saints to warn you that the time is near for him to take on his attributes, when you can see a difference between one who serves God and one who serves man. When he comes on the clouds of heaven, with his mighty angels, with flames of fire to take revenge on all who know not God, and are not obedient to the gospel of our Lord Jesus Christ, that is the one who was sent from heaven in these latter days, and the one whom we preach to you. He that has ears, let him listen to our message. He that has eyes, let him read our publication for himself. Indeed, we say to you, your eyes will see that it is true; choose life and goodness, then, so that you may live in paradise and glory.

PARABLE.

ON *Christmas day* a certain *King* held a wedding feast for his son; he prepared a dinner, and he resolved to give him one of his territories on his wedding day. The *woman* that was to be his bride was exceptionally beautiful; her finery consisted of a magnificent crown with *twelve diamonds* set around it, and she wore it on her head. In her hand she carried a *shining sceptre*, from which the sun's rays were reflected on the *diamonds*, until the road ahead of her was lit day and night, and she never walked in darkness, rather in the brilliance of the noonday sun. Her countenance was fair and pleasant; purity, innocence, and love could be seen imprinted on her beautiful cheeks. Her favorite work was to administer comfort and joy to all around her; she surpassed all the women in the kingdom in wisdom, faith, and the like virtues and graces. But, the *inhabitants* of the territory became jealous of her; they conspired against her and her chosen spouse, and in the end they succeeded in exiling the Son from their borders, which caused great sadness and prolonged grief to the bride, until she was comforted by the King's promise to restore the Son back to his rights. And since those treacherous subjects had ignored and refused the *dinner*, he prepared a *supper*, and he invited all the inhabitants of the province to it, and he crowned his son King over the whole land;—he caused the beautiful sceptre in the hand of the bride, to reflect until all the lands in the territory were filled with a great light; inasmuch as this son was his only heir, he announced that all the kingdoms of the territory at this time were under his rule.

The bride was sustained by this joyful news, and she fought through many hard battles, until in time the Emperor of the warring nation changed his war tactics, and he declared a general peace. He expected, through this trickery, to succeed in gaining possession of the sceptre, for he expected it would be the sceptre that would reign over all the nations; he embraced the woman lovingly, until she was overcome by cunning and treachery. But at this important and dangerous time the king himself came forward to the place, and only barely in time, to save the woman when she was about to give her authority to the emperor: he took the sceptre from her hand, and he took the empire unto himself, and he saved the woman from the hand of the treacherous emperor, by hiding her in a neighboring wilderness, so that her life would be spared. This angered the disappointed emperor, and he declared a fierce war of revenge on the woman, proclaiming his own greatness, and he asserted that he would have the authority of the bridegroom from the woman, putting to death everyone who doubted him. The woman wandered sadly in the wilderness for many days, having lost the *diamonds* from her crown, having been plundered from her sceptre, with no light by which to see her way except the beams of the moon shining through the branches of the trees. She lamented and wept greatly because of her sudden widowhood, longing for the return of her exiled husband. Nevertheless, she was comforted in the hope of the promise, and she sat alone in the woods waiting attentively, and listening to the rustling of the leaves and the songs of the birds, and she heard the heartening news, "Behold, the bridegroom cometh, go out to meet him, array yourself in your wedding dress that I gave you; put your pearls in your crown as before, and put on all the wedding adornments that he prepared for you, so the marriage may be completed; and let no one who has refused this, his second and his last invitation, partake of this great supper." She waited for a messenger to arrive directly from the empire of the great King with this good news, according to his promise, and her sceptre was restored to her, together with all its splendor and its greatness thereunto appertaining; and authority was presented to her to proclaim in the name of the great King, through all the provinces and kingdoms of the territory, and to every kindred, tongue, and people throughout its borders, saying with loud voice, "Fear the great king, obey his laws, seek the wedding dress, and come in to his supper; for behold he is about to bring all his strong armies with him to avenge, and to destroy all the rebellious inhabitants of the territory, and none will be spared except those gathered for the supper. And he will crown his only son and heir king over all the territory." Now, reader, what is the parable? Search it in detail, for you and we are in it. The following references will enable you to comprehend it.

The *King* and his *Son* are the Father and his only begotten Son, Jesus Christ.

The *Woman*—the Church of Jesus Christ.

The time the *dinner* was offered was when Christ and his apostles offered salvation to the Jews.

The *traitors* that exiled the Son of the King—the Jews. "We do not wish this man to rule over us."

Persecutors of the Woman—The Church of Rome.

The *emperor* that embraced the Woman—Constantine the Great, when the church was linked to the government of Rome.

The *shining sceptre*—The priesthood after the order of the Son of God, which was given to the church.

It was taken from her—in the year 570 A.D., when the Pope in Rome declared himself head of the church throughout the world. (See Rev. xii, 4-6.)

The *twelve diamonds*—The twelve apostles.

The wife comes from the desert again (Rev. xix, 7-9), dressed in all her former adornments.

The time the Bridegroom is crowned—As soon as the woman is ready, and her friends have gathered to the supper.

The place where the woman is now—On the American continent, calling the guests from the four corners of the world, by sending her servants with loud voice to call, "Come to the Lamb's wedding feast, for the woman has made herself ready."

The manner in which she is recognized among all the women of the world—By her priesthood, her twelve apostles leading her, and all her officers according to the primitive plan, and being led by revelations from heaven, that is the only light that leads the church of Christ, or the people of God, in every age of the world.

The jealousy of all the women of the world towards her—This is proved by their cruel and persecuting acts, yes, all the women unite to shout, "Highway prostitute" at her.

The ones who refuse the dinner—The Jews refusing the gospel of Christ and his apostles.

The ones invited to the supper—The gentiles, when the apostles turned to them from the Jews. Acts xiii, 45-49; Rom. xi.

The dinner—The gospel that was first offered to the Jews, so that the first could be the last; and the second time to the gentiles, so that those who were last could be the first.

The ones that cannot partake of the supper—All who refuse that gospel again, when God sends his fishermen and hunters to gather them together—when he establishes his church on the apostolic plan—when an ensign is raised to the gentiles from afar, preaching the eternal gospel to every kindred, tongue, people, and nation, saying with a loud voice, You, all the inhabitants of the earth, listen when God speaks to you from heaven, for he has sent an angel with the everlasting gospel for man on earth, saying, "Fear God, and give glory to him; for the hour of his judgment has come; and worship him who made heaven and earth, the sea, and the springs of water."

The *messenger* that was to return the sceptre, is that angel that John saw in the midst of heaven, having the everlasting gospel, to present to those that dwell on the earth. Rev. xiv, 6.

Now, the parable is true, and its interpretation certain.

EPISTLE OF ALEXANDER, THE COPPERSMITH,

TO ALL HIS FELLOW CRAFTSMEN THROUGHOUT WALES,

Showing the best way to oppose the "Latter-day Saints," and defend our crafts.

"RESPECTED" GENTLEMEN,—It is well known to you all, now, the remarkable success of the old Saints throughout our country, and that the people are running after them. You must also know that they are the worst enemies of our great goddess in this age and country, as before. And I understand a considerable amount of their trickery, since my fathers before me were famous and very successful in doing them harm, ever since the days of the old deceiver Paul and his followers, as he himself admits in his second epistle to his fellow heretic, Timothy, chap. iv, 14—"Alexander the coppersmith did me much evil," he says. And since I fear they will become too numerous for us to be able to subdue them, if we do not awaken against them quickly, and that there is no hope of seeing practically anyone returning having once swallowed their deceit,—these considerations, together with my duty to keep up the memory of my fathers and their honorable craft, compel me to address you through this epistle. You will remember the praiseworthy epistle of our renowned leader, Demetrius, who wrote from our meeting place in *Diana Square*; and doubtless you are troubled to hear through it of the failure of all the *schemes*, the plots, and the stories we invented against the Saints; and indeed, gentlemen, neither we, nor our zealous leader, nor our fellow craftsmen, are at fault for that, because you know that we have preached bravely from the pulpits, and proclaimed every invention in the publications; but, no matter what we do, they are flourishing everywhere. The people are at fault certainly, because they do not believe our stories, rather they listen for themselves; and as soon as they do that, farewell to them; before we see them again, they have been baptized by them, and are as zealous in the cause of their deceit as any one of them. And now, Oh brethren, what shall we do to them? It would not be any use for us to declare any of the old tricks, or fight them with the old weapons that were successful in the days of our fathers, because these old Saints, through some device or another, have come to know us too well for us to succeed further. And I am very pained to inform you that they have, in their cunning, come to understand all our most secret stratagems! Yes, they have got their hands on the eloquent epistle of our immortal Demetrius as well, for I read it in its entirety in their monthly publication, "*Prophet of the Jubilee*," for *October*, 1846, page 101; and so they rip the veil from the eyes of the people, so that they see us in our true colors! Oh, what shall we do? How did this happen? Pity you were not more secretive. There must be some "Achan" in our camp, and some traitor in our midst, surely. Search him out, and bring him before our commendable court quickly. I heard that some of our giants, and some of our high councilors, have fled to their side recently; is that possible? However, do not despair, for I have good news for you—a new way, an excellent way, yes, the best of the lot, to annihilate the Saints. We shall succeed now, surely. It is a way that has been greatly acclaimed in our meeting place also. (And for the sake of your lives, keep it *secret* from the Saints!) Our Assembly was held on the day after the last of the month of Ahithophel, in our main office on *Copper Street*, *Diana Square*, CARDIFF. A considerable number of our theological patriots came there on the praiseworthy occasion, to devise some plan to oppose the saints. Our chief apostle Demetrius was elected president, your obedient servant as vice president, and our revered trumpet, that is the clapper of our iron bell from Cardiff, as scribe. After various eloquent and heated lectures, and exhortations to carry on with our war until we conquer, the following was decided unanimously:—

1st. It was decided to change our method of warring with the Saints from now on, completely; not to persecute them in any way, nor talk about them, but to praise them; socialize with them, and admit that they are, at least, as good as we; and say that we are all going hand in hand to the top of the mountain, and that we shall all reach heaven, although there is a bit of difference in a few minor and insignificant matters. Speak fairly to their faces, because you know that we could never stand against them to their faces, and then what good is it gnashing teeth at them? We fervently exhort everyone who is in union with Demetrius's family, to behave as falsely and unanimously as possible, and lend a chapel to them every now and then to preach, until we have won their trust.

2nd. That the most highly regarded men, one from each craft, are to form a *committee*, such as our general from Dowlais, our *corporal* from Abercaniad, our *drum major* from Cardiff, and our *whipper-in* from Merthyr, &c. That they are to bring a *petition* before the committee of the "Evangelical Union," in their next *hodgepodge*, requesting that the Saints be allowed into the union like others (but for goodness's sake, keep this secret); and all of you are asked to *sign* the *petition* without hesitation, and to pray for its success, for it is certain that the success of our crafts depends on bringing them into this quandary. Do not utter a word against their miraculous gifts, nor anything else, for they will not give them up for the sake of coming to our numerous family. But once having got them into the Demetrian family, we shall make the best of these things. Shhh! be wise as serpents now. If they enjoy these things now, they will disappear as soon as this knot is tied between us. Let us take this forward, dear boys. Do you not remember that this is how my fathers caused the spiritual gifts formerly, and that power of God that was poisoning our crafts, to disappear from the apostolic church? The hotter the persecution the more they flourished; but the moment they persuaded Constantine the Great to take the reigns of their church, and to unite it with the state, the great and the rich and the whole lot flooded in, and turned the poor, lowly saints out of their jobs, gradually changing the ordinances, and losing all society with the Spirit of God, until it all conformed completely to our crafts; and it is wonderful how clever our fathers were in closing up the great gap, lest the people notice the lack of the spiritual gifts afterwards, by asserting "that they were not needed any longer." That is a smart device, and that saying continues to this day, with no one but the troublesome saints daring to say otherwise; but shh! do not give into tricks, or the cat will be out of the bag again.

3rd. It was decided to send an epistle to our dear brother Havard, to warn him not to take that *petition* any further from house to house along the roads of Lacharn, to prove that the Saints are those "false prophets" that the scripture says are to come in the last days, nor to try to get people to *sign* that they will not listen to them when they come there. We are glad to see our Calvinist brothers waking from their slumber to join this good work; for indeed they are further behind in this than others, although not as indifferent as the Wesleyans either in helping us against these mighty enemies, for they, like their father Wesley of old, are too generous and innocent to persecute anyone, whoever it may be. Some of the great ones of the assembly judged that the *petition* of their brother Havard was an excellent device, and worthy of emulation, and that he deserved praise for his zeal and faithfulness; but no matter what, the effect it had on the people afterwards was completely the opposite, like every previous device; the people were not satisfied without hearing them for themselves. There was also considerable pleading as to who this Havard is. Some insisted that he was the one whose mother kept the old "Elian's

Fountain!" while others did not know; but it was agreed to warn him and everyone else not to do anything of the sort until we see the effect of our *petition* in the Evangelical Alliance. The attack of the Methodist Treasury on the Saints was also condemned. It is so foolish, accusing them of "professing perfection of persons!" Every lad who knows anything about the Saints knows that that is a completely false accusation; and then, what good is it to our cause to be so foolish as to tell such obvious lies against them? That is how the people find our weakness, and leave us. Be clever, be valiant and brave, and we shall preach at the funeral of the Saints before long, bringing peace throughout our country, and success to our crafts as before; and may the Spirit of our zealous fathers' God support us against this troublesome people who are trying to turn the world upside down, and bring disgrace and bareness to our great goddess, is our prayer, Amen.

I am, your zealous fellow craftsman,

ALEXANDER, JR., THE COPPERSMITH.

Main College, corner of Copper Silver Street, near Diana Square, Great Cardiff.

THE LATTER-DAY SAINTS *VERSUS* SECTARIANS.

OFTEN it is asked of us, "What is the difference between you and the other sects in Wales?" We answer simply, that it is exactly the same as the difference between the sects and the holy scripture! But to be plainer still, we state that is it too great a task for us to find space or time to show the difference among the various sects; consequently, the easiest way to show the difference is to show what we believe to be the first principles of the gospel, and allow the reader to compare them with the creeds of the sects, and then form his own opinion that would hold sway in the scales of truth.

We believe that the gospel of our Lord Jesus Christ is the "power of God unto salvation," and that it has an influence on the mind of man today, as it did eighteen hundred years ago. That it is essential for one to have the right or the authority, and a divine mission from God, and receive it through a better medium than paper and ink, in order to preach "the word of life" and to properly administer the ordinances of the gospel (as it was with the apostles), before we can be saved, or become members in the church of Jesus Christ, "which is the column and foundation of truth", through which we are perfected, sanctified, and prepared to inherit a fulness of the blessings of heaven, a part in the adoption, that is the redemption of the body, and to be able to reign with our blessed Jesus on the restored earth, when the King of kings shall come, and his angelic host with him, and after which we can be forever with the Lord.

What we utterly fail to believe, yes, even though the claim is made by all the sects of the world, is that it is possible for us to receive the gospel in its purity and its saving power from anyone, without their having been authorized by God, that is their having received the ministry of the covenant, or in other words having received a dispensation unto themselves from God, as Aaron received; and we believe that they need to be sent in behalf of, or in the name or authority of Jesus Christ, which authority is considered in the scriptures as priesthood. You may be angry or not; but we cannot believe this no matter how hard we try, and that because the claim offers not a grain of reason or scripture as a foundation on which our faith can act; and we must admit that we are too stubborn to believe a single thing in this world, or in the next world, without a sufficient foundation on which to hang our faith; and the required foundation is the true testimony of those who know the thing; and if that testimony is not logical and scriptural, it cannot be truthful, and thus please excuse the Saints because of their inability to believe.

However, we can easily believe that there is the same animosity in the hearts of the human race now, against God and his gospel, as there was in the time of Jesus Christ, and that the idea of the flesh is just as hostile to the order of God now as when the apostle declared it. We also believe that it is as necessary for God the Father, Jesus Christ, together with the Holy Ghost, to act now for the salvation of men, as it was for them in the days of Peter, Paul, and others; and consequently, that the duty of man is similar now, that there is need for similar endeavors, obedience to the same order, with faithfulness throughout, in our days, before we can arrive at the same "goal" by running the same "race." Since we believe this, we are different from those who go about teaching, for commandments, the traditions of men, professing "a form of godliness, but denying the power thereof;" and out of love for them, in an attempt to convince them, we say as did John of old, "If there come any unto you, and bring not the doctrine of Christ, he hath neither the Father nor the Son," &c.; or as Paul says, "Though we, yea, though an angel from heaven, preach any other gospel unto you than that which we have preached unto you, let him be accursed;" and because of this the sectarians are offended greatly by us, and with many excuses they move sideways as far as they can from us, and then they shout, "Oh look, there is a great difference between us and the Saints." That is exactly what the sectarians of the first century said against the same religion. But if anyone comes to us preaching the pure gospel, the one which is the power of God, he will offer it in its original power, promising (if he knows that he is a servant of God) a promise to his listeners of "*the gift of the Holy Ghost*,"now as before, on the following conditions:—

1. Faith in Jesus Christ, and his revealed word, that he is the Son of God, and a sufficient Redeemer for sinners. To believe in Christ is a task no more difficult than the sufficient testimony that is heard about him; thus, what keeps you from believing a word just as true about him, when the word of untruthful men is frequently believed? It is an easy thing to believe in Christ, and a reasonable thing as well, but not any easier than it is to obey his commandments after believing his truth, and the importance of them—after believing that Christ is a Redeemer, and you a sinner; then, as a sinner it is easy to repent of your sins against your merciful Redeemer, that is to determine between you and God, in the name of your redeemer, to be a subject of his government from then on: furthermore, this is a task of fewer than five minutes. Then the next thing is to fulfill that promise or that oath, and the first step toward the water is the first to that, without which it is impossible to fulfill, and then come to make the covenant binding which you promised on your word. "Be baptized, and wash away your sins." And yet one more thing this time, I say to you, if your motives are pure, by the laying on of

hands of the servants of the living God you will receive *the gift of the Holy Ghost* from God as before, which will work powerfully in you and through you, to sanctify you and to lead you in the center of the light; and he will impart to you heavenly gifts in his own time, and that as soon as they will benefit you, such as *the spirit of prophecy*, *tongues*, *interpretation*, *the gift of healing*, *discerning of spirits*, *revelations*, or any other gifts, for it is *He* who "divides to every man [on these conditions] severally, as he will;" yes, it is he who knows best.

Now, reader, you see already that there is considerable difference between us and the sectarians, yes, more than anyone thinks; but we pray you, what difference do you see between this and the scriptures? If any, we wish to know what it is. If none, the choice is life and goodness. If you doubt the truth of the tales of the country against us, come and see: *there is a welcome for everyone*; yes, put us to the test honestly and thoroughly, and if you can find deceit, show it to me, for the sake of my soul, and I shall leave it then and there. *Come and see, then, before it is too late ! !*

MERTHYR TYDFIL CONFERENCE.

On the first Sunday and Monday of January, a Conference was held by the Saints in the Cymreigyddion Hall, in the above town. The meeting started at half past ten, through singing praises and praying as usual. Then Captain D. Jones addressed the listeners warmly on the occasion, and he opened the conference by proposing that brother John Taylor (one of the apostles who came over from America recently) be the president. He said that he was very glad to have the honor of making them acquainted with Mr. Taylor, in Wales for the first time for him or any other apostle to visit our country—that his thoughts on this occasion, were being transported over the depths of the Atlantic Ocean to the far corners of the western land where he worked together with Mr. Taylor for years in this work—to the persecutions, together with the pleasure and the blessings they received together there; he had the honor of being a fellow prisoner with him for the gospel of Jesus Christ and for the testimony of Jesus, whom they preached together from the jail to thousands of their persecutors; and he was not far from him when four bullets were shot into his body. His thoughts and his desire ran quickly at that time toward the land of his ancestors, thinking of the time when he would be able to see his brothers and his sisters of the same blood after their having obeyed this eternal gospel, and in a conference in the hills of Wales, rejoicing together under the guidance of the Holy Ghost, and that today his expectations had been exceeded by the presence of this our brother. He rejoiced with the listeners, because this happy day had come to them, and he expected all to pray with him for the presence of our God to be with us throughout the conference. The proposal received unanimous approval.

Then Mr. Taylor took the chair, and he addressed the conference briefly and succinctly. He had joy in meeting with so many brothers and sisters in the Lord in a foreign land, and although they were not of the same language, they were under the guidance of the same Spirit, bound together in the same eternal covenant, and traveling together on our spiritual course toward the same western paradise, where we shall all better understand one another, when the pure tongue is restored to everyone, we shall all according to our faithfulness meet together in Zion, around the table of our God, to sing the song of Moses and the sweet song of the Lamb for over a thousand years, without worry, pain or sorrow. He earnestly beseeched the God of the Saints to bless his children in Wales with more of his Spirit to keep them in the unity of the faith, love, and joy;—that his heart was full of blessings, and that he will bless every man who is honest of heart. After that he requested that brother Jones carry on with the matters of the conference in Welsh, which was done as follows:

Glamorganshire Conference—Number of branches, 30; elders, 28; priests, 50; teachers, 25; deacons, 19; baptized since the last conference, which was held here July 12, 287; total membership 841. Monmouth Conference—branches, 8; elders, 6; priests, 11; teachers, 10; deacons, 3; baptized since the previous conference, 54; total membership 138. The total for these two conferences is—Branches, 38; elders, 34; priests, 61; teachers, 35; deacons, 22; baptized in the last five months, 341; members, 979. The following persons were called as elders:—Daniel Evans, Hirwaun; William Jenkins, Cardiff; William Hughes, Merthyr; Samuel Evans, Clwydyfagwyr; Thomas Hughes, Machynlleth; William Clark, Harlech; David Roberts, Ffestiniog; Richard Griffiths, Rhosllanerchrugog; William Evans, Dihewyd; Samuel Morris, Merthyr; Joseph Davies, Aberdare. Also called were 15 priests, 17 teachers, and five deacons; the president ended the morning session with prayer.

In the afternoon session the holy supper was administered to a large crowd; afterwards brother Taylor, and brother Webb from Bristol sang songs which they had composed in praise to God for the occasion. Then the president addressed the Saints warmly in relation to their great privileges, and their responsibilities to live more proper, spotless, and godly lives than everyone else, and to take heed not to sadden the pure spirit of God, but to nurture it through prayer and faithfulness in the appointed practice and manner, and keeping all the commandments of Jesus Christ—to be careful to nurture brotherly love in the unity of the faith, &c. He explained in an excellent manner the purposes, the great importance, and the usefulness of this holy ordinance; and he closed the meeting by praying to God to bless his Saints, &c.

In the evening, Mr. Taylor preached the gospel in his zealous and warm and clear manner, by drawing to the crowd's attention new and old treasures, on which they feasted (judging by their cheerful appearance, and their attentive listening) with relish and great eagerness. He was followed by Capt. Jones, with a short and warm oration, suitable to the occasion, with sincere and persuasive invitations for the listeners to come in to the kingdom of God (those who had not yet obeyed the gospel), so they would have the spirit of adoption to guide them to all truth, to testify to them the truthfulness of our heavenly call, so they would be sanctified and prepared to inherit the glory of the Saints in the light, &c.

Monday, three meetings were held, in which the splendor and great importance of the various church offices were shown, the responsibilities of the officers and the Saints, together with their privileges, and the hope that has been set before them. Many of the officers who had been called (and who were present), were ordained by the president and brother Jones, in English and in Welsh.

In the evening, the president bade farewell to the large crowd with a short and comprehensive address, which no doubt lodged itself in the hearts of the Saints. He left his blessing with them, with the expectation that they would meet again in Zion, after coming out of the great affliction, and their garments having been made white by the blood of the Lamb. He said he would like to have stayed with them longer, but that he had to make great haste to call on other conferences in England, &c.; he had come about seven thousand miles lately, to visit with the Saints; that he had left his family with the Saints who had been exiled from Nauvoo, in the middle of the western desert, hundreds of miles from white people; that the savages of the forest were behaving in a more loving and Christian way toward them than many of the professed Christians [! !] and that he was about to sail from England in a few days toward America, to join with his family and the Saints by the time their camp began its move toward California. He was pleased to see so many of the Welsh who had obeyed, and who were happily enjoying the privileges and gifts of the fulness of the gospel; and he expected that shortly thousands who were honest in principle would come into the church of Christ yet, &c. It was easy to detect the love nurtured in the hearts of the Saints toward him, and the benefit they received, through their cheerfulness, and the welcome he had received from everyone. He blessed them again, and left on the *railroad train* to Cardiff.

Thus ended the most well attended, the sweetest, the most worshipful, and the most edifying conference, that we have ever had in Wales; and we think, judging from the hosts of the world who came there, from their attentive listening, from their cheerfulness, and their courtesy through it all, that they received great light and happiness, and from the readiness of the admissions old persecutors were sorry for having believed the false accusations of the preachers and the writers for so long; they saw now that it was all lies of wicked men, and they admitted that God was no doubt in our midst, and several said that they would be in our midst before long ! And certainly all principled men who love the truth and who wish to have it from all the committed and the uncommitted, would say the same, if they were to listen for themselves, instead of believing the false witness of our persecutors; and the gracious Lord, whose work this is, will cause it to be so, for their benefit, and for the glory of his name, Amen.

William Davies,
Edward Edwards, } *Scribes.*

N.B. It would be too long to give a report of the excellent sermons of brother Taylor here, although it would be desirable for the Saints to have them. We know, under the blessing of God, that they have benefitted and have given great knowledge to those who heard them, for the fruit is beginning to spring forth already; and although only nine were baptized in the following two days in Merthyr, we hear that several have obeyed the gospel already, and that the nine who were received in the first meeting after the Conference are only the first fruits of an abundant harvest of valuable souls who are about to come to the kingdom of God. I hope those prophets who prophesied from chapel to chapel of the death of Mormonism, some within six months, others before the end of the year, &c., will read these accounts, and ask themselves which sect among them has experienced a similar increase in the same time! Let them, and the preachers and authors who are preaching the funeral sermon of Mormonism, contemplate a bit until she has died, for up to now she is not even sick, nor is there any likelihood of that either! I wonder if by now they will confess that it is they who are the "false prophets of the latter days?" But whatever they do it makes no difference, for "by their fruits shall they be known" after all. It is useless for them to shout *false prophets* at the Saints, in order to blind the people, when their own prophecies prove so clearly as Nathan said to David, "*Thou art the man.*" But go on, you poor wretches; vomit out your desires, and the wickedness of your hearts, through prophecies; we shall go forth, preaching the gospel, to save souls, until, through the power of our God, our country will be filled with knowledge from God through "Mormonism," and all those whom you have deluded will hear her, and they will be released from their tiresome bondage to the glorious freedom of the children of God; their shackles will be broken, and their heavy burdens, and their taxes and excessive loads, to maintain the great sectarian goddess of this age, will be cast down. Soon the light of the Jubilee will banish their names and their priesthood from our country.

MISCELLANEOUS.

THE PLAGUE.—The newspapers of England tell us that the plague called the *Cholera Morbus* is fast approaching Europe, and we fear that the consequences will be dreadful.

COMFORT OF THE SAINTS.

WE LAUD our privileges, O united brethren;
And we sing songs joyfully each one:
It is lovely to journey in unity and peace,
Along the wilderness to Zion and her feast.

Despite the crosses we bear now,
O let us not be disheartened—the reward is great;
Let us lift up our heads, relief is nigh—
Our course will end in peace ere long.

The sun, the moon, and the stars will be darkened,—
All the powers of heaven will be shaken, by God;
But this will be a sign to the faithful throughout the world,
That soon the Lord will come to gather them together.

How sweet is the thought of living without pain,
In a land without affliction, in the presence of the Lamb:
The *thought* is pleasant, but better is the *enjoyment*;
A thousand times better is the *possessing*, than the *talking* about the land.

If the bliss is so great, what ought we to be?
Keen or complacent, to reach the goal?
Let us strive bravely—God gives strength—
If faithful we strive, the striving becomes reward. J. D.

WAR IN NAUVOO AGAIN.—We are informed through additional effects, and even more grievous, of the matchless madness, and of the inhuman cruelty of the rioters who live in the environs of this city. Almost all the Saints had left Nauvoo before the start of this riot, and the Americans from various states had purchased their possessions, although at their own price, and were inhabiting them, and the few remnants of the old inhabitants (that is the Saints) were about to leave. But it is seen that the enmity continues, and the opposition increases more and more against the latest inhabitants, and that because the *mobs* are losing their purpose, losing the prize they expected from the beginning, that is to get those fair inheritances through violence, and possess them themselves. A letter from our friend Joseph A. Stratton, of St. Louis, informs us that because of the election of some man by the name of Carlin to the office of peacekeeper, that this war began. This peacekeeper, together with a large number of rioters, went to Nauvoo, under the pretense of seeking one Pricket as a prisoner, but their objective was to plunder and destroy the city. Within a few days Carlin had gathered about 700 armed men in Carthage, and he put them under the leadership of Colonels Singleton, Chittendon, and others. Finally, after much fuss, they were sent to the inhabitants of Nauvoo, to inform them they had better yield to the rioters, that they were too strong for them: or if they wished to fight, a man should be placed to lead them. The rioters came nearer, and they camped within three quarters of a mile where the defenders of the city waited, and after shooting some number of balls without much effect, the rioters retreated. The rioters numbered about 800 now, but those on the side of Nauvoo were only about 300 without many weapons. The next day there was another battle, and the rioters were forced to flee, leaving fifteen of their number dead on the field, and among them General Smith. Only one of the people of Nauvoo was injured. The fighting continued the next two days also, but the same ones kept the upper hand. But the fifth day a number of armed men landed in the place, to decide amongst themselves without further loss of blood; and the decision was reached—that all the Saints and inhabitants of Nauvoo give their arms to the rioters, and flee from the state within five days. And so it was; the Saints, poor things, left completely, and left many of their possessions behind.

THE SIGNS FOLLOW THE BAPTISTS!—A few days ago, one Mr. W——, a respected minister with the Baptists, not a hundred miles from Llanybydder, was heard testifying in the presence of several that the signs mentioned in the commission, followed in his church. He said they cast out devils, through which wicked men became good men; that they spoke in new tongues, through which many who were ungodly came to pray; and that they healed the sick, through his laying on his own hands on the heads of his children whenever they complain, and this took them to their place immediately!!!

POPERY.—There is not a week that goes by that we do not hear of some of the priests of the Church of England turning over to the old mother church; and no less often young preachers of the nonconformist sects turning to the Church of England. This, together with a multitude of other things, leads us to think that that time is near, when it will not be permitted for anyone to buy and sell without the mark of the beast on his forehead.

CONTENTS.

MERTHYR TYDFIL:

PUBLISHED AND FOR SALE BY D. JONES, AND ALSO FOR SALE BY THE SAINTS IN GENERAL.

JOHN JONES, PRINTER, RHYDYBONT.

PROPHET OF THE JUBILEE,

OR

STAR OF THE SAINTS.

No. 8.] FEBRUARY, 1847. [Price 2*c.*

FAITH.

Since it is upon this strong axis, namely *faith*, that even the first and most excellent principle of the revealed religion is founded, and every stone of that heavenly city, "the architect and builder of which is God," has been built above upon this, it is beneficial for us to research into this precious principle, to properly understand it, and to increase in it, which we will do as well as we can, beginning according to that which Paul says in Heb. xi: 1:—"Now faith is the substance of things hoped for, and the evidence of things not seen."

What is faith? ask several. Well, here is a very clear answer, namely, that it is that principle which assures or testifies to its possessor the existence of things, places, or persons, besides those that his eyes have seen. When another is heard relating the story of things he has seen, or that he has heard another say, man is of such a composition that he will believe or disbelieve that story to the degree he considers it worthy of his attention. Well, without faith it would be impossible for him to believe or disbelieve; for the innate faculty that is brought into operation by the testimony of someone else, of necessity gives its verdict of acceptance, or of condemnation, of everything it considers. The fact that man believes anything, is proof that he possesses such a faculty; and his dealing with the one thing, is sufficient proof that he can believe the other thing, yes, everything he wishes; or then, if he cannot, his Creator has not given him control over his own powers, which leads to even worse confusion, and makes man a powerless and irresponsible machine. Many in our country say they cannot believe such a thing, when they cannot show one reason why, except that they have no faith. It is obvious that those people do not know themselves, nor can they understand what faith is. It is not possible that one reasoning creature can be without faith, without proving a great defect in his composition! Except that a man have faith, his ears and his tongue would be of no use, for the purpose of the Creator in creating the one and the other, and arranging them so conveniently, is, so that one can hear the testimony of the other; and what use is it to hear that, if it cannot be believed? and how can it be believed, except that such have faith? Perhaps some oppose this, from what the apostle said, "For all men have not faith." But we would answer him through the words of an apostle that are just as true—"Giving faith to every man," &c. How can that be, without contradicting each other? I shall answer the last, that the one way through which God has given faith to every man, is, through his endowing him with that innate faculty which is brought into action as a result of believing; and after that, he sends his servants to proclaim "good news," the sound of the words of those who are effective in bringing that faculty into action, if given fairness. This shows how reasonable it is for Christ to send his servants. "Go and preach," says he. "Those who believe in me through your *speech*." Paul says that "faith comes through *hearing* the word of God." Also, "Because our *testimony* among you was believed," says Paul. Again, "It pleased God by the foolishness of *preaching*, to save them that believe." "And he that believeth not is condemned."

The failure to believe how, and to which place, or from which place faith comes when heard, is the cause of the different opinions on this subject, we would suppose. We prove in this way, that it does not come directly from God to the unbelievers. Yet, Paul says that faith *comes*. Does it not come out of the listeners, in its effects, as streams from a fountain? Reasonable enough; and the cause of its flooding over its banks, is the agitation of the source (the innate faculty) through the testimony of the speaker. The fruits of faith are obedience; and without that, it is foolishness for anyone to claim that he has faith, "for faith without works, is dead."

Another way that God has given faith to all to be saved, is, through organizing a way for that, by placing a middleman as an equity, and by sending others to invite everyone to believe in that equity; or, in other words, he laid the foundation for his faith to work, or to give birth to obedience. On the other hand, not all those pagan nations to which Paul referred had faith, for they did not bear the fruits of true faith, namely the spiritual gifts, godliness, &c. If it is not like this, it must be that a new faculty is created in man when he believes; and if a faculty is created when he believes in one thing, why is there not an additional one created for everything he believes? It is obvious that it is man's duty to believe in Christ; proof that a righteous judge may, or that he may not, punish him for not believing. If he does, he has that faculty of faith. And furthermore it is useless for anyone to excuse himself in that way. "I cannot believe," is a contradiction; "I choose not to believe," is what such a person means. Not only does man possess faith, but it is impossible for him to do anything temporal, or spiritual, except it be the effects of faith. Yes, I say, faith is the provacative and original cause of every act, and of every effort. Without faith, the body and the mind would lie *dormant*. Consider, reader, what caused your infant attempts to walk, and to quarrel with your playmates? Why did you try to learn in school, unless you believed that you would become a reader, then a writer; after that you made more and more effort to be a good scholar; and after that, onward from degree to degree in knowledge. What motivated everything, yes, every movement, but faith, namely *believing that you could*? What causes a man to leave the land of his birth, his relatives, and everything, to cross the Atlantic Ocean, in a small ship, towards the distant west, except the certainty that he has from a testimony, of the existence of America, perhaps, and believing also that he is in a better country, and that he will arrive there to enjoy it? Well, if he did not believe that, he would make no effort to reach it. Would the farmer throw his wheat so carelessly upon the face of the land, unless he believed that he would have it returned a hundredfold in the harvest? Oh, no, he would take his seed to market instead, where he knows he could receive payment for it. Who would send a costly ship, with its cargo, and its sailors, among angry waves of the *Indian Ocean*, unless he believed that he would return with a great increase? Who would work a day for his fellowman for wages, if he did not have faith that the other would pay him his wages? Who would pay to plant a vineyard, unless he expected to eat its fruit? No one; the cause of this faith in these circumstances is, through practice from age to age; and the first cause was, because of the command of the Chief-president of the elements to do such and such, and such and such would be the consequences, and so it was, and so it will be; and the promise of this indissoluble connection between cause and effect, is the basis of faith, in spiritual things as well as in temporal things. This is the secret of what Jesus Christ said—"He that believeth and is baptized shall be saved," Mark xvi, 16. Just as we receive all our temporal things by putting our faith into action, so also all our spiritual blessings are enjoyed through faithful efforts in the righteous practices and the appointed methods, and no other methods, for the promise has not been linked to any others; thus faith cannot possibly exist except it be based on the promise, for "faith is the substance of things hoped for," and "hope that is seen is not hope;" thus it is seen that every man has the ability to believe in himself, and the logic evident to him from the testimony he hears from another, or that he may read, is what stirs his faith to action, and the action, from this principle, is worthy of the effect, and that because of the connection, or the promise given of that. This is the reason why the sick receive health, namely through the faithful use of the means that were organized for that purpose. This is how they enjoyed the spiritual gifts, yes, every promised blessing, as they performed their duties; and through continuing to obey faithfully the divine instructions, they shall enjoy eternal life.

Again, *Faith* is, not only the motivating principle of every movement, but the power, or the strength through which every act in heaven and on earth is fulfilled. Paul proves this in Heb. xi, 3, "Through faith we understand that the worlds were framed by the word of God," &c. The reason that God said the word "Let," was, because he knew that it would be according to his request, and that because of his omniscience concerning the laws of all the elements; and to the extent that men attain any knowledge, their ability extends to fulfill (through the use of the means that he commanded) their objectives, yes, even that which is considered to be *miracles* in the opinion of the unbelievers, namely through their unshakeable faith prompting them to action, and the fact will make obvious the faith of man, and the power and faithfulness of God according to his *promise*. Neither unbelievers, nor the disobedient, can use faith to carry out the act, because they do not have the *promise*.

It is obvious, that because of the faith that God possessed he was able to organize the shapeless and empty *chaos*, of every good and evil, to be a paradise so beautiful and desirable, that her creator said, "Behold it is good." Through his faith he placed her on her axes, and they support her until the present day; and through his faith he perfects her and her fulness. And thus, to a corresponding extent he perfects the faith of all her reasonable inhabitants that obey him, for the glory of his name and their benefit.

To this Jesus Christ himself testifies, in Matt. xvii, 20, when his disciples asked him why they could not cast the devil from that man; he answered, "Because of your unbelief; for verily I say unto you, if ye have faith as a grain of mustard seed, ye shall say unto this mountain, Remove hence to yonder place, and it shall remove; and *nothing shall be impossible unto you*." Here it is seen, when the sufferer is not able to have faith, for lack of reason to believe, that that is required not only in the one who ministers, but in the observers also; for Jesus chastised the latter because of the deficiency; see v. 17, "O faithless and perverse *generation*, how long shall I be with you?" In a similar fashion to this all the inspired writers testify, and they teach the same principle to their contemporaries. "By faith Abel offered unto God a more excellent sacrifice than Cain, by which he obtained *witness* that he was righteous, God testifying of his gifts." He had faith to believe that God had commanded that; and on that foundation he obeyed. "By faith was Enoch translated, that he should not see death." "Before his translation he had this *testimony* [through his faith], that he pleased God." "By faith Noah, being warned of God of things not seen as yet [he believed on his word, and behold the act, namely], he prepared an ark to the saving of his house." By faith Abraham offered Isaac; he believed God, and it was counted [his obedience, namely the act of his belief] to him as righteousness. Had he disobeyed, he would have been condemned, even though he believed. By faith they passed through the Red Sea, the walls of Jericho fell down, the sun and the moon stood still at the command of Joshua, yes, and what more shall I say? For the time would fail me to tell of Gideon, and of Barak, and of Samson, and of Jephthah, of David also, and Samuel, and of the prophets, who through faith subdued kingdoms, wrought righteousness [namely obedience to God], and obtained promises, and stopped the mouths of lions, quenched the violence of fire, escaped the edge of the sword, out of weakness were made strong, waxed valiant in fight, turned to flight the armies of the foreigners. Women received their dead raised to life again; and others were tortured, not accepting deliverance, that they might obtain a better resurrection. It is said that all these things were done through faith.

Had it not been for Joshua's faith, he could have spoken to the sun until his tongue stuck to his palate, and on would go the sun as usual; and except for Joshua's understanding about the laws that governed such things, and their connection with the promise, it would have been impossible for him to get a sufficient foundation for his faith. Faith, then is the agitating principle for every movement, namely the power that fulfills every act. Faith is a required principle that is woven in all things, to a greater or lesser extent; yes, without faith, it is impossible to please God; and thus, let us seek knowledge for its foundations, that it might increase more and more. Let us have sufficient faith to obey the commandments of God, believing in his promises steadfastly; for he who doubts is like a wave of the sea, which is thrown and scattered by the wind. Let not such a one expect that he will receive anything from God.

It is so unreasonable and contradictory for the religionists to condemn the Saints for presumption, for they say that they have received approval before God, when, in fact, the Bible does not give us the story of any saint who is destitute of the necessary degree of faith to receive such a witness! "And these all, *having obtained a witness* through *faith*, received not the promise." The key of the mystery of sectarianism, and the axis that binds its associates to its altars, to grope in the darkness like the blind man for the wall, is the lack of faith to receive such a witness from him that they are his children, which proves their impoverishment of the Spirit that co-testifies with the spirit of the saints, through obvious facts, that they are children of God; and this deficiency is caused because the servants of God did not lay their hands upon them for that purpose, and that because they were not baptized for the remission of their sins, and that because they did not request them to do so, bringing forth fruits worthy of repentance; and they did not do that, because they have no faith, or, rather, insufficient faith to show it in deed, namely by walking to the water. And thus it is seen that this principle, namely faith, is a complete remedy, its beginning and its end meeting together, the motivating cause of the first movement, and the acting force to the last hour. Only he that continues in the faith to the end will be saved.

ELDER

Is one of the lesser offices of the Melchizedek priesthood. Apostle is another office in the same priesthood; every apostle is an elder, (2 John i; 3 John i; 1 Peter v, 1;) but an elder is not an apostle; before any man may have this office, he must have come through the door in an orderly fashion, and governed himself as such until he is called through the Spirit of God. See Acts xiii, 2, 3; and after that he is not in the office until he is ordained by some one, or more, who received this office earlier. Tit. i, 5. It is difficult for a man to present to another that which he does not himself possess. A stream cannot run higher than its source. A traveling elder has the right to ordain elders, if he is not within the boundaries of some conference; or if he is, he must do that in an assembly of the conference, Acts xiv, 23; 1 Tim. iv, 14, and then it is expected, that if anyone has anything against him, he must make it known immediately, or forever afterwards not utter a word; he who is called must stand before the church to testify of the hope that he has of his worthiness of the office. The duties of the elders are as follows:—"Baptize, ordain elders, priests, teachers, and deacons, and administer the bread and the cup—the symbolic emblems of the breaking of the flesh and spilling of the blood of Jesus Christ—and *confirm* those who have been baptized in the church, through the laying on of hands, for them to receive the baptism of the Holy Ghost and of fire, according to the scriptures. [1 Peter v, 2, 3, 4, 5]. Also to preach, expound, explain, exhort, and baptize, and watch over the church; together with confirming the church through the laying on of hands to receive the Holy Ghost, and to preside over all meetings." 1 Tim. v, 17 .

"The elders are to conduct the meetings as they are led by the Holy Ghost, [Acts xiii, 4], according to the commandments and revelations of God." *Doct. and Cov.*

Another duty that pertains to this office is, to go to the Saints who are ill, and anoint them with the consecrated oil if they ask him, and lay on hands and pray for the Lord to heal them. See James v, 14. "Is any sick among you? let him call [the duty of the sick person is to call] for the elders of the church; and let them pray over him [then it is not they, but God, as they administer the ordinances, who gives health], anointing him with oil in the name of the Lord, (15). And the prayer of faith shall save the sick, and the *Lord* shall raise him up [from his bed of affliction], and if he have committed sins [after receiving forgiveness of previous ones through baptism], they shall be forgiven him." The blessing will not be accepted every time, nor indeed any time if they are guilty of sins, namely transgressions of the laws of the church, and are trying to conceal them; the elder should take care that this not be an obstacle to the sick person in receiving health; for "he that covereth his sins shall not prosper." Therefore, "confess your faults one to another," says Paul, "and pray one for another, that ye may be healed. The effectual fervent prayer of a righteous man availeth much."

It is a transgression among elders to refuse to do this, and the sick person who neglects this firm commandment, sins against him who gave it. The one and the other must have faith; and indeed how can they do less, since the promise on these conditions is unique; for he who promised the blessing is faithful. It is he who imparts the time he wishes, but not without obeying; the instrument is nothing but the office which binds in heaven and on earth the knot on this rope of three yarns.

We thank God for such an honor and privilege; we conform every time and in all things, so that we will be enveloped with the spirit of our offices, praying always with every prayer and plea in the Holy Ghost, so that we may be temples fit for the spirit of our offices to dwell within us continually.

The office of elder is a very important and glorious one. He is the shepherd of Jesus's flock: under his care he entrusts his lambs; and the Chief shepherd expects his flock from his hand when he comes to his main fold, when there will be but one shepherd and one fold. He should be watchful over them, loving them as Christ loves them; and with all his strength feed them with the guileless milk of the word, so that they may increase in the most holy faith, so that they may understand the wiles of the devil and his wolves, that they may recognize and follow the voice of their shepherd, that they may have victory over all the temptations of perdition—so that all may be led to work together to perfect his flock. Dear brethren, look therefore upon yourselves, and upon all the flock, upon that which the Holy Ghost has placed you as overseers, to shepherd the church of God, which he purchased with his own blood.

No accusation of any transgression against this office will be accepted except from two or three witnesses, which are in the church, but not from the world; neither will the accusation be accepted from anyone except before a council of the elders; yet, if a brother or a sister sees an elder in transgression, it is their duty to go to him themselves. If they utter a word to others first, they are transgressors. It is better to refrain from saying a word to another about his transgression, unless it derives out of love towards, or from a desire to benefit such, otherwise there is danger of making the divisions even greater: but more on this in "rules of discipline."

Frequently we are told that no one has the right to lay on hands for giving the Holy Ghost, except for the apostles. I asked one who hung his argument on this hook, whether that Ananias who laid his hands on Paul for him to receive the Holy Ghost, was an apostle? (see Acts ix, 12, 17); and he became mute!

All the elders should meet together in the conferences to organize properly all the matters of the churches. There they shall receive certificates to prove that they hold the office; and no one shall be accepted as such, without such evidence signed by the president. Let everyone make sure of this!

Now, elders of the Latter-day Saints, you know your circuits; remember that it is to you that this grace has been entrusted, the stewardship of the "eleventh hour"—the keys of salvation of your contemporaries—"the ministry of the covenant"—namely this treasure in clay vessels, that has been given to you by God, who has called you with a holy calling, not according to your works, but according to his own purpose and his grace. Preach this form of doctrine that has been given to you by the holy apostles; be instant in season, and out of season; convince, reprove, exhort with all long-suffering and doctrine; do not dispute about words, something that is beneficial only to overwhelm listeners; be diligent and honest workers, properly imparting the word of truth. Beware of foolish and unlearned questions, for they give rise to disputations, and a servant of the Lord should not dispute, but is to be courteous to everyone, edifying, patient; in meekness teaching those who oppose, to see that God may give them some time for repentance to recognize the truths you teach, so they may come to righteousness out of the snare of the devil. Put on the girdle of love, persuade even your enemies, while knowing the love of Christ, who when reviled, did not revile in return: pull them along with the cords of love. You know that you have received part in the dispensation of the fulness of times, in which all things will be gathered together in Jesus Christ. You are the ones he has sent to the high roads and the fields, to persuade all to come in to the feast. Oh, persuade honestly, before closing the door: consider the worth of souls, the privilege you received of coming in yourselves, and may the loss and the danger of being outside prompt you to diligence. It is better to be without the office (the talent), than to hide it after receiving it. Remember the fate of the one who misused the "one talent:" he was thrown into outer darkness. How, then, was the one dealt with who neglected the "five talents?" Remember these things always, teaching your flock to deny ungodliness and worldly appetites, and to live soberly, and justly, and devoutly, in the world that is now; waiting for the blessed hope, and the appearance of the glory of the mighty God, and our Lord Jesus Christ; so that you may be able to give your accounting joyfully, and hear the invitation, "Well done, thou good and faithful servant; thou has been faithful over a few things, I will make thee ruler over many things; enter thou into the joy of thy Lord." Until then, brethren, these things speak, counsel, and persuade, according to the power and authority of your office, trusting in him who has entrusted your offices to you for the necessary qualifications to fulfill them. Since God is on our side, it matters not who is against us; from him is our sufficiency. Watch and pray, so that he who initiated this good work in us may finish it in the day of Jesus Christ, when those who turn many to righteousness will shine like the stars of heaven forever in glory, so that we may say to the Lord of the harvest, Here am I with my sheaves gathered into the barn, and to the Chief shepherd, Here am I with the flock thou gavest me to watch over—I lost not one. This is our privilege and our duty. May the Spirit of God strengthen us to fulfill it.

"DEFENSE OF THE MORMONS."

THE FOLLOWING is a copy of that which was sent, under the above name, to the *Congregational Treasury*, which is published by the Rev. J. T. Jones, in Carmarthen:—

MR. EDITOR,—Since you published, in the June issue of the *Treasury*, an article by one Didymus ab Gwilym, the truth of which is testified to by Thos. Hopkins and Evan Davies from Ystradgynlais, containing that which they named "Profession of Faith of the Mormons;" I hope that the same medium will continue to be as "Independent" as to allow me, in behalf of the "Mormons," as they are called, to inform your readers that we do not believe such things as that "profession" contains. There is nothing except one tenth of that, that is not considered by us as erroneous; and I shall say, having had greater opportunities than anyone we know in this country to know what Mormonism is, I have not read, nor have I heard from any of them, such errors as the aforementioned "profession" contains. But, despite that, we do not wish your correspondent and his witnesses to think that I am accusing them of deliberate misrepresentation; and yet, I am sure that either they have received a misrepresentation, or they have greatly misunderstood, and it is not impossible that that "profession" is the fruit of the one and the other. We do not profess perfection: yet, we do not admit to our having seen any of us so imperfect as to give such a misrepresentation as that of our faith; and we admit also, if we get hold of such a man, that we will endeavor to instruct him better. Nevertheless, it is unfair for the repute of any society to suffer such an injustice because of the misrepresentation of any one person. The "shibboleth" of that profession testifies clearly that its father and that of the little anonymous treatise published in Merthyr, and which was proved to be utter, hateful slander, are one and the same. The profession of faith of the Latter-day Saints, in a word, is read in the Testament.

As for the "Apostle" your correspondent mentions, we know nothing; but we are certain that there is no one in Wales, having anything to do with us, who claims nor has that high repute. But, lest I weary you with length, I shall not venture to note the other great differences that exist between the "*profession*" in question, and the doctrine that we profess, rather I shall simply direct those of your readers who wish that information to the various books that have been published by us in Welsh, which can be obtained from our brethren in general, yes, even in YSTRADGYNLAIS itself; and no doubt your correspondent and his witnesses saw them there, and knew better than that hideous profession! If they wish to understand our "profession" in them, why do they not believe it in our own words, instead of the words of our enemies? Who knows best?

I am yours humbly,

D. JONES.

This defense was sent to the *Treasury*, and the "reverend" Editor admitted to having received it; and what use did he make of it? According to the normal custom of the biased and slanderous editors of our land, rather than give fair play to the truth, to us, and to his own readers, by publishing it, he accuses us of "boorishness!" But we cannot find it thus, nor any other man who may be *sober*, we would suppose. If true what is heard less than a hundred miles from Carmarthen, more "boorishness" was delivered by a drunk from the pulpit, yes, to the point that he had to be escorted out; and his "reverend" does not find fault with a word of such a thing as that. But, Oh, the *Treasury* has become too saintly for an entire denomination of believers to be able to defend the religion through which they hope to obtain life—yes, against the disgraceful and ungodly false accusations that the same Editor of the same *Treasury* published, of filthiness against them without foundation! He was excused the first time to some extent, thinking that he could be sufficiently dull as to believe that the Saints believed such a "profession;" but now he knows better, and he does not let his readers know; which is what proves that false accusations and slander satisfy his taste better than the truth. Let the innocent and the truth suffer a strong blow from his bow; and it is good that they are just rush arrows. Let his readers judge him.

A very easy way, and far too common, for authors who may be ashamed to show their faces after doing wrong, is for them to escape through the back door, shouting "Blasphemy" at everything that exposes their shame: so it is with this one also who escapes to his hole, by announcing on the wrapper that the above defense is "BLASPHEMY!" He knows much better; and this trick is too old and well-known to succeed, by now. Expecting that, we kept this copy; and let the reader judge which is the "blasphemy" or the "boorishness" that it contains. We waited for month after month for that "profession" to find its own *sink hole*, namely the *Baptist*—the source of every filthy stream—the father of all the false accusations, and the messenger that tells every false story about us; yes, to be sure, we gave our word to several at the time, that either the *Baptist* would find this *carcass* through its foul taste, or the skeleton would crawl as far as Cardiff to be buried; we did not know how in the world, but it was either through the ravens of this *rookery*, or somehow, we believed that its fate before the end of its course would be to have a welcome in its mother nest, namely the *Baptist*; and when we were about to admit that our prophecy was false, here it is in the *Baptist*, sure enough, like a shooting star! But who does not understand the tricks of this Editor? Not any of his readers, we should think. A short time ago these two "reverend" Editors and their factions were at loggerheads with each other; but now, here is an excellent way of removing the barrier between them, and mutually reconcile themselves to persecute the Saints, and that which one accuses will be verified by the other!

As for the Editor of the *Baptist*, we did not intend to lower ourselves any more to take notice of his odiferous rubbish; but for yet one more time, we shall take a glance at his unfairness. He had refused a defense one time, but after delivering his lies about us, he shouted that he would have nothing to do with us, and he promised to leave us in peace, but he discharged the filthy story that appeared in the next issue; then he closed his press against any defense, &c. Yes, even in the issue before this one that contains that "profession," he refuses shamelessly to allow some Gwilym of Monmouth to defend the Saints, against the false accusations of David Williams, Abercanaid. (See the Wrapper.) "We do not wish to see these two quarrel with each other with respect to the Saints," he says. Oh, no, certainly not, if Gwilym of Monmouth quarrels a word in their favor, or if he points out a word of his dear partner's deceit; but hey Davey! ho David! you and everyone else can quarrel against them all you wish through the *Baptist*, and if they quarrel back, I shall put coal on their mouths, as much as I can. This has been his language and his behavior and his drivel for years. "*Now you shall, now you shan't*," is his vain talk.

Oh no, dear reader, that "profession" is nothing more than one of the bugbears that make our enemies prone to persecute, like all the other things published against us in the sectarian chronicles and treasuries of the country. Do not believe them, lest you be deprived of the truth. It is obvious that they do not want their readers to understand our principles, otherwise they would use that which we believe from our own books. Is it we, or rather our enemies, who can explain our tenets most correctly, I wonder? If we believed the aforementioned "profession," would there be any reason for us to deny it publicly? Would we not be judged liars by those who come to us from every faction? and I wonder if they would then stay with us by the hundreds, through every scorn and persecution, as they are doing?

A surprise is such inconsistency——which has been formed,
Without a line as an answer;
After long experience with his foolishness,
Owens has gone lower than anyone.

THE PARABLE OF THE LAMBS AND THE BEASTS.

On a lovely summer morning, we see some old, infirm mule wending his way along the road, foraging along the sides until he comes next to a lush and lovely meadow, in which there were a number of innocent lambs grazing, and since hunger was cramping his stomach, he broke through the hedge, and he ate his fill of the lucious grass. And after that, we see him trampling the rest under his feet;

and raising his hornless head in the air, with his large ears sticking straight up, he opened his huge mouth, and he began to bray and shriek like a *mule*. I understood that his objective was to frighten the lambs and stir up the animals of the neighboring forest to come there to prey upon them. The resounding of his shrieks served the purpose of bringing them all from their caves, but the wisest of them understood that it was just the braying of a donkey, and they returned to their caves; but the wolves, the foxes, the owls, and all the monkeys took fright at their own voices, and they gathered together; and at that behold a huge lion from the eastern corner of the forest came in a big hurry, his huge head and his tail held high, roaring after his prey; he invited the *jackals* and all the other petty beasts to follow behind him to the meadow, from where he could hear the telltale sounds of prey. And despite how cruel their expedition, and how frightful their bleatings, we cannot help but laugh seeing the lively monkeys chasing each other from the branches of the trees to the ground, their teeth *chattering*, and pulling faces in their eagerness to follow behind this *zoological* retinue, into battle. But when they came to the meadow, they saw to their great dismay that the shepherd, who had heard the noise of the donkey, and expected the effect that that would have on the beasts, had preceded them, turned the donkey back to the road, and stood in defense of the lambs. When this spotted lion saw this, and fearing the scorn in the sight of the petty beasts who followed him if he were to flee, he went ahead after the lambs, inviting the others to follow him; then they were given a voice like the voice of men, and they threatened to prey on the lambs for causing such an uproar, and for causing them the trouble of coming there. Then the shepherd showed them that the poor lambs had not caused any disturbance to them or anyone else, but merely grazed quietly in the green meadow where they had been put, but that it was the mule he had turned back to the road that was the cause of the *false alarm*, and let it be between you and him, he said. At this some dropped their heads down in shame, while the rest reproached each other. They had been so foolish to let the braying of a mule make them the laughing stock of all the other beasts, that they could not expect from a mule anything better than braying, whether there was a reason for it or not! The majority turned back to the forest in shame, with their tails dragging along the ground. But the lion had become more and more infuriated by now, and he encouraged the others to take revenge on the poor, old mule, threatening that they would see their chance to prey upon the lambs after the departure of the shepherd. The next thing we see is the lion dragging the mule by its tail; the others, some by its ears, some by its feet, and others by the skin of its stomach, till they brought him braying himself hoarse to the ditch of the hedge, with his feet up! Then they turned their backs to him, and they buried him as if he were a carcass; and each one returned back to his den. The parable is true, and already more than half fulfilled, and the following interpretation is its key:—

"*The lambs*," are the Latter-day Saints. "*The lush meadow,*" is their church. "*Their pasture*"—the spiritual gifts. "*The mule*"—that execrable thing that has trampled their pasture, and brayed through the *Baptist*. (See the October issue, &c.) "*Lion of the East*"—the lion with the teeth of iron and the nerves of brass, that echoes the braying of every mule, wolf, fox, and owl, from Cardiff, to Holyhead, and invites every filthy creature of the forest to follow them to get revenge on the lamb! "*The wolves*"—The persecuting preachers and autors throughout the principality, whose dens are in Dowlais, Abercanaid, Cardiff, Llanelli, Carmarthen, Dolgellau, Liverpool, and other caves. "*The monkeys*"—are the *jacks* who echo the howlings of the wolves and the lion in the taverns and the chapels from Llanfaircaereinion, to the ends of the principality. "*The burial of the mule's carcass*," has not been completed until now, but will be shortly. Amen.

SIGNS OF THE TIMES.

TO THE Saints, those who are looking for the promised signs of the last times, one need only refer them to the remarkable and multitudinous forerunners who fly so swiftly on the wings of the elements to every corner of the world, to remind them of their responsibilities to watch and pray, since the day of their deliverance draws nigh, that their God has set forth to battle, to fight as he fought in the day of the battle, and that the destroyer of the nations is on his way.

Our Messiah, while he was on the earth, gave undeniable proofs of his foreknowledge, and his goodness to his children in the detailed description of the signs, the wonders, the wars, the diseases, pestilences, the plagues, and the judgments, the earthquakes, the revolutions, and the famine; the hearts of men will fail them with fear and trembling because of the things that will come upon the earth. The lightning, the thunderings, the sea with its waves roaring and overflowing its shores; furthermore, there would be warnings of the astronomical beings like an angelic clarion witnessing to the world, that their King is coming as a conqueror of conquerors, to visit, with his steadfast and mighty sword, with the kings of the earth on the earth, and to execute his vengeance upon all the ungodly of the earth, and all who did not *acknowledge* God, and who did not obey the gospel of our Lord Jesus Christ, will be gathered as prisoners in a dungeon, and they will be imprisoned—when the mountains will leap like rams, and the hills like lambs; and the earth will be moving and swaying like a drunkard, and she will shake like a shack; and her transgression will weigh heavily upon her, and she will fall, and she will not rise again. O wondrous time! The Apostle appropriately called it the "perilous times of the last days;" yet it is obvious from the words of Christ that men do not realize that regardless of how clearly they see, feel, and suffer under these judgments, they will not return to give the glory to God, rather they will blaspheme him because of the plagues, the pestilences, &c. But "as the days of Noah were, so shall also the days of the coming of the Son of man be." They were eating and drinking, marrying and giving in marriage, and casting far away the dreadful day, until the day that Noah entered into the Ark. "Thus" it is now. "Where is the promise of his coming," they say. And they did not know until the day that Noah entered into the ark, and the flood came and took *them all* away. Despite how clear the signs of the times are, yet no one except for the children of God understand them now, any more than they were understood by the children of the world in the ancient days, for they in their wisdom count them as effects of some causes that they see as entirely natural; they comfort themselves from time to time that there is no danger, for such things have happened many times before, they say. Peace, peace, is always their cry. "Then he cometh as a thief in the night," or "like sudden destruction upon *them all*." But "you," says the Apostle, are not children of darkness, that that day should overtake you, rather ye are children of the light.

"Therefore be ye also ready: for in such an hour as ye think not the Son of man cometh."

But there is no reason for us to think that all these things will come to pass at the same time, rather beginning gradually, this year in this corner, and afterwards in some other corner of the world, increasing more and more, hotter and hotter, and more frequently, and more insufferable to the same extent that the nations, the kindreds, and the tongues, have had opportunities to obey the important message that God sent them through the mouths of his servants, for it would not be just to destroy them before offering to them a way of deliverance; and there is no way of deliverance except through obedience to the "eternal gospel." And that is as it is preached by the messengers of God "in the power of God to salvation," temporal and spiritual; and we are not aware that God has judged the world in any age, without providing temporal as well as spiritual deliverance, if they obey his call, and thus in the dispensation of the fulness of times he gathers together everything that is in Christ Jesus, either to Mount Zion, or to Jerusalem, for only there will there be deliverance from the plagues of great Babylon; and let the Saints remember that it is through obedience to the call, namely, "Come out of her, my people, &c.," that deliverance is promised. How can they expect to escape if they remain within, then? And in order to warn the Saints to prepare, God shows through remarkable signs these tumultuous and dreadful times, that he remembers his covenant with the fathers, "he will cut short his work and he will do it quickly in righteousness," and all these things are like a number of witnesses that the hour of his judgment has already begun on the disobedient inhabitants of the earth, and his sword will not return to its sheath until the intentions of his heart are fulfilled.

John says that the red horse would follow quickly on the heels of the white horse; and are not the whinnies of the red horse the sound of wars and the thunder of weapons resounding from the steep cliffs of Circassia, Russia, and Poland? Was it not his steps that trampled to dust hundreds of our fellow countrymen, and thousands of the Chinese, the Hindus, and the Bengalis, lately? Did he not gallop from there through Africa to Portugal, leaving thousands lying in their blood? And behold him now having put the western continent like a boiling cauldron under his feet. Santa Ana rode him for years through the states of the *patriots*, &c. Now, horse against horse, and steel against steel, and thousands of the Americans thirst after the blood of men. And all this so quickly after the white horse, namely the ETERNAL GOSPEL which was brought by the angel to men in the year 1830. Why can we not expect the third horse, namely the black one, with his cruel famine to follow on their heels? Will the two come so clearly, and the third not follow them? What is the lament, the mourning, and the groaning that are heard throughout the world? We see, we hear, or we read the news of the age. Food—Food—Famine, is their cry, until all the kingdoms of Europe are racing to engage in clever competition for food from the far countries, and are preparing for famine. In Poland, Russia, &c., the people are greedy for the rotten potatoes, the unripened corn and the hay, and are living on animal feed in order to stay alive.

But it has come still closer than that! Yes; his whinny can be heard loudly from his black nostrils in Ireland, and his severe wound can be seen on the face of our sister island next to us. It is grievous to hear through the newspapers of our country, from here and there, about strong and once fit men—wives and mothers, together with children, by the hundreds making their way along the roads, like shadows of what they were, their outward appearances proof all too obvious that hunger grips their stomachs and who are still without hope for any remedy. Thrown together by the tortures of famine, the people swarm together in some places by the thousands, and they storm the food shops, rushing in to snatch a loaf of bread, or any food they can get their hands on; and the government has sent an army to defend houses, shops, and the very lives of the upper classes lest they be killed and destroyed before the ravenous appetites of the perishing. Neither the carts of the bakers nor the butchers travel along the roads except they be defended by soldiers. Some are killed there every day, either in their homes, on the roads, or else trying to defend their storehouses.

In the city of Dublin, over a thousand of these wretches walked the streets under the name of "The starving rioters;" and the feast they got was the imprisonment of twenty-two of them by the soldiers, and the others were chased away to die of starvation, or to survive if they could.

In Tipperary, it was feared that the food which the government intended to present to the town was too late to save the lives of many, as they were dying of starvation daily; and at times it is impossible to get food for money. From Cork one reverend writes that sixteen have died from starvation during one week in his neighborhood—that over 600 families are without work or food, and the children as well as their parents are starving; and for the sake of filling their cups with wormwood the tenants have to sell their furniture and their possessions for the rent, and they are turned out to die of exposure, with hardly any kind of bed to lie on, or any shelter over their heads except for the clouds. In the *Poorhouse* in Dungarvan, eight hundred have been squeezed in, over two hundred more than the house is suitable to hold; yet, if it were four times as big, it would not hold the applicants who come to it to save their lives. In Mayo so many are dying that not enough coffins are to be had to bury them all! Over sixteen, says another, have died of starvation in his own parish in ten days. We could quote similar reports from the newspapers from every corner of Ireland or deaths because of starvation, murders for food, and dreadful massacres of this black horse. But we add the following as an example of the tortures and pangs of hunger. In Bautry, and its environs, there were hungry rioters who had become so cruel as to kill several who opposed them. The soldiers chased them to the mountains, &c., but to no avail, until hunger finally forced their leaders, one by one, to come to the town and give themselves up to the *Police*, confessing that they did not expect anything less than their hanging, but they would choose that in preference to the death by starvation that stared them in the face if they remained any longer, with any hope of food gone, and that they would have to die somehow! They had come to look so thin and weak that their old friends did not recognize them unless they made themselves known. Other infections and diseases are beginning from lack of food, clothing, and shelter, as natural consequences; and nothing less can be expected in Ireland than a great many more dying this way. To the potato plague, most particularly, is this hunger attributed. It is said that there are shortages of turnips and corn, especially wheat, in places. Who can foretell the results when other elements of our diet increasingly fail, from one year to the next! Who considers and understands this? The prophet spoke the truth,—"The wicked will go before them worse in their wickedness; but the wise will understand the signs of the times, and they shall lift up their heads in hope, for the time of their deliverance is nigh." No one considers that it is because of their rejection of the white horse and their contempt for him, that the red horse and the black horse take their revenge on them; and before long the pale horse, in his turn, will also come, to kill with the sword, and with famine, and with the beasts of the earth.

Several of the pastors of the people deny that all this is the hand of God, but through other happenings they confess God; and they take courage, but not to search out whether the foundations of their beliefs are divine, and based on the word of God, rather they take that for granted from the traditions of their forefathers; and all the judgments of God have no effect except to bind them more tightly in their nets, and to cleave closer to their beliefs. Then they proclaim fasting and prayer, yes, all the conflicting religions, as if God would accept all in their own ways. Prayer and fasting are good in their appropriate time; but we think it would make more sense for the papist priests to proclaim a feast than to proclaim further fasting, to the wretches who are already fasting of necessity, to the point of dying by the scores!

But why must we talk so much of the sound of the black horse so far away as Ireland! It draws closer to us still! Yes; it has crossed the *channel* already, and it is galloping through the chief towns of England, grating on our ears with the groans of the wretched, too numerous to count. He who holds his reins will tighten his bridle, and keep him from rushing upon us, the Welsh, unprepared!

BAPTISMS BY THE SAINTS IN JANUARY, 1847.

Merthyr.—Baptized by the Saints in January, only 31. One for every day!

Penydarren.—In this branch, not as successful as usual. Only three were baptized last month.

Dowlais.—Namely the chief den of the father of our persecutors, eighteen were baptized in January, and additional hosts believe, and are at the door. Now as they scrutinize us, instead of looking at the false portrayals of our persecutors, the people are coming to understand who we are, and what we believe. Hosts will yet come.

Cardiff.—Under the nose of the *Baptist* that slanders us, ten were baptized in January, several from the Baptists there, with others daily promising to obey. Great will be their blessings.

Nantyglo.—For quite some time in this place there has been a fiery war with "believers" persecuting the Saints, gathered in their houses, throwing stones at the doors and windows—following them to the water of baptism, shouting and mocking, throwing dogs and stones, &c., into the water at them; some threatened with being cut off if they go to listen or if they associate with the Saints; yes, even if they are close relatives to them! There is constant preaching against them. Several have been turned away from the door for obeying the gospel! Nevertheless, the spirit of their God comforts his children, and adds to their numbers—their love and their gifts wondrously. Eighteen were baptized there in January. Despite everything, the Valley is ablaze with a longing for the truth. May they soon grasp it.

Cwmbach.—Seven were baptized in January, which are rejoicing in their privileges.

Blackwood.—Five were baptized last week, and more will follow soon.

[There are several others besides those mentioned, such as four or five in Rhymni, but we will not count those until we receive a report from the hand of the one who baptized them. We know that there is an increase of over one hundred per month, but we do not know of any other denomination in the country that is not decreasing, by their own admission. It is with the Saints that God is.]

ASSIGNMENTS OF THE PREACHERS.

ELDER John Morris went on a mission to Pembrokeshire; there was a call from there from eight of the same place who wished to be baptized.

Elder Thomas Pugh, and priests Evan Rees, David Matthews, and Thomas John, moved from Cwmbach to Cwmbychan, and we are glad to hear that they have begun to proclaim their important mission there already. Success to them.

Elder Hopkin Matthews has moved to Treforris and is preaching in those environs with hopeful signs of success.

Elder Benjamin Jones went to the town of Carmarthen to live, and great is the joy of the church there because of that. They have been under more disadvantages and privations than they will be from now on, we hope. Several are about to obey there.

Elder Abel Evans began on his journey through the North to visit the churches throughout the various northern counties.

Elders John Phillips and Dafydd Rees have moved, with their families, to Cyfyng, near Ystradgynlais, for the sake of the gospel, and may God be with them.

Elder William Hughes and his family have gone to live near Llanelli, Carmarthenshire, in order to preach the gospel in those environs.

Elder William Henshaw has gone to preside over the Garway conference.

Elder Jacob Watkins and priest John Carver have gone there with him.

Elder William Evans, Dihewyd, has gone to Pontypridd, and others with him; and the gospel is being preached there weekly.

Elder Ebenezer Morris is about to move to Llantrisant soon; and several preachers, in addition to those named, are preparing to move to other places soon in order to be able to sow the good seed more abundantly.

In the aforementioned places, and many other places, there are thousands of immortal souls who have not heard the word of the eternal gospel, rather unfounded stories of the preachers and sectarian authors against it; and in every place there are beyond argument those who are honest in their principles, of good intent, and who will embrace the gospel as soon as they have the opportunity.

Dear brethren, since this treasure has been entrusted to us in such poor vessels, we will trust in its giver, we will be faithful, and he will crown our labor with success; but woe betide us if we are slothful stewards. The accounting will come shortly. The foregoing brethren wish for an interest in the prayers of the Saints, and we all say Amen.

CONTENTS.

MERTHYR TYDFIL:

PUBLISHED AND FOR SALE BY D. JONES, AND ALSO FOR SALE BY THE SAINTS IN GENERAL.

JOHN JONES, PRINTER, RHYDYBONT.

PROPHET OF THE JUBILEE,

OR

STAR OF THE SAINTS.

No. 9.] MARCH, 1847. [PRICE 2*c*.

CATECHISM FOR THE COLLEGES OF THE "*REVERENDS*."

WHAT is the *Gospel?*—The plan of God to save man.

How many plans, or gospels, does God have to save men? The same number as he sent Christs to the world to organize it, namely *one*; and that one is so skillful, complete, and perfect, throughout, that it is suitable for everyone in every age and country, without change by taking away from it or adding to it one jot or tittle.

What is the first principle of the gospel?—Believe that its Author is truthful, crucified, and resurrected.

What is the second responsibility that man has?—Covenanting with God that he will obey his commandments the first opportunity he has, and that he will strive to shun evil, and please him.

What is the third thing?—Go with one of the preachers of the Latter-day Saints straight to the first water he can find, and receive his baptism in it "*for the forgiveness of sins*."

What is the fourth thing?—Receive the Holy Ghost through the laying on of hands of the elders of the church, as in the days of the Apostles. Anyone who does all these things based on the correct principle will be Saints, or children of God, through the gospel of Jesus Christ; and if they continue in the confines of this sound doctrine, they will be able to rule with the Redeemer, Christ Jesus, on the restored earth, in a blessed state, without ever dying again.

And can the worst sinner obey all these conditions as soon as he understands them, without help from the Holy Ghost?—Most certainly; otherwise he will never obey them, for God did not promise his Spirit to help the sinner to believe that Jesus is the Christ, or to repent, or to walk to the water, because he gave *testimony* through his servants and reason to judge the first, natural ability for the second, and feet to obey the third, &c. Therefore, he cannot expect God to believe, repent, and be baptized for him, nor force him to do that. *After* receiving forgiveness did Peter even give the promise of the Holy Ghost. See Acts ii, 38, viii. 15-17, xix. 5, 6.

Is it any use to pray for God to convince them, and give to them, while they refuse to obey the gospel?—No, not one bit. In vain do they call Lord, Lord, without obeying his commandments. Not everyone [or anyone] who says, Lord! Lord! will enter into the kingdom of God, rather he who does his will. In vain will they try to worship him, through teaching for *doctrine* the commandments of men. God calls man to him, but our calling God to us, and according to our schedule, is what that would be! Which of the two is right!

Is it not required of the Lord to do something different from what he has done before we can come?—No, or else he is at fault for not doing that *something*, and he would be choosing our salvation. What else can he do? If anything, he himself, and not we, will determine when that day comes.

Does not Paul say in Eph. ii, 8—"By grace are ye saved through faith; and that not of yourselves: *it is* a gift of God?"—Quite right, and it proves that the salvation of man depends on his own faith to believe the plan to keep, namely the gospel, which was given through the grace of God to men. The *gift* is his Son, and not faith.

Are you saying that all the sinners of Wales can obey the gospel as soon as they hear it preached intelligibly, and thus be adopted as children of God?—One greater than we assures that, namely God. "Look unto me [that is through obeying the gospel], and be ye saved, all the ends of the earth."—God. "Come unto me, *all ye* that labour and are heavy laden, and I will give you rest."—Jesus Christ. Well, that is sufficient, come now, then!

Since this is how it is, what would the servant say to God as he gazed at the rejoicing, and the shouting for religion that is in the sectarian meetings? He would say as Ananias said to Saul of Tarsus,—"And *now* why tarriest thou? arise, and *be baptized*, and wash away thy sins, calling on the name of the Lord."

And then, if they were not to obey what would be the consequence?—He would say that "he that saith that he loveth God and keepeth not his commandments, is a liar, and the truth is not in him." Also, "he that knew his Lord's will, and did it not, will be beaten with many stripes."

Is it not possible for them to have religion by praying so fervently for it?—According to Christ's word, it is not because of their long-windedness, with a show of long prayers, that any will receive his religion. Yes, if he were to pray as long and as often as the scribes, or those four hundred prophets of Baal.

Did not the Apostle say to the keeper of the prison "believe on the Lord Jesus Christ, and thou shalt be saved, and thy house?"—Yes, he said that believing it was the first step, but not the only thing; but he, Paul, "spake unto him the word of the Lord, &c.," and see what that word is in Mark xvi, 16. Then see his obedience before the light of the next day; Paul placed such importance on the baptism that he did not dare to delay any further. Thus let all do.

What would be the result if he had refused to receive his baptism after believing?—He would be worse off than before, inasmuch as the gospel is "the savour of life unto life, or of death unto death, to each one who hears it."

Does not Paul say, "That if thou shalt confess with thy mouth the Lord

Jesus, and shalt believe in thine heart that God hath raised him from the dead, thou shalt be saved?"—Yes indeed, that is how the church was to whom Paul wrote, namely the Romans; for they had been baptized already on their acceptance into the church, and Paul would not speak to them in this way, and in a different way to others.

If baptism is indispensable to gain forgiveness, why does Paul give thanks that he had not baptized any of the Corinthians?—If he himself is to be believed, he says in the following verse, "Lest any should say that I had baptized in mine own name."

Does he not say, "Christ sent me not to baptize, but to preach the gospel?"—Yes, and he says that others *watered* those he planted. Through preaching the gospel he laid the foundation for their faith to act, but he made sure that others built higher up.

Did not Cornelius receive the Holy Ghost before his baptism?—Yes, to eliminate the center-walls of the difference that existed between the Jews and the Gentiles, so that this first one of the latter could obey the gospel. This was God's exception. There was no *promise* to him of that, or to anyone else before or after. But despite that, his sins were not forgiven through that, nor did it make baptism unnecessary; for after that Peter commanded them to be baptized for forgiveness, and to be accepted into the Church.

Was not the "thief on the cross" saved without being baptized?—If so, he did that not through the gospel, but to the corresponding extent as it applies to the pagans without law, who are a law unto themselves, who are excused because of lack of opportunity. Besides this, that commission, "he who believes *and is baptized* will be saved," had not been given at that time; furthermore, it is necessary to prove that "Paradise" and heaven are the same place before the salvation of the "thief" can be proved, which is a never-ending task!

[*To be continued.*]

DUTIES OF THE PRIEST.

"THE priest's duties are—to preach, teach, expound, exhort, and baptize; also to administer the *sacrament*, and visit the members in their houses,—and exhort them to pray vocally and in secret, and attend to all family duties: he has the right to ordain priests, teachers, and deacons. He is to take the lead of meetings in the absence of any elders; but when there is an *elder* present, he is to take the lead, and the other is to assist, by carrying out the other duties mentioned."—Translated from the *Doc.* and the *Cov.*

This is one of the offices that pertains to the lower priesthood, that is the Aaronic, and it is just as indispensable, useful, and glorious in its place and its proper purpose as any other office. Every sect that we know about doubts the necessity of this office in the church now, except for the "established church," and we cannot agree with them with respect to the assertion about the required qualifications, or the responsibilities pertaining to the office any more than in the consequences of it. It is not surprising that those who deny offices such as the apostleship, prophets, &c., together with the ordinances pertaining to them deny this also; but, from our part, we thank the fountain of light that we have not been covered by such darkness; it is easier to believe the present need for all "gifts" placed by the head perfectionist in his perfect machine, namely his church, until they answer the purpose, that is to perfect the Saints,—Eph. iv, 4-14, until the very last one of them has been perfected. We have a firm testimony of the angels of heaven of the existence of this office in his kingdom on the earth,—Rev. i, 6, v, 10; "And priests; and we shall reign on the *earth*." This will be fulfilled in the future, of course, and since no one held any office except those given to them which they fulfilled in this life, and since each one receives according to deeds performed in the flesh, how can anyone join with his golden vessels this praiseworthy *chorus* that existed after the apostles, if there is no such office for them to earn and fulfill. Not at, but *before* the coming of the bridegroom does the bride adorn herself, "for the woman *made* herself ready," will be said at that day. In this way will the church of Christ be governed perfectly in its original plan, and consequently it will have this office and every other office that has ever been, or that ever will be in it, except one, *before* he comes himself to fill that office. The existence of this office does not show, as some suppose, that sacrifice is needed as the law of Moses commands, for the shadows have been swallowed by the coming of the great reality himself. This office has the right to lay hands on the sick, calling on God to heal them, as Philip did with the Samaritans in the early days, but not to administer the ordinances of "anointing with oil in the name of the Lord," nor to lay on hands for receiving the Holy Ghost, any more now than Philip did with the Samaritans; see Acts viii; or on the Eunuch; administering these two ordinances is something that pertains to the Melchizedek Priesthood, that is to the elders, and above. James v, 14.

Although a priest has the right to ordain others to the office of priest on down, it is not wise or usual for him to call and ordain others while an elder is available: nor for the one or the other to do the one thing or the other thing without putting it before the church, and if there are problems there, let the matter be brought before the council. The branch president is responsible for this, and in the council, or the conference, they should be approved at least, if circumstances call for their service before that, and if the divine leader directs. For the sake of proper order and to prevent the Saints' being deceived in Wales as they have been in other countries, by evil men pretending to hold this office, certificates pertaining to it have been printed and no unknown person is to be received without this identification as a rule.

Finally, dear brethren, remember the counsel of your leader Paul, preach the word, be instant in season, and out of season; convince, exhort with all long suffering and doctrine—consider the great importance of your office—strive to be cloaked with the spirit of your office so that your labor will be crowned with success, and you and those who hear you will have entrance to eternal bliss.

THE AMERICAN PRESS SIDES WITH THE SAINTS.

THE following is quoted from the "*New York Sun*." This publication like many others has been very diligent in publishing false accusations against the

Saints for years; and influencing others to reprint articles of the enemies, the oppressors, the ravagers and murderers of the Saints, who through doing this intend to throw a cloak over their own inhuman deeds at the expense of the innocent, and the purpose was answered remarkably well, to the point of exiling many thousands of the children of God to the midst of the uncivilized and the animals of the western desert; but soon the deeds of darkness were brought to the light of the sun. Isaiah describes these people as follows:—"Woe unto them that seek deep to hide their counsel from the Lord, and their works are in the dark, and they say, Who seeth us? and who knoweth us?" This editor published the letter that was translated and published as good news in the "*Baptist*," namely the one which was professed to have been written by Emma Smith, widow of Joseph Smith, putting a great insult on her own husband, and on the teaching she confesses that he sealed with his own blood. But although that letter carries its own refutations, yet we proclaim that every syllable of it is false, that Mrs. Smith had nothing to do with it, nor any knowledge of it until she read it in that paper, whereupon she put the law on its author; a verdict of slander was brought against him, with a large amount of compensation to the victim. But whether the editor of the "*Baptist*," and the other authors in Wales, are as honest, as humane and just, as the American editors, to undo the harm they did, when things are rethought, and reason and truth are shown to them, is among the things of the future, yes, and it will either raise them up on the pinnacle of warranted greatness, or be one "more nail in their coffins."

"A strange excitement and sympathy is gaining ground in favor of the Mormons, throughout our land. The peculiar nature of their tenets, the strange origin of their faith, and the singularity of the personages selected for their prophets and leaders, together with the books, &c., published against them, had an influence on the popular opinion of the age against them for years. They were represented as unmoved in disgraceful habits, and it is most remarkable that the Mormons hardly opposed these charges [they did, we say, for we know they did all they could in that matter, and we also know that while truth was lighting its match, falsehood would set the world ablaze, and our defenses would be thrown there; not to the newspaper columns, but as in Wales, to the back of the fire without being read]. When a cruel mob rushed into Carthage prison and killed Joe Smith, and his brother Hyrum, the atrocious act shocked the country for a while, but it was soon forgotten. Subsequently a mob gathered in the state of Illinois, under the name of Anti-Mormons, with the aim of exiling them from their community, and compelling them to abandon their farms, their houses, and all their possessions, as well as the costly temple which they had built, as plunder for their persecutors. For this purpose they collected their cannons, and their arms of war against Nauvoo. The position of the Mormons attracted the attention of the other states; but as Illinois, their own state, gave them no assistance or protection, but rather commended the violence of the persecutors, it was believed that their characters were so bad as to merit the treatment they received, and their exile to seek a place of residence somewhere else. [What evil could they have committed to deserve exile from a republic, I wonder?] The Mormons defended their homes as well as they could, until they were overcome by the numbers of the rioters, and having the state against them, and public opinion; and when they had no aid and no protection from anywhere, they said, 'We will go,' and they did go into the wilderness, men, women, and children; some on foot, some in wagons, carrying with them the remains of their furniture, and leaving their homes, they fled to the wilderness. Some [500] joined the army bound for California, and another part went west of the Mississippi river. Thus 12,000 or 15,000 persons, from a state of comfort and prosperity, were driven from their homes to lie down on the banks of sickly rivers, or to deal as well as they could with savages and beasts, on the vast *prairies* of the west. But it now appears clear enough from various testimonies worthy of our belief—some are intimate with the Mormons, and have closely observed, and scrutinized their conduct and behavior, that great injustice has been done to those unfortunate people, so oppressed, robbed, and abandoned quite defenseless by a sovereign state which was bound to protect their rights. The late Capt. Allen of the *U. S. Dragoons*, who had 500 of the Saints in his army, testifies that they were all not only spirited and brave, good and faithful people, but describes them as wonderfully pure and unexceptionable in their moral conduct, frugal, careful, industrious, and self-denying, and manifesting heroic patience in suffering, worthy of the noblest Christian character. Again, one of the worthiest correspondents of the '*U. S. Gazette*,' who has travelled and lived among the Mormons, writes that chastity, virtue, and love, together with a spirit of unity, and effort for family happiness, form absolute characteristics of this outcast people, as well as their temperance, orderliness, industry, courage, and steadfast determination in the objects of their desire. If this be so, words are inadequate to portray the incomparable injustice and cruelty they suffered in the state of *Illinois*. One can excuse the cruelties suffered by the Goths and Vandals, to some extent, and the persecutions of the dark ages; but that a free country such as America in these enlightened times, with all its institutions to ensure freedom for its citizens, should exile about 15,000 [over three times as many] of its citizens, without being proven guilty of any crime, through the power of arms, from their homes, and their possessions, and that the strong arm of the state should not be held forth for their protection, is a stain on our annals and on our country, which will take years to wash out. There is no parallel to it in the history of our country. And this is not the worst of the story either; *riots, drunkenness, and crimes, are the results of the victory of the Anti-Mormons!* A reckless body of people violated all the Mormon property, took possession of their farms, and desecrated their temple; the poor, the sick, and the aged, like the innocent children, were driven half-famished into the woods, and all their safeguards, and their livelihood, were outraged and cut off.

"If strong statements about the condition and character of the Mormons be true, the state of Illinois is bound in *honor* and by its own laws to restore these innocent victims to their homes, their property, and their rights, and the legislature, for the sake of justice and humanity—for the character of their state and their institutions, should direct the governor to issue a proclamation inviting the Mormons to return to their homes, and guarantee them protection against every attack on them. They are now, by the injustice of the state, dying in the wilderness of starvation and cold; or are prey to the savages and the beasts. Hosts of them are now lying on the earth on the banks of the Mississippi river, opposite the city they built through industry, and now see it all in the hands of the worst kind of robbers. Let Illinois awake to this good work before public opinion of the whole country *demands* for the Mormons justice for what has passed, and protection for the future."—(From the *New York Sun.*)

We feel very grateful to this editor for his sympathy at last for the people he has been persecuting and falsely accusing, and through that helping with his drops to fill the pail, until giving birth to their natural fruits, namely cruelty and devastation, but better late than never for the sake of their character, and their religion, and for the sake of the souls of the rest who search for the truth for him to have called back the opposition, and who can say what joy he would now have, had he researched those things before publishing them! But we would be most grateful to the editors of the *Baptist*, *the Star*, *the Treasury*, *the Times*, and the authors of our own country also, if they would be so thoughtful as to consider what use they make of their influence and be as honest on the side of truth as the Americans, and review the untrue and harmful stories they have published, half believing them perhaps, under the flowing *infatuation*. They can see the results of such comportment there in a mirror, they will read about similar things in the early days, and if they continue to fan the sparks until they ignite an ardent flame in Wales, it will be useless for them to feel pity for the blood of their victims while they are suffering, except the natural consequences of their pointless persecution. Oh no, it will be too late to shout *hold!* enough! at that time, and that they were not thinking, or intending to cause such a thing; such an excuse will not be valid, and they will be held responsible by the Judge of the whole earth, and the "King of the Saints."

The Saints thank their supporter that they are not suffering so severely as the foregoing portrayal, although for others it would be just an unavoidable wait. And while there is sympathy throughout the world for their oppressed, and for the starving wretches of Ireland and the eastern continent, and all have refuge and a place to put their heads down to rest on the tender bosoms of some sympathizers, who have "the splendid ones of the earth," "the Saints of the Most High," those who have denied themselves all things, and who have consecrated themselves and all they have for the good of the world; and they have suffered the stress and heat of the day to build the kingdom of Emmanuel, as a city of refuge to all who may come; will these brave ones suffer everything, to have all plundered for their testimony of Jesus, and the word of God, without sympathy in this country; can Wales turn a deaf ear to such a call—is it possible that one Welshman will not share a little bit to alleviate their needs? Oh no, we hope that if there is one heart so cold as that, that it is not the heart of the reader. As for the Saints, there is no need to say anything to you, except to inform you of their need for assistance. The Council decided in Merthyr, that the President of every branch throughout Wales is to explain this matter to the Saints, and send whatever is collected here to Merthyr, every month, so that all can be sent according to the direction we received from Brother Orson Hyde. The Saints will go forward until they reach the end of their journey, and you know that they are our forerunners to prepare for us when all of you will be repaid an hundredfold for every assistance that you extend to your brothers and sisters in the Lord, yes, in this life, and the short time of its trials; and in the last words of our dear Brother Hyde before taking his leave of me, I say, "The Lord will bless the one who considers this call." Amen, we say, with all our heart.

SIGNS OF THE TIMES.

THERE is a multitude of these arrows that continue to circulate throughout the world, changing and multiplying as the world acknowledges, and the time is drawing nigh. The dispensations of him who holds the fate of the nations in his hand prove the truthfulness of his servants as loud as the sound of thunder,—as common as the light of the sun, and as close to thousands as is the feeling to the heart, and despite all this hardly anyone was considering this thing or taking it to heart, or recognizing who is at the helm.

The news from Ireland informs us that the famine, and consequently the wretchedness, and the deaths are increasing daily, "until this minute (says one) famine, sickness, and disease are increasing all around; and even in the northern parts. Their condition is worsening daily. The *workhouses* of Bedfort, and Omagh have been overflowing with poor people. And begging and stealing are multiplying even in the places that were practically free from them. From every corner of our country the mournful news that is heard about deaths from hunger is too numerous to record." The *Cork Examiner* says that "fourteen have died from hunger in Bantry, today." The *Southern Reporter* says the same. "It is our duty to publish that the deaths by starvation have increased so greatly, and such numbers are reaching us daily, that by now it is too great a task for us to publish them or to find space for them in our columns. Our correspondent sends the story of the 15th who died in Bantry, yesterday of hunger, and he says that another 20 have died this week; they are too numerous to hold *inquests* on them. We heard today of *inquests* on the 11th in Mallow, who died of hunger. Mournful news pours into our office from every corner, so that we cannot publish the tenth of it. According to the Police, over 50,000 have died of hunger already, besides many they do not know about." And indeed, we ourselves admit the same, that our small publication does not have space for the mournful news we have heard, and seen, and read daily, for it is obvious that it is not only in Ireland, although in the forefront in heartrending suffering, but the disease is also crossing the seas—rushing through the continent, and many thousands are feeling its agony in France, Spain, Germany, Austria, Prussia, and Russia, to the point of being forced in some places to try to feed on grass like animals, and on bread, (as they call it) mixed with moss. It is not surprising that they are driven together by a master as harsh as hunger, as rioters in their final pangs to try to sustain life by plunder, despite the death that faces them. There are Roman provinces, together with others to some extent that are within the grasp of this strong conqueror. And needless to say that its influence is increasing in England, Scotland, and to some extent in our midst, although as if from afar the sound of its cannons are yet heard by those who flee here before it by the hundreds.

In addition to this warning the God of War speaks, through rivers of the blood of men to the inhabitants of the countries, and even louder he sends his pestilences abroad, beginning in the east. It is said that the *cholera morbus* is busy destroying the Turkish nation before it, as if sharpening its arrows for others, and it is not know who will escape this time. Also, a pestilence has broken out in Cain, Mecca, &c., in Egypt, which in the space of nine days swept to the spirit world no fewer than 15,000 people! Despite how lamentable it is for us to publish the foregoing, yet it is more grievous still to have to acknowledge the fulfillment of the following prophecy in the face of everything. "And the rest of the men which were not killed by these plagues yet repented not of the works of their hands, [for they are a punishment for such things] to give glory to God; but they gnawed their tongues for pain, and blasphemed the God of heaven because of their pains, and repented not." Oh what a wretched and obstinate condition! if signs and wonders were effective in convincing men, the world would soon be convinced; but thank heavens, a better way has been provided for that, namely through preaching the gospel as a seed of grace.

GOOD NEWS FROM CALIFORNIA.

THE ship *Brooklyn* from New York, has landed her passengers in San Francisco [in California]. Part of the emigration from the United States have reached the Sacramento valley, and many more are on their way, which are expected there within a few days. The very bears, the deer, the *antelopes*, and the wild horses are puzzled and frightened at the visit of such hosts of strangers as these in those unfamiliar valleys and forests. Sometimes droves of the latter gallop through the horses of the immigrants, attracting some to follow them; and it is a great hardship to catch them afterwards. These Saints intend to settle in San Francisco, in a land where they can have plenty of the finest land in the world, without payment, rather as a reward from the government for settling the country. The climate here is remarkably temperate. Neither the heat of the summer nor the cold of the winter here, as in other places of the same latitude, cause extremes of the one or the other, and that because breezes, called *trade winds*, blow from the north for the six summer months, and from the south during the other part of the year; and because of this, together with the excellent aspects of that paradisiacal country, it is said that disease and pestilence are unknown there save in name only. In Monterey, one of the main towns of that land, a newspaper is published, which informs us that they have built some small ships that sail along the shores. They are building houses, mills, and erecting schools, &c., after the American fashion, and the whole country is alive, with clothing of every kind, and exotic goods, the price of which has fallen by half since the United States have taken possession of the country; and they have taken away the *duties*, which amounted to more than the present price. We are glad to know that the Saints have had a good welcome there, and that popular opinion is in their favor, although they are exiles from their own country. A paper by the name of "*Friend*," published in Honolulu, says,—"We feel it our duty to make a few observations with respect to the Mormons, with whom we are acquainted. We lived in Illinois, not far from the Mormons. At the time of the last war, many hard and incredible things were said about them: probably, much of it true, though many things have been highly colored. At all events, they have landed here in our midst. Here they will make their home; and those of us who preceded them have not the right to prevent them; and whatever faults they may have had before, it is hoped that all will be corrected here; and we plead with our friends that they will be able to secure favor and harmony with everyone. May God rule their councils in wisdom." This is an example worthy of emulation by the editors of Wales, namely praying for us, instead of constantly cursing us and falsely accusing us; and this one will have his wish also, by seeing that "God does rule over the councils of the Saints in wisdom" for his glory, and the good of the whole world.

Another newspaper tells about the position and hopes of the Saints who have arrived there,—"It is said that they number in the hundreds of thousands, very many of whom have come off from other denominations. This is true of the company who came now on board the *Brooklyn* at least; for many are seen in their midst who were with the Baptists for years, others with the Methodists, the Independents, &c., yes, every denomination has its representative among them, and all are in unity of spirit, purpose, and cooperation now, under the wing of Mormonism. It is our understanding that California is the central rendezvous of their campaign; and especially it is in the beautiful valleys around San Francisco that the Latter-day Saints will begin to settle. And leaving aside the exaggeration used to describe the beauty and excellence of this place, one must confess, on every consideration, that it is a lovely, advantageous, and blessed place,—the best location to settle a colony to be found along the borders of the country. The natural facilities of the country and the bay conspire to show that flourishing cities and towns will rise up to beautify the scene before many years elapse. The watchword of the Mormons now is '*California*.' The few who have come already are but a fraction of those who are yet to come soon. We believe, from the accounts we have had, that over 25,000 of them are already on their way here from the United States. We have heard also that a ship filled with them has started from Liverpool, as the first-fruits of the numberless hosts who will come from the eastern continent."

"Whatever views different classes of Christians may form of the tenets of this people, one thing is certain, that this general and remarkable movement from the four quarters of the globe to California contains a new and beneficial chapter in the colonizing of a vast, fruitful, and sparsely inhabited region. These people will have an influence on California, and they will contribute wonderful civil, social, moral, and religious improvements to its destiny. We cannot but hope for a brighter day, and most certainly we are far from taking a dark view of the subject."

"Before closing, we consider ourselves duty bound to give publicity to the testimony of Captain Richardson of the ship *Brooklyn*, in regard to the behavior and character of the emigrants who came on board the ship during a long voyage round Cape Horn. He greatly extols their conduct and their character, which was beyond anything he had ever seen. He says they live together in more unity and love than he had thought anyone could under the same circumstance; they were cheerful, peaceful, and very orderly, without exception. They came here with determination to work the land, with all necessary preparations for that, such as ploughs, carts, wagons, scythes, and all kinds of husbandry implements, and tools for building ships, houses, mills, &c. And they have not forgotten to bring with them materials for schools, instruction, &c. Captain Richardson informs us that during most of the passage they maintained orderly and beneficial worship services; and that they continue to tend to their religious duties constantly on shore, after leaving the ship. This numerous and lively company are soon to establish their new homes; and may they enjoy more peace and justice than in the ones they left. Although we think differently from them on several doctrines, ceremonies, yet our best wishes and prayers are with them. May the providencial tenderness and cheerfulness of the Most High God rest upon them. They are to lay the family, civic, and religious foundations in our midst. And O, may they be such that coming generations shall rise up and call them blessed." "Monterey, August 13, 1846."

It would be wonderful if more of those who hold the keys of popular opinion had such accurate spectacles, and a heart as honest and sensible as this one; no doubt the coming generations would call them blessed. And we are certain, that if the writers and editors of the United States had been as free of prejudice and as patriotic as this one, they would not have caused their charmed ones to behave so inhumanly, to spill so much innocent blood, or to suffer so severely the fruit of their deeds; but the Latter-day Saints would have forever caused their overloading with temporal and eternal blessings. Oh, that others would be wiser in the day of their influence, taking warning, and giving fairness to the truth, wherever its source.

We take great satisfaction in informing our readers of the safe arrival of the ship *Brooklyn* at the desired port. It will be recollected that we announced its departure from New York in January 1846 with the company under the leadership of Dr. Brannan. No doubt gratitude will rise from the hearts of the Saints in Wales also to him who holds the sea as in the palm of his hand, and the wind in his fist, for his fatherly care over our brothers and sisters, during their voyage, requesting an extention of his goodness for their needs in the future, until they turn that desert into a meadow-land, and into a refuge for thousands of people of the Saints of the Most High from the judgments of the world. And may pleasant breezes of heaven blow sweetly on these flowers, so that their godly examples and teaching will perfume the entire continent, and the world as well.

NIGHT VISION!

"On the 16th of December, I preached to a large gathering in Bolton, on the resurrection of the body, and after that I went with one of the brethren to sleep that night. After a while, I viewed myself travelling in company with two or three of my brethren in the ministry, conversing on the things pertaining to the kingdom of God, when all at once a very fine looking stranger fell in company with us, and he said, 'Well brethren, how do you all do?' We looked at him, and we answered that we did not know him. Then he said, 'If you keep my name secret whilst I am with you, I will tell you who I am.' We promised we would. By then we had arrived at the home of the brother where we intended to take lodging; and after we had all gone in, and were seated in a private room, the following conversation took place: 'My name,' said the stranger to us, 'is James. I am one of the apostles that were on this earth in the days of the Savior. You now see my resurrected body. Handle me and see; for a spirit hath not flesh and bones, as you see me have.'

We then viewed him very closely, and O that I had words to describe the beauty and glory of that body! His flesh and skin looked so pure and shining, and his cheeks were like the rose. I then put my hand on his cheek; and then he said, 'Be careful! for I am very choice of my heavenly body.' I asked him, 'Brother James, how did your contemporaries treat you?' He answered, 'Very much the same as the people of this age treat you and the apostles at the present time. They mocked and derided us, casting our names out as evil. The priests contended with us, and they told the people we were false prophets, and impostors; that we were not fit to live on the earth; truly like the people say about the twelve that God has sent in this dispensation. And the truth is, that the people are the same now that they were in that age; and they will not receive the pure principles of Christ from you now, any more than they believed the truth from our mouths. In our days, only a few believed our testimony; and but few will believe your testimony.' Said I to him, 'Brother James, the people have got a large and splendid chapel reared to your name in this country; I wonder if they let you preach in it.' 'Oh no,' said he, 'they would not let me preach in their chapel, any more than they would one of the twelve of the present age; and if they were to allow me, my preaching would be in direct opposition to all their false traditions. You know my writings; what little they have of them, they do not practice; and they are not nearly so plain as when I wrote them. They have changed and lost the plainest parts of my writings; and if I should tell them of it, they would not believe me. Thus, all that you can do is to preach wherever you can get the opportunity, and gather out the honest in heart from among them; after that the disobedient will be cut off from the earth; for all the Lord does is to warn people, and if they reject his warning, he will destroy them with his judgments.' Then I asked him what he thought of the twelve apostles who lead the Church of Jesus Christ of Latter-day Saints now? Said he, 'They are good men; and if the Saints will obey their counsel, they will be exalted in the kingdom of God.'

Said I, 'They have come to understand many of the glorious principles since the organization of the church.' 'Yes,' says he, 'but they are but babes yet to what they will be when they get their immortal bodies, as you now see me have.' 'When did you get your resurrected body?' To this he did not answer definitely. I said, 'Oh, I wish that I had an excellent and immortal body like the one you have.' He answered, 'It will not be long, if you continue to be faithful, before you and all the Saints will have bodies like this body.' At this, we were called to supper in another room; then he said, 'If you promise not to reveal who I am, I will take supper with you.' At this I awoke; and behold it was a dream! Perhaps some will think that this is just imagining; but to me, in fact, it was tangible, substantial, and glorious; something I shall never forget, in time nor in eternity. It took place truly just as I have described, and it makes my heart rejoice every time I think of it. O! human language cannot portray the beauty and glory of that body! I am willing to suffer every contempt, and scorn, and persecution in order to obtain a glorious resurrection. May it be so. Amen. I am, your brother in the eternal gospel, M. SIRRINE."

"When we first read the 'vision' of brother Sirrine, we considered it similar to a ficticious vision; but after that, we saw brother Sirrine, and he assured us that it was not ficticious, rather a substantive vision, as he truly worded it. Joel says, 'And in the last days, your old men will dream dreams; and your young men will see visions.' And the wise man says, 'Where there is no vision, the people perish.' May the heavens permit the veil to be parted from our eyes, all of us, so that we may know as we are known. ORSON HYDE."

[From personal acquaintance with brother Sirrine for years, on this side and the other side of the seas, that his name is attached to the foregoing "vision" is sufficient seal of its truthfulness.— ED.]

THE IVORITES EXCOMMUNICATING THEIR MEMBERS BECAUSE OF THEIR RELIGION!!!

IT has been said, "there is nothing new under the sun;" and perhaps the following story is not new, rather another fulfillment of the oppression and cruelties of the persecutors of the dark ages; for, may the entire race of Gomer listen! There are some of their tribe who claim to be the chief patriots, and philanthropists of our age, and are themselves spreading the veil over the Goths and the Vandals! It is quite true that the committee of Lodge 299, Ivor-Hael Lodge, Carmarthen Union, Ivorites, have excommunicated a party of religionists from their society, on the admission that it was because they dared to worship the God of heaven consciously according to the holy scriptures! But, it is worthy of the others of this generous and respected society to publicly inform the circumstances, and the persons who caused them this shame; and it will be seen who of them is so philanthropic and just as to take their broom to clean these foul stains from out of their remembrance. Three days before this remarkable period in the history of the Ivorites, as the Latter-day Saints were preaching (by permission of the owner) in the hall of the *Yew Tree*, Blaina, one of the "Reverends" of the Baptists again, by the name of Thomas Evans, stood up to face them; and by doing so he showed his foolishness, bringing the reproach of the crowd on him, and causing the listeners to disregard him; and then he rushed out in shame. Nevertheless, that did not answer the purpose, except to get more and more angry, not knowing how to get additional revenge on the Saints; but the third day after that the following persons were seen gathering under the name of committee of the society, which had been called for that purpose, and that "reverend" was the chief councilor and *dictator* as to what should be done with the Saints (in their absence, notice, but as one of them came to know by accident), and his brother, namely Dafydd Havard, one of the Baptists, was placed as chairman, and Dafydd Thomas as assistant-chairman. Then one other of the Baptists, by the name of W. Williams; George Davies, Wesleyan; John Daniel, Wesleyan; James Mark, Independent; Thomas Griffiths, Baptist; and John and Benjamin Thomas, as this committee in the Ivorite inquisition, *alias* Sectarians! Let the reader imagine the vengeful "reverend" on his throne now; and the first step was to divest the robe, namely the job, from off one of the Saints, and put it on himself. With this, he swelled more and more like the "toad who was trying to imitate the ox," until he collected enough brass in his face to twist and torture the publications of the Saints, in a way that has them denying the divinity of the scriptures; and the proof that he gives of this is because they believe the Book of Mormon to be true! And consequently, admitting the truth of the New Testament is denying the divinity of the Old! Yes, according to this reasoning, admitting the truthfulness of the one epistle of the Testament denies the divinity of the other! Yes, it would be the same thing for this "reverend" to assert that believing the last witness in court is to deny the one before, although they be as compatible with one another as the Book of Mormon is with the Scriptures.

But it was of no avail whatever defense was put forward, they agreed to cut off all the Saints without warning, and without returning their money, although some of them had been paying into them for years, without ever getting a cent of it back; and one, whom they knew was with the Saints, had paid to them 9*s* in the last meeting before being cut off. If a more appropriate name can be had for such work as this than *wholesale swindling institution*, we would like to know what it is. Whether this is an example of Welsh Ivorism, or of oppression and the transgression of this *clan* of their rules, is proved through facts that undo the transgression, or their conformity through their tolerance of that. But we hope that there is enough virtue in their brethren who belong to other *lodges*, either to administer justice, or to separate themselves from unjust oppressors, for whoever says, "God is generous" to them, is a participant in their wickedness. Until the above fact is proved to the contrary, let the Welsh remember (and we shall be more fair than they by telling others), before heaping up money in the chests of the Ivorites, they must give up every right to free agency, and their own opinions about religion, and hand over, not only their money, but the pearl of greatest price, and the best of God's gifts to men, namely an *independent mind*, into their hands. What is the slavery of the most enslaved Negro in comparison to the Ivorite slavery of the fairest Welshman who dares to choose his own religion in his own free country? What can they do but appeal to the reason of their other brethren for the justice that is out of reach of the laws of their country to win it back for them!

Vainly every Ivorite—hopes to block
The Mormons so forthright;
They have no sense, no insight
To know that God gives us might.

BAPTISMS BY THE SAINTS IN FEBRUARY, 1847.

Merthyr Tydfil.—Twenty were baptized in this branch in this month, who along with all the other faithful members are greatly enjoying their privileges, and are in the comfort of the Holy Ghost.

Nantyglo.—Despite the depth of dust and mud that have been thrown in the faces of these brave lovers of truth, they are increasing in love, patience, gifts and graces, as well as in numbers. In this young branch of the church of Jesus Christ, 16 were baptized in the month of February, on their profession of faith in the Son of God, and his gospel; although they are greatly threatened, they are solid in the faith that was once given to the saints, and they are greatly rejoicing in the comfort of the Holy Ghost in the midst of oppression, magnifying their privilege of being worthy to bear all things for the sake of the name of Him who laid down his life for them.

Penycae.—Two were baptized, and others have promised to obey soon.

Tredegar.—One was baptized. Also there is regular preaching in the "*Gen. Picton*," Sirhowy.

Blackwood.—One more; and many are gravitating to the Hall to hear the gospel preached.

Abersychan.—Despite the opposition here, through the generosity of the owner permission has been obtained to preach every Sunday in a convenient Hall; and here, as in every other place in which the people are able to understand what we profess, instead of that which we deny, our gospel is winning their love according to their honesty; and do not our opponents understand and confess this, by threatening and chastising their members, to prevent them from listening to us, and falsely portraying our religion? Despite all this, five were baptized this month, on their profession of their faith in Jesus Christ.

Cwmbach.—Here, only three obeyed during the month.

Llwyni.—Two were baptized, and it is hoped the resistance will open the eyes of many others.

Cwmbychan.—In this new place also, our brethren are preaching diligently, and two have been baptized already during this month, despite how much the Sectarians warn everyone not to listen to the "babbling of the false prophets," &c.

Rhymni.—Two were baptized from the Baptists, and it is strange how their former brethren persecute them.

Cardiff.—Five were baptized, according to what we have heard, the majority from other religions.

Dowlais.—This town is like a boiling pot, between two factions as different from each other as are Sectarianism and Apostolicity; the former as if about to die defending the mantle they have drawn over the faces of their worshippers, and becoming enraged every time the latter lift the veil to allow others to see things as they are, especially when their members, and their deacons who are honest in their principles, escape to the light, shouting, Life! Life! Although we have not had a letter, more than fifteen have been counted to us who were baptized here this month; and we give thanks to the fountain of light, that the dawn has broken through this wretched obscurity.

Elder Morris baptized some in Pembrokeshire; and elder A. Evans has sent comforting news of the success and joy of all the churches throughout the North; brother R. Evans informs us the same also; and it may be seen that we have many reasons to thank Him whose work this is, together with exhortations to diligence.

[N.B. We repeat our request for every branch president to send to us the number that were baptized, at the end of each month!]

ARRANGEMENTS OF THE PREACHERS.

PRIEST John Price has moved to Risca, and has received a warm welcome. Priest James John intends to go there also soon.

We saw Elder Robert Evans in Wrexham lately. He is diligent and successful in the North, and has baptized several lately, and sends greetings to the Saints in the South, wishing for an interest in their prayers.

Two were baptized in Rhosllanerchrugog at the beginning of the month, and the branch is blossoming.

Elder W. Davies, Rhymni, went to Brecon to preach, and he intends to be in those environs for some time. Success to him.

Priest John Richards, Merthyr, has migrated toward Llanelli, Carmarthenshire, for the gospel.

GLAMORGAN CONFERENCE.

THIS Conference will be held in the CYMREIGYDDION HALL (White Lion), Merthyr, beginning Sunday, the 18th of April, at 10 o'clock in the morning.

MONMOUTH CONFERENCE.

THIS Conference will be held Sunday, April the 25th, in the CAUKER'S ARMS HALL, Nantyglo.

It is requested that the presidents of all the above branches and Conferences come there, so they can represent the numbers, growth, and condition of their branches. Food may be obtained from Mr. Evans, Caukers' Arms.

N.B. It is expected that President F. D. RICHARDS (lately from America), from Liverpool, will visit the two Conferences.

CONTENTS.

MERTHYR TYDFIL:

PUBLISHED AND FOR SALE BY D. JONES, AND ALSO FOR SALE BY THE SAINTS IN GENERAL.

JOHN JONES, PRINTER, RHYDYBONT.

PROPHET OF THE JUBILEE,

OR

STAR OF THE SAINTS.

No. 10.] APRIL, 1847. [Price 2c.

CATECHISM FOR THE COLLEGES OF THE "*REVERENDS.*"

(Continued from page 39 of the March Prophet).

Are you sure that there is not another gospel or plan through obedience to which man can be saved, except through believing, repenting, and being baptized for the remission of sins, and the laying on of hands to receive the Holy Ghost?—Neither our Christ, his Father, or anyone of his servants has said a word about another one; and thus I conclude that they do not know of any plan but this one. If there is another one, it has another author, and some other bible that shows it. To say that perfect Christ has organized more than one perfect plan to take us to perfect heaven, is to say that all except one of them are imperfect; and since the work of each one proves it, that is an imperfect Christ, and that plan is to be without Christ in the world; and being without a perfect Christ as an acceptable sacrifice is to be without God; and to be without God is to be without anything; consequently, every man who claims that there is more than one plan to save mankind is a deist to that extent; yes, in spite of what they profess, their zeal, their long faces, and their frequent prayers, and their devotions!

What! are all the believers and preachers throughout the world who have not obeyed this kind of doctrine, deprived of the eternal gospel, like unto the pagans?—I cannot point out any difference, except that the former believe historically in Christ, and in teaching morality, &c., through the scriptures, although they do not understand the gospel.

Is it not possible for even the learned theologians of our colleges to have part in the first resurrection, and be with Jesus Christ, and be like him, through some of the new and convenient ways they have invented, without obeying this gospel?—Christ himself answers,—"Verily, verily I say unto thee, except a man be born of water and of the Spirit, he cannot enter into the kingdom of God." How, then, can anyone be saved in the kingdom of God if he refuses to "go into" it through the door? You will have the treatment, or the welcome of "thieves and ravagers" if you go to it any other way!

What will become of all those who are living on the earth, and who refuse to obey the gospel, at the second coming of Jesus Christ?—The

Bible says that Christ will come with his mighty angels. and a flaming fire taking vengeance on them that know not God, *and that obey not the gospel of our Lord Jesus Christ.*

How is it that the Christian world (as it is called) has been so long deprived of the justice of the eternal gospel?—In fulfillment of many of the prophets, such as Daniel, and John; namely, that grievous wolves have come into the church after the time of the apostles, have brought in destructive heresies, transgressed the laws, changed the ordinances, &c., and are "making war with the Saints [who were authorized by God], *until they overcame them.*" Then they claim to this day that divine authority is not necessary, and they do not want it either; instead may everyone do the way he wishes!

How have the Latter-day Saints come to understand, and have the privilege of being instruments in the hand of God to restore the fulness of the gospel back among men?—Not because of any qualification, virtue, or worthiness in them more than in others; but, because the fulness of times has come, according to the design of the great God of the early council, for the gospel of peace to be preached to all the inhabitants of the earth, to prepare the way for the second coming of his Son, to prepare appropriate people, and invite them to the marriage supper of the Lamb, lest he come and smite the whole earth with a curse; for he does not delight in the death of the ungodly, &c.

How did they receive this gospel, and the right to preach it?—God sent that holy angel that John saw coming with the everlasting gospel to preach to every nation, kindred, and tongue, saying, "*The hour of his judgment is come.*"

Will not anyone who refuses this gospel be saved from the judgments that will come on the earth?—The same number as were saved from the old world after refusing the message of Noah! If one who refused him is saved, why not more? If so, it was useless for God to send him.

Are you not narrow-minded in your opinion, and very unkind toward the other religionists, who are so zealous in worshipping God according to the light they have, in saying that to them?—If Christ was unkind to the more zealous believers of his day when he called them "hypocrites;" and when he said,—"Generation of vipers, how can ye escape the damnation of hell?" He who sees the evil that is coming on the country, and warns them clearly and honestly according to "the law and the testimony," is kinder toward them, and benefits them more than ten thousand of those who shout "Peace, peace," prophesying goodness all the time, when sudden destruction cometh upon them.

What is the condition of all those who died from the time the gospel was taken from the earth until now?—They will be judged according to the works they did in the flesh, before a just court, according to the light that was offered to them during their lives, and the use they made of it; for those who have no law, are also damned without the law, and doubtless thousands of them will rise in the judgment against this generation, and will condemn it; for had they received the advantages and the offer of it that this age has, they no doubt would have embraced the fulness of the gospel readily. Many of them desired to see the glorious light of the last days, and they could not; therefore, do not worry about them, for each one will give his own accounting to God. The harvest of your soul is now; the summer day of the gospel has dawned for you; and O, may you not close your eyelids against the divine rays of light of the Jubilee.

***Composed for the service of the Students of Oxford College, and others.

DUTIES OF THE TEACHERS.

"THE teacher's duty is to watch over the church always, and to teach and strengthen the members, seeing that no one of them fosters any iniquity; that there is no hardness with each other, lying, jealousy, or backbiting, giving rise to the root of bitterness in their midst; to see that they are not negligent in their meeting together; rather that the church meet together often; and that all the members do their duty. He is to take the lead of meetings in the absence of the elder or priest; and the deacons are to assist him in all his duties, when he requests them to do so; but neither teachers nor deacons have authority to baptize, administer the sacrament, or lay on hands; they are, however, to warn, expound, and teach, and invite all to come unto Christ."—*Doc.* and the *Cov.*

The office of teacher is one that is essential and very important; essential, we say, because there are so many temptations put before the Saints who are young in the faith. The devil-enemy is a tyrant, and in their weakness he attacks them the most, to try to subvert their souls, because they have escaped the clutches of the heretical spirits to the kingdom of God. That is the time he uses his tricks and his most frequent and most effective temptations, because of their weakness. That is the time he leads his priests with their fabricated stories, their false accusations, and their threats, blaspheming the things they know nothing about, as in primitive times. Thus the necessity for the teachers to watch over them as if over their flock moving the obstacles from their way, explaining the hard-to-understand things, feeding them with the guileless milk of the word, so they will increase daily. Let every teacher understand the worth of the souls, together with their weakness, who are entrusted to his care; for they are worth the blood of the great chief Shepherd; the danger is that they will lose their first love, and become confused with the things that are contrary to godliness; and let it be remembered that this will turn a sinner from the error of his ways, saving a soul from death, and hiding a multitude of sins. Take care not to strangle them with food too strong in their weakness, for "strong meat belongeth to them that are of full age." We fear that not everyone is teaching in wisdom; thus we exhort such to sympathize with the weaknesses of the new members in the faith, remembering that such were we at one time. The baby does not become a man immediately, nor the acorn an oak, nor do we become of full age thus; rather gradually, as the light of morning increases, until it reaches the brightness of mid-day. We know that there is an immense difference between joining the church of Jesus Christ and everyone else who professes the name; even at their first coming the enemy does not miss one opportunity to whisper in their ears the bad about this thing, and they use every chance to cause them to doubt the other thing; and we know from bitter experience that the stories of the backsliders, and now flooding their minds are the false accusations of the enemies of the truth, which we heard earlier, almost to the point of overcoming our frail faith; nevertheless, others have given light, and God has given us his patient spirit to cling to until our faith has been tried, something more valuable than perishable gold; and O how we give thanks by now for the rescue we had at that time from slipping; and thus we consider that others can be, and we strive to visit them frequently, and strengthen the feeble knees; so our "fruit will be holiness, and the end everlasting life." The great importance of this office is seen in its divine position, in the benefit that flows to the Saints through the faithful application of it, and also in the accounting that needs to be given to the Giver for the use made of this talent. A wise, alert, and zealous teacher will make the Saints thus also. He is their nourishing father, under the leadership of his superiors in offices. He ought to know the condition and the spiritual trials of his flock, and see that there are no bitter roots among them causing hatred, which is a poisoned arrow from the bow of the enemy; see that they live peaceably, and have family worship as often as possible; for the most effective way to fulfill their other duties is through prayer. If they cannot worship together and pray at the family atlar, they cannot receive gifts, or great growth in holiness, or beauty to their vow. We fear that slipping in this place will end in withering and grief.

The teachers should visit everyone who has neglected three church meetings in a row; and if there is not good cause, let him counsel with the branch president; then with this transgression, as with every other transgression of the members, it should be placed before a council of teachers when it convenes, if it is convenient to the place where such a council has been established; or send the accusations to a council of the elders; the transgressor is to be notified of the matter, and he is to be invited there, if he elects to defend himself. But, take care that every move originate from love, and a true desire to restore such to the right path so they can be saved, and rejoice together in the love of Christ.

Finally, dear brethren, be careful to give good examples and good teaching to the flock over which the Holy Ghost has placed you as supervisors, by keeping yourselves and your flock blameless and unspotted from the world, with a good conscience before God and men; and you and those with whose care you have been trusted will have a glorious entrance into the main fold, when the good shepherd gathers all his shepherds, and his scattered flock, to hear his voice in the blessed place of rest which is still only for those who suffer together with him, those who continue to the end, and those who await and love his appearance.

NEWS FROM THE SAINTS IN THE WILDERNESS.

LATELY a letter came from the apostle in their camp, near *Council Bluffs*, to the east of the Rocky Mountains; dated January 23rd, 1847. Our columns do not allow space for the entire comprehensive letter; but the abridgement is as follows:—

"In our last letter we portrayed the city we planned to build, but it is already one we feel the benefit of. It contains about 700 houses, built of logs, mud, willows or clay, and covered with straw, and are comfortable and healthful dwellings for the *Saints*, although they will not endure the thaws, rain, or much sun in the summer.

This our great city was built much like "Jonah's gourd," which sprung up in a night as it were, in the middle of this wilderness, with 22 wards. A bishop and his counselors were organized to preside over each ward so that no one suffers for want of food or raiment; and if they suffer, it is their fault for not asking for it; or, if they are too lazy to work. But the fact that so many houses have been built in so short a time is proof to everyone of unusual industry, the kind that will bear comparison with the history of any nation in any age or country! We decided to build a water flouring mill here while wintering; and our dear president, Brigham Young, offered himself for the task of superintending the work, and behold the barley ready for grinding already. It is true that he has more cares before him than ought to be given to one man; but "the greater the toil, the greater the glory," is our motto. He does not hesitate at anything that tends to gather Israel, or to promote the cause of Zion. He sleeps with one eye open, and one foot out of bed at night; and whenever there is a call, he is the first one to go forth, and his counselors are of one heart with him. He frequently mentions the mission of our dear brethren Hyde, Pratt, and Taylor, particularly the gathering of the Saints from the isles of the sea, and the best way for them to come from the four corners to their places of abode. Dear brethren, don't you forget this important matter either, whatever else you do; it is not our fears that say this, rather we bring this to your remembrance. A company of 300 forerunners is being sent as soon as the weather permits, toward *Yellow Stone*, at the foot of the mountains, with everything necessary to raise a crop from the earth for some two or three thousand of the Saints who should follow after them; and those who remain there are to labor and to prepare for the coming of another camp; and thus the Saints who come will have sufficient without going so far as *Missouri* to purchase food. The sellers in this country imitate everyone else in trying to starve and exterminate the Saints by raising the price of wheat from 40 to 50 *cents*, and *Indian Corn* from 20 to 25 *cents* per bushel, ever since we arrived here.

On the 9th of October, when our wagons returned to the banks of the Mississippi, across from Nauvoo, they found the rest of the Saints lying on the banks of the river, without houses, beds, furniture, food, clothes, or anything; but death from starvation was staring them in the face! They had been driven out of the city by the mobs without pity, or warning, or mercy, besides many being afflicted with the illnesses and diseases of that country at the time. They did not have anything to live on there, or anything with which to start their journey. While in these distressful circumstances, they turned to the Lord, and he sent them a great flock of *quails*, which lit in their midst, on their beds, and by their feet, until the sick and everyone could catch them with their hands, until they were satisfied; thus their tables were laden with meat, morning and evening. Not only the Saints saw this, but the world also. A steamboat was passing by within six rods of them, and they saw them, and the travelers on it marvelled greatly; others on the shore (not of the Saints) marvelled when they saw such a sight; but you will marvel further still that those birds had followed the Saints along the road when they began their journey, lighting on their wagons, and under their feet, offering themselves as a voluntary sacrifice to save the lives of the Saints under the oppression of their persecutors. Declare this to the nations of the world! Tell the kings and leaders ! ! Proclaim this to those who profess to believe that God brought Israel through the wilderness in the days of Moses, so they may believe also that there is a God in these days, and that he is just as caring of his children *now* as at that time; *and that he will yet feed them when the oppression of the enemy is unbearable.* He is the God of the whole earth; before him bows every knee, and every tongue confesses to the name of Jesus Christ."

"Since the foregoing was written we are informed through the news that General Taylor, and Santa Ana, have agreed on terms of peace between Mexico and the States, allowing California to have religious freedom, and to choose their form of government for the present time. It is said also that 200 *Dragoons* that travelled with the "*Mormon battalion*" have been called back, and the Mormon army is going forward to the desired place."—*(From the "Millennial Star.")*

THE MOST REMARKABLE WONDERS OF THE SEVEN MILLENNIA !

THE chief wonders of the first millennium of the age of our world were, the transgression of our first parents, who were driven out of the garden, and which opened the door for all the degeneration that is seen on the earth, its things and its inhabitants; the building of Zion; and Enoch, together with all its inhabitants walking with God for three hundred years, and the taking of them and their city from the corrupt earth.

In the second millennium, the world and its inhabitants were drowned, except for Noah and his family; foolish men built a tower to climb up after Enoch; the languages were confused; the world was divided into seas and continents; its inhabitants were scattered across its face, and America was first populated by the Jaredites.

In the third millennium, Pharoah and his armies were drowned in the Red Sea, when Israel, the chosen people of God, went through on dry ground, and they were led by the brilliant glory of their Jehovah in a cloud of mist and a column of fire; and a temple was erected in Jerusalem to the Lord.

In the fourth millennium, the ten tribes of Israel were led away captive from Canaan, by God, to some country the Gentiles have not been able to find to this day: all the Jaredites were destroyed for their wickedness, and Lehi was led by God to the American Continent.

In the fifth millennium, the Savior of the world was born, crucified, and resurrected, and the majority of his apostles were martyred for declaring his message: and Jerusalem was destroyed, with over a million and a half of its inhabitants; the rest of the nation was scattered through the four corners of the world until this century.

In the sixth millennium, America, the most excellent country of all the countries of the world, was settled by the gentiles; the fulness of the gospel was presented, through the Book of Mormon, to mankind; the kingdom foreseen by Daniel was established, which has filled the whole world; and the Saints began to gather together in preparation for the second coming of their Messiah on the clouds of heaven, with all his angels, with a flame of fire, to take vengeance on all who refused his gospel, so that in the seventh millennium the earth could rest, its fulness restored, and the remainder of its residents free from all oppression, and pain, and death; each will sit under his vine and his own fig tree, without anyone to frighten him or to harm him, worshipping unanimously their Savior for a thousand years, when he will be the King of kings, and there will be no other king except by his appointment, and voluntarily humble to him; at that time all the kingdoms of the world will of necessity have come to belong to our Lord, and his Christ; and he will be a visible King to his Saints, when none of them will say I am sick; but during this last millennium, all the Saints will be perfected to be suitable residents of the new heaven, and the newly perfected and unchangeable earth; and he will finish the perfection of his work on this small earth, and move its sphere to a more brilliant light, and he will bring this his kingdom up to his Father, so that God will be all in all, and all like unto him!

Hail to the good times to come,
  We shall see our own Jesus
On a white cloud, great his splendor,
  Coming to reign.

DESCRIPTION OF CALIFORNIA.

"THIS country lies to the west of the 'Rocky Mountains', to the south of Oregon, to the north of Mexico, and to the east of the Pacific Ocean, which washes its coast, from 18° to 42° northern latitude. The appearance of this country is very attractive. Along its borders there is a fairly high plain, with splendid fruitful valleys, of different sizes here and there; to the east of the above *range* there is a plain reaching from 20 to 150 miles in width from east to west, and south to north the length of the country. This is without argument, one of the most luxuriant and fruitful found in the world; it produces abundant crops naturally of oats, clover, and flax. Sweet and pure grass grows commonly, which the animals enjoy greatly, but the oats often grow to five feet in height, the clover to two or three feet, and the flax is excellent. The soil of this valley is of deep, black and rich clay; but the upland is lighter and sandy. East of here there is another smaller valley, but just as fruitful as the other, along the borders of which is a row of fairly high mountains; and to the east of these is yet another very fruitful valley.

The produce that has grown there most abundantly until now is wheat, which produces in a normal season 30 to 60 bushels from one acre, and after sowing one bushel. I am informed by an honest farmer that he once had 133 bushels from sowing one, and the second crop from the same land 61 bushels without sowing; and despite how incredible this may seem to people in this country, I have no doubt of its truth, and it is not stranger than oats growing without sowing to 5 or 6 feet. I travelled (says the historian) through thousands of acres of such oats. The wheat is of a good and heavy species; and the main difference between it and the type we have is that several ears grow on the same stalk! This is one reason of its fertility, although the climate is the main cause, perhaps. Indian wheat, beans, peas, barley, *tobacco*, and all kinds of vegetables grow here in abundance; and I do not think there is any more suitable climate in the world for *rice*, *cotton*, and *sugar cane*, than that of California. The fruits are apples, pears, *peaches*, *figs*, *almonds*, *olives*, *dates*, *oranges*, *lemons*, *citrons*, *pomegranates*, and *grapes;* in a word, all the fruits found even in the southern hemisphere are easily found here. Some complain that there is a shortage of trees in comparison to the meadowlands which has nothing but grass and crops growing on them; but I judge that there are plenty of all kinds of trees for the use of the country, however numerous its inhabitants, besides being able to grow there quickly wherever wished.

The *climate* of this paradise is practically a continual *Spring*; at least one scarcely feels the cold of winter, or the heat of the summer. The reason for this marvel is the "*tradewinds*," which blow from the north for the six summer months, and from the south the other six months. Sometimes it is more temperate in some parts even at 28° northern latitude in the season called winter. Running water has never been known to freeze there, nor still water to freeze to the thickness of window glass. There is no need for fires in the houses in winter, except for the service of the house, namely, boiling or baking food. The "rainy season," as it is called, begins in November and lasts until February, during which period beneficial rain showers occur, and the rest of the year is dry, lovely, and healthful weather. Wheat is sown throughout the winter, and several kinds of vegetables remain green throughout this time. When the "rainy season" begins, the valleys and trees sprout, and all nature is clothed anew. It is possible to get two crops of some kinds of corn in the year. In October and January the vegetables are in full bloom; and it is appropriate to say of this country that "October is as lovely as May." During this time numberless flocks of tame and wild animals are seen collecting together, leaping and bleating, from the mountains to these grassy and lush meadows and valleys, and greedily grazing their sweet vegetation with apparent happiness, and rejoicing in the complete enjoyment of the abundant preparations of nature for their sake.

As for the *pastures* of this land it is needless to say they are beyond anything I have ever seen. Here and there are seen numberless herds of cattle and horses. The farmers own from 1000 to 20,000 head of cattle, and sometimes as many horses! The prices of the former are from one to five *dollars* a head, and of the latter from two to ten. Usually whoever wishes to is permitted to slaughter any number he wishes provided he return the hide to the owner of the *brand* that is on it; and if there is no *brand*, it is all his. Their main reason for raising the cattle is for their hides; and thousands are slaughtered just for their hides. Thousands of horses here are killed because they are too numerous. There is here an abundance of pigs; and the sheep are countless; and they have young twice a year. There is here an abundance of game, such as *elk*, *deer*, *antelope*, *bears*, *foxes*, *martins*, *beavers*, *muskrats*, *seals*, and *raccoons*. On my journey through the valleys, I sometimes saw thousands of *elk* at one glance, and no fewer *antelope*. In the winter season the geese, ducks, and many kinds of waterfowl gather together like clouds to the straits, rivers, lakes, and to the fields of labor; and the cackling of their different voices and their giddiness are practically unbearable at times.

Large and navigable *rivers* are in this country also; the largest is the *Sacramento*,* which nature has made navigable for over 300 miles.

Every kind of *fish* can be found in large numbers in these rivers and straits.

As for *merchandise* in California, it would be difficult to find better advantages with respect to ports, &c. It is said that the strait of St. Francisco† alone could safely contain all the navies of the world, and there are several other safe and convenient anchorages, such as Monterey, St. Diego, Bodego, &c. In every one of these places there are towns being built rapidly; and before long there will no doubt be seen here and there cities that will put to shame some that are a hundred years old.

The *inhabitants* of California do not number over 8000, two thirds of which are civilized Indians; and the rest are *Spaniards* or *Mexicans*, mostly negroes mixed with every blood, color, and class; and besides the Europeans and the Americans who are in their midst, the inhabitants are quite uneducated. It is estimated that there are only about 500 or 600 white people in this country,‡ which are greatly respected.

To encourage immigration there, the government allows all who come, their choice of land, and on the condition that they live on their land and work it. From three to nine square miles can be obtained, according to the size of family. All those who came here with me have settled in the places they chose.

Lastly, I declare that I do not think there is a country in the world that contains such attractions, nor which offers such hopes and advantages for the immigrants as does California, and there is no country under the sun that nature provides so much for, to assist, please, and prosper its inhabitants."—*(From the "St. Louis New Era.")*

N.B. The account of this country will be entertaining to our readers, although some may think that this portrayal is too good to be true; to these we answer only that none of it appears to be too incredible for us to believe; also it has not been disproved by those who have the chance to discover that it is not true.—ED.

PORTRAYAL OF THE RELIGIOUS WORLD IN A DREAM!

WHILE traveling from place to place through the country, trying to benefit my fellow nation, and getting a lot of scorn and opposition from them, one day I turned off the road to a pretty grove to rest. While meditating on the scenes I

* Here the first camp of the Saints will gather, and some have arrived already.

† Here the first shipful of Saints who went from York around *Cape Horn* have landed.

‡ This historian wrote this about three years ago. Thousands have gone there since then.

saw, the divided and mixed up state of the religious world, and its similarity to what it was like in the time of the apostles, suddenly I was overtaken by sleep. I saw myself in a great field, among the innumerable host of people of different classes, ages, and colors, all walking back and forth in opposite directions scowling at each other and being cross. In amazement, I asked one of them standing nearby, what could cause such a scene? Who were those people and what were they trying to do? He answered that they were people from all the countries of the world, and that those were their forms of worship, and that they all expected to arrive at the same place in the end. After observing the pains, the punishments, and the cruelties that were used by the pagan part of them on themselves, and on each other, I turned away in deep sorrow, to see the behavior of those who professed Christianity. As soon as I conversed with them, I was asked if I had a religion, and to which sect I belonged. I explained my condition impartially to them, expecting to receive guidance to the right path. By then, several had gathered around me; and to my great surprise, one said, it is over here;—no, said another, we are the ones who are right;—Oh no, don't believe those people; we are the ones who are treading the right path, said others: and so, they went head to head with each other. I was even more surprised when I heard all of them, though contrary to one another, trying to prove their beliefs through the scriptures! I was so disappointed because of their contradictions, that I was about to turn away in hopelessness, when others came up to me to comfort me, sincerely inviting me to join with them; and they said that what the others were quarrelling about were just small things, unimportant, and unnecessary; and I could choose whether to believe them or not, if I felt like it; and all I had to do was to join with them and everything would be fine. Although I liked their generosity, logic taught me that they were too generous at the cost of the organization that was established, whatever it was. I knew that I would have to keep that one rather than the one I or they would have chosen; nevertheless, through their eloquent descriptions of the glory of heaven, the love of God, and the benefit of being Christian; through their gentle voices, and their singing, they charmed me into following them for a time; but soon I heard others quarreling, giving dire descriptions of the pains of hell, and threatening all who did not join them, that such would be their fate. Others claimed that there was no such place as hell, rather that all were imaginary pains; and there was no subject that one professed that another would not come along to deny. This disgusted me, and I announced my intention to leave them and their contention, and that I would not trouble myself any further about religion, if that sort of thing was what they called Chrisianity. At this, they urged me to inquire of their learned ones, promising that I should have light and a satisfactory explanation from them. But when I visited with the one and the other of them, they tried to explain the scriptures according to their own beliefs; and as proofs of what they said, they referred to some large books, which were completely different from each other, which, they said, contained the thoughts and opinions of the most famous theologians of the country; and indeed, their skillfulness in inspiring and explaining their own interpretations was so prompt, and their eloquence and their gentleness were so attractive, and like plaster on every wound, and my own desire for religion so great, that I decided to join the most popular ones, and swim with the biggest stream, in peace and respect. I left aside searching for myself, and I endeavored to believe and to obey them; but, before a partial spirit could plant its talons so deeply in my heart, so that I could not listen to anyone else, the scene changed, and I saw my danger. Suddenly they were all covered with a large cloud, and it was a wondrous sight! Some loud and frightening sound was heard, and despite the level of the tumult of the people before that, it silenced them and filled them all with fear, as they gazed intently on it. And behold a person like unto a man was coming from it toward us. Frightened, everyone tried to guess who it was, and what would be the results of his coming. Some said that it was a sign of the end of the world; others said, no; but the majority believed the former, because no one was to come henceforth from above, they said, until the end of the world. At that the bright being stood in their midst; and along with others I pushed toward him to hear his story, from whence he came, &c. But the only answer to be had from him was that he had come from some distant planet. I paid close attention to his behavior, together with what he said, this stranger; for he spoke the same language as we spoke. The learned of the various denominations drew near to him, and they asked him if he believed in and belonged to the Christian religion? He answered that he did not know anything about it, and that he had never heard of such a religion before; but he seemed desirous of understanding. The various factions endeavored to persuade him that they had the true religion. Then he became very displeased at these contentions, and he asked for their rules, or the standard of their religions, to bring the discussion to an end. They extended the Bible to his hand, praising it greatly, that it was the book of books; and that in it that which they had told him could be confirmed, and that he could have the pure gospel; and that it was the fountain of light and knowledge, which created in him a great desire to read it carefully.

After reading the book impartially, he liked the doctrine that he read, especially after reading the story of Jesus Christ, the purpose of his coming to the world, the gospels, and the letters of the apostles to the churches. His breast was filled with joy when he read the great promises they made on conditions so attainable. But when he read 1 Cor. xii; Rom. xii; Eph. vi, and other places where he understood that God had established a church on the earth, and set apostles, prophets, &c., in it to lead it, and promised to his subjects forgiveness, and justice, and that he would give the Holy Ghost to them in its gifts, such as healing the sick, speaking with strange tongues, interpreting through the Spirit, prophesying, visions, and ministering of angels, &c., he decided, at the expense of everything, to obey the conditions, and become a member of such a glorious church as that. It did not occur to him to doubt the existence of such a church, and he could not imagine that those who professed such zeal for it, and had presented him with the valuable book they confessed to be a standard and rule for their churches, did not enjoy the sweet gifts it promised. He asked some of them to take him to one of their apostles, as they talked with him about these joyful promises. They answered him,—"Apostles, indeed! there are no such strange beings as that in our churches in these days, nor any need for them either." We saw the countenance of the stranger go pale, and he did not say a word for a moment, so great was his disappointment. Then he again asked the same thing, for he could not believe that he had understood their answer correctly; but he was forced to believe them the second time, since all of them testified with a scornful smile that it was foolishness to inquire after apostles in this age. After recovering somewhat from his surprise, he said, "Well, well! if I cannot have the privilege of talking with apostles, I have a degree of hope yet: the book that you recommended to me says that the officers next to them are prophets; take me to one of them, then." The answer to this was again similar to the other. Again, like a man running for his life, he inquired of the one and of the other, who among them had the church that possessed the offices and the gifts that good book described; for each one claimed to have it, and each claimed to believe the book; but not one of them possessed, or believed in, or even saw the need for those apostles, prophets, or spiritual gifts. The stranger accused them all of having deceived him cruelly, by putting a description of such a church in his hand, exhorting him to read the book, and he, by doing that impartially, believed they had these things; and now, here they were denying them! and cutting him down from the highest degree of hope and joy, to the extremes of hopelessness, by claiming that they did not enjoy those gifts. Yet, they all claimed to operate according to that book! At this, he said that the inhabitants of this planet were a hypocritical and deceitful people, more so than the people of his own world. You are all, said he, saying one thing, and thinking something completely contrary to it; and not in one single thing do you agree with one another, except in denying the book you profess to believe! He said that he thought, when he had hope for that religion, that by changing his country, he had gained something worth more than the planet where he used to live; but now, to his disappointment, not only had he lost hope of ever finding it, but these new and strange friends vex him the most, since he did not know what in the world to believe of anything they said. He asked whether it was the custom of this country to say everything backwards! This excited the multitude against him, especially when they saw that he was too logical to join with any of their factions. He upbraided them for their hypocrisy, and said that he did not want the thing they called Christianity; if he could not have the religion the book described, he would be without any excuse. At this, they despised him and shouted after him that he was a deceiver; others said that he had gone crazy, &c.; and all the bad boys in their midst threw rocks at him; and the most quarrelsome of the learned men shouted from their high places in the crowd that they should beware lest they be deceived by that wicked man; and when they told the people that he, by refusing their religions, was insulting greatly all their godly fathers and indicating that they were going to hell, they shouted in one great, loud voice for over two hours,—"Away with such an impudent deceiver from our country; great is the great goddess our fathers worshipped." The stranger escaped to the top of a mountain, to a secret place, naked, hungry, and wounded. Upon seeing the treatment he received, without any cause, I took pity on him, and I tried to defend him; for I, upon hearing his defenses, and upon reading the book, had come to believe in, and tried to show the others the necessity for all the offices and the spiritual gifts in the church, before it could be the church of Jesus Christ; and the corners of my eyes were already beginning to open to see the harmful effects of the apostasy from that form of doctrine delivered to the world by Jesus Christ and his apostles; and the more I manifested that to the people, the more their pastors were jealous of me; they called me a dangerous heretic; and, without any other accusation against me, they turned me out of their midst, warning others not to come close to me, that I was affected by a plague more dangerous than leprosy. At this, they pointed their fingers scornfully after me, and told false stories about me, trying to blacken my character; and then the boys shouted—"That's the man who believes in the need for apostles, prophets, and miracles." "There's a false-prophet," said others; and at last some proper "Reverend" came there from somewhere else, and he shouted—"Beware of this wicked and deceitful man there, for he is a *Mormon*." With that name coming from his mouth, behold it coming through all the mouths that were there, until, amidst their noise, and seeing everyone holding a rock, I and a few others who believed the Bible fled from their midst for our lives. At this I awoke, and behold it was a dream!

AN EXAMPLE OF OPPRESSION ON THE SAINTS.

THAT which follows is worthy of being chronicled among the feats of our religious age:—Lately, a mob of rascals, for the most part, if not all of them, sons of believers, attacked a house in Cwmcelyn where the Saints were preaching, breaking the windows and doors with rocks, in order to disturb the worship. At last, the man of the house went to fetch the constable by the name of William Owens, one of the Baptists, and an Ivorite, to defend his house against the persecutors. And after the the rioters had fled, the constable came, to be sure; and the way he defended the Saints was by *demanding a crown for his journey !* And despite everyone, and everything, he would not go, and he did not go away except to return, until he got it! The excuse he offered for his endless importunity was, "because he had insisted from the beginning that he would want a crown," he said, and he would rather plunder his neighbor than break his word! We hope that no one else is found throughout Wales holding to his word as firmly as this man. *Too much of the good thing is good for nothing*, says the Englishman; thus can the sufferer admit, that the word of the other had cost him a crown.

AN EXAMPLE TO PROVE THE DIVINITY OF MORMONISM!

A YOUNG girl by the name of Margaret Jones who was employed at the works of Thomas Brewer, Esq., Nantyglo, was baptized by the Saints, on her profession of faith in the Son of God. When the *steward*, William Munkle, understood that, he told her that he would turn her out of the works if she did not deny her religion! The girl answered that she would not deny her Lord, despite losing her job. "Well," said he, "go away this minute; for Tom Brewer and I are determined that not one Saint will have employment in these works while our two eyes are open!" It is difficult for us to believe that a gentleman, of the character and influence of Mr. Brewer, has lowered himself to take vengeance on some who are so dependent, through such persecution as this. Yet, the fact forces us to believe that, against our will, because of his servant. Despite it all, the worst of our wishes toward him is, that He who sustains his "eyes open," will be long-suffering with him, until in time he will come to see that it is hard to kick against the pricks, and that he will come to see that that which concerns the children of God is near to his own heart. We are reminded of the words of Christ,—"All that will live godly in Christ Jesus shall suffer persecution."

TO OUR DISTRIBUTORS.

YOU know, dear brethren, of many of the obstacles in our way to publish our principles, and to defend them, as the giants of tradition defend their fortresses, and aim their cannons against us from the four winds. You know how small our circulation is, and that cash has been our motto from the beginning (nor could it be otherwise); and while we extend to you our heartfelt thanks for your help until now, we earnestly beseech you for your assistance and your cooperation in the future, by striving to sell the *Prophet, &c.*, as much as you can; and, especially, you would facilitate our way, by sending the money for them as soon as you can, to publish the multitude of treatises that we have on various doctrinal topics, &c., already prepared for the press, and a great need for them; for profit is not our objective, rather the spread of truth throughout our country. Most of the money for the previous volume has yet to reach us, but it will have a hearty welcome when it does. We are all fellow workers in this last vineyard; and no doubt it will be according to our faith in this, as in the fulfillment of every other duty, that each will receive his "penny" at the end of the great harvest under our hands.

The first complete volume can be obtained, if they are requested soon. If there are any of the first issue on hand that cannot be sold, please send them back at your earliest convenience.

Every effort will be made to answer questions of the distributors with respect to doctrine, teachings, and anything else that is of benefit to the Saints, not to contend with words, and endless questions, but to present every ray of light, and do the good we desire for everyone, to the extent that our small publication is able.

*** *Address to Capt. D. Jones, George Town, Merthyr Tydfil.*

ANNOUNCEMENTS.

A MAN by the name of Morgan Thomas, one of the members of the Merthyr branch, was excommunicated some time ago, because of disgraceful and unrepentant transgressions. He is well known among the Saints for the great trouble he has caused; and it is so indisputable that he has felt as much of the mighty workings of the spirit of God as any man, by his being delivered from the hand of the enemy; and despite all this, we have heard that he is now a cruel persecutor. Pity him; the word is verified that says, that "it is a fearful thing to fall into the hands of the living God."

John Pugh, formerly of Llwyni, wishes to announce that he is calling back, with all his might, the false accusations that he declared against the Saints, that he perceives his sins to be atrocious, and that he desires forgiveness from the Saints and God, together with having the privilege of coming back into the church, and an interest in the prayers of the Saints, so that his behavior and his confession may co-testify to all that he is bringing forth fruits meet for repentance. He came before the council, and made satisfactory restitution to all. He has written to the church in Llwyni, for the same purpose, regularly; and we are pleased to announce that they have accepted him and his wife back.

We would wish all the Saints' most earnest attention on the plight of our American brothers and sisters who are exiles in the wilderness, by the thousands, because of their testimony of Jesus, and the word of God, on the plan that was drawn up by the council to assist them in their great and varied needs.

N.B.—Newly published by us in Welsh, a pamphlet, proving from their fruits, who are the "*False prophets of the Latter Days*."—Price a Penny. Also, "*What is Mormonism?*"—Price a Halfpenny. A defense in the face of the insolent accusations of the "*Cuckoo of Ton*," in the Star of Gomer.—Price a Penny.

*** The following English books can be obtained here, with a large reduction in their prices for cash; namely, *The Book of Mormon*, 3*s*.—*Doctrine and Covenants*, 2*s*. 6*p*.—*Hymn Books*, 1*s*. 6*p*., besides several small pamphlets. Also, the *Millennial Star* may be obtained monthly with the *Prophet*, by sending names and money, price *3p*. each. It is published on the 1st and the 15th of every month.

BAPTISMS IN MARCH.

WE are sorry to inform our readers that we are unable to publish how many, or even close to how many, were baptized last month, because of the negligence of the presidents in sending the number to us. Until now we have not received word from half of the places where we have heard that some have been baptized; but we hope this is the last time that we shall have to offer this excuse; and we shall announce the ones we know.

Merthyr.—Nine were baptized for the confession of their faith and their repentance.

Dowlais.—Eighteen were baptized. The "man of sin," shows in many ways his jealousy for the truth here, and having failed to prevent the honest in heart from embracing it in another way, he regroups, as he did in America when on the verge of dying, by indicating, suggesting, and prophesying that the Saints are doing, saying, or thinking something or other treasonable against some civic organizations, wishing through that to raise a riot, or some excuse to avenge their anger on the innocent; and we will be disappointed if this spirit increases in their evil bosom where it was nurtured, until it is believed by others, yes, even by themselves finally,—until they consider that they are serving God by perjuring themselves to try to prove it! Marvel as you will, we have seen this spirit giving birth to such villainy before now, more than once, yes, to the point of practically drinking a stream of innocent blood.

Penydarren.—Three were baptized last month.

Rhymni.—We have heard of six being baptized. Some who were members, and others who were preaching with other denominations, with approbation and influence. Great is their privilege.

Nantyglo.—We have heard of some; but we do not know how many, or in any place throughout the Monmouthshire conference.

Llwyni.—Two were baptized, with hopeful signs that others will love the truth.

Cwmbach.—One was baptized here, others promising, and still delaying.

Treboeth.—Brother J. Matthews announces that he has baptized two, and that there is a great call for preaching in those environs, and more than they can fill.

Dihewyd.—Five were baptized, with cheerful expectations for more soon.

Cardiff.—We cannot give a number, but we think we can say that more here than in any other branch this month; and perhaps because of the hotter persecution there the success is such. We are glad that everyone there is happy and firm in the faith despite it all. May it go forward.

Llanybydder.—*Daniel the Blind* and his booklet have caused quite a stir lately, and great are the crowds who have been listening to the preachers of the Saints, and many are believing our religion, after reading his booklet and ours. Last week two were baptized there. There was a large crowd there cheerfully and respectfully listening to the preaching, with signs that many believe. Three others promised to obey the Sunday following that one. Thus it is seen that the false prophecy is that of *Daniel the Blind*, where he proclaims, "Everyone will leave before long," although that is as true as nearly all the rest of his booklet. Pity him, let him go ahead if he wishes; his worst, and that of all his supporters, tends to increase "Mormonism."

Brechfa.—This is another place near Daniel; yes, where he is well known. Six have been baptized since he began to raise his arm against us.

Carmarthen.—In the place where his booklet was printed, and despite the influence of his *partner* also, everything is working together for the spread of the truth, which proves that we are baptizing more in the places where they are the most well known, than was ever done before in the same amount of time. Six were baptized, and hosts have been gathering to listen, ever since their persecution began; and thus we expect the reaction to be in these works also, and in every place, to the extent that they read our defense, and compare "Haman" and him without bias, and judge the two sides according to the scriptures.

Rhosllanerchrugog.—Three were baptized lately. Elder R. Evans baptized some here and there through the North. Abel Evans reports, after visiting the majority of the churches throughout the North, that they are all, nearly without exception, warm in the spirit, and firm in the "faith which was once delivered unto the Saints," and enjoying the gifts and great blessings abundantly in every branch, and going forth toward perfection. May He who began the good work in them sustain them until the day of our Lord Jesus Christ is our prayer for all of them. Amen.

CONTENTS.

MERTHYR TYDFIL:

PUBLISHED AND FOR SALE BY D. JONES, AND ALSO FOR SALE BY THE SAINTS IN GENERAL.

JOHN JONES, PRINTER, RHYDYBONT.

PROPHET OF THE JUBILEE,

OR

STAR OF THE SAINTS.

No. 11.] MAY, 1847. [Price 2*c*.

THE "*HATER OF DECEIT*" PROVED A *LOVER*,

A MAKER, AND A PUBLISHER, OF "DECEIT" HIMSELF.

In the May issue of the *Revivalist*, pg. 144, &c., is seen a lengthy essay under the title, "*The Mormons are Deceivers*," composed by someone who calls himself, "*Hater of Deceit, from Blackwood*." Although for any thoughtful man the writing throughout contains sufficient proofs that its author is deserving of the character we have given him, still we shall glean some of the ears of corn from his labor, to show more clearly the kind of harvest that one can expect, together with the filth of the field that produces such cabbages. The first leap the splendid author takes to attempt to prove that close to 1500 of his fellowmen in Wales, not counting hundreds of thousands of others, are deserving of the above heavy accusation is to shout with all his might from the top of the crag, "*False*," and he continues to shout "*false*" no fewer than four times in his beginning to battle. On this axis he bases all his preliminary false accusations, as if he had already won the battle without firing a shot! Is it a small thing in his sight to condemn without proof that religion on which so many rest their souls? If so, this proves how little it would matter to him for others to do the same with his own religion.

THE "MORMONS ARE DECEIVERS."

Because, is it? *Because* what, I wonder? Is it *because* they are deceivers? But slowly does it, you swift galloper, first prove that, and then we shall have reason to thank you; but until you can do so, it would be just as appropriate for us to shout, "*because* you are a deceiver, yes, so is everyone else." Having founded his aerial castle on the word "*because*," he piles up a heap of false accusations instead of stones, and he fuses them together with lying liquid instead of *mortar*; and so, it is no wonder that they collapse in confusion, and bury him in their ruins, for it is said that he who digs a pit for his neighbor will fall into it himself. Making his bed in the minds of his readers (as does the pig in the dungheap), he sings the old *tune* of every deceiver, namely that the whole thing is "not out of envy for the Saints," rather out of "*love for his fellow nation*," lest they be deceived, &c. But by their fruits shall we judge him, regardless of that; and let the reader judge from the following examples of his guileless and loving sentences! whether he is a *hater*, or a lover and deviser of deceit and false accusations. "They claim to be able to work miracles, &c.," says he. If he has followed them to the extent of being able to have the advantage of understanding their deceit, as he claims he has, he must also understand that those are deliberate and totally unfounded false accusations; or, whether he has or not, he has been caught lying in this matter, and he ought to try to gain a better understanding of what the Saints believe, before daring to proclaim it to the world. Is he so thickheaded, I wonder, that he does not see the great difference between the profession of worshipping that God who was formerly admitted as the author of miracles, and who is still admitted as unchanging, which is the same as admitting that he (not men) works miracles now, and that men claim miraculous power?

Let him understand the difference there is between his assertion and the truth. Love for what compelled him to do this, I wonder? He says also that he saw them failing to heal one small child, and he offers that as proof of their deceit! According to that logic, he condemns all the apostles because they failed to cast the devil out of that man! Yes, he proves that Paul was a deceiver half again as bad as the Saints, because he failed to heal two that we know of, if not more, namely Trophimus and Timotheus. Oh, poor thing! here you have proved yourself so much a "*hater of deceit*," that you have reasoned yourself into a deceitful deist, and placed the Saints on the list of the apostles. We thank you for placing us in such company. Further on, you admit that the Saints imitate the apostles, through their obedience to the godly rites of anointing with oil, the laying on of hands, &c. But what deceit is in that, any more than the general claim that every denomination makes about the other apostolic rites? You suggest that it was deceit for the mother to try to get the elder to anoint her child to heal him; all right, we shall attribute the "deceit" to James, and let it be between you and him, for it was he who instructed, chap. v, ver. 14,—"Is there any sick among you, let him call for the elders of the church, and they will anoint him with oil," &c. Here you are, like every other deist, head to head with an apostle, by scorning the Saints for obeying him! Now, is it the Saints, or you, who are the deceiver professing a form of godliness, but denying its power? You blame the anointer, for asking the mother if her faith was strong enough for the child to be healed. What deceit could there be in that, without admitting that there was as much deceit in Jesus Christ, when he asked the same thing to those blind men,—"Believe ye that I am able to do this?" he said, Mat. ix, 27-30.

"According to thy faith be it unto you," he said. To another, Luke xviii, 42, he says also, "THY FAITH (not my faith, but *thy own faith*) hath saved thee." Further, Paul did not dare to tell the lame man in Lystra to walk, until after "stedfastly beholding him, and perceiving that he had faith to be healed." No wonder you call the elder a deceiver like them, since he used the same words.

"The elder drank some of the oil himself," you say. *Well done!* very careful indeed, lest there be some harm in it to the child. As for the "pouring" on the child's head, that was a bit of a *slip* of the tongue, like "*Daniel the Blind*" who says that the oil ran all over his clothes, when in fact, they meant to say, or ought to have said, anointing with a fingertip. What deceit is in this again? Since trying to get to grips with the deceit is our work, so that we can correct it, we shall look astutely, for until now Mr. "Hater of Deceit" has failed to reveal to us anything except his own sectarian deceit. "Having prayed the prayer of faith, he said that the child was healed," you say. Well, would he be so foolish as to say that, unless the child was healed? What good would it do? Would not everyone see that it was not true? Here is an acknowledgement of the power of God sealing their obedience to his ordinances by healing the sick. Very good, Sir. You acknowledge also, reluctantly, that "perhaps he was" well. That you saw him sick the following Wednesday is not any proof that he could not have gotten better three times in the meantime. Furthermore, had he not gotten better, whose failing would it be, the anointer's? If so, it was Paul's failing that he did not heal Trophimus and Timotheus, yes, Jesus Christ's failing, says your logic, for not healing the eyes of the blind man the first time he put clay on them; thus you still couple the elder with apostolic company, and he should be very grateful to you for the honor you give him. After scrutinizing the example, and failing to see anything similar to deceit of the Saints, now we shall show clearly the deceit and its promoters, like this,—"I saw them fail in their attempts to heal the sick," says he. Compare this with the testimony that he admits the mother gave to him. She says she believed, and her reason was that her other child had been healed by the elder's using the same means. If the testimony of the mother is true, which he does not attempt to disprove either, (and how can he?) then the deceit is seen clearly; yes, here is the deceit, and the great *bogeyman* he refers to, but with this difference at the same time, that Mr. "*Hater of Deceit*" is its father, and to him also is attributed the lying deceit. Thanks to you, Mr. Deceiver, for showing yourself so publicly, so that we may be saved from you!

"THE SPIRIT OF PROPHECY."

As for the "Dark Daniel," you mention, read his story which we have published already, and you shall see your persecuting *partner* like "*Haman hanging from his own gallows*," so that every lover of the truth will loathe him and his evil tricks; and it is true that more of his acquaintances joined with the Saints, than before his pranks, accordingly. All things work together for the good of truth. Next, our author mocks the Saints for professing the "Spirit of Prophecy." But let us go slowly here again, until we scrutinize his own rule, in order to see whether it is the *deniers* or the *professors* of the spirit of prophecy who deserve the verdict of deceivers. We ask, what is the "Spirit of Prophecy?" John answers, Rev. xix, 10, "for the testimony of Jesus is the spirit of Prophecy." How can anyone claim the one and deny the other, then, without contradicting himself, or John? Paul says in 1 Cor. xii, 3, "And no one can say (i.e., testimony, or knowing) that Jesus is the Lord, but by the Holy Ghost." Jesus Christ says in John xvii, 3, "And this is life eternal, that they might *know* thee the only true God, and Jesus Christ, whom thou has sent." Thus, the *denial* of the "spirit of prophecy" is sufficient to prove the ignorance of the denier of Jesus Christ, and by that his unfamiliarity with God, for no one cometh unto the Father but by me, says Christ. Thus the denier proves his own spirit of prophecy without Christ, without God in the world, yes, without anything except for hypocritical deceit to this point! Doubt the logic of those scriptures if you can, or take back your mocking assertions, Sir. By now, here we are about to hang this atheist with his own rope, having already unwittingly brought all his sympathizers and supporters onto the same *scaffold!* Pity the "Reverends" who have published their own sentence in their '*Revivalist*.' I wonder if they would not *revive* were their readers to let go of the cord from around their necks once again? For our part, we cannot release them, and neither can the Bible, until either they admit the spirit of prophecy, or cease to climb to their pulpits to shout out with long and hypocritical faces, that the Mormons are deceivers, and that they are the ones who are witnesses of Jesus, servants of God, &c. Asserting the latter, and denying the former, has to be a complete contradiction! I wonder whether the *Reverend* Editor will be ashamed ever again to claim to be a servant of Jesus Christ, until he gains the indispensable qualifications for so being, namely that "Spirit of Prophecy" that is so much denied? We turn again to Mr. "*Hater of Deceit*,"—"The Saints claim that they know things that have been, that are, and that will come," he says. Well, they do not thereby, claim anything except that which their faithful forerunner promised them in accordance with their need, John xvi, 13. He promised, "when he, the Spirit of truth, is come (namely the Holy Ghost, namely, the 'Spirit of Prophecy') he will guide you into *all* truth." Further, "and he will shew you things to come." If this does not contain a promise of knowledge of "things that have been, that are, and that will come," it is all suggested in the following: "But the Comforter, which is the Holy Ghost, whom the Father will send in my name, he shall teach you *all things, and bring all things to your remembrance*, whatsoever I have said unto you." Again, he says, "The Spirit of truth, which proceedeth from the Father, he shall *testify* of me." Why, Sir, do you not allow it the same freedom to reveal what it desires to the Saints now as before? Answer, whoever can! By the sacred volume we venture to challenge all our readers to answer why! Up to now the 'hater of deceit' admits the profession of the Saints scripturally, and by his own denial he is proven a denier of the scriptures! because remember that it is the *profession*, and the *denial* of the Spirit of Prophecy that is in question so far. Next, we shall note his refutations, and what are they? Only his *assertions*, which have already been proven unworthy of belief. In order to catch him in his own net, we shall admit even that, and we shall get some *one* (out of hundreds of thousands) prophesying that a certain number would be baptized at some specified time. In the same breath he admits that six of the number had been baptized. Very good, is it not! Could he himself foretell so much truth, I wonder? The omens are bad now. And if one were to come forward, what better proof would that be that the "Mormons are deceivers," than proving him a deceiver would be proof that all the Independents were deceivers? Or would not the same logic prove that every column in the *Revivalist* was slanderous false accusations because of those columns that he filled thus! That would be twisted logic, would it not? again, here is his best logic to prove the Saints false prophets. Bear in mind as well that not even Paul claimed prophetic perfection; rather, "we know in part, and we prophesy in part," he says. The Holy Ghost was not imperfect, but his own stubborn spirit fought against the divine influences, because of the corruption of humanity, and this is what equally numbs the increase of his understanding of the other; and that was the extent of the correctness of his prophecies. Still I do not think that any of the Saints would tell him that they had prophesied anything similar. If they had, it is the first we have heard of such a thing; and despite questioning everyone, almost, we failed to find a foundation for his assertions, or that such a man had been in the church of Blackwood, Victoria, or any other place, unless he lives in Dowlais, the *factory* in which such nets are made cheaply.

With respect to Elder Jones, whose name you take lightly, this is only one in those environs, and he will deny it to the extreme, that he knows of the least foundation for your assertions. As for that 'W. Thomas,' who makes such an effort to 'clarify the deception'; may he go forward, poor thing, as quickly as he can; he is striving to clarify his own deception as are you. We expect to see him coming with his deceit at his tail, or like a shooting star through the atmosphere of the *Revivalist* as soon as he can be caught, in accordance with the common practice of those we excommunicate. It is surprising how they flash one after another through the religious *chronicles* of our '*religious age*,' everyone out of '*love* for their fellow nation,' of course! But rub your eyes, readers, and you will see where they have all gone. All like shooting stars into the depths of the universe in the midst of the things that have been, leaving behind them nothing but a foul smell to stain their remembrance; and thus will it be again. Everything we are told by the existence of such a man as that W. F., contains like the *Almanacs*, 'some truth and some lies' about his remarkable success, so that the Saints cannot '*deceive*' anyone else there; it is true for the most part; because they have not tried to '*deceive*;' their religion did not '*deceive*' anyone there, and furthermore, it is impossible for it to deceive anyone there, or in any other area; because it is its own proof of its truthfulness to every honest man who tries it out fairly and without prejudice, as dozens of the Saints will testify even in *Blackwood* to your face, Sir, and to the Mr. Thomas you mention: and what are your assertions in the face of more than ten to one experienced and acceptable witnesses? But still, in the syntactic meaning that you give to your assertion, it is an untruth known to you Sir, because you and your neighbors should know that the Saints have baptized more in the time since you and your *partner* have been persecuting them than ever before! Do you not know that they have baptized five recently in a period shorter than that number of days, besides many at other times? And why do you dare to proclaim that they cannot get 'ANYONE *in that area?*' Yes, to the face of all your neighbors who know better, or should! Therefore, you two cannot deceive anyone to stop them from obeying the truth; that's all; and then you take revenge through the *Revivalist*, do you not? worse still, you do all that out of 'love' as well!! Keep everyone from such '*love*,' as from a dragon's poison! Or on with it until it stirs all honest men and lovers of the truth to prove it and embrace it more and more; because there is no danger that you can deceive any of their kind. Another example of your untruthful deceit is your assertion 'that the Saints when they baptize someone, call a council and prophesy to what office God called him.' We challenge you to prove that for once somewhere! You cannot. But we do not have to disprove it; our rules, which we have already published in Welsh, and which are before the public, prove that our preachers are not called upon except in our conferences; and then not by the prophesying you mention. If you have ever been with the Saints (which is greatly doubted) you must know better than your assertion. In the name of truth whither did you exile your logic when misrepresenting your fellow men like this? prove your *love* by calling it back.

OBVIOUS DECEPTIVE REASONING.

As for the T. Smith who you say was ordained a priest immediately, it is as true as the others of your assertions; instead of getting drunk and being excommunicated after *two months*, as you say, that was not for as many *years* as that! And instead of being called and ordained '*immediately*,' he was not called nor was he ordained for two-and-a-half years after his baptism! Was it not '*jealousy*' of them that compelled you to do this, Sir? Who will believe you! There are hundreds who will testify to this throughout these environs to the present day. But, if he had been called as soon as you say, would his sin that he committed *afterwards* prove his *previous* unsuitability? If so, your logic condemns even Jesus Christ for calling Peter or Judas; certainly the crime of the one shows the deceit of their calling like the other! Here you are, having placed Jesus Christ worse than the Saints because he called *two such men!* Weigh the preachers of other denominations in the scales in which you weigh T. Smith, and he will get considerable company, yes, not only Peter and Judas, but also David, Solomon, Lot, Noah, and Adam. Still further, register 'Lucifer, the morning Star,' on the same list as those. Strange company, is it not? Was every one of them evil before sinning? If not, how will he whom you name be proven unsuitable then? We thank you unanimously for admitting the temperance of our rules, by admitting that we do not allow membership to a drunkard, much less an office in our moral and pure church. Rather *strict* rules, are they not? I wonder whether our discipline is not as severe against other sins? And so where is the deceit? we ask again: but still in vain. It is so easy for deceivers to shout 'deceit,' 'false prophets,' 'false teachers,' 'fanatics of the town': thus it is for you. You stand by your fruits, you who have been proven guilty of what you accuse the innocent of. Next he depicts a church meeting of the Saints on Sunday afternoon; we shall strive to get hold of the *deceit* in that thing then. He admits that the priest began the meeting by *reading* and *praying*; if that is deceit, all religious people are as much deceivers as the Saints. This is the first time a man who dares to call himself a '*hater of deceit*,' teaches us that *reading* the Bible and *praying* are deceit. Still, this must be deceit, because he says that it is 'obvious that EVERYTHING they (the Saints) have anything to do with is deceit!' According to this logic the Reverend editor who published this is proven a deceiver, at every meeting he holds. You do not blame them more than others for 'striving to color [the truths they believe] in the most beautiful way to attract their listeners to love them'; for this is their privilege as well as the privilege of others, 'after threatening them terribly, because they love the darkness instead of the light, which they were showing to them,' he says. Here is a correct admittance of the light: what darkness do they warn one to beware of? Not traditional darkness, because their presence there proved that unnecessary; what else but transgressions against the sacred rule they read at the beginning of the meeting, where they warned to beware of them! Very good again, remembering that you admit all this out of jealousy. What deceit is there in exhorting people not to sin! Paul exhorts Timothy to be instant in season and out of season, to preach, reprove, rebuke, &c., because he foresaw the time when they would not endure sound doctrine, but after their own lusts would they heap to themselves [not sent by God through the Spirit of Prophecy, &c.] teachers. Since their ears were itching from the truth, they turn their ears away [as does Mr. 'Hater of Deceit,'] unto the fables, namely such fables as you and other sectarians publish out of '*love*,' *alias* HATE, for the truth. Now, Sir, we ask, and you will answer the truth for your conscience, if Paul were your neighbor in Blackwood, then, could he portray you more accurately, do you think? Despite denying the prophecies of your contemporaries, you must admit the truthfulness and most detailed fulfillment of Paul's, on your own condition. Where does the deceit meet?

[*To be continued.*]

"MOTHER'S GIFT," OR THE FIRST CATECHISM FOR THE CHILDREN OF THE SAINTS.

WHAT is man?—The race of God.

Who is Jesus Christ?—Our brother.

What is man in his beginning?—A helpless baby.

What is he in his stature?—One of the sons of God.

What is he in his moral perfection?—Like unto Christ; and Christ is like unto God: and they are all one society.

How many lives does a man have?—He shall live in three lives.

What is the first?—Spiritual life.

What is the second?—Temporal life.

What is the third?—One that is immortal and eternal.

How did he begin to live in the first?—He was conceived and born of God.

How did he begin to live in the second?—He was conceived and born of the flesh.

How shall he begin to live in the third?—Through resurrection from the dead.

What is his eternal destiny?—To be in the image of God, and with him.

What is man like without revelation?—Like a ship in the fog without rudder or compass.

What is he like when he receives divine revelations?—Like a *lamp* full of light; he shows the truth of all things.

What is the Spirit of man?—The candle of God.

How is it lit?—By the Spirit of God.

How many Gods are there?—"There are many lords, and many gods, but to *us* there is but one God."

How many heavens are there?—They are without number.

Where will the heaven of the Saints be?—*On the earth;* and on every perfect star and planet.

Briefly, what is Mormonism?—A plan of divine truths.

How old is it?—There is no beginning of days or end of its life span.

What is its destiny?—To fill the earth and the heaven with knowledge and perfect love.

Who is Joseph Smith?—He is the brother of Jesus Christ.

Where did his authority come from?—From the third heaven through angels.

What was he sent to do?—To establish the everlasting kingdom of God, preach the gospel of peace, and to announce the dawn of the great Jubilee to all that believe.

What success will his mission have?—General success, until the knowledge of the Lord covers the world, as the waters cover the sea.

What if men try to oppose him?—They will not succeed; rather they will be like the fine dust on the scales.

Why is that?—Because the great and powerful God has awakened as if from the sleep of ages to do his work.

What are all the political forms of the world?—The great idol that Nebuchadnezzar saw.

What are the religious forms of this world?—That spiritual Babylon that John saw (when he was on the isle of Patmos,) which was full of blasphemous names.

MERTHYR CONFERENCE.

WHICH was held in the *Cymreigyddion Hall*, Sunday, and Monday, the 18th and 19th of April, as follows:—

At half past ten o'clock in the morning unanimously elected president was Capt. Jones, who had begun the Conference as usual, by singing praise and praying, and he addressed the crowd warmly, expounding on the importance and godliness of the glorious work that was entrusted to us; and he showed the great difference that exists between the human plans and the perfect plan of the kingdom of God. He proved that men are equal to their wisdom that the former have composed and perfected; but, that this latter plan is to perfect men; or that the one perfects its subjects, and the others are perfected *by* their imperfect subjects! That the latter is as unreasonable as it would be for man to try to raise himself from off the floor,—only according to the wisdom they possess can anything be expected from men,—no one can organize a plan to perfect himself, or consequently perfect another better than himself, any more than the stream rise any higher than its source. According to this reasoning, the president showed that *Mormonism* was established on a divine foundation, and that that life and power were in all its veins, its sinews, and its joints, from its head to its foot; and that it benefits everyone through, and according to the correct understanding of it and the correct use of it. At that time president F. D. Richards came in from America, besides J. Holliday, Kendall, Webb, and others from England, and they found the hall filled with cheerful and handsome listeners. The president called on the representatives of all the branches to report their numbers, their condition, &c., which was done as follows:— Number of branches in the Glamorgan conference is 18; Elders 34; Priests 48; Teachers 38; Deacons 17. Baptized since the previous conference (3rd and 4th of last January) 220. The total represented in this conference now is 965. The presidents showed that the situation and condition of their branches were comfortable, successful, and hopeful; and that all, nearly without exception, were in unity, love, and the bond of peace, and enjoying gifts and comfort of the Holy Ghost according to their faithfulness and their diligence. After that Brother Richards addressed the meeting briefly and comprehensively in English, and the morning meeting ended with prayer and singing.

At 2 o'clock there was a church meeting for the Saints only, and the Hall was very full of them. Three who had been baptized were received into the church, and then the ordinance of the Lord's Supper was administered to the numerous company, who delighted themselves in the enjoyment of the love of Christ in their hopes, and in the happiness of the Holy Ghost. Brother Richards explained the purposes and usefulness of the ordinances, and exhorted the Saints to unity, faithfulness, and love. He showed the goodness of God toward his Saints in America, through wondrous deliverances from the hand of their enemies,—miraculously feeding them in the wilderness, and comforting them in all persecution; and the president addressed the meeting on the same topic in Welsh, and he ended the meeting with prayer.

The evening meeting was begun by elder Thomas Pugh. The president addressed the numerous crowd, inviting them to obey the eternal gospel with haste; he was followed by Thomas Pugh on the nature and offices of the apostolic church, &c. Then Brother Richards pointed out who are the children of Abraham, according to those who follow in the footsteps of their father Abraham, who are of the faith of Abraham, and who carry out the works of Abraham; that Abraham left his home to look for a country, but that no one else had done that except for the Saints. Abraham and his family were led by divine revelations, so it is with the Saints: the former suffered every affliction; and through faith, which was proved through works, expected a 'country,' namely the place of rest which is yet to come for the people of God. All religionists except for the Saints expect an imaginary heaven, '*beyond the bounds of time and space*.' He went into more detail on the similarity of the 'Latter-day Saints,' to Abraham and his seed, and that they will imitate him more and more, until they can sit with Abraham, father of the faithful, in the kingdom of God, namely the blessed place of rest on the earth, and that he died in hope of enjoying. After him the president interpreted the greater part, making additions and exhorting the listeners to prove our plan in an honest and unbiased manner, since that is how God would prove it truthful to their satisfaction. He thanked the crowd lovingly for their gentleness and their cheerfulness during the day, and he persuaded the Saints to live spotlessly before the world, to strive in every way to spread the truth, and to do good to all, especially to the family of faith. Brother Richards ended the day's labor by asking God to bless them.

Monday at half past ten the Hall was overflowing with people, and the president and Brother Richards spent the meeting showing the scriptural way of calling and ordaining to the different church offices—the duties, and the necessity for the different offices like before; God would not pour out his judgments upon the world now before sending his servants to warn them and to offer them safety. Then two were called to be elders in the Merthyr branch, one in Dowlais, one in Penydarren, one in Rhymni, and one in Risca. Twelve were called to be priests in Merthyr, three in Rhymni, two in Carmarthen, three in Cardiff, one in Cwmbach, and one in Cwmbychan. Teachers—three in Merthyr, one in Rhymni, two in Cardiff, two in Carmarthen, one in Cwmbach, one in Llanybydder, and one in Penydarren. Deacons,—Rhymni one, Cardiff two. In Dowlais, six were called to be priests, four to be Teachers, and two to be Deacons. Then brother Richards ended the meeting by praying.

At half past two o'clock the Hall was full again, and in this meeting the majority of the officers that had been called were ordained, and it was agreed that the rest would be ordained in their respective branches; the president counseled and warned those persons emphatically to respect the proper use of their valuable offices, with an eye on the coming day of reckoning; he exhorted them to open their mouths in wisdom, and for all they do to stem truly from love toward, and a desire to benefit men; but for them to refrain from arguing with stubborn men, or to debate about words or ungodly questions; and he sincerely beseeched all the Saints to pray for them. Then president Holliday, from Bath, and after him president Kendall, from Bristol, addressed the meeting, and after them, elder Webb; after that the last two sang a hymn in remembrance of the martyrdom of Joseph and Hyrum Smith, and their godliness, and the meeting was brought to a close with a prayer by elder Henshaw.

At half past six elder Thomas Pugh preached in Welsh, Brother Richards in English, and the president after him in Welsh, and all with great power and persuasion; and it was clear by the attentive listening, and everyone's cheerfulness, that they received pleasure, light, and happiness of the heavenly Comforter.

Thus this lovely and useful Conference ended under the blessing of God, to open the eyes of many to see the glory of the kingdom of God, and to strengthen the Saints in the holiest faith; we have never seen more signs of unity, brotherly love, and a determination to go forward through all persecutions and obstacles, until reaching the supreme achievement in Christ Jesus. May the gracious Lord strengthen all of us to continue faithful, until we arrive in the company and glory of all the faithful with our Father in the kingdom of God, is our prayer through Jesus Christ. Amen.

WILLIAM DAVIES,
EDWARD EDWARDS. } *Scribes.*

PARABLE OF THE TREE THAT BEARS NINE KINDS OF FRUIT!

ONE day a certain wealthy vinedresser *(a)* visited his vineyard *(b)* in a distant country, and he planted some wondrous plant *(c)* that he had brought with him, which had become a tree that bore nine *(d)* kinds of excellent fruit. He chose, *(e)* and taught *(f)* his servants *(g)*, how to tend and look after it so that nothing would harm it. He had brought a few *(h)* of each one of the fruits with him, so that his servants, and some of the people of the vineyard, could taste them; and then he went back *(i)* to the distant land. His servants, after tasting the fruits, and understanding that they were excellent and healthful nourishment, as well as medicinal for every illness, endeavored day and night to tend the plant according to the instructions they had received. Their diligence was crowned with such remarkable success that numerous verdant branches sprouted forth, and it was enshrouded with beautiful sweet flowers; and in the first summer the tree was overladen with fruits like the one the vinedresser had brought at first. Soon its fame spread throughout the vineyard, and the people journeyed from every direction seeking the fruits. The servants took many of the plants to other parts, and everywhere they were planted (if treated according to the directions of the vinedresser) the same kinds of fruits were brought forth; nothing less, and nothing different; and to everyone's surprise, it bore fruit on the tops of the most rocky mountains as well as in the lushest valleys, in the frozen poles as well as in the *torrid Zone;* in short, it was never seen without a single one of the nine fruits.

There was a certain oppressor *(k)* who had come from a distant land a long time ago, who claimed a certain right to the vineyard, and many of the people believed him and served him; but not one of those kinds of fruit grew on their trees, which caused his servants to complain to the oppressor, because the excellence of the fruits of the others brought nearly all the people of the vineyard to their markets, and that hope for their own profit was fading. Upon hearing this, the oppressor promised that he would journey to a distant land for a plant *(l)* just as good, if not better, than those they had; and when he returned, and planted it, and the time came for it to bear fruit, some fruits were seen on it that were similar to the others; but to their disappointment, behold they were deadly poison *(m)* to everyone that tasted them. The oppressor, and his servants, became more and more jealous of the others because of this, and because they were too proud to ask them for the plants, they attacked them, and killed them, thinking they could get the tree and its fruits, and that everyone would come to them to buy afterwards *(n)*. But to their surprise, and the great loss of all the people of the vineyard, not one of the earlier fruits grew on the tree after that, because they had not been taught by the vinedresser or his servants how to tend it; and soon its branches withered, its freshness dried up, and trunk rotted *(o)*, and all the people hungered for the fruits for a long time, and there was none to be had *(p)*.

In the meantime, the tree of the oppressor grew very large, and instead of fruits, all the unclean birds of the land overburdened its branches, making it their nesting place, and preying on everyone who came that way. At last, one of the eagles *(q)* of the oppressor, who was much better than the others, taking pity on the sufferers, got hold of some ancient book *(r)* written by the servants of the vinedresser, describing the old tree, and its toothsome fruits, which created a desire in him to get a tree similar to it, but nowhere could he find a plant to get started. In the end, as he was gazing down from his nest on the corpses of the multitudes who had died around the trunk of the tree, he saw there some green *suckers* growing from the roots of the tree, and he thought he could, with the directions in the ancient book, nurture one of those to become a fruitful tree; but he knew that his life was in danger if the other birds understood his objective, and through cunning, he succeeded in getting a *sucker*, and fled with it, and planted it in the furthermost part of the vineyard, and it grew to be a strong tree. Others, upon seeing his success with his tree, ventured to do the same, and were as successful as he. In time, *suckers* grew from those *suckers*, which he planted in a like manner, until those trees were very numerous through the vineyard; and although they were quite similar to the old tree at first glance, yet not one of the nine kinds of fruit was growing on them anywhere, although each one claimed that his tree was of the same species as the fruitful tree. Since there was a severe famine throughout all the land, when the people heard that there were so many fruitful trees in their midst, they gathered to them in multitudes, shouting for fruit, so they would not die of hunger. At this, the birds stretched their heads over their nests, and in a voice like the voice of men they persuaded the people, saying, "Oh, the primitive fruits are no longer necessary. It is true that nine kinds of fruit grew on it in the beginning, and their only purpose was to show that such a tree had existed [!], and the only comfort you can have now is to journey to our trees when you feel hungry, and look at them more stedfastly the more the hunger pangs tighten your stomach; and we shall read from this ancient book the story of the feasts that men enjoyed from the fruits of the primitive tree, for faith is everything that is required to keep you alive without nourishment, just believe the story without enjoying, and journey here to look and listen. What! can you not live on the strength of *imagination!* for after arriving in the far country you shall have those nine kinds of fruits *(s)*." In this manner they deceived multitudes to journey to them, and though weakening and starving, the children followed after their fathers to the death, until their bones could be seen whitening across the face of the earth around these trees.

But the *most sensible (t)* of the people opposed them, saying that they were deceiving them, and that the groans of the dead, together with the excruciating pains of hunger on their own bowels, were proven facts that they could not live without enjoying the fruits of the tree themselves; and since they claimed that such fruits did not grow on the tree now, they could not believe that such a tree had ever existed, or borne the nine kinds of fruit their ancient book described; for (said they) the inseparable connections with which the chief naturalist tied every effect to its own cause, together with examples of all the other trees of the vineyard, bearing the same fruits now as they bore at that time, prove your foolishness in claiming that you have that tree now, while yet denying its fruits. This caused pitched battles between these factions. All the armies of the former united against the latter, although not infrequently they killed each other, and flooded the vineyard with the blood of their beguiled. The whole vineyard was in this sorrowful condition for a long period of time. Finally, the vinedresser took pity on their wretched state; and since the end of the harvest was drawing nigh, when he intended to possess the entire vineyard himself after putting it in order, he threw the oppressor into prison, together with all his servants who sided with him, and he sent one of his servants *(u)* from the distant country with a plant like unto the first, so that those who wished could eat of its fruit, so that all would not die of hunger before it came. The servant planted it in a lovely and secret glade, he chose and taught those assigned to him *(v)*, and he set them to watch over, and to tend the tree carefully (for he knew that there was deadly enmity between him and all the unclean birds), and he returned home. Through the faithfulness of the servants to do everything as they were commanded, this tree brought forth an abundant harvest of exactly the same fruits as the nine kinds that grew on the original one. The joyful news went as if on the wings of the wind among the people, and great was the gathering there to seek after the fruits, and all who came feasted on them without money and without a price. But when the oppressor heard this, it frightened him greatly, for he knew perfectly well that that tree could not be obtained from anyone except the vinedresser, and he also understood that his time was short *(w)* to rule over the vineyard. At this he remembered the trick that had succeeded in destroying the said tree before, and he stirred up his servants to persecute the others. He told them to persuade the people that the fruits did not grow on their tree, but that their claims were lies. He also told them to persuade those who had tasted of them already, that they were the poisoned fruit that grew on his old tree, and to warn everyone they could not to believe them, or to associate with them, because it was nearly impossible to get anyone to leave them once they had tasted of the fruits, &c., *(y)*. And in this manner his lies succeeded until he killed the earliest servants* who had looked after the tree; but to his great disappointment and that of his servants, the tree had taken root so deep, that a number of plants from it had transplanted themselves across the vineyard, and were bearing the fruits so abundantly, that hosts of those who denied the existence of the primitive tree, together with some of the wisest and most honest of the others, defended them, so they could not succeed; for these cruel enemies, like the other tree, were those who received much gold, silver, respect, a luxurious world, and colorful garments, from the other trees. They foresaw that their hope for profit would fade if the people got to taste the fruits; and also, when the wind blew from one of these trees toward their trees, it struck them with such a blast, that their leaves drooped, their branches shook, so they could not support the birds that nested in them; and since the people did not gather there to be plundered, some of the birds fell to the ground, together with their nests, and they could no longer fly, but they chewed the bark in their rage†. Seeing by this that this would be their own fate before long, the other birds of prey became even more angry, and they all joined together in a mighty campaign to get revenge on the servants of the vinedresser and their followers; and although they had always been hostile before, they made peace with our old mother-family at last, in this last place of battle, and they succeeded in forcing all those who did not obey them to gather to their trees, and they refused the fruits (but they did not kill anyone), and they went away in a large group in many ships across the great sea‡, and they returned to their nests, and great was the rejoicing throughout the land because of their victory. They sent gifts of joy to each other for having got rid of their enemies, and they boasted that they would have all the prey in their clutches before long§. Suddenly, they were frightened amidst their rejoicing by the roaring of thunder, lightning, and the sound of a terrible storm. The vineyard shook, the hills danced in fear, and the entire vineyard swayed like a drunken man. The sun was dressed in sackcloth of hair as mourning apparel, and all the elements were mixed up, like soup in a vat, which they boiled, and all the trees of the vineyard, together with the unclean birds and their beguiled ones, which was heard from afar like the crackling of brambles under a pot, and they snarled at each other, shouting, "Oh, that we had listened to the voice of the servants of the vinedresser! Oh, that we had partaken of their fruits, so we could live eternally! But the summer has ended, our harvest of believing your enchantment is over; you promised us peace, but O! now we are being punished in this flame!"|| At this, behold the vinedresser himself, and his innumerable retinue, come in aerial chariots of fire, setting fire in the eastern corner, which spread quickly and annihilated on the right and on the left everything before it, like dry stubble, so that all that was understood of this horrible massacre was groaning and crying aloud.¶ And this scene was closed up by the loud sound of a trumpet from the midst of the chariots, declaring, "And the smoke of their punishment will rise up forever and ever."** And it echoed like the sound of harps through the atmosphere, "Rejoice because of it in the heavens, and your holy apostles and prophets, for God has avenged you."†† And they all joined in the *chorus*, "Just thou art, O Lord, King of the saints; for they have spilled the blood of saints and the prophets." He that reads, let him consider this parable! In order to understand the parable, read the following references:—

(a) Jesus Christ, see Isaiah 5, 1—7; Mat. 20, 1; 21, 28; Luke 13, 6—8. *(b)* The earth. *(c)* The gospel. *(d)* The nine gifts of the Holy Ghost, 1 Cor. 12. *(e)* John 15, 16. *(f)* Mat. 28, 20. *(g)* The apostles, &c. *(h)* The miracles that Christ himself did before establishing his kingdom. *(i)* His ascension into heaven. *(k)* The devil enemy, Mat. 13, 25. *(l)* The Church of Rome. *(m)* False miracles, Mat. 24, 24; Rev. 13, 13, 14. *(n)* Those who killed the successors of the apostles. *(o)* When divine authority was taken from the earth, and the church went into the wilderness, Rev. 12, 5, 6. *(p)* The famine for the gospel through the "dark ages," Amos 8, 11, 12. *(q)* The first who opposed the church of Rome, and established his own church. *(r)* The New Testament. The *suckers* are all the daughters of the "old mother," and their daughters, Rev. 13, 18. *(s)* All who deny the necessity of the nine kinds of gifts of the Holy Ghost throughout the world, and claim their commission from the book, and that the purpose of the gifts was to prove the truth of Christianity: see the *Baptist*, the *Star of Gomer*, and the *Revivalist*, &c., and then 1 Tim. 4, 1, 2; 2 Tim. 3, 1—9; and 4, 3, 4; Judas 4, 10, 12, 19. *(t)* The atheists opposed sectarianism, 2 Peter 2, 11, "because of those that blaspheme the way of truth." *(u)* The angel that John saw bringing the everlasting gospel back to the earth, Rev. 14, 6. *(v)* Joseph Smith, &c. *(w)* Rev. 12, 12. *(y)* All who plot, who publish, who preach, or who deliver, any of the "thousand and one" unfounded tales, and the false accusations that flood the country about the Saints. * Those godly martyrs in the Carthage jail, and dozens of other innocent Saints on the continent. † The *blast* that has begun, and is increasing more and more so the excellence of truth will be understood. The withering of their leaves, the shaking of their churches, and their rottenness, have become too obvious to hide any longer. Their decay is so rapid in America, and their judgments are increasing, until they hold meetings of fasting and prayer to try to freshen their trees of powder, yes, when the innocent blood of the martyrs of Jesus is dripping from their hands! And in Britain, the *blast* is more harmful on their followers than on the potatoes. They begin to see that some "part of a hand" has written "Mene tekel" on their trees deeper than the bark, yet they shout, they fast, they pray after a fashion, and then they become enraged to curse, persecute, and falsely accuse the children of God for their religion! But the greater the withering of the tree the more they chew the bark. Oh yes, the rottenness is too clear to deny, and even the *Baptist* for once is sufficiently honest to admit it: see the February issue, pg. 69,—"The wind [the Holy Ghost] blows wherever it wants," says this persecutor: and so it is, but the signs are very poor if it chose to blow on him ever since we have known anything about him. "This saying is entirely descriptive of the Spirit of grace in these days. It shows [to him] that the churches of the saints, for the most part throughout the world, especially Britain and America, have angered the Spirit away [which spirit? when? how did he know that, when he impudently denies the need for the Holy Ghost, by denying its gifts!], and the Almighty says (says he), 'I go, and I shall not return to my place until they acknowledge their fault:' [but all the signs and threats of God are completely opposite. "The destroyer of the gentiles is on his way,"—"And he shall smite the earth with the rod of his mouth,"—"When they shall say peace, peace, then sudden destruction cometh upon them," says the Bible,] under this sentence (he admits that) corruption is being nurtured in the home, (the 'tree') truth is multiplying, and love of many is growing cold;" i.e., many are leaving his tree, and enjoying the fruits of the good tree, which he calls poisonous; but this is no wonder, for evil is the good, darkness is the light, and truth is the worst lie,

according to his intrepretative rules toward us continually. Here he suggests that persecuting churches such as his are worthy of the character of *Saints*; while on the other hand, he admits that grave flowers have crowned the other denominations besides his own, and he shows that the Wesleyans, despite the labor of close to ten thousand preachers, have diminished over one hundred and fifty last year. His portrayal of the churches of the "Saints" is not true, for instead of becoming empty, and angering the Holy Ghost, the comforter in their churches is more fervent than ever, and more fruitful. Though they do not have one preacher for every hundred of those who are diminishing, or hardly a chapel that they can go to comfortably, or a house, or an audience, if they can prevent it, despite it all the Holy Ghost frequently crowns their labor with success at something over two hundred per month. The foregoing confession proves their disappointment, in spite of all their effort, in the plan they made some time ago to receive the Spirit, and no wonder either, for they are not willing to come down to God's plan to get it, as the Saints have received him, and they will be deprived of that also, we suppose, as the Editor confesses, "until they acknowledge their fault." Thus the sooner the better for him, to do so and call back the shameful false accusations that he has published about the Saints. ‡ The Saints fleeing to Zion. § Rev. 11, 10; Psalm 11, 6; 68, 2; 110, 5, 6; Isaiah 9, 18—20; 13, 6—9; 24, 6, 17, 21, 22; Jer. 30, 23, 24; Zeph. 3, 8; Mat. 4, ; 2 Thes. 1, 8—11; ‖ Rev. 19, 23. ¶ Rev. 18, 20, 24; ** Rev. 16, 5, 6, 7.

LLANYBYDDER BRANCH.

ONE was baptized, and others have promised to obey soon, despite how much that Daniel the Blind has kicked against us; but it is hard for him to kick against the pricks of God now. We heard that he is in very bad condition, and no one can understand what illness he has. He drinks a lot of cold water, saying that he hears his bowels on fire, and he asks others to pour cold water on his body, which was done for hours and days. He would rush out of his house from the heat of the supposed fire from within, and he would run to lie in a pool of water in order to cool down. We heard that the doctor said that he did not know what in the world is wrong with him. We would request all the Saints to pray that he might be brought to the right path out of the snare of the devil.

CONTENTS.

MERTHYR TYDFIL:
PUBLISHED AND FOR SALE BY D. JONES, AND ALSO FOR SALE BY THE SAINTS IN GENERAL.

JOHN JONES, PRINTER, RHYDYBONT.

PROPHET OF THE JUBILEE,

OR

STAR OF THE SAINTS.

No. 11.] JUNE, 1847. [Price 2*c*.

TENETS OF BAPTISM.

"Only those who humble themselves before God with a broken heart, and with a contrite spirit, bringing satisfactory evidence to the church that they are truly repentant of all their sins, and are willing to take upon them the name of Jesus Christ, having a determination to serve him to the end, are worthy of being baptized into the church of Jesus Christ."—*Doc*. and the *Cov*.

The elders and the priests should be very careful not to administer this important ordinance, or any other, to any who are unworthy. It is all too true that there are men who are so presumptuous and hypocritical, even in the land of the bibles, who profess to believe it, yes, so presumptuous as to plot with each other to deceive the servants of God for the sake of mockery and degradation, such as that Methodist in Machynlleth who testified to the preacher that he believed, that he was repentant, and that he was desirous of being baptized; and not until he went into the water, when the presumptuous rascal tried to throw the preacher into the river, threatening to drown him, did he reveal his treachery; and by then the hosts of his ungodly partners, who had hidden themselves in the bushes beforehand, rushed on the preacher threatening to drown him, and not without earnest efforts was he able to escape alive from their clutches, and they following him like bloodhounds. What reasonable creature, not to mention *Christian*, would not dread to mock a godly ordinance in this manner? Could not the preachers of every denomination be thus deceived? And although we have not the right to prevent anyone who obeys the conditions from getting baptized, yet things such as this, and others we could name, warn us to look more closely for fruits meet for repentance. Others, such as *Daniel the Blind*, can dissimulate practically with our knowledge, and yet we have no proof of that, and a delay would be much better; for it is much better for them not to be baptized than to come as do some, to spy on our freedom, and to try the use of slander, and so they can falsely portray us; from such defiled lips as these come nearly all the false accusations that flood the Pharisaic articles of our country against us.

We would wish for every officer to remember that the day is coming in which it will be asked what use he made of every talent he received, and if the fruit of his labor is not there to be found, it is in vain, if not worse than in vain. Not according to the number he baptizes, will a man be rewarded; but according to the number he turns to righteousness, and who keep to the paths of righteousness and godliness to the end; these will have entrance into, and will shine like the stars in the eternal resting place of our Lord Jesus Christ.

ZION. ITS LOCATION, &c.

THIS is the subject of the song of the patriarchs, and the object that absorbed the love of the prophets, and the hope and desire of all the saints through the ages. They took delight in the portrayals of it, and to the extent that they had the spirit of its King, like the skilled swimmer extends his hands to swim, they frolic in the seas of boundless love, the purity, and the unsearchable riches that are stored in her for the time when all her children will come to a suitable age to enjoy her forever. They described the salvation the children of God will have when his judgments come upon the world. Much of the history is written in the holy volume until this day, and is read constantly; and yet, the mention of "building Zion," "gathering" towards there, and the blessings that are enjoyed in it, is so strange to some extent in this age that it is as if nothing had been portrayed about her. After all that was said about Zion, we do not know of one of all the religions in the world, except for the "Saints," which is building, gathering to, or which understands anything with respect to its location; and they know nothing better than to mock them and to persecute them because of their belief in, and their efforts to gather together in, Zion, just as they mocked the antediluvian Noah and his family because they made preparations and went into the ark.

That a city by the name of Zion was to be built and adorned magnificently before our Lord comes to his kingdom, has been indicated so clearly by the prophets (that is if one believes them), that it is of no use for us to elaborate now. Let their prophecies testify, together with the fulfillment of them to some extent through the signs of these wondrous times, together with the voices of the servants of God, of the necessity of it in these latter days. But our purpose in that which follows is to show in which part of the earth the prophets foresaw the great Zion of the latter days established.

There was a city by this name in Jerusalem; and so it is understood to which one the prophets refer in that which we quote, it would not be unprofitable to show the difference between the two cities, as well as the different places they will be. Sometimes they called the Zion that was in Jerusalem, "the highest city." It was separated from Jerusalem by a great wall that surrounded it.

Historians say that it was Melchizedek who founded Jerusalem, and afterwards called it Salem. Paul says, Heb. vii, 2, that Melchizedek was the king of Salem; whether he was the one who founded Zion, is not clear; but there was one in existence at least in the time of David; for it is said that he, when he took Jerusalem from the Jebusites, "took the strong hold of Zion: the same is the city of David." 2 Sam v, 7. We acknowledge that many of the inspired writers refer to this Zion; such as, Isaiah 30, 19,—"For the people shall dwell IN Zion AT Jerusalem." We ask, if he did not have some other Zion in mind, why did the prophet use the preposition "at?" Was it not to show the difference between that Zion and another Zion that God was preparing as a refuge for his children in the latter days? But, says someone, if they knew about the latter, why did they call that city by that name? We answer, even though the scripture does not explain this, yet we venture to suggest what *we think* about the subject. The name Zion is of great antiquity, and signifies the pure in heart, or the dwelling place of the pure in heart. Through revelations, we understand that Enoch in his day had built a city of that name, which was taken up from the earth, and perhaps it was to this one that Paul referred in Heb. 12, 22, 23,—"But ye are come unto mount Sion, and unto the city of the living God, the heavenly Jerusalem, and to an innumerable company of angels," &c. To the antediluvian saints most particularly belongs the title of "church of the first-born;" and since they and their city have ascended to heaven, and Paul calls it the "city of God," why could it not be to this that John refers, Rev. 21, 10, where he saw the "great city, the holy Jerusalem, descending out of heaven from God?" If it was not to the earth that it came, how could the nations of them which are saved walk in the light of it? "And the kings of the earth do bring their glory and honour into it," says John, ver. 24-26. It is obvious that it was to the new earth, and not to the restored one, that this city descended; and that it is after, but not before, nor during, the thousand years. Is it, one wonders, where the spirits of them which are saved dwell, to wait for "the adoption, to wit, the redemption of our body," together with the resurrected and transfigured angels? If not so, we do not understand Paul, John, or the prophets.

But to return to the history of the "City of David." Perhaps Melchizedek, or whoever settled it, when organizing the sections and boundaries of Jerusalem, out of respect to some Zion that existed before that, named the highest city, and this beautiful scene, "mount Zion," just as cities, many chapels, and persons, to this day are named in memory of, and out of respect to those who have gone before. After David, it was named "the City of David." We have no doubt but what this Zion will yet be built when Jerusalem is built, but not under the construction, or according to the portrayal of the prophets of Zion of the latter days; rather in connection with Jerusalem. Now is understood the difference between the two cities, and the two countries where the two Zions were and yet will be. Among the host of witnesses we have to prove that it is on the American continent that God commanded his people to build a city of refuge for those of his children who gathered there, we notice, to begin with, that which David says in Psalm 48, 2-3,—"Beautiful for situation, the joy of the whole world, is mount Zion, on the *sides of the north*, the city of the great King." "For, lo, there the *kings were assembled.*" Thus it is seen that it does not refer to the first small city, but some great Zion in the sides of the north, where many kings would come. Compare this to that which Isaiah says about it, chap. 17. He shows that mount Zion would be on some land sheltering [figuratively speaking] with wings, beyond the rivers of Ethiopia, which was to the west far from the place where he stood as he spoke, where he shows that the Lord will lift up an ensign to all the inhabitants of the world, and he will blow a trumpet; and from which country they send ambassadors by the sea, namely to show the "ensign" [which denotes the kingdom of God], and to bring treasure to the Lord, namely many people coming to Zion in obedience to his call, like doves to their windows, "to the place of the name of the Lord of hosts, the mount Zion." Furthermore, see Psalm 132, 4 —18: "I will not give sleep to mine eyes, or slumber to mine eyelids, until I find out a place for the Lord, an habitation for the mighty God of Jacob: Lo, we heard of it at Ephratah; we found it in the fields of the wood." "For the Lord hath chosen Zion; he hath desired it for his habitation: I will abundantly bless her provision; I will satisfy her poor with bread." Yes, they will have their fill with their remnants of food in Zion, when all those who have fought against her and her inhabitants will die of want. As for the "fields of the wood," if the reader had traveled with us through the *prairies* of America, he would be ready to acknowledge that David of old had seen them, and was very familiar with them according to his portrayal. Not in the "fields of the wood" was the "city of David." In America the fields are like valleys or meadows twenty miles in length and width, sometimes less and sometimes more, and they are surrounded with trees. Isaiah says that Zion is a wilderness.

Notice the portrayal of Micah, chap. 4, of the Zion under consideration,—"But in the *last days* it shall come to pass that the mountain of the house of the Lord shall be established in the top of the mountains, and it shall be exalted above the hills; and people shall flow unto it. And *many nations* shall come, and say, Come, and let us go up to the mountain of the Lord, and to the house of the God of Jacob; and he will teach us of his ways, and we will walk in his paths: for the law shall go forth of Zion, and the word of the Lord from Jerusalem." Admittedly there would not be room for so many in the "city of David," which was not even a mile in circumference. It is obvious that this is unfinished work, from ver. 7,—"And the Lord shall reign over them in mount Zion from henceforth, even for ever," that is, personally. But read the rest of the chapter, and it will be seen that the prophet is portraying the distress of Zion before this her last victory, while gathering, preparing, and building their first cities. "And thou, O tower of the flock, the strong hold of the daughter of Zion, unto thee shall it come, even the first dominion; the kingdom shall come to the daughter of Jerusalem. Now why dost thou cry out aloud? is there no king in thee? is thy counseller perished? [we answer, yes, he was killed in the Carthage jail,] for pangs have taken thee as a woman in travail [because of that]. Be in pain, and labour to bring forth like a woman in travail, for now [soon after killing her counseller] shalt thou go forth out of the CITY [no need to ask which "city," for we know of but one city in this age that professes to be built under the direction of God through her counseller], and thou shalt dwell in the field ['fields of the wood,' the wilderness of America perhaps, where scores of thousands of the Saints were exiled from their city last year, after their 'counseller' was innocently martyred]; and thou shalt go [out of the boundaries] even to Babylon [that is the mother of the whores of the world, and from among all its families]; there shalt thou be delivered; there the Lord shall redeem thee from the hand of thine enemies. Now also [notice that it is in the 'last days,' when the Saints will gather to, and will build Zion, this is to be] many nations are gathered against thee [which nation has not mocked and scorned the concept of building a temple or cities by the command of God in this age?], that say, let her be defiled, and let our eye look upon Zion," says everyone, especially those who name their chapels by that name. "But (poor things) they know not the thoughts of the Lord, neither understand they his counsel; for he shall gather them as the sheaves into the floor. Arise and thresh, O daughter of Zion," for the last time ever, for after that, "nation shall not lift up a sword against nation, neither shall they learn war any more." There is no need to say that this is not fulfilled, nor any likelihood that it will be soon. Zechariah says, chap. 9, 9,—"Rejoice greatly, O daughter of Zion; behold, thy king cometh unto thee." When? Verse 10 answers,—"And the battle bow shall be cut off; and he shall speak peace unto the [believing] heathen, and his dominion shall be from sea even to sea, and from the river even to the ends of the earth." This is not fulfilled either, rather it has only begun.

David proves through the following, beyond all argument, that the building of the Zion he refers to would be work as late as our age, Psalm 102, 13—16,—"Thou shalt arise, and have mercy upon Zion; for the time to favour her, yea, the set time, is come." "So the heathen shall fear the name of the Lord, and all the kings of the earth thy glory. When the Lord shall build up Zion, he shall appear in his glory." Who will affirm that the Lord has appeared in his glory up until now? When he comes, "the Lord my God will come, and all his Saints with him," say the prophets. If they have come, where are they? If they are not to be found, then it must be admitted that Zion has not yet been built either. Also, notice that the Zion that was in Jerusalem was in existence when David spoke these words; and he says, "This shall be written for the generation to come." We have already proved in the first volume of the *Prophet* of the going over of part of the tribe of Joseph to America as a fulfillment of many prophecies; the history of the Book of Mormon, and the gathering of the remnants of Joseph and the tribes of Israel to Zion. It was proved also that God prepared two centers of places for his children to gather in order to have deliverance, as Joel and others say when portraying the destruction that will come on the ungodly of the whole earth, when Judah will be returned from its last captivity, and build Jerusalem, "for in *mount Zion, and* in *Jerusalem* shall be deliverance, as the Lord hath said, and in the remnant whom the Lord shall call." And having considered these connections, why does it not appear as logical to every impartial mind that Zion is to be built on the western continent, and the remnants of Joseph who are living there will gather to it, as it is to admit that the tribe of Judah will gather to, and build Jerusalem on this continent where they will be delivered? And in fact, who can believe the scriptures, and doubt the one or the other? For our part, we believe that to be impossible.

Since our task of proving the place of Zion depends on her disconnection from that Zion that was in Jerusalem, we have the difference of location clearly from Isaiah, chap. 62,—"For Zion's sake will I not hold my peace, and for Jerusalem's sake I will not rest, until the righteousness thereof go forth as brightness, and the salvation thereof as a lamp that burneth, and the Gentiles shall see thy righteousness, and all kings thy glory. And thou shalt be called by a new name, which the mouth of the Lord shall name. Thou shalt also be a crown of glory in the hand of the Lord, and a royal *diadem* [not an *empire*] in the hand of thy God." Many states can be under one kingdom. Not some small place, and not one, or two, or a hundred cities will be in Zion, if we know something about her; but there will be plenty of room there for many nations to live and exist, and plenty of land for each one to have a vineyard of his own, and to eat of its fruit, with no one to make afraid.

Some fail to understand why Zion can be in America, when the prophet says that when Israel is restored they will be one nation on the mountains of Israel, and not part of every side of the great ocean as the Saints say. And we admit that it appears to be a rather difficult knot at the outset, yet even moving that ocean from between them is but a simple thing to keep truths constant! Isaiah said much on the part of the Saints before this; and since it is he who led us to this net, if in fact it is a net, we expect him to take us through it also; and no longer than the request, here he is forever nearby, ver. 4,—"Thou shalt no more be termed Forsaken; neither shall thy land any more be termed desolate; but thou shalt be called Hephzibah, and thy land Beulah; for the Lord delighteth in thee, *and thy land shall be married*." In the days of Peleg the earth was divided, Gen. 10, 25. When Moses says, Gen. 1, 9, that God gathered the waters under heaven to one place, was not all the land of necessity in one place? And when the times of the restitution of all things come as Peter mentions, in Acts 3, and others, all the islands and the continents will be joined together as they were. John drives this nail to a strong place, and seals the subject up for our part, Rev. 16, 20,—"And every island fled away," for without seas it is impossible to have islands. And not on a *mountain*, but on the *mountains of Israel*, will be the delivered, who will be numberless, as far as we know. That which is proved is that there will be *one king, and his name and his government will be the same over all the earth*. And thus our subject is proven despite having to dry up the seas to do so!

Having presented brief evidence this time that it is in America that Zion will be built, we shall attempt on another occasion to show the necessity for her, her usefulness, her splendor, and her glory, together with the call to gather there, and the danger of not going, &c.

THE "*HATER OF DECEIT*" PROVED A *LOVER*,

A MAKER, AND A PUBLISHER, OF "DECEIT" HIMSELF.

(*Continued from pg. 75 of the March Prophet.*)

YOU admit also that they commemorate the death of the Lord with the

Sacrament; very good again, for our other persecutors claim that we do not; but they will believe you, we hope. This is counted as virtuous in everyone; and we hope it will not be counted as deceit in the Saints. You also admit they did not dare to partake of the emblems until they had been blessed. Go ahead, friend, the Saints are certainly improving. After this act, the priest beseeched his brethren to pray with him for God to give a manifestation of his 'Spirit,' you say. Better still! The more manifestation of the Holy Ghost they received the better, is it not? No one but an avowed atheist would mock them as deceivers, because of this their acknowledged godliness. It would be good if you and your kind would imitate the Saints more in this, and spend less of your scarce time misrepresenting them and mocking them. But fair play on every side. Perhaps you consider the use of water in the communion sufficient deceit to condemn ALL they do, indiscriminately! Well, we shall weigh this also in the popular scales of the age, to begin with; and then in the truthful ones. You admit that the contents of the cup are a representation of the shedding of the blood of Christ; all right, so do we; but, did not "WATER and blood" come out of his holy side; why do you not have a representation of the two, or the one as well as the other? Answer this question or someone else for you who has more human wisdom if he can. Furthermore, which is the purest and most suitable to represent something as pure and undefiled as the blood of Christ, pure water, or a filthy and poisonous mixture of *logwood*, liquor, and other intoxicating *drugs*? I wonder whether God would be more accepting of filthy wine than clean water in the communion? Yes, he would, says the drunkard alone. Having lost the logic of '*representation*,' you flee to your deceit shouting, "there is a commandment in favor of using wine." Well, we shall follow you there also, for we have a word or two on that still. The word "*cup*" is in the scriptures where you say "*wine*;" and although some argue from the chastisement of Paul to the Corinthians, that an intoxicating drink was in that cup, that is not proof that that is what Jesus Christ used or commanded; if they had been deceived or misled about the *sort* of wine in Corinth, that was not their only transgression. Christ proves in Luke xxii, 18, that he chose "fruit of the vine," unfermented, at that time; that is, of the same nature and purity as he will drink with them AGAIN (why *again* if not before?) and anew in the kingdom of his Father, when they will eat at his table in his kingdom. We do not think anyone would dare to say that an intoxicating drink will be there; and so they cannot say that the other one was intoxicating, because the two cups are similar. Thus is it a liquid, or an intoxicating drink that our accusers use in the communion? If it is a commandment you want, come hand in hand with the Saints to keep the commandments, or half of them, before you condemn them. Yes, there are definite commandments to "covet to PROPHESY, and FORBID NOT to speak with tongues." Where are you now, friends? Come along again, there is a commandment to anoint the sick with oil, and lay on hands to receive health. Who is ahead now? The Saints go forward again quickly; God placed in his church apostles, prophets, and all the spiritual gifts. The Saints obey all of them. Have any of you received the right to abrogate them? If so, answer; if not, who among you can throw a stone at the Saints for representing through a pure emblem, the water that came from the pierced side of their Lord? By now I hear all of you singing the old *ipse dixit*. "Those things are unnecessary in this enlightened age." Well, there you are in your own net, then; who was condemning an entire denomination as deceivers previously for what you consider an aberrance of one of the emblems pertaining to one ordinance! And now able to abolish almost the whole thing yourself! this is, in our estimation, a prime example of "straining at a gnat and swallowing a camel!" But we shall come closer still to ending the debate; the Saints believe *every* commandment, as well as the one under observation; they believe that the fruit of the vine would be the most suitable thing in the communion, and that is what they use when they can get it: until then they have permission from the reasonable founder of the rite to use the emblem next to it in purity; yes, and sufficient facts to prove their God's acceptance of that. And you should know that the earliest centuries of the church did the same as we are doing. The Saints know what they are about, even though their foolish scoffers blaspheme the things they know nothing about, and are bringing upon themselves imminent destruction. By now, the "deceit" has disappeared from this also, and it is the truth that shines the more it is dealt with. As for your babble that the priests may sleep whenever they wish, for as long as they choose, alternately, and that they must lose their own spirit so that the Spirit of God may borrow their tongues, &c., needless to say that you are the father of that; it is seen on its cheeks that it is a brother by the same father to the others. Who has seen men that could do that? if true, there is a miracle for you! We never knew that a man's spirit leaves him when he sleeps! *Fie*, man!! The examples you give of speaking in tongues are examples of an incredible memory also! You find the mocking of sacred things like this very entertaining! And you admit at the same time that you did not know what in the world they were, but *you knew* that Beelzebub understood them! how did you understand that? Remember that it was the most arrogant and hypocritical servants of Beelzebub who shouted *Beelzebub* the loudest, even in the face of the Son of God. Your persecuting brethren, namely Cuckoo of Ton, &c, have proclaimed that the Saints do not make any display or exhibition of the gifts in their meetings, but that their public profession of this is a lie; but as for you, thanks to your stupidity, your testimony is in favor of the Saints, and it is expected that everyone will believe you in this as in all other things. That proves our similarity to the apostolic church, upon which we pattern everything. Well, that is sufficient to end the debate in our favor forever, we hope. It is not the ignorance of the persons concerning those things they were speaking in strange tongues, that proves the deceit of the Mormons, any more than that of the Corinthians proved them deceivers; i. e., if it is any use to offer you the words of Paul any more. In 1 Cor. xiv, 13, Paul proves that those speakers did not know one syllable of what they were saying;—"Let him that speaketh in an unknown tongue *pray* THAT HE MAY interpret." If they could, why exhort them to *pray for ability*! In ver. 14, he says that his "understanding is *unfruitful*," when he spoke in tongues. Your deceit and the Saints' correctness are seen even more clearly in ver. 2, "For he that speaketh in an unknown tongue speaketh not unto men (why do men condemn for not understanding then?), but unto God; for no man understandeth him; howbeit in the spirit he speaketh mysteries." How do you expect to understand, then? This was not speaking Hebrew to a Greek, or English to a Jew, as your theological stupidity explains;

but the speaking was entirely unintelligible to everyone, until it was interpreted through the "gift of interpretation" through the Spirit of God. If the unbelieving could understand the tongues, they would not have said "that they were mad." See ver. 23. Oh no, mysteries belong to God, and only he can explain them through the interpretation. So say the Saints also. "Wherefore tongues are for a sign," not to cause some to believe, but a sign of their being sealed in unbelief; and "yet for all that will they not hear me (namely, through other lips, or other tongues), saith the Lord." Thus it is no wonder that you, poor thing, harden more and more upon hearing the same sign; for that is the way it was, is, and will be, "saith the Lord." "The natural man understandeth not the things of the Spirit of God, for they are foolishness unto him; neither can he know them, because they are spiritually discerned." Because of your lack of the Spirit of God, namely *the spirit of prophecy*, you mock such sacred things; for the things of God no one understands except through the Spirit of God. Thus with every word you prove the truthfulness of the Saints, and their religion, despite publishing your own deceit! As for the secret plans you say the Saints have to make merchandise of people; it is like your assertion, "they claim to be the successors to the apostles," without one syllable of truth in it, as you must know if you have been with the Saints. If you could publish anything worse, no doubt it would be sweet for you to do so. "*Merchandise*," is it? everyone deserves this more than the Saints. But it is useless to go on, because for the life of us we cannot find any deceit through it all, except your deceit. Let Mr. Rees also take a few of these *pills* with you; yes, let all our persecutors swallow their *dose* so the filth may be purged from their stomachs, for their good, and bring them to love truth instead of loving lies is our desire, that's all.

LOUDMOUTH "MEIRIADOG" FROM LLANFAIRCAEREINION FORFEITING HIS HEAD TO BE A FOOTBALL ! !

IT will be remembered that the above man wrote to the *Baptist*, a shameful epistle against Robert Evans and the Saints, challenging him to debate with him through the *Baptist*. R. E. refused, because the *Baptist* would not publish defenses, except all bad things against the Saints. "*Meiriadog*" doubted this so strongly that he promised before witnesses "that he would allow his throat to be cut, and his head to be a *football*, if the writing of R. Evans were not allowed to appear in the *Baptist* as does the writing of others." He added that R. Evans should send his correspondence to him, and he would insist on having it included there. But it is seen from what follows how he fulfilled his promise, although at the cost of his own head:—

MR. ED.,—"The readers of the *Baptist* for *September* last year are aware, through the description of Mr. *Meiriadog* himself, that a debate was to take place between him and me through the *Baptist*, the sum of which was,—That he was to prove the existence of a church of God without the spiritual gifts in it: and myself, from the other side, to prove the promise for, together with the necessity of the spiritual gifts before it can be worthy of the character of being a church of God. He promised that if I would send my letters to him he would send them to the *Baptist*, and he would send the first letter there to call me to the battlefield. But instead of that, he sent a list of bad names that referred to me, such as "*deceiver*," "Penny-pinching face," "arch-deceiver of the north," preaching "miracle of slime," and that I was going to destruction, &c., &c. Yes, this is how he began the debate before offering one proof of his subject! At first I thought, together with everyone I heard, that his blackguardism and his quarrelsome false accusations did not deserve an answer, and that it could not be expected to convince such a liberal man, with scripture or reason. But toward the end *Meiriadog* prophesies that he would not ever hear a word from the "chief deceiver of the north," or so he thought! It was probably to lower himself beneath my notice that he unleashed this disgraceful, slanderous, and unchristian-like *broadside* to begin. And by the time he finished it, he thought that he had succeeded in that. But I wrote to him a defense of that which I had promised, together with observations on his writing; I requested him to send it to the *Baptist* according to his strong promise. I had plenty of reason to understand that he had received it, and I expected month after month to see it in the *Baptist*; but I saw nothing! Like this, since that time, many moons came and went without a *hew* or a *mew* from the great *challenger*, or my defense! ! Neither did I hear of his death, but several here and there are heard saying that *Meiriadog* has *forfeited* his head to me, much more than did John to Herod. And it is not unlike him to do this in his great desire to prove his foregoing false prophecies; namely that I would not answer him!

"I have a copy of my letter, and I intend to publish it if that which is quoted from his letter is deemed worthy of setting before the public. So much for the promise (*a head's worth !*) of Little Meiriadog of the big mouth! He should have known better of the *Baptist*; he had plenty of proofs to the contrary. "Best the learning that is bought," goes the old saying. Let him remember either to release my letter through the *Baptist*, or not to be so ready to pledge his SKULL, lest he vow to give it to those who go around the country looking for *skulls*. What if those kept him to his word! As for me there is nothing in his skull I covet, and I give him permission to have back the right of it that he gave to me on the condition that he make better use of his head from now on than to blaspheme the things he knows nothing about, and that he chooses not to understand concerning them!

"*THE latter days* now are all dawning,
The angel's expounded the plan;
And Jesus has chosen his servants
To further his message to man.
Today he addresses the lowly,
While wise men retreat to one side,
But when he himself comes to Zion,
His enemies all, woe betide!

R. EVANS, *Glan Conway*."

NEWS FROM THE "FIRST CAMP."

Two of the brethren who were in the camp at "*Council Bluffs*," were on their journey as far to the west as *Pueblo*. There they found 170 of the "Mormon

Army" wintering, and the remainder of the 500 who invaded *El Paso*, which contained about 5000 inhabitants, and in which place they hold the key of passage through the Rocky Mountains; and an army cannot go from Mexico to California except through that narrow gap. Since the winter was getting worse, they stayed here, building ramparts, and strong defenses, under the supervision of Elder A. Babbitt, who was selected by the government, and was rewarded with a high rank in the American army. They were all healthy and comfortable when the historians left them. Upon returning, during about a quarter-year's journey through the forest without road or leader, they were plundered three times of their horses and their supplies by the Indians, who gave them mules in their place. Practically their only food throughout the time was the meat of the *Buffalo*, which they saw in multiple herds throughout the country, and remarkably tame. All the camps of the Saints throughout the wilderness and the states are preparing to migrate toward the west as soon as the weather permits.

EXTRACT OF A LETTER FROM ONE OF THE "TWELVE."

"CONTINUE in well doing; you are part of an excellent work. Thrust in your sickle like a man of God, and reap—not as a *thunderbolt*; yes, as a thunderbolt, but in meekness, and testify of the sayings of the beginning of the religion of Christ. And after faith, repentance, baptism for the remission of sins, and receiving the Holy Ghost through the laying on of hands. When the people inquire, what next? tell them, "Oh, Jerusalem, Jerusalem," &c., gather, gather. What next? Gather. And what next? Gather yourselves together, O ye children of the kingdom, to the place the Lord has promised deliverance; yea, prepare yourselves for the hour of your departure for the house of the Lord, for the resting place of the Saints."

THE GATHERING TO ZION.

MUCH great wisdom and goodness of God to his children are seen in every age preparing temporal and spiritual deliverance, when all the human wisdom of those ages believed in, and praised the *spiritual* deliverance, they say, and at the same time mock and discredit those who prepare to receive the *temporal* deliverance, twisting the purposes of it to their own destruction, by refusing to gather with children, according to the commandments of God. God's custom is to warn the world, or such part of it that he is about to destroy, and the way he does that is by sending his servants to preach the gospel to them, or the order that will bring them to an agreement with God and Christ; and after that the order of God is manifested to them to deliver them from the judgments that God will bring upon those disobedient to his call, and who disrespect his servants; and thus their *spiritual* deliverance depends on their belief in, and their obedience to the *temporal* deliverance. After the servants invite, preach, exhort, and earnestly warn, in season and out of season, in every other manner, and in vain, the *last* sermon, the *highest* testimony, and that which seals up everyone who sees it is *the flight of the Saints ! !* This testifies that they know what they are doing. This testifies that danger is at the door, and is inevitable by waiting. This testifies that it is not hypocrisy that causes people to leave their country, their relatives, their possessions, and all that they esteemed as worth having. This is the testimony that sealed up the Sodomites. This was the last testimony of the Saints to those in Jerusalem; "when ye shall see Jerusalem encompassed with armies, *flee to the mountains.*" Thus do the Latter-day Saints also testify through their gathering from every country and nation as one family, and they flee toward the Rocky Mountains, and the far west, to search for the deliverance that is promised from the judgments, the famines, the plagues, &c., which are to follow as if at their heels. This last flight will continue to flow by the thousands from every language and nation to the center point of their campaign, or the *loadstone*, namely ZION, until the honest of heart come to hear of, and to obey, the message of God through his Saints in this dispensation of the fulness of times, the purpose and objective of which is to gather together in Christ Jesus all his chosen ones, namely his Saints, from the four corners of the world to Zion. The spirit of gathering has already brought its thousands from the isles of the sea, as well as from every state throughout the continent. Lately 150 natives of the *Sandwich Islands* landed in California, the firstfruits of the abundant harvest who will yet turn their faces from the Islands of the South Sea toward Zion for deliverance. These are but a few in contrast to the rest of those natives who have obeyed the fulness of the gospel already, despite the opposition of the sectarian missionaries also, remember. Do not all the signs of the times prove to you, Saints, the necessity there is for some safe hiding place from the threatening storm? That there is need to flee to their rooms for a brief moment until the disturbance has passed? Ask all the wise men of our age, where will there be deliverance? And there will be no answer. Ask the weakest of the Saints, where will there be temporal deliverance? He will answer, "*Mount Zion*," says God, and he will know where that is! That is the place that delighted the Lord as a dwelling place for himself; "He will abundantly bless her *provision*, and he will satisfy her *poor with bread*." Also, remember that "beautiful for situation, the fairness of the whole world, is mount Zion, on the *sides of the north*," says the Bible. You children of Zion, raise your heads above all the tribulations, although you are scattered throughout great Babylon; your deliverance is nearing faster than her destruction, despite that. Prepare, prepare in every way to pay your debts to the world; strive to warn all of their danger, and let your good examples testify to everyone wherever you are, that you seek a better land; yes, one full of every goodness.

MONMOUTHSHIRE CONFERENCE.

THIS Conference was held at Nantyglo, Sunday, the 25th of April. At ten in the morning, the Hall was overflowing with cheerful people, and hundreds going away because they failed to find room to come in. Capt. D. Jones was elected president, who, after thankfully acknowledging the great honor and trust they gave him, showed the importance and responsibility of such a presidency, and he desired the help of the faith and prayers of the Saints for him to fulfill it properly, and he opened the conference through singing and prayer. He addressed the crowd warmly and enthusiastically with respect to the work at hand, &c., and then he called on the presidents of the various branches throughout the conference to represent their churches, which was done as follows:—Number of branches, 8; Elders, 8; Priests, 16; Teachers, 10; Deacons, 5; the number baptized since the last conference, 114. Total, 236. The presidents portrayed the condition of their branches as very comfortable and hopeful; that love and zeal increased as the persecution heated up; that the Saints were increasing in spiritual gifts as well as in numbers, and that the most earnest and pious were receiving additional gifts, although some who came in for false reasons had transgressed and had returned to their own place after a while.

In the afternoon meeting, after partaking of the Lord's Supper, 2 Elders were called; 7 Priests; 4 Teachers; 4 Deacons; several children were blessed; and the president showed in English and Welsh, the great importance, usefulness, duties, and responsibility, of the various officers. Then president F. D. Richards, a missionary from America, came forward, and he greeted the Saints briefly and very sweetly, showing the hope that was placed before them, and the surety of their enjoying the path of their duties, &c.

At six, Elder Wm. Davies, Rhymni, preached the basic principles of the eternal gospel, and brother Richards followed him, portraying with remarkable skill and eloquence the glory of Zion, and the great benefit of her inhabitants, the holy influences of the Holy Ghost on the Saints, how it fitted them to be saviors on mount Zion, &c. But, it would be too lengthy here to attempt to do justice to his speech, which lifted the hearts of the Saints delighting them in their hopes. The president made a brief and appropriate speech to the Saints, to the cheerful listeners, and then he greeted our persecutors (who were at the time throwing rocks through the window to his side) and prayed for them; and he then closed this comforting conference which was a great blessing to many besides the Saints.

DAVID JONES, *Clerk.*

PROPHECY OF MR. WESLEY ABOUT MORMONISM!

FROM the visions of Daniel, says the American "*Times*," the pious Mr. Wesley expected that a new era in the religious world would begin in the year 1827, which he calculated by giving the "time, times, and half a time," i.e., 1260 years that the church would be in the desert, to the number 567, that is the time when it went there; and he said that in the year 1830 would begin that great work that would usher in the Millennium ! ! Strange how accurately he counted; for in that year, namely 1827, the light of the fulness of the gospel shone on our earth, for the angel came that John saw, Rev. xiv, 6, and he restored the keys of the kingdom of God to our world, and the "Book of Mormon" was brought to light from the hiding place of ages, it was translated through inspiration and by means of the "Urim and Thummim;" and in the year 1830 The Church of Jesus Christ of Latter-day Saints was established, on the foundation of Apostles and prophets, with Jesus Christ himself as the chief cornerstone. At that time there were but six members in it, and by now there are hundreds of thousands throughout the four corners of the world, and the islands also who are living in hope of enjoying the peace and blessing of the great Jubilee that Mr. Wesley said was to begin at this time. Hundreds, if not thousands, of his followers have obeyed the fulness of the gospel, and see that his prophecy is true; and the greatest wonder is, how any one of those who believed him in other things can doubt him in this, or refuse this godly light when it is offered to them! We believe that Mr. Wesley would rejoice in this blessed news were it offered him. He walked according to the best light that he could obtain, and no doubt great will be his reward. One wonders whether he will be a witness against even those of his followers, who refuse this gospel, especially when he left behind his testimony of it!

SAFE LANDING OF THE TWO APOSTLES.

No doubt the Saints will have great pleasure in hearing that the apostles P. P. Pratt and John Taylor have landed in New Orleans well and comfortable, on the 10th of March, and they have obtained a steamboat there to carry them up to their brethren and their families. Thanks to the Savior for sustaining them.

PLENTY IN THE MIDST OF FAMINE!

In Egypt there were seven years of plenty before the seven years of famine. We do not say it will be thus in America; yet, if it is not quite similar to it there, that will be proof that we understand neither the prophecies nor the signs of the times. The United States have shown great and very commendable generosity to the starving sufferers in Ireland. They have loaded warships with food, and have sent it for free across the ocean to the subjects of this country! Very good. But they suffer hundreds of thousands of their own subjects to be driven without cause from their own homes, from their lands that they purchased from them, to die of starvation in the wilderness as far as they care, without any to take pity, or to extend an arm to sustain them, and there is no mention of giving them food or anything else. *Charity begins at home*, is the old saying; but not so towards the Saints. Will they not be measured with the same measure that they mete?

Nearly half a million *dollars* were collected for the Irish in that country in less time than they were plundering the Saints in the same country of property worth five times as much, besides the priceless lives that were taken as martyrs, and the other sufferings that were inflicted on the Saints! They have shown this great tenderness toward *foreigners*, and the other great cruelty and injustice toward their *brethren of the same country*! They filled the needs of those who were suffering for lack of the things of this world, and they passed by the children of God, those who suffer it all for the testimony of Jesus Christ and the word of God, turning their heads, and leaving them in the wilderness as food for the wild beasts as far as they care. They prove at least one word in this, namely that "the children of this world are in their generation wiser [in helping one another] than the children of the kingdom," although not in accordance with their ability either.

In a letter we received from apostle Orson Hyde, who wrote on his arrival there from Liverpool, he says that in the entire city, namely New York, there was not enough flour to feed its inhabitants for four days, because they had sold out so completely to the European markets, expecting the rivers and canals to open earlier, but had been disappointed. Besides this, it is understood also that the buyers of corn and flour from the various countries, outside the eastern states, have flocked to the west through the valley of the Mississippi, and have secured most of last year's crop that was in the country, and intend to take it in boats to the eastern world. If so, it is not unlikely that their flour, &c., will be as scarce in the eastern states as it is here before the next harvest, especially when it is remembered that during the past five years so many have emigrated there from other countries, continuing to do so this year, all of whom will assist in consuming whatever may be left, of course. But again we say, what will their situation be if the corn fails in the next harvest? One must also bear in mind the great appetite of their numerous armies along the borders with Mexico. When all the things that have been said to them come to pass, then they will remember, hopefully, and they will look at their bloody hands, and they will understand that the blood of their dead, and the lament of the widow and the orphan whom they plundered of their food and all their possessions, have reached the ears of the Lord of the Sabaoth.

AMERICA AND MEXICO.

It appears that the former have been very successful in killing thousands of the other wretched ones in their own country. They have won several cities lately from Mexico, and after taking Vera Cruz they are advancing toward the capital city of Mexico. It is said that Santa Ana has been sworn in as president of Mexico. And news reports are that peace is to be made between the two countries, by Mexico allowing the Americans to have the Californias.

IRELAND.

It is said that swords follow quickly the footsteps of famine. We read pitiful stories of so many dying that not enough coffins can be obtained to bury them. It is said that the corpses in some families lie in the houses for a long time without anyone in the family with enough strength to bury them; and some have been buried somehow in the gardens, or along side the roads in the country, and starving dogs eat them afterwards! Their situation is dreadful, and may he who holds the fate of nations in his hand have mercy on his children until the way is opened up for deliverance. One of the London newspapers calculates that two million have died of hunger in Ireland in one year! which makes 5479 in a day, 228 every hour, and close to four every minute!

TO OUR DISTRIBUTORS.

Dear Brethren,—Behold the *Prophet*, through your assistance and that of other readers, has lived to be a lad one year old. You can hardly comprehend his usefulness to you yet if you support him until he becomes the size and age of a man. I am confident, dear fellow workers, that you will make sure the money finds its way to the Press that sends it to your midst; and although it is made of iron, you know that it cannot live without money. *A hint*, we hope, that will do the trick in this regard to the faithful.

GLAMORGAN CONFERENCE.

THIS Conference will be held in the Cymreigyddion Hall, (*White Lion*), Merthyr, Sunday, July 11th.

The *Anniversary of the Missionary Society* will be the following day, namely Monday the 12th. Tickets can be obtained for one shilling each from the presidents of all the branches, and others, and an earnest appeal is made to all the well wishers of this beneficent society to do all they can for it, hoping that the gentle sisters will not be one whit behind with their customary zeal, efforts, and faithfulness.

N.B. The feast will be on the table by half past two in the afternoon, and lectures will be delivered in the evening.

PRIZE FOR SELLING BOOKS !

WHOEVER sells the most of our books by the end of the year will be rewarded with a bound copy of all the pamphlets published by us during the year, together with a volume of the *Prophet*, in calfskin of the most handsome available. Now, dear brethren and sisters, who will win the prize? It will be a pleasure for the *Prophet* to proclaim the winner to the world, and pay their warmest thanks to whoever achieves the highest feat.

CONTENTS.

MERTHYR TYDFIL:
PUBLISHED AND FOR SALE BY D. JONES, AND ALSO FOR SALE BY THE SAINTS IN GENERAL.

JOHN JONES, PRINTER, RHYDYBONT.

PROPHET OF THE JUBILEE,

OR

STAR OF THE SAINTS.

No. 13.] JULY, 1847. [Price 2c.

DUTIES OF THE SAINTS AFTER BAPTISM.

"The officials should have a sufficient time to explain to them their church duties as much as possible, previous to their being confirmed by the laying on of the hands of the elders [wherever there is a church; otherwise, they may be confirmed in the place they are baptized] and before their partaking of the sacrament. The members should manifest, through their faith and their works, together with their godly walk in the presence of all, and their pious behavior before God, that they are worthy of a place within his church, and a share of its privileges."—*Doc.* and the *Cov.*

Dear Saints, remember "that ye were not redeemed with corruptible things, as silver and gold, from your vain conversation, but with the precious blood of Christ." Remember that you are a mirror to the world, and that even the other professors of religion who defend their systems at the expense of people's failings, are ready to condemn the gospel believed by us all because of the smallest blemish they see in any of us. We remember that the whole world, its flesh, and its lusts, and its passions, and all the principalities and authorities of the kingdom of darkness are against us; therefore, put on the whole armor of God, so that you may be able to withstand all the fiery darts of perdition. When you are persecuted and falsely accused, in your patience take hold of your souls, trusting in the justice of him who said, "Vengeance is mine." Although the love of Christ persuades us to testify to others of the assurance we have, the blessings we enjoy, and persuades us to invite them to obey the gospel, yet we must endeavor to do this in wisdom, clarity, soberness, and discretion, lest they not understand, and lest you cause them evil instead of convincing them. Above all we counsel that every counsel and attraction to them derive out of love for them.

We are persuaded before this to believe that the Saints have brought persecution on themselves at times unwittingly, by testifying to the world about which gifts they and others have received, &c. How much better is that for those who do not believe the emphatic words of Jesus Christ, when he said, "He that believeth and is baptized shall be saved;" "And these signs shall follow them that believe," &c., than it would be to "cast pearls before swine." What else can be expected than for them to "turn again and rend you?" Let everyone seek after every other gift, *wisdom*, and with all his strength let him try to understand, so that he may properly use the other things.

We counsel all the Saints, especially the new in the faith, (rather than argue or act stubbornly with the perverse ones of the world, that try to provoke your spirit, so that you transgress, and they have cause against you, or with those who blow the old baseless stories in your faces), to associate at every opportunity with those who are strong in the faith, those who have received and who walk in the light and comfort of the Holy Ghost, so that you may increase daily in the most holy faith. Remember that evil conversations corrupt good morals; and since no one stands except through the strength of God, watch that you not go into trials by meeting with temptations, and thus grieve the Holy Spirit of God. We counsel the Saints to be very careful that the mote they see in another not be a thorn in their hearts, establishing itself there as a root of bitterness, and festering to the point of poisoning their freshness, and cooling their initial love. The best treatment against this is, not to spread it throughout the district, or to utter a word about anyone before going to the one who caused offense, and in love reproving him; and, that is usually the end of the obstacle, especially if one possesses that Spirit that *hides* a multitude of sins, instead of that accusing and harmful Spirit that reveals other faults. Avoid that as you would a viper! The world expects, and not without reason, for the Saints who profess such a valuable, heavenly, and incredible testimony to make a different stand in all good causes, and God expects them to live more godly lives than anyone else under the sun. We do not doubt that they are doing so already; yet, it is useless to deny that there is room for improvement in the best of us.

"Every member having children is to bring them to the elders before the church, who are to lay their hands upon them in the name of Jesus Christ, and bless them in his name." "No one can be received into the church of Christ unless he has arrived unto the years of accountability, i.e., he can distinguish between right and wrong, and is capable of repentance."

WISDOM IS POWER.

THE truth of this is proved in many ways, times, and countries. It is admitted that the wise have superiority over the unwise. Well, follow that reasoning to its extremes, and the power and worth of wisdom will be seen. The power of men to reach the objects of their affection is proportionate to their understanding of such; and the extent to which the patriot understands the situation of his country, and the craftsman his craft, is proportionate to the wisdom each possesses that his power and his strength (in the proper use of them) will be of benefit; so says the wisest of men, "Righteousness exalteth a nation;" and wisdom contains righteousness, and this is power!

It is obvious that there are two kinds of wisdom; for in their turn many have possessed great power, even over empires, and yet have not been righteous. These two kinds are often at odds with each other, namely the wisdom of men as opposed to the wisdom of God, and the wisdom of this world as opposed to the wisdom that is on high, which is noble, and easily dealt with. It is said that God has made the wisdom of this world foolishness, and that the foolishness of God is wiser than men. The cause for this was, because the ways of God are different from the ways of men; and the more that men possess of that which they call *wisdom*, the more they oppose the manner in which the wise God carries his work forward. They are often jealous because the wisdom of God has chosen the foolish things of the world (or those who are considered such), to confound the wise, or those who are considered such. The extent of this difference compared to the extent that man has become estranged from the "only wise God," and the opposition of man's wisdom to God's wisdom, proves the extremes of his own corruption, his foolishness, and, as a result, his *inability* to oppose the work and the servants of God. It is obvious that because of their pious wisdom the "children of wisdom" understood how to overcome their more foolish enemies; for example, Joseph was the wisest man in Egypt; Moses was wiser than the astronomers of Egypt; David was wiser than all the servants of Saul; Solomon was the wisest man in his day; Daniel was wiser than all the wise men of Babylon; the Apostles in their wisdom (as their leader ensnared the doctors while still a child) trapped the rabbis and the chief wise men of the world, only because of their wisdom, and the extent to which their wisdom reached; and in every circumstance, to that extent would be their strength, or their power to fulfill their own purposes through wisdom, even though the others envied them, persecuted them, and killed them, and thereby proved through facts, their own foolishness, and the wisdom of the sufferers, which proves that righteousness contains wisdom, and that because of their wisdom the wise would suffer, foreseeing righteousness follow in the scales of their righteous and *wise* Father. Thus wisdom is justified by her children in every age and country; foolishness is jealousy, stemming from an evil root, and its fruit is hatred, persecution, vengeance, &c. Here is the "shew of wisdom in *will* worship [that is in their own mind], and humility [apparent], and neglecting of the body," that Paul mentions: this is not the right kind of wisdom. But James shows clearly the difference between them,—"Who is a *wise* man and endued with knowledge among you? let him shew out of a *good conversation* his *works* with *meekness* of wisdom." Not calling their fellowmen deceivers, false prophets, and satanists, &c., without offering one proof of that, as if saying it were enough, for thus do the foolish. "But if ye have bitter envying and strife [even] in your hearts, glory not, and lie not against the truth [as I foresee the foolish mockers of the latter days doing]. *This wisdom* descendeth not from above, but is earthly, sensual, devilish, for where envying and strife is, there is confusion and every evil work." What wisdom can be there! "But the wisdom that is from above is first pure, then peaceable, gentle, and easy to be intreated, full of mercy and good fruits, without partiality, and without hypocrisy." Having shown as much as this concerning the difference between the two wisdoms, namely the godly and the human, the source and inclination of each one can be seen, as well as their drawing toward the original source; for the stream imitates its source to the extent that it is raised; thus, to the extent the children of God increase in wisdom they imitate their Father in power. The unsearchable wisdom of God has taught him how to create the countless thousands of worlds, and that is his omnipotence to rule over them; he understands the laws that govern the elementary life; because of this he commands them to go, come, or mix together, as he wishes; and thus it was, is, and will be. This is proven if one reads Jer. x, 12, 13; Psalm cxxxvi, 5, 6; and to the extent he imparts this wisdom to others, the elements will obey them as well, as Paul proves to anyone who believes his account, see Heb. xi. Joshua and others knew this very well; and thus did the sun and the moon come to understand soon, and the *secret* of all power is *faith*, for there can be no faith with a *foundation* for it, which is *wisdom* or *understanding* with respect to such things; and how do they understand except someone teach them. Who could teach them except him who understood, namely God? How did he teach them except through revelation? Well, here again, the foolishness of the mockers of revelation is seen, for they do not want wisdom from its source through its own godly pipes; and the result is, "the world by wisdom knew not God," and they do not wish to, because foolishness (they say) is the way to know him. Thus it is seen that no one who denies revelations from God "knows" him; and not knowing God is to be deprived of eternal life; for "this is life eternal, that they might know thee the only true God." But Paul prayed for the complete opposite of all the *orthodoxy* of the 19th century, for the Ephesians; he prayed "That the God of our Lord Jesus Christ, the Father of glory, may give unto you the spirit of *wisdom* and REVELATION in the KNOWLEDGE OF HIM." If it is admitted that the wisdom of God is beyond that of everyone else (which is not to dare to deny even a word of it, we suppose), that is to admit that "those who understand the most about his mystery imitate him most closely in wisdom;" and thus, those who associate with him most, understand most about his purposes. Here also is seen the foolishness of the wise men of this world glorying in their understanding of

God, glorying also that through their strangeness to him they found him out! The great difference that has been, and continues to be between the wisdom of God and the wisdom of men is that the one is taught by the head scholar himself, through revelations, and the other by men, who were taught by other men, who all deny the necessity of a direct lesson, mocking, hating, and persecuting those who were thus taught, accusing them of being fools, &c. Thus has it been practically from the beginning. When God accepted Abel's offering, was that not a revelation from God to him? Doubtless Cain believed the revelations his father Adam received, and he did not accept additional revelation; and thus out of jealousy he killed his brother because of it. Noah was the wisest man on the earth in his day, and the way he proved that was through receiving the ability to save himself and his family; he received that wisdom in purity from its source, and yet who of his contemporaries believed him; it is likely they believed all those the earlier ones received, but it was foolishness to have more, because they were not necessary. Abraham also came, professing that he knew something about God and his mysteries through experiences; but who would believe him? What, say the wise men, some wandering stranger like that possessing wisdom! and bringing some new religion into our midst: with respect to the revelations Adam, Abel, Enoch, and Noah received, there is no doubt, but as for this foolish Abraham, claiming to have received new revelations, it is foolishness, say all the wise men. What! say the zealous, the man says that he has seen God on the plain of Mamre! that he has seen angels, and those were eating and drinking!! O such impudence, away with such a deceiver from our country with his revelations.

Notice Moses also coming in haste from God himself with new and wondrous revelations, destroying their enemies with judgments; despite that it was the wise men of Egypt who opposed him most, as did Cain with Abel, the *Magi* and the wise men with Abraham, because they could not savor the new revelations from heaven. The priests of Egypt and Canaan admitted the truthfulness of those who had gone before according to what they saw, yet the old cloak of darkness, namely the hypocrisy and hotheadedness of former times, covered them, until they all sank back into the sea, before they would admit the truth of the revelations of their contemporaries. How could they receive much wisdom, then? The same thing is seen through the history of the children of Israel; namely, that the smaller and older the revelations, the more that human wisdom increased (of necessity at the expense of wisdom from above), until they stoned practically everyone who uttered new revelation because he would be certain to reveal the foolishness and deceit of the wise men. When that "just" one himself came from God, who was without sin, and no deceit was found in his mouth, all the "wise men" of the nation were found racing to whitewash and confer dignity on the graves of the prophets of old, and believing, reading, and explaining very wisely, the revelations they had received; and in the next breath they condemned unsparingly the message of God to them from the mouth of his dear Son, and they shouted, away with such a man from the country; he has a devil, &c. Later on, the apostles' testimony of Christ was believed, and thus they received "POWER to be sons of God," namely wisdom as to how to be, but who of their contemporaries believed that the Apostles received revelations, visions, &c. Was it not for that profession that their followers were killed by those who professed to believe the revelations the apostles received, and from then until now woe to anyone who dares to come with a message from God saying that he has had a revelation; the profession of that is considered worthy of the verdict of deceiver immediately. We remember the saying of Jesus Christ, "I am come in my Father's name, and ye [wise men] try to kill me; if another shall come in his own name [in the name of some *college* or party], him ye will receive." The wisdom of this age uses exactly the same language and behavior against the "Book of Mormon," and the revelations of God to his children: those who profess the most college, pulpit, and authority wisdom, those who are most zealous over every word of the old revelations and the prophecies the former prophets and even the apostles received, are the ones who said, "Beware lest ye be deceived by this people; they claim to have revelations, visions, &c., as did the former Saints! O! such deceit and impudence! (they say). Away with such deceivers from the country, &c." What is this but "filling up the measure of their fathers," proving the truth of the religion that was opposed similarly by those in every age and country, and proving that which was said, namely that mockers would come in the last days, "having a form of (professing) godliness, but denying the *power* thereof," namely its strength, its godly wisdom, the spiritual gifts, and the priesthood, through which he was Christ, the *power* of God, and the *wisdom* of God, to those that were called; and thus they spoke the wisdom of God in a mystery, even the hidden wisdom, which, says Paul, "none of the princes of this world knew; but God hath revealed them unto us by his Spirit, for the Spirit searcheth all things, yea, the deep things of God." Again he says, "The things of God knoweth no man, but the Spirit of God." Here again is seen the foolishness of those who are sufficiently wise and want no further revelations through the Spirit of God. How is anything received from the Spirit of God without that being a revelation? Also seen is the foolishness of professing one kind of revelation, and denying another kind, such as the gifts, or the ministering of angels. O the weakness of human wisdom! What foundation do men have for wisdom? Nothing better, according to their admission, than the *history* of the wisdom of others; and the *power* cannot be in the *history*, rather in the *enjoyment* of it, to the extent that the Spirit teaches the wisdom of anyone who has it. Through this they speak the "word of wisdom;" not with the words learned from human wisdom, rather those that are learned from the Holy Ghost. While the words of the one were like sounding brass, or a tinkling cymbal, the words of the others were the power and strength of God, and that because of their connection with God.

The great mystery and power of wisdom from on high are made manifest through their good behavior, their suffering, and the fact that in every age and country, from Adam to 1847, they have received wisdom from its source, and knowledge of things past, present, and future, through the gifts of the *Spirit, wisdom*, and *revelation*, like Paul, and through the Comforter that Jesus Christ promised, which no one, not even the *princes* of this world, can receive, or compreehend, rather they judge it as foolishness; but to as many as have received it, he has given them *power* to be sons of God; and if children, they are heirs of that same *wisdom and strength* that closed the mouths of the lions, that suppressed the heat of the fire; others wandered in sheepskins, and put to flight the armies of their enemies, and they were harder than the edge of the sword, stronger than the spirits of darkness, or the shields of kings, yes, than anything that opposed them. Through the proper use of this wisdom they were enabled not only to sacrifice their lives joyfully, to prove the goodness of the word of God, and the strengths of the world hereafter, to come to mount Zion, the city of the living God, to myriads of angels, to the church of the first born, to God the Judge of all, and to Jesus, the Mediator of the New Testament, and the blood of the sprinkling, which speaks things better than the things of Abel; but they will be enabled also to receive the adoption, namely the redemption of the body, and to gain entrance into the eternal kingdom of our Lord Jesus Christ; yes, further still, their power will increase in proportion to the increase of their wisdom, until they all become one, having drunk from the fountain until they are swimming eternally in the middle of the sea of wisdom and power like the Father and the Son, which is proved by Christ himself: "The works that I do, he that believeth on me, shall he do also; and greater works than these shall he do;" yes, greater than creating and perfecting this small earth. *According to their wisdom was their power.*

INTELLECTUAL POWER OF MAN.

THE human mind is such that it can gradually be enlarged, and widened until it encompasses not only the globe and its fulness, but also in a second it can be shot to the heights of the firmament. It wanders in the midst of strange worlds, the planets, and their countless moons, like the swallow through the rarified air. It brings the frozen poles to the same place, the sun from its sphere to the palm of its hand, and the moon beneath its feet; and it penetrates through the depths of space like a shooting star, and back on its throne practically before it is known it was gone. It discerns the wretchedness of the wretches of the whole wretched world; then it jumps up through the abyss to the firmament above, and under the veil of darkness it gazes cheerfully at the ages to come. It smiles in the company of countless angels, and contemplates the wretchedness of its contemporaries, and the next minute it is seen carefully scrutinizing the substance of the unorganized chaos before moving from the self-impelled mass on the face of the void; yes, before anyone but the watchman of the morning council awakes; and again in a second, there it is on a white horse, with a golden crown on its head, on a calm sea as if made of glass, a numberless throng with it in glory, yes, having placed this football in the midst of its sisters who are crystalized to run their orbits perfectly around their *centre of attraction*, namely the great "*Kolob*" itself! Yes, what can it not do! A man who does not know himself is someone who says that his mind cannot contain such things. O man, thy mind is almighty to the extent that thou puttest it into smooth operation. Once free from the iron shackles of false tradition, lifted from the ashes of the heresies of the country, to fresh air, to breathe, like the *Phoenix* of old; to socialize with intelligent beings, it can reach forward, again and again from truth to truth, and clutch the void like the morning light. It understands past mysteries, and unlocks the eternal doors to peer through the mist of future millennia, until it portrays before it all the vast creations of its Father, and it drinks deeply from the unsearchable treasures of wisdom with eternal increase.

As the stag thirsts for flowing waters, so does the mind of the wise for wisdom; and whoever gets it, like the grave for its prey, he shouts louder and louder, "Give, give," forever, after he grasps the key of wisdom and understanding, namely the Spirit of prophecy, the Spirit of revelation, the Spirit of light, namely the Spirit of God.

REVIEW OF THE PRESS.

Now off the Press, by CAPT. JONES, *price a Shilling, and it can be obtained with the Prophet inexpensively,* HISTORY OF THE LATTER-DAY SAINTS, *from their Establishment in* 1823, *until Three Hundred Thousand of them were exiled from America in the year* 1846.

HISTORICAL accuracy is the chief motto of the author in this book, and in addition to the advantages that he had of being an eyewitness to many of the scenes he describes, he has spared neither cost nor trouble to search for reliable testimonies, such as those given under oath in courts, and which were made public to the world for the most part, and which stand irrefutable to this day, and which the author keeps carefully in his library for the satisfaction of the doubter who asks to see them.

The author did not know of a better way to disabuse his fellow countrymen than by presenting them this history of the holy religion that is falsely portrayed so much throughout our country. It is well for the reader to secure a copy soon, for through a misunderstanding on the part of the printer, fewer than half of what we expected were printed. We quote to the *Prophet* the two following segments, so the reader may better understand something of the nature and quality of the book:

CHARACTER OF JOSEPH SMITH.

THERE are hundreds of thousands in the four corners of the world who know that Joseph Smith was the godliest man on the face of the earth, yes, who know this, we say, beyond dispute, apart from the countless millions who must yet confess this; and fearlessly we dare anyone in Wales, or in the world, to prove to the contrary. Let those unacquainted with him think what they will of our testimony, that matters nothing to us; we are answerable to God and men only for what we say, and we say only what we know.

This is also proven through the great work, and the wonderful preparations he made for the restoration of pure religion, and the gathering of the remnant of Israel according to God's covenant with Abraham and others. In what country or age, we ask, was such a revolution in the religious world created, was the cause of Zion furthered, and was the world flooded with such heavenly light, as Joseph Smith brought about in less than twenty years, from the time the angel first appeared to him? Yes, let it be remembered that he was an uneducated young lad, a husbander of animals in the woods, barely seventeen years old,—as the willow on the river bank withstands the fury of the waves of the flood tide, this lad faced and conquered all the human wisdom, popularity, wealth, and obstinacy, of a perverse and adulterous nation, yes, and this without any ability, experience, wealth, or influence on his side, or anything but divine power, incontrovertible truths, self-evident facts, and divine revelations containing so much light, and so much of the Spirit of God in them, that they could not be resisted from the lips of his servants; but which shoot their beams of heavenly light and divine love into every honest heart that receives them, and reflect like the brilliant rays of the sun off a glorious mirror, and animate, adorn, and glorify, the one who possesses them.

Despite the best efforts of the enemies of truth to blacken the character, and stain the memory of Mr. Smith, the columns of our history are as unsullied by them as the white snow; and in order to adorn the picture of his life and death more gloriously still, he fearlessly and bravely took the brush in his own hand, and painted a *border* around it of scarlet, that is, *with his own blood!* Worthy of such adornments is only he whom God made a monument for the nineteenth century of the perfection of his power through a poor instrument such as Joseph Smith! He came out of the middle of about fifty furnaces heated for him by persecutors, before courts of law, on charges of some crime or other, ten times hotter than for others; and of them all God saved him, like those three young men, without singeing a hair on his head (that is, his character), nor the smell of fire on his clothing. His enemies will have a poor excuse when they stand before the Lord God of Joseph Smith, and their Judge, for shedding innocent blood. At that time they will have to confess the truth in public, which is that it was out of jealousy for his godliness, and envy for his greatness and incomparable glory, that they killed him. No doubt it was fear of Joseph Smith's sincere righteousness, and alarm at their own merits, among other things, that incited them to martyr him.

Because of his gentleness and his guilelessness in judging everyone to be as honest as he, some cunning and selfish men slipped in among Joseph Smith's friends, who, in his greatest trouble, behaved toward him like that serpent which some man found on the road almost dead from cold, and warmed in his bosom until it revitalized, and the way it repaid his tenderness was to bite him to his heart. So they could not stand in the midst of the wheat before his powerful fan, when he blew transgressors from his presence like chaff before a rushing whirlwind. No doubt false brethren, or rather let them be known by their proper name, which is "apostates," greatly influenced others to deprive him of his life. They had seen his greatness, and they, like Delilah with Samson, knew of his weaknesses too. Yet their victory over him is a disgrace to the state and the nation, and has done them eternal harm. They cannot outgrow it; they cannot outlive it; and they cannot undo it, wash it away, or *outdie* it either. The verdict has been inscribed with a gold pen on the hearts of millions against them, from the one who conformed to the one who shot the fatal balls in Carthage jail; and in every bosom where dwell honesty, humanity, love of life, or freedom and happiness, thence also will righteous "anathemas" be breathed against the "Carthage butchery." The vengeance and wrath of a just God and good men will dog the steps of all the guilty ones and their supporters with terrors, as Milton describes the entrance gates of the Gehenna itself,—

"———*grating harsh thunder*."

Our Lord said, "It is impossible but that offenses will come: but woe unto him, through whom they come!" According to the way that the whole Christian world, as well as ourselves, professes to tread, which is the holy volume, it is seen that it is in keeping with our God's gracious custom to send prophets to the world in every age when he had particular work to be done; and more clearly still he says explicitly through his servant, "the Lord God will do *nothing*, but he revealeth his secret unto his servants the *prophets*." The same accurate mirror also shows that they all received the same cruel treatment, from Abel to the last mentioned, yes even his own dear Son, as the cruel treatment received by these their last brethren in Carthage, and all their lives. And it is no less strange than true either, that the nation which professed most zeal without knowledge, most illusion of godliness while denying its power, and most college and pulpit wisdom and human devotions instead of divine ordinances, were, and are, those who have the loudest voices, the greatest application, and the sharpest spears and swords to shed the blood of the divine envoys [i.e. that nation]. This is why the pagan nations will belong to the Lord in the days of his strength, namely because they will not be guilty of shedding the blood of prophets as is "*this enlightened age*," and the other "*enlightened age*." Their "conscientiousness" does not do this for God as they imagine, rather it tightens their bonds, and increases their sentence, because they should have looked into the thing before condemning it, or opposing it! But on to the story.

JOSEPH SMITH had foreseen that his end was at hand, and in preparation for this he had been for about four months almost daily (before the beginning, or any signs, of the last disturbance) teaching the apostles, in their councils, about the mysteries of the kingdom of God, and the manner and means to carry on the work after his departure; and, having finished giving them their endowment, he said clearly, "The kingdom of God now rests on your shoulders; take heart to spread it all over the world; it no longer matters what becomes of me, or how soon I may go to rest, &c." He publicly informed about 15,000 people so clearly that everyone understood that he was shortly to leave them. He said that he would not live to see the temple completed, but that he had presented the essential keys for giving the endowment, and everything else to the apostles. A few weeks before the beginning of this disturbance, all the apostles but two, Willard Richards and John Taylor, went according to his advice, to preach throughout the eastern states, "for," said he, "your lives are not safe in Nauvoo, or in these parts;" and that is where they were when he was killed. They returned to Nauvoo as soon as they heard; and on the 8th of August an assembly was held in Nauvoo to organize things for the future, and to bring into effect the measures arranged through Joseph Smith; but primarily for the apostles to stand in their proper place at the head of the church on earth, in the absence of their former leaders. There were between twelve and fifteen thousand Saints gathered there, and arranged in districts according to their offices. Brigham Young, Orson Hyde, P. P. Pratt, and others addressed the crowd warmly and effectively, so that everyone perceived that the mantle of the prophet had truly fallen on the apostles; and the whole crowd without exception manifested their approval of the apostles as leaders of the church by raising their right hand.

ADDRESS OF GOVERNOR FORD TO THE PEOPLE OF THE STATE OF ILLINOIS.

"I DESIRE to give a brief but true description of the disgraceful affair which took place in Carthage, in regard to the Smiths, as far as my knowledge extends. The Smiths, Joseph and Hyrum, have been assassinated in jail; I do not know by whom, but I will know. [He could not have forgotten the names of those who threatened that to his face!] I had pledged myself that they would receive protection, and on that basis they surrendered as prisoners. The Mormons surrendered all the arms in their possession, and the Nauvoo *Legion* submitted to the command of Capt. Singleton of Brown County, willingly and obediently. And I had sent him there for that purpose. The rioters required all this to prove that the Mormons were peaceably disposed; but it appears that every obedience and submission on the part of the Mormons proved ineffective in bringing them [the rioters] to peace. It was not I alone that gave the pledge of security to the Smiths, but my officers and men assured me that they would assist me in protecting them. [So much the worse then was their crime and their treachery, and he should have known better from their previous "*honor*" than to entrust men's lives to their bloody hands.] If this deed was committed by these people [we answer that it was, and how did he not know?], they have added treachery to murder, and have done all they could to disgrace the state, and sully the public '*honor*.' [! ! Whose "*public honor,*" I wonder? Where was it hiding before? Was it in the bosoms of the murderers?] On the morning of the day the deed was committed, we had proposed to march the entire army to Nauvoo; but I discovered clearly that the army would not be satisfied with less than the utter destruction of the city [and still leaving the prisoners in their hands after discovering that much!]; and that once we arrived there, pretexts would not be wanting for commencing hostilities. The Mormons had already complied with everything required of them, and had submitted to more than should have been asked of them. An attack on our part against them in the present season, with the harvest on our hands, would be as impolitic as it was disgraceful [and so, having killed the two best, it appears that the thanks of the other thousands for their lives were not due to him, but to the harvest which called them!]; and because of this [that is the 'harvest,' and not because of justice, and the desire to prevent the shedding of more innocent blood], we decided in a council [of traitors] to disband the army [so that they could be more free, and less responsible for the murder], except three companies; two of which were promised to guard the jail [only 70 in all], and with the other I went to Nauvoo to address those people [he did, poor things, and he was a worse comforter than Job's too], and to tell them what they might expect in case they designedly provoked a disturbance [yes, he threatened that their houses would be in ashes, and that their wives and children would be burned in the bonfire, and that he could not defend them! ! but he would not, is what he meant]. I think I performed this duty keenly and fully [says he; yes, in a way that no one since the days of Nero, except his partner Clark from Missouri, has done]; and having returned about 3 miles towards Carthage, I met a messenger from there who informed me of what had taken place there. I hastened on to that place. I am told that the *guards* did their duty [but it was proved to him later that there was a clear understanding between them, and that the *guards* had written a letter to the other rioters, telling them the best time to fire, and of course that they would empty their barrels into the air above their heads! The letter came to hand later]; but that the majority were overpowered [if so, how was not even one from either side wounded?]. Many families had fled from Carthage, and others were preparing to follow them; and as I considered there was danger of the Mormons wreaking vengeance, I supported this. Gen. Demming volunteered to remain here with a small number of soldiers, to defend property from damage as far as he could. I decided to proceed to Quincy, to prepare a force sufficient to suppress disorder. I have hopes that the Mormons will not start, or cause any disturbance. But I may be disappointed in this [if he had been, it would have been the first time for them to disappoint him]. I fear the opposition will not be satisfied. They may recommence their atrocities. I am determined to preserve the peace as far as I can, whatever the consequences. I think I have sufficient pretext to summon up an army, to be ready at my disposal at a moment's warning. Establishing myself at Quincy will enable me to get all news with greater celerity.

"THOMAS FORD,
"*Governor, and Commander-in Chief.*"

HOW CAN THE HUSBAND MAKE THE WIFE GOOD, WHATEVER SHE BE?

MUCH is blamed on the wives, poor things, that they are ill-tempered, unloving, or disobedient, when, on the other hand, if the husband could see how unreasonable it is for him to expect perfect obedience from his wife in her present imperfect situation, or until he himself learns to give perfect obedience to his head, namely Christ, half the argument would be over. He like her should learn obedience before being fit to govern. Having learned this lesson, namely obedience, his wife will have no need to say afterwards that he is an oppressor, for he will love her as Christ loved the church, and with an alluring and loving spirit he enlivens the warmest feelings of her nature towards him, and he will overcome her with gentleness until she will take care not to grieve him. From this principle of love that he nurtured in her towards him spring all the obedience and virture that a reasonable man expects from his wife. A wife is an intelligent and sociable being, who was created to be a suitable helpmeet to her husband; not to govern over him, nor to be scorned by him, rather to comfort him in his sorrow, to minister to him in his need, and to love him and respect him as her head. The wife cannot bring happiness to her husband except to the extent that she achieves her own happiness, and one who is so sensitive, with a heart so tender, with her sights so decidedly set on the affections of her husband, as is the nature of a virtuous wife, cannot be happy when she feels herself in captivity under the oppression of a man who is unworthy of her.

All must feel a degree of freedom before they can be happy. The yoke of Christ is easy, and his burden light. The reason for that is, because he governs through love for our benefit, without asking for our obedience in anything except in that which will make us happy. In a word, Jesus obeys his Father because he loves him; the husband obeys Jesus because he loves him; and every wife should love her husband until she obeys him with pleasure and willingness. Love begets love; for example, Christ loved his Father because his father first loved him; we love him for he first loved us; so should the husband, through his tenderness, his compassion, his nobleness, and his goodness, draw the warmest affections of his wife to the same image and spirit; and then she would not consider it captivity to serve him cheerfully in every way she can. After he creates in her trust in him as her wise and philanthropic head, she will love him and repose on him, as does he on his head, namely Christ, willingly.

It is evident, if this principle, namely loving persuasion, were a governing element, understanding, wisdom, goodness, love, happiness, proper order, and perfect obedience, yes, life in a world of bliss, would flow; from the life-giving fountain blessed virtue would run through every branch of every human family, until every *link* in the great *chain* is found, from the highest throne in the heavens to the poorest family of love on the earth, willingly joined as one. Behold a happy family.

What husband is so unfeeling as he who does not sympathize with forebearance with the weaknesses and failings of the friend of his bosom! Every man should remember that he took his wife in the beginning "for better and for worse." That is an admission that she is not infallible, and why is the husband so disappointed when he finds this to be true? You husbands, do not be so many masters, but rather, master in this way as much as you wish, namely through love, and the more the better.

There is much reproof and blame placed on poor old mother Eve, because she was the first to transgress, and Adam followed her. But for my part I cannot place so much blame on our old mother, for I consider that she is the least to blame of all the women of her age who came after her. And as for old father Adam, he was not much better. He dined with his wife in a way that proves his respect for her taste in her family preparations. When it was learned that she had partaken of the fruit of the forbidden tree, he behaved in a manly and patient manner with respect to her transgression without malice or anger toward her. Neither the one nor the other was half as blameworthy as the best of us in this age. They lived together, they transgressed together, they were exiled together, and they died together, and they will rise together, and they will yet reign together. Undoubtedly the eternal God will bless the white-haired Ancient of Days, because he did not become angry with his wife or reject her because he found in her a small fault.

We end for now by offering an *infallible way to prevent quarrelling!* Let both covenant when they are in a good mood that the one who blows his top have time to cool down from it before the other answers one word back. Thus will the words of Solomon be verified, namely, that "a soft answer turneth away wrath, but grievous words stir up anger." *Patience*, *patience*, above all else try *patience*. Think twice before saying an agitated word and you will be happy.

AMERICA AND MEXICO.

THESE continue to battle bloodily, according to accounts we receive. The *New York Herald* says that the Americans have won eighteen notable battles during the past year, and in each one many precious lives were lost. It is mentioned that Mr. Bankhead, the British envoy there, is trying to make conditions of peace between the parties. Success to him at length.

MORMON SETTLEMENT IN CALIFORNIA.

THE *St. Louis Union*, of the fourth day of May, informs us that following the trek of the *Mormon Batallion* to California, a newspaper is being published by them in *Yerba Buena*, in which the principles of the Latter-day Saints are explained. The success of this army shows considerable bravery, devotion, and great capability, in their leader and president, to be able to overcome such great obstacles as those that were in their path. The distance from Santa Fe is over 1100 miles, through rocky mountains, and through tangled wilderness, where they could not obtain water or food for man or beast. Furthermore, most of the army were foot soldiers.

The chief camp of the Mormons who were exiled is near Council Bluffs. They suffered much from want of food and comfort without doubt during the hard winter they went through, but they will be happy to hear of the safe landing of their brethren in California and that will encourage the rest to follow them.

The foregoing is delightful news, and we are glad to hear that the public acknowledges the incomparable bravery and capability of the Saints, who, although under the greatest disadvantages, have traveled almost miraculously from one end of the continent to the other, over rough mountains, in the midst of wild beasts and dangerous savages, through or over bridgeless rivers, and have established a successful settlement through it all, and better still we hear that they consider Mormonism not only worth taking with them through everything, but also worth proclaiming to that new world so soon, and also so zealously. When there are famine, wars, and death, in so many ways feasting upon men, there is no doubt but what the Lord looks after his covenant people, keeping them safe from their enemies, feeding them with "quail," and opening his hand to quench their thirst miraculously as in the days of old. We pray that he will continue thus until they who are on the way, and all his children of the whole world, have reached the end of their journey.

SAINTS IN THE STATES.

APOSTLE Orson Hyde, writes from New York, where he arrived on the 6th of April, that one large camp of Saints were about to leave from there after their brethren towards California the following Tuesday, and that hosts of others throughout the eastern states are preparing to follow them. He thinks that if about a hundred zealous and faithful preachers could go through that country now, that the resistance is so great, and the prophecies of the Saints are being fulfilled in such obvious ways, and all the signs of the times have caused the people to open their eyes, that thousands would soon embrace this gospel. The news from the camp was good, and everyone was healthy.

APOSTLES PRATT AND TAYLOR.

THESE two brethren reached New Orleans, Tuesday the 10th, after a more pleasant voyage than they had ever had. It took them only 30 days from England to there; and there were no crosswinds, nor any cause to take in one sail except for one time, for a few hours. They went past all the ships they saw, and some who started from two to three weeks before them arrived there after they did. We do not have space for this lengthy, comforting, and informative letter in our small columns, yet we give a brief quote to satisfy our readers. After giving his excuse why he did not publish his *farewell* to the Saints, namely his great haste in getting underway, and enlarging on the purpose and results of their mission through Britain, the pleasure he had, and the hope he has, &c., he says in one place (which will show the Welsh that he has not forgotten them),—"Elder P. P. Pratt and myself journeyed together to visit most of the churches all over Britain, and we left them all in a prosperous state, and obeying our teachings. In the leading Conferences, such as Manchester, Liverpool, Birmingham, Sheffield, and Glasgow, they were exceedingly prosperous; nor were they less zealous, industrious, and loving, in most of the smaller ones. I visited London and Edinburgh myself, and left them doing well. I also visited Wales, and was very much pleased with the delightful situation of things there. I found the Welsh church in a most flourishing condition. Elder Jones is publishing a monthly paper, which circulates quite extensively for its beginning; and he has also published many thousands of tracts, and circulated them throughout the length and breadth of his native land. He has taken a very wise and judicious course, and in his publication he ought to be encouraged and assisted. In speaking of him and the good done by the American elders, I would not forget the English and the Scotch, for I have found many of them desirous to do all they can to propagate the truth, and to build up Zion, and who will yet shine bright in the kingdom of God."

More of the interesting counsels of this brother will appear in the next Issue of the *Prophet*.

GOSPEL OF THE ANGEL.

Tune—"*Eliseus.*"

WHAT was seen in the heavens?
An angel flying down.
Did he have something to bring?
Yes—the gospel of great Jesus.
That is to be preached
To every nation, kindred, and tongue—
To all the people on the seas,
And on the face of the great earth.

Did we not have a gospel?
Yes—nearly as many as the grains of sand.
Well, what is the new gospel?
The old gospel that existed before.
Here is the one that Peter preached,
Here is the one Paul preached;
Here is the one we also preach,
In authority after them.

Where was this gospel for so long?
In its "forsaken state."
What became of those who did not have it?
God is a righteous judge.
One seeks not a crop where nothing was sown,
Nor the light of day where there is night :
Now light shines forth—
Let no one see wrongly.

J. D.

CAPT. JONES ON MORMONISM, IN 1846,

CONTAINING

The first volume of *Prophet of the Jubilee*; the *Old Religion Anew*; the *Reply*; the *Scales*; the *Defense*; and the *Millennium*; and *Proclamation of the Twelve Apostles*; bound in one handsome volume, 12fold. Price Three Shillings.

It is better to secure a copy right away, for not one of the aforementioned can be obtained anywhere except in the Volume, without the Volume of the *Prophet*, for they are out of print, and we do not intend to reprint them any time soon.

GLAMORGAN CONFERENCE.

THIS Conference will be held at the Cymreigyddion Hall, (*White Lion*,) Merthyr, Sunday, July 11th.

The *Anniversary of the Missionary Society* will be held the following day, namely Monday the 12th. Tickets can be obtained for a shilling each from the presidents of all the branches, and others, and we earnestly plead for all the wellwishers of this beneficient society to do their best for it, hoping that the dear sisters will not be one whit behind in their zeal, their efforts, and their previous faithfulness.

N.B. The feast will be on the table by half past two o'clock in the afternoon, and lectures will be delivered in the evening.

CONTENTS.

MERTHYR TYDFIL:
PUBLISHED AND FOR SALE BY D. JONES, AND ALSO FOR SALE BY THE SAINTS IN GENERAL.

JOHN JONES, PRINTER, RHYDYBONT.

PROPHET OF THE JUBILEE,

OR

STAR OF THE SAINTS.

No. 14.] AUGUST, 1847. [PRICE 2*c*.

WHO IS THE "ANCIENT OF DAYS?"

THIS is a frequent question, which is answered in as many ways by the human wisdom of our age, as is nearly everything else that pertains to the "mystery of godliness." Anyone who reads without bias the visions of the prophet Daniel will easily perceive that it was the "ancient of days," who fills the character, holds the office, and fulfills the greatest, most wonderful, and most glorious work, except ONE, that Daniel saw through the whole majestic scene. Daniel was informed of the future situation and destiny of the world before then; he saw the one who "reveals mysteries," beneficially showing him the beginning, the growth, and the destruction of four of the empires, varied and strange, which were in their turn to stretch their iron rod across the world. In a previous vision he saw the four kingdoms shattered into ten parts, and still further he saw the tumults, revolutions, and massacres, of all the kingdoms of the earth for many ages and generations; last, and most remarkable of all, he saw the origin of the fifth and last kingdom, the one that would shatter all the other kingdoms and sway the imperial, godly, and golden sceptre over all the boundaries of this great creation forever.

He saw the setting of this last one, not done like all the previous ones, through earthly wisdom, covetousness, or power, rather "the GOD OF HEAVEN set up a kingdom," says he, Dan. 2. 44, indicating that he had nothing to do with the others before then; and after this the King did not say how in the dispensation he revealed himself; "My kingdom is not of this world," *now*, as if he were saying; nor will it be until the time that Daniel refers to. In order to satisfy the thirst and the desire to understand more that these scenes caused, especially about the glorious kingdom that would continue for eternity, once more wisdom flowed from its inexhaustible fountain through its overflowing pipes, displaying before him a more detailed portrayal of the object of his love, which through the help of former manifestations now shone forth in a brighter, clearer, and more glorious way, to his inspired and piercing sight; he perceived not only the wasting away of the widest monarchies that destroyed the crowned heads like the fine dust of the balance; but in wonder he perceived, in majestic splendor, his garment as white as snow, the hair of his head like wool,—crowned and sitting on the throne that was like a fiery flame—its blazing wheels consuming before it everything that opposed it, like stubble before an ardent flame:—before it ran rivers of fire, just like the boiling *Volcanoes* flowed, and preceding it an escort of a thousand thousands, and myriad myriads of the mighty ones of heaven, and the brave and splendid ones of the earth through the ages, the prophet saw the "ANCIENT OF DAYS ! !" Dan. vii, 9, 10.

After his coming to the earth he is seen organizing a chosen council from among the selected councilors of all the previous dispensations,—wearing his judging attire and adornments, with his royal sceptre in his able hand, and sitting as the *Chief Magistrate* over it all, and giving just sentences on every matter dealt with there. Among the first things that were deserving of his detailed scrutiny, having brought forth and opened the books, were the condemnation and execution of some of the highest and most able authorities that the previous emperor of the earth possessed, and his chief president was the first thrown into the eternal fire, [ver. 11]; the next thing is to impart more wisdom (which is strength) to the chosen officials so they may learn all the tenets of the victorious kingdom in every mystery, wisdom, and understanding that are attainable for their perfection and to prepare them to bear, and to be able to enjoy the unspeakable glory in the appearance of the great king himself to reign over his kingdom, ver. 18. "But the Saints of the most High shall take the kingdom [from their king through the 'ancient of days'] for ever, and for ever and ever." It will not be a small task to perfect everything by the time of this sight!

The purpose of the King of kings in sending the "ancient of days" and his heavenly retinue, is as forerunners to prepare the way before him to rule over his kingdom more perfectly,—to make the people ready, so that those who escaped from the "great Babylon," and who came out from the great affliction, would be able to stand in the midst of the numberless multitude with him on mount Zion, their garments whitened like the garment of the ancient of days, and so they would be taught what is, and how to sing the song of Moses and the sweet songs of the Lamb with one voice, metre, purpose, and heart; for the king will not come to *prepare* his bride; his servants will do this beforehand, "and the wife that *prepared herself*," will be said at that time. Who will not see the great work of his servants to teach such a multitude to that extent!—Such efforts will depend on the scholars, and also on the association that must be between them and the great chief Schoolmaster before they can understand what to teach! Who will believe that the school door has closed, and that the lips of the schoolmaster have been sealed up forever! We respond, that there is no one who understands anything about the remarkable period to which we refer. O, that will be a blessed day! O marvelous time!! hasten to come, when everyone [of those who are left alive after the plagues, &c.] will know the Lord; they will have been taught by his servants until all come to the foremost class to be taught by him. No wonder that old Daniel fainted from the joy and brilliance of this scene while yet a slave. And what tongue can tell,—what mind can portray; or which angels can proclaim the thousandth part of the happiness, the glory, and the joy of the righteous people who are living on the earth when all these things will be brought to pass!

Still it is asked, Who is this "ANCIENT OF DAYS" who will accomplish such a feat beyond all the godly visions of the last days? It is impossible for it to be the "Son of man," because *after that* "the Son of man came with the clouds of heaven; and came to the *ancient of days*, and they [the escort] brought him, [namely the Son of man] near before him," that is before the "ancient of days." It is obvious that there are three characters here, all different with respect to office and glory. These two cannot be one and the same person, unless he is brought before himself! which would be an absurd extravagance of language. Although they are all one in purpose, cooperation, and love, yet they are different *persons* filling different spheres. There is no doubt as to who is the "Son of man," but who is this "ancient of days" who will be *second* to him, who is hiding from the sight of multitudes among the other mysteries of the kingdom of God. Neither is it God the Father; for if the Saints were fit to withstand the brilliant glory of the Father, what need would there be for all these great preparations to fit them and prepare them for association with the Son? is not the glory of the Father above that of the Son? Also, it is not the Father that prepares the kingdom and its fulness for the Son, rather it is the Son who will do that, so that after he finishes perfecting it the Son may give it up to his Father, so that God will be all in all.

Still we are searching to know, Who is the "ancient of days?" We presume that it would be someone of great age; yes, the oldest who dwelt in flesh perhaps: his name in English, namely *Ancient of days*, suggests the oldest in days, which is a sufficiently distinct characteristic to distinguish him from all the others who were, who are, and who will be. We know of no logic or anything that disproves this.

But thanks to God who is in the heaven, and who reveals mysteries to his Saints on the earth, as gracious now as in the days of Daniel, and his other children, that he has not left his Saints in ignorance of this thing either, but has restored and revealed through his servants the prophets, assurance about this also as of the wondrous and glorious things he will yet reveal to prepare a people fit to meet him. Through these means we are informed that the "ancient of days" is none other than ADAM himself, namely the first Adam who placed the crown on the head of the second Adam who won it. Thus is seen the great diversity of the wisdom of God and his plan to bring many sons to glory. He sent the first Adam, with his first mission, in the beginning of the first dispensation to the world to preside over a few; and he will send him again at the end of the last dispensation to bring order to the chaos it caused; and as the last excels in grace through the second Adam, so will the glory of the "ancient of days" excel even more in numbers of his subjects, which will be unnumbered millions to present them all in one to their savior and their worthy King; after that he will present himself and his all to his Father, "so that he may be all in all." Amen.

THE "REV. W. R. DAVIES, FROM DOWLAIS," AND HIS CRUEL AND SHAMEFUL PERSECUTION AGAIN!—AGAIN!!

WE remember as a boy the harmful red hot overflowing of *Etna and Strombulo*, when they spewed from their *crater* the contents of their self-agitating hot belly, rivers of fire and brimstone, until they destroyed every flower, blade of grass, and every living thing within the reach of their furious fiery waves!

We have seen the overflowing floodwaters of the *Nile*, the *Mississippi* ("the father of waters"), the rapid *Missouri*, the majestic *Niagra*, and the splendid *Ganges* rushing over its *cataracts*, and its banks, sweeping houses, yes, towns—peoples, and animals, on the swell of their cruel waves in massacre into their bottomless vortex. We have heard the sound of earthquakes that swallowed mountains and whole cities almost into the mysterious depths of the land of oblivion! It is known, nearer home, about the subterranean fires which at times blow our dear neighbors in a second to the other world, whether they are ready or not!

But never (to this extent) have we seen a more detailed imitation of the above phenomena than the overflowing of the unclean bowels of the above man now and again through the press and over the pulpit, against his innocent neighbors, because of their religion! Like the *Volcanoes*—he pours forth one unclean bellyful only to empty the pit of his dreadful heart in order to collect an even more unclean stream: and when about to burst with malice and envy, out flows another scandalous stream as through the *crater* from an inexhaustible pool. I wonder in all seriousness whether there is not some sort of underground *gas*, or *foul air* that *electrifies* surface creatures around Dowlais. Certainly, the disturbances and overflow from the bowels of the "*Caersalem*" *Volcano* are not dissimilar at times! By now the people of Dowlais can tell when he is about to burst, and spew his filth over the town from his aches and pangs, as those who live near *Etna and Vesuvius* know, from their *grumbling* and their thundering.

From the least of these, his friends (if he has any) should notice if there is some *electric gas*, or the power of an anarchic element exerting such a strong influence on their self-motivating *Volcano*, so that he cannot help spewing out his evil and his folly; and persuade him to move from Dowlais to the land of Nod, the desert of Ethiopia, or some other desert place to spew up his filth, lest he should *burst* as Judas once did (who was a much more truthful man) and soil the moral climate under the noses of his neighbors for any longer to his shame! It is sufficient excuse for the harshness of our scourge to remember that we are *defending* our good names and our religion.

He who doubts the accuracy of the above comparisons, and their aptness, let him read the endless feats of libel, filthy stories, inventive, immoral, harmful, and persecuting false accusations of this man in the columns of the "*Baptist*," &c. Since the Saints first came to Wales, and their first preacher refused to be hired as a preaching servant to him, he has not stopped blowing out his hatred and his malice against them. In addition to this if he did not *send* his contentious devotees to disturb their meetings, he *agreed* to that, and out would go some fawning, deformed story through the press, carrying the name and language of its father on its forehead. Despite all this, the Saints were succeeding, and at last out he came himself like a shooting star through the country purposely to misrepresent and persecute the Saints from any pulpit he could; and it is fair to admit, that his rubbish is too poor in the sight of reasonable men to allow him to ascend into their pulpits to proclaim it. As though determined to be chief bully, or the *champion* of persecutors of his age, as were Goliath, Herod, Nero, and Adrian, in their ages, he continues to invent some new stories almost as regularly as the new moon; and in a word it could be said that he is almost "*the father of lies*" that are told even today about the Saints; he is their progenitor, and he will yet have to be accountable for them! Having disgusted his listeners with his cruel tongue, and worked his scandal-mongering machine out of use, he has collected his old lectures into a treatise in order to get even more use out of his blackguarding, and has called it "*Substance of a Sermon ! !*" And since he admits that the *substance* of his sermon is there, no one need doubt who sent it to be preached ! !

I reviewed his *treatise* carefully and fairly in "*Star of the Saints*" from September to October. There one can see his deceit, his dullness, and his evil so clearly that he has not to this day dared to disprove one bit of it. I did all this in case he was stupid enough to publish such things out of ignorance; but by now it is seen that he published it all knowingly since he admitted that he read "*Star of the Saints*," and thereby must have seen his errors, and instead of taking them back and repenting of them or leaving us alone to worship the God of our fathers, as all the other children of Gomer are allowed to do in this enlightened age, and as any man would have done who had a grain of conscientious honesty, or a desire for his fellowmen to have the truth, it all has no effect in restoring him from his madness, or in leaving them alone, but worse and worse, as though he were in a hurry to fulfill the measure of his iniquity, he rushes again like a wild horse into battle by revamping his "substance of a sermon" as a Catechism to trick and blind the poor little children of the Sunday Schools into his darkness. But what we are concerned about is this, that he is preparing and presenting destructive weapons, namely his false accusations, into the hands of the young rising generation, which to the extent they are believed nurture such hatred and envy that they thirst for the innocent blood of those who dare worship God according to the New Testament in their own country! We have seen before, to our chagrin, such an accusing and lying spirit as this quaffing the blood of godly martyrs in floods! Even in a Catechism for Sunday Schools, this gentle "evangelist" cannot find better names for his religious neighbors than "SATANISTS ! ! !" "*Deceitful atheists*," and "*bloody old Chartists, &c. ! !*" Since I reviewed his treatise in such detail, and answered everything that merited attention, and as his Catechism is only a revamping of that, having had done to it what some *ladies* do to their *bonnets*, or the *dandies* to their old coats, that is to turn them and bring them out in some new fashion, we will not be expected to review his Catechism here until he offers to refute our previous review: yet, let us take note of the above accusations to see if it is he, or we who merit them at all. This man accuses the Saints of trying to "Entice the uneducated and the unbalanced, for the purpose of attracting their money, and living in idleness at the expense of the weak-headed ones who believe them," says he. This would be considered a very weighty accusation if it came from any mouth but the soiled lips of Mr. Davies of Dowlais; yes, one who needs strong proofs before he would be believed: but it is vain to expect any sort of proof, example, or reason from him to prove it, any more than he provides for anything else; otherwise it would long ago have been out in public. Is it Mr. Davies who brings this accusation! From how many chapels does he himself receive his salary, I wonder? Who lives in such idleness at the expense of his devotees, and *electioneers* so much for money, money, all the time as our accuser? No one we ever heard of. Who attracts the money of the weak-headed of Dowlais to his shop? Also, who was that stubborn, red man who was seen in such a frenzy in his pulpit that, while searching his pockets in alarm for his sermon, he brought out fistfuls of *tickets* of the "*New debts act*," ready to sue his customers who could not pay their old *accounts*! Who was that, Sir? Name him so that the public may know, but even so the people of Dowlais know that it was not one of the Saints who was found in such a *dilemma*. Living in idleness at the expense of others, is it? Which of them prove themselves guilty of this by building new houses, &c.? Who was the man who was *off* for three months without preaching once in any of his chapels, and on his return got £50 from his devotees at home! Name him, Mr. Davies! What money do the Saints attract, poor things? Oh no, although over a hundred of us preach more often than you, I should think, yet I would challenge you to prove that among them all, yes, from one end of Wales to the other, they attract as much money for that as you yourself demand in Dowlais. There is a fair offer for you; now make use of it. Before accusing others of attracting money, a *rich man* like yourself should set a good example by preaching free, without any payment, as the Saints do. Or if your hatred is for avarice, new houses, shops, &c., are poor signs to prove it. Instead of trying to reform those you call "SATANISTS," start nearer to home, and no doubt you will have enough work with your own respectable denomination, if the letter of your own assembly that was held in *Cwmtwrch* on the 17th and 18th of last June is telling the truth. This shows that your assembly considers avarice to be almost the chief Lord of your sect. Mammon is considered so highly that they make him the main subject of their confidential letter, and we do not blame them for that, but we blame you for not reforming yourself and your faction before you accuse others. Do you not see your ailment in that mirror as your brothers see it clearly? "The harm of worldly affections," is their subject, and they admit it, that is, your brothers, remember, not the Saints: "And he [namely mammon] militates against our spiritual good, and threatens our destruction; [this is an admission that he is quite high up with the Baptists!] this accusation is so pertinent to us," they say, that is to the Baptists, remember! and why do you seek to attribute it to the Saints then, Sir? Having labored hard throughout the lengthy epistle to loosen the pursestrings, and unbutton the pockets of their devotees, so that the tokens would come out more easily, the *cloven foot* appears as clearly as yours. "But we consider [they say] that God [*alias* a Baptist preacher!] has the FIRST RIGHT, [here it is ! ! !] and every member should give the FIRST PLACE to him." How they can claim that giving to them is giving to God is a source of endless astonishment! Again, notice who is claiming the FIRST *right* to the treasures of their devotees, lashing them and us for avarice if we complain at all about such oppression. Fie on such shamelessness. They suggest that he who claims the first right to his own purse is an idolator, miserly, and doubts God's providence, &c.; without considering that they themselves by claiming the "first right" are sacrificing themselves to their own idols! Without doubting the suitability of their subject, we ask how they, let alone Mr. Davies, dare throw stones at others while living in glass houses themselves! Having registered Balaam, Achan, Gehazi, and Judas among their devotees; having spoken of their short measure, their light weights, and their despoiling the Sabbaths, &c., they grumble sadly like this: "some people's riches are increasing, and yet their contributions are scarcer than before!" Yes, here it is again, always eyeing the wealth! The scriptures warn us that men would heap up teachers unto themselves in the latter days, turn to fables, &c., and are they not these assembly letters? Is this not making merchandise of their devotees under a pretence of evangelizing? and are these not the ones who are living in idleness at the expense of the weak-headed ones who believe them? Our accusers assert that "contributing generously to God's cause (*alias*, the Baptists) is the way to keep wealth safe," and indeed, it is very "safe;" yes, too "safe" even for the interest ever to come back. "We (that is you) are earnestly called upon to make an effort to sustain the home ministry," they say. Well, that is more of a bum-bailiff than the Saints do to anyone, and their own words are appropriate for such people, namely, "It is vain for you to attempt to convince them (the world) that your treasure is in heaven when they see that your heart is on the earth." All true. "*Charity begins at home*," Mr. Davies. You, accusing the Saints of trying to get people's coin indeed! Put your *spectacles* on your eyes once again, and read the *decisions* in your "assembly letter;" after undoing the *pursestrings*, the mammon is seen rearing its head through three of the six decisions, tinkling for tokens, and collections for something or other. Physician, heal thyself and thy brothers. Afterwards comes the splendid "plan" under seven headings, and all but one of those tinkle like bells for money, until they grate on the country's ears! And although we do not care how much they get of the money of those who are foolish enough to allow them the *first right*, yet we are very surprised how these guilty ones can attribute their "love of money" to the Saints who work with their hands so they can preach the gospel for nothing!

As for the building of ships to go towards Jerusalem that he mentions, he knows very well that none of the Saints has any intention of going there, because he read differently in that "damnable" book as he calls it, *Star of the Saints*, yes, that little publication treats him *just right* ; and it is a bad sign to see a dog chewing the rod that beats him. So much to prove who attracts the money of the weak-headed, and lives in idleness at the expense of their deceit.

[*To be continued.*]

TRUTHFUL MARRIAGE.

HE who ventures to marry the truth will be disappointed if he expects to have her other than an unendowed and unadorned maiden; she marries on behalf of that which is in herself, and is like that lady who had covenanted with a soldier to marry him when he returned from the battle; but the next letter she had from him was one freeing her from those conditions to marry someone else, because he had lost his four limbs on the battlefield, and was so badly mutilated, that he was not worthy of her. She answered him back as any wise person will upon hearing the truth, namely "that she was willing to marry him for better or for worse, despite his having lost his limbs, yes, even if there was only enough of his body to sustain life, and then she would hold him to the first condition." When one marries truth, one should covenant to love her, nurture her, and obey her, not only to death, but beyond that; for this union will continue not just until death, but longer than time, which overcomes death. The lover of truth is above the vile rubbish that glitters around him, strong in the midst of temptations, bold and brave in the midst of treacheries, his pearl before him attracting his love after her. Prejudiced men will envy him, only because he is without prejudice; they shout expensive bargain at him, because he cannot be bought; every partisan opposes him, because he is not a partisan; rather he is a groom who loves and follows his heavenly bride, who is an exquisite and beautiful lady, of divine ancestry, and of royal blood, and her name is truth.

GOOD NEWS FOR THE SAINTS.

House of Commons, Monday, June 14.

"LORD M. Hill appeared before the *bar*, and said that he on that day, by request of the house, had visited with her Majesty, and presented for her notice the speech the house had made on the *colonization*, and to this he was pleased to have from her Majesty the following gracious answer:—

"I have considered the speech of my faithful House of Commons. I am quite sensitive to the good that would come from the best measures to facilitate colonization, and I shall request that a more detailed search be conducted into the matter, to enable the Parliament to draw up some measures that will free the emigrant and the colonies from the damage of impulsiveness in this concern."

"It was ordered that her Majesty's response be recorded."

Although we do not think that the measures the Saints desire will be brought to the front directly, or on the first time, yet they seek nothing but justice, and that which will be for the benefit of all, without loss to anyone, in their recent request to her Majesty, and since the the hearts of all are in their heavenly Father's hand, all these considerations and others exhort us, and we would wish for them to comfort the hearts and strengthen the faith of every one of the faithful Saints to believe that God remembers his promise, and in due time he will open the way for his faithful people to gain deliverance. He promised that if kings and queens were not fathers and mothers, they would be nursing fathers and nursing mothers to his children, and it is likely through providing measures to gather his children together from the four corners that they are fulfilling this prophecy; at least, we believe this firmly, none of them will be held back because of their poverty, if they are but rich in the Spirit, and faithful in their duties.

That which most discourages the government to send its subjects to its new and distant colonies is the danger that they will be in need there before being able to grow a crop from the earth, or the great cost of supporting them until then, together with the cost of taking them there. The latter is nothing, and the former is but small after understanding the means. If the government would give 320 acres of land, which is only half a *section*, they could get merchants in this country who would transport them there for an interest in that land, and thus they could furnish food for all they had here, and then they would be free subjects in a fruitful land, with a healthful climate, where none would suffer want or hunger. Besides that, some of her Majesty's colonies, such as Oregon, Vancouver, Australia, &c., are in such a temperate climate that they will produce many kinds of food in a few weeks, and two crops of corn annually, besides the abundant game to be found there. And thus, if her Majesty were to allow just as many acres of land there to each male of age, she would put such in an independent state, yes, in a state of happiness and wealth, and their posterity after them; and thus future generations will call them blessed. We are confident that she will see fit to do this, so that anyone who chooses will be delivered from the famines, the afflictions, and the harsh judgments that are coming on all the ungodly of the earth.

SIGNS OF THE TIMES.

THE correspondent for one of the newspapers of New York, close to Galena, writes, dated May 18:—"I have heard many times of large hailstones, but had not seen any until yesterday. About four o'clock in the afternoon, a thick, black cloud came from the north, and poured upon us wind, hail, and rain. Some of the hailstones were the size of goose eggs, or *turkeys*. I did not have at the time a chance to weigh them, nor did I think to measure them; but I picked up some within 3 hours after they fell, and within 16 hours after they fell one of them measured 4 3/4 by 3 3/4 inches. A gentleman told me that he had measured some within about an hour after they fell that were 10 1/4 in circumference; and another that he measured was 9 1/4 in circumference. I understand that the crops in the path of the cloud from the north were badly damaged, and to the east of here they have suffered greatly. I assure you that the hailstones were as big as anyone would ever wish to see, filling the face of the earth under the center of the cloud."

The *Marietta Helicon* for the 20th of May says that a shower of large hailstones has come down in their town, and their county, Sunday night, and has destroyed much of the corn and the fruit. And on Monday night there was another heavy shower for about half an hour, and it cooled the atmosphere until a fire was not only tolerable, but a pleasure. In other places it is said that the Indian corn and cotton were completely destroyed even in those places of the southern States where the shower reached, until the farmers are reploughing their cotton land for crops of something else. A publication of Lagrange says that hail ranging from the weight of bullets to the size of hens' eggs had fallen, and some pieces weighed several ounces; that they had completely destroyed entire fields of Indian corn, wheat, &c., and had blown and beaten them level with the ground, together with the *rail* fences, the woods, and everything that was in their path. It is impossible to tell the extent of the loss, they say. This storm arrived through the state of Alabama, laying waste everything in front of it, and filling the face of the earth with hailstones several inches thick, and about six inches in circumference.

We are informed also that a fierce shower of hailstones remarkable in size rushed through the state of Georgia about the same time, causing great calamity, especially to the trees, fruits, and the crops. It is a very unusual thing to hear of hailstones such as the above. And, would we be considered presumptuous, I wonder, if we ventured to ask, Is the voice of the Creator of the elements speaking through things like these to the obstinate inhabitants of the earth? Job says that the Lord reserves hailstones against the time of trouble, against the day of battle and war. The Psalmist says, Psalm lxxviii, 47, that the destruction of their vines with hail was the judgment of God on Egypt. The prophet Isaiah, chap. xxx, 30, says that the hailstones, and the devouring fire, are proof of the glorious voice of the Lord. He also says he will fight with hail against the enemies of his people Israel in their final restoration to their land, as he did with their enemies previously. See Ezekiel xxxviii, 22. It is seen also from Rev. viii, 7, that hail will be in the midst of other things of the materials that God will use to vent his anger on those of the family of great Babylon who refuse his gospel, disrespecting his servants: and in past centuries in what country have they done that to the extent they have in the country where the God of those servants begins to visit it with such great hailstones? although this is only the beginning of the worries. God said to his servants upon sending them through that land,—"After your testimony cometh the testimony of lightnings and thunderings, HAILSTONES, floods, and fires," &c. And it is remarkable that this is being fulfilled there already so much more than in any other country, especially ever since they drove the children of God from their midst!

John says, in Rev. xvi, 21, that he saw great hailstones the weight of talents falling from heaven on men, and that despite all that, men blasphemed the God of heaven because of the plague of hail, for exceeding great was their plague. It is obvious that plagues are not to convince men, rather it is the servants of God who are to convince men through preaching, and it is God who takes vengeance on those who reject them through plagues, &c.

Another marvelous sign that mighty God is preparing his destructive instruments against the day of spoil, when he will call together not only vultures, but all the birds of the air, to feast on the flesh of kings and princes, and on the flesh of all those who worship the beast, or who have received his mark, is the following:—The newspapers of the state of Missouri (namely the state that without cause or mercy exiled the Saints from their borders) contain strange stories of the appearance of a large host of vultures flying from the north to the south through that state. They extended in width about two miles, &c., from the north to the south, as far as the eye could see. They flew as close to the ground as the tops of the trees, and so high in the sky, that they were seen as one thick cloud, and as close to each other as they could fly. So dense were they and their shadow that they blotted out the light of the sun until it was like the darkness of Egypt beneath them. The inhabitants were greatly frightened at the sight, and great was the wondering as to the cause, together with what would be the results. But if this small thing frightens them, what will become of them when the God of the Saints gives their flesh as food for the birds of heaven?

Although signs will be in the heaven, and on earth blood, and fire, and hail, and famines, wonders, and pestilence, &c., yet all this is only the beginning of the afflictions: it is not "the end of the world" yet, as some say, nor will it come until "THIS gospel of the kingdom" has been preached throughout the world as a witness to all nations—until the earth is bathed in blood—cities are burned to ashes, or swallowed up into the bowels of the earth—until the nations are covered with paleness and with fright—until the others of the holy prophets and apostles are killed for their testimony of Jesus, as their brethren were killed earlier—not until the clear sign of the Son of God is seen in the heavens will the end of the world come. All the others are forerunners.

NEWS FROM CALIFORNIA.

FOURTEEN hundred emigrants landed in the valley of San Francisco last autumn. Two hundred of them were Saints, who had come around Cape Horn, and the others had come in 180 wagons under the leadership of governor Boggs across the mountains.

The trail is improving annually from the states to here. The first house they see on their path after leaving the states is that of Mr. Johnston, an Englishman, then that of Capt. Sutters, which are making better preparations for the immigrants in the coming years; and others intend to settle along the way, so that before long the immigrants will not have to want for anything. All are encouraged to use oxen to travel, instead of horses or mules. Those who brought provisions with them are selling them easily for high prices. The emigrants who went there with Col. Fremont had a splendid opportunity to sell their horses, saddles, guns, and everything they wanted, and they received 25 dollars a month in wages for 6 months.

They expect from 3000 to 4000 immigrants in the Sacramento valley this year. The natives are praised for their incredible skill in fighting while on their own horses, because they have been taught to do that in their own way very skillfully.

"On the 9th of January, General Kearney joined with Colonel Cooke, in San Diego, and the Mormon army with them. They were greatly praised for their orderly and well-organized arrival. It is said that all their soldiers were in good health and good spirits, with their weapons as shiny as the day they began their journey—in excellent discipline, and without suffering any losses. Soon after arriving here they went on toward Monterey, where they arrived safely. Two regiments of infantry joined with them there. Commodore Shubrick had joined Gen. Kearney there also, but their purpose could not be known, for the one and the other alleged their right to preside over the territory."—*St. Louis Republican.*

The *California Star* (a Mormon publication) gives an account of the tumult that took place in Santa Clara:—"As one of the navy officers, with an escort of six soldiers, had gone on business to the country, they were imprisoned by the Mexicans. The captain of the ship sent two regiments to fetch them, who pursued the Mexicans as far as Yerba Buena, and through their cannons they forced them to request conditions of peace."—*St. Louis Union.*

"We are informed through the *Californian* that 60 emigrants suffered great hunger as they tried to cross through the Mountains of California. Of the nineteen who started toward the valley, only seven arrived, and they had to eat the flesh of the others of their number, after they died, to keep from dying! Among those who arrived there were two young girls. A public meeting was held in Yerba Buena on the occasion, and 800 dollars were immediately collected, the worth of which was sent in food with a company to those who were yet in the mountains. The cause of this misfortune was that the immigrants have lost their cattle and their animals on the Salt Plains near Hastings Cut Off, a way that should never have been traveled."

This is the occasion for people to say, "that the Saints are eating each other in the wilderness." But thanks to the God of the Saints, despite the world, and despite the eagerness of everyone to eat them up, not one of the Saints was in that company. They are under better leaders than those.

"THE MORMONS. The Mormons who came to San Francisco have settled in two separate townships, and in this wide and unpopulated land, no doubt that will be better for the good of everyone than being in the same place. They have industrious practices, which they can make very useful in this land. They are a hard-working, thrifty, and honest people, and completely undeserving of the shameful characters given them by some prejudiced publications."—*Californian.*

"IMMIGRANTS.—Over the past several weeks, we have noticed hosts of emigrants going through this city toward the west. We were surprised at their neat manner of dressing, and their gentlemanly behavior almost without exception. The greatest part of them are from the class considered the most respectable and substantial of the eastern states. Never before have we seen so many immigrants of such a good appearance. And to our great disappointment we were informed by a gentleman who knows, that nearly all of them are Mormons! Pity that such wise and prudent people, with so many large families (for they were very large), have been beguiled by such deception."—*Pittsburg Gazette.*

Pity that he himself was not sufficiently humane as to examine their principles as much as they had, before condemning their religion as deceit. Pity such Editors! They did not ever have sufficient patience to search anything out for themselves, rather they snatch what they can from whatever comes along on the wings of the popular breeze, and off he goes like feathers before the whirlwind. Is it he, or the people who had experienced the religion who could best understand concerning it? But this is the custom of such almost throughout the world.

NEW AND NEARER WAY TO CALIFORNIA.

A WEALTHY company in London has taken the *charter* to join the Atlantic Ocean and the Pacific Ocean together at the Tehuantepec isthmus. It is said that they intend to begin the task as soon as peace is restored in Mexico. This way will save several thousand miles, besides the unpleasant weather of Cape Horn, for those who go by sea to California or Oregon. We wish them every success to complete it soon.

EXCELLENT ADVICE.

THOU man know thyself! understand thy nature, learn the powers of thy physical and spiritual faculties. Search into thy beginning, the purpose of thy present existence, and thy eternal destiny. Dig for the fountain of true happiness until thou findest it, and pour its streams into the bosom of all those around thee. Teach all that thou art of divine ancestry through thy virtues, prove that royal blood is in thy veins, not with thy tongue, rather by thy example. Reach for every chance to widen thy abilities, as a drowning man reaches for a straw that is within his grasp. Refuse not one ray of light because of the candle that gives it, for light is light, come from where it may, like truth. Continuing to do this, thou wilt fill the sphere in which thy father has set thee, thy name will be in remembrance in the chronicles of the house of thy fathers, thy brethren will call thee blessed, thou shalt sit on a white throne, a crown on thy head, a sceptre in thy hand, with endless generations to wear them!

DISEASES IN AMERICA.

THE *Patriot* for June 17th says that there is considerable excitement, and great fear through the main cities of the eastern states, because of the appearance of some disease in their midst they have named the Plague of the Ships. It is said that it is very deadly in New York, and kills some daily, not only of the immigrants, but also several others who caught it from them. There are several hundred in the hospitals, and in one place six of them died in the space of two hours. Nearly every ship that lands in Europe with emigrants on board tell of from fifty to sixty, or seventy, deaths from it during the voyage. In Boston, the government prevented some ships from landing their immigrants because of it, and in their hospitals some die from it daily. It is making a great carnage in Baltimore, and in Quebec and Montreal the hospitals are overflowing. From 40 to 70 are dying on every ship that comes in. There are 224 sick on board four ships, in the river near Montreal, and some more or less die every hour. It is said that this plague is as deadly as the Cholera, and it is rare they live more than a few hours.

GLAMORGAN CONFERENCE.

THIS Conference was held in Merthyr, Sunday July 11th. Twenty-seven branches belonging to this conference were represented, containing 124 preachers, 70 teachers and deacons, and all the total number of members was 1153. There were 142 baptized during the past two-and-one-half months. Four new branches were established, and about fifteen were called to the ministry. The meetings were orderly, the crowd of listeners very numerous, and much good advice and edifying teaching were given to the Saints throughout the day, which was borne out by the great cheerfulness and the attentive and polite hearing through it all.

Monday, at ten, a meeting for the Saints was held, and especially for the officers. At half past two the tables were spread with the finest china, and laden with the dishes prepared for the feast of the Missionary Society. And from then until eight o'clock over a thousand people feasted. We heard not so much as one incident of ungentlemanly conduct, or one unkind appearance throughout this entire orderly crowd; but everyone we saw had smiles on their faces, indicative of the joy of their hearts the whole time. More food was prepared than was used, so that everyone had his fill, and the remainder was sold for close to two pounds. After finishing the feast, the pleasant crowd was addressed by president Jones, Elders Henshaw, A. Evans, and Mitchell, in a warm and interesting manner.

The scribe read the numbers of the Missionary Society, namely its receipts and bills, how much was received for this feast, its costs, and also how much money is in the treasury at present. We were pleased to understand that the tickets and the bills, and all the numbers met with everyone's approval. At the end of the feast, thanks were given on behalf of the Saints to their kind and gentle friends from the world, and from other denominations, for their cheerfulness, their company, and their assistance in this blessed work. And after singing praise, the president dismissed the crowd with the blessing and protection of the gracious God; and no doubt this gathering was beneficial to eliminate much of the prejudice that was in the bosom of the listeners, to convince many, and bring them to believe the gospel, besides edifying the Saints in the most holy faith. May the gracious Lord hasten the happy day when the whole Welsh nation can unite to love one another, and agree without exception, and go together toward the same divine objective in Christ Jesus, is our fervent prayer for all our dear fellow-nation. Amen.

Tuesday, the committee met to apportion out what was on hand for the needs of those preachers who went to the North, and to Pembrokeshire, and other places, to assist them to continue preaching through the remainder of this season. It was brought to our attention that some of them had been suffering great want. We hope the Saints will strive in their monthly meetings to make contributions for these brethren who are giving their whole time in Christ's vineyard, without purse or scrip for the journey, for they are in the middle of a very stiffnecked and devotional generation; yes, so pious that they consider it a sin before God to give a meal, or a night's lodging, to his servants! O, such disappointment those charmed wretches will have when they have all gone to their own lodgings!

MEXICO.

THE Mexicans, after their strong armies failed to stand in the face of the braver armies of the States, who put them to flight with the loss of several thousand lives, in about 18 consecutive battles, have changed their strategy of waging war. Instead of bringing their soldiers face to face, and forcing them to kill their fellow men in this way, it is seen that President Antonio Canales has published his address to all the Mexicans, ordering each one, noble and lowly, old and young, in the towns and in the country, who are able to stand under arms, to gather together in small bands, and choose their leader, and attack or completely destroy every American, whether armed or not, mercilessly; and also, for them to look for every opportunity to rush upon and kill all those they find separated from the American army, searching for paths, seeking for food, &c. He orders that everyone who does not obey this call within eight days is to be considered a traitor to the government, to be killed without inquiry, and that all his possessions will belong to others. The president is serious, it is thought, about destroying lives. This way will not answer the purpose he desires, for the Americans will look out for them, and keep together; and where they succeed in killing some of the Americans who settled there before, they will bring a threefold revenge of the army on their heads. The former manner of waging war was sufficiently bloody as could be expected, when thousands on each side were being killed, but this manner is even more brutal. The excuse the Mexicans offer for starting this "*Guerilla*" war is that the Americans have been unfair with them, and have killed some number without trial. Many tales are published through the Mexican newspapers against the Americans, to create animosity against them; and they cannot expect less, for that is an old American trick. It is they who taught the world how to turn the flood of publicity against their enemies through the influence of the press, when all other ways had failed. This is what the American press did with the Saints for nearly twenty years, until succeeding through their baseless tales in getting the whole world to think ill of them; and is it any wonder that the Mexicans pay them according to the measure which they have meted out to others.

General Scott has published a proclamation to the Mexicans, in which he defends the character of his army, and denies the allegations published against them, and accuses the gentry and officers of Mexico of oppression and great unfairness to their subjects. He gives notice that he is on his way from Jalapa to Puebla, a very large town in Mexico, and from there to the capital city of Mexico. Some of the leaders of the country are urging that the city be burned rather than allow the enemies to possess it, and more of this important news is expected shortly.

ARRANGEMENTS OF THE PREACHERS

IN addition to those who were there already, the following persons have gone or will go shortly to the following places:—

Monmouthshire.—Robert Evans, William Davies, and Chason Thomas.

Caernarfonshire.—Eliezer Edwards, and Lewis Jones.

Denbighshire, and Merionethshire.—Abel Evans.

Flintshire.—John Jones.

Cardiganshire.—Several are on the verge of going soon.

Carmarthenshire.—Benjamin Jones, Howel Williams, John Roberts, Morgan Richards, and John Floyd.

Pembrokeshire.—E. C. Mitchell, J. Morris, John Davies, and John Price.
Cwmaman.—John Griffiths and James Phillips.
Cyfyng.—David Isaac Jones, and Daniel Williams.

We are pleased to understand that several other brethren are arranging their circumstances preparatory to going out to warn their fellow-nation, and to invite them into the kingdom of God. Dear brethren, be diligent, purchasing the time, for the days are evil. Now is the harvest, and we hope that no one will be caught sharpening his sickle, especially those of our brethren who have no worldly or family cares in their way. We receive frequent and earnest calls from many places where no one has ever preached, in the different counties, for preachers to preach to them the word of life: and, O brethren, those of you who can go, do not let them call in vain; rather send your names to us, and we shall inform you of such places. May the Lord give success and blessings to whoever obeys this call.

CAPT. JONES ON MORMONISM, IN 1846,

CONTAINING

The first Volume of *Prophet of the Jubilee*; the *Old Religion Anew*; the *Reply*; the *Scales*; the *Defense*; and the *Millennium*; and *Proclamation of the Twelve Apostles*; bound in one handsome volume, 12fold. Price Three Shillings.

It is better to secure a copy right away, for not one of the aforementioned can be obtained anywhere except in the Volume, with the exception of the Volume of the *Prophet*, for they are out of print, and we do not intend to reprint them any time soon.

CONTENTS.

MERTHYR TYDFIL:
PUBLISHED AND FOR SALE BY D. JONES, AND ALSO FOR SALE BY THE SAINTS IN GENERAL.

JOHN JONES, PRINTER, RHYDYBONT.

PROPHET OF THE JUBILEE,

OR

STAR OF THE SAINTS.

No. 15.] SEPTEMBER, 1847. [Price 2*c*.

THE SONS OF GOD.

The sons of men are called sons of God, because 1. God is the "father of spirits" before they came to our earth and had contact with flesh, Heb. xii, 9. 2. As his creations. 3. They are sons by adoption to him after being separated from him through the transgression of our first parents in some respect; and also, "all have sinned, and come short of the glory of God," having reached a knowledge of good and bad. After we became "foreigners and strangers," our Father organized a way to adopt his rebellious sons as sons of God, and in this way it is seen that all the saints are "sons of God." It appears that there were persons of this character on the earth from a very early time, Gen. vi, 2, 4. The patriarchs were called sons of God, i.e., adoptive sons. Abraham, Isaac, Jacob, and others, are seen as sons of God, and it appears that many of them were on the earth in the time of Job, chap. i, 6, "Now there was a day when the sons of God came to present themselves before the Lord, and Satan came also among them." The following scriptures show the conditions of adoption, or that plan which God has to adopt sons, namely the gospel. Because no one in this sense can be sons of God without forgiveness of sins, and receive the Spirit of adoption, through which they cry, Abba, Father, it is seen that the same gospel in its ordinances for the same purposes is had by the first one as well as by all, until the last one is adopted as a son of God; and also, that the "children's bread" or the spiritual gifts, and the direct association with their father, are promised to all as well as to any of his sons in any age; for he is no respecter of persons.

THE "REV. W. R. DAVIES, FROM DOWLAIS," AND HIS CRUEL AND SHAMEFUL PERSECUTIONS AGAIN !—AGAIN ! !

(*Continued from page 123 of the August Prophet.*)

WHAT more malicious accusation can one evil man proclaim over and over again completely without foundation, than that we are "*bloody old Chartists*?" He is trying in this way to incite the state against us, for he knows very well the punishments, the scorn and the exile suffered by those against whom the same accusation was brought! Doubtless the nobility of our country as well as the common folk have tired of and understood his lies; otherwise he would have drawn their wrath upon us before now; we thank them, but not him, that we have life and liberty to worship God, and live among the graves of our fathers. Letters have been written to the aristocracy of the country asserting that the Saints are "*Chartists*," seeking revenge against them! We do not guarantee that it was he who wrote them, but we will say this, that we do not consider that the man who dares proclaim this in the *Baptist*, the *Star of Gomer*, his Treatise, and his Catechism, and from the pulpits of the country, is a jot above writing that even to his Majesty himself, if he could; and that he who does the one thing would certainly not be above doing something even worse to try to prove it as well! We do not have anything to do with Chartism, nor with any matters of state, or of politics; only the eternal gospel as it is seen in the holy scriptures is our confession and our creed, and why can we not be left in peace now by our cruel persecutors? Yet, we proclaim fearlessly, and we challenge you to allow us a fair trial, and let our accusers, yes everybody with their refutations, come forward,—

THE SAINTS ARE NOT "CHARTISTS."

All we have to do with the laws and institutions of our government is to give full obedience to each one, and every respect to their administrators, as the scriptures command us and everyone to do, "Having your conversation honest among the Gentiles (the sectarians): that, whereas they speak against you as evildoers (calling you "bloody old Chartists"), they may by your good works, glorify God in the day of visitation. Submit yourselves to every ordinance of man for the Lord's sake, whether it be to the king, as supreme, or unto governors, as unto them that are sent by him, for so is the will of God, that with well doing ye may put to silence the ignorance of foolish men," such as Mr. Davies, from Dowlais. He is trying to hide his own disgrace by bringing this accusation also against us, as is seen from what follows:—A few days ago for the first time ever in the country, the Chartists' publication was put into my hand, and almost the first thing that drew my attention was the correspondence of someone very contentious filling several columns, militating with all his might against one of the main state institutions, namely the church; and the surprise was seeing the full name of our accuser at the bottom of it as its author!! I could scarcely believe my eyes that there was a man who had been a fervent correspondent of *Chartism's Trumpet* and who was shameless enough to accuse the innocent of being "bloody Chartists;" but, when I remembered that "W. R. DAVIES, DOWLAIS," was the man, the surprise vanished then and there, for that is his *habit*! Plainer still, toward the end were words like these,—"Success to you (says Mr. Davies to the Chartists, note!) and your publication (namely to proclaim Chartism!!) is the HEART-FELT WISH (of our accuser!!!) of your well-wisher.

Dowlais, Merthyr. W. R. DAVIES.

Yes, reader, the same W. R. Davies who was that much of a *Chartist* at "*heart*" at that time, is now assuming the form of the angel of light to accuse others of being *Chartists*, when some of them did not know that such a thing as Chartism had existed, until it was dead and buried! This is one of Davies's own miracles when he was a *Chartist* at heart! Come forward, Sir, and see who is the "*Chartist*;" you were not ashamed to attest with your hand in public that you were a *well-wisher at heart* of Chartism!! If you deny this, we will prove it in black and white: yes, I have it carefully filed away also, as it will likely come in handy again. If anyone doubts whether this is possible, let him read it in No. 9, Vol. 1, of *Trumpet of Wales*, and then let him say to our accuser, "*Thou art the man*." "Physician heal thyself," again for shame.

Again, he says, "one would think from reading that accursed book that is called "*Star of the Saints*," that they are numerous." How wonderfully do these things, these titles, sound through the splendid chapels when they are answered in one voice by the scholars! And oh, how he laughs up his sleeve while rejoicing in such revenge! Next for the refutations he brings to prove that book accursed and untruthful, what are they? Oh, the same proof as he brings for every other assertion, i.e., no proof whatsoever; nor any pretence of a proof! Only shouting three little words of ten letters! This is all he offers to prove hundreds of his fellowmen to be liars, shouting, "THEY ARE NOT." He must be duller than the school children if he expects them to swallow his *ipse dixit* as the truth without proof, or perhaps he considers himself some sort of infallible being, so that he is not expected to lower himself to attempt to prove anything he says, although every accusation is as full of poison to the characters of better men than he, as the fangs of the asp or the viper are of venom. And yet, if we were not numerous, that is no proof against us, i.e., according to Mr. Davies's own rule of interpretation, which is seen yet in the columns of Chartism as follows:—"Note that it is not the mass or the state that *legitimizes* any institution, rather justice and the tendency of the principle to benefit its subjects." *Well done*! And so he knows better than to condemn us if we are not numerous, then. It is fair to bring his own scales to weigh him, is it not? Yet, he said when a *Chartist* at heart, "Only three were to be found on the plain of Durah who did not bow to the state religion." "The three young lads, Elias and others, would be merely the objects of scorn, apparently, to Sir R. Inglis and his brother Mr. Prejudice," he says. So the Saints are merely the objects of scorn to this *Sir* W. R. Davies, because he shouted "*They are not*" numerous! What would you say about that, Sir? Are you not imitating those you condemned? Yet, the argument is ended by fair *statistics* about our increase and that of our accuser. Surely you will be satisfied by what your own *assembly letter* says, Sir! Well, it says on page 7, that 87 is the addition to your Glamorgan Conference in the past year. They also admit, "This year's increase has been caused *mainly* by moves from other counties." Not through baptism. Compare this with the letter of the Glamorgan Conference of the Saints, and it will be seen that 295 were baptized in the past year!! without counting the "move-ins." This is almost four times the increase of the denomination of the man who cries "*They are not.*" "And in their midst there is not one *responsible* man," says he. What! not one! Sir. It is useless to expect to attract enough money from them to buy ships, and "live in idleness" very long, since there is not "one *responsible*" man in their midst, for responsible and wealthy are synonymous to you, I should think! Are not some of your old members who came to the Saints "*responsible?*" What is responsibility? Is it going up into pulpits to shout "Satanists," and *bloody old Chartists*, &c., at his neighbors that makes a man responsible, then? or is it by publishing all manner of false accusations, and lying, evil tales about religious people that responsibility is gained, according to your *Dictionary*? If so, you are the most responsible we know, and great will be your responsibility in days to come!

The poor Saints! Not one responsible man or woman among so many hundreds of those who were respectable members, zealous deacons, and gifted preachers with other religious denominations, some of them for thirty to forty years—not so much as "one responsible" person! They have baptized about a hundred in Dowlais in a few months. Mr. Davies, did you search them all for a responsible man? There are nearly five hundred now in one branch of the Saints in Merthyr, Mr. Davies; do you know every one of them? If so, why do you say "*They are not*" increasing? If you do not know *every one*; yes in every place where the "*Star of the Saints*" gives their story, how can you be sure that there is not ONE *responsible* person among them in some part of Wales? Poor Davies, we are afraid he has gone mad; at least "his speech accuses him" of it. We have his own words to throw in his face very nicely again. "When Sianco tells a lie, he always tells it so clearly that everyone knows it is a lie;" since the *cap* of the little old lady from Cardiganshire is in fashion and fits you so well, wear it Mr. Davies; and thank you for telling your lies about the Saints so clearly that everyone can see that they obviously are lies.

We ask, in the name of justice, what is to be done with a man like this? We have tried every way we can devise through arguments and scriptures, to defend our religion from the disgrace he tries to bring upon it: we have scourged him with his own whips so painfully and so often that we think he is so *callous* and unfeeling, his face so shameless, and his conscience so seared that it is useless to try to impress anything upon him, or to restore him any more; he will not be persuaded by facts or reasons. Yet he does not cease blowing out his threats and slaughter against the innocent. There is no peace for our characters to worship God! What more can we, or are we expected, to do for him? We were previously blamed for not putting up defenses against him; and having put up defenses, his brothers refuse to read them, but boast that they have often thrown the defense into the fire before reading it; this is done not infrequently! Yes, we have prayed a great deal for him, until we had sufficient facts to prove that it was knowingly and stubbornly that he published the ugly false accusations about us out of enmity for the truth! Now, our hands are clean of him and the results of his persecution. With easy consciences we can refer him henceforth to special care, and to the eternal arms he fights against; it is obvious that he has worked himself into such firm error, that he prefers, yes he is determined, to believe lies and reject the truth, after having a fair offer of both. Does he not prevent everyone he can, in every way he dares, from looking into, and finding the truth: no doubt there are many more of the honest in heart and lovers of the truth who have been blinded by him than dare search: may merciful God have pity on such ones, we say with all our heart, and shatter the *cast iron creeds* that oppress them. But as for him, he must know, or at least he had sufficient opportunities to know better; so we are now satisfied for the sake of those who are in two minds, and our accuser should jump onto the scales first. What say you, Sir? are you prepared for the one who can judge correctly to end the argument between us, so that everyone may understand which of us serves the God of heaven? You shouted a great deal for "*a miracle*," *a miracle*, and a sign from one direction or another; well now, Sir, we join you in prayer that he who possesses miraculous power should please you so much as to give you a sign all the same, at a time he wishes himself, remember. It is a pity that you have not had some little sign by now!

We have better things to do with our valuable time than notice the wrangling of such contentious men as these if they would leave us in peace; yet, it would be doing an injustice to our religion and our nation and everyone if we were to suffer defenselessly like murderers or thieves. A short time will bring an end to the argument, whether we know what we are dealing with, or whether we are practicing religion at random like our accusers.

THE "HATER OF DECEIT" PROVING HIMSELF A FALSE PROPHET AGAIN ! !

THIS anonymous accuser has filled various columns of the *Revivalist* for July, with his foolish false accusations against the Saints; and of the two it is more stupid than in the May issue, which in the eyes of every reasonable man, it would be supposed, was proven in the *Prophet* for May and June, to be beneath common sense. He admits that his skin is smarting quite harshly under the treatment he got, which signifies that he has not become completely without feeling; the truth is *harsh* in the eyes of a number of men, and who will console him! Instead of admitting his false accusations after receiving proofs of them, and taking them back, as every "*hater of deceit*" would do, he goes on stiffnecked to pile up a heap of stupid assertions without foundation again; without proving that the saints deserve one characteristic of all he says. He complains very pitifully that he has been proclaimed a "*deceiver, a deist, and an atheist, &c.*, so that it is plain to see (he says) that it is by Beelzebub that they cast out a *devil, if they do*, and thereby show how little of the Saints' principle is being shown." We raise the last part of this disjointed sentence up to the wind, and we hold it before the eyes of our readers as an example of deceitful reasoning, the most foolish that could be got from the mouth of a babe. How does proclaiming you a "deceiver," &c.,

prove that it is by Beelzebub that the Saints cast out a devil, Sir! What do you mean? Why put that *if*, having closed the assertion up already? This is stupidity too bad to get a place in any publication, we would have supposed. Concerning that first part of his sentence accusing us of calling him the above names, it is an example of his previous false accusations, and proves that these are his best weapons this time again to fight against us. We challenge him to bring forward the sentence, the page, and the words that prove that we call him names. Oh no, that is his work. We did not give him those names, but we showed that he proved himself thus, brought his article before him, and through fair reasoning we proved that "thou art the man" who is guilty of those characteristics. "Thine own mouth condemneth thee, and not I; yea, thine own lips testify against thee." Why struggle then? He should stop putting the cord about his neck, if he does not want to hang himself. He should not blame us for putting it there, because that is where we found it. See how little of the "principle of a Saint" (not truthfulness) is in him in this matter. Listen reader to another example of our persecutor's madness, and we are surprised that he was able to get a place in any publication! "But I thank him (he says, that is, he thanks us for whipping him "quite harshly" as he says); my *only* wish was to get him to oppose me," and so, poor fellow, here you are not only having got your wish like everyone else who opposes our dear religion with lies, but also hanging yourself again with your own words like this;—In your first attack you asserted that it was not out of jealousy of the Saints, nor with any evil purposes, but that your *only* wish was to save your dear compatriots; then your next *only wish* was "love of the truth", when it was proven that your *only wish* was to tell about a dozen lies of your neighbors, and your *only* wish now is to add evil to the deceit, and strive to tell lies horrible enough to excite men's feelings, and bring them out to oppose you!! Well, that is what *blackguards* do when they are drunk and want to start a fight, and bring others out to oppose them, namely like you, planning the accusations that will excite us the most. This is the confession of a *bully*, you poor fellow, since that is your "*only wish*", what will you win? Only shame and rebuke. Why is it necessary to publish these lies about our religion for the sake of getting us to oppose you, Sir? You also admit here, that you are one of the stubborn, corrupt-minded arguers that Paul talks about, not having the truth, and he urges us to retreat from such men, and we admit, if we had thought that this "hater of deceit" did not have a better reason or principle than what has appeared so far, that we would have left him to fight his own imaginary goblins. A very unworthy purpose for such a masterpiece, is it not? Why did you not get hold of some principle that we wrote about, poor fellow, since we publish so many principles so frequently, and so contrary to your traditions, and leave people's characters in peace? That would be the nicest way by far for a man as zealous as you to expose deceit, instead of shouting *deceit*, *deceit*, *deceivers* all the time at the top of your voice, and threatening to show it, and only threatening, and then giving into passions for falsely accusing, and never proving any assertion true; you imitate that foolish shepherd who shouted "wolves, wolves" in order to frighten people, when there were no wolves nearby, and then he laughed in his sleeve, but the day of reckoning came to him before long, as it will come to you if you do not repent of your hypocrisy and evil. Who are you, poor thing, who shouts "*Mormonism is deceit*," and then expects everyone to believe your babble without any proof, and then you blame them if they do not follow your lead to shout as you do; reasonable men judge you only by the contempt you show yourself; cannot everyone else judge our religion when they hear it, as well as you can? Your stupidity stinks in the nostrils of the readers of the *Revivalist* according to what we hear. You hear the sore threatener again; "He [that is, little old us!] and his religion will show themselves in their true colors before long." Goodness gracious! What will become of us then! it will be the end of the world for us or worse, he supposes; apparently it will be better for us to *settle* our *accounts* and make ourselves ready to *exit* since this great Goliath is putting on his arms, and putting them before him like this!! "before long," is it, Sir? only a short time for us and our religion to live, it appears. You poor thing, you remind us of the old saying, "*barking dogs seldom bite*." You have long been threatening to publish our deceit; and trumpeting all the time that you are going to reveal something very terrifying. And so far you have disappointed us completely. Yes, you have been lent as much of the *Revivalist* as you wished; it did its part for you to fulfill your promise, and no doubt there is the odd man who has been expecting you to show something evil by now against the people you threaten so severely, and persecute so cruelly, but so far not one proof of any deceit or heresy of the Saints, no, not one! Neither can he, although it is seen that he would find it sweet to do so. *Poor fellow*, you want to get us to oppose you, do you, only to threaten and falsely accuse us. No wonder you refuse to reveal your name just like every deceiver or slanderer. Oh evil man, hiding in his black hole like the fox, gnashing his teeth from there at those who go by; is this fair? Give your name to the world, so that they understand who deserves the whip, and who are our accusers. We are never ashamed to own our names in public under what we publish in support of the truth, as you are ashamed to own up to your ridiculous lies! You asserted in the previous issue that you had been a member with the saints, which is greatly doubted, unless you are that Thomas Jones who was in one meeting only, but who joined another group in order to get higher pay from his master. If you are not he, you have been caught lying in your first assertion that you have been with the Saints. If you are he, you have been caught lying before witnesses denying the denomination; furthermore the letter written to people in Blackwood is still extant, and it condemns you as lying whichever way you turn, or whichever person you are. And your truthfulness has been completely forfeited; was it for the purpose of doing this that you hid your name, Sir? Shame on the man who falsely accuses his neighbors because of their religion, and does it under the cover of the city, with his name hidden! Another example of our persecutor's stupidity is the "proverb" he quotes, that is, "When thieves fall out with each other an honest man gets the account of his property." You suggest that you are a good thief, yes, you admit that when you admit that you yourself are one of the parties who are "complaining aloud!" For our part, we deny the suitability of the comparison to us completely, and it is not we but you who are accusing yourself of stealing the goods of an honest man; where are they? Hopefully you will tell their owner, so that he can retrieve them! Is this the sort of man who shouts deceit about his neighbors' religion! And he is the one who said a while ago that his "ONLY *wish*" in all his attacks on the Saints was to get us to oppose him. Then after everything we proved that he is a lover and publisher of deceit; we have shown that he has proved himself a *deist*, a false prophet, and guilty of about a dozen intentional lies, and we have done all this to him fairly and unanswerably, but instead of admitting his faults, as an honest man would do, now he runs into his hole, shouting, "But since his wrangling [no, fair and irrefutable arguments, and scriptures not a one of which you can refute, Sir] is beneath attention [oh yes? beneath attention after you have got your only wish, is it? It is easy for every boy along the roads to shout this when he cannot give any other excuse] I shall not tire the reader this time by making any notes on it," this aggressor says, yes, even having got his "only wish!" No rebut! Not one argument left in your defense! Is it not worth your trying to wash the dirty stains that you daubed on your character before! or any effort at all, I wonder? Oh, he is very poorly off, when he admits that he cannot make the least little effort against all the whipping he has had, after he has admitted it was HARSH. Where are his dear partners now? they will help him to clear his character somehow, poor thing, since he is the aggressor: we are on the field, with our full armor on all the time defending ourselves from the arrows of all our false accusers, and the slanderers, and the apostates, and the traitors, who make us a target for their rush arrows, and still our basket is full of the arrows of truth, although our persecutors' baskets, one by one, are emptying; and the emptiest bag of them all, we suppose, is this last one, which is without so much as one arrow to shoot back; still, there is not enough humanity in him to admit that, but he continues to assert to the last what he said at first. "Beneath your attention," is it? Like this was that little corgi who barked at the moon until he cracked his voice, and then he turned with his little tail wagging boastfully, suggesting that the moon was not worthy of his attention any more! Poor thing! what's the difference if that dog or this one barks on, or who tried to get them to do so, and what good is the bark of the last any more than that of the first? The way this man tries to prove the Saints deceivers, and false prophets, is by quoting a list of scriptures from the Old Testament and the New, and asserting completely without proof that they refer to the Saints, when, in truth, he has stolen those, together with the observations about them, almost word for word from the little essay called "*False Prophets*," in which we proved the Saints completely innocent in the face of everything; and not one of the characteristics the scripture gives as the fruits of false prophets, or false teachers, is to be had amongst the Saints after a fair examination; and since we have proven our accuser guilty of them clearly, every one, he tries to turn them back with assertions without any proof. This is the Irishman's logic,—"It is said that there is a thief in the town, and you must be he," he says to the first one he meets on the street. Concerning the godly man whom you (reviler) call "that *deceitful monster*, namely Joseph Smith," you know nothing about him but the mendacious stories of our enemies, and you cannot prove to us that any one of the characteristics of a *monster*, or an evil man, belonged to his character, for we knew him better than that personally for years, and thus we are witness to what we know about him, which you cannot be; and we testify also that he was a good and godly man, despite the fact that you and your ilk, blasphemous revilers, try to falsely accuse him as you do to everyone more godly than you, practically. Regarding the prophecy you quote from Jeremiah, it does not refer to us, but to our accuser. You great prophet, we ask you, When did you see 301,000 reasonable men "*jointly testifying to lies, and striving together to deceive!!*" Oh man, do you yourself, on your baseless assertion alone, dare to condemn the religion of so many, in the face of over three hundred thousand opposing witnesses! Prove your foolishness, before trying to get anyone to believe you, rather than the whole lot.

When will the following accusing prophecies you make be fulfilled? "And when they become numerous enough, then their fruits will prove it." Wait till that time comes, then, or stop denying the Spirit of prophecy. What prophet wants to prophesy evil and slander, as you do? "And when the *Shareholders of the Joint Stock Company* become numerous enough, then the principle of Mormonism may be seen," you say. Oh, such eagerness you show to blacken this religion! Under what spirit did you prophesy, Sir? The saying has it that "it was an evil man of the heart's evil treasure that brought out evil things" about others. Yes, the good principles of Mormonism will be seen, when you and all its mockers have gone to oblivion. As for the "*Joint Stock Company*," there is not, nor has there ever been, any connection between it and Mormonism; and if you did not know this, you should have known before publishing your stupidity to the world. The former was a trading society only, which had been established according to the laws of Britain, and had been duly *registered in the Chancery*, like other lawful societies; and if it had been connected with our religion, would the government have defended it when our religion is not connected with the government? Oh, no, you are showing your eagerness to blacken our religion again with this, but failing. Mormonism is above your unhealthful odor to insult it. It is your shameless hypocrisy that causes you to pretend to pity so much the "dear Welsh" as you call them.

Love for the truth, and your own immortal soul, compels us to testify boldly that you are through this "galloping towards the land of woe!" And as for the rest of your deceitful hypocrisy, let it testify against you to your shame.

TO THE ONE WHO CALLS HIMSELF "THE TRAVELER OF NANTYGLO, OR WILLIAM WILLIAMS."

SIR,—In a small essay of yours, you accuse *Prophet of the Jubilee* of containing an article, in which there were the "most impudent and shameless lies that man could possibly imagine." Our respect for that publication, together with our great desire for everyone to have the truth, compels us to call for proofs of that heavy accusation. We consider from both sides that we are worthy of this favor from you, for we would not wish for anything that anyone would lie under any kind of false accusation through the *Prophet* any more than we would suffer the *Prophet* to lie undefended under such an accusation as that one. We readily admit that we, like any other fallible editor, are prone to being wrongly informed; and if we were deceived in the story to which you refer, we plead, we demand, yes, humanity will force you, since you have made that accusation, to bring convincing and fair proofs that this story consists of impudent lies. A reasonable man will not consider "you are lying" as one proof of the matter in a debate. Oh no; nothing less than witnesses, or facts, will satisfy him who seeks the truth. The accusation that is brought in the March issue of the *Prophet* is that "the Committee of Lodge 299, Ivor Hael Lodge, excommunicated religionists from their midst because of their religion." This is the subject under discussion: and so stand to it. You assert that it is an impudent lie, and if you will but send proofs of that, your defense will have the most prominent place in the columns of the publication that you accuse; and what do you want that is fairer than this? Now, we will stand on this until your accusers are brought to the disgrace that every attacker on other persons deserves: but, on the other hand, remember that if you do not do this after such a fair call and offer, the disgrace will fall on your own head. We consider this a generous and fair way to end the small debate under consideration, without wasting many words. Yet, we vow that neither you, Sir, nor anyone else, will ever be falsely accused through the *Prophet* while we are associated with it. But remember also that we, upon opening the columns of the *Prophet* to defend, that defending is what will be done, yes, defending in humane and gentle language and spirit, with good intent, and not for any quarrelling, or for the use of sentences such as, "these rogues, when spewing their blasphemy against their betters," or "these rogues have a mouth to swear, but no teeth to chew," or "secretive sneaks, despite scorn, slander, and reviling." What good are names like these to prove a point, or to enlighten the mind of any wise man? Well, we say, for goodness's sake, leave such language where it belongs, namely in debauchery. Please understand, and may all our readers understand, that truth is what you and they will get through the *Prophet*, or else we will not be at fault. Understand plainly also that this matter is not in any way between the Saints and the Ivorites, for the article in question admits in the following words that the Ivorites were not blamed, page 49,—"But, it is worthy of the others of this generous and respected society to publicly inform the circumstances, and the persons who caused them (namely the "respected society") this shame (namely the excommunication of their members because of their religion); and it will be seen who of them (namely the others of the Ivorites) are so philanthropic and just as to take their broom to clean these foul stains from out of their remembrance." Therefore, Sir, it is obvious that this was a personal matter, and something considered against the rules of the Ivorite society; and so you cannot be a defender for the Ivorites, but only for those persons of the Ivorites who are accused of excommunicating some other persons because of their religion. The only suggestion that is in the article for the society is these words, page 50, "Whether this (namely the excommunication referred to) is an example of Welsh Ivorism, or of oppression and the transgression of this *clan* of their rules, is proved through facts that undo the transgression, or their conformity through their tolerance of that."

This is fair enough, and stands as a firm standard. And so you cannot be a defender of Ivorism as appropriately as can your exiled brothers. What depends on you now is to prove that such a committee as your accusers mention was never convened, or that no persons were excommunicated because of their religion, which if you do will bring the names of your accusers to the world as publicly as your own names. This is what you ought to do in your essay; for a thousand essays, if they do not contain this, will do nothing but cause you to sink deeper into the bog; and this can be done (if in fact it can be done at all) without sinking into evil and shameful passions. Is it jealousy for a few persons whom you accuse of the aforementioned cruelty that causes you to revile and reproach the beloved religion which hundreds of thousands of people as wise as you depend on for eternal life? Is this humane? Is such temperament Christian that calls your compatriots, those who were born as free and independent, and received just as good an upbringing, and who are considered just as responsible as you, "SMITHITES," instead of the name they profess? Do they not have a right to choose their name, and to have it without being reviled, equal to the right of the Baptists, or any other denomination? What if they called you Waldenses, or Mennonites, or some other nickname out of scorn, would that be pleasing to your ears? Please consider that others have natural feelings also, and that it is to God they are responsible for themselves. As for the printing press that published the article, leave it alone until you prove, or until you offer as much as one proof, that it did not print the truth, and you will see that it will be as ready to publish your refutation, or your defense, as it was to publish the accusation. And until you do this, your surprise that your exiled brethren complain about their cruel treatment, will be like the little old woman who caned her son severely in case he did something wrong, until he cried, and then she caned him even worse for crying! So it is with you, say your brethren, for treating them so severely, and depriving them of the money they paid into your pockets, and now you revile them and mock them for expressing their complaint to their other brethren! Did they not have a right to complain when there was no law to defend them? Who would not do the same thing? And if you are not the guilty ones, it is easy for you to prove that, is it not? If you cannot, your previous defense proves to all men of discernment that you are defending yourself and your accused partners for excommunicating your brethren, and not defending one principle that is found in Ivorism. The article is not, as you say, "murdering society," rather it is publishing the *daggers*, and showing the wounds that the assassins of society give to it like the *Italian Assassin*, by denying that, and twisting it against the society that is defended from him. Now, Mr. Williams, you see that no one uses pseudonyms, nor does anyone hide names, through the *Prophet*. You know the name of the one who urges you lovingly and earnestly, either to defend yourself, or to take the blame like a man. The one or the other now you cannot but do.

To you, Ivorites, we lovingly direct a query also, namely, Is it true that the "Saint David True Ivorites, Ivor Hael Lodge, No. 299, meeting at the sign of the Yew Tree, Aberystwyth parish, sent the following [aforementioned] defense, so that the Welsh in general will beware of SECRETIVE SNEAKS and murderers for the confidence and comfort of society, namely the *Latter-day Saints*"? Is it possible to have a lodge of Ivorites among barbarians, not to mention having them in the land of bibles, and in enlightened Wales, yes, in Blaenau, who profess religion, and who dare to revile, and behave so boorishly toward a party of religionists? If this is true, here is proof that the principle that defends and the principle that excommunicated are the same, and there is no need to blow much on this spark in order to have an ardent flame! If it was the Ivorites who sent out the aforementioned "defense," what additional proof is needed that they excommunicate their members because of their religion, for to defend this is to confess the deed. But we will believe better of Ivorism for a while yet, than that they all hired this man and his little essay as a Goliath to defend them; otherwise their cause is a poor one in our sight! If their principle is just, they would defend the expelled, poor things, instead of defending those who expelled them! A character even worse for the Ivorites is this. We repeat, what knowledge we possess of Ivorism requires additional proofs, before we will believe that the society knows about, or that it approved the defense, any more than they knew of the aforementioned expulsion. A short time will prove whether the men will be restored according to their rights. That is the best fact. Or, whether the greatest Goliath will be praised, the one who scorns society most by defending its greatest enemies.

GARWAY CONFERENCE.

THIS Conference was held in Orcup, Sunday, July 18th. It was presided over by elder Henshaw. Nine branches were represented in a rather successful condition at present, and the officers unanimously proclaimed the success of the gospel. The number of members is 130. In the afternoon and the evening the crowd was addressed by elders Davies, Rhymni, and J. Morris, together with other visiting elders.

Hosts of listeners had gathered together, and appeared eager to hear the gospel, and there are good prospects for success yet in these environs. Some came forward at the end of the Conference requesting baptism. All the decisions of the Conference were unanimously approved. May the Spirit of the Lord lead us all along the paths of peace, is our prayer.

W. HENSHAW, President,
W. LEWIS, Scribe.

ACCOUNTS.

AMERICA.

CAMP OMAHA, May 30, 1847,—Apostle O. Hyde arrived here in good health on the 12th, and found his family well and in good spirits. He reports that apostles

Pratt and Taylor arrived there in time to start with president Young, with a company of several hundred, to cross the Rocky Mountains to search for the best place to settle, which matter must be determined before the emigrants can be counseled to come there from Britain, unless the government agrees with the previous petition. They will probably be followed by two numerous companies, or three, during this summer, over the mountains. There are tens of thousands of acres of Indian corn planted on both sides of the Missouri river. The work that was done in the desert, and the crops that were put into the soil, are almost unbelievable. Under the blessing of heaven not one of the Saints will lack food when their harvest comes. All the wilderness, from Nauvoo to the Rocky Mountains, is alive with Mormons, with multitudes preparing to follow them from all the states. Great is the excitement that is in the west.

ENGLAND.

We are very pleased to announce that president Spencer is improving from a heavy fever, and through the mercy of God he intends to fill his important office soon. Conference statistics show that the Saints in England are increasing by more than one thousand every quarter. Yet, their enemies shout, "They are declining, still declining."

IRELAND.

It is understood from an account of the Belfast Conference that the gospel is gradually increasing in many places in this country.

SCOTLAND.

Some are being baptized in the Glasgow conference almost daily, and there is constant increase in the Edinburgh environs, &c.

FRANCE.

Several additional preachers have gone to this country lately, and several have obeyed the gospel, with hopeful signs.

WALES.

Merthyr.—This branch is on a constant increase, with hardly a week that some do not come in, to the point that the members here number over five hundred faithful Saints, in a unity of the faith and a bond of peace. Some poor little man has been agitating Georgetown constantly on Sunday nights for several months, bringing with him a crowd of the same persuasion as himself, for the express purpose of deriding the Saints, and they are most zealous! Poor things, they unwittingly produce scores of people to hear the gospel for every one that used to come there. Among the persecutors are religionists who claim to be quite prominent with the denominations, running from the communion table, and gnashing their teeth worst in the faces of the preachers! The most gentlemanly procedure of their Goliath is to jump on a chair near a preacher of the Saints, and continue to shout with all his might, "*You are a liar, you are a liar*," &c., constantly. When the Saints move to another place, he moves after them, and does the same thing there. And he is not ashamed to announce that he is determined to follow them and persecute them as long as he is able, wherever they may go. The greatness of God's patience is remarkable in suffering such a thing for so long. We are reliably informed that religionists hire him for money to do this! Since we have heard that this man has asserted in public many times that he has spoken with us, and found us to be liars, and many other allegations, we announce to our readers that every syllable of it is an unfounded lie, that we have no recollection of our eyes ever having seen the man before, and that we do not know him from all the people of the world; nor are we anxious to see such an intractable wrangler. He has not been deserving of so much as this of our attention before, and we would be loathe to lower ourselves from our important calling to quarrel with a man, or men, so unprincipled and liberal. Our God will take care of such when they have done all the good they can for his work, by calling the attention of the honest in heart to the gospel through their persecution. "I will repay, saith the Lord."

DOWLAIS.—The preachers in this town are awake in earnest now against the Saints, because almost all of them are losing a number of their members. The old tricks of these (with some respected exceptions) were to preach against the Saints, and publish every shameful and unfounded story about them, but they have a new method now, since their previous persecution only brought men to listen to the Saints for themselves, and the result was, if they were honest in heart, for them to believe the truth, and they joined with the Saints. Now, everyone who goes to hear the Saints preach is sorely threatened! And great is the excommunication after some come from their midst to the Saints, making them an example to frighten the others. But this did not succeed, for the people came to the Saints constantly; and the new device afoot now is to choose a select number of the most impudent brawlers from the different schools and chapels, and send them after the preachers of the Saints to oppose them wherever they are preaching, rather similar to the Spaniards' sending their bloodhounds after the natives of America in the past, and great was the barking and hubbub they caused to keep the listeners from hearing the gospel. But let them go ahead, poor things, for their stupidity becomes obvious to all, and they cause hosts to come to listen, and many to believe. Despite "the father of lies," and all his devices, the truth prevails until well over a hundred have been baptized by the Saints in Dowlais in a few months; and those being some from among nearly all the sects, and who would not for the world go back to the "empty husks" they left. May the gracious and good Lord yet tear the veil from the eyes of hosts there, so they may see this godly light.

CWMBYCHAN.—The sectarians work more cunningly through the works here than in some places. Here biting the heel is their *game* to turn the Saints from their work. Yet there are here attentive and dignified listeners searching for the truth, and embracing it despite every scowl and scorn also. We are informed some time ago that 11 have been baptized there since the last Conference (less than a month ago), and that several others have promised to obey soon. And lately several additional preachers went there, and some from the environs.

LLWYNI.—Excitement here once again has been blown up through persecutions and threats; nevertheless, the Saints are faithful and determined, and many have been baptized lately. We heard that false religionists have succeeded in getting some nearby gentleman to turn the Saints from their work because of their religion; but we hope, for the sake of humanity, freedom, Christianity, and reason, that within the borders of enlightened Wales—evangelical Wales, that there is no man as cruel as that.

LLANELLI.—The Editor of the *Revivalist* says that the Saints in his town are some insignificant little things, and that all one has to do to kill them is to pretend not to hear them. This is a prophecy that proves its author a false prophet! Remember it! But the Saints, despite it all, have caused great searching and excitement to take place in Llanelli, yes, even in his own chapel, that he will never extinguish, although he tries to smother it for a while. The Saints baptized 12 there last month to begin with. Rather good, is it not, Mr. Rees?

PONTYBEREM.—Elders H. Williams, Edward Thomas, and Ephraim Rowland are very diligent in these environs, and there is much call for preaching. We heard that they baptized two women lately. Success to them.

PEMBROKESHIRE.—It is the persecutions of the antagonistic preachers that are bringing hosts of listeners here also, and we are informed by brother Mitchell, and others, that some have been baptized since the Conference.

CARDIGANSHIRE.—Elder W. Evans, from Rhymni, and priests James Edwards, and J. Price, have been diligent throughout this County for some time, and are having a splendidly good hearing.

MACHYNLLETH.—We received a letter from elder A. Evans from there lately. The Saints are increasing in unity and love, and like all the congregations of the Saints, great are the gifts and blessings of God in their midst.

FLINTSHIRE.—Elders John Jones, and J. Parry, from Birkenhead, are presently assisting the previous preachers in this County, and several have been baptized. They complain that the family of Demetrius is stirring against them over toward the north, and that they are arming themselves with unfounded tales invented by its Sanhedrin here in the south. Here is proved true the old proverb that says, "A lie sets the whole province on fire while the truth is lighting its match;" yet the truth will be proven, and in time will overcome the sanctuaries of lies.

DENBIGHSHIRE.—Several hard-working officers are preaching the everlasting gospel very successfully in this area also, and many people are searching into it.

CAERNARVONSHIRE.—Elder E. Edwards and priest Lewis Jones are very diligent in this County. We have had several letters from them recently, showing zeal and determination not to turn back. The first stubborn opposition was around Bethesda, &c. The best weapons his enemies had were the lying stories of the newspapers against the character of Joseph Smith, and other elders of the church. We thank God for a doctrine from which they cannot budge one principle. We are also grateful for the certainty we possess that the accusations brought against the vessels that established it are unfounded lies. He says that neither he nor Lewis Jones have suffered from want of any necessity; and the two of them wish for us to announce that Lewis Jones had no intention of coming back, as the enemies of the truth had thought, but that he is preaching boldly and diligently everywhere throughout those environs; and using his own words in a letter lately from Bangor, he says, "I have my heart's desire, and am determined to go forward with this godly work, let them say whatever they wish about me; I have been disappointed in them; and I send my best love to all the Saints." I wonder whether those who caused such persecution to this faithful servant of God will be ashamed, when time proves their lies in their faces!

ANGLESEY.—Elder Robert Evans is preaching his best, and he says that some rascals called the "*Sons of Anglesey*" sent a request to him in one place to leave the County, or his life was in danger! He answered them that he was satisfied, if that was their desire, but that they should remember that his blood would be required of those "*Sons of Anglesey*" eternally. And he is still preaching bravely.

TO OUR DISTRIBUTORS.

THE first part of the "SCRIPTURAL TREASURY" is off the press, price one shilling, and it can be received with the *Prophet.* The work contains about four or five segments sixpence each, in addition. We earnestly beseech you, dear friends, to continue your former diligence in spreading our publications, especially the *Treasury*, and returning the money as soon as possible. One need see only the first part to see the great need for such a book as an instructor to the Saints; and especially so the preachers can understand what we believe on all the topics it contains, and have the thoughts of the inspired writers gathered together at their service, so they may defend them against the attacks of their opponents. The *Treasury* will enlighten our fellow nation concerning our doctrines, which they oppose in their ignorance, for we believe that the publicity of our religion is proportionate to its success in persuading lovers of the truth to embrace it. It is our duty and our privilege to publish it; and the more we do of this, the more we benefit our fellowman, and we shall be rewarded by him who owns the divine work that has been entrusted to us. Now is the time to work, before the days of tribulation come!

*** *We beseech all our distributors to prepare to settle all their accounts by the end of the year, and if there are some books or Prophets on hand that cannot be sold, to return them at that time.*

*** *We have on hand several "History of the Saints," price one shilling, and we hope that not one of the Saints will be without one.*

*** *We also have a selection of nearly twenty kinds of pamphlets of different prices, from a halfpenny to three shillings, which we have published in Welsh lately, and which can be obtained if you hasten.*

*** *Also, a variety of English books, such as the "Book of Mormon," and the "Voice of Warning," "Millennial Star," fortnightly,* 3c.

CONTENTS.

MERTHYR TYDFIL:

PUBLISHED AND FOR SALE BY D. JONES, AND ALSO FOR SALE BY THE SAINTS IN GENERAL.

JOHN JONES, PRINTER, RHYDYBONT.

PROPHET OF THE JUBILEE,

OR

STAR OF THE SAINTS.

No. 16.] OCTOBER, 1847. [Price 2*c*.

APOSTLES.

To prove that there were more than twelve in the church of Jesus Christ in the first age of Christianity, we offer the following:—

Luke ix, 1,—"Then he called his twelve disciples together, and gave them power and authority over all devils, and to cure diseases." Here are seen the twelve disciples. Luke ix, 10,—"And the apostles, when they were returned, told him all that they had done. And he took them, and went aside privately into a desert place belonging to the city called Bethsaida." The same twelve are found here under the name apostles. Luke x, 1,—"After these things the Lord appointed other seventy also, and sent them two and two before his face into every city and place, whither he himself would come." Seventy of what office were these? Were they elders? There has been no word of mention about that title or any other title earlier than this except for apostles: he had not sent anyone else. Why was the word "other" used, if they were not of the same order as the others? We cannot understand what name to put on them except apostles, and if it were said, seventy other (apostles), it would be just as clear, for apostles were being talked about before. The reason why some argue there were but twelve apostles at that time is, we suppose, so they can prove that there is no need to continue them in the church of Christ, rather that they were necessary only to establish it or to be witnesses for Jesus in that time. That argument is older than our fathers, we think; and if it could be defended, that would close the great chasm that is in every congregation that professes to be the apostolic church, and yet is destitute of apostles. But read the following:—Rom. xvi, 7,—

"Salute Andronicus and Junia, my kinsmen, and my fellowprisoners, who are of note among the apostles, who also were in Christ before me." What divine peculiarity could have been in them to deserve praise, more than those of a higher office? if in fact it was higher. 1 Cor. xv, 5, 6,—"And that he was seen of Cephas, then of the twelve. After that, he was seen of above five hundred brethren at once; of whom the greater part remain unto this present, but some are fallen asleep." I wonder if the seventy apostles were not in the midst of this multitude? Had they turned away, such a thing would have been worthy of recording. 1 Cor. xv, 7,—"After that he was seen of James; then of all the apostles." Here it is suggested that it was not known how many were meant by the phrase "all the apostles." The twelve did not include all of them, for he had already indicated in ver. 5, that the twelve had seen him. 1 Cor. xv, 8.9,—"And last of all he was seen of me also, as of one born out of due time. For I am the least of the apostles, that am not meet to be called an apostle, because I persecuted the church of God." Acts xiv, 14,—"Which when the apostles, Barnabas and Paul, heard of, they rent their clothes, and ran in among the people, crying out." Here Luke definitely acknowledges that these two were apostles, even though they were not numbered with the twelve. Rev. ii, 2,—"I know thy works, and thy labour, and thy patience, and how thou canst not bear them which are evil; and thou hast tried them which say they are apostles, and are not, and hast found them liars." If there were supposed to be that number, namely twelve, it is seen how foolish it would be for anyone else to claim to be an apostle. We shall not consider the counter arguments that seeing Jesus Christ, having a personal commission from him, or that each one should have miraculous power, or should have been with him from the beginning, &c., together with having the power to miraculously speak every language, constitute indispensable qualifications in order to be an apostle, rather inconsistent assertions of those who claim "that apostles are among the unnecessary things and gifts." It is seen that it was not possible for all the above apostles, or anyone, to have all those high qualifications, according to what we read. Indeed, we do not understand that there were but four or five working more powerful deeds than the other preachers, or the Saints, and not everyone could be expected to work miracles, any more than it could be expected for all to be apostles. 1 Cor. xii, 29, 30. That one apostle is endowed with such a gift does not keep God from giving the same office to another who does not have that miraculous gift, for the one and the other are a gift from God. "According to his will" is everything.

REVIEW

OF THE LECTURE OF THE REV. D. JONES, CARDIFF, ON "THE EXCELLENCE OF THE CHRISTIAN RELIGION."

THIS lecture was delivered in the Bethania chapel, Dowlais, on the 3rd of September, following the Rev. E. Roberts from Rhymni.

The first step that the lecturer took was into the job of Chairman, and the first thing that came from his mouth was the cruel sentence that follows:—"My brother [E. Roberts] has shown quite clearly that Mormonism is deceit, and only deceit;" when at the same time his brother had not disproved any principle that belongs to "Mormonism," but made horrible hobgoblins out of his own work, and that of others of the same taste, and torturing them alternately; yes, stories, we say, and assertions that were as inappropriate to the Mormons as to the *Baptists*, if not more so. It was not Mormonism they had in their hands, nor its shadow, but the imaginings of its enemies; i.e., if it is admitted that we understand something about it; and if we do not know something, having had years of its society, there is a poor chance of expecting these men who never knew the first thing about it to understand anything of it. Who, seriously, ought to understand it best? Still, we say, that it was not "Mormonism" that was being tortured so mercilessly in Dowlais; for it is more alive and successful today than ever. And we prophesy that it will live forever, despite all its opponents; it has in it divine life, and it will increase the more they martyr it and its followers. Yes, it has in it "the strength of everlasting life," and "the eternal arms are beneath it." No arm of flesh will succeed against it. Next he asserted that "only the Book of Mormon or the Bible can be true, because their contents clash with each other." He did not see fit to note the places, or give even so much as one example to show that clashing, nor can he or anyone else prove that one sentence of the Book of Mormon is contrary to the scriptures; for there is not one. On the contrary, there is complete accord between the two books, and so those who admit the veracity of the one, should admit the veracity of the other also, or prove that the two truths cross each other. He thought that none of his listeners had read anything of the Book of Mormon any more than he himself, and while he could hinder them from reading it, they would not see otherwise. Another assertion of his is,—"The Old Testament ended with an opening to the New to come into our possession. It was prophesied at the end of the Old Testament that there would be another; and at the end of the New Testament the great God, through the mouth of John, locked it forever, so that whoever adds to the words of the prophecy of this book (that is the Old Testament and the New) or who takes away from them, there are only these plagues to fall on his head." See Rev. xxii 18, 19. We have published enough on this counter argument already, to prove that John was not referring to the Old Testament or the New; but as he says himself definitely in the words in question, that is "the words of the prophecy of *this book*," namely, the book of Revelation; that is, the writing he had in his hand at the time on the isle of Patmos, and which contained the words of the prophecy he had received there alone. Does Mr. J. not know that the writings of the apostles were not collected into one book until centuries after John had been on the isle of Patmos? How then could he refer to the volume in the above words? If he forbade adding to the Bible as Mr. J. says, then John became open to the plagues himself, because the critics say that he wrote his three Epistles and his Gospel in Ephesus, after leaving the isle of Patmos; and yet they are in the volume. But concerning this see *Reply* pages 5, 6. *The Scales*, page 15. And yet, what addition to the Bible can the Book of Mormon be unless it is collected there as well, and professes to be a part of it? Is it not a book on its own? and it cannot be an addition to John's words unless it claims John as its author. A child's reason teaches it better than to bring that counterargument against the Book of Mormon; yet that is the mightiest he can think of; and it is good that he gets something against the book he hates without having seen it, is it not? His "brother" referred to this various times before him, and thereby they showed the vanity and stupidity of their arguments and proofs. This is a strange way to display the "excellence of the Christian religion," is it not! They themselves admit that its former "excellence" was its adherers' enjoyment of divine revelations, visions, &c., and Paul prayed to God to continue to give even to the Gentiles "the Spirit of wisdom and *revelation* in the knowledge of him." Yes, he prayed for a continuation of this in the church "throughout all ages, world without end. Amen." Christianity like that was excellent, but the Christianity of Caersalem and Bethania, Dowlais, is more excellent now, without *revelations*, or any of its early power except the form alone. Still Mr. R. had admitted the previous evening "that Christianity is unchanging," namely its "revelations," and the whole of it; but here, against himself, he labels those who profess the gospel that brings revelations as "deceivers." Is this not a fair example of those who say of the darkness that it is light, and of the truth (according to their confession) that it is deceit? That "Spirit of wisdom and revelation" which was the chief excellence of the same Christianity is denying revelations. Yes, they did all this with the Bible before their eyes, affirming the complete opposite in more than a hundred places. How these deniers and scorners can claim any part or share of the "Christianity" of Jesus Christ and his apostles, is a matter of surprise, particularly when despoiling and shaming it publicly! We ask Mr. J. to direct us to the chapter and verse in the Old Testament that promises us a book like the New Testament? How many books, or epistles or letters, chapters and pages were to be in it? We do not know of any prophecy in the Old Testament describing a *book* like the New Testament; and he cannot show any. True that there are there many prophecies about the coming of the Messiah, the great work he would do, the treatment he and his servants would receive after him, apart from many other things; but not one promise of the coming of such a book regarding size, &c., as the New Testament, as Mr. J. asserts. And if the prophets had described a book like the New Testament to appear, their description of it would be very different to what the book is now; because they would have described it as containing the following letters and epistles, (however many more) which, although he admits their veracity like the others, are still lost; such as Paul's *first* Epistle to the Corinthians. See 1 Cor. v. 9. His Epistle to Laodicea, Col. iv, 16. Judas, "about the general gospel," Jude, ver. 3. Enoch's prophecy, ver. 14; apart from many others, says Luke 1, 1, &c. So it is seen that Mr. J.'s assertions so far are completely erroneous. Let us see further whether we can get any truthful assertion from him. He says that the Old Testament has been ended as well, but he does not say by whom; but since John has locked up the New with the above words, why is it not that Moses locked up the Old Testament with the similar sentence in Deut. iv, 2? And if so, Joshua, David, Solomon, Isaiah, yes, all the later prophets, and their work get excommunicated and denied by Mr. J. in the same way as the Book of Mormon and the entire New Testament! This is his logic! He locks himself up in the same dilemma again by asserting that the Old Testament is complete, as he did when he asserted that the New was complete; because if it is fitting to offer to him the Old Testament as proof, it will be seen that it as well is very far from being complete. The book itself admits over a dozen other books as divine as those that are in it; and yet not one of them is in the Old Testament. We refer to some of the many, such as Josh. x, 13; 1 Chron. xxix, 29; 2 Chron. ix, 29; Chap. xii, 15; Chap. xxxiii, 19, &c., &c. How can you claim that the Old Testament is complete, Mr. J., until it contains all these, at least? And having got these, perhaps they will give an account of others then. What, is it the two covers that make a book complete, or your assertion that it is thus? Does not the book itself say completely the opposite of your assertion in various places, how God would give more revelations from age to age, if men did not twist his paths, and deny revelations, &c, yes, that he would reveal his mind "line upon line," precept upon precept, here a little and there a little? And he is doing so in this age for his children through the Book of Mormon, through the spirit of revelation, and the spiritual gifts, &c., despite the fact that you deny that, and oppose the things you know nothing about, as did Cora, Dathan, and Abiram before. For the sake of your souls, and the souls of your listeners, do not be so eager to get the wages of injustice with that Baalam of old. What but this excites you and your persecuting brethren, to assert such foolishness and lies against the truth? Next, note Mr. J.'s comparison. He says that the light of the Mosaic, Patriarchal, and Jewish ages are like the light of the stars, the moon, and the sun, "but Joe's light is like the *light* of a candle." Thank you for admitting that "Joe" has as much light as that; because you were asserting first that he had *only* deceit, and there is not even the "light of a candle" in deceit. Light is the same; and it is good, from wherever it may come. Your comparisons neccessarily signify divine light, and so of the same sort as that of "Joe." From whence did "Joe" get that light of a candle? From whence do you claim to have received the light of the sun? Is it not from the New Testament? If so, was not the New Testament of "Joe" as good as the one you have, and as a result could he not have received the light of the sun that you claim, i.e., if it is to be had in the book; and here is your profession, and the only axis to your structure, since you deny the spirit of revelation. If the book is the source of light, from whence did the authors of the book get their light before composing a book? If the book was not the source of their light, how can it be a *source* of light now? It is said that "God's holy men spoke the scriptures as they were moved upon by the Holy Ghost:" and not as they were moved upon by a *book* or *books*. Again, if the book is the source of light, why do you and all your fellow preachers with your opposing words not come to agree and jointly teach the divine principles of the New Testament, instead of being at loggerheads with each other every day, even regarding the important and unchanging ordinances of the gospel? There is hardly anything in which you pull together, apart from denying the spirit of the light, and persecuting and slandering the children of the divine light, and calling them "deceivers," "children of the darkness," "satanists," &c. Since we are to know men by their works, what is more obvious than that your works and assertions prove you children of darkness? The scripture says that men in the latter days would have a form (that is only a profession) of godliness, and would deny its power, (that is that spirit of light and revelation that was a "*strength* and great certainty" in the Saints of old;) who would not wish to come into the light, because their works would be evil.

[*To be continued.*]

QUOTATION OF THE LETTER OF APOSTLE O. HYDE.

THE following letter was written from St. Louis, dated August 5, to O. Spencer, Liverpool:—

"June 22nd, Elders Pratt and Taylor started from Horne, together with a company of Saints, with about 600 wagons, after the first camp. When returning from the Bluffs toward St. Joseph, five days ago, they met with 5 *battalions* of the Saints that had joined with the American army, returning to meet the camp, which had not yet arrived there. They and some others from the Fort went after them. A messenger came here recently informing us that the first camp had reached beyond the Rocky Mountains, through the "*South Pass*," all well.

The rest of the army have settled in California. Several messengers returned to meet with the first camp, who had been looking over conditions in California; and thus through the goodness of God all will meet together in a council near the foot of the mountains, at which time the focal point of their effort will be determined, &c. To God be the thanks! His own spirit began this work, and has guided it forward until now; otherwise all things would not have come together in such a remarkable and convenient manner to join together the ends of the earth, without the sound of a hammer. The crops of the Saints in the land of the Indians are bountiful and splendid; practically everywhere the face is turned, great fields of Indian corn, &c., are seen throughout this wilderness. A week ago last Sunday, I preached at my encampment in the woods to a large congregation of attentive listeners, and eight were baptized at the end, in a pool that had been made on the *prairie;* and although we are exiles, we have many lovely and sweet Sabbaths.

"Our camps are followed by hosts of people from the world, who enjoy our company; and many are being baptized all the time along the way, in the wilderness, &c., and others stream after them.

"I heard that the Pratt and Taylor company was within 150 miles of *Fort Laramie* on the 17th of July, all well. I have been preaching and holding Conferences for an extent of 50 miles on both sides of the Missouri river from *Council Bluffs* to *St. Louis*, besides laboring with my own hands until I have a field of over 50 acres fenced, and 30 acres in cultivation. It is an easy task to place a crop in these *prairies*, and it bears fruit splendidly.

"When a message returns from the twelve, you will be timely advised concerning emigration, and I hope the Saints will be patient a little time longer. If the Saints in Britain assist us here as much as they can, that will be all the better for them as well when they come here; for this is not personal work that we have, rather everyone cooperates to benefit the whole temporally and spirtually. I have come down here presently on business relating to the church, and to train the Saints here; and it is not impossible but that I may run over to Britain again, when I have a whole day to rest. Yet be that as the Lord and my brethren will.

"Tell Capt. D. Jones for me that Zion's banners are nailed to the top mast, waving proudly over the sons of Joseph, lighting up their sad visage with a generous degree of hope that "the day spring from on high hath visited them." My warmest greeting to him and his family, and also all the brethren and sisters over whom he has been called to preside. May heaven's choicest blessings rest upon them,—and his favor distil on the Cambrian hills, like the dew on mount Hermon, or the fresh showers of dew upon the mountains of Zion. I remember Scotland also, brother Richards, and a thousand others just as good. May their God bless them.

"Greet all the godly and dear brethren and sisters lovingly for me; those in England, Scotland, and in Wales.

"I am, your brother in the Everlasting Covenant,

"ORSON HYDE."

GREETING TO THE SAINTS.

DEAR SAINTS,—Here we are, once again, through the medium of the *Prophet*, and more earnestly than ever before, seriously calling your attention to assist the Saints that are in the wilderness. We remind you of our promises to them, by calling your attention to what has been said before of their troubled and suffering circumstances on their long journey. We remind you of the relationship that is between us and them through the bond of the new covenant, to exhort you to fulfill our duty and our privilege toward them in their present distress; and, that it is our duty to assist them, not with our prayers *only*, but also through "bearing one another's burdens," for "faith without works is dead." The fact that it is for our comfort and safety, yes, for our temporal and spiritual salvation, as much as for anyone else's, they are striving, compels us to say that we should bear as much as we can of this great burden. Also the tumultuous and pitiful condition of the world in general, and our country in particular, proves to "those who were given to know the signs of the Times," that freedom, enjoyment, yes, in a word, all the comfort of the children of Zion, depend on their success in building the gates of the daughters of Zion, as a resting place for her children, when forced to flee from the borders of great Babylon and all its daughters, before the days of tribulation come, in which the vials of the wrath of God are poured out upon them. All the persecution, the lecturing, the false accusing, the threatening, and the cruel and unfounded attacks that are upon us in these days, especially in these environs, remind us that that spirit that makes Babylon drunk with the blood of the Saints, is now working busily in her children to fill the measure of their lies; and to be the objects of the righteous judgments of God upon them; and no doubt their rage will increase to the same extent that the godliness of the Saints increases, with the great power of God in their midst, in other places besides here. All will remind us that we are foreigners and pilgrims, even in the land of our birth, and that there is no city with foundations for us in their midst, and proving as plainly as the sun the absolute necessity we have of securing our part of the "city which hath foundations, whose builder and maker is God," and that we have no time to lose if we desire "the resting place that yet awaits the people of God." Doubtless the Welsh will need it as much and as soon as any other nation. Let us remember that those who request our assistance now are our servants and our forerunners, and no doubt it will benefit us to help them. "For on Mount Zion, and in Jerusalem, there will be deliverance." Well, may all these considerations move us to help them along with all our might. Not many shillings have been contributed in their behalf by the Welsh for several months, I am sorry to say; and the previous faithfulness and readiness of the Saints lead us to believe that the fault was ours for being so silent about the matter, or perhaps it was the fault of the various officers, through neglecting to put the plan that was designed for this purpose into operation. Let the Saints give their contributions to their presidents according to their means, and in a book especially for that purpose, let the name of every contributor and the amount given be recorded, and that will be in remembrance of the future time, and the names found in the "book of the law of the Lord." It is true that the Missionary Society calls loudly for our assistance, to spread the gospel in the midst of our fellow nation; but in face of the present circumstances, what is a fellow nation in comparison to dear brethren and sisters, which are bound in the same eternal covenant—children of the same heavenly father, and joint heirs of the same heavenly resting place? Brethren before strangers,—children of God before children of the world, and *builders* of Zion before its *mockers*, may this be the motto of us all. Again we say, you officers—you gentle Saints above all other things now, remember this call, and let all of us strive together to fulfill our promise as a nation. The possessor of all the earth will repay an hundredfold to all who give, we say.

THE SIGN OF THE PROPHET JONAH.

MR. EDITOR,—The people of this country are seeking signs, but they will not receive any except for the "sign of the prophet Jonah." Yet no one accepts that one either! Not everyone understands what kind of a sign it was. Some think that because the prophet was in the belly of the fish it was a sign, but Christ said, "so shall the son of God be to this generation." Therefore, if the Ninevites saw Jonah after he had been in the belly of the fish, that generation did not see the resurrected Christ, for he himself said, "ye shall not see me henceforth, and the world seeth me no more," and he said that he gave it to make it clear to *chosen witnesses*, &c. If so, the nation did not see him after he resurrected; therefore, the miracle was not the sign. But Christ said that the Ninevites listened to the preaching of Jonah, and that for that reason they condemned that generation. Consequently, the preaching of Jonah was the sign, and not his being swallowed by the fish. Thus it is with Christ also, as Isaiah said, "Behold, I and the children whom the Lord hath given me are for signs and for wonders in Israel." Therefore, their coming as messengers to the people made them signs, did it not?

So it is in this age. Men have been sent by God to preach the sermon that he spoke to them, and not something they imagined; and not in excellence of speech, or in outward appearance, for if Jonah had a tidy appearance at the outset, his clothes had been soiled and dirtied in the belly of the fish. Next, Jonah knew what to preach; likewise with the servants of God always. Not one like this, and another like that, but each one preached that which he received at the beginning. What is the reason that men go through the country in this age, and that without money or majesty, but poor of appearance, and uneducated, yet testifying that they have been sent by God to warn the people for the last time before his judgment comes. What, I say, are these men? No doubt, this is a remarkable sign! Who would not say, What can this be? Who would not accept their word with all readiness of mind, "searching the scriptures daily, to see if these things are not so." Therefore, let the Welsh know assuredly that these his servants are sent to preach to you this gospel, which will testify greater things than this to whoever receives it.

The Spirit of God like a fire's ablaze,
  The latter-most days have now dawned in this age;
The Lord has extended by heavenly rays,
  Eternal deliverance, his word to engage.

That on Cumorah's hill the truth was revealed,
All backwoodsmen also will one day believe;
And when California their blemish has healed
Much peace and rejoicing at length they'll receive. R. EVANS.

THE LATE REV. JOHN WESLEY A MORMON!

CONCERNING the spiritual gifts the church of Jesus Christ enjoyed in the days of the apostles, the scriptures show too clearly for anyone to deny to this day, that they had them at that time, as in 1 Cor. xii, &c. They show so clearly that their purpose and their effect were to perfect the Saints in this life, Eph. iv, that it is seen in the same context and other places that they were necessary in the church until all the Saints had come to a unity of the Christian faith,—after being baptized with the same baptism, after drinking of the same spirit, and coming to an agreement of the same principles, and walking the same paths, or spiritual journey, until reaching the objective set before them, namely the payment of the reward. The promises of these things, we say, are as clear as are the conditions on which they were received formerly, and despite all that, nearly all who claim the ordinances agree to deny the gifts associated with them. They claim the right to the tree, but say there is no need of the fruits now. That no one needed those beneficial fruits except for the contemporaries of the apostles. Furthermore, the only purpose for which those fruits grew on the primitive tree (or the church) was, not to feed the soul of the Saints, but to satisfy the eyes of the world, and to prove that such a tree had existed. From what follows, it is seen that this tradition is older than Mr. Wesley, and perhaps almost as old as Calvin, Zuinglius, Menno, Peter Waldo, or Melanethon, but whatever of that, it is too popular now, yes, even among those who harbor great zeal for the name of the godly Mr. Wesley, and we hope that counsel from the mouth of their father will be beneficial to convince them of the absurdity of such an assertion, and to bring them to believe more of the principle of the one, although dead, who yet speaks to them about this. The following is quoted from his 94th sermon on the "*More excellent way*."

"It does not appear that supernatural gifts have continued generally in the church, except until the second or the third century. Rarely do we hear of them after that destructive period, when the emperor Constantine called himself a Christian, and through his selfish whim he intended to spread Christianity by piling wealth, honor, and power on the Christians in general. From that time they disappeared almost completely; at least, it was most unusual to hear of them after this time. The reason why they stopped was not as the common folk (*vulgar*) say, that they were not needed any longer, because all the world had embraced Christianity. This is an unfortunate misconception! There was not the twentieth part of the world who were Christians at that time, even in name. The real reason [why the miraculous gifts did not continue] is because of the cooling of the love of many—the Christians had not more of the spirit of Christ than did the other pagans! The Son of God, when he visited his church, could hardly find faith on the earth. This is the original cause for supernatural gifts of the Holy Ghost not being found any longer in the Christian church, because the Christians turned into pagans after that, with nothing but the dead letter remaining."

It is seen that we are not the only ones who call those who deny the need for spiritual gifts "*vulgar*," and an "unfortunate misconception;" but here is the revered Mr. Wesley saying that, yes, even above his own mistaken children; and is it not high time for them to return at his call to the church that has those gifts, as we are certain that he would do if he had the same opportunities as they? His honesty compels us to believe this of him.

THE SPIRITUAL GIFTS.

OUR able correspondent "Daniel ap Iago," is of the same belief as Mr. Wesley concerning the gifts, it is seen, although not one more than the other was in touch with Mormonism. And who, indeed, of those who profess to believe the scriptures, does not agree with what is so clear!

"A great surprise if there is one man—in Gwalia,
Who does not see this as a standard:
This is the power of every commandment,
Good will, and benefit to man."

"God gave signs in his primitive church, 1 Cor. 12, 38.
To keep it sound and orderly on its way; Eph. 4, 12, 13.
But in the present age these are as thorns,
To those whose faith is smooth and easy.

And since God gave them from his true infinite grace,
Woe to anyone so insolent as to try to extricate them;
Whoever does not avow all the gifts ardently,
Has nothing but a mirage of religion, having denied its power. 2 Tim. 3, 5.

To whom is the promise? Is there a place to know this?
Yes, yes, within the scriptures to be seen in black and white:—
To you and your children first, but here is better news. Acts 2, 38.
You see the promise reaches all afar. 39.

While God is calling, this promise
Stands firmly as a privilege before us;
But though it is God who calls, there are thousands in our age
Who deny the promises by cruelly contradicting. 2 Tim. 4, 1.

Human traditions, without order of the true kind, 2 Tim. 4, 3, 4.
Instead of enjoying the pure rules and rites of our God,
Lead some astray, with every kind of evil bigotry, 2 Peter 2, 1, 3, 12-19.
And hold them in the midst of foolishness, against the order of grace.

Upon the heads of those who follow scripture true,
Every foolish curse and woe will be proclaimed. 2 Peter 2, 10.
A partial explanation will satisfy some
Better than the teachings from the mouth of God himself. Jude 8, 15, 16, 18, 19.

If anyone mentions that gifts are to be had within thy gates,
The people begin to shout, why do not you do miracles?
Thus can their spirit be seen, proving it unfailing,—
The chronicle of their devil father asks the same thing. Mat. 4, 3.

There will be, I am sure, no miracles, to please the whim of man;
When asked, Christ himself refused. Mark 8, 11, 12.
The Holy Ghost gives the power without doubt,
To those he wishes, and wherever he will. 1 Cor. 12, 11.

Say what is the cause, is this not strange,
That we do not believe the prophets while they are in our midst?
In centuries to come, they will be believed by every class.
But while they are among us, they're useless if not killed. Mat. 23, 30—34.

The foolish arguments among all humanity would cease,
If they would be taught, fairly by the Spirit of God, Eph. 4, 3—18.
And receive the testimony he spoke, every bit; Mark 16, 16—18.
It is strong on the earth, and strong in the judgment to come." Mat. 24, 35.

CATECHISM OF THE SAINTS.

TUNE—"*The Prophet Daniel.*"

Who is busy shaking the earth,
In boldly preaching without dearth,
And for their work meet scorn or mirth?
Saints of the Most High God.

Which is the party many shun,
Which is attacked by everyone,
Which after whom abusers run?
Saints of the Most High God.

Who is hated by the gentiles?
At whom do they aim their missiles?
Who is cursed in their ranks and files?
Saints of the Most High God.

Who are sought by the so-called wise
For empty signs before their eyes,
While gospel graces they despise?
Saints of the Most High God.

Who "confound the minds of many"—
Claiming they're as wise as any
In mild Jesus' tesimony?
Saints of the Most High God.

Who are thought to be but "sweepings,"
Or just dregs, or poor spoilings,

Fools, "deceivers" in their teachings?
Saints of the Most High God.

But who is it has a promise
In the Lord of holy solace,
Many blessings given to us?
Saints of the Most High God.

Who shall have prophetic spirit,
Who do knowledge, faith inherit?
Who will speak in tongues about it?
Saints of the Most High God.

Who'll express the Spirit singing?
Who its wonders are performing—
Every gift, including healing?
Saints of the Most High God.

And with whom do apostles stand,
Preachers and teachers as one band,
Helping their charges understand?
Saints of the Most High God.

Who expects one day to gather,
Jesus being the convener,
In perfection with our ruler?
Saints of the Most High God.

And who each day should therefore strive
To be as one in love alive,
Of their creation joy derive?
Saints of the Most High God. J. D.

NEWS FROM THE ELDERS.

We would have great pleasure in setting before our readers quotations of the comforting letters of our traveling brethren from the north, if our columns permitted, but we must be brief. We received several letters from our dear and faithful brother Abel Evans from various places. The most distinguishing characteristic throughout all of them in nearly every place is the unfailing adherence of the Saints to the gospel through every obstacle. Their increase in love and wisdom, together with all virtues, are clear to him each time that he visits them, says he, and this is as it should be with all who are under the guidance of the Spirit of grace. He says that many have been baptized lately through the different counties of the North. Elder R. Evans is very diligent in Anglesey, and has baptized some there lately. We would be glad to see the face of our beloved brother in the South for a while this winter, if he agrees. Elder Eliezer Edwards gives very hopeful news from Caernarvonshire, and says that he also has baptized some; he in his turn will come to visit his brethren and sisters in the South before long. He raises longing in our heart to see all the cheerful Saints when he writes their stories like this, and raises even more longing to see the happy day when we shall all meet in Zion, with no one pulling the opposite way, rather all with their harps in tune to sing to him, the one who loved us and washed us in his blood, &c. May it hasten. Amen.

STATE OF THE CHURCHES.

MERTHYR TYDFIL. This mother branch is going forward steadily and successfully. Although not as rapidly, yet more faithfully, warmly, and unitedly, than ever, and in fuller enjoyment of the spiritual gifts, and other promises of the great head of this church. Five have been received in the church this week already, on the profession of their faith and their repentance.

DOWLAIS. We hardly know what to say of this town! There is general agitation through nearly all of it, like a boiling cauldron, between the lectures of Mr. Roberts, Davies, Jones, and other Reverends, from their pulpits (which will be reviewed in a TREATISE, and in the PROPHET); and besides these, some number of quarrelsome men are following the preachers of the Saints, and disturb them rudely wherever they preach. And among others there is some man by the name of Mr. Evan Lewis (although we do not know him from all the people of the world), who continues to hold meetings at the corners of the streets to lecture against the Saints, and proclaim the old customary false accusations against Joseph Smith. But after washing that old stock over and over, until souring the minds of his listeners, it is said that he is as zealous as can be in telling baseless tales about our own character; one example is the story he told to a crowd, namely, "that a woman in Dowlais was ready to swear that we tried to rape her;" but by the time that other men from Dowlais went to question that woman, she had confessed that there was not a word of truth in the matter! We had never exchanged so much as a word with her, and we assure you that we would not know her if we were to meet her on the street! Many find fault with us for tolerating such slander and blasphemy without seeking redress, and yet they would be more ready to blame us if we did, that it would be revenge, and unchristian behavior, &c.—As for the Saints who are in Dowlais, they are more determined and united here, as in nearly every other place, the more they are persecuted. They happily enjoy the spiritual and gracious gifts that were promised them, and this strengthens them to endure every attack joyfully.

MONMOUTHSHIRE CONFERENCE. There is growing excitement throughout this conference lately, and several have obeyed the gospel, especially in Nantyglo. We have heard of additional hostile fruits of Sectarianism around Beaufort lately. Two men, who claimed to be constables of another parish, got hold of three preachers of the Saints, one after the other, when out preaching on Sunday, with a large crowd listening respectfully until these rude and unlawful agitators came there, and under the pretence of civil authority they locked the three preachers up!! How long will the just God suffer such oppression and violence, in the name of Christianity? The men were released from prison at some time, and without either reparation or inquiry, or without knowing why, until now.

LLANELLI. Elders William Hughes, Morgan Richards, and others, are diligent and successful here, and in the environs, however much the Editor of the *Revivalist* proclaims that they are a bunch of illiterates, and that their religion is a small, insignificant thing, &c. Yes, there are from thirty to forty there who have been baptized by them in the last two months, and nearly that many in the two months before that, until there are over sixty Saints now, and almost all of these were with the different denominations of that town, and they were, it seems, considered to be of impeccable character before they received membership with them, and all of these were "deceived" by an illiterate and stupid man, were they not, Mr. Rees? If they were deceived, great was your neglect toward them for years; otherwise, you should have taught them better than to be deceived by such men as those! One of two things is acknowledged in your accusation in view of the fact of their success, either your negligence, or that it is illiterate men who are the most effective in convincing men. The latter was true previously; for example, remember the "fishers" of the sea of Galilee, and why not so now? Well, cease to boast of your college education any more then, and do not blame the illiteracy of such successful preachers. Who but Mr. Rees shouted in the Parks Chapel a short time ago,—"Nothing should be judged prematurely. When we judge beforehand, our judgment is erroneous, and we draw false conclusions." And he has substantiated that himself very clearly through his death sentence on that small, insignificant thing that is attracting the mind and heart of about thirty of the most honest and wise hearts that are around him. Yes, and many from his chapel also, without his knowing, supposedly by his speaking. But the people of Llanelli are too intelligent, and consider their souls of too much value to be persuaded that light is darkness, and that truth is deceit, despite all the priests of Baal on the walls of Llanelli shouting that.

PONTYBEREM. Elder Howell Williams, and several others, are laboring successfully in these areas round about. They are receiving an attentive and numerous hearing, and many are believing the gospel, and are calling for more preachers. And we would be happy if some of the priests who are in these areas could go there to help them. They praise the people of that land greatly, for their courtesy and their graciousness. Seven have been baptized in those environs lately, according to what we have heard, and we expect to hear of more daily.

CWMAMAN. Two elders, and one priest, have moved there to live and to work, for the purpose of being able to preach the gospel of Christ freely to those good people; and great is the hearing they have, and the cheerfulness that is shown them by almost everyone; and according to what we hear from nearly everywhere, the people, after being so long in wrangling with respect to sectarianism, are disgusted; and when they open their ears to hear this everlasting gospel, at times they shout, "This is it," and we answer, "Yes, dear friends, this is it," indeed! This is the godly religion you have searched so eagerly for; embrace it, and you shall find the treasure of treasures in it.

YSTRADGYNLAIS. Several have been baptized here and the environs also, and are rejoicing in their privileges. There are four preachers here also laboring diligently and boldly.

CWMBYCHAN. There is here a continual increase, and they are baptizing frequently in the neighborhoods. All the officers are in unity and love through the entire council, and the Saints lovingly enjoy abundant gifts, and are increasing constantly.

PEMBROKESHIRE. Elder J. Morris is baptizing here now and again, and sometimes in the midst of heated persecution and rock throwing; but despite it all, the kingdom goes forward here as in other places, until it has been offered to all.

CARMARTHEN. The zeal and love of these Saints are greatly praised to us also, and we have heard that elder B. Jones has baptized there lately. Onward, onward, dear Saints, you have hosts of honest people, seekers of the truth, around you.

LLANYBYDDER. The zeal and faithfulness of these Saints have been very noteworthy recently, and they have baptized 10 or 12 around Brechfa, &c., a short time ago. May the gracious Lord, who began this godly work in our midst, increase them more and more, and pour out a greater abundance of his Holy Spirit upon his Saints.

ANNOUNCEMENT.

We have for sale a number of volumes of
CAPT. JONES ON MORMONISM, IN 1846.

For sale, newly bound, available with the Prophet, or as indicated for the following prices:—

	s.	p.
Bound in linen beautifully	3	0
" Half in calf skin	3	6
" In sheepskin	4	0
" Completely in best calf skin	4	6

*** *Thomas Jeremy's question answered in "Doctrine and Covenants," page* 330.

*** *D. Jones, Bagillt, answered in "Doct. and Cov.," page* 200. *Also in the Prophet, No.* 12, *page* 92.

*** *We beseech our distributors to prepare to settle all their accounts by the end of the year, and if there are unsold books or Prophets on hand, to return them at that time.*

*** *We have on hand several "History of the Saints," price one shilling, and we hope that none of the Saints will be without one.*

*** *We have also a variety of nearly twenty kinds of essays at different prices, from a halfpenny to three shillings, which we have recently published in Welsh, and which can be obtained if you hurry.*

*** *Also, a variety of English books, such as "The Book of Mormon," and the "Voice of Warning," "Millennial Star," fornightly,* 3p.

We ask for the patience of our other Correspondents for a little while yet. Our Prophet is a small one, with many attacking it.

CONTENTS.

MERTHYR TYDFIL:
PUBLISHED AND FOR SALE BY D. JONES, AND ALSO FOR SALE BY THE SAINTS IN GENERAL.

JOHN JONES, PRINTER, RHYDYBONT.

PROPHET OF THE JUBILEE,

OR

STAR OF THE SAINTS.

No. 17.] NOVEMBER, 1847. [PRICE 2*c*.

REVIEW

OF THE LECTURE OF THE REV. D. JONES, CARDIFF, ON "THE EXCELLENCY OF THE CHRISTIAN RELIGION."

(Continued from page 154.*)*

FOR the sake of reason and consistency, do not claim "the light of the sun," since you have been born blind, and have not come to see any of the light yet. Do not think that this is too hard a statement, Mr. J.; for your deeds prove it. Your admittance that you have not got hold of the source of the light (that is through the spirit of light), but have mistaken it for the book, and denied the spirit of revelation, which alone enlightened the Saints formerly, is also a fact to prove that you are one of the children of the dark. And since you have already admitted that "Joe" had light of the same sort as the light of the sun, it is better for you to accept just this tiny bit to begin with, rather than stay in that pitch darkness any more. The path of the just is like the light, increasing more and more until midday; the young little Saints got the light of a little candle formerly, which increased, and perhaps thus was the candlelight of "Joe." Mr. J., do not try to extinguish it then, because there is no danger for the honest man to get too much light; it is deceivers who take fright at the light, as you take fright at the little candle of "Joe." No wonder that you shout so loudly "reject his candle, &c.," because to the extent to which it is had it would expose your heresies and those of others; but the greatest surprise was hearing a man with both his eyes closed, and in the middle of the black night, shouting at the top of his voice, "come into the light of the sun!" And on coming there, what was his *sun* but a book describing the sun which some others had seen eighteen hundred years ago! I can imagine hearing someone who had a grain of *common sense* trying to persuade him to come out of his black hole, and open his eyes, so that he might see the same sun now for himself; but he refuses the invitation, asserting that the book has been set in place of the sun, that there is no need of the sun now, and that it was only meant to enlighten the inhabitants of those ages; and that reading about it was "*more excellent*" now than enjoying it. And he boldly asserts that the other is telling lies, although his eyes see the sun; and he would be able to see it, if he were to open his eyes, but despite everyone he would not, lest anyone understand his previous blindness! So Mr. J. prefers to persuade everyone to stay in the darkness, to coming into the light of a candle to start with, which would increase until the sun of justice came over the public, and filled the world with light and knowledge of God, as the waters cover the sea. Well, one has pity on him, because he is depriving himself, poor thing! Next, note Mr. J's prayer. "Let Joe's candle be extinguished *as he was extinguished*." "Joe's candle" is his religion, necessarily; because the light of his candle is now in Dowlais, frightening and discomfitting Mr. J. and his brethren wondrously. Next, note how "Joe was *extinguished* (that is, he died)." Mr. J. and the world know, yes, the heavens know as well, that he was trampled by bloody murderers in Carthage jail, because of his religion. Well "*thus*" in effect this "Evangelical" "Reverend" prays for the people of Dowlais, to kill the Saints in Dowlais, and everyone everywhere who professes the same light as Joseph Smith! J. Smith was killed after giving himself into the hands of the government and under its protection, in order to have a fair trial; for he knew that the law of the land would acquit him, and his murderers knew that; and so they shot four bullets through him and his brother before getting a trial. Well, *thus* Mr. J. prays in his manner, for us to be murdered in our country, because of our religion, and without having a trial. Men are the candles that show his light according to the comparison of Mr. J., and so it is men he wishes to kill as Joseph Smith was killed, and not its light, namely its religion: because that cannot be killed in the same manner without that. We know from experience that scores of those who professed the same ministerial craft as he, and under the influence of the same Spirit have led the bloody armies of the *mobs* to kill scores of our dear brothers in America. Yes, they were the first instigators of the persecution there, as they are here; they continued to breathe their threatenings and their false accusations from the pulpits, &c., until they got a party of their followers cruel enough to follow them to kill the Saints, and burn down the houses of others about their heads, and exile thousands from the land of their birth without trial or mercy; yes, the Reverends did all this; and they will have the pleasure of drinking the dregs of the horrible cup of blameless blood which they themselves filled. And yet, brothers of theirs with the same father are to be found even in enlightened Wales, "in the land of the Bibles," and "the garden of Christianity," praying from pulpits for the committing of such *wholesale butchery* of their fellowmen! Trying to close the ears of the people from listening to us,—closing their chapels to those of our members who come to listen:—charging 6p each for their fellowmen to be allowed to come to their chapels to hear us and our religion being falsely accused! Yes, these men, having done everything they can, are trying to close the Press to us, and deprive us of the freedom of this the only way we know of in this country, which is free to publish anything for us. And now they are completing the *picture* of our horrible persecution by praying for all of us to be murdered as was Joseph Smith!!

We wonder if the papal "*court of inquisition*" of old would not blush, before releasing such sentences over their pulpits. Read it on paper before your eyes, and the eyes of the public, Mr. J. "Let Joe's candle be extinguished as he was extinguished," is it! This sentence will be remembered, Sir, and its author will be remembered by godly Saints, when wallowing in their blood in the mountains of Wales, probably. You will remember it, Sir, and it will be imprinted on the lintel over the door to your eternal prison, unless you call it back and repent of it, before it gives birth to its bloody offspring, namely the shedding of innocent blood. Oh, dear Wales! What is the matter? Teaching like this flooding from the pulpits of our land! What! in this "enlightened age?" What will be the results before long? whose life will be safe? Shh! the groans and voice of our perished fathers who were martyred here have scarcely ceased echoing on the crags of our country,—their graves are still new under our feet; and the ruins of the crosses, the prisons, and the altars where they were sacrificed are still staring us in the face. And despite all this, behold some of their own children trying to blow the sparks of the old embers to burn their brothers of the same blood for their religion. And worse still, they do all this under the mantle of "Christianity." Yes, this is the "excellence of Christianity," say these men. Oh paganism, hide thy altars for shame; because thy *animal* sacrifices do not compete with the *human* sacrifices of these people! Why talk further about the papal *inquisition*, the druids, or Juggernaut himself, because a *selection* of those victims would be made; but as for the altars of this sort of "Christianity," they will not be satisfied except with the blood of Saints, without trial or defense! And however much it drank deep of the blood of our godly brothers and sisters beyond the sea, behold its priests here still thirst for ours. And their open mouths are like the grave *here* still, shouting "*give, give.*" If they are asked "give" what, the answer is to be had from Mr. J. and his partners, namely "give" us more sacrifices "*like*" that of Joseph Smith, so that the same thing can be done with them. You dear Saints, be grateful with all your hearts for the laws of the land, to defend us from the altars and priests of this bloody "Christianity"!

Is it not to these people the apostle refers when he says "by reason of whom the way of truth shall be evil spoken of?" Doubtless there are hosts in our country saying, on seeing the unchristian acts of its professors, and on hearing the persecuting lectures and sermons of those who claim to teach "Christianity," "Give us atheism rather than that kind of Christianity." Why take the trouble to review the assertions of such a bloody man as this? We would not consider it worth notice were it not for their assertions of Christianity, and their influence to shame that divine religion, and to deprive our fellowmen of the blessings. This lecture also shouts often for people to embrace Christianity rather than Mormonism, and not to touch the Book of Mormon but to read the Bible. What is this but to try to get the people to believe we do not believe the Bible? But we thank his "brother" before him for admitting that we "believe in the Old Testament," even though this one denies that. Let our work defending the principles of the Old Testament and the New, from the denial and distortions of those aggressors, prove whether we believe the scriptures, or whether we do not: and let that testify whether it is we or our accusers who are the infidels, the deceivers, the *idiots*, the satanists, the *baboons*, and the *monkeys*, yes, and who really deserve all the other misnomers they give us. And let the reader and the public judge, whether it is we or they who have the excellent Christianity that the scriptures describe; because by its fruits you will ever know it. If reviling their fellow-men with the respectable names above is its fruit; if denying the spirit of revelation and all the most excellent gifts of Christianity is its fruit, then they most certainly have it. If Christianity teaches men to persecute, to make the freedom of the Press captive, and to raise riots, and to urge men to murder each other over it, then we shall easily admit that they are the Christians, and that Mormon Christianity does not know anything about these things, nor does it choose ever to understand anything about a religion that has brought forth such fruit. And may the great creator of the Christianity of the Saints save them and everyone, from the talons and altars of such a religion and its priests. But if the words are true of him who said, "ye shall be hated of all men for my name's sake." If the principle that Christianity's founder taught is true, namely, "all that will live godly in Christ Jesus shall suffer persecution," and if that religion is "unchanging" as Mr. Roberts admitted, then the truth is that the "Mormons" are the only Christians to be had in Wales; and if the tree is unchanging, so is the fruit. The fruits of Christianity formerly were the "spiritual gifts;" why not now? Another fruit of that time was that all the Pharisees and false religious men of the age condemned it as deceit, and slandered those who professed it as false prophets, devilish men, traitors against the government, fanatics, ignorant men, and the filth of the world, and the offscouring of all things, &c. Why does the same Christianity that caused such men to persecute it not bear similar characteristics in this age? Consider, gentle reader, does not the religion of the Saints bring forth fruits quite like those of early Christianity? Were it not of divine derivation, it is unlikely that men like this would persecute it so much. He does well to counsel everyone to embrace the Bible, and thus do we say with all our heart, but again, we say, there is as much difference between shouting "embrace the Bible," and embracing the doctrines it teaches as there is between Mr. J.'s "Christianity" and the religion of the Bible, or Mormonism; and whoever does not see this difference, we have pity on his condition. But enough now of such false Christianity. Let the scriptures be searched, and let their divine commandments be obeyed, and then God will prove that "Mormonism" is truth, and that it is the Saints that have the "Excellence of Christianity," by contributing its divine gifts and its promises into your possession. Do our persecutors promise this? Oh, no; that is because they do not have the spirit of "Christianity" nor "*her power.*"

Thy spirit, mighty Lord—
Possess me in accord—me to perfect;
So that the world's base way
Shall end without delay:
Desires of flesh and falsehood I reject.

The errors of my days—
In truth, your words erase:—give me advice
Whereby I gain new strength
To drive them out at length;
Extolling thus your precious sacrifice.

EXTRACT FROM THE LETTER OF JOHN BOWEN FROM LLWYNI.

WE beg your indulgence to publish the following letter, because of the principle it contains, although it was not written to be published. It is easy to perceive from the research of its author into both sides whether Baptists or Mormons have the true Christianity. It can also be seen what harmful effects the writers cause who publish all this rubbish against the Saints.

"Dear Brother,

"The best news I have to inform you, is that I was baptized "for the remission of sins," by the Latter-day Saints, on Saturday, a week ago today. You will remember, that I was zealous in persecuting them when I wrote the previous letter; I did this out of conscience, and out of zeal for the church of God, as I supposed, and I believed that I was serving God by so doing. The reasons that prompted me to do that stemmed from my having heard so much against them from the pulpits, the schools, and also from the monthly publications, especially the *Baptist*, for which I was a distributor. Now, I know that it is practically all false accusations, that which I read against them; and great is my sorrow for giving credence to them before searching for myself. Now, after God by his grace and his goodness has granted me time to repent, for calling me "from darkness to light, and from the hold of Satan to the kingdom of his beloved Son," namely to the church of the Saints, I say as you yourself said to me repeatedly, "Thanks to God for the opportunity." I say to you that God gave me a testimony through his Holy Spirit the first time I went to the church of the Saints, "that the house of God and the gate to heaven were there." Several things testify to me that the church of the Saints is the true church of Jesus Christ; apart from the fact that the signs which Jesus Christ promised follow these believers, the united efforts of nearly all the other denominations to persecute them with lies, prove that they are not of the world, were it not that the world has loved its own. Your work in so earnestly testifying to me that the Saints are in possession of the spiritual gifts caused me to search carefully the scriptures to determine whether these were promised, or, as nearly all our teachers say, whether "They were not to continue except to the end of the apostolic age, and that only to establish Christianity, and they are not needed now, &c." It was not until I learned to believe the scriptures themselves instead of the explanations of men about them, that I was able to understand them. I read Mark xvi; Acts ii, 38, 39; Romans x; 1 Cor. xii; Eph. iv; and many other places where the spiritual gifts are mentioned; and I was greatly amazed at my previous blindness, failing to see the absolute necessity of the spiritual gifts, and the apostolic plan to be the church of God, all of which is obvious to me now; and immediately "I did not wrestle with flesh and blood," but I informed my brethren the *Baptists* of my decision to leave them, and to join with those I believed were more similar to the truth. When they heard that, and although I left them with my head held high, yet I never had so much persecution from anyone during the eight years I was with the Baptists, as I have already suffered from them during this past week. May the gracious God forgive them. Those who professed to be my dearest friends before are my chief enemies now, and that only because I obeyed the commandments of Jesus Christ according to the scriptures; and in this are the words of Christ verfied, namely, "Ye shall be hated of all men for my name's sake." I realize now that I deprived myself greatly by delaying for so long my joining of this religion, and compassion now fills my heart, when I consider how many hundreds who are probably with my old brethren yet, hiding in the lying sanctuaries that were published against the Saints; and my fondest wish for each one of them is in the words of Jesus Christ to Nathaniel, "*Come and see;*" and I assure them that no one who is honest in his principles who is searching for the truth, and who comes to the church of the "Latter-day Saints" will be disappointed; for God is with them in truth. That our entire nation will embrace this excellent religion soon, is my prayer.

"David and myself greet you and your family together with all the Saints there. I am, your dear Brother,

JOHN BOWEN."

BAPTISM.

THERE have been so many arguments among the wise of the various factions, and so much has been written by the one side and the other of them, that we do not consider it beneficial to take much notice of this subject here; not that we do not have more to say to them than we have read from them; not that we do not consider the method of great importance to understand and practice either; but because we have a much better, surer, and shorter way to put an end to this debate, and although it is a very old way, yet until lately it is entirely new to this age. This is to prove the one as fair as the other, and the one that is accepted by God, and that alone will bring the man who is honest in his principles in possession of the spiritual gifts that Christ promised, Mark xvi, 17, 18, as Christ promised,—"If anyone will *do* the will of my father, he shall *know* of the doctrine, whether it be of God, or whether I speak of myself," and then, if the promises are not received that Christ gave to the truly baptized through the one baptism after a fair trial, we counsel all men to try some other baptism, and so on until he discovers the right approach which will bring him within reach of the greatest light and blessings. Some oppose this, because the scriptures say that there is "one baptism." We answer that we understand that there is one *true* water baptism for forgiveness; and recognizing that each one claims that their baptism is that *one,* we exhort everyone to be baptized, never mind how often, until they have the right one for sure. For it does not matter how often or how infrequently a man is baptized in the other ways, he cannot be considered baptized in the sight of heaven, unless it be that only one commanded by the author of the plan. For a man to obey something that some man calls a baptism, and stay with it to the point of refusing a better one is unwise, for when the true baptism is obtained, it will prove itself, independent of human witness; or rather its author will prove it true, by imparting the blessings; and to be destitute of all such blessings, after being baptized, is to admit either that we were baptized with a false baptism, or that the promise of Christ is void. Also we do not believe that God intended for the Bible to be the only way through which men may come to a knowledge of the truth. Understand us rightly! God did not intend for the world to be, nor did the apostles imagine that the 19th century would be without any church rule better than their writings. With all due respect to them, and belief in them, I shall say this in their own words. They said that the church (not the Bible) is the pillar and ground of the truth. 1 Tim. iii, 15.

The chief leaders of the church were the officers, who were and shall be inspired while it remains the church of God, and so they will be taught how to administer in baptism, and in every other ordinance, not by some ancient writings belonging to their fathers, despite how many beneficial examples, and profitable counsels there were in them; that was not their standard, but the Spirit of God which brought everything to their remembrance, and which was precept upon precept, line upon line, here a little, and there a little, according to their needs, a day's portion in its day. This is why the manner of administering other ordinances besides baptism is so obscure in the scriptures.

Again about baptizing more than once, that does not make more than one baptism if a hundred baptisms were performed, any more than going through the same door of a house a hundred times makes a hundred doors. And if a man trying to go to his friend's house had gone through some door to another house, would that be sufficient that he had gone through some door? If not, a man's obedience to what some call baptism, would not be sufficient to go into the kingdom of God; for in someone else's kingdom he would be without doubt, or, as Christ said, he would have come some other way besides the proper baptism, or the lawful door, and he would receive the welcome of a thief or a robber. The man who follows this counsel and who tries every kind of baptism until he gets the correct one, is much more rational for his own good, than the *bigots* who refuse the correct one, as a result of their own insincerity.—*From the Scriptural Treasury.*

THE PERSECUTION OF DOWLAIS, AND THE GOOD IT HAS DONE.

THE threatening and self-stirring storm that has been in this town and its environs lately, has already gone past, and the bright light of the gospel of peace is shining more fervently than ever. Many of those who believed the curses of "Simei" have wearied at his untruthful and blasphemous tales, and are saying as some said at that time, What does this dog do in barking, my lord? And now, when second thoughts are enthroned, they will say, let them spew out their filth until their folly is obvious to all.

It was thought from the wind of the great bellows of Dowlais in the *Star of Gomer*, the *Times*, &c., that the sparks that he blew to start would have increased to a fierce flame by now, and that it would utterly consume "Mormonism," so that soon only its ashes would be left. And we did not see anything more like this than the drunkard who came to his house, in the middle of the night, and searching for the fire he saw the light of the moon shining through the keyhole; he grabbed the bellows, and there he stayed blowing without seeing his mistake until he became sober! Thus do these blow their great bellows and their small bellows in all the keyholes, chapels, and houses, that they can get around Dowlais, and just as completely useless as the blowing of the drunkard; for, it is not Mormonism that is before their bellows any more than the fire was before the bellows of the drunkard. The lying and cruel *ring-leader* of this persecution wishes for the readers of the *Star* to believe that *Mormonism* has received a "*homestroke* forever in these areas," yes, he asserts that this is the "unanimous decision of all of the listeners." How did he know this, one wonders, if there are there as many thousands as he suggests? But we know, and hundreds if not thousands know this way better than that; and we say also that we have never heard such heavy criticism placed on anything as placed on those lectures against Mormonism by the listeners, and hosts have wearied of such contradictory rubbish they heard there, and are searching into the principles of the godly religion that was so hideously and falsely accused. Time will prove that all things, including this, work together for the good of this eternal gospel. One sees an example of the shameless impudence of the lying persecutor in publishing in the *Star* that "two of the chief elders of the Mormons left them the following week, and others with them," he says. Oh, how pleased he would be if this were true. But we say in truth, that it is a complete lie, and affirm that not one of the elders of the Saints left them after that; no, not one kind of officer left them, neither are there any signs of that! And as for one of the two members to which he refers as holding meetings, &c., he was never in but one or two of the biggest church meetings of the Saints; and he had evil and dishonest intentions in coming at that time, namely to seek an occasion to falsely accuse before the world. He had been excommunicated several months before the lecturing that took place in Caersalem. And the slanderous inclincation of the aforementioned man is seen in that which follows:—A secret council was held in Dowlais by the chief leaders of the persecutors to devise plans to persecute the innocent Saints; among others there were some who had been excommunicated from the Saints, because of unchristian conduct, as members of the council, and the aforementioned man in particular, when the following conversation took place.—As each one told his hideous and lying story in his turn; to select the best ones to tell in their public meetings, this *Iscariot* said that he had seen a dog in a meeting of the Saints, dressed in white, and beautifully decorated, and that the Saints said that he was an angel, &c. But this was too hideous for another who was near him, and who had been with the Saints for a long time, to tolerate; and he accused him to his face that that was a completely unfounded lie. "Hush, hush," said the first, "what does it matter, we must tell lies about them, otherwise we shall not succeed, and we will not have anything to say, is that not right Mr. President?" "Oh most certainly," said the president, "it makes no difference whatever, for it brings scorn on the Saints!" Yes, these are the witnesses that are believed by those who are of the same taste, although contrary to the testimony of scores of truthful people, who are with the Saints. Why believe false accusers now more than the backsliders from the other denominations are believed?

Backsliding is disgraceful—but in Saints,
It seems, not so awful:
Each blow, they hope, is harmful,
Our foes are heeded in full.

As for the other backslider he refers to as being an "elder," and speaking with tongues, &c., along the roads. It is true that one very young and weak member was beguiled by the evil persecutors to cast his "pearls before swine," and to recite such sacred things, and to speak with "strange tongues" before the dogs, and the result was as Jesus Christ rightly said, "they turned and devoured them." What stronger witness than this is possible to have that the Saints enjoy the spiritual gifts that were enjoyed in the early church of Christ, and which the New Testament promises to the church, while it remains the church of Christ? Behold a confession of our professed enemies of that, and examples of them made public!! Well, we hope that that is sufficient to hold them without excuse if they continue to refuse them then. Besides that, the man referred to has come to see his sins, and has sincerely repented for being persuaded to make such misuse of sacred things. And from reliable witnesses we report that he is earnestly seeking to keep from being excommunicated from the church. And so, the victory of the noble Mr. Davies, and others, is false every word, yes, so that there is not even one member, much less "two elders and others," who have left the Saints yet. But, the truth is, instead of the Saints being a "*blasphemy and a curse*," as Davies says, and instead of some leaving them in Dowlais, not so much as one has left them since this last persecution began! And furthermore, let the world understand that there has been *more success and growth among the Saints, even in Dowlais, since that than ever before!* Instead of our meetings dwindling to nothing afterwards, as is said, the hundreds who come to listen will testify that our Hall there is more full of respectful listeners than it has ever been, and so far from receiving the *homestroke* and dying, that some, more or less, have been baptized by us in Dowlais every week since the aforementioned uproar; and whoever doubts it, can see on the books of our church that not so much as one week has passed since then until now in which some new people have not been accepted as church members by the Saints there; and time will prove that everything, yes, the worst that our enemies can do and say, is for the benefit and spread of our religion, for the multiplying of its subjects, and for the strengthening of the Saints in more unity and love. We thank him whose divine work this is, and not our persecutors, and we plead for strength from him to continue in it, patient and industrious until the day of the coming of our Lord.

Fondest brothers, fondest sisters,
This is Jesus's creed revealed,
Ushered in to raise the lowly,
Who can but in joy be sealed?
Here's the spirit that was promised,
Here's its blessing, such delight:
All its gifts by name acknowledged
Poured upon us in their might!

DESCRIPTION OF CALIFORNIA.

THE following was quoted from a letter from the above country, which was published in the "*New York Herald:*"—

"With respect to California (said one writer), despite all it has been praised, not half of its advantages, its climate, and its fruitfulness have been described—it is a country that providence prepared in Eden for the children of freedom. Yet, there is need for many things to organize this paradise as a happy dwelling place for man; it is true that there is already a name of government, but only a name. The head Hispanics in the country do not understand what a free vote is, and election to office through the voice of the majority is unknown here. General Kearny is busy organizing the previous disorder with respect to the government; and his fatherly kindness to this point causes the inhabitants to look to him for protection and justice. Under his administration unity and brotherly love have been created between the immigrants and the old inhabitants to some extent. They associate with one another in feasts, with the flags of America waving victoriously overhead; and if the armies of the United States were recalled now, the inhabitants would defend themselves as a republic independent from Mexico.

"With respect to the quality of the land of California, the soil is usually black and fertile to a depth of about four inches, and it produces abundantly every species of corn and vegetables that grow from the earth in any place. There is not one country that rivals this one for growing *tobacco*, *hemp*, *flax*; and as for the fruit of the vine, it is far superior to every country that I have ever seen. I saw here several vineyards of the Hispanics, but they are too lazy to tend them. I say that not many years will pass before the whole world will fetch their wines from California.

"As for its suitability for raising animals, it is difficult to have better; nutritious grass, and wild oats, grow abundantly in every part of it; even now the hills and meadows are covered with green grass two feet high, where at one glance one can see thousands of head of cattle voraciously grazing, and continuing to do so all the year round, for this land continues to be green every season, and has been thus since the beginning of time. You in the states boast of your breeds of cattle, such as the Durham, the Devonshire, &c., but come here, and you will see two or three thousand oxen fattening along these meadows, and then you will admit that this country is better to raise animals than any country under the sun. And although no one takes care of them here, yet they grow here into the biggest and the fattest in the world. Every lake and river is alive with every species of fish, especially the *Salmon*. There are in these mountains and woods countless hosts of *Elk*, *Deer*, and every species of reptile; and the geese and several kinds of duck fly in clouds through the air. Diseases are unknown here, and a lifetime lasts until it becomes a burden. The mountains are rich with valuable ore; and iron ore and copper can be seen along the face and sides of the mountains; in a word, an abundance of everything grows here except for loaves of bread; and these idle Hispanics are too lazy to work for them. The price of flour here now is 20 dollars (over four pounds) per barrel, and is very scarce nonetheless. *Beef*, *beef*, is their motto; and they practically live on meat only; they work together, they dwell together, and they lie down together with their animals, and the chief wonder is that hooves, horns, and hair are not growing on every Indian and Hispanic that are in this country!

"Send farmers here instead of soldiers; and tell them that a beautiful and abundant Eden is to be had, if they come to this place where it is located. If the inhabitants of some parts of the states were to come here, doubtless the change would cause the old to dance, the sick to get well, and the thin to get fat on the fat of this land. As for the doctors and lawyers of your country, it is better for them to stay there, for there is no need here for the one more than the other. But farmers, merchants, printers, cobblers, tailors, and all honest and industrious craftsmen can become rich here quickly. There is a great need here for all kinds of workers, and they should bring the tools with them, for there are no craftsmen here to make such things. Lately 300 wagons from the state of Missouri landed here (in the Sacramento valley), but it is easier and more comfortable to come by sea, not to mention that this way you can bring with you the things you choose.

"In this valley, namely Sacramento, is the most numerous settlement of Americans of any region of California, and this large and luxuriant valley is quickly being filled with people. Silence spread over it during the passing centuries, except for the gentle songs of the varied feathered families, which sounded through its woods intermingled with the sounds of wild beasts, together with the sound of oars and songs of the red inhabitants of the forest when they rowed their *canoes* laden with *furs* down its crystalline rivers. Recently the first *pioneer* landed here, with his axe and his rifle on his shoulder, until the banners of our country waved in the air; and already the desert is blossoming like the rose. The sounds of the happy ploughman are whistling after his plough—the songs of the milkmaid amidst the lowing of her cattle, and the merchandising signs of the hammer, the saw, and the axe, echoing on the walls of homes from the quiet waters of the straits of San Francisco to the chalky rocks of the lumpy white mountains; and before long these splendid and dear valleys of this land will be a happy homeland to thousands more of free sons and daughters, who, in ease and fulness will take paradisiacal shelter under the branches of the *Freedom Tree*. Although there is as much merchandising in Monterey at present as there is in San Francisco, yet because so many navigable rivers pour into that strait, the latter will probably be the chief market port of this country. But the days will surely come when the railways will be driven through the mountains, the lowlands will be raised, and the need for fiery engines will be seen, which will run with the speed of the wind from Vancouver to Panama, and when the inhabitants of the wilderness will thank the God of freedom that they are also free."

To whoever considers the above description as too colorful, or too good to be literally true, we say that it is a literal translation of the words of an eyewitness. That is all, and if it were only half true, who would not wish the enjoyment of part of it! We are glad to hear that such a paradise is before us, and already under the feet of some of our exiled brethren, and although it is not one of them who is this witness, we hope we can say, after hearing his story from them, like the queen of Sheba, for another thing, namely that "the half has not been told us" of its goodness.

PROCLAMATION TO THE SAINTS.

Dear Brethren and Sisters,—We feel a desire and responsibility to present to you, through the medium of the PROPHET, especially to those who are scattered throughout the country, and under many other disadvantages, interesting counsels and directions, and we hope they will be received, and we pray they will be as beneficial to you as is our wish.

It is an unspeakable privilege to have membership, and even an office, in the church of God. It is a privilege that bestows the right to all the other good and godly privileges that God has promised, and which are not to be had in any other place. But it is expected that we be in the church circle not only in name, but that our behavior will be heartfelt and in accordance with the responsibilities of that circle, and in a spirit of grace and prayer will we enjoy the promises. It is true that many obstacles are on the path, and the temptations are strong and numerous; neither is that any wonder when we consider we have the "old man" to crucify, together with his lusts and his desires, and that the enemy is losing his hold on us. Yes, he has many ways to try to pull us back, one to some old sweet sin, and the other to popularity or worldy wealth; but the most cunning and most destructive for the true Christian is the influence of the hypocritical spirits, those who assume the form of the angel of light. Beware of those that come to you in sheep's clothing, with the appearance of humility, uttering words of puffed up vanity, with great compassion, and fairly crying, "because you were beguiled to such heresy," as they call that which they know nothing about. Not infrequently they will offer to pray for you, and they will tell tales and deathbed testimonies, in order to tug at your feelings, and make you feel nostalgic, not for the truth as much as for the sweet old fellowship, and the old Pharisaic tune. Beware of them, we say again; the fact that their tales bring discomfort and melancholy to your heart, proves that they do not have the Spirit of God, for that brings joy in the Holy Ghost, and nurtures love for all truth, and not for the old traditions of man. "Believe not every spirit, but try the spirits whether they are of God."

Another very popular method the enemy has to prevent you from going forward in the godly work, is to send his servants from one corner of the country to another like shooting stars, their bag full of an assortment of blasphemous stories; and sometimes one person will swear that some fellow or other performed them in one place and that he was there, and another person will swear that it was someone else who caused them to happen, but in a completely different place, and the whole thing is verified! And often these things are heard from the pulpits! To the Saints who are scattered, again we say, "Believe not every spirit," and especially believe that the false prophets are those who shout that the Saints are failing here, and dwindling to nothing there. That is their desire, but it will not come to pass eternally.

Another trick the enemy has after failing in every other way, is to try to cause a rift between the flock and their pastors. They know very well that the strength of the Saints originates from God through his Holy Spirit. They know that "Do all things properly and in an orderly fashion," is his motto, and consequently that the growth of the Saints depends on hearing the voice of their teachers, and keeping a unity of the Spirit in the bonds of peace, as every member's physical growth depends on the nourishment he receives through his mouth; and if the enemy, through reporting lying tales about them, through diminishing or betraying the trust of the members in their pastor, he can expect great plunder. We understand that the enemy now has a host of agents throughout Wales on this errand. They say that they are well acquainted with "Capt. Jones," and others, and that they have debated such and such with him, and surely have defeated him, and rendered him mute. They will say many things that were told to them, so they say, and from tales with not one word of truth in them. And as incredible as this may seem, it is abundantly true that we have walked together with some who professed to go along the country preaching the gospel, and who professed a perfect knowledge of us, and we found out from their heart such a mixture of lies that it is not decent to repeat them! And at the same time, when we made our identity known, they shouted in our faces the name by which we are known. Some of such a family are those who gossip so much about us in Llwyni, Pontyberem, Llanelli, to Monmouthshire, and in places throughout the North also. Do not believe them; there is not a word of truth in their rubbish or their false arguments. We are not aware of ever having exchanged two words with such persons, and we do not think that our eyelids have ever opened on one of them, nor did we know of their existence, until their boastful tales, and their names came back to us. Whose character is safe under the breath of such slanderers as these? And who of their beguiled ones would not consider themselves to be serving God by killing us, as their brethren did to our own godly brethren in America recently? Oh men, if you know nothing about the worth of a good name, consider your responsibility in the days to come!

To the Saints we say, Though we do not claim perfection, yet the Spirit will jointly testify the truth together with your spirit, through its gifts and its many sweet blessings, and it is the Spirit that feeds you with the genuine milk of the word. Your growth in every good deed, and spiritual comforts, together with the hopes you hold, that "evil men of evil treasures of the heart, bring out evil things" against their betters. To our sorrow we admit that even the best at times slip, yes, even those who ought to be examples to their flock, yet we say, those evil men referred to, and the like, are not the agents in the hand of God to set straight such as these, nor is that the way for you to understand that, rather your privilege is to gain knowledge from God through his Spirit according to his plan, and then to hold fast to that plan, and not to persons any longer or because they belong to that plan. It is necessary for you to have a test of your faith in this regard, as in all other things, before you are perfected in faith. But when in the midst of temptation, "in your patience possess ye your souls." You have a Father to watch over you at that time. You know the way to him, and there are courts in his house where all will have justice. Oh to have patience until that time then. Be prudent and gentle, praying always, especially in secret, with every prayer and request, for God your Father to keep you from the clutches of heretical spirits, to comfort you and perfect you in every good deed, remembering the proverb that says, "Avenge not yourselves (but rather suffer wrong); vengeance is mine, I will repay, saith the Lord."

NEWS FROM THE SAINTS WHO ARE IN THE WILDERNESS.

CAPT. Drake and Mr. Campbell report through the *St. Louis Republican* for August 24, that on their journey from California toward St. Louis they met with hosts of emigrants going toward the west. They met with the first company of the Saints beyond the Rocky Mountains hastening to go to the *Great Salt Lake* to search for the best place to winter. After that they met with the second company, containing from five to six hundred wagons. They were moving along very successfully, and peacefully together. A few days before our reporters met them, the Saints had hunted and feasted together very amicably with the nation of the *Pawnee Indians*. The travelers came past the place where the aforementioned feast had been held; but they considered themselves quite fortunate that they had not met up with the Indians despite that. This proves much in favor of the Saints, not only that "the envy of Ephraim is departing" quickly, according to the prophecies, but the behavior of these barbarians proves that they like justice, and repay goodness to the Saints for their fairness to them. Further, our reporters say, "that the Mormons have plenty of pigs, chickens, geese, and fat cattle with them, together with an abundance of provisions to last for a year-and-a-half!" This is so contradictory to the stories that were published recently and flew on the wings of the breezes, and that were considered sweet in the mouths of some we knew, namely "that the Mormons are eating each other in the wilderness, and an end to them will be had before long, &c." But we thank our gracious God, that is the sustainer and leader of the Saints, and not of the Christians (in name) who have banished them, neither their brethren of the same taste as they who rejoice in their cruelties, and imitate them even in Wales, to whatever extent they can. This is like practically all the other accusations against the Saints, and more truth is to be had in them if they are taken completely opposite from what they state.

With the Latter-day Saints
    Is the most divine religion now,
And this will be proclaimed
    Until it fills the whole earth.
But when they depart
    Such war and pestilence will be seen!
If the gentiles knew of their prosperity,
    They would not talk of moving the Saints!

MONMOUTH CONFERENCE.

THIS Conference was held Sunday, October 3rd, in the Hector Hall, Nantyglo. The hall was overflowing with listeners by ten o'clock. Capt. D. Jones was selected as president, who, after beginning by singing and praying, addressed the crowd warmly about the necessity of having a religion that would bring them a knowledge of God, and the enjoyment of his promises; and he showed the difference between that and the bigotry of the doctrines of men, or a religion of whim and feelings only. He rejoiced greatly upon seeing such a numerous and noble congregation of his fellow nation, the majority of whom if not all, were in possession of such an excellent religion, which is self-proving, and which gives the power of God to its possessor. He said that the purpose of this Conference was not to change or improve the religion, but to strive to come to a more correct knowledge of it, and to organize the best means of spreading it among our fellowmen, and also to perfect unity and love among the Saints. After that the different presidents represented the eight branches of the conference, and they described their circumstances almost without exception as being in unity, and increasing in the enjoyment of the gifts and joy of the Holy Ghost. They showed that there were better signs of growth, and hopes of multiplying, and that the Saints were more fervent and energetic through it all than they had ever before been. The number of elders present is 12, priests 25, teachers 18, deacons 8. Baptized since the previous Conference 24. The number of all members is 209. A great number has moved to other parts of Wales, and are sowing the good seed with increase.

At two o'clock, the meeting for the Saints only was begun, although there were there several of our friends from the world by permission. After partaking of the ordinance of the supper of the Lord, the president showed its excellence and its usefulness, &c., in English, and he gave many sweet and beneficial counsels in Welsh also, until it was thought that every bosom was rejoicing, and every heart cherishing more and more the splendid religion, which brings them such enjoyment and hopes. Afterwards one was received into the church, and four children were blessed. Elder W. Phillips from Merthyr was chosen unanimously to be the president of this conference, because the previous president, elder J. Morris, was laboring successfully in Pembrokeshire, and this was agreed upon unanimously. It was agreed also that every branch would choose its distributor of the PROPHET, and to pay for it monthly for however many members there were—that all the distributors would pay the conference president, and that the profit from them was to be for his support; and it is earnestly requested that all well-wishers of this divine work will do all they can to spread the PROPHET, and pay for it.

It was agreed also to do all we can to aid and supply the needs of the American Saints who are in the wilderness, and to send the money collected from now to the end of the year with the missionaries who will be returning to America at that time. This sweet and beneficial meeting ended at five o'clock with prayer and singing.

At half past six, the evening meeting began. Elder Eliezer Edwards, D. Jones, Penycae, and Thomas Giles, Merthyr, preached in a lively and clear manner on various principles, and they were followed by the president, who showed that the earth is the happiest heaven and the eternal destiny of all the godly of the human race—that here will be the "resting place which is kept for the people of God." He proved that this was the expectation of the patriarchs and the prophets, together with all the Saints, and that the chorus of the gentlest anthems of the angels was, "and we shall reign on the EARTH," Rev. 5, 10. He also showed the necessity there was for a godly emissary to establish the heavenly kingdom on the earth, and to bring men to be subjects of it in preparation for the great restoration, and the coming of the king to his kingdom. He proved that this work, or the establishment of this kingdom, had a small beginning like the "stone that was cut out of the mountain," and it will increase gradually until it fills the earth with the knowledge of God, as the waters cover the sea; and the whole earth at that time will have become heaven for the resurrected and transfigured Saints. After that the president testified that this heaven had already begun on the earth—where, and how, and he earnestly invited everyone to hasten to obey its laws, so they could have enjoyment from it. It is not here possible to do justice to the talks that were delivered in this meeting, but it was easy to understand from the respectful and attentive hearing, together with the happy faces of the whole crowd, that their hearts rejoiced in the hope of enjoying these glorious promises. Success, I say, to it until it fills our country, and crowns our fellow nation, and the world, with his joy. Amen. DAVID JONES, Scribe.

The kingdom has come, in its time,
Without an end to it, ever more;
It was cut as a stone, from the mountain,
And will roll forth, over the nations.

ANNOUNCEMENTS.

TO OUR DISTRIBUTORS.

SINCE there is just one more issue of the *Prophet* to come out this year, all distributors are earnestly requested to prepare to settle their accounts for the year for the other books as well as for the *Prophet* by the Conference.

N.B. We would be glad to buy back our own books, namely the following, and pay full price for them, if they are clean, that is the *Old Religion Anew*, the *Reply*, the *Scales*, the *Proclamation*, and no. 1, 7, 8 of the *Prophet*. Whoever has them, let him send them here, and he shall have the money, or other books, in their place. Not every author will do this, nor does this wonderfully increasing demand for our books testify that our religion is in decline in the least!

*** We have books of Welsh hymns bound for sixpence each.

NEXT GLAMORGAN CONFERENCE.

IT is intended to hold the above Conference in the Cymreigyddion Hall in Merthyr, Sunday and Monday, December the 26th and 27th, that is the first days after Christmas.

*** Visitors from America are expected at the Conference, and all the Saints are earnestly requested to strive to fulfill the promise we made to assist the Saints who are in the wilderness, by that time.

We expect that the various presidents throughout Wales will take care of this.

CONTENTS.

MERTHYR TYDFIL:
PUBLISHED AND FOR SALE BY D. JONES, AND ALSO FOR SALE BY THE SAINTS IN GENERAL.

JOHN JONES, PRINTER, RHYDYBONT.

PROPHET OF THE JUBILEE,

OR

STAR OF THE SAINTS.

No. 18.] DECEMBER, 1847. [Price 2*c*.

"SPEAKING WITH TONGUES" OF THE NEW TESTAMENT, AND MORMONISM !

Mr. Ed.,—Some questions were directed at me in the September *Star*, by one Independent Reverend from the North, and I wrote an answer for them, being sure in my mind that I would receive the same fair play that the inquirer received; but to my disappointment, I was told that it was too poor, that there was none of the "*cleverness*" in this article that I had shown on other occasions, and that the aforementioned Reverend would take no notice of it. The only thing I shall say is, that I did my best. Now, I set my cause before you, and begging the fair play that was denied me in the place where it should have been received.

Yours humbly,

J. D.

[*Copy of the Article sent to the Editor of the* Star of Gomer, *under the above name*.]

Mr. Gomer,—About last February when I sent you an article on "Speaking with Tongues," which appeared in the Star for June, little did I think that anyone would be so perceptive as to see that it was defending Mormonism; for it was nothing more than an investigation into the New Testament to know what is to be understood by "speaking with tongues." But within two months, here is H. Tegai (see page 258) writing as follows:—

"I saw in the June Star, an article of one J. D., on '*Speaking with Tongues*.' If J. D. wishes to come forth to defend Mormonism, let him come to the root of the argument at once, by answering, 1. Did Christ and his apostles work public miracles? If they did, 2. Do the Mormons do so in the same way? Let J. D. answer as he may, and then I shall have a word to say to him."

Now, I would wish the reader to take the trouble to reread the article on "Speaking with Tongues," in case he may have forgotten it. It is trying to prove there not that which H. Tegai and his friend from Porthyrhyd think is the "speaking" in question; but that it was a gift from God to the church, to edify it, and that it was to be imparted as the spirit willed. H. Tegai does not indicate that I have erred in that; but he says, "If J. D. wishes to come forth to defend *Mormonism (!)*, let him come to the root of the argument at once." What is that? Was "speaking with tongues" Mormonism in the days of old? That was the subject I dealt with, remember. If Mormonism was the "speaking with tongues" then, and if it can be shown that the "speaking" continues to this day, no wonder that such a sect as the Mormons exists. Now, it would not be a foolish trick to try to set Paul to prove that the "speaking" was to continue until these days, and perhaps further. He says—"Charity *never* faileth: but whether there be prophecies, they shall fail; whether there be tongues, they shall cease; whether there be knowledge, it shall vanish away. For we know *in part*, and we prophesy *in part*. But when that which is *perfect* is come, then that which is *in part* shall be done away." (1 Cor. 13, 8—10). Are the speaking and the prophesying things in part? Yes, say all. Well, is that which is in part to be done away before that which is perfect comes? No. When is that which is *perfect* to come, then? Yes, that is the question. And not when *we* shall "see face to face;" for it is not likely that they (namely the early Christians) will be made perfect without us. It is seen, by now, is it not, that the speaking and the prophesying are to continue until the last ones on earth are perfected, but not longer, for then that which is "in part" will be swallowed by "that which is perfect." Now, Mr. Tegai, is that Mormonism, again? If so, the Mormons will be glad to hear it.

Next, since I have come forward to defend the "speaking with tongues" of the New Testament, that which H. Tegai calls Mormonism, he calls me "to the *root* of the argument at once." What constitutes coming to the root of the argument? Oh, "by answering, 1. Did Christ and his apostles work public miracles? If they did, 2. Do Mormons do so in the same way?" I wonder whether we would not come to the root of the argument just as well, by answering, 1. Did the apostles speak with tongues? If they did, 2. Do the Mormons do the same? What if we, through searching into those two subjects, were to find ourselves convinced that the speaking with tongues of the Mormons is true and their miracles are deceitful? The Mormons profess the one and the other; consequently, to say that the "root of the argument" that pertains to both (and to others that can be noted) is in one of them, is quite inconsistent. What of that? Paul, a man approved by everyone, sets down a rule far more excellent than "coming to the *root of the argument*"—i.e., to judge whether it is a false religion and deceit that the Saints have, or not. He says—"But though we, or an angel from heaven, preach any other gospel unto you than that which we have preached unto you, let him be accursed," (Gal. 1, 8.) By finding out that the Mormons do not preach or profess that which Paul and his brethren did, is the best procedure to prove them deceivers. If they deny anything, or profess anything differently, about that which Paul had, they are sure to be preaching something else, and worthy to receive the anathema. But at present I shall not go to look into whether the Saints are following Paul, for H. Tegai does not consider that to be the "root of the argument;" and consequently, I shall now answer his two questions the best I can.

"1. *Did Christ and his apostles work public miracles?*" It may be asked also, and many do that, did they work miracles at all? We have a history, namely the New Testament, that contains mention of some strange things being fulfilled many years ago; but it has all been written by biased men, and one must believe it all, or not, without having one proof of its truthfulness. If the fact that the "Mormons," who are alive in our own times, claim miracles in their midst is not a proof that they occur, then it stands to reason that the fact that Jesus's disciples, in the earlier ages, claimed also that miracles occurred in their midst, is no proof to us in this age that they did. Indeed, except that men receive supernatural knowledge, it seems to me quite natural to doubt that Christ and his apostles worked miracles; and that because Christ said that signs would follow the *believers*, which is as good as saying they would do so in our age. He has said also, that whatsoever thing we asked in his name, we should receive. Well, it has been so many times, among the Independents, at least, for those are the ones with whom I was most familiar, as they sought in his name to heal some sick person; and after asking, no answer came. Many times also they have imitated Elijah of old, asking in the name of Christ for God to forestall the rain at harvest time, and at other times for him to give rain; but no notice was taken of them by the One who promised to give if they would ask. But, said one Independent, *We have received our answer many times*. Well, well! Where is H. Tegai now? There are "public miracles" in our age and our country at last, yes, by the Independents, not the Mormons! The old "false-prophets," are they not? But wait! I am straying from the subject; the questioner wants to know whether Christ and his apostles worked miracles *in public?* A glimpse can be had at the public nature of Christ's miracles then from what his brethren said to him. "Depart hence," they said, "and go into Judaea, that thy disciples also may see the works that thou doest, for there is no man that doeth any thing in *secret*, and he himself seeketh to be known openly; if thou do these things, shew thyself to the world." We can also conclude that the miracles of Christ were not very public, otherwise, learned men such as the scribes and the Pharisees would not have been ignorant of them; for, perhaps, if responsible men such as those had had the least proof of his miracles, they would have believed. We note that which they said to him while he was on the cross—"Let Christ, the King of the Jews, descend from the cross, that we may *see*, and believe." If he normally worked miracles in public, why did he not do so at that time, when men of such influence, were present,—yes, men who had they believed would have turned the world after them. There are also men in our days who are so honest, that they would believe the Mormons at once, if they could miraculously feed the five thousand, &c. It is not likely that the Mormons can do such a thing, or they would not be so stupid as to refrain from convincing men like that; and it was not likely that the apostles were able to work miracles in public, or they would not have been so unwise as to refrain from showing their power to men at that time. But despite that, it is said in the New Testament, that miracles had been performed by Christ in public (and in secret); but it is given to understand that he performed them among "his own," and only among the believers of such also. Likewise it is said of a few of the apostles also. It is quite obvious that many of the miracles that are mentioned were performed in public, without any intention that they would be thus; and very often their performers tried to hide them. Now, after all the foregoing reasoning, I cannot come to a sure decision as to whether Christ and his apostles performed public miracles, but I shall just say that the New Testament mentions their performing such things. After giving an answer like that, the other question comes to my attention, namely,—

"2. *Do Mormons do the same?*" In this, I suppose, is the "root of the argument." Although, by answering the first question, I have become quite unbelieving about the miracles of old; if I find out that there are similar things among the Mormons now, it is logical for me to believe the truthfulness of the Bible about the works of Christ and his apostles. Neither do I consider that the miracles of the Mormons have to be as big, or as public, as the miracles of Christ and his apostles, before they can be miracles, and true miracles; for there are none among the Mormons who profess so much faith as Christ had, and there are none in Wales who hold offices as high as the apostles held. If it can be proved that some sick person has received health miraculously, by the laying on of hands, the principle of miraculous power will be proved; and consequently, according to how the Mormons are able to operate by the rule, "All things whatsoever ye shall ask in prayer, *believing*, ye shall receive," by that shall they be empowered, not to work miracles as great as those of Christ and his apostles, but much greater, such as even being able to move mountains! Now, among many such circumstances, we can note one that happened in Merthyr Tydfil, to a man by the name of William Hughes, who was working in a coal mine. One day, he happened to break his leg in two places: and he was carried home by his fellow workers, when the doctor set the bones in their place, and bound them up. That night the man called for one of the elders of the church to come to him, and he administered in his office, at which time the injured man received a complete relief from the pain. The third day after that, he called for another elder, and he administered again; and the result was that the injured man jumped down from his bed in the presence of several *impartial* witnesses, and walked around in their presence! Mr. Tegai can have the complete story in the publication of the Mormons, called *Prophet of the Jubilee*, for July, 1846, together with the witnesses. They are now alive; and the man who was healed is in Llanelli, Carmarthenshire, and he is willing to come to face everyone to prove the truthfulness of the matter. This was all public, but not everyone believes, especially the learned; and thus it was in the days of old. Several healings are happening among hundreds of observers, but the Mormons cannot help it if they are made up of Christ's "own," any more than the apostles could. The greatest testimony I could give to H. Tegai would be to assure him that I myself received healing miraculously more than once; and I testify that that has happened. But, now, I imagine that Mr. Tegai is ready to say, if he himself were to see such things take place, it would be no time before he would join with the Mormons. That would, however, be difficult to believe of him; for if he is one of the "elect," it would not be *possible*, even if he were to receive a clear sign from those he considers to be "false-prophets,"—it would not be *possible,* I say, to bring him to believe in a doctrine different from that which he now believes, namely Congregationalism, I mean. But in case he is not one of the "elect" that will not be deceived, those who have a testimony of Jesus, I am of the opinion that a testimony for himself would be the most acceptable to him, and the most convincing also. How to get that, I wonder? Like this:—"If any man will do his will, he shall *know* of the doctrine, whether it be of God," (John 7, 17). To *know* is the main point. Our friend could be a witness of a miracle, and not *know*, despite that, whether it was a miracle from God, or from the "false-prophets." Now, the Saints, like Christ, offer that knowledge to every one who does that which they teach; and H. Tegai has the opportunity to take them at their word, and test them. That is all I shall say at present about the second question. Next, and last, our friend says this:—

"*Let J. D. answer as he may, and then I shall have a word to say to him.*" This thing looks like a *trap* or a net; and if the words are taken "spiritually," they mean, in my opinion, that Mr. Tegai has determined beforehand what he will say; yes, even if I were to convince him of the complete opposite. But that makes no difference: for I hope, that when our friend lifts his net, that a miracle will take place (as in the time of Christ), and instead of capturing me, he will have captured the truth, and that as it is in Christ. Amen. J. D.

THE "TIMES" AND ITS LYING SLIME ON THE SAINTS AGAIN! AGAIN!!

THE "Reverend" Editor of this paper greatly imitates the miller of the American *corn crackers*, for the latter carries nothing in his hopper but "*corn*," which is nothing more than food for swine in comparison to wheat. So the former will drop nothing into the hopper of the *Times* with respect to the Saints but *swinish lies;* and sufficient facts have been had before this to prove that not one of those is too hard, slanderous, or harmful for him to publish; and immediately when the truth is offered him in defense, down closes his hopper every time; and as soon as some sufficiently hideous false accusation comes along, in it goes then! Who has ever heard of the Editor of the *Times* having permitted any of the Saints ever to defend themselves against his lies? Who has ever heard of his getting any story against them that he found too disgraceful to publish? What is this but an invitation to all the slanderous liars of our country to bring their full sacks forward and pour them into his hopper! Read the following. From the *Times*, Nov. 4:—

"NEWMARKET.—The Mormons pay frequent visits to this place. It shows that the disciples of Joe Smith have a great liking for the place, and more of a desire to get the inhabitants of Newmarket from the reach of the destruction of the world to safe California, than to get the inhabitants of any other neighborhood in these parts. A woman was jabbering some nonsense here on Monday night. The application of soap and water on her skin and clothes would not have been out of place, as she had great need of it. The following Tuesday night this woman's husband attacked a young girl, in an isolated spot about a mile-and-a-half from the village. Very fortunately for the girl, someone happened to come past in the meantime, and so she was spared. He was followed, and caught in a tavern. It is said that he had on him several sharp weapons and *plasters*. He tried to put plaster on the girl's mouth to keep her from screaming, and in the struggle he missed the mark, and he put it on her cheek. He is now in the Flint jail "suffering persecution." It will be seen whether the family of miracles succeed in getting an angel to open the doors of the jail, and to lead this 'saint' out."

Now, with respect to all this "jabbering," we say that there is not one syllable of truth in it in connection with the "Mormons" (as they are called); and we challenge the Editor and his *correspondent* to prove that any kind of connection or anything similar between the aforementioned woman or her husband exists with the "Latter-day Saints," or has ever existed. Can you deny this Mr. Editor? Perhaps you will again escape to your old vulpine hiding place as you have done before, and shout from there, that you cannot be held responsible for the lies of the correspondence that is sent to you. But this will not do, for read your refusal of the defense, hard-faced as before:—

"No space can be given in the *Times* for the long letter of Mr. J. P. in defense of the Mormons, or the "Latter-day Saints;" for there would never be an end to the debate on such a subject. Our correspondent can have his article, if he calls at our office."

"Before speaking ill of anyone, we should ask ourselves three questions: first, Is it true? Second, Is it kind? Third, Is it necessary?"

This J. P. was present when the aforementioned woman delivered that "jabbering." He and another preacher of the Saints declared publicly after she finished "that there was no connection between her and the Saints." But perhaps your storyteller was not there at that time you say. Whatever of that, we can prove that the accusation is a known lie, for it is true enough that the woman herself declared publicly more than once, and as understandably as anything she said, "that she had no connection with any denomination or party." Your storyteller must have been there, else how could he have known that there was great need for water and soap on her skin and her clothes? If his eyes were there to see her filthiness, why were his ears not there to hear her confession, which is completely opposite to his story? Does not this, together with every other sentence of his report, reveal that heartfelt enmity toward the religion he falsely accuses is the cause of it all? This was a sweet pause for revenge, especially since he knew that your hopper is open for such rubbish, and not open for any defense. Will you allow this, your slanderous and dangerous little servant to hide himself secretly from the public longer? Why did you not publish his name to the world, so we can see who is this *mad dog?*" Whoever gives someone freedom to say what he likes is an accomplice to his evil deeds, remember; and perhaps it would not be unprofitable to give you a dose of your own pills since you are the sickest one that we know. The *dose* is just a small one! only three of your own pills; yes, in the same issue, and only the thickness of the paper between them and the root of your illness. Here they are, Sir,—"Before speaking ill of anyone, we should ask ourselves three questions. 1. Is it true? 2. Is it kind? 3. Is it necessary?" Very good counsel! A pity that you did not remember to do one of them yourself, for if so you would not have published the above tale. Since it is not *true*, and if it were true, it is not *kind*, much less *necessary*. The saying "physician heal thyself" is equally appropriate to you.

Oh, how you laughed derisively, I am sure, when you saw in your columns "that a Saint was in jail suffering persecution." We thank the God of the Saints that his angels keep the Saints from going to jail except for their religion, and that is not too much for them to suffer, however much your blasphemous scorn is like that of the children of perdition earlier under similar circumstances. Did you not know, Sir, that our church rules do not permit a woman to preach? You ought to know that before attacking to battle against us, for it has been proclaimed more than once in your language, "that we do not acknowledge a female priesthood." But what we say is not worthy of your notice, for it is as much as you can do to search for accusations and lies against us, to be sure. Yes, you are an entirely one-sided man, and your fondest work is to "accuse the brethren." Well, you poor thing, go on as you please, but remember, if you were as free as the wild donkey, the "season" will come when you yourself will be tamed, and your shackle will be as short as that of any other donkey. Yes, the day will come before long that will blow away the shelters of falsehood—when all shall have the truth.

MORE CORN HUSKS IN HIS HOPPER AGAIN! AGAIN!! AGAIN!!!

While writing the foregoing defense the following issue of the *Times*, namely the November 18th issue, was thrown before us, and the first thing practically that attracted our attention, in place of the defense of the previous accusation, was the following:—

"William Smith, the Mormon prophet or patriarch, is now about to be tried for odious immorality."

Now, Mr. Slanderer, is it "kind" to publish this even if it is true? Is it "necessary" to devour the dear religion of our fellowmen by ransacking the world for the faults of people? Would it be kind for us or another to publish the atrocious lies and the wantonness of the *Congregational* preachers, and raise to the wind how many have been imprisoned, and executed, and exiled out of the boundaries of a Christian land; not to mention those who have not yet received their due! If this were to be done according to your own logic, the *Congregational* religion would stink in the nostrils of the public seven times worse than does Mormonism in yours.

With respect to the "William Smith" you mention, did you yourself not tell us through the *Times* that he had left the Mormons about two years ago? Yes, yes! and that he was about to reveal to the world some monstrous *hobgoblins* about it, &c. You did not mention a word about his joining with them afterwards, until you get something bad—worse, worst:—shameful, most shameful, yes, "repugnant" to say about him; and then, surprise! behold him a "Mormon prophet or patriarch" immediately! Oh what evidence we get from him against Mormonism!

Grime in his bag and no gold—only husks
That are withered and old.

We do not consider that we tell you anything new by saying that the above W. S. is not a Mormon through any kind or connection, much less a "prophet or patriarch;" and consequently that his virtues or his failings are not the fruits of Mormonism, any more than that of Congregationalism or any other *ism*.

We know of no better *pills* to cleanse your slanderous illness from your stomach, and from your bones (if they are medicinal also) than your own *pills* again, which you have in the same corner of the previous story;—

"Not one word that is spoken for the truth, falls in vain. Tell the truth; work out the truth; testify for the truth,—and leave the consequence to God."

"Our first duty to truth is to believe it; our next duty is to submit to it."

And despite testifying constantly, you never provide space to the truthful testimonies of those you accuse. Nevertheless, "we testify" wherever we can; and according to your counsel "we leave the consequence to God." Since you love lies rather than the "truth," you cannot blame us for leaving you in the hand of that God against whom you fight so stubbornly,—his "truth" and his own: for,—

Stiff-necked aggressive villain—defamer,
Of lies you are spokesman;
You are ensnared, are fallen,
Are trapped, muddle-headed man!

From now on be yourself just as consistent, and leave us and our religion in the hand of the same God; for it is him we serve, and to his judgment-seat we are responsible, thanks be for that, and not to the court of the one-sided and persecuting *Times*. We heard much mention of some "minister" who preached "obey my commandments but not my examples." But we did not know for certain that "*thou art the man*" until we had read the counsels you gave, and compared them with your slanderous deeds. Your continual and increasing false accusations verify your own motto, which follows:—

"That which is good, can expect to get better; and that which is bad, fear to get worse; for wickedness, virtue, and time, never stand still."

You also verify that which the Preacher says, chap. viii, ver. 11. "Because sentence against an evil work is not executed speedily, therefore the heart of the sons of men is fully set in them to do evil." What greater evil can you do than to falsely accuse a religion, and persecute the children of God? "He that toucheth you toucheth the apple of his eye," will be proved true in your own fate unless you repent, as sure as those in truth are those you falsely accuse. May the gracious God allow you time to repent, is our prayer, if in your ignorance you do all this; if not, may it be done as seemeth him good in his sight.

THE *STAR OF GOMER* AND ITS RELIGIOUS BLASPHEMY!

THIS one also has learned the old trick nearly as well as the *Times*, and its columns constantly pour some shameful slime on her neighbors because of their religion. But she is as much wiser than the *Times* as she is older. She has released occasional little pieces in defense of her accusations against us, so that she can claim some kind of right of being two-sided; while, at the same time, she intends to kill two birds with the same stone by so doing; and while she was doing that she was just behind the curtain loading her heavier cannons to attack us. It was very Starry fairness to publish a challenge, as H. Tegai did to J. D., to come to the field, namely the field of the *Star*, and then refuse space for the defense ! ! ! Who else of the children of Gomer have been treated like this in a publication that professes to be free? Yet, this is not the first time for her to play the *Yankee trick* with the Mormons. In the same issue she confessed that she purposefully left out very interesting things to provide space for others to malign us and misrepresent us wholly without provocation, namely the false story of the "Lectures of Dowlais," &c. You editors of Wales! what is the cause that nearly all of you have the bellyache at once? Why bark so much at a religion so unknown to you? What did any of us do to stir you like wolves from your holes? Say, if you can, what is the cause? If we are guilty, why do you not publish that, then, instead of publishing lies about us from one year to the next? Would you not, we wonder, publish some transgression against us, if you knew of one? Your eagerness to publish false accusations, proves that you cannot find truthful things to harm us.

What reasonable man can find worthy words to show the atrocity, the slander, and the sinfulness of that article that appeared in the *Star of Gomer* for November, under the title of "*Proclamation of the Latter-day Saints to their Compatriots!*" Was it not bad enough to publish lies about us under pseudonyms, and no names at all, and then this last and ungodly deed of forging our names? Having the audacity to publish such slanderous rubbish in our own names!! That has really done it. This is worse than publishing that "Profession of Faith" a while back. If the Saints had some proclamation, I wonder if it would get to appear? Oh no, it would not. Well, in the name of reason, is a filthy fake-proclamation, forging the name of an entire party of religionists, better with respect to influencing the public, or sweeter to the taste of the publisher! What if people believed that that proclamation is what it professes to be, namely belonging to the "Saints?" Who would come to listen to them? and who would come to listen to the Baptists either, if some wicked man forged the name of their party to falsely portray them as much as this proclamation does us? Why is it not considered that our religion is just as good and just as dear in our sight, as is yours to you? Again, we say, do as you please, for God is on our side despite all the ugly howling of all the wolves!

THE SAINTS IN CALIFORNIA.

[*From the "Millennial Star."*]

"*Lately from the Mormons.*—We understand from letters received lately from the first company of the Mormons, that they have reached in a safe and comfortable condition the edges of the great Salt Lake, where they have settled for a while, and their cattle and their flocks are feasting on the lucious grass, and the pure waters, which are so typical of those parts. They made a new way from the Omaha Indians to the foot of the Rocky Mountains, which will no doubt greatly facilitate the way for other immigrants who come after them from the United States. This is to the north of the Oregon trail—and more direct—they have built strong bridges over the main rivers. Opening this trail is evidence of hard work and much suffering. After they reached beyond Grand Island, they had plenty of wild cattle, to strengthen the fibre of these brave men. They came into the midst of about ten thousand at once, or as one writer counted, "that there were eight or ten million pounds of beef there." [A very abundant and cheap market for the exiled children of God in the wilderness!] When the railway is made from Missouri to the Pacific Ocean, no doubt the government, or whoever does it, will have better overseers and workers from among the Mormons, than they can get from anyone else—the strong sons of constant persecution, those who overcame and gave no heed to all obstruction and danger as things of naught. A new printing press is on its way to them.

"O. B. H."

This is very sweet news to the children of Zion throughout the world, and to the Welsh also. We give thanks to their sustainer for his great tenderness toward them. Behold the firstfruits have reached the grainery; what can hinder the main crop? Nothing on the earth, or under the earth, we say, while they keep the law of Zion! Neither let the Welsh think that they have arrived beyond the need for assistance. Oh no, but now when they are beginning to settle in a country so new, under so many disadvantages, at the cost of using up their goods, their money, and their clothes, &c.—now, I say, is the greatest need for assistance in order to repair, to get building materials, clothes, seed to put in the ground, and the necessary things to work the land, and carry on with the various vocations necessary to be mutually beneficial. Consider how advantageous and lovely it will be to arrive in a country where everything necessary is available, different from going as they did to a place where there is nothing of the kind except what they themselves established. Let this cause us to be sympathetic with them, until we will all "*long pull a strong pull, and a pull altogether*," now, for their sakes—the work that they have done, and for the benefit that we expect from the fruit of their hard labor and sufferings. We are very confident that we will be able to fulfill our promise to them in the next Conference. What do you say, children of Zion? If you are all of the same mind, we shall not be disappointed.

We understand that many other thousands of Saints are on their journey from the states toward California, like doves flying to their windows. There is now more earnest and successful searching into the principles of Mormonism throughout the states than ever before. This last testimony, namely the departure of the Saints from their midst, in addition to the voice of "the blood of holy prophets and apostles and saints," is having a strange influence throughout the land, and shows that God earnestly wishes "to do his work, his strange work," and he wishes to gather his children together "to their rooms for a small moment, until the calamity has passed." Not everyone understands the signs of the times in this age of light, any more than they did in the days of Noah, or in the days of the destruction of Jerusalem, for not everyone is going to the place which God has prepared to be a place of deliverance from the judgments of the last days, any more than everyone went into the ark—or else everyone would go from Jerusalem to the mountains. Oh no, no one but those Saints understood through the Spirit of revelation for themselves where their deliverance would be. By this also is seen the great blessing to be had, yes, the absolute necessity there is for receiving divine revelations and more in our age, as in all other ages in which God does his work. "Surely the Lord God will do nothing [in this age any more than before], but he revealeth his secret unto his servants the prophets." Listen to their voice, and harken to their call, so that we will inherit not only temporal deliverance, and delightful rest from all oppression and hunger, but also so that we will receive our holy endowment in the temples of our Lord, so that we will be made fit through the perfecting of our understanding and our sanctification to enjoy His beneficent association—patriarchs and prophets, together with the blessed heavenly family; and so that we will receive an abundant entrance into the joy of our Lord when he comes to his glory in his saints. This is the way to reach the mark. Dear Saints, run this race speedily, and you will enjoy, step by step, "the payment of the prize."

We anxiously await from now to the end of this year for the good news from our presidents about the opening of the way, and instructions for us to journey out to join them; for, no doubt they watch over us also. Hail! yes, call, we say with all our hearts.

THE BEST TREASURE.

SEEK first the kingdom of our God,
Not earthly wealth or pride;
Let this best treasure be your bond;
All else is dross beside.

'Tis better for the soul of man,
Than all the world's excess,
To serve the purpose of our Lord,
And in this find success.

This is a treasure which will last,
Man knows not its extent—
To gain the Zion of our God,
Where saintly days are spent.

With songs of Moses and the Lamb,
All fears will be released;
New wine may freely be imbibed,
In Jesus's wedding feast. J. D.

THE STATE OF THE CHURCHES.

WE are pleased to inform you that all the accounts that reach us, not only from every part of Wales, but also from England, Scotland, America, and everywhere the gospel is being preached, give evidence of rapid and sustained growth of this divine work; and that there is not only a large increase in numbers, but also an increase in unity, zeal, and holiness is evident among the Saints, and a continual and more abundant enjoyment of the gifts of the Holy Ghost. We have not read of so much persecution and opposition anywhere as there is in our country in these days. Despite that, do not be disheartened, dear brothers and sisters, for our mighty God is on our side, and is presiding over all that must be in order for us to complete our task, of warning our nation, and inviting it from the grasp of destruction in a short time. Thanks be to our God that we know what it is that we are about, and that we know that our labor will be crowned with success, yes, with a thorough victory, if we bravely maintain confidence in our profession for yet a small moment. Lift up your heads, and look at the "signs of the times!" Listen closely to the news! It is the sound of wars here, and the shedding of the blood of men by the thousands is heard from afar! Famines, pestilence, and diseases, are circulating around the world:—markets of the world, and their richest merchants will find themselves worse than worthless with but a few hours of warning;—and the greatest hearts of the world will shake and shudder from fear from what they expect;—food rising in cost, and the wages dropping, together with many other things showing that our world is in confusion—that the judgments of God are quickly following on the heels of his servants and their godly mission for the last time; and everything, we say, testifies to those to whom "it is given to know the signs of the times," that the time of their "deliverance is nigh." We thank our Savior that we know of the place of refuge, where God provides full deliverence for his children against all evil; and we shall strive to complete our task quickly, so that we will be ready to go when the important invitation sounds in our ears, namely "Come out of her, my people, that ye be not partakers of her sins, and that ye receive not of her plagues." Let us remember that we are strangers and wayfarers here, and those who are striving for a better land, and let us take comfort.

MERTHYR.—It is too great a task for us to be able to inform you how many were baptized here last month, for many are baptized night and day, and at times as many as ten in a week; but this we will say, that we remember hardly a meeting of the Saints in a long time that did not receive some in. And further we say, that the number of this branch is at, if not over, 600 faithful and zealous members, and great is the joy that is in their midst, and the growth in every good work. We ought to thank our persecutors (if we really should) for causing among other things some unusual excitement here, and causing more investigation than ever into the doctrine that we preach; and not only those who profess no religion, but also those who do, yes, and those who have been respected leaders and preachers are coming near, and are listening, and believing, and obeying, and are saying they would not take the world for their conversion. May others hasten to do likewise, we say.

DOWLAIS.—The truth is growing here; and the tumult has subsided like summer thunder, and it brings sweet showers in its wake, to the joy of the Saints, and additions to their numbers nearly every week. This, like everything else, proves that the false prophets are those who prophesy that the Mormons have received the *home stroke*, &c., for we assure you that she is more alive and glorious than ever. We thank her author for this.

CARDIFF.—Eight were baptized here during the past month, with good signs for more; and we are very glad to hear that the Saints are unanimously more energetic than they have ever been. We hope they will take care as if before the teeth of the lion.

ABERDARE.—This branch is scraping the moss away from itself, and we expect to see it soon blossoming like the green branch in the summer. Two were added to their number this week. Hosts will come, for there is yet room.

ABERSYCHAN.—After beating for so long on this adamantine stone, it has finally broken into splinters. Nineteen were baptized here in the same week, and 24 in fewer than that number of days, and according to all the signs there are hosts at the door; and the Saints are happily enjoying the blessings of the children of God according to the promises of Jesus Christ, and are gaining strong and varied testimonies that God and his work are the same as they were in former days. Among others who were baptized here, there is a tavernkeeper and his family, who gave an example of his honesty and his desire to serve God, by taking down his *sign* immediately, saying, that he would not try to serve God and Bacchus, and that a religion as glorious as this one deserves every sacrifice in its cause. Here is one example to prove that in his religion there is strength and influence, although not of the same nature as our accusers say. Although our church rules do not absolutely command this, yet it is an example worthy of emulation when this or any other business prevents a man from worshipping God. May the Lord reward this brother an hundredfold, we say. Among the host of instruments that God allows to exist to purify and perfect the patience of his children, there is near here some surly, old, Pharisaic tailor who is very busy, yes, often before finishing dressing in the morning in following after some of the weak and newly baptized, especially the women, and challenging them to perform miracles, &c. But finally, the old tailor met his *match* very nicely! He intruded like this into the house of a woman who had been baptized the day before, and he asked her to cast the devil out of him! But another man who happened to be there at the time asked the old tailor if he claimed to be a child of God? "Yes sir," said the tailor very stubbornly, "for over 17 years." "Well," said the other, being much more reasonable, "it is very strange that an old child of God like yourself is seeking such a thing from a child who is not as many hours old as you are in years, is it not!" The next thing that was seen of the old tailor was his tail dragging behind him into his hole. And if he is heard coming out again on the same business, you will know who he is, and more of his story. It is surprising that his brethren have not taught him better manners!

BLAENAU GWENT.—Five were baptized here recently, and the work is going forward quite successfully. There was some man here, and the same man has been in other branches, who professed to be a member with the Saints in Scotland, and who crept into the meetings, and into the homes of the Saints, asking cunning questions, and trying to trap them into giving some topics for him to write lies about them to the world; but he was caught in his treachery. Do not believe every spirit that rushes into your midst, even though they come at times very flatteringly like this one; but test them properly before they have part in your love-feasts. They are spots and blemishes, coming in to spy on your freedom, so they can devour you in the presence of the world. Do not give sacred things to the dogs. There is no freedom for anyone to come to the church of God except through the door, namely baptism, and those who come some other way, are considered thieves and robbers now as before.

NANTYGLO.—Five were baptized here recently, and this sister branch has already developed breasts, and has received the honor of nursing brave and useful sons, which have taken their good seed to several parts of the country, and it is sprouting wonderfully, promising an abundant harvest. On may they go.

PENYCAE.—Two were baptized recently, one of whom was a respected deacon, and of great influence with the Baptists for years; and there will be no end to his thanks, for he has chosen the better part, if he continues faithful in it.

VICTORIA.—Six have been baptized here since the Conference, two of which again were from the Baptists! one with the Wesleyans, besides more that believe.

TREDEGAR.—Two were baptized here last week, and we hope that those are but the firstfruits of the second crop in this populous place. You Saints, be careful of your conduct, that there be nothing in you to prevent the honest in heart from coming to the family of God, for "woe to those by whom the offence cometh."

BLAENAVON.—Two have been baptized, and several are at the door here, and if they had the advantages that are to be had in other places, they would come in. We trust that the Conference president will succeed in getting a zealous and diligent elder to go there before long, who can properly impart the word of truth to those who are dying from lack of knowledge about the plan of God to save man.

PONTYBEREM.—-Four have been added to the numbers of the Saints here recently, one of which was 91 years of age. Elder H. Williams, and the other preachers, greatly praise the noble and honest investigation of the inhabitants of these environs. Not only did they come to listen attentively, but they carefully searched the scriptures themselves, and great is their joy when they discover that the promises of Jesus Christ are for them to enjoy the spiritual gifts, and the blessed association of his Holy Spirit as before. Several others have promised to obey the conditions of the gospel before long. The Saints are very grateful to the masters and overseers of these works for their kindness to them, and their freedom to worship God, as others have, and for their not believing, as some do, all the tales that are brought to them by gossiping men, for the purpose of persecuting them out of the country. We pray for the God of the Saints to repay them an hundredfold for their kindness to his children.

CWMAMAN.—-Elders J. Griffiths and R. Davies earnestly beseech help in preaching in these environs. The call is so great and earnest that they hardly know where to go first, and it is increasing more and more. Although only two were baptized there during the past month, yet according to the present signs, those are but the firstfruits of an abundant harvest of souls for the church of God. The masters and overseers here are also greatly praised by the Saints.

LLANELLI.—-We are continually informed of baptisms here, and 41 have been baptized since the Conference. Almost all of these have been carefully searching among the religions of the age for the true religion, and they have been, for the most part, members with the Baptists and the Independents for years, and with hardly a blemish on their character; nevertheless, as soon as they became true disciples to him who said, "Ye shall be hated of all men for my name's sake," even their brethren fulfill this prophecy by persecuting them, especially their former pastors, who fed on them instead of feeding them; and especially a minister of the Baptists, by the name of James Spencer, is trying to devour those who feed him richly! He sees that he will not get any more of their fleece, otherwise he would not be so eager to tear their skin: but no one fears the length of his teeth, for they are rotten. Is it not a clear sign of the remarkable blindness of men like these, that they think to keep honest and reasonable men under their clutches in the darkness, by maligning those who bring them to light, while having so many facts to prove that his persecution has the entirely opposite effect? Very often we are asked, "In the name of reason, what is the cause for the Baptists everywhere being so terribly bloody to the Saints, more than everyone else, and insisting on being at the forefront in all persecution?" We have an answer to give to that before long, but it would be too long here.

We are pleased to report that all the Saints are united despite everything, in fervent love toward their God and his work, and happily enjoying of the "the children's bread," that their increase is so great in godly wisdom, and all godliness. We say to the Saints of Llanelli, for their comfort, that their "Balaam" has returned to his old place of cursing, but he is not able to curse Israel one bit. He, poor wretch, has died away, as has been the case and will be the case with every shooting star that has cut across the orbits of the planets; his sparks are not seen, and his odor has been blown away. You heard true that his backbone was broken under the hammer of the bailiff!

CWMBYCHAN AND BRYN.—-We have heard from several that some large multitude was baptized here recently, and all the preachers are very busy at their work. Perhaps this is the reason why the president has not had sufficient time as to inform us for a long time about their number or their state.

CARMARTHEN.—-This branch is blossoming anew, and the number of Saints has increased through the baptism during the past two weeks of four. Elder B. Jones tells us from there that scores of others there believe this gospel, with hopeful signs for an increase soon, especially in the surrounding areas for several miles, where there is a great call for preaching, and an attentive hearing. They have secured a convenient hall in the town, where there is continual preaching to a crowd of noble listeners. They wish for a portion of the prayers of the Saints, especially their mother branch in Merthyr, and I say Amen.

PEMBROKESHIRE.—The work is on a continual increase throughout this County. Elder J. Morris reports that he has often received uncivil and hateful opposition, especially when baptizing. Even when administering this godly ordinance attacks were made on his person, and stones were thrown at them while in the water, &c., yes, this was done by those who professed religion, among which were even some of our friends the Baptists! And had it not been for the kindness of some unbelievers, it would have been worse for the Saints! The Saints wish to acknowledge the defense of the gentlemen of the country, chiefly Mr. Owens, with gratitude. And who would not give thanks for freedom to worship God, when those who profess religion attempt to prevent them, and sometimes compel them to go for miles in the night secretly to have a quiet setting in which to administer one of the ordinances of the house of God! In what pagan country is anything similar to this to be found, not to mention that it is among the "Christians" of enlightened Wales? Great is the patience of our God; we are grateful that everything is under his care, and that all will turn for the good in the end.

LLANYBYDDER AND BRECHFA.—Several have been baptized in these places lately, especially in the latter; and among others, some deacons of the Baptists, and some elders of the Calvinists, until there are there now 25 who have all obtained, and who continue to have edifying testimonies from God of their acceptance before him. There is a great call for additional preaching in the environs, and several have decided to take up their cross, and follow Jesus through all scorn and obstacles. Our dear brother, elder T. Jeremy, has been very zealous and successful, together with elder T. Harris, and others, and God is blessing their labor, to the comfort and edification of the Saints, and he is bringing godly light to the eyes of the world. They have caused anew a wondrous searching into the scriptures throughout those areas. T. H. says, as proof of this, that the people said it is difficult to find clean houses wherever the Saints go, because the old dusty Bibles that had been closed up about their houses for a long time are opened and handled busily, "to see if they can find in them the strange and wondrous scriptures the Saints are reading from their Bibles!" Well, people who cause searching of the scriptures are not so bad, even though they are "Saints!" May the searching increase, and we do not fear with respect to an increase of the Saints where there is honesty. The commotion is among the old as well as others; for example read the following: "There was some man selling *spectacles* out that way, and he was urged to go to the places where the Saints were preaching, since there was hardly any need for *spectacles* except where the people were searching in their Bibles because of their excitement." For his own benefit it would be good for the salesman to hasten, lest the Saintifying enlighten their eyes so they are able to read without *spectacles*, if they obey it. We are reminded of what was done to "Dark Daniel" according to his own testimony, namely that he could see the candle on the table clearly the first time the ordinance was administered to him! And may his pitiful fate be a warning for all to refrain from mocking and falsely portraying the work of God!

We are sorry to hear of the alarming accident that happened to brother Jeremy through a gunshot, which wounded his head so seriously, that those present said that he was beyond treatment. We were very happy to hear also that he was so full of faith and trust in his heavenly Father and his treatment, so that he wanted nothing else, and that the only call that was to be had from his mouth was for the elders of the church. This is a fact to prove the divinity of his religion when in dangerous and dire circumstances; would he have done this, had he not believed he would be healed through the oil and the laying on of hands? This is not the first time for him to see that God is true to his promise. He was administered to in the presence of a crowd by elder *Thomas Harris*, and although not all at once, and although contrary to the expectations of the onlookers, yet he received healing to a great extent, and he is improving quickly after that. We thank our heavenly Father, and we pray continually for him.

COUNTIES OF THE NORTH.—Our dear and hardworking brother, elder A. Evans, informs us of more joyful news than we have space to publish here concerning the growth of this divine work throughout the North. Though there is no miraculous growth in their midst, yet some are getting baptized frequently. Some were baptized lately in new places also. The Saints are unusually faithful and determined to go forward through all contempt and obstacles until they achieve excellence in Jesus Christ. We expect to be able to aid our brethren of the North after this Conference by sending a host of gifted preachers from the South to plant their vineyards.

ANNOUNCEMENTS.

TO OUR DISTRIBUTORS.

SINCE no other issue of the *Prophet* is to come out this year, we earnestly beseech all the distributors to settle up their accounts for the year for the other books, as well as the *Prophet*, by the Conference.

N.B. We would be glad to buy back our own books, namely the following, and pay the full price for them, if they are clean, that is the *Old Religion Anew*, the *Reply*, the *Scales*, the *Proclamation*, and no. 1, 7, 8 of the *Prophet*. Whoever has them, let him send them here, and he shall have the money, or other books, in their place. Not every author will do this, nor does this wonderfully increasing demand for our books testify that our religion is in decline in the least!

*** We have books of Welsh Hymns, bound, 6p. each.

*** Review of the Lecture of the Rev. E. Roberts in the Isaf Chapel, Merthyr, will appear in the next, or as a treatise as soon as it can be printed.

*** Those who wish to have back issues of the *Prophet*, or the *Millennial Star*, send here without delay.

NEXT GLAMORGAN CONFERENCE.

IT is intended to hold the above Conference in the Cymreigyddion Hall in Merthyr, Sunday and Monday, December the 26th and 27th, that is the first days after Christmas day.

*** Visitors from America are expected at the Conference, and we earnestly beseech all the Saints to strive to fulfill by that time the promise we made to assist the Saints who are in the wilderness.

We expect that the various presidents throughout Wales will take care of this.

CONTENTS.

MERTHYR TYDFIL:
PUBLISHED AND FOR SALE BY D. JONES, AND ALSO FOR SALE BY THE SAINTS IN GENERAL.

JOHN JONES, PRINTER, RHYDYBONT.

1848

PROPHWYD Y JUBILI,

NEU

SEREN Y SAINT;

YN CYNNWYS

EGWYDDORION "GORUCHWYLIAETH CYFLAWNDER YR AMSEROEDD,"

MEWN

TRAETHODAU, LLYTHYRON, HANESION, PRYDYDDIAETH, &c.

"YR ARGLWYDD IOR A LEFARODD, PWY NI PHROPHWYDA? CANYS NI WNA YR ARGLWYDD DDIM A'R NA DDANGOSO EI GYFRINACH I'W WEISION Y PROPHWYDI."

CYF. III.

MERTHYR-TYDFIL:

CYHOEDDWYD AC AR WERTH GAN D. JONES, AC AR WERTH HEFYD GAN Y SAINT YN GYFFREDINOL.

1848.

1848 title page, courtesy Harold B. Lee Library, Brigham Young University

PROPHET OF THE JUBILEE,

OR

STAR OF THE SAINTS;

CONTAINING

PRINCIPLES OF THE "DISPENSATION OF THE FULNESS OF TIMES,"

IN

TREATISES, LETTERS, ACCOUNTS,
POETRY, &c.

"THE LORD GOD HATH SPOKEN, WHO CAN BUT PROPHESY? SURELY THE LORD GOD WILL DO NOTHING, BUT HE REVEALETH HIS SECRET UNTO HIS SERVANTS THE PROPHETS."

VOL. III.

MERTHYR TYDFIL:

PUBLISHED AND FOR SALE BY D. JONES; AND FOR SALE ALSO BY THE SAINTS IN GENERAL,

1848.

FOREWORD.

DEAR SAINTS AND FELLOW COUNTRYMEN,—We hereby present to you the third volume, and the last also, of the PROPHET, giving our warmest thanks for the support you have given to him. Not because he cannot come to you again, is the cause for his suspension; but we consider that by now he deserves to go to his "resting place," since he has run his race, and kept the faith. From now on we intend to trumpet after you in ZION'S TRUMPET, shouting every month, "Come out of her, my people." Frequent mention will be made of the excellencies of Zion, and the law that will come forth from there, together with the best route for everyone to go toward that country. Now, may you listen to the TRUMPET as you did to the PROPHET; and show your respect for the latter by buying for him the best leather clothes, so that he will be handsome in his place and in his appearance.

Yours in the truth,

THE EDITOR.

December 15, 1848.

CONTENTS.

PROPHET OF THE JUBILEE,

OR

STAR OF THE SAINTS.

No. 19.] JANUARY, 1848 [Price 2c.

A GREETING AT THE BEGINNING OF THE NEW YEAR.

We have great pleasure in greeting our readers through the *Prophet* at the beginning of the year 1848. And our desire will not be less than before, nor our devotion, nor our zeal to benefit them, nor shall we tire of imploring the grantor of all good gifts to bless them temporally and spiritually. Each year as it follows on the heels of the other is more replete with wonders and changes ever since the establishment of the church in 1830. Great have been the commotion and the changes among the kingdoms of the world!—the moral earthquakes that have shaken societies, and have completely overthrown the organizations founded on human wisdom. And the spirit of prophecy teaches us that all this is just the beginning of trials and struggle, and they will increase, and pestilence, famines, and revolutions will follow on the heels of the missionaries of the "dispensation of the fulness of the gospel," until the Son of Man sets his feet on the Mount of Olives.

The best time to treasure historical knowledge is when such things are being fulfilled. Of necessity, the history of the church for the coming year will contain many important, beneficial, and interesting, if not incomparable facts. The situation of the "twelve" leaders, the church in the wilderness, and the establishment of the "ensign" to all nations are among the wonders of the past ages. Zion, having bled through all her pores, and for over seventeen years having nearly drowned in the deluge of oppression and tribulation, has at last planted the banners of freedom on the tops of the mountains, and sent her missionaries throughout the world to invite the wretched of the nations to a fulness of joy. The foundation of the strongest empire that has ever been on our earth has been set in the place the holy prophets have foreseen for centuries. A more hopeful year has never dawned on the church than the year 1848. The church has wandered in a strange land for a long time. Strangers, foreigners, and enemies have encompassed it on all sides.

State officials without mercy have scourged her to satisfy their passions. Fanatical priests of Babylon, and slanderous gentile editors, have persecuted her with their slime and their hatred, like *Spanish bloodhounds* on the heels of the innocent natives of the forest. But, thanks to the Head of the church, who comforts her, her deliverance has come at last; safe, they have gathered themselves to a place of refuge, from which neither all the armies of perdition, nor authorities, nor the principalities of darkness can chase them. Fearlessly, we record this prophecy in public columns, namely that the church will never again leave its home in the valley of the mountains, even if the world and hell camped against its walls. No matter what happens among the gentiles, or however many empires cease to be—or however many of the elements they enrage as if head-to-head to destroy each other, or whatever may be; the strong defenses of the daughter of Zion have been chosen by inspiration; and the islands will flee, the mountains will jump—the hills will leap like lambs—the stars will fall, and the heavenly bodies will shoot out of their orbits, before the strong towers of Zion are overthrown.

Now a campaign toward Zion such as has never before been seen is expected on our earth. The rich as well as the poor from every nation, country, and clime, are desirous to greet a redeemed land, where the banners of truth and freedom wave victoriously and delightfully above a peaceful, happy, and holy people.

The gathering and building of Zion will contain a field sufficiently broad where the zeal, bravery, and virtues of the most generous can operate. The wise, distinguished, and brave people of the age among every nation and land will understand that the God of heaven has at last indicated to them a land and a blessed and permanent home. It is the inheritance of the meek, and the refuge of the oppressed.

The tumultuous, and suffering, yes, the pitiful, and threatening situation of the world now testifies, that this is the only way there can be a Jubilee for all the pure in heart. Nothing less than one that brings temporal salvation, yes, *present* and spiritual, can satisfy the present needs of the countless wretched of our world! For the past six thousand years, no doubt such banners as these have never before waved in such a hallowed environment in our world. The course for never-ending glory and joy has been opened and paved by deity. All are invited to run along it—and no doubt countless thousands will achieve the lofty goal and payment of the prize. Everlasting crowns shine in the distance. Tin will no longer deceive our eyes. No, but the great reality of all the protections at that time will each one of the blessed family feel over his head. Tried and faithful people will run the course—and they shall win the prize, and they shall return to their earthly brethren in godly chariots, dressed in shining robes, and immortality, to invite the sons of men to the glorious campaign. The heavenly excellent ones will already have, at that time, possessed the crown, and "yet there is room!"

The walls of Babylon are already shaking to their foundations, and the hearts of its kings and their subjects are weakening from fear and the dread of the things that are hanging over their heads, and without hope for deliverance. But also the sound of the broken shackles of their beguiled can be heard here and there sounding like the golden bells of the great Jubilee after them. The pure in heart are gathering. Their homeland has been indicated by the finger of God. Angels of heaven have been sent to gather the righteous, and to harvest this land which is ripening quickly for the judgments and plagues of the Judge of the whole earth. Rejoice heaven, and be happy, oh earth, for the wise understand and prepare for their rooms until the wrath is past. But the wicked do not understand, and fall worse and worse to wickedness, like the ox to the slaughter, or the bird to the net. The history of these times, of which 1848 is the center point, teaches experience and wisdom to the future ages. Whoever does this and understands, will enjoy the goodness of the Lord, and will continue on his course to the higher spheres in the world to come.

Behold the *Prophet of the Jubilee*, or the *Star of the Saints*, appearing again in the atmosphere of Wales, at the beginning of the year 1848, and offering its ray of light of the coming Jubilee to light the footsteps of its readers onward towards the source of light, namely the *Sun of Righteousness*. In it will be an account of the great deeds of God through his children in these wondrous days in Zion and its branches throughout the world, things the hearts of the Saints thirst to hear—things that will perfect their unity, and will increase their knowledge. The remarkable growth of the Saints in Wales, while practically every other sect is decaying and weakening, merits our attention, and encourages us to strive to instruct them in the glorious principles, although new and strange, that pertain to the family of Zion. Through the help of the Saints, through their faith and their prayers, we are confident that the *Prophet* for 1848, will contain more new and old things to benefit them than ever before, and we are confident that, through their efforts, hundreds more will be able to read it, and receive the benefit it aims to do for all. The increase in its circulation already in the face of so many obstacles, together with the countless testimonies we have received from various places of its usefulness, heartens us to publish it, and to pray for it to be a means under the blessing of our Lord to bless our dear fellow nation.

"MORMON MIRACLE."

UNDER this title, the "Reverend" Editor of the *Revivalist* took care, to make room in the December issue, for the following; and no doubt his *spectacles* through long practice with strong taste, draw his attention first to all the filthiest and most lying tales in every little paper against "Mormonism."

"The *Ottaway Free Trader* gives the following account *with assurance of its truth*:—'It appears that the prophet Strang needs a house, and he decided that his followers get to build it; and after calling them together, he said, if they would build the house for him, that the Lord would authorize him to promise them an uncommon gift. The house was built immediately, and the gift was requested: the prophet took them to the church, and after going through several ceremonies, of washing feet, anointing the head with oil that smelled funny, he took them to a dark room, and when they were all there, all their heads were shining as if with the brightness of the sun, and great was their joy; but the prophet William suspected a deceitful trick, and he took some of the oil, and found out that it was nothing but oil and *phosphorus* mixed. He availed himself of the first opportunity to expose the deceit before all the brotherhood. Strang did not deny it, rather he admitted the whole deceit, and he preached a sermon to justify the deceit, and to prove that all the miracles of Moses and Jesus Christ were accomplished the same way, through natural means. William broke off all relations with him, but Strang was *snug* in his house despite that.'"

Now, Mr. Rees, why would you not say what was the "assurance" your reporter gave you of the truth of the above story? Your assertion is the assurance. Remember, even though any assertion of any blemish against the Saints is sufficient "assurance" of it to cause you to believe it and to publish it, yet not all your readers are of that mind; actually no one is except those who like yourself love lies rather than the truth. The next thing expected from your hand is, either to prove there is a connection between the aforementioned deceit with Mormonism, or we expect you to confess, if there remains one grain of honesty in your bosom by now, that it is jealousy for the religion of your neighbors that has caused you to falsely accuse them again this time, and that because your disciples practically by the dozens are getting fed up with your empty husks and your loud cries, and are embracing "Mormonism." Ouch! ouch, as for "this insignificant, innocuous, little thing" as this wise Editor said "all one need do is to pretend not to see it and it will die of its own accord;" even that "illiterate" thing is such a threatening monster to the *craft*, and the popularity of the Reverend, that he not only considers it dangerous for him to publish its defenses, but that he is obligated to publish all lies about it that reach his grasp from far and near! Did you perhaps have a look through the wrong end of your *magnifiers* when it appeared so *small* and *innocuous* to your synagogue, Mr. Rees? It was probably because you turned your lenses the wrong way that you changed your opinion of it, and your behavior towards it so impulsively and thoroughly. Well, take care that your lenses are in the proper *vanes* this time, then; otherwise your readers will think that you are a "*cock of the smoke*," or that *Chameleon* is the appropriate name for that which gives you such a bellyache; and not Mormonism. If so, you lose your vindictive purpose.

Again, what if we were to categorically deny that the above was not a "Mormon miracle," and there is no more connection between the aforementioned "Strang," or the aforementioned "William" and Mormonism, than there is between Mr. Rees and Mormonism;—than there is between the miracle of "Newmarket" and Mormonism! What would you say, Sir, if we were to say that you know that the above persons have no kind of connection with the Latter-day Saints? Was that not published throughout Wales over a year ago, from one end to the other, and how could you not know? What if we were to challenge you to prove that Mormonism has anything to do with the above, any more than with the Independents? What would you say? You would have to become as mute as that man became who was deprived of his "wedding garment," despite exposing your shame.

Despite how deceitful and ungodly is the anointing of this "Strang" (if the story is true) his *endowment* is not much more inconsistent than that of the Sectarians! The latter receive their endowment in their academies without anointing and without (divine) right, and the former through anointing with phosphoric oil in the darkness. Query! Which of the two is the brighter? This is a case of the "pot calling the kettle black!"

Strang and William Smith are called Mormons, by the sectarians, in the same sense that the Turks call everyone Christian who live within the boundaries of a Christian country. They do not have any other basis to link them with the "Latter-day Saints."

Since Mr. Rees is ransacking the Newspapers of the world so diligently for, and with such enjoyment to find a story of a "Mormon miracle," we feel a bit of craving to please him [for he will be very pleased to hear that miracles are being performed, of course!] by translating the following story as a sample of the many we could quote and declare the powerful deeds of the Spirit of God among his people, and in fulfillment of the promises of His Son, Jesus Christ. Most assuredly it will be just as easy to "assure" the truthfulness of the following accounts to the Reverend Editor as it was for the preceding; besides, there is no need to go so far to inquire after the latter as for the former; and so there is no danger for them to change so much in their translation. Here are some stories for you, Mr. Rees, straight from the source, from the mouths of eyewitnesses, and which are published in the exact same place, and are irrefutable. Yes, here are some public miracles for you after shouting for them.

"LETTER OF W. ATHOLL MC. MASTER TO ORSON SPENCER."

(Quoted from the *Millennial Star*, Dec. 1, 1847.)

"Wood Mill Street, Dunfermline, Nov. 8, 1847.

"Dear Brother Spencer,—

"By means of this letter I wish to tell you how the Lord is working with us here by confirming the word with signs, which follow them that believe.

"On the 29th day of September, a brother came to me in a prayer meeting, who had burned his arm terribly, by helping to put out a fire, about 12 years ago; he was in great pain,—he wished for me to administer to him the ordinance of anointing with oil, and the laying on of hands in the name of the Lord. See James v, 14, &c. In the administration the pain left him completely, and his arm has been completely well since that time. Again, on the 6th of October, he brought his wife to me, who had been struck with a *fit* of the *palsy* about ten months ago, through which she had entirely lost the power of her speech. I anointed her, and I laid hands upon her in the name of the Lord, offering a prayer; and the woman received her speech immediately; and since then she has been speaking as clearly and understandably as ever, and rejoicing in the work of the Lord. Again, on the 11th of the same month, I was called on to visit a brother who had been afflicted with a sore sickness, and with blindness. He was living in the town of Oakley, from 4 to 5 miles from Dunfermline. I was first told about him by brother Brown, and nearly all his sickness had left him when he administered to him, except that he still remained blind. Brother Brown and the son of brother Mackinley, (for that was the name of the sick man), came with me to his house; when the son saw the blindness of his father, he told him, thinking to comfort him, "well, father, you can hardly expect to be anything but blind since you are so old." (His age is 73.) I answered that I did not believe in such a doctrine as that; and I would not believe it at least until I could see what the Lord had in his storehouse for him. I asked the sick man if he believed that God could bless the appointed means so that his sight would be restored to him? He answered that he believed. Then I anointed his eyes with oil, and I laid hands on him and prayed in the name of the Lord; and the result was, that the night before I left his house, he received his sight. And I left him greatly rejoicing in the salvation of God in his behalf. Again, Nov. 8th, I was called to visit another brother, that was struck stone blind. When I arrived at his abode, the house was full of people, and he was in his bed. I pushed forward to the side of his bed, and I asked him if he wanted me to administer the church ordinance to him? He said he did. Then I turned to the onlookers, and I said, "When the Saints obey the commandments of the Son of God in the administration of his ordinances, they are accused of trying to work miracles. I showed that our duty is to pray according to the plan set up by Jesus Christ for the sick; that it was not less of an obligation on them than on others, which if they agreed to do until the Lord answered us by healing the sick, it would be a great blessing for him, and glory to God, and not to any man. This alone is our purpose." They all knelt to pray, and after rising I anointed the eyes of the blind man with oil, and then his head; elder Huggar laid his hands with me on his head, and as soon as we had finished administering and took our hands from his head, he received his sight as before. At this I turned to the crowd and I addressed them emphatically and soberly; I called on them to see, and to consider, and recognize the power of God thankfully for his goodness. I said, "Behold the power of God, and who of you can deny it, or doubt it." And all were amazed and did not utter a word of objection. Now, tell this to the nations of the earth,—yes, tell it to the kings and the great men of the 19th century,—yes, let the hireling priests of "this enlightened age" understand, and they will know with certainty that Joseph Smith is a prophet of the most high God, and that God in fact gave to him, and others through him, the holy priesthood, and the lawful right to properly administer the ordinances of His kingdom, and that the power of God is going forth with his servants to the nations of the world, and that he is hastening to bring out the honest in their principles from among the various families of great Babylon to his own church.

"I am, your brother in the everlasting covenant,
"WILLIAM ATHOLL MC. MASTER."

Now, Mr. Rees! Yes, now Editors of Wales; you who are so eager to publish the "Mormon miracles," as you call every bit of lying trash; here are some true things to gild your columns! You, those who insist that God be glorified, publish this to His glory, and acknowledge his faithfulness in fulfilling the promises of his beloved Son to his own, and return to him with a broken heart and a contrite spirit, and your eyes will be opened, and you will understand more of the revelation of his power than this. Yes, you yourselves may be the means, and it will be sweeter to you to be instruments to bless than to falsely accuse your fellowmen, we hope.

TEA PARTY OF THE AMERICAN LADIES FOR THE BENEFIT OF THE MORMONS.

"THE above feast took place in *Carusi's Saloon*, in the city of Washington, U.S., October 28, and an excellent feast it was also. We will have several complimentary comments about it tomorrow. At present we simply report that ladies of all the various denominations throughout the entire city had gathered there, led by the mayor and the clergy, hand in hand. Among the gentle ladies was the venerable Mrs. Madison, wife of the late President Madison, Mrs. Polk, (wife of the current President of the United States), wife of Nobleman M. Comb, and hosts of others of the most influential, most respected, and the finest of the capital city, all energetically united in this generous and praiseworthy work; and when the diligent efforts of these gentle ladies are made known with precision, together with their contributions and their generosity to the Mormons who are outcasts in the western wilderness, wherever there is a heart to feel and a recognition of true charity and generosity, there will their memory of this deed be as cheering as the sunshine of a summer morning."—*New York Herald.*

"We consider the above tea party as one of the most praiseworthy things, and as one of the most hopeful signs for the Saints, that have ever taken place on the continent. The wives of two Presidents of the United States acting so zealously and successfully on behalf of the Saints, despite being subjects of the same government that cruelly exiled them from their country to the woods, totally without cause! These, together with the widow of the late and famous Macomb, who was commander over all the armies of the country, deserve much praise, and their names can be found wherever this gospel is preached. They dared, despite the many obstacles, to come to the field boldly and effectively to show their sympathy for the oppressed, not only in word, but also through their generous contributions to the Saints, sufferers of incomparable persecutions, which are rapidly attracting the attention and sympathy of humanitarians throughout the world. Neither will the influence of this praiseworthy example end with this tea party; but hopeful signs are already seen that it, together with other things, is having an influence on other ladies in the greatest cities of the country; and these sweet streams will flow from every city, and town, and state, we are confident, to satisfy the needs of those people, to whom the birds of the heavens by the thousands offered themselves as sustenance, together with wild animals of the forest, through divine command: when no human arm, or anyone's hand were open to sustain them or save them from starvation. We are very willing to name this deed as *true benevolence*, although the Saints were brought to this state of suffering by inhuman mobs; and although the government should punish them, and restore the Saints to their possessions; yet, through the above act, these ladies show, together with their co-workers, just as Pontius Pilate showed by washing his hands, at the exhortation of his wife, that they have no part or portion in this bloody oppression on the Saints. We are confident that the time is not far when the British ladies will show—her Majesty leading them—their disapproval of these wicked persecutions through acts, which will be like pearls in their crowns. Not without strong foundations have we formed a respectful and high opinion of the generous and benevolent character of her Majesty. When the authorities of our country come to a proper consideration of the growing influence of the thousands of British Saints with their sights set on Oregon, no doubt their defense and their generosities will set a deathly rebuke to the ardent and degenerate persecutions that flow now and again from the pens of the prejudiced authors, and the hireling priests."—*Millennial Star.*

EXCERPT OF THE LETTER OF APOSTLE O. HYDE TO O. SPENCER.

"*Hyde Park, Council Bluffs, Nation*
"*Pottawattomie,* Oct. 7, 1847.

"Dear Brother Spencer,—My family and I are enjoying excellent health. There is hardly anyone sick in the camp at present, neither throughout practically all our numerous settlements. Our crops are more fruitful than ever. There has been no frost until now; and our Indian corn, and our *Buckwheat*, will ripen before it comes according to the signs. We have a great abundance of a variety of vegetables. Our herds and our animals are all fat; and peace and unity reign without exception in our midst within and without. Thanks be to God who giveth us the victory through our Lord Jesus Christ.

"We are daily expecting the return of President Brigham Young, &c. They have established their location in the vicinity of the Salt Lake, and Utah Lake, on the east side. At least that is what I have heard. But, when they return here, you shall have the account officially and fully; and also concerning emigration. I do not feel authorized to direct till I see them.

"I think sometimes that the council will send me back to Britain, but these are my thoughts; perhaps another will come, or you will remain.

"The 'Mormon battalion' is returning from California. A few have arrived, and the rest are on their way.

"May the powerful hand of the Almighty keep you and all the churches in Britain for good, is the prayer of your brother in the New Covenant,

O. Hyde." *(Millennial Star).*

Now, you dear Saints throughout Wales, here is the news that you have waited long to hear! Behold the place, yes, the refuge for deliverance has been found, the one which from now on will be the centerpoint for all the children of Zion from every nation, tongue, and people, to gather to—who is ready to get under way? Not who is desirous is the question, rather who are those blessed ones who have been so just and paid their debts to the world? Who has been faithful in warning everyone they could; yes, who is innocent of everyone's blood? Those who can expect payment of the reward. Let us awake, and let us prepare ourselves with haste.

"DWELLING PLACE OF THE MORMONS."

"YESTERDAY we had the advantage of chatting with a person who had come directly from *Council Bluffs*, who informed us of the arrival there, on the day he left, of a messenger who had been sent before the *Mormon twelve*, who were on their return journey from the *Salt Lake*. They had sent a small group before them to the *Bluff* twenty days earlier, for the purpose of arranging for carriages and provisions to meet them, since they had left everything they could by the Salt Lake. Our informant tells us that the Mormons have marked their primary gathering place half way between the *Salt Lake* and *Lake Eutah*, in California, on the banks of the river that connects the above waters. The distance between the lakes is about 60 miles—an exceptionally fruitful and lovely valley stretching the entire length. There they have laid the foundations of a city, and they have already begun to build it. They are in the middle of the Indian tribes, namely the *Blackfeet*, *Utahs* and the *Crows*, who are peaceful and very favorable to the settlement of the Mormons in their midst. The lead Mormon company which started from the Bluffs arrived in June as far as the *Green River*, over 200 miles beyond the *South Pass*, through the *Rocky Mountains*, by the end of July. They traveled toward there freely and without obstruction, and they drove forward quickly toward their new dwelling place."—*St. Louis Republican.*

The remarkable love of the uncivilized Indians, especially the above tribes, toward the Saints, fulfills the prophecy that says, "The jealousy of Ephraim [namely these Indians] will depart," when the "fulness of the gospel" [namely the Book of Mormon] is brought into their midst. The *Blackfeet* are called the "Arabs of America," because of their cruelty to everyone, but now the Saints consider them as well as the others, not as slaves, rather as brothers, yes, as heirs of the covenants and the endowments.

GLAMORGAN CONFERENCE.

THIS Conference was held in Merthyr, Sunday and Monday, the 26th and 27th of December. The morning of the first day the Hall was overflowing with listeners, many having come from the different Counties of the South and North to the Conference. Capt. Jones was chosen as President; W. Davies from Rhymni, and E. Edwards, Merthyr, as Scribes. After the meeting was begun in the usual manner by the President, he set out the business of the Conference, and after a warm greeting on several matters pertaining to the different areas of the church, he called on the Presidents of the different branches to represent them, which was done as follows:—

Number of Branch.	President.	Num. Eld.	Pr.	Tea.	Dea.	Bap. since July.	Total.
1.	Merthyr, W. Phillips	13	20	16	3	110	606
2.	Penydarren, T. Griffiths.	3	3	2	1	4	53
3.	Dowlais, Alfred Clark.	4	10	7	2	36	145
4.	Rhymni, William Davies.	4	6	4	1	2	58
5.	Cwmbach, John Price.	1	1	2	1	8	33

Number of Branch.	President.	Num. Eld.	Pr.	Tea.	Dea.	Bap. since July.	Total.
6.	Aberdare, J. Davies.	3	1	1	1	4	30
7.	Hirwaun, Daniel Davies.	1	"	1	"	9	22
8.	Dihewyd, J. Richards.	1	2	1	"	2	13
9.	Cardiff, W. Jenkins.	1	2	2	1	18	38
10.	Llwyni, Samuel Davies	3	4	1	1	14	28
11.	Cwmbychan and Bryn, T. Pugh	1	5	4	1	50	63
12.	Treboeth, J. Matthews.	2	1	"	"	1	21
13.	Cyfyng, Wm. Davies	1	5	1	1	3	17
14.	Cwmaman, J. Griffiths.	2	1	"	"	2	12
15.	Pont Yates, H. Williams	2	2	"	"	33	39
16.	Llanelli, Wm Hughes	2	10	4	1	62	103
17.	Carmarthen, Ben. Jones	1	4	2	"	5	37
18.	Llanybydder, T. Jeremy.	2	1	2	1	11	29
19.	Brechfa, David Jeremy.	"	1	1	"	22	30
Conf.	Monmouthshire, W. Phillips.	11	20	14	6	96	262
Ditto	Pembrokeshire, J. Morris.	1	5	2	"	11	40
Throughout the North		9	22	5	5	19	109
"	Garway, W. Henshaw.	6	7	"	"	20	145
Number represented		74	133	72	26	542	1933
Number in the last conference, namely July 13.		45	79	50	20	142	1157
Increase in the last five-and-a-half months.		29	54	22	6	400	776

All the Representatives testified together that all the Saints are without exception in unity, brotherly love, zealous and faithful: and that not only have we increased *seven hundred and seventy six, in the last five months*, but that they are increasing in gifts, good deeds, and in all godliness excellently, and they have better hopes for success in the gospel in the future than ever. There was not from among the lot one accusation against anyone, nor one unpleasant matter to bring before the conference from anywhere. Thanks be to God for such unity and faithfulness. Among who else is such to be had in our country, or in the world, in this tumultuous time? The following places were established as branches of the conference, and the following pesons to preside over them:—Bryn, Thomas Pugh; Cyfyng, William Davies; Cwmaman, John Griffiths; Pont Yates, Howell Williams; Brechfa, David Jeremy. Several were called to the different offices of the priesthood, especially in the distant branches.

President Orson Spencer, recently from America, visited the Conference, and taught in the different meetings through the two days many heavenly principles, interesting counsels with respect to the different duties of the different quorums throughout the church, especially about the necessity of obeying the priesthood; that through so doing the greatest influence of the Spirit of God is to be had to strengthen us and comfort us on our journey, and that in this manner will we be able to benefit our fellow nation the most. He elaborated skillfully and gloriously on the gathering together in Zion as a refuge from the things that come on the ungodly, and to have the more abundant privileges of the kingdom of God. He persuaded the Saints to reflect again on that, since there is nearly a daily expectation for more detailed information about it, together with the manner and the itinerary, together with the best time to emigrate. He proved clearly the superiority of a gospel that brings godly revelations to its subjects over the form of religion that has not its power, and many other beneficial and goodly principles were explained by President Spencer, for which the size of our little *Prophet* will not allow space at present.

President Jones gave a detailed accounting of the sum of money received to assist the Saints who are outcasts in the American wilderness, and the way it was sent to them, and he said that there was a notice in the *Millennial Star*, together with and through letters in his possession, that every penny had been presented for those righteous and worthy purposes. He showed that he had published 22 volumes of various sizes and contents, containing 850,000 pages in all, 12-fold, and that over a hundred pounds of the money owed for them is now owed to him from the various branches, and he and President Spencer earnestly exhorted all the Saints to be faithful in distributing the publications and paying for them. Over £22 were collected in one meeting to fulfill our commitment to the Saints that are in the wilderness, and that made up the required sum.

We must leave out the eloquent and beneficial lectures of Elders A. Evans, Thomas Pugh, Robert Evans, &c., &c, for lack of space, despite how sweet they are. During the conference more principles were taught, and also more glorious than ever before; and judging from the attentive listening of all the crowds throughout the long and overflowing meetings, joy and a desire for divine wisdom concerning the things of God were perceived, cheerfully smiling on every face until the end of the conference. It is unquestionable that the Spirit of the God whose work this is rested on his children there in abundance, and that they went away saying they were glad to have been there.

May the beneficial impressions made by all the work of this lovely conference bear fruit after many days, and give birth to their proper fruits, namely eternal life to the Saints, and glory to God, is the prayer of your servants in the eternal gospel,

WILLIAM DAVIES,
EDWARD EDWARDS. } *Scribes.*

THE WELSH PLEDGE TO THE AMERICAN SAINTS.

IT is with great pleasure that we inform the Saints throughout Wales, that the aforementioned pledge to aid our exiled brothers and sisters who are in the western desert, was fulfilled in the last conference here. We cannot find words to express our gratitude for their generosity, their compassion, and their love for the afflicted children of Zion. Great will be the gratitude of the sufferers when they enjoy the comforts that you have provided for them—great will be your reward no doubt in the kingdom of God, when the King says—"Inasmuch as ye have done it unto one of the least of these my brethren, ye have done it unto me."

All the gifts were sent with President Spencer, and the public acknowledgement of that will be seen in the *Millennial Star*. He will send them to the camp the first opportunity, and no doubt prompt acknowledgement of that will be had from President Young, so that all will see that the law of justice presides in all the spheres of the Saints. Again, we express our thanks for our dear brethren, to the Welsh Saints, for their great faithfulness; and we earnestly beseech the God of the Saints to bless them an hundredfold for that.

PETER THE BARD IS A MORMON !

UNKNOWN compatriot—I call you "unknown" although I am aware of your name as a man, and I am aware of the character you have as a professor and defender of the unchanging order of the Son of God for the salvation of mankind, namely that of deceiver, false prophet, and one of the toads of the bottomless pit, &c. I am confident that you will not mind my being so bold as to greet you in these few lines. I am a constant reader of your small monthly publication called *Prophet of the Jubilee*, or *Star of the Saints*.

I supposed that I had arrived at the best religion in the world, until I began to listen to, and converse with some of your brethren, together with reading your sundry publications. But now I am without a religion. The Bible has been taken completely from me, the only standard I thought I had that would shatter all the strongholds of the other Sectarians into small pieces. But to my great surprise, I have come to see my mistake, and also to discover by reading your publication and others of the Sectarians, that some of the founders of the Sectarians, such as John Wesley, and others, were of the same opinion as that held by the old sect of the Nazarenes, about the Church of God, its gifts, and its officials, which was and is everywhere spoken against. Therefore, I suppose that to present information of that to their old brethren, who love their principles, would tend to diminish their prejudice, rather than to increase it; thus I was inclined to put at your service another testimony, later than that of John Wesley for the kingdom of Christ with respect to its gifts and officials, namely that of Peter Jones, of Liverpool (Peter the Bard), in his poem on the unity of the body of the church, which was well received by everyone, especially the Bards who sang his praise.

"You eagerly pierce through him;
Everything inside him is honey."

A part of this is as follows:—

"God has a holy, fair Church;
Yes, a true and exquisite Church
In the world (not one without a yoke)

P.S. Honey of the Muse is the name of the book, and until now, I have not heard that anyone has complained of tasting any bitterness by devouring the Honey.

With visible members.
The body of Christ through belief and baptism;
Brethren, confessors of one faith.
A favorite work of an effective call
Will bring them to a worthy right.
One Holy Spirit, comforter,
Is among the Saints to unite them.
He gave them several offices,
For their benefit truly to improve them.
One of privilege beneath his honor,
And another that exceeds it.
Some have more public work,
And some lesser in station.
Gifts, offices are to them,
Of benefit, of different kinds:
But of one body despite a hundred gifts,
Of wondrous men, they will be.
One Christ in every sadness,
One prosperous Lord still,
From an excellent river they drink,
One Spirit will they all receive.
There are strong, gifted men,
And shining saints in the Church of the LORD.
Worthy pillars, Apostles,
In height, and their joyful radiance;
Prophets and their earnest tune,
Of fine sort, and Teachers;
Healthful countenance, gift of healing,
And talkative tongues;
Governors, brave men;
No Elders were found wanting.
They are servants duly promoted
In the house by the Father.
Not all are of staunch purposes,
Excellent and renowned men.
All have their work, but not every man,
Who is a worker is a preacher,
Perhaps the one is not a president,
Nor the other an elder;
Nevertheless, they are all parts,
Beloved members are they,
Of the body of Christ who grieved over them
From pain and treachery on the hill."

I do not doubt that it will be a pleasure for many of the Saints to see these lines in the *Prophet*, and for many others also who have not yet joined with you; but whatever of that, here they are at your service to do with them according to your wisdom. Much success to you and all the faithful Saints in Christ Jesus.

I am, your well-wisher,

Harlech, *October* 26, 1847. WILLIAM PUGH.

No doubt it will be sweet to the lips of the Saints to suck the honey of Peter the Bard through the *Prophet*, although it flowed through the pipes of our Calvinistic friends: for like the industrious bee the Saints suck honey from all substance, yes, even from the rock at times; truth is their honey, come from where it may. Nevertheless, that of Peter the Bard tastes more delicious because of the personal acquaintance we have had with him for so long; and who of his Calvinistic brethren will say that his honey is growing bitter in the hive of Mormonism? Who of the readers of the bard will not see that Mormonism was his muse? Who can prove that the true muse, if given her freedom, is ever otherwise?

We are not surprised that a man of the experience, sense, and understanding of our correspondent perceives consistency, and is sufficiently human and free to acknowledge his love for truths which are so self-evident as those of Mormonism; but, the greatest wonder is that anyone, especially of his old brethren, who all claim to be the frontrunners in striving for the truth, fails to perceive, or delays in embracing a plan that is so full of blessed truths as that of the Latter-day Saints.—Ed.

ANNOUNCEMENT.

THOMAS Harries has been excommunicated from the church of the Saints, by consent of the Glamorgan Conference Committee, which was held Jan. 11th, in Merthyr.

A *policeman* near Aberaeron arrested Thomas Harries, when he was standing before a large crowd to preach, on the accusation of stealing a Welsh and English Dictionary; and then he was imprisoned. Jan. the 4th, he was sentenced to suffer two months of prison, without hard labor. The disciplinary rules of the Saints excommunicate from their association all transgressors of the laws of the land, in the emphatic words that follow:—"He who steals shall be excommunicated, and he shall be delivered up to the law of the land."

Many testimonies were brought forward at the trial to prove the excellent character of the prisoner, until the time that the Judge told the *jury*, that he did not acknowledge the transgression as stealing unless it was deliberate. He enlarged greatly on the excellent character of the prisoner; and when, after long waiting and contending, while several other trials continued, the *jury* said that he was guilty, the Judge asked again whether they were sure they were all of that opinion? The unexpected verdict caused considerable surprise and sympathy throughout the place.

We do not say the verdict was unjust, according to what the *jury* knew; yet, after carefully examining all the considerations of the matter, we believe that it was an error. It would have been easy for him to put the book in his pocket by mistake instead of his Bible, when the two were on the table to end an argument his opposers had brought before him; and just as easy was it for some blackguard to put the book in his pocket without his knowing it. The fact proven at the trial that T. H. did not know the book was in his pocket until he arrived at a house about three miles from there, and his admitted surprise at taking a dictionary out of his pocket thinking he was pulling out his Bible, together with the fact that he announced at the time that it was not his, and that he paid a woman to return it to its owner at the time—all this, and much else that could be said, teaches us to believe that he did not take the book intentionally. It is said that he denied having the book, and it is true that he denied that he *stole* it; yet, he did not deny it, rather he admitted that the book was in his possession. Not at the request of the owner did the *policeman* go after him, for he had not said that the thing was deliberate; rather it was some professed persecutor of the doctrine that Harries preached, by the name of Morgans, who came to the house soon after Harries had gone away, and who asked to see the dictionary, and before they had hardly searched for it—"Oh!" said he, "you can be sure that it was the Saint who stole it, &c." This Morgans went out to fetch the *policeman* at once, and after he had returned with him, and questioned the owner at length, he had some hint of admission that the book was lost, and that likely it had been stolen. At this the *policeman* rushed out, even though the entire family begged him not to arrest Harries, for they expected that he would surely bring the book back. But, it was all in vain: the *policeman* went after Harries, and took him to prison in the most public way. It had been only a short time since that *policeman* had been restored to his office, from which he had been deprived for something; and this was his first prey of this kind, to prove his faithfulness to the government, and to win fame. Why in the world did that Morgans come in immediately to inquire after the book? Who cannot see that Harries had behaved through it all, exactly like a man would do who found the book in his pocket unexpectedly? for it does not appear that the behavior of the man who was mentioned, nor the *policeman*, is very much like men whose only *business* was to find out the truth, and to punish the guilty fairly and without tricks. Every praise is due the chief magistrate for his attempt in every possible way to get the prisoner free from the condemnation of *intent* in the act; but that is what a visiting preacher can expect when men prejudiced against his religion sit in judgment on him.

Let it be understood that Thomas Harries is not being excommunicated for intentional theft; but because of his neglect for the honor of his religion under these dangerous circumstances, which were known to him. He should have turned back the minute he realized that another man's property was in his possession, and not allow his enemies to have the chance to accuse him of theft, while he had left the book in the hands of that woman to return it. He has fallen into great difficulty, despite through whom or in what manner it came about; and it is obvious that he has demonstrated considerable carelessness for the honor of the ministry that was entrusted to him through the circumstance. Let each of us take a lesson from this sad tale, to be watchful over our pockets and our characters, every step of our journey through this perverse generation. There are no doubt hundreds of things more similar to intentional theft than the above that have been allowed to go unnoticed in our country, yet the Saints should not think they will receive the same kind of mercy that others receive. This is the first transgression proved in any way against any of the Saints, since we have been in the country, and we hope that this is the last. There is much watching of our footsteps to trip us up, so that no one of the Saints can die without someone striving to try to prove that something in the religion caused the death. A *post mortem examination* was held for a man here lately, who had suffered from a *liver complaint* for two years. The Saints, in obedience to the scriptural commandment (see James v, 14) had been administering the holy ordinance of anointing with oil and praying for him; and the enmity of some is so great toward the religion of Christ, that they tried to prove its followers were murderers; yes, on the profession of their obedience to it; thus it was here, and we are grateful to the doctors for recognizing that it was not the holy ordinance that caused his death; would not this slanderous people accuse the Son of God himself of murder for administering such ordinances? Lately the Editor of the *Carmarthen Journal* dared to publish about one old man who died that he was a "*victim* of the *wicked faith;*" that is, for obeying the commandments of Jesus Christ faithfully. Lately also a sister near Brechfa died of smallpox, testifying on her death bed of her peace with God, and her desire to go to her heavenly Father, and her thankfulness for having the true religion, &c. It was spread through the country on the wings of the breeze that she was repenting for having obeyed the doctrine of the Saints, and that she was leaving them, &c., completely contrary to the truth and to the statement of her mother. Here also, some showed such enmity to the religion of Christ as to say that the holy ordinance was the cause of her death. A most nosey *policeman* came forward, and tried his best to sound important, by asserting that the oil was poisonous, but he failed completely this time; what will they not do next? Dear Saints, be watchful.

CONTENTS.

MERTHYR TYDFIL:
PUBLISHED AND FOR SALE BY D. JONES, AND ALSO FOR SALE BY THE SAINTS IN GENERAL.

JOHN JONES, PRINTER, RHYDYBONT.

PROPHET OF THE JUBILEE,

OR

STAR OF THE SAINTS.

No. 20.] FEBRUARY, 1848 [Price 2*c*.

REFLECTIONS ON THE YEAR GONE BY.

The year one thousand eight hundred and forty-seven is now numbered with those that have passed. Its hopes, its fears, its pleasures, and its sadness are over, yes, over forever! The unfailing chronicler who records temporal things for eternity has placed in the heavenly record vaults for safe keeping for the day of judgment, one more volume of the history of the yearly deeds of every owner of reason, good and bad. There they will stay in unchanging colors recorded on imperishable materials, so that not one sentence nor one iota of the factual register can be taken away or changed. Oppression, wars, and the injustice of nations toward each other—pride, prodigality, and the violence of kings, princes, and rulers—hypocrisy, deceit, and misanthropy of those who claim the title of *Reverends*, and who profess to be the leaders of the people, the sins of all peoples, and especially the *lies* of the religious zealots, who have concocted, who have declared, and who have published concerning the poor Saints, they are all printed on unchangeable chronicles, waiting to be read again in their faces, to be heard by the countless myriads, in the day of visitation. Oh what a sober thought! Yet, entirely factual! Where, at that time, will the ungodly hide? What giant rocks, at their call, will spring on the liars and the persecutors to hide them from facing the truth? Doubtless they would consider the mines of the world as but little to give for changing one sentence, or blotting out one word! Yet, they have no hope for that.

While their oppressors sleep, the groans of the bondsmen under their burdens, who starve while the former feast—the sighs of the troubled and the afflictions of the needy, the widow, and the orphans, have ascended to the ears of the Lord of Sabaoth, and testify against ungodliness in places on high, when there are also tears, and blood, and fatigue of the Saints, who have suffered because of the testimony of Jesus—their wondrous mission, shouting together in one loud *chorus*, "When wilt thou avenge us, Lord of justice, &c.?" On the other side, patience, virtues, works, meekness, brotherly love, charity, zeal, diligence, and the faith of the Saints of the Most High, have been recorded also, and they will continue in remembrance until that blessed day comes when it will be said to them, "Come ye blessed children of my father, &c."

Happy indeed is the man who can say upon reading his own history for the year, that all is as he wishes. Who (even among those who wish to do good) can read his history for the year 1847, line after line, and the one sentence after the other, without wishing to change many of them, if he could? But that cannot be done—what is past is past forever, and, "that which is written is written."

All this teaches us one particular and useful lesson; that is, let us take care that our history in 1848, is such that we will be glad to read it in the day to come, and likewise the history of every year that will be granted us until the word "end."

The year 1847 was notable in its connection with the history of the Saints in Wales. The missionaries of the Most High have been zealous in fearlessly raising their voices and repeatedly declaring their message of peace within the hearing of thousands through the various counties of our country; and despite the shackles being removed that were on our brothers of the same blood—despite how frequent the false accusations that were declared and published about the children of God and their mission—and despite the wrath of the prince of darkness and his children, hundreds of the honest in heart have embraced the truth as it is in Jesus—have come to see the great light, and we have more reasons to be grateful to him who owns this work, because of his increasing readiness to seal such a blessing on the message—for confirming the word with such a host of divine witnesses, of wondrous signs, and of continuing circumstances of his own power. Also, we thank him for the health and the temporal blessings which he so abundantly imparts to us, together with the unity, the remarkable love, and the additional hopes which are in the possession of all his children throughout the land. Certainly the Saints have never been here in such a flourishing, loving, and successful condition as they are at present; yes, we can hardly bring to mind even one single exception. We give thanks for this. But, at the same time, despite how much has been done, who of the Saints—who of the officers, could not convince some other sinner? Who is that happy person in our midst to whose conscience the Spirit of truth testifies, "All thou couldst have done, thou hast done?" Hosts, yes, entire areas through our little country, have not yet heard our message, and the preciousness of their immortal souls, and the glory of our God, calls loudly for those who have accepted the divine treasure to strive more and more in the coming year than ever before, as the troubled days are approaching, in which the good seed cannot be sown here. Inasmuch as this small vineyard has been entrusted to us, we shall strive to properly use our talents, and thus we, and those who believe our testimony, shall have a swifter and more abundant entrance into the eternal resting place of the faithful.

However, it was not only in Wales that the year 1847 was noteworthy with respect to the success of the gospel; but even on the American continent. Despite the cruelty of the one part, thousands of the other part of those inhabitants have obeyed the gospel, and hosts have taken up their tents like Abraham of old at the call of God to leave Babylon lest they receive her plagues, rather choosing as did Moses of old the hideous wilderness with the people of God, than to dwell in the tents of cruel persecutors. And there is more call for preaching, greater hearings, and higher hopes throughout the States now than ever before.

Happening on that continent is one of the most remarkable events not only of the year, but of the age; yes, the latter ages, namely the exile of thousands of the Saints of the Almighty to the western forest. Happening there are miracles of their God as in days of old, extending his generous hand to feed hundreds of them with the birds of the sky, and with the wild animals of the forest, together with his strong arm keeping them from all their enemies, despite their numbers—to climb over every obstacle, though they lift their heads as high as the cloudy cap of the Rocky Mountains. He tamed the anger of the wild beasts, and even the incomparable rage of the "*Blackfeet*" (the Arabs of the forest) for their sakes; and he caused the savages to treat them with brotherly love, yes, he led them by the right hand until by the thousands before now they reached their chosen homeland; and there he feeds them with his goodness, as a shepherd feeds his flock. May their God multiply them and prosper them!

Several thousand inhabitants of the isles of the South Pacific became subjects of the kingdom of God also last year, and they are gathering in large numbers to greet their brethren of every color in Zion.

Great was the stir among the camps of the enemy throughout Britain, and thousands, or nearly that many, have *enlisted* under the banners of Zion during the past year, which diminished the sects of the age, although several of them decreased by 5000 last year! In short, the increase in number of the Saints throughout the world last year was no less remarkable than was their growth in godliness and good works; and the one and the other were no more remarkable than the false accusations, the persecution, and the enmity which false religionists cause to keep step with our progress. We thank our God for the well-known victories we won in the year 1847; and we trust in the same strong arm for more in the coming year. No doubt "a short work will the Lord make upon the earth" through us, if we take courage for his sake. May the mighty God, who gave us success with his work in 1847, lead us with his spirit, and give us more success in the coming year to gather his wheat into his garner. Amen.

PROOFS OF THE NEED FOR THE "GIFT OF HEALING" IN THE CHURCH OF THE BAPTISTS.

SINCE the establishment of the Baptist mission in China until the present time, 26 of the female missionaries have died; the average missionary time was only four years and four months. Of the men 13 have died; the average length of their missionary warfare was seven years and six months. Twenty-six of the missionaries were obliged to leave their field of labor to search for health in some other climes; their average time in the field was five years and four months.

This is quite different from the average age of those missionaries Jesus Christ sent in his day; and it proves the preciousness of his promise to them, "Behold I am with you alway even until the end of the world." When some of them were sick, they would call for the elders of the church to anoint them with oil in the name of their Master, and the prayer of faith would save the sick, unless their period of warfare had been completed. They believed the promise of their Master in their behalf, namely "they shall lay hands on the sick, and they shall recover," rather than fleeing to another country, and leaving their flock open to wolves. Who can read the foregoing failure? who can contribute so much money to send them so far, and keep them there at such cost? who says that the salvation of the souls of the pagans depends on hearing and believing their mission? yes, we ask who in their senses can think that the above missions have been sent by God, and think at the same time that the "*gift of healing*," by the laying on of hands, anointing with oil, &c., (James v, 14), is not absolutely essential? Yet, we ask, who says "that those gifts were only for the establishment of the gospel, and that they are not needed now?" Let the sufferings of the aforementioned sufferers, poor things, say whether there is need for the "gifts of healing" in the church of God, yes, among the *missionaries* in this age. Let all the thousands of pounds that are taken from the destitute and widows, and the poor, and the Sunday school children of Wales, year after year, to pay the expenses of the aforementioned sick from every corner of the world, and from one climate to the other atmosphere in search of health;—let all this testify to the truth, and then the worth of the "gift of healing" will be told, or if the need for it continues to be denied in the face of these clear facts, let the collection of money as a *substitute* for it cease for shame. And yet, if the need for the gift of healing is admitted, its deniers will foresee that they will be asked according to the same logic, why are all the gifts Christ promised to the church not needed? And then the Baptists will foresee that that would be the same as admitting the fact, namely that their church is destitute of the gifts, and admitting that it is not the church of Christ, rather the church of Simon Menno, that is their church! And if so, all the collections, and consequently thousands of their *livings* would be ended. Ouch! to be spared such a fate!

The wretchedness we saw our compatriots suffering in foreign countries, and our personal acquaintance with the missionary stations in various distant countries, cause in us compassion for their sufferers, but yet our reason together with the scriptures, and these and other facts, prove to us that the latter should not go there on such errands until God sends them, which if they did this, doubtless he would send the "gift of healings," and the other gifts with them. Surprising the suffering that zeal without knowledge causes! Also, if the spiritual gifts were given to establish Christianity, it is surprising that the same God would not give them now to establish the same Christianity (if in fact it is the same) among the pagans; or it is surprising, if God sent these missionaries to establish it! Doubtless if a servant of God went to these sick ones, and offered to them the ordinance of the laying on of hands, they would excommunicate him as a DECEIVER because of it!

A PEEK AT THE SLUGGER, AND THE DOWLAIS SHOPKEEPER.

(A scene from real life behind the curtain !)

HENGIST and Horsa were no more fervent on the day of the "treachery of the long knives," than the above Reverends appeared according to their ability in the following scene; and through this little mirror it is easy to see who is the pivot, branch, and root, and whose are the delicious fruits that fill the most beautiful branches of Jerusalem!

One beautiful, summery day recently, when the *Slugger of Independia* was sadly making his way along between the agonies of colic and headache, because of cursing the Saints so much on previous evenings, he came within some hundred yards of *near the bridge*, and a certain "Reverend" Shopkeeper, red and corpulent, was seen striding toward him as fast as "*Tobit*" once crawled after the bird that took out one of his eyes when he lay drunk on the road; but what shaking of hands! Oh! such joyful eyes! They hardly went a hundred yards in the same direction, as all birds of a feather flock together, before it was understood that they were some of the Daviesite carrion crows, not only by name, but also through a shared taste for carcasses.

Shopkeeper.—"Well, dear partner, how goes the business of persecuting the old Satanists these days?"

Slugger.—"Indeed I do not really know how it goes, but quite badly in some ways; to tell you the truth, I am almost losing heart, for they are increasing the more they are opposed, despite the fact that we are all shouting at the tops of our voices that they are dying out."

Shopkeeper.—[Halting rashly and alarmingly on the road, shouted] "What! losing heart did you say! Oh! no, one dare not lose heart or grow weary; on with it, follow them to every service, tell everyone to shout Satanists after them on the streets, and they will be sure to tire before long. The Satanists are preaching on the street tonight, near Caersalem; yes, they are blowing their old ram horns at our walls. Go there, and disturb their meeting, and I will send some of my noisy boys there, to *cheer* you, whatever you say. We must, Oh we must devote ourselves to persecuting them, otherwise they will reveal the feet of our great Goddess, and the hope of your profit too will fade like ours, and all of Dowlais will follow them. And also, listen brother [and looking about him he put his head near his ear], that is an excellent way for you to win fame, and who knows but you may win one of the fine temples of our Goddess if you are faithful for an instant. You see that every child who persecutes these Satanists wins respect through the publications, and soon earns a *living*. That is how I would have climbed up to a pulpit anywhere, but I can operate more successfully from behind the *screen*, you know, and have the occasional lecture in the chapels, and the publications against them, for in that way they will never be able to answer back."

Slugger.—[Who pricked up his ears, and rejoiced from his head to his heels when he heard about the synagogue and the fame] "Oh! I feel my hatred for the old Satanists being kindled under the weight of your advice, and if only you would promise to write an account of the occasional debate for the publications, with my name victoriously attached, of course I would decide to persecute them with all my might, for you know how to fix them. Yes, that is a *noble plan* in order to climb up; on with it. But what subject, or scripture, is the best to cut them down?"

Shopkeeper.—"Subject! do not try to discuss subjects with them; otherwise they will certainly beat you, and about the scriptures do not say a word, for they will turn them all in their own favor. The best way I found was to shout that miracles had ended—and to tell all sorts of old fables against the people, and I have a sackful about Joe Smith that I could get for nothing. This is the best way, and the only way to oppose them."

Slugger.—"I am of precisely the same opinion as you, brother; and Oh! now I remember [rubbing his scarf], I have a new and very delightful story about them at present."

Shopkeeper.—[Standing up again so as not to miss a word] "Well, what is it? Tell me quickly, for I will not take another step until I hear it."

Slugger.—"No, come on, I am in a hurry, so that I can go to their meeting tonight, and start before they get there; and so I will be sure of a chance to speak. Well, [walking forward slowly], one of the Saints' preachers in Llanelli said—"

Shopkeeper.—[Contradicting him indignantly] "No, do not call them Saints; do you not know that I have named them Satanists, and that I am energetically teaching everyone to call them by that name? a much more appropriate name for them, but go on with the story."

Slugger.—"Very well. Satanists they shall be then. Well, that preacher said that an angel was to come to the service one evening, and he invited everyone to come there to see it. There was great excitement and everyone gathered to the place; and after the appointed time had arrived, with the people waiting eagerly, the angel rushed into their midst from some other room, wearing a white robe, and the women screamed, and fled in fright, and the others fainted, and the angel swayed! But, so much the worse for him, some of the wise lads of Llanelli had come there, expecting that there would be some tricks there, and they grabbed the angel, and dragged him out, and began to kick him, and the angel began to cry out, and beg for his life! But they gave the big Satan a good thrashing for calling himself an angel, and then they left him. And the few weak-headed fools who believed them have left them because of it."

Shopkeeper.—[His stomach heaving like a bellows from laughing] "Very good, that is a splendid story; send it on."

Slugger.—"But it is rather too plain for anyone to believe it like that; would it not be better to alter it a little; and I cannot on my conscience verify it."

Shopkeeper.—"What! believe it indeed! they will easily believe it from your lips. Do you not know that the title reverend at the end of the story sanctifies it in the eyes of the people, whatever it may be. Say that some minister from there wrote it to you as true. What does it matter if it is lies, if it serves a good purpose. All weapons are legitimate in war. Oh yes, I know that that is true enough, for it is very like the Satanists' tricks. I have heard it before, and have written it down, and am going to publish it as true through every publication that accepts it, and those who doubted it before will believe it from there, you know. That is what I did before. Did you not read the stories of those women from Penydarren, and the account of their meetings, in the *Baptist*, and the tale of the man who broke his leg, and many other things, which would do great harm to our craft if the people found out the truth about them; and one must color a little at least, in order to prevent the people from going headlong to hell. Although many strange things have taken place in their midst, yet I will not believe even if they were to perform the greatest miracle ever. I have decided to persecute them to my utmost ability as long as I live; for I have done too much already to give up now."

Slugger.—"Certainly I feel my old zeal rekindled by your advice, but I must go this way now; I shall see you again tonight." And after shaking hands *exit* the *Shopkeeper* laughing up his sleeve at the fun he would have at the expense of his "*cat's paw.*" And the Slugger for his part strode the other way, chewing his cud and thinking about this new way to fame, and whispering to himself, "*Synagogue,*" "*living,*" *&c.* The next view of the Slugger was at the top of the place where the Saints were due to preach. He had been as good as his word and got there first, and was busy shouting the "story of walking on the water," &c., &c. And the reverend Shopkeeper was in the crowd, smoking a long pipe and laughing every now and again, until the mantle of darkness fell, and hid them from men's eyes from shame!

If you happen to meet the "Shopkeeper"—beware
Of his kicks, he is a traitor;
Out of shame the man presents
His *sledge* to the Slugger's head.

The "Slugger" also sledges,—at anyone
The jail is extremely cold;
It is too clear that a frown meets
The cultivators of all lies.

PRAISE FOR THE REVIEW OF CAPT. JONES

ON

The lectures of the REV. E. ROBERTS, *Rhymni, and his supporters, against Mormonism.*

HE raises his head no more a Captain—joyful
Sovereign—praiseworthy;
Though their tempest was terrible,
A giant of strength, he beat them.

Your brilliant REVIEW—gentle and wise,
It deserves acceptance;
Doubtless it goes to show
Man's power in his Father's hand.

Reigning like a proper lion—a genial
Lamb too for a purpose;
A happy man full of grace,
Steadfast for his kingdom.

You shattered all their castles—vile things,
Without making mischief;
You revealed and pulled down
In dreadful shame their odiousness.

They scratch true professors of faith—awful and fierce,
They may not dwell in peace.
Doubtless, if shown in daylight,
They will see their naked shame.

Mr. Roberts, in the *Apostolic Witness*, says that it is too much of a compliment to the devil to interfere much with the Saints, in the form of writing or lecturing. And I say,—

The deadly enemy will not tangle—with the Saints,
If our *Witness* is prospering;
Roberts, it is well known;
In his deceit is worse than a d——l.

No man is found to hear him—who is
In his right mind and senses;
To men with buttermilk brains,
Very dull, he is quite a man.

The reverend men vomit—in vain,
Poisonous slime;
For profit the devilish ones
Incomparable, bear their grudge.

An impartial consideration of the disgraceful behavior of some of the preachers of the age (especially the Baptists) towards the Latter-day Saints, compelled me to compose the above, and to offer it for your public use, and I hope it will be convincing to many of the devotees of the said persecutors, so that they are not misled by their fabricated tales. What but Satan is stirring them up so that they do not leave their innocent and conscientious neighbors in peace to worship God as they please? Yet, I have not heard that one of the pious and respectable attackers has offered to disprove any of the Saints' principles; they only revile them, tell the unfounded stories of their professed enemies about the characters of people who are dead, and others who are thousands of miles away from us;—revile them as *Satanists*, *deceivers*, *false prophets*, *witches*, *&c.*, *&c*. Whether the free reviler or the willing liar is worse, is a difficult question to decide, because they are two brothers with the same father; the age of the one is six, and the other's is half-a-dozen. No doubt he whose tongue is unclean enough to revile his fellowman, out of malice against his religion, is also black-hearted enough to form lies, and deliver them as truth even from a pulpit, to seek vengeance on him that way too! Poor even in their own minds are the false religions of those who have no better way than this to defend them, and to keep their devotees under their paws. But you innocent flock of Jesus, fear not the gnashing of the teeth of all the wolves, nor the blasphemies of all the priests of Babel the great, for the heavens rejoice at your incomparable courage, and smile upon you, multiplying you more and more; and no doubt hundreds, if not thousands, like myself, have been convinced that you must be of God, for all the old persecutors who were always at loggerheads with each other, to persecute you as zealously as they do now. There is no doubt about your religion, that it is the powerful actions that the Spirit of God brings you through it, that are disturbing the enemy's kingdom, and alarming his servants against you. Go on, there is long life and happiness before you, and hosts almost without number are beginning to run after you, in the Mormon race for the highest feat.

May it go on with ease—through the ages,
With Jesus as protection;
Were all the strong and wise of faith
Against you, who shall deliver you?

I am your well-wisher,
Rhymni. DANIEL AB IAGO.

LETTER OF J. JAMES, VICTORIA.

DEAR BROTHER JONES,—I am pleased to inform you that our branch is going along successfully, and some are obeying continually the ordinances of the gospel, with evident and successful signs throughout the conference in general of the constant goodness of our God toward us in his work of imparting his several spiritual gifts in our midst. I have one particular and very strange example to tell you about, and think it worthy of being chronicled in the *Prophet*. Last Sabbath night, at the end of our evening service, I went with a newly baptized brother, whose daughter was lying ill. Her age is about 16, and she was totally unaware of our principles; and her mother and the rest of her family is in the same perilous situation until now. The girl referred to was suffering from excruciating pain, with pains shooting through her whole body, so that it was necessary for her to stay in bed. Another brother and I went to the room where she was lying, and through our prayer to, and our faith in, the Savior, she received an immediate release from her pain. There were there six unbelievers as eyewitnesses of the power of God in her healing, and they marvelled at what they saw. Also, yesterday was a remarkable time here; the power of God was made manifest in a very obvious way in the preaching of the gospel by our dear brother John Pugh from Blackwood. He received some unusual assistance in preaching in our meeting at six, and he had the joy of seeing two who had been pricked in their hearts, and seeking part in Salvation; and afterwards they bore witness of the Son of God by giving obedience to the commandment that says, "Repent, and be baptized every one of you." There are yet here many more who have promised to follow them; may the gracious Lord strengthen them, so that Zion will become a joyful mother of children, with hundreds of the race of Gomer among them. Your humble Brother in the Gospel of Christ,

JAMES JAMES.

P. S. Seven were baptized last week, which should be added to the number that brother W. Phillips has.—J. JAMES.

"NIGHTINGALE OF THE GLADE" AND MORMONISM.

MR. EDITOR,—Recently I happened to meet some poet who calls himself "Nightingale of the Glade," and I had the opportunity to explain to him something of the principles that are believed in our midst, which he did not oppose: but I heard that after that, poor thing, as many do, he disregarded godly things, and used his talent to malign and falsely accuse the Saints, as follows, according to what I heard,—

"Latter-day Saints—I understood,
Were completely deceived,
By a poisonous fiendish knave,
Far to the left of the deepest pit."

I wrote the following as an answer to him:—

It is awful to give a verdict—the damning
Condemnation at once;
The main point for the man is to prove the work,
And useless without this is the law.

Oh fair "Nightingale" wait for a moment—watch now,
And take back your verdict;
We challenge the bards and the best in the world
To scrutinize us and overthrow us.

Answer you, not opinion either—it is this,
Has the law changed?
No, and yes, is your language,
Answer—not in supposition.

If the "Nightingale" says yes—next
He will show the true side;
A true one had to be there,
Now it is one that knows no change.

The second Adam is our ruler—he
We claim is a man of God;
Whoever strays from his teaching by just one degree,
The foolish waverer is a godless person.

Our teacher does not turn back—learning
That does not bend its rule,
Our faith is not, foolish wretch,
Of a Being that is changeable.

Note the mistakes—of the author
In the creed of the Saints;
Excellent "Nighingale," if there is falsehood,
Explain with fluent words.

In his life Jesus gave—a promise,
Unfailing to his family;
We hold, the Saints that follow,
Will you change and give in?

Will you admit that which belittles—as deceit,
To blind us, wait,
"From the deepest pit," slow down,
The oppression is too thick.

If there is blasphemy in the disciples—this,
For claiming the signs,
Wholly well of this blasphemy
The apostles will not escape.

We still remain—to walk,
Along the old paths;
In one age is it false,
To another the best lesson?

Llwynygell. DAVID ROBERTS.

LETTER OF ABEDNEGO WILLIAMS, NANTYGLO.

RESPECTED EDITOR,—One of my chief aims in this letter is to inform your readers that I am the one who published the song that is being sung against the Saints of the Almighty through the fairs, the markets and along the streets; that is, the song that was printed in Brynmawr, the one that maligns the dear Saints as "Smithites," &c. Yes, I myself with sincere remorse say that I was so bad as that; and O! if I could delete all that, and undo the harmful influences that it has no doubt caused; yes, if I could but move the obstacles I put in the way of the weak in their search for the truth, it would cause me the happiness my conscience now refuses me. Here I am making one more effort to call that rubbish back, and I earnestly beg some space in your columns for my sad confession so that I shall be free from the consequences of the influence of that song, at least in the sight of your readers. The only excuse I have for having published such a thing is that I was in darkness, and after composing it under the influence of prejudice of the teaching I had from the pulpits, the publications and from the heads of ministers who should have known better. But now, I understand that such is an insufficient excuse here; but O, what about being sufficient before the court of truth in the day that comes! For goodness's sake, forgive me, and allow me through your columns to beg humbly for all the Saints to forgive me. I pray constantly to the God of the Saints whom I persecuted, through Jesus Christ, to forgive me also. The way in which my closed eyes were at last opened, and by which I understood that the people of God in truth are those whom I scorned, was the following: I confessed that I was blind, and I was spiritually drunk, yes, dizzy; while in this state I did this great evil against you, and for this have mercy on me, dear Saints. If a drunk man, especially if he were blind also, were to trample on your feet, I know that you would excuse him if only he were to pull away and ask your forgiveness. In a like manner I also seek your forgiveness. As an occasional word will have a greater impact than others on the drunk man, so my own consideration was attracted to the saying, "Prove all things, hold fast that which is good," together with another saying, "Repent and be baptized every one of you in the name of Jesus Christ for the remission of sins, and ye shall receive the gift of the Holy Ghost." I went to listen to determine whether the Saints promised this priceless gift, or whether they say as do other sects, "that such a thing cannot be had now, that it is not necessary, &c." And to my great surprise I heard from them the gospel of the Son of God, and they promised as did Peter of old, that I myself, the lowest of all, could have forgiveness, and that God would impart the Holy Ghost in his gifts to me on the aforementioned conditions. This was too fair an offer to refuse, and nothing short of obedience could calm my troubled conscience. I was baptized, and through the laying on of hands of the servants of God, thanks be to Him forever, I received the influences of the heavenly Comforter, and of the association of His Holy Spirit. Again, I am thankful for my salvation to the point of getting the chance to come into the kingdom of God. I made terrible scorn in that song because of the testimony of the Saints; but by now I myself testify humbly and soberly, that I have received many supernatural witnesses to prove that the Church of God is the Church of the Latter-day Saints; and since I have this knowledge, I am completely willing to suffer, through the help of my Heavenly Father, all the anger, and to profess in the presence of my compatriots that they might also hear the way to inherit the kingdom of God and its blessings. I suggested also in that song that you make Mormonism a profitable venture by charming money from the charmed; but now I know that that is as completely contrary to the truth as anything I published. I know that I and all of the Saints I know received this glorious plan and its heavenly gifts for free.

O, that I could see hosts of my dear contemporaries come in, so that they could receive and inherit the fulness of the promises of the Son of God, then they would know that He is true and unchangeable, and they would get his Spirit to bear simultaneous witness with their own spirits that they would then be the children of God; and if children, heirs also, that is the heirs of God, and joint heirs with Jesus Christ. I earnestly beg a share in the prayers of the Saints so that the enemy will never entice me to bring shame on this holy name, and so that we all arrive at the crowning achievement in Christ Jesus.

Latter-day Saints—the purpose
In my life, I see,

Is to find my God, the light of the Lord,
The true high God Almighty.

Your humble brother in Christ.

Nantyglo. ABEDNEGO WILLIAMS.

WHO IS READY TO START HOME ?

GENTLE SAINTS,—After a long wait, behold the desired time has come for whoever wishes to begin his way toward the object of his affection. After frequent asking—"When can we go toward Zion," here is a full answer. And who is ready to get underway? Thousands of our brethren before this have through every obstacle arrived at the place which their Father indicated as a place of refuge for them—"until the wrath has subsided." Thousands of others are on their way in the wilderness, and the western states; about three hundred are starting from Liverpool, and a similar number to follow them in March, &c. And the way is open to whoever is ready to follow them as quickly as circumstances permit, in *righteousness and order.* The awaited time has come for the gentle Welsh also to have temporal deliverance from oppression, violence, persecution, famine, and destructive judgments. Who is ready, we ask? The center point of the gathering is the valley of the mountains near the "*Salt Lake*," in *California.* The recommended way is through New Orleans, up the *Mississippi* river, and the *Missouri*, to *Council Bluffs*, and from there overland in wagons, to the end of the journey. Those who do not have sufficient means to carry them further than *Council Bluffs*, will receive houses there built for them by their brethren, and small farms cheaply, prepared by other Saints who have gone ahead; and where everyone will be able to raise plenty of food, &c., very easily to assist them in going further; and thus they will have establishments, namely dwelling places, small farms ready to be worked, mills, and everything necessary at their service. Further on, over, and over, they will have the like until they reach the end of their journey; thus, no one will have to suffer hunger or much of the fatigue compared to what the first *pioneers* suffered. In these generous and beneficial arrangements and preparations are seen the love and the unity that are among the Saints and their brethren throughout the world, their strivings to benefit them, and their care for them temporally, and spiritually. Also seen is the great wisdom that governs all their movements! In time we expect to be able to provide a detailed account of the lovely country where the Saints dwell, together with the cost of going from here to there, &c., &c. But to come closer to home at present, we ask again, who is ready to start? The question is not who wishes to go, for we know that the extent to which the Saints receive the Spirit of God, their eyes will be opened to understand the absolute necessity for them to have this temporal salvation as well as the spiritual. As for anyone who does not perceive this now, let him be patient, and stay where he is; but, if he prays to God for the Holy Ghost, that Spirit will be as certain to draw his heart toward Zion, as his fondest work is to lead to a unity of the faith. As for anyone who does not agree with this emigration now, the time will come when the *signs of the times* will testify to him all too clearly concerning his misunderstanding, that "On Mount Zion" will be his only deliverance. Yet, we say, and we wish everyone to notice, there is no compulsion for anyone in this regard, any more than with respect to any other principle pertaining to the kingdom of God, but complete free agency, and each one can choose his time to go if he wishes; not in haste, but in an orderly way. Yet, we foresee that more wisdom will be necessary to carry out this emigration in an organized and beneficial manner, than with anything else at this time. And upon studying the best, cheapest, easiest, and surest way for the benefit of everyone who goes, we can do nothing less than pray frequently—"O! Thou who didst begin this good work, give an abundant portion of thy Spirit to thy children, in wisdom, love, and humble spirit to guide them in the right way." No doubt some will have a greater test of their faith in this matter than they have ever before had. Let not anyone expect to receive a recommendation from us to go, except on righteous principle. Righteousness, and the respect we have for the name we profess, together with the success of the work here, and the character of the Saints who stayed behind for a while; all this compels us, we say, to inquire as to who is free from worldly debt. For, let everyone understand clearly, that we cannot recommend emigration for anyone while still in worldly debt, except he be able to reach an agreement with his creditors first. And further concerning this, inasmuch as we are going to the place "where righteousness dwells," it cannot be expected for them, neither will they, suffer injustice from anyone throughout the world; we know of some who were sent all the way from Nauvoo, back to England, just to pay their debts to the world, or to leave the church. But to exhort the Saints, we say, In all things, act righteously towards everyone, and pay what you can, and perhaps you have been paying your money for so long previously to philanthropic, just, and generous men, whose hearts the Lord will open at your petition, to forgive you that amount which you cannot pay (if such is the case after every effort and diligence); but let not anyone shame the holy name that he professes by trying to practice unrighteousness. With this still in mind, we ask, *Who is ready to start?*

God expects honesty from his Saints in this also, namely in warning our dear compatriots of the danger of staying in Sodom. Inasmuch as he out of his goodness has imparted the dispensation of the gospel to us, doubtless our nation will request it from our very hands; and let all the Saints know, especially the priesthood, that whoever neglects opportunities to warn his fellowman, and to invite him to shelter in time, is behaving, not only unrighteously, but also unkindly toward such, and his conscience will be pricked, and there will be sorrow in his heart because of that, even after arriving in Zion, and he will have a desire in his soul to return again, perhaps, to complete those of his duties he neglected before starting from here. With this still in mind, we ask, Who of you Saints is ready to start?

No doubt many obstacles, and some very large, or will be considered thus, will be thrown in the way of some as they are about to start; such as, children of some parents who are dragging behind, or parents weeping before their children; their old neighbors as the cruelest opponents, or the most earnest in persuading them to stay. No doubt the thousand old tales invented by the father of lies, and which were proclaimed by his servants, about the emigration, &c., will come to the memory clearly; yes, it is indisputable that the devil and all his children will strive as much, if not more, to keep the Saints from obtaining this deliverance, as they strived to prevent Lot from going out of Sodom, or Noah and his family from going to the ark; and in time let it be remembered by such ones of the Saints that God's call is to them, saying,—"Come out of her (Babylon), my people," &c. And also, let the words of Christ be remembered, "He that loveth father, or mother, or relatives, or houses, or lands, more than me is not worthy of me." Furthermore,—"Through much tribulation shall one enter into the kingdom of God." And also, "He who endures to the end will be saved."

Let the poor pray to God, their Father, to open the hearts of their religious brothers and sisters who are rich to help them to pay their expenses to Zion, and once there they can repay them with interest. That is how the American Saints did—that is how the Saints in England did and are doing—and we hope that the Welsh Saints will not hold back in their readiness and their generosity in this. Although all the Saints, like others, are free to do as they wish with their possessions, with no church compulsion; yet, we do not hesitate to say, that those who do this for the poor and faithful Saints, are deserving of more of the fruit, blessing, and interest, from their money, than they will receive through any other way that we know of; for there, *labor* will be worth more than money. The instruction we received is, serve our nation for one more year, which we are content to do, although it would be much more attractive to go, as soon as possible. And also, we counsel all who can, to prepare themselves for that time, and perhaps we will be allowed the pleasure of their company as we leave this weary captivity!

DISTRIBUTORS, TAKE NOTE!

WE earnestly implore your efforts to spread the *Prophet* again this year; and we hope that no one will be satisfied to let the numbers of subscribers diminish, but rather to increase, as the need for it increases, and as the interesting news increases that of necessity comes through it. We ask for every distributor to question carefully, and often, how many he can sell this year, in case we send too many to any place, to rest on the hands of the distributor when they would be of greater use in some other place. Send, then, at the first opportunity, for whatever number of the *Prophet* that is needed, that is the number they can sell; and it will be expected for them to continue at the same number for the entire volume; otherwise the rest that remains on hand will cause confusion with the volumes.

There is more than the whole subscription for an entire year of the *Prophet* owing us for books, which were received this past year; either from the subscribers, or from the distributors, or perhaps from both! Yes, dear Saints; consider, for there is as much as that in your hands of money that should by rights be assisting to carry out this work faster! We ask you, What, seriously, is this if not binding our hands from publishing? You do not realize, perhaps, while only a little bit for one, and a little bit for another is owing, that that is a lot; while it rests on a small operation like ours to bear up under it all; and also, that pays in advance for everything that is printed! There has never been a publication, we believe, that has been carried forward through so many obstacles as the *Prophet*, and we hope that its distributors will not be guilty of starving it to death, by refusing to pay for it.

Also, since we intend to leave this country for a spell before very long, we call the attention of the whole world as far as we can, Saints and everyone else, to this, namely,—If we are indebted to anyone anywhere, *bring one, and bring all* of them forward to us, and we shall pay them! Pay close attention to this, and let the backbiting enemies who are spreading their blasphemies about us be silenced, and we shall close up their way for this before starting; and we challenge the whole country to prove that we refused to pay one penny that we owed when it was demanded. Let our enemies pattern their behavior according to this honesty before saying a word to anyone else; and let every one of the Saints strive to imitate this, if no other example is worthy. Since we proclaim such a fearless challenge to the world, we are fearless also to exhort our debtors to pay us as soon as at all possible.

ANNOUNCEMENT.

WE have volumes of "Capt. Jones on Mormonism, in 1846," for from 3s. to 4s. 6c. Also, volumes of the Treatises we published in 1847, for from 3s. 6c. to 5s. 6c. Also, the two volumes of the PROPHET bound together, for from 4s to 6s., according to their binding. The distributors can get the foregoing with the PROPHET if they send the money. We also have a variety of English books and the Millennial Star, biweekly, for 3c per issue.

*** *Direct letters, prepaid, to* CAPT. JONES, Wellington Street, Merthyr. *No one can expect a response, if there is no stamp on the letter. We are tired at last of paying postage for everyone!*

CONTENTS.

MERTHYR TYDFIL:

PUBLISHED AND FOR SALE BY D. JONES, AND ALSO FOR SALE BY THE SAINTS IN GENERAL.

JOHN JONES, PRINTER, RHYDYBONT.

PROPHET OF THE JUBILEE,

OR

STAR OF THE SAINTS.

No. 21.] MARCH, 1848 [PRICE 2*c*.

PROPHECY OF SAINT THOMAS, THE MARTYR.

TO CAPT. D. JONES

SIR,—Would you be so good as to provide space for the following in your correct and useful *Prophet*. My reason for sending it is because I, after questioning many men who professed to have much knowledge, have failed to find satisfaction. And since you avow that religion that leads to every truth, we are confident that we shall have the correct interpretation of it, which will satisfy several besides your well-wisher,

DANIEL AB IAGO.

Translated from Latin, and quoted from the "Magazine," 1793.

"The Lily *(a)* dwells in the best parts, and invades the land of the helpless Lion *(b)*; and the creatures of his own kingdom will tear his skin with their teeth *(c)*, and he will stand in the land, to the purpose of triumphing over the thorns of his kingdom. The Son of Man *(d)* will come with a great host *(e)*, going across the waters *(f)*, bringing the beasts in his arms *(g)*, and his government will be in the land of the wool *(h)*, and will frighten the whole world. The eagle *(i)* will come from the east spreading his wings over the sun, and with him a large host of people to assist the Son of Man *(k)*. In that year the camp will be left empty, and great fear will be in the world *(l)*, and in one part of the kingdom of the lion, there will be war among many kings, and a spilling of blood *(m)*. The lily will lose its crown, with which the Son of Man will be crowned *(n)*. And during the following four years there will be wars among the followers of the faith *(o)*. The greatest part of the world will be destroyed—The end of the world will come to the earth—The Son of Man and the eagle will triumph, and then there will be peace in the whole world *(p)*, and after that the Son of Man will see a great wonder, and he will enter the land of promise *(r)*."

THE INTERPRETATION.

The following is the most correct interpretation we can think of at present. Despite our having obtained, mercifully, "that religion that leads to every truth," yet we are far from possessing its infallibility thus far, and we are very pleased for anyone who can improve on our interpretation.

(a) The "Ancient of days," Dan. vii, 9, 10. *(b)* The "beast," Dan. vii, 7. *(c)* Dan. *vii*, 12. *(d)* Ver. 13. *(e)* Ver. 10. *(f)* Zech. x, 5—18. *(g)* Isaiah xl, 6—9; and lxv, 25. *(h)* The American Continent: see history of the *Peruvian Sheep*. *(i)* Those of the House of David who go from Jerusalem toward Zion, Isaiah xviii; Jer. iv, 6, 7. *(k)* Jerusalem. *(l)* Battle of Armageddon, Zech. iii, 8; Ezek. xxxviii. *(m)* Dan. vii, 13, 14, 25. *(n)* The thing most likely to this is the period of prophecy of the "two witnesses," Rev. xi, if their days are counted at 360 in a year, it is seen that the 1260 days make from three to four years. *(o)* Dan. vii, 18, 27. *(p)* Zech. xiv, 9. *(r)* Rev. xi, 15.—Ed.

A PAGAN PROVES TWO OF THE SECTARIAN RABBIS LIARS.

"*And they shall speak with new tongues*," says Jesus Christ. Our purpose in the following is not to prove that such a self-evident doctrine as the gift of "speaking with strange tongues" is to continue in the church of Christ while any other gift continues; but the following true story is an example to prove how similarly the children fill up the measure of their fathers now compared to what they did in the time of Christ; and it proves also that it is the same class of craftsmen, namely sectarian rabbis and doctors, who are the most cruel enemies, and the most impudent persecutors, of the same godly religion now as in the days of the apostles, whatever their hypocritical profession.

A few days ago, one of the persecuting Rabbis of Independia came arm-in-arm with one of the haughty *students* of Trefecca, into the home of one of the saints, who had himself been a sectarian preacher, until he saw their deceit and tired of it, and embraced the truth, together with his wife. After expressing surprise and insulting the saint at length for having "been so foolish as to be charmed into such unpopular deceit;" and after dispairing in their attempt to charm him back into their deceit, they insisted that the Saints do not speak in tongues through the Spirit, but that it is all a bunch of nonsense or *gibberish*. And at that the following conversation took place:—

Saint.—What proof do you offer of that, namely that the strange tongue that the Saints speak in their church is a bunch of nonsense or *gibberish*?

Rab.—Oh, that is what we believe.

Saint.—But I know that they speak tongues understandable through the Spirit of God, for I have witnesses that have heard them. One told me that he had heard the Saints speaking in six different languages that he understood, and that in one meeting; and also he testifies that others interpreted them, as far as they were interpreted correctly in English, when neither the speakers nor the interpreters understood one word of those languages of themselves.

Rab.—We do not believe that; and if it is true, tell us where we can get hold of that man; for we would search all over Britain, whatever the cost, in order to have the truth; and if that is the truth, we ourselves would become Mormons at once.

Saint.—Well, remember your promise. But you will find him sooner, and more easily than you expect, perhaps; at least, you will not have to go outside the borders of Wales to find him.

Rab.—All the better; bring him forward, and we shall believe at once.

Saint.—Do not forget your promise, then, when he comes.

Rab.—If you can, say who he is, and where he can be found; otherwise we shall not believe you.

Saint.—Be calm; you do not have to wait days, hours, or many minutes, or go out of the village of Aberdare, or even from this house, to have proof of the matter.

And then, opening a door leading to another room, he said in English, "John Shack Mamoth, these gentlemen wish to interview you." At his call there stood before them, sooner than their expectation, a large, black, and cheerful Hindu, in the dress of the eastern countries, with his *turban* on his head, and gazed intently into their eyes. They looked like two simpletons who had lost their way in the fog. They had no idea what to do now, for they saw that they were about to fall in the ditch they had dug for the honest and the innocent. If the man proves he understands the strange tongue, they were obligated to become Mormons at the cost of their popularity, and all their merchandise, or break their vow, and through that admit themselves voluntary liars. A man-size trap to catch them! An accurate mirror to show whether it was the truth or lies they loved most. The whole time they were in shock, and looked at each other, there was the living witness standing before them ready to answer for himself. At last, they went ahead with the interview to look for an escape from their snare. The Reverends asked the pagan the following:—

Rab.—How many languages do you understand?

Pagan.—Sixteen [and he named some of them].

Rab.—Do you understand Arabic?

Pagan.—Do you understand Arabic?

Rab.—Yes, and several other languages.

Pagan.—[Taking a book from his pocket, containing Arabic, and handing it to them] Prove that you are telling the truth, by reading this [but the two were struck dumb!], or ask me something in Arabic, and I shall answer you in the same language; or else, you answer me.

But no answer. The pagan proved that he was a better linguist, and more of a doctor than the learned and proud *rabbis*, and he also proved that he could tell the truth better than they, which was no great task. The *rabbis* struggled greatly, trying to escape the trap, by turning the story to something else, but the pagan held their noses to the lie until they became terribly angry, and let go inhuman passions, and in this rage, the following came out:—

Rab.—How many languages did you understand the Saints speaking through the Spirit in their meetings?

Pagan.—I understood a few in nearly every meeting, and as many as six in one meeting.

Rab.—An impudent lie (!) is every word you speak, and you do not understand a word they say.

Is that so? Are these the men who were so desirous of having the truth a few minutes ago? Are these the ones who promised to go to the nethermost corner of the country to question him, and to seek him at any cost? And here he is looking them in the face right then and there irresistibly, and the reception he gets is an allegation that he was telling an *impudent lie*, while their own lies had hardly finished echoing from the walls. All this substantiates the proverb that says that "the most impudent liar shouts lie first at the truth." Is this the best *polish* that can be had in the academies, I wonder? After their clamour subsided somewhat, the pagan defended his truthfulness bravely and irrefutably, and challenged them to put him to the test before linguists whenever they wanted. And with his hand he gave an appropriate scoff to the contentious self-wise men, informing them "that the pagans of his country did not consider it proper manners to come uninvited to the home of a stranger, and accuse anyone under that roof of telling lies. You are too much of a blackguard for me to speak with you; but before you leave I shall testify again that it is true that the Saints speak with different tongues through the Spirit of God, while not understanding a word of those languages on their own. But you and your ilk build splendid synagogues with the money of the poor, and eat the bread of the orphan and the widow, so you can ascend to your pulpits to tell lies to them, and to teach them to reject the true gospel, and to persecute the children of God. And it is not enough for you to do so in your own country, but you send your brethren across the great sea to our country, to try to proselyte my honest compatriots to your false religions, teaching them to tell lies as you yourselves do. You have been proved wicked men here; and this you cannot deny."

Then the pagan left them, and went into the other room. They tried to excuse themselves for their poor manners. But the man of the house was obliged to give them a few *lessons on ethics*, to prepare them to behave properly next time in the presence of a pagan, and they went away in their shame, refusing the truth after everything, as do all seekers of miracles, despite all their promises. And in all likelihood the next scene in which they can be seen is one in which they have ascended to the top of some pulpit, above a crowd of their fellow travelers toward judgment, and are there cursing and blaspheming the Saints of the Most High, and twisting the gospel of Jesus Christ, under the false profession of their preaching. May the gracious God take pity on their wretched and deluded ones, and may he shatter quickly their traditional and ruinous shackles.

The aforementioned Hindu was convinced a few months ago to believe the gospel, through hearing in our meetings of the "great works of God in the language in which he was reared." He was baptized, and he, poor thing, despite the blackness of his skin, greatly rejoiced in the eternal gospel. Should not the zealous Welsh blush on hearing this pagan defending Christ's true religion in the face of all their errors! Who else can bring so much proof as this of the godliness of their cause? If the spiritual gifts the Saints have are not true, how does the Hindu understand them? And he is not the only one who understands them. If these gifts are not true how does he give the same interpretation in English of the utterance as others give through the Spirit in Welsh, when the latter do not understand English, nor he Welsh? It is useless for the Reverends to shout that this is a lie, for there are hundreds of witnesses of its truthfulness in Wales! Let the sign-seekers make rightful use of this fact then, or let them be silent from asking for more.

RETURN OF THE PRODIGALS.

AMONG others who were unfaithful, and who returned repentant, came Herbert Walters, of Dowlais. This is the man about whom there was so much commotion through the *Star of Gomer*, and some other publications. This is he whom Mr. Davies called one of "*two of the chief elders* of the Mormons (!) having left them, and speaking with tongues, and exposing the disgrace of the system, &c." This is the only one they could tempt through all the lectures of Mr. Roberts, in these environs at all. Yes, this is he, poor thing, the only one from the midst of all the Saints who turned to them, and O! if they could hear him now telling of his bitter experience; from the sufferings of a guilty conscience day and night because of what he had done; and if they could understand his great and sincere desire for returning, no doubt they would confess the truthfulness of Christ's saying on this subject, namely that "it were better that a millstone were about their neck, and were sunk in the depth of the sea, than for them to offend one of these little ones." He earnestly wishes for the forgiveness of the Saints for that which he did against them, and for a part in their prayers for God to forgive him and keep him in the face of all temptation ever again. Where now are the claimed victories of our Dowlaisite persecutors? Where are those who declared "that Mormonism has received a *home stroke*," that it is a sacrilege and a curse, &c., &. Let them read our conference statistics, besides many who were baptized in Dowlais since that time, and there are better signs than ever for growth; yes, let them open their ears or their eyes, and then they shall see and hear facts to prove, not the ruin of Mormonism, rather to prove clearly that our persecutors are the false prophets who prophesy lies against us. Several others of the chief persecuting backsliders are earnestly pleading to be allowed to come back to the church this way.

WHAT IS THE MATTER ?

THE principality is on fire—its usurper is striking up for volunteers—the priests of great Babylon are on its towers blowing their horns, long and loudly, to gather all their armies to do holy sectarian battle against the Saints—their foundations are shaking—their armies are fleeing before the cannons of the truth—the giants of the principality are falling before the two-edged sword of the Spirit, and the others are enraged in the pangs of death—the devil is losing subjects in every battle—the hind parts of the great goddess are being bared—her worshipers are retreating from her temples in shame and enlisting under the banners of the King Jesus—the treacherous tricks of the chief leaders of the usurper are coming into full public view—his crown, and the hope of profit of his priests are about to fail ! !

It is surprising what wars and rumors of wars are throughout our country in these days! From the preparations and noise of their enemies one would think that the Saints were about to turn the principality upside down, and that these agitators fear that it will fall on their toes and hurt their corns or something worse! From nearly one end of the principality to the other the goatherds of Babylon have become frightened as the mountain rams are frightened at the echo of thunder in their own twisted horns. And they dart across hills and dales, blowing their shrill horns against their innocent neighbors, just like the shooting stars go to the reaches of outer space, and their place cannot be found. What is the matter? Why all the noise, the chatter, the lecturing, the publishing of lies, and the big *yoohoo* that grates on ears in the south and the north in these days? Why can every vain man, from the schoolteacher to the editor and from there to the highest benches of the Colleges, be seen scouring their old weapons, and each one with his old rusty sword on the whetstone of malice? Certainly something is wrong! Has not some archenemy dangerous to all their crafts just landed on the shores of our country? Something must be threatening to destroy them before they would prepare so busily for war. What is the cause of all the commotion? Who can say? Let the generals of the attacking armies answer the question themselves. Come Mr. *Times*, your horn is going to sound loudest in this massive campaign. Tell us, of whom are you so greatly terrified? "*Joe Smith* and *Mormonism*" are still the target of your reed arrows, are they not? Some "Mormon deceit," "Saint in Prison," or "chemical oil," are staining your columns constantly. As the movement of the straw indicates the direction of the breeze, so your actions show in which army you are.

Next, Mr. *Revivalist*, you have shown which side of the battle you are on. Yes indeed, you have devoted as much as the enemies of Mormonism wanted of your columns to slander it, and you yourself help a little at times, says your *shibboleth*. After everyone had cried shame on you, and not before, you gave a backward kick, it is true, to the "Hater of Deceit from Blackwood," and likewise to others after getting all the slanderous material their lying hearts possessed. Is it those few "illiterate and bad little men" who are frightening you now? Is it that "most harmless and insignificant little thing" which by now has charmed toward Mormonism many of the best and most able people that you had? Is it because of this that you listen intently for every distorted story to publish it against them? And after failing to get anything else, behold a *fresh edition* of the "walking on water" story, the hundred and second *edition* of the *Spaulding Romance* about the Book of Mormon, and finally, and just as true and logical as anything else of your chatter, you publish a story about some "dove as big as a *horse!*" "And *looking* just like a *horse!*" Bah, man, where have your senses gone? It is easy to perceive that *poor* Joe, even though he is dead, is the *common foe* of these editorial and Reesly Reverends.

The *Star of Gomer* also, and its thousand forked and slanderous tongues, proves of what army it is the trumpet. It is like a bellows, blowing wherever there is a spark of the fire of malice, and away it goes until it sets the whole state on fire with all its might. This is its favorite work; and the sons of Gomer understand, especially those who are of the same taste, that their slimy slander will be welcomed here anyway, as long as it is something dirty to smear *poor*

Joe and *Mormonism.*

The *Apostolic Witness.* It is marrow to thy bones, and honey to thy mouth under a pseudonym, like all false apostles and false angels, to show the length of thy filthy tongue against Mormonism forever; if there were no better, there would be "laughing" work for thee at the lying scoundrel in Machynlleth, who, although he professes zealously with thy great goddess, testified that he wished to be baptized, when he was just joking with one of the important ordinances of the house of God, and had announced his treachery to his blasphemous partners, who gathered secretly to the place and tried to drown the preacher!! Yes, this is what the presumptuous *infidel* calls a "*laughing*" matter! That is sufficient to prove to whom and to what thou art a "Witness."

And the *Educator,* which is one of the chief trumpets of great Independia, itself shows its side at time, and its cannons roar to the point of startling the goatherds and the goats of Cader Idris, and driving them over the cliffs. Cader Idris is not a sufficiently strong tower, it would seem, to keep you from the terror and fear of these "*illiterate* and *foolish* little men" who are called Mormons. In spite of that, they must be more immortal than the "young men of Snowdon;" otherwise some of your giants surely would have killed them before now. But the roar of your cannons is an admission that they are alive, and that your craft is in danger. Besides the editors, pick up the work of any recent author you wish, and one can see that the aim of their arrows is the same thing.

The last, and the dirtiest also, to come to our attention is Mr. *Baptist,* and its tasty stories about the "the Saint a thief." But we have not heard it publish a word about that Baptist preacher from Bethesda, who was exiled to *Botany Bay* lately for *wholesale* thievery, nor anything about the one who broke into the St. Asaph church Sunday night after he had finished preaching and stole almost up to his throat. Nor was there a word about the thefts or the murders of anyone of the Baptists to be sure; however, every imaginary mote among the Mormons it holds up to the wind, but the huge beams that are in the eyes of its partners it hides. Your mistake, Sir, is to say that that T. H. had "scratched out the name of the owner of the book" or to admit either that he had stolen it. How in the world do you come across every lie and fail to ever get the truth of things? The name was on a loose page, and it was lost. He admitted that he had the book, but he denied having *stolen* it, nor did he know how it came to his possession. That is what was proved by the investigation. But this has nothing to do with Mormonism any more than your confessing that all Baptists are thieves because those mentioned and many others are. If you had been a contemporary of Judas, the readers of the *Baptist* would have plenty of proofs from you, and those as solid as the aforementioned, to prove the Son of God a deceiver, and his religion as bad as Mormonism!! Those who live in glass houses should not begin to throw stones at others. We are reminded of this one's filthy old tales some time ago about those chaste women in Penydarren, Rhymni, &c., things that anyone else would be ashamed to publish out of respect to womankind, but from the most wanton hearts flows the filthiest wantonness, and from the carcass the unclean bird feeds; so it is here. This one spies, eavesdrops and searches all the dirtiest papers from the "*Warsaw*

Signal" to the back issues of the *Baptist* for lewd stories until at last he received a tasty morsel from some American paper mentioning some kind of wives who are called "spiritual wives!" Well, could it be that he denies that all wives are spiritual? Listen, wives, this one doubts the existence of your spirits, it seems! Take care, women, lest your husbands join the Baptists; otherwise, who can tell if they consider you any better than their animals. Yes, and according to the logic of the *Baptist*, we warn the husbands also. Watch, lest the preachers of the Baptists in Wales steal your wives, not to mention those in America! Surely, it is dangerous, and only a few days ago a man's wife was enticed by one of their members. And even worse, she stole his money and all his furniture she could get her hands on, and all this just because of the poisonous fangs of the Baptists in the religion of the husband. Some dangerous monstress to family society is this one. J. S. was accused of much because of his fatherly defense to the "weakest vessel" when under oppression of a hot-headed man, and the thanks he received was to be accused of wantonness by wantons; and thus accused are all humanitarians who save the life of a woman by divorcing her according to the laws of the land. Pity that they cannot tell some bad story by now, after trying so long!

It is obvious that Mormonism is the *target* of all these *crusaders*, and that all of them from Abergavenny to Anglesey, and from Cardiff, Abercanaid, Dowlais, Llanelli, &c., &c., to the borders of Wales. Why so? We answer that it is clear fulfillment of the prophecy that says, "Ye shall be hated of all men for my name's sake." It proves that Mormons are subjects of one kingdom. But of all the vain men who have been on the field against their *common foe*, the most stupid, the most impudent, and the most shameless, is that one who blows his strident horn from the Rhymni Valley. That one claims that despite the failure of all the giants who shouted that they had killed Mormonism, &c., that he is the great *champion* who is going to put an end to it for sure—that he has the "sling," or "the jawbone of an ass," and he will bury its skeleton in the Rhymni Valley, that he will erect on it a tall monument to immortalize his name, and he will carve on it, "*I was the big lad who was the death of Mormonism.*" And off he goes to battle like a fool, with his quiver filled with reed arrows. He lectured his slime in Dowlais to the point of making Mormons out of scores of his listeners, yes, and some of them members with Davies, Caersalem, himself; and they testify to this day that it was upon hearing those lying tales that their minds were inclined to examine it. Now that's no way to kill Mormonism! Again he vomited his sick stomach out in Merthyr; and greatly did he sweat and shout, "down with Mormonism," when he was here. But despite everything he did, things improved by leaps and bounds that week, and went along as heedless of him as the moon is in its orbit, in spite of the little corgi dog barking at it until his voice cracked. His rage was boiling hotter and hotter. We heard that he promisied to kill Mormonism in Rhymni on Christmas day and bury it the next. But by the time the day came for it to die, its alleged murderer was bound between the sides of his bed by the cords of him who has the power of death, it seems. It was necessary to ask someone else to fill his pulpit that time. Again, the gracious God allowed him to get up, and one would think that he had kicked enough against the divine pricks, but on he went battling against the Saints still; and not only were all the Saints who were there to hear him strengthened in Mormonism, but the eyes of many others were opened to see his tricks and his deceit. He failed to kill it or to hurt it on any of those occasions anyway. Rather it was he himself he hurt every time. We refuted his lying tales so completely in two treatises that he has not tried to answer either of them to this day, neither can he. He saw everything, but to no avail, rather he loved lies. It did not make any *difference* to him whether it was true or not, for he had learned his one story, like the *parrot*, and that which he said first, he said last.

Since Mormonism was succeeding in Aberdare, with one of the chief preachers with the Baptists there together with his wife, and several others having joined it lately, that was a good opportunity for him to show himself, and satisfy his passion; and there he went as greedily as the wolf goes after the innocent lamb. We can imagine seeing him listening intently to the tinkling of the tickets, for no one would get to hear the *secrets*, certainly, without paying sixpence. Pity the poor; because they lacked the sixpence, he would let them "be charmed by Mormonism going headlong to hell." These Reverends had the *policeman* drag one respectable man, like a dog by his neck, from his own pew, for which he paid regularly, and this man's wife was a member of that chapel. Great was the battle that ensued between the reverends and her by the door. The woman announced the deceit of their craft, and they were forced to flee to their hiding place, where no one could utter a word except themselves. Those two were not the only ones of the members of the Baptists who decided that they would not go near them again, but that was the general prediction that was heard throughout the listeners at that idiotic lecture; and the Saints have baptized more there in a few weeks than they had baptized in months before the lecture.

After getting all the sixpences he could for delivering his rubbish, he is riding another *speculation* now, as did his foster father of the same taste from Dowlais, that is to publish his lectures as a pamphlet. And great is the placarding of the walls, and the *puffing* they do about it, and then they failed to get *rid* of it without getting it peddled from door to door by those who plead poverty as their excuse for selling it! That is frequently the murderer's excuse. But his treatise stinks in the nostrils of everyone we know without exception; in spite of that, one sees this *puff* after *puff* going up on the walls. One would expect that he could *afford* to pay the printer without all this, and give more than 24 pages for sixpence, since he has received so many sixpences here and there for his lecturing, besides the eight pounds each month that he gets at the same time for the *use* of his tongue at home; or else, pity the poor Mormons who do not charge eight pence, or even eight halfpennies in a year for preaching, and who even paid sixpence to those who came to listen to his lectures get torn to bits. Facts such as these show who is making commerce of the souls of the people at the cost of their pockets. And yet, here is this one, in his own opinion, threatening and supposing that he can hinder the success of Mormonism. *Poor fellow !* time will tell: let him do his worst, for the gnashing of his teeth does not frighten the least, rather it strengthens the youngest of the Mormons in every place. Yes, poor thing, although against his will, instead of killing Mormonism, he enlivens it and causes people to listen. Not so much as one has turned back in spite of all his jabbering; rather hundreds have joined the Saints in these environs since he began his cruel *crusade*. Let him go forward and thrash as he will; he is nothing more than a *splash in a wash hand basin !*

This last one, as his brethren before him, must be totally ignorant of the divine powers of Mormonism to expect to be able to hinder its pace. But, bah! what good it is to review or take notice of their treatises or their ridiculous lectures. Our reviews are already across the country by the thousands, and are plainly giving the *homestroke* to their rubbish;—but we will say this again, after spending much more time writing than we had intended to spend with their kind, if all the priests of Babylon were to come like a herd with their spinning wheels to spin lies as fast as the breeze, and if they got assistance from all their persecuting partners, from Pharoah, Maximus, and Nero, down to their American brothers, yes, let them do whatever they will, they have slept too late, and there is too much daylight for the birds of the night to frighten anyone who has eyes in his head. Succeed is what Mormonism will do until it brings the lovers of truth out from Babylon. And after all our persecutors are buried in the graves they have dug for Mormonism, the Mormons by the thousands will sing:

I shall climb through the persecution, up above the King invites me;
Depite the cruelty of my enemies, I have not yet been killed.
Regardless of the obstacles on my path, my journey will never be reversed;
Blood will not do except for a witness, *victory*, will be the result in any event.

It is true that prejudice can kill, it is true that the world turns away
Yet if they were all unified, a Saint would *never* come back.
Were there a thousand for one of them, were the obstacles myriad for one,
Yet at the calls of the King, the Saint himself would go forward.

The world calls from the right and the left, that I am stupid, that I am a fool;
Sin calls on me to stand, hell calls me back;
The enemy calls for his libel—let him call, and for his fire!
While the King of heaven is calling, the Saint forward must go.

Let all the great giants come with their scheme—bitterly,
And let them strike against Mormonism;
Let them try to wound us, but what use, what difference,
Until they deal with our testimony?

Misfortune does its work quickly,—and flaunts;
But strange how powerless it is!
We are raising the cross of the age—
We are running and succeeding.

EXCOMMUNICATION OF PHILLIP SEIX, BLAINA, MONMOUTHSHIRE, FROM THE CHURCH.

WE are sorry to announce that this person has sunk to such depths to the influences of the devil, that our rules of discipline have obliged us to excommuniate him from the church, and that he now has been taken by civil officers to the *Lunatic Asylum.*

According to our understanding, through a detailed search into the painful circumstances, and truthful eyewitnesses, it took place as follows:—

The afflicted was of a gentle and meek nature, with a natural inclination to depression. About three months ago, he believed that he had sinned greatly by disobeying the counsels he had received, and by neglecting his religious duties. Finally, he went in secret, to pray for God to send a messenger to inform him if there was any forgiveness for him; and while there, some being appeared to him (or so he said afterwards), and told him that all his prayers were in vain, because he had committed unforgiveable sins. This had a worse and worse effect on his mind, until it nearly drove him insane. After his religious brethren understood what was troubling him, they persuaded him not to believe any such thing, that it was the influences of the devil, to do him harm. According to the commandments of Jesus Christ in such a circumstance (see Mark xvi, 18, &c.), they rebuked that evil spirit from him by the laying on of hands and the prayer of faith, and God heard their prayer and restored the afflicted to his former senses. After following his calling for a while, a stone fell upon his head at work and injured him greatly. Before wholly recovering from the effects of this, he fell into such influences as before. He received deliverance once again in the same way as before, and many times afterwards. After coming to his senses, he admitted that the fault was his because he did not oppose the influences of the devil with greater bravery, and promised to do so from then on, &c. But again, and again, he was possessed by the same or worse spirits. Finally, Elders W. Phillips, together with A. Evans, visited him, and through their administrations of the above ordinances, he was restored to the possession of his full reason, and went with them to Nantyglo. They counseled him to remain there for a while, until he was strengthened from his physical illness, and the Saints there promised to keep him for free; but the next day, he insisted on returning against the will of them all. He was warned, that if he went, he would be possessed once again by a worse spirit, until he would be bound hand and foot, and under the care of the *police* before long; but nothing had any effect—back he went. He continued in his full reason until the next afternoon after returning. At this time he was called to a neighbor's house, and he was invited to the table to drink *tea* with the others. These accused the religion that he professed of having caused his sickness; and they persuaded him to leave it, &c. This agitated his feelings to such an extent, that he arose to his feet in the presence of them all, and he testified that it was not the religion's fault, rather his own—that it was the true religion of the Son of God the Saints professed, and because of that he had been healed a number of times. This opposition caused such agitation in his mind, that he hated them out of zeal for his religion, and sinned because of that. At this he was possessed worse than ever, and they all ran from the house in fear, and he after them howling and frothing, and others after them through the streets, causing quite a stir in the place. Finally, he was got into a house, and bound. While in this situation, W. Phillips visited him again, and in a few minutes, he was restored to his reason and was as good as ever. He arose, washed himself, ate, and took comfort, thanking God greatly for his deliverance; and he escorted his visitor about half a mile, and he said he would go to work the next day. The second day he gave way to temptation again, roaring like a lion, and frothing; and he tried to injure whomever he could. By this time the *police* came, and a host of people as well, and they bound him, taking him soon afterwards to the aforementioned place. They were obliged to carry him about three miles before getting a carriage; and all the way, until they shut him up, he testified that it was not the Saints or their religion that were at fault, rather it was his negligence that was the cause of everything, and he begged them sincerely to leave the matter between him and the Saints, saying that he would surely receive deliverance once more, but all in vain. Like this he went, the first of the Saints ever, to our knowledge, to such a place, and doubtless it was his fault; for he fulfilled the above prophecy despite our best efforts, and because of this transgression and its consequences, he has been excommunicated. From this grievous circumstance, let the Saints learn faithfulness, courage, and obedience to the counsels they receive, so they are not overcome by the same false spirits, that are overflowing our world, seeking anyone they can swallow. Our constant prayer is, that the Spirit of God will encircle his children.

This circumstance has created among the Saints a new determination to cling to their God, and to fulfill their duties. Several of the honest in heart believed the gospel when they saw the great power of God manifest in the matter, and several were baptized in those environs afterwards as a result. But as for the other part of the people, especially the most zealous and fanatical false religionists, we understand that their tongues are like a hellish spinning-wheel, spinning and twisting every color, shape, and species of lies, in order to blacken the character of the Saints. Yes, lies we say, which are almost too disgraceful for us to repeat; and their utterers are guilty of blasphemy by their arrows, despite their being so sweet to their loathsome appetite, without mentioning the wickedness of inventing such lies to shame the people and children of God without cause. His word that says,—"He that toucheth you toucheth the apple of his eye," is as true now as before. And these slanderers prove that they are under the influence of worse devils than the foregoing wretch. We and our brethren have suffered long and quietly every kind of lie against us because of our religion, until we do not believe that God will ask us to suffer like murderers or *thieves*, while law is to be found in the land, and man to administer it. Therefore, we announce our decision to bring, and we earnestly implore the Saints, and everyone else who has one degree of feeling for his good name, for humanity, if not for our dear religion, to help us bring those incomparable scoundrels to prison before the civil court, namely anyone who says that we, or W. Phillips, have robbed the above Phillip Seix of his money, or of a single penny either ! ! There is no foundation to such allegations except in the minds of their slanderous inventors. We challenge any man to stand and accuse us to our face of getting one penny, or anything worth a penny from him, or ever trying to get anything; rather it is completely to the contrary, as he is in debt to us, and to W. Phillips, and we have witnesses who heard him say, that no one of the Saints was in his debt, but that he was in their debt. It never cost him a penny for food whenever he came this way, and the reward we have for our generosity to him is to be accused by his enemies, enemies to every good thing, of plundering his belongings, is it! But we shall not tolerate it any longer.

STATE OF THE CHURCHES, AND THE BAPTISMS.

Merthyr Branch.—Thirty-five were baptized here during the past six weeks, several of which were formerly members with the sectarian denominations. All the Saints belonging to this branch are almost without exception, faithful, and increasing more and more in every gift and blessing, and if the Saints remain strong in the faith and faithful, we believe, from the hopeful signs we see, together with the numerous and attentive audience here, that hosts will come soon and become subjects of the kingdom of Emmanuel.

Dowlais.—There is here such an increase in the number of listeners since the great commotion caused by Messrs. Roberts, Davies, Lewis, &c., that the Hall the Saints had at that time has become too small; and they now preach in the convenient Hall of the *Marquis of Bute*, which is overflowing with polite listeners on the Sunday. This is how Mormonism became a "sacrilege and a curse" in Dowlais. Nine have been baptized there since the beginning of last January, one of which was the *right hand man* to the Rev. W. R. Davies! He was a scribe in his meeting house, one of the *trustees*, &c., and very staunch in their sight. Their persecution and their unceasing lies are what caused him to look into Mormonism; and the honesty and love that he possessed towards truth caused him to embrace it as the treasure of treasures; and now he values the Mormon religion more than the world and its fulness. Two others of Mr. Davies's members were baptized after him, and several before that, despite Mr. Davies's assertion that only one old woman left him for the Saints. More will yet come before long, yes, all who have love in them for the truth. Doubtless there are among them also many who are searching for the truth, and it is a shame that they are losing time, and depriving themselves from so many blessings, and divine light, by allowing anyone to pull a blind of darkness over their eyes at the cost of their purses and souls. Yes, the Saints baptized the man and his wife who were living in one of the houses of Mr. D., yes, next door to his own door, and above his shop! And yet, this is the giant who was going to kill Mormonism with one blow, a short time back. Oh, no, it is hard to kick against the pricks of Mormonism, Sir. It is not Mr. Davies's fault that his members join with the Saints, for he does his zealous best against them, not only in the meetings, but he walks the houses while the men are at work, and by the time they return their once peaceful hearths are from then on a hell to them, just like his own bosom. Now his wiles come to view! Now many understand what and who was the root of their family discord; and having rid themselves of the evil they dwell in peace.

Tredegar.—Five have been baptized, two of which were respected deacons with other denominations for years—one with the Baptists, and two with the Wesleyans, and everyone had a good word for them. One other, who had great influence in the midst of the Wesleyans, and was the head Sunday school teacher, had been baptized a while before that. Another came from the Calvinistic Methodists, in addition to others not connected to any denomination. And great will be their joy for changing their religion for the better. And after their long search for the religion of Christ, they say now, after obtaining it, that they would not take the world to return back to empty husks.

Penycae.—Two. A while before that one of the deacons of the Baptists and his wife were baptized; they are now rejoicing daily in the happiness of the Holy Ghost, and are grateful for his bringing them from the dark mist to the freedom and light of the children of God. Their former brethren are ever their worst persecutors and false accusers as usual.

Victoria.—Nine, nearly all of them from the Baptists, besides many who have come from the Baptists a short time back. Among others, a minister came to visit with one of the women who had joined the Saints from his church. After he made a prolonged attempt to persuade her to return, but in vain, she testified to him that she was better off than anywhere in the world for having left him and his church, and coming to the Saints; for now, she said, I know in truth and surety that I have the privilege of coming to the church of God, where he imparts his Spirit in his various gifts, which I did not have while I was with you. This sincere statement greatly enraged this reverend, and he said, "Well, it was your unfaithfulness that was the cause of your not having it." "Surely not," said the woman, "for I was as faithful as I could be, and prayed as much as I could, for years, and despite that I never had, and I do not believe you, or any of your members, had anything like the love, the joy, or the light, that can be had through the Holy Ghost and that is with the Saints." That was enough for the Reverend; he saw that he was finished, and the end of his story was to shout, with his hands up, as he went through the door, "Oh! you have sinned against the Holy Ghost." And the next scene in which he appeared was from his pulpit on Sunday cruelly and shamelessly proclaiming his anathemas over the wretched woman, as he excommunicated her for, said he, "sinning against the Holy Ghost." These tricks constitute one of the chief practices of this group of people. It is high time by now to make an example of them, since nothing else shames them. Since the devil himself appears as an angel of light, is it strange that his hireling servants imitate him? Does not the scripture warn us that they will come in sheep's clothing, speaking swollen words of emptiness, trying to entice back the honest in heart who have escaped from their heresies, the judgment of whom, for their hard words against his children, does not slumber.

Nantyglo.—Eight, mainly of no previous religious affiliation, and this branch is flourishing in love and the spiritual gifts as well.

Blaina.—Two. The Saints here are more determined than ever to fulfill their duties.

Abersychan.—Nine, two of which were members with the Baptists, and the others of no previous affiliation. The divine sparks have opened the eyes of the honest to catch a glimpse of the church of God, and its superiority over theirs, until several of them are like a boiling cauldron, and nearly spilling over.

Cardiff.—Twenty-eight have been baptized since the beginning of January, and others promising daily almost. Some of the above came from the Baptists, and other denominations, and this is what causes the filthy *Baptist* to have colic and shoot its loathesome stories at the Saints, thinking to keep the rest under its paws; but those who have come have gained so much by changing their religion, that lies will not keep the others back for long.

Llwyni.—Seven were baptized in the same week, with many (we do not know the exact number) before that, and afterwards. Those people are beginning to come to their senses after the cruel persecution there.

Swansea.—Elder Joseph Matthews baptized two last month.

Bryn.—Many (we are told) were baptized there after the Conference.

Llanelli.—The president delayed informing us by letter how many were baptized here in January, but we heard that it was about a dozen at least, through the frightful assistance of Mr. Spencer, a minister of the Baptists, and others. May he go forward successfully, and may he proselyte more of his flock to Mormonism.

Pont Yates.—Here, and in the neighborhood, the Saints have baptized 19 since the Conference, and they are all rejoicing in their privileges and their hopes.

Llanybydder.—Eight were baptized here recently—two from the Baptists.

Brechfa.—Four have been baptized since the Conference, with signs for many more.

We have heard of others baptized in different places; but those presidents have not sent the number to us. We expect that every president will do this regularly each month.

Behold over a one-hundred-and-fifty increase among the Saints just in the places named in about a month! This is how it is going! Thanks to him who sustains this work, and we pray for more and more success on it constantly. Amen.

*** *Direct letters, prepaid, to* CAPT. JONES, Wellington Street, Merthyr. *No one can expect a response, if there is no stamp on the letter. We are tired at last of paying postage for everyone !*

ANNOUNCEMENTS.

IT is intended to hold the Monmouth Conference in *Nantyglo*, on the last Sunday of April.

We expect to see there a number of the Saints who can come, and especially the officers, and all branch presidents, prepared to represent the branches, their number, how many baptized since the previous Conference, the number of the various officers, together with the spiritual condition of the Saints, &c.

***We warn the Saints to beware of oppressors and deceivers. A woman has been this way recently professing to be one of the Llanelli Saints, saying and doing much deceit, when in fact she was not at that time, nor had she ever been in the church. Only a short time ago some were claiming to be preachers with the Saints in England, or Scotland, and expecting to receive here a welcome of such. Let the Saints and the officers take care to get certificates from the presidents of their branches, or else they will not be received in another place, unless they are well known.*

***Elder Jacob Watkins has been stripped of his office until he satisfies the council in Merthyr of his behavior.*

BOOKS.

WE have volumes of "Capt. Jones on Mormonism, in 1846," priced from 3s. to 4s. 6c. Also, volumes of the Treatises published in 1847, for from 3s. 6c. to 5s. 6c. Also, the two volumes of the PROPHET have been bound in one, for from 4s. to 6s., depending on their binding. The distributors can obtain the above with the PROPHET if they send the money. We also have a variety of books in English and the *Millennial Star*, biweekly, for 3c. per issue.

CONTENTS.

MERTHYR TYDFIL:

PUBLISHED AND FOR SALE BY D. JONES, AND ALSO FOR SALE BY THE SAINTS IN GENERAL.

JOHN JONES, PRINTER, RHYDYBONT.

PROPHET OF THE JUBILEE,

OR

STAR OF THE SAINTS.

No. 22.] APRIL, 1848. [Price 2*c.*

A NEW AND EXCELLENT WAY TO SPREAD KNOWLEDGE OF THE GOSPEL.

We exhort the Saints to apportion the towns and areas where they live, so that he who is able, may have as many houses in his area that he can visit all of them every Sunday. Buy a few different pamphlets of the Saints, and lend one to each house that will accept it, urging all to read them, and keep them clean, then call the following Sunday to exchange them for a different one. Take that one to the next house, and take the one you get there to one door further on; and so on until you go around them all. Then the one that was in the house last Sunday can go to the first house the next Sunday; and so on until every house has been offered the entire selection. Back issues of the *Prophet* are very useful to loan in the area with the others, and *for that purpose* they can be had for a *penny each !* The other pamphlets also can be had, for this good purpose, for as cheaply as they can be printed! Profit is not our aim; rather to spread the godly truths that have been entrusted to our care. According to this plan, every pamphlet will get much more reading than any other way, and without must cost to the distributors, and none to the reader (unless he chooses to purchase some one or other), and *all* will be read by *each one*.

Dear Saints,—We trust that this will not be too much cost or trouble for you to do on behalf of your dear neighbors, which, especially those who are so unfortunate to be under the yoke of sectarian oppression, are almost completely ignorant with respect to our religion, except for the lying tales, and the disgraceful false accusations, that are declared and preached to them from their pulpits, in their schools, their societies, and their publications. You know, through undeniable facts, that such are wiles from the father of lies, and that to blind the minds of the lovers and seekers of truth, and to entice their immortal souls to darkness and perdition. Remember that we were the same before we had light; and now, let your light shine forth in this way to our gentle neighbors. You know that they are threatened with eternal excommunication by some of their "pastors," if they come to listen to the preaching of the gospel! for until now, we do not know that it is an unforgiveable sin for them to read our books, if they get them for nothing; but hasten, who knows how quickly they will follow your heels in this also, as soon as they understand you are doing good.

God has already prospered this plan in some of the areas beyond the expectations of the distributors; and He will crown your labor with success proportionate to your diligence. Let no one say he has nothing to do until he fulfills this. If the pamphlets are fairly clean after finishing the one circle, let their owner sell them to another, and let that one begin in his neighborhood so that others become free. If the branch president does not have enough on hand to start, let him send here for some; but use those that are on hand to begin with, and more will come off the press before long. You will most likely encounter the occasional Pharisee who will consider that you are breaking the Sabbath by doing this, but Christ says it is permitted to do good on the Sabbath. You will no doubt meet a few bitter, cantankerous, and proud rascals, but do not quarrel with them; leave them behind you, and be patient. Perchance, the books will answer all their questions.

Zealous sisters,—Here is a place for you also to work, so that you may be blessed, and be a blessing to others. We all remember that our time is short to warn our nation, and that the day of tribulation is at the door.

EPISTLE OF THE TWELVE APOSTLES,

TO

The Church of Jesus Christ of Latter-day Saints, scattered throughout the world ; proclaiming :—

DEAR BRETHREN,—At no period have the Saints, since the organization of the church on the 6th day of April, in the year 1830, been so extensively scattered, and their means of receiving information from the proper source so limited as since their expulsion from the state of Illinois; but the time has come when it will be profitable for you to receive such information, by this our Epistle, as our Father wishes for you, and which he has made manifest by his Spirit.

Knowing the designs of our enemies, we left Nauvoo in February, 1846, with a large company, for the purpose of settling in the place where the Saints might gather, and dwell in peace. For the first part of our journey, we had excessive rains, and very unfavorable weather, which, together with the scarcity of provisions, compelled us to leave a portion of the camp in the wilderness, to settle in a fertile land we called *Garden Grove*, where we made a large enclosure containing 16 houses; and soon after, from similar causes, we made another settlement in a place we called Mount Pisgah, leaving another portion of our camp there to tend the crops we planted in the soil. After making a road, building a bridge over a multitude of streams, for over three hundred miles, mostly on lands of the Pottawatamie Indians, we arrived near Council Bluffs, on the Missouri River, during the latter part of June, where we were met by Capt. J. Allen, from Fort Leavenworth, soliciting us from the government to *enlist* 500 of our brethren in the "Mormon Battalion" on their journey toward California, under command of Col. J. Allen, leaving hundreds of wagons, families, &c., destitute of assistance on which they depended, and that on the open *prairies*, in a savage country, far from any abodes, and farther still from the place they intended to settle.

Our camp, although aware of a cold winter approaching, with all inevitable consequences, namely discomfort, famine, poverty, sickness, and every undesirable thing; yet, in the face of it all, we obeyed the call of the President of the country with the alacrity that is due from children to a parent; and even though the best and the flowers of our camp had taken their departure in the battalion, yet the widow and the orphan, the old and the infirm, in full hope and faithful determination, went forward on their journey. A small portion went as far as the *Pawnee Mission*, where, finding it too late to pass the Rocky Mountains, they stopped to winter; but the majority stopped to winter in this place, which we call *Winter Quarters*. In under three months we built here over 700 houses. In July, there were 2000 wagons on the way from Nauvoo following after us.

In October, 1846, a cruel mob, clad in all the horrors of war, fell on the few remaining Saints who were in Nauvoo (who, for want of means and opportunity, had not been able to remove), and they murdered some, and they drove the remainder mercilessly across the Mississippi river, where they were totally destitute of houses, tents, food, clothing, money, or practically any of their own possessions, or anything to sustain their lives but the providencial care of their Father, and a few contributions from some benevolent and generous men from Quincy, St. Louis, and other places, whose names and kindness will never be forgotten. At that period the Saints were obliged to scatter to the north, south, east, and west, wherever they could find shelter and employment. And, hard as it is to write it, yet it is true, and it must ever remain a monument on the columns of history,—While the flower and best of Israel's camp were risking their lives to sustain the wings of the American Eagle in a foreign country, their fathers, their mothers, their brothers, and their sisters, and their children, were driven by mob violence, out of the borders of a sister state of the same union; yes, they were obliged to flee from the fire, the sword, the rifles, and the cannons, as from death. From that time to this the Latter-day Saints have been roaming without home, from Canada to New Orleans, and from the Atlantic Ocean to the western Pacific Ocean, and many have taken up their abode in foreign lands. Their property in Hancock County, state of Illinois, was little or no better than confiscated. Many of their houses were burned up in flames by the mob, and they were obliged to leave most of those that remained without sale; but some received whatever others felt like giving them for their possessions, for the objective of their enemies was to depreciate possessions to the lowest extreme, so they could obtain them and everything under the excuse of paying the cost of their self-agitated war; and many of those who were living in abundance and independence received hardly enough for their handsome and valuable estates to assist them on their journey from the place; and there are thousands since that time who have been wandering to and fro destitute of the necessaries to sustain life, many of which, and their families, unable to endure such hardship, have sickened, and died, while the temple of the Lord is left in the midst of our enemies, an enduring monument, to testify to heaven and earth, and everyone who sees it, the faithfulness and diligence of the Saints.

On April 14th, we, together with 143 of the brethren, began our journey toward the west. We made a new road for close to one thousand miles, until landing in the *Great Basin*, where we arrived in the latter part of July. We found ourselves here in an extremely beautiful valley, of some twenty by thirty miles in extent. To the east there is a high mountain range, capped by perpetual snow. There is a beautiful line of mountains in the west, watered by showers of abounding rains. Utah Lake is on the south, hid by a range of hills, with a delightful prospect of the waters of the Great Salt Lake to the northwest as far as the eye can reach, interspersed with islands of different shapes and sizes. The valley reaches further to the north, along the eastern shores, for about sixty miles, to the mouth of the Bear river. The soil of the valley appears to be extremely fertile, although the moisture is not always sufficient to produce certain kinds of vegetation. Many streams run through it; and among others, the western Jordan (which runs from Utah Lake) at its height runs through the center of it from south to north. The climate is healthful and lovely—not too hot, rather dry and summer-like. Salt abounds at the lake. There is a variety of springs—warm, hot, and cold, coming up from the earth in several places; and there are excellent advantages with respect to streams to turn mills and machines of every kind and size. Timber is not very abundant across the valley; but plenty of *box*, *fir*, *pine*, and *sugar maple*, *&c.*, trees may be found on the mountains, for present needs, until more can grow.

In this splendid valley we have established a city, the name of which will be, *Great Salt Lake City*; and for convenience of the Saints, we have instituted here the *Post Office* pertaining to the *Great Basin*. The city was surveyed, and divided into blocks of ten acres each, and each block has eight lots. The streets will be 45 yards wide, crossing each other at right angles.

One block is reserved for a temple to be built on it, and several more in different parts of the cities as places to build public buildings.

Soon after our arrival in the valley, a portion of the battalion, who had been stationed at *Pueblo*, together with a company of the Saints from the state of Mississippi, came here, and they helped us to plough, plant, and sow near one hundred acres of land with a variety of seeds; and in building a row of houses around a ten-acre block, and nearly completing the same on one side. Building materials, such as stone, bricks, &c., are very abundant, and easy to get here.

After tarrying four or five weeks, we (that is, the high council) commenced our return, nearly destitute of provision. We were accompanied by a part of the battalion, who were quite destitute of provision, except for a small quantity of *beef*. We left there all the people, and the provision we could, to prepare places and food for others who were to come. All we had to depend on for subsistence was hunting for wild animals, such as the *buffalo*, *deer*, *antelope*, which were at that season of the year very scarce. Between the Green and Sweetwater rivers, we met 566 wagons loaded with Saints on their journey to the aformentioned valley. From there we passed Fort Bridger, South Pass, Fort John, and across the north bank of the Platte river to *Winter Quarters*, where we arrived the last day of October, all well, having completed this long journey, with oxen and horses, without much food except wild flesh, without losing a single man, although many were so sick and feeble when they left, that they were nearly unable to walk until they reached over half way.

Dec. 11, fifteen of the batallion arrived here, with a pilot from the valley, through much tribulation. These informed us that all the battalion had served out their time, and were discharged in California, and that a portion of them under the leadership of Capt. Davies had re-enlisted to sustain a military post in that land—that some had arrived in Salt Lake City, where they found the emigrants healthy and happy, except for just three deaths that had transpired in their midst.

The Saints are bearing all their privation in meekness and humility, doing all they can in preparation for their removal westward. Their hearts, and all their inclinations, are drawn toward the setting sun; for they desire to be so far removed from their oppressors, that there shall be an everlasting barrier between them and persecution. Although we as a people have been driven from state to state; although Joseph and Hyrum, our prophet and patriarch, were both murdered in cold blood, after giving themselves up to the hands and protection of the government, and the governor, together with his military leaders, after vowing they would have their protection, and a fair trial; yet we believe that in that state, and in other states, there are honest and noble men, who loathe being guilty of shedding innocent blood; and were it in their power, they would wipe away the bloody stains from their nation. If such wish to become innocent before God and the public, let them speak out against such oppression, such atrocities and thirsting for the blood of the Saints and the prophets in the country. The cause is between them, their country, and their God. But we reiterate what we have said many times before, and what we have ever shown by our conduct from the beginning, namely that we as a people, despite our sufferings and our persecutions, are faithful subjects, and are more ready than anyone else to defend the laws and institutions of our mother country, and we shall do our utmost for them, if we are permitted; and we exhort the Saints throughout the world to be obedient to, and respect, the laws that protect their persons, their property, and their rights, in whatever government and country they may live, suffering wrong, rather than doing wrong to anyone. This we have ever done, and mean still to continue to do. We anticipate sending a petition to the government as soon as circumstances will permit, to request the right to establish a territorial government in the *Great Basin.*

Now, brethren, we have given you a brief idea of the most salient things that have transpired among us since we were driven from Nauvoo, the present situation of the Saints in this vicinity, and our views in general, as preparatory to answer your important question, which is asked us constantly from every part of the world, namely, "What must *we* do?"

We answer,—Gather yourselves together speedily, to this place, and if possible be ready to start from hence by the first of May, or as soon as grass is sufficiently grown for the animals, and to go to the main city, carrying as much provision with you, if possible, as will sustain you until you produce more from the earth. Let all the Saints who have been scattered from Nauvoo, and other states, gather immediately to the east bank of the Missouri river, bringing with them all the stock, and other young animals, that they can buy. Also let all the Saints in Canada, and the United States, come as quickly as circumstances permit, together with their wealth, and all the things needed for the purpose of colonizing in a new land. Let the Saints buy all they can of young cattle and horses as they come along the way here, for they are greatly needed nere, and will be ready sale; and when here, let all who can continue on directly over the mountains; and those who cannot go further, let them work the land here, raising all kinds of crops needed for provisions, and so they can sell to others who may come, and through that prepare themselves to complete their journey. By interchange of labor and their brethren, even the poor will be able, not only to provide sustenance for their families, but to obtain animals, and to build wagons. By sale of their improvements and their increase to those who come after them, and who will be desirous of purchasing, all will be able to emigrate comfortably to the end of their journey, and their permanent home. It would be good for all the Saints from everywhere to prepare themselves also with an abundance of warm and heavy clothing, instead of some that is too light, since they experience various kinds of weather before they cross the mountains.

We have named the lands of the *Pottawatamie* Indians as the place to meet, because the journey is so long, that it is not only desirable, but necessary, to have some rest; and this is the nearest point that is convenient for that; and since it is wilderness country, it will not infringe on the rights of anyone; and also, this place is more convenient because it is so close to the borders of the state of Missouri, so that only a few days travel are necessary to be able to trade in every needful thing.

To the Saints who are in England, Scotland, Ireland, and Wales, we say,—Emigrate as speedily as possible to this vicinity, looking to, and following the counsels you receive from the presidency in Britain; take ships to New Orleans, and steamboats from there directly to *Council Bluffs*, which will save much expense. Those who have but little means, nor hope of getting any, will soon exhaust that means if they remain where they are; therefore, it is wisdom that they remove without delay, for there is here an abundance of land, on which, through just their labor, they can speedily better their condition. Let all who can of all the Saints from every part of the world come, and bring with them all kinds of seeds, vegetables, flowers, and plants of all kinds of trees; in short, of everything that will please the eye, and gladden the heart, and cheer the soul of man, and that will grow out of the earth. Also, the best variety of technical machines for farming or technical use, yes, everything that tends to comfort, bless, and promote the success of any people in the world. So far as possible, however, bring drafts or plans of the machines, and they can be made in the places where they are used, through which great expense in transportation can be saved.

The brethren must recollect that their journey from this point will be through a savage country, and that not only their safety will depend to a great extent on their having an abundance of good firearms, together with powder and lead, but those will be necessary for hunting along the way; otherwise there is no certainty but what some uncivilized rascal will try to steal their animals from them.

Let the branch presidents read this epistle to those who are entrusted to their care, giving instruction and counsel abundantly as they are led by the Spirit, exhorting them to live in all things according to righteousness, and to walk humbly and piously in the fear of God, and to do his will in all things, so they may have his Spirit to lead them and to assist them speedily to the gathering place of the Saints. It is the duty of all parents to train up their children in the way they should go, instructing them in every correct and useful principle so fast as their understanding increases to receive them; and setting an example worthy of imitation; for all parents are responsible for their children until they arrive at the age of accountability. Mothers should teach their little ones to pray as soon as they are able to talk. Those who preside should be particular to instruct parents concerning their duty, and the teachers and the deacons should see that they do it faithfully.

It would be desirable for all emigrants to bring with them a copy of all books that are practical, historical, technical, and all other kinds that may be for the benefit of the rising generation. We have a printing press; and it would be of great benefit for all who can to bring writing and printing paper with them. Useful also will be all kinds of musical instruments, &c. Let every elder keep a journal, so the church historian will have historical facts concerning the church and the world.

Since Joseph Smith was murdered, many false prophets and false teachers have arisen, and tried to deceive many; but we have mostly tarried with the body of the church, and seeking to watch over, and lead the Saints to safety, leaving those false prophets to run out their race themselves, and die a natural death. And now, we intend before long to reorganize the church according to the original pattern, under the supervision of a first presidency and a patriarch. We feel that it will be the privilege of the twelve, after that, to spread out across the world, not to hinder, but to promote the gathering, to preach the gospel, and to gather the honest in heart from the four corners of the world. We exhort all the elders throughout the world especially to remember and conduct themselves according to the "Doctrine and Covenants," preaching nought to this generation but repentance; and those who have faith to repent, lead them down into the waters of baptism, lay hands on them for the reception of the Holy Ghost, and confirm them in the Church of Jesus Christ of Latter-day Saints, comfort their hearts, teach them to behave uprightly towards their fellowmen, administer to them the sacrament in remembrance of the death of Jesus Christ, and if they want further information, tell them to flee to Zion,—there the servants of God will be ready to wait upon them, and teach them all things that pertain to salvation; and everything different from this in your teaching cometh from evil, and it is not required at your hand, but leads to snares and temptations. Should any ask, Where is Zion? tell them in America. If any ask, What is Zion? tell them the pure in heart.

It is the duty of the rich Saints, according to their ability, to help the poor to emigrate; and if they choose, they may covenant with each other to be repaid at the first opportunity. It is also the duty of the rich to strive to lead out, rather than delay coming, so they can set up useful machinery, *factories*, and whatever jobs they choose, which will give work to the poor, and produce all kinds of clothing and things necessary for the comfort, growth, enjoyment, glorification, and happiness of the Saints; and no one needs to be ignorant in these matters, if he walks sufficiently humble before God, as to keep and understand the still small voice of the Holy Ghost within him continually.

Let all the Saints who love God more than their own dear selves—and none are Saints unless they do this—gather without delay to the place appointed, bringing with them of all things within their reach, to build, adorn, and glorify the house of the Lord, together with wisdom and skillful knowledge, carved work of all woods and metals, and anything that ever was, or is, or is to be, for the exaltation, glory, and salvation of the living and the dead, temporal and spiritual, for time and for eternity. Come then, walking in righteousness before God, and your labor shall be accepted; kings will be your nursing fathers, and queens will be your nursing mothers, and the glory of the whole earth shall be yours in connection with all those who shall keep the commandments of God; or else, the Bible will fail, the ancient prophets, which the present generation professes to believe, for the time has come for the Saints to go up to the mountain of the Lord's house, and the name of the Lord shall be there,—and the excellency of the Lord will be there, the glory of the Lord will be there, and the exaltation of his Saints will be there. There he will hold them as in the hollow of his hand, when the scourges of Jehovah flow through to depopulate the earth, and to lay waste the nations because of their wickedness, and to cleanse the earth from pollution and blood.

We are at peace with all nations, with all countries, with all governments, and with all authorities under the whole heavens, except the kingdom of darkness, which is from beneath; and we are ready to stretch forth our hands to the four quarters of the globe, extending salvation to every honest soul; for our mission in the gospel of Jesus Christ is from sea to sea, and from the river to the ends of the earth; and the blessings of heaven are upon us; and when every other arm shall fail, the power of the Almighty shall be made manifest in our behalf, for we ask nothing but what is right, we want nothing but what is right, and God has said that our strength shall be equal to our day; and we invite all presidents, emperors, kings, princes, judges, and rulers, from every nation, country, and tongue, under the whole heaven, to come and help us to build a house to the name of the God of Jacob, a place of peace, a city of rest, a habitation for the oppressed of every clime, yes, for those who love their neighbors as they do themselves, and who are willing to do as they would be done unto. This we are determined to do, and we will do also through the strength of our God; and we will help those who sustain wholesome laws to nurture and defend purity, virtue, and goodness, and to punish doers of evil.

The kingdom which we are establishing is not of this world, but it is the kingdom of the great God; its fruit is righteousness, peace, and salvation for every honest soul who receives it, from Adam down to the latest who receives it. We have good will towards all men, and we desire to clothe them with temporal and eternal salvation; and we will do them good so far as God will give us the power, and men will permit us the privilege; we will do no evil or harm to any man, but if men will rise up against the Almighty to overthrow his cause, let them know assuredly, that they are running on the thick bosses of Jehovah's buckler, and as God lives, they will be destroyed.

Come then, ye Saints; come, ye honorable men of the earth; come then, ye wise, ye learned, ye rich, ye great, according to your riches, your wisdom, and the knowlege ye have of Jehovah and his work, from all nations, kindreds, countries, peoples, and tongues, under the whole heavens, and join the standard of Emmanuel; help us to build the kingdom of God, and to plant and nurture the principles of truth, life, and salvation, and you shall receive your reward among the sanctified, when our Lord Jesus Christ cometh to make up his jewels, and no power on the earth or in hell can prevail against you.

The kingdom of God consists of correct principles; and it mattereth not so much to us what a man's religious faith is, whether he be a Presbyterian, or a

Methodist, or a Baptist, or a Mormon, or a Campbellite, or a Catholic, or an Episcopalian, or Mahometan, or even pagan, or anything else, if he will bow the knee, and with his tongue confess the Lord Jesus Christ, if he will support wholesome and peaceful laws, we hail him as a brother; and we will stand by him while he supports us in these things; for every man's religious faith is a matter between him and his God alone; but if he shall deny the Jesus, if he shall curse God, if he shall indulge in debauchery, and drunkenness, and crime, if he shall lie, and swear, and steal, if he shall take the name of the Lord in vain, and commit all manner of sin wantonly, he shall have no place in our midst, for we have long sought to find a people that will work righteousness, and distribute justice equally, that will acknowledge God in all their ways, who will respect and obey those ordinances and laws that are recorded in that sacred book called the Bible, which we verily believe, and which we proclaim to the ends of the earth.

We do not claim pre-eminence; we want no pre-eminence; but where God has placed us, there we will stand; and that is, to be one with our brethren, and our brethren are those who keep the commandments of our God, and who will do the will of our Father who is in heaven; and shoulder-to-shoulder we will stand, and with them we will dwell in time and in eternity.

Come then, ye Saints of Latter-day, and all ye great and small, wise and foolish, noble and ignoble, rulers and ruled, who are on the face of the earth, who love virtue and hate vice, and help us do this great work, which the Lord hath required at our hands; and inasmuch as the glory of the latter house shall exceed that of the former, then ye shall be rewarded an hundredfold, and your rest shall be glorious. Our chief motto is, "*Peace with God, and good will to all men.*"

Written at *Winter Quarters*, *Omaha Nation*, west bank of Missouri river, near *Council Bluffs*, North America, and signed December 23, 1847, in behalf of the *Quorum* of the twelve apostles.

BRIGHAM YOUNG, *President*,
WILLARD RICHARDS, *Scribe*.

We were obliged, because of the shortness of our small columns, to omit some things of this lengthy Epistle: but nothing, however, that bears any connection with the Welsh Saints; but such parts as have direct reference to those who are in other countries, and under different circumstances.

We beseech the most serious attention of the Saints, and especially the officers, to the important things that are in the above Epistle. We trust that the presidents will make this known in an intelligible manner to the Saints who are under their care; and if there is something unintelligible in it, ask for a clarification, and you shall have it to the best of our ability through the *Prophet*. Behold the awaited time has come, and again we ask, "*Who is ready to start homeward*?" We would be pleased to hear from those who are eager to start next February, as soon as they can, namely what their circumstances are, and whether they can get seven or eight pounds for each member of the family after preparing here to start? for not much less will take them to *Council Bluffs* from here. Those who choose to go at that time, and who can afford to help others of their poor brothers and sisters, inform us how many, &c. Let the Saints remember that "a short work will the Lord make upon the earth." Let everyone remember also that each one has his free agency to go or to stay, and that everyone has a complete right to his freedom, his rights, and his own *possessions*, so that the poisonous tongues of our perverse and lying enemies will be stifled with respect to this glorious gathering; for no doubt neither Noah nor Lot ever heard a hundredth part of the lying and baseless tales, when going to the ark, or fleeing from Sodom, that numb the ears of the Saints in their emigation, which, together with a thousand other important reasons, cause us to long night and day to escape somehow by the skin of our teeth from the stupor, oppression, and recalcitrance of this wicked and perverse generation, to settle once again in that place, and among those blessed people, "where righteousness dwells." Ringing our bell loudly, and making a lot of noise about our going, will not facilitate anyone's departure, and perhaps it would be best not to make extensive preparations, such as selling possessions, &c., which is too rash, before having personal advice to that end, or until delving thoroughly into the relevant circumstances. It is indisputable that there is a need for wisdom, careful organizing, and faithfulness, to carry forth this great procession in an effective and beneficial manner for all. "In your patience possess ye your souls," is very pertinent counsel in this matter also. "Do all things in a proper and orderly manner," is our motto in this as in every other thing. There is nothing wrong with having someone come with you if he wishes, even if he is not a church member, but it is not permitted for a man to leave his wife in order to go, regardless of how oppressive she may be, nor is the wife to go without the permission of the husband. Let those who are yoked so unequally, pray and strive more that their unbelieving spouse will be convinced through them, and receive salvation.

NAUVOO.

Who lives at present
In Nauvoo?
Are they Saints of the great King?
Says Nauvoo.
I was owned by the children of God,
But their enemies came.
And the Saints in anger they drove,
From Nauvoo.

The Saints are on their journey
From Nauvoo.
Along the vast wilderness,
From Nauvoo.

They lost, yes, their city,—
But when God sees fit
They shall own the heavenly kingdom,
And Nauvoo. J. D.

THE PERSECUTION IN PEMBROKESHIRE.

Pembroke, March 17th, 1848.

DEAR BROTHER,—I have baptized but four since I last saw you, i.e., two months ago; but we are suffering a bit of persecution here also, especially in Haverfordwest. The practice of our religious neighbors has been for some time to disturb our worship in the chapel; but last Sunday, when I was preaching, the chapel was filled with men and boys, who began to scream and whistle, until it reached a great shout of *hurrah*, and prevented me from preaching. When I came out of the chapel Sunday night, the street was full of rioters maligning me and threatening me, and some of them flung dirt at me. Some of them closed the door, and were holding it shut, while others were inside; they tried to extinguish the light, and you may judge to what purpose, but through great effort I prevented them from doing so. I got hold of one of those who were holding the door, thinking to get his name, but soon his partner wrested him from my grasp. Our custom is for one brother to stand by the door to watch that these wicked lads not come to disturb us. Last Monday night, we met in the chapel to hold a worship service, and one of the brethren stood by the door; the rioters rushed at him, and they pushed him over the stairs to the street, and they beat him badly; he shouted out for his life, and when I reached him, several had hold of him on the ground, kicking him, &c., and he was covered with blood. The next day, he showed himself to the magistrate, and asked for protection of the law, and the magistrate counseled him to get a warrant for the attackers; but to our great surprise, when the guilty parties were brought forward, and they were proved guilty before the magistrate, they received neither punishment nor chastisement, nor did our brother receive a bit of compensation or protection, rather he was *obliged to pay all the costs himself ! !* Expecting that the magistrate would counsel them not to disturb us further, I explained to him their constant tricks, and that these were the main leaders of the continual rioters. The magistrate asked whether the chapel was registered, and I answered that it was; but they would not believe me unless I went to the clerk of the court to obtain a copy of that; and without a word of blame to the rioters, he said that the only thing I could do was to warrant them to appear before the Quarter Session, which would cost me about 20 pounds, they said. I went to the clerk of the office where the chapel was registered, and asked for a copy of the *license;* but he would not trouble himself to search the books for it. This is how the connection is between the great and the small, the noble and the common, the officers and the subjects, the believers and the unbelievers, all one against us testifying that they are children of the same father, and that because our religion is godly, and endangers the kingdom of the devil, he stirs everyone up against us. The rioters felt stronger with this support of the civil officers, so that they threatened in my face that they would do worse outrage in our chapel the next Sunday than ever before, and that they were determined to persecute us, until they overcame us somehow!

One of the magistrates asked me at the time, what we thought about the expression he had read on one of our letters of invitation, "authorized by Jesus Christ?" I answered that it was a commission or divine right to preach the gospel of Jesus Christ. At this he said mockingly, that he would be very sorry to hear that any of his relatives were beguiled by such heresy; and they turned me out of the room! Like this you see, Dear Brother, how those who profess to have a mission from God in this enlightened age, and this Christian country, are received! This reminds me of the words of our blessed Master, namely, "I come in my Father's name, and ye try to kill me; if another shall come in his own name [in the name of some Missionary Society, church, or reverends], him ye will receive." Quite similar, is it not? But despite it all, I and all the Saints give thanks for being counted worthy to suffer a bit for the sake of him who suffered so much for us, and we thank him more and more for the divine testimony we have of what we are doing, and that we have the divine treasure, namely the gospel of the Son of God, in clay vessels. Oh, brethren, pray for us, that our Father will hear us.

Your brother in the gospel,

JOHN MORRIS.

REMARKABLE HEALING OF BROKEN BONES.

ESTIMABLE EDITOR,—There is much shouting about signs, and challenging for as much as ONE example of the spiritual power of God among the Saints; and with your indulgence, I will inform you of one great blessing among many that I have seen, and I testify in truthfulness of spiritual healings that the children of God have received through the exercise and ordinances of the Church of Jesus Christ, which took place before my eyes, under my hands, and within my own family a few days ago. Yet, I am not so unversed in the wiles of the devil, and in the unbelief of this age as to expect this obvious fact to be a means of convincing those of this age who hear it (for it is not the case with those who see with their own eyes), any more than the powerful works of the Son of God convinced his contemporaries of his divinity, which is obvious from the facts of his challenge to them to believe him because of his works; despite that, the more miracles he performed the more they stoned him, yes, and crucified him finally because of them. I do not doubt that their anger would be such to the extent that they were able to see the powerful works of God through his children; if one were to rise from the dead, they would be just as desirous to kill him again, for fear of his influence, as were those to kill Lazarus whom Christ had raised from the dead.

My purpose in offering the following story for your publication, is so that the Saints may rejoice and give thanks together with me and glorify God for his goodness, who is the only Provider of every bounteous blessing. Only he deserves the praise. The story I propose took place as follows:—

Two months ago, my eleven-year-old boy was crushed between the *trams* in Cyfarthfa Colliery, so that the bones of his leg were broken in two places. He was carried to my house; and, according to the rules of the works, the doctor hired by the works came there soon, and set the bones in place, and put splints around the leg. The doctor said the bones were broken in two places. Soon after the doctor left I administered to the boy the divine ordinance according to the scriptures (see James v, 14, &c.), and he was eased of all pain at that time, and the boy testified that he was completely well, and earnestly begged to take off the splints and get up from his bed; but we refused him this, lest we be punished by the doctors, as we and several other Saints who had been divinely healed had been threatened. The third day the doctor visited him again; and after looking at the leg, with great surprise he testified that the bones had knitted already. Again the doctor admitted that the bones had been broken in two places, and that he had never seen such healing before; for he did not know of the administration of the ordinance. After this another doctor came to the house, and questioned the women that were in the house in a very surly manner about "the oil they had put on the boy's leg, that he wanted to see it," &c. The women answered that they had not put oil on his leg, which was a truth in itself. He begged every day to get up and go outside, assuring us that he was quite well. Then we allowed him to go around, provided he took a stick in his hand and took care not to let the doctor see him outside; and he was so pleased with the freedom that we could hardly keep him in the house another minute, except when the doctor was expected. Like this he went around Merthyr with the splints hanging around his leg, and he did not dare to remove them. On the eleventh day the doctor came and asked where the boy was. My wife answered that he was in the field playing with the boys with no stick or anything. He had to see before he would believe; then he said that he was healing so well the last time that he had thought of allowing him the next time to get up to the fire, with his leg on pillows; but to his surprise there the boy was before him! My wife said to the doctor that some of the neighbors, on seeing the boy walking so soon, said that the bones had not been broken, and others said that "only the *small bone* had been broken." The doctor replied that he was not a bit surprised at their disbelief, because it appeared to be such an incredible thing to see the healing of broken bones so soon; and it would be difficult for the doctor himself to believe, except that he knew for a fact beyond all argument that the bones had been broken. He refused to take off the splints, nonetheless. The next day the boy went past the shop of the doctors on his way to Merthyr, and they looked at him through the window in astonishment; and as soon as they took the splints off his leg, the boy went back to work completely well, where he has been working since that time until the present.

About two years ago this boy broke his other leg in a similar fashion, and received similar healing; but despite all the threatening and scolding on the part of the doctor, around the boy went, and eventually to work without the doctor's permission. Let anyone who wishes tell whatever tales he chooses about this thing, as they did about the leg of William Hughes, &c., &c., yet not one man would dare to stand to my face and refute the above truths. There are hundreds of others that know that it is true; and I acknowledge the Almighty God with gratitude for the blessing.

I am, your brother in the gospel,

45, *Cyfarthfa Row*,
Georgetown, *March*, 1848.

THOMAS REES.

These are the names of those who heard the testimony of the doctor,—

DAVID X JOHN,
MARY X JOHN,
MARGARET REES.

A REMARKABLE DREAM AND ITS FULFILLMENT.

"WHEN in a deep sleep one night, I found myself in a large field amidst a large crowd, and listening to some stranger preaching, and speaking much about some book that he held in his hand. After he had finished, I approached him, and asked him what book it was. He gazed intently into my eyes for a moment; then, extending the book into my hand, he said, "Treasure this book in your memory, and print it in your heart; and while you keep hold of it, all the spirits of the court below cannot harm you." I took the book and went (according to the instructions of the man) into a dungeon that was nearby. He bade me knock on the first iron door I came to, which, after I knocked, opened on its rusty hinges; and the first greeting was a huge lion leaping towards me, roaring and opening his jaws as if he would finish me at once; but I noticed that he was restrained by a great chain, which heartened me to go on past him. At this he saw the book under my arm, and in a voice like a man's voice he persuaded, begged, and begged earnestly, and pleaded gently, and in every way, to get possession of the book. He promised surely to give it back to me in a while. But I remembered the advice I had been given, and that my life depended on keeping hold of the book. And after pressing it closer to my bosom, I ventured along a narrow road, as through the middle of a den filled with every kind of beast on chains, and all wanting the book from me, but in vain. After reaching the furthest edge, I knocked at another iron door, which opened to a room very similar to the last, but its inhabitants were snakes, scorpions, and the like. I soon understood that they had in them a strong attraction toward the book to destroy it and myself, I supposed; but I held onto it with my hands until I reached safely through to the third room, which to my surprise, except for the road which was through the middle, was full of men, most of them naked, standing up in chairs on every side, obviously in great pain. At times, they gnashed their teeth, but they could not reach to maul each other. My attention was drawn from this heartrending sight to a large man who came along the road from the furthest edge towards me slowly; and as loud as were the cries of the rest, the cry of this one pierced my heart even more keenly;—groans every step—his hands folded—his hair white, and his gown long and black, frightened me as he drew nearer to me; but when he was close to me, I took heart, and asked him what could cause such pains and excruciating torture as that? Then, he lifted his head a little, and gazed at me in astonishment, as if he had not seen me before; he opened his clothing, and then I saw his breast shining like a blazing fire, and immediately he closed his garment again; and all he said was, "If I had that book, I would not be in these pains;" then he went past groaning as before. But I chose to turn back; and through difficulties and great dangers I came out of their midst safely.

I awoke, and behold it was a dream; yes, a dream that affected me more than any other thing ever before. I imagined and pondered much about what it signified, and what book that was, but all in vain, until in a few months when in another part of the country, over 200 miles from there, I went with my friends on a Sunday afternoon to listen to some stranger who was preaching some new and strange things in a nearby field. As soon as I arrived, I remembered my dream. I recognized the scene at once. After he finished, I asked him to see the book he held in his hand; and after gazing at me with the same eyes as I saw in the dream and in a similar voice, which pierced through the marrow and the bones, he handed the book to me, reciting the above words about it exactly as I had dreamed. This affected me until I almost fainted; despite this I quickly opened the book, and read, for the first time ever, the title "BOOK OF MORMON." As soon as I found it, I believed it, and I obeyed it, and thanks be to its divine author for the enjoyment of its precious promises."

ANNOUNCEMENT.

IT is intended to hold the Monmouth Conference in *Nantyglo*, on the last Sunday of April.

We expect to see there a number of the Saints who can come, and especially the officers, and all branch presidents, prepared to represent the branches, their number, how many baptized since the previous Conference, the number of the various officers, together with the spiritual condition of the Saints, &c.

CONTENTS.

MERTHYR TYDFIL:

PUBLISHED AND FOR SALE BY D. JONES, AND ALSO FOR SALE BY THE SAINTS IN GENERAL.

JOHN JONES, PRINTER, RHYDYBONT.

PROPHET OF THE JUBILEE,

OR

STAR OF THE SAINTS.

No. 23.] MAY, 1848. [Price 2c.

LETTER FROM WILLIAM DAVIES.

Llanelli, Carmarthenshire.

Dear Brother Jones,—

It is with pleasure that I make use of this opportunity to inform you of my feelings and my decision about the glorious religion that I profess at present, namely the religion of the Latter-day Saints, after being for many long years zealous with the Baptists, the belief of which was very different from what I think of it by now, and different from the true religion of the New Testament.

Dear Brother,—It was not until I heard and obeyed this religion that I understood a little in relation to it, and I saw its divine and unchanging truths shining its rays of light through its preaching, although those who declared it to the world appeared very poor; yet, by this they bore the same character as their brethren formerly, those whom the Son himself chose from amongst men to preach his gospel, namely the apostles, and their fellow-brethren of that time, who were pleasing to heaven, but poor in the sight of the world. However, I was not without feelings with the Baptists, but they were very different from my present feelings. How much all this difference is I cannot say; but I shall tell a little of it, namely that it is as much difference as between sound and substance—between light and darkness—between day and night—between truth and falsehood—between fantasy and the power of religion; yes, as much difference as there is between being a member of the church of Jesus Christ and being an outsider. Also, it is easy for me, in this church, to understand the New Testament upon hearing its doctrines being taught, its ordinances being administered, and the promised blessings in it being divided "to every man severally as he will;"—earlier we had a church in one place, and the Testament in another, being impossible to recognize the Testament by the church, or the church by the Testament, without distorting the Testament through explaining it, &c. But in the church of Jesus Christ, the one which is among the Latter-day Saints, to read the Testament is to read the church,—to go to the church is to go to the place where the promises of the Testament are *fulfilled*, or where the will is given to the heirs by the Head of the church, who is Jesus Christ. My determination is to go forward with this religion, through the strength of my Father who is in heaven, and do whatever I can to spread it, let men say whatever they wish, "that I am not so zealous as I was before," despite that I will go forward, and intend to do my best to put down the false religions of the world, and to build up the religion of the Lamb. Although I tried my best with religion for about twelve years, I failed to obtain one conviction of my acceptance by God; but at best it was practically all fears and doubts; but after getting hold of this one, there are no fears concerning the plan, rather great certainty through the Holy Ghost that this is his church. There are many different religions in the world; but among them all, this I shall say, that

This is the best religion I have seen,
And that I have liked in the world;
This one brings to all men
Who come to it with obedient mind,
All knowledge, for perfecting
Them on their journey to their land,
And they will have the Holy Spirit,
To lead them to their Father.

Oh, that all my former and honest brethren, would come and experience this! They will receive a reward a hundred thousand times better than they now have, and in the end eternal life. This is the wish and the earnest and constant prayer of their well-wisher,

WILLIAM DAVIES.

MIRACLE OF THE INDEPENDENTS ! !

MR. ED.,—I suppose it will be good, if not new, for you and all your readers, to hear of the noteworthy miracle that was caused here lately. This is not a "Mormon Miracle;" otherwise, I would expect to have read about it in the *Revivalist*, and all the other publications throughout the country; but this is a miracle that puts an end to the debate with respect to the age of miracles forever, I suppose, the way it proceeds. Neither can one claim that it is deceit because one of the *Satanists* performed it. Oh no, one of the ram's horns of great Independia is the worker of these miracles; and even more remarkable, Sir, this is the *Slugger* who would follow the Saints from house to house, from one street to the next, all through the last season, practically, to disrupt their meetings, and who would come to the place before them, and take their publications from them, &c. His main chant at that time was, "Miracles have ceased," "Miracles were unnecessary after the age of the apostles," yes, he sounded his screeching horn almost as loudly as another Davies from Dowlais, that no one but the "Satanists and the Mohammedans claim miracles, and that is the same thing as Infidelism." But now behold the same man with the same tongue praying to God publicly from his pulpit, and begging him to remove those who posed an obstacle to the peaceful decision on the Dowlais *lease*; namely out of this world through judgment of course, he means, ready or not! The news came back that the *Marquis of Bute* had died quite suddenly, and great is the chatter through Dowlais of this, that it was the fulfillment of a miracle. "There is a challenge for you Saints to perform a miracle; there is a miracle for you," says the family of Independia.

But for my part I believe that performing miracles like that constitutes a craft akin to and suitable for thieves! I wonder whether this slugger-like preacher believed that God would answer such a prayer from his mouth? It was even worse then for him to say it if he did not believe that; yet I would like to know what is the difference between the principle of that man who prays for God to kill his fellowman, and his doing that himself if he could? He who would do the one thing would do the other if he had a chance, I suppose; or else he shows great foolishness in asking God to do what he will not do himself! Also, what is the difference between claiming the praise for this miracle and claiming the praise for the murder? How much greater a miracle would it be for him to pray the *Marquis* back into the world than it was for him to pray him out of it? Let him try that again, and no doubt it will be better than ever. Forgive me for answering the fools according to their foolishness this time, for their contradictions around Dowlais here are too shameless to answer in any other way; but we hope that despite this that this Independent miracle turns them to their senses, and that they will admit the age of miracles from now on, though they be different miracles from the foregoing that we mean. Behold the *Shopkeeper* and the *Slugger* head-to-head, nose-to-nose, and tooth-to-tooth, in this miracle also, and it is unlikely that they will finish the argument any time soon. May the God of heaven open the eyes of the men of Dowlais, to discern the true from the false, is the wish of your, &c.,

LEM. WILLIAMS.

TWOFOLD MIRACLE !

MR. ED.,—Inasmuch as there are many different stories being spread through this valley and other places, with respect to the misfortune that befell me lately, I consider it my obligation to the truth, and its lovers, to give a truthful report of the circumstance, and many besides myself wish for it to have space to appear in the columns of the *Prophet*, and I hope that you agree with our request, and that all the Saints will strive against giving way to similar unbelief and suffering.

On Saturday morning, the 18th of March, I was severely burned, especially my face and hands, by the *damp* in the coal works. My fellow-workers were very sympathetic and covered me against the breeze when I came to the surface, and led me to my house, and put me to lie upon straw in the corner, and soaked cloths in oil for fire burns, according to the usual practice, and I was in great pain all the time. One of the Saints went to Aberdare to fetch oil from the church, and brought back elder W. Howells with him, who having arrived, found me in the situation noted, and he began to teach those that were in the house that it was not only a privilege and a custom, but also an obligation on the Saints, to obey the divine commandments to anoint with oil, to lay on hands, and to pray to God to heal the sick, which the brother did with me, and I testify in thankfulness to God, that immediately the pain left me completely, and I got up in the sight of them all, praising God for this precious blessing. There were many in the house at the time, and they marvelled greatly. We held a meeting of prayer and thanksgiving to God for the healing, and everyone was very happy, and none more than I myself. About an hour afterwards Mr. H. and the Saints went away, and I intended at that time to return to the coal works; but because it was the end of the week, &c., I did not go. By the afternoon, the matter had caused an unusual commotion throughout the area, and the common assertion was by those who had not seen me, that I had not been burned, but that the whole thing was ficticious to deceive men. Many came to my house, and having seen that I was well, and completely without pain, they affirmed decidedly to my face that I had not been burned. Some religionists accused me of daring to purposely claim such a thing to deceive men. Some cried before me, especially one woman who was my neighbor, and begged me not to tell such a lie that I had been burned. The more I showed them my healthy skin, and my hair and eyebrows that had been burned, the more they were infuriated against me, gnashing their teeth at me. I remained completely without pain until the assertions of the impudent unbelievers began to affect me, so as to cause me to disbelieve the fact to a considerable extent. At about six o'clock I began to feel the burns of the fire coming back a little, and they continued to increase, until by Monday morning they were burning as much as they had been before the administering of the ordinance, and they blistered badly. After those who alleged that I had not been burned saw this, they could no less than believe to the contrary of their former allegations, and then they blamed me for neglecting to get medical treatment. By now the public gossip, namely that I had not been burned, had turned completely, and now they asserted that I had not been healed, but that it was all a lie of the Saints, which many believe to this day, because I was for about a fortnight unable to work because of the excruciating pains of the burns. Whatever may be said to the contrary, this in brief is the truth of the matter, and I advise all the Saints to take care not to listen to such heretical accusers, and sin against God, and by that bring shame on this holy religion; and my prayer is to have strength by the day, to continue in it to the end. I am your brother in the gospel,

EVAN DAVIES.

Cwmbach, April 21, 1848.

I also testify that the foregoing account is true. I was one of those working with E. D. I saw him in the fire, I followed him from the mine to his house, and I myself put the burn oil on him first. I was there while Mr. Howells anointed him, and prayed over him, and my eyes saw him rising from the straw immediately, and my hears heard him say that he was completely healed, and he praised God for his healing, and prayed in the meeting that was held in the house after that. I believed that he was well; I heard him say that he was about to return to work; and after going through the neighborhood, and leaving him well in the house, I told everyone who asked me that he was better, and that he would be at work as usual on Monday, and the reason he did not come was what he said himself. My witness is true, although some doubt me; and although I am not one of the Saints, nor do I believe their religion, yet I testify to the truth for the sake of those who wish to know the truth of this remarkable story. I am, &c.,

DAVID MORRIS.

There are many peculiarities in the foregoing account that are worthy of attention, such as;—

1. It proves very clearly that men do not believe miracles now, any more than in the age of the apostles, despite their seeing them with their own eyes, which gainsays the popular heresy which says "that the purpose of miracles is to convince unbelievers:" and it shows the foolishness of seeking a sign to cause anyone to believe, for this incident indicates quite the opposite, as in hundreds of other miraculous circumstances that can be noted amongst the Saints, even in Wales. In spite of this, *they do not believe so*. But when they fail to disprove the incident entirely, they prefer to give all the glory to the devil instead of to God, which proves very clearly children of which of the two they are.

2. The foregoing account shows the skill of the devil in attempting to blind men, and to put to scorn the children of God; and the truth of the matter is almost too incredible for the world to believe.

3. It proves the truthfulness of Jesus Christ when he says, "According to thy faith be it unto thee." Who cannot see here the indispensable necessity for faith in every reasonable creature, to be worthy of the miraculous blessings from God? Furthermore, says the scripture, "Without faith it is impossible to please God."

4. Beware you Saints, lest the devil tempt you also through similar unbelief, and take the blessing from you; for, if he cannot prevent you from receiving it, he will not hesitate in attempting through every craft, to steal it from you afterwards; and the greater the blessing, the greater his temptations.

5. One can see the folly, the loss, and the disgrace that are caused by listening to and believing our professed enemies and their lying allegations. "From such turn away your ears."

6. Let the Saints learn experience and patience from this, to suffer all the lies of their enemies without commotion, looking forward faithfully to the court of judgment where even the "*Saints*" will have the truth, which is vain for them to expect in any other place.

7. One sees that the more the children of the devil see of the power of

God before their eyes, through the mighty workings of the Holy Spirit, the more they become enraged against them, like the most impudent servants of Beelzebub of old, who, the more they saw of the power of God through his Son, the more they shouted in his face,—"He hath a devil." "Faith comes through hearing," and not through seeing, according to Paul's truthfulness. The ear is the means, and not the eyes—the word that is believed convinces, and not miracles; for "we walk by faith, not by sight," as all the scripture instructs us. May we have sufficient faith to accept and to hold onto every temporal and spiritual blessing that we may need.—ED.

LETTER OF ELDER ABEL EVANS.

Ffestiniog, April 24th, 1848.

DEAR BROTHER JONES,—

The best news I have to tell you in this letter is that some agitation has begun in the North, and the people are generally listening, and some are also obeying.

Mr. Parry, from Liverpool, came with me to Mostyn to work, and in a short while he and his sons are coming to Wales again to live, to work, and to preach. I baptized eight the week before last near Newmarket, a man and wife who live in the *Light House*, *Point of Ayr*, and five from Newmarket, and one from Llansaint; and John Parry is the president over all of them there. Mr. Davies, an Independent minister there, tried to create a division in the family of John Williams, coachmaker, by going there and saying that the Saints had come there to eat the food of his children; but he got a *tidy* rebuke for that from the man and his wife. I went to Rhosllanerchrugog last Wednesday, and Mr. Jones (from Liverpool), a Wesleyan minister, had been speaking against the Saints on Tuesday night; but it was necessary to pay sixpence to come and hear him. Robert Evans happened to be there that night, and he went to listen to the lecture by paying sixpence. He asked permission from the chairman to review the lecture, which he received. But he was stopped before long, because he was gaining influence over the people to perceive the lies of the lecture. After being stopped, he announced that Wednesday night he would review the lecture completely and in detail, at which time hundreds came to listen, and he smashed Mr. Jones's lecture to bits.

Seven from Cefnmawr were baptized the week before last, and five promised me on Friday that they would be baptized in public today, Easter Monday. Thus things are on fire in Rhos and Cefn. I am on my way now to request copies of the *Prophet*. I shall send another letter at the end of the month with a more complete account. We desperately need preachers in Bethesda, Caernarvonshire. The Saints are firm in the faith, and filled with the spirit almost without exception throughout the North, and enjoying the gifts of the Holy Spirit. Please be so kind as to remember me to all the Saints there. I am your brother in the new covenant,

ABEL EVANS.

We have received several letters from this faithful brother lately, showing baptisms in several other places. We are pleased to hear of their success and their faithfulness, and that the same Spirit that gladdens the hearts of the Saints of the South, leads and directs the Saints of the North to a unity of the faith also.

Gentle Saints, do not lose heart because the priests of great Babylon curse your religion. Neither their curses, nor all they can lecture and publish in the North will do you any harm, nor prevent the success of your religion, any more than did all they could do and say in these parts; and we are sure that they cannot say anything that prevents reasonable people from obeying the gospel; and those that believed their foolish tales would be of little benefit to you, nor would they be of any glory to God, if they came to you. It is necessary to gather the tares out of the midst of the wheat with such baskets as these. The lies that our persecutors utter against us are not enough excuse for one reasonable person to refuse our message; because if they were to come humbly to obey the conditions of the gospel, our God would prove to them beyond any doubt that all is baseless false accusations. What reason to believe them, then? What use to devote much of oneself to disprove them either, since God will do that for us, and in a much clearer fashion also?

Let us take heart in the face of it all then; and like the above uproar in the Rhos, so it is in every other place; they do good to the truth by drawing men's attention to it, and then embracing it. It is true that all things, especially such lectures, work together for the benefit and success of *Mormonism*. Let them lecture, gnash their teeth, blaspheme, shout and yell, make and scatter their claims, as they wish, for we have more for us than against us, namely God, despite all the ugly howling of the wolves. The death pangs of their great goddess are these howlings, namely the lecturing and similar things that are directed against the Saints.—ED.

GREETING OF THE "*PROPHET OF THE JUBILEE*."

Prophet of the Jubilee beware:—too harsh
To the sight is thy course;
And thy nature, in Noah's language,
Like a summer's evening.

Thou nurturest some empty imaginings;—not the word of God,
Rather thy purposes lead astray;
And thou shoutest some blasphemies,
Thou hast renoun from Abergavenny to Anglesey.

Keep to more definite things,—the Bible,
For the peoples who are disappointed;
If thou wilt insist in having an age of enjoyment,
Avoid speaking about the Saints.

The dear language of Matthew and Mark and Luke;—now,
Through an oath, as John,

Hand in hand *will* have a pure gospel
Exactly as she came forth.

Promising after the apostles,—to all,
Throughout the world, of her faithful,
That they would receive gifts—these rights,
To the extent of *signs*. SINGER OF THE TUNE.

VERSES OF D. JAMES, VICTORIA.

M. N. 8 and 7.

I HEARD the voice of the harps of heaven,
Resounding out above the sky,—
"Oh, for strength to remember daily
The man who was on the tree."
It is high time for us to awaken,
And to cease being cowardly,
For Jesus is telling us
That the time is drawing nigh.

M. N. 7 and 6.

My beloved Jesus will come,
Singing to meet his Saints;
The glorious morning will dawn,
And great will be our privilege.
The golden harps will sing,
Up above the sky;
And then Hallelujah,
I will sing forever, Amen.

THE SAINT OUT OF PRISON, AND HIS DEFENSE.

Ynysybont, *March* 25*th*, 1848.

OUR DEAR BROTHER JONES,—

We are happy to inform you that we have come to this point successfully. While on the way, we were informed by a responsible minister that he had heard from honest men that Thomas Harris had been a light-minded, lying, and ungodly drunkard, in Aberaeron, Llanddewi Aberarth, Cribyn, Talsarn, &c. That caused much grief to me, W. Evans, and I pressed Thomas Harris hard to tell the truth, and he testified that he was not guilty of such a thing. Then we decided to go to those places to find out if those accusations were true. Cribyn was the first place we went to. I, W. Evans, asked the people how T. Harris had behaved when he had come there to preach? the answer from everyone was, that they had never seen anyone more proper in every way than Thomas Harris, and that they had not heard from anyone that he was a drunkard, &c., and that the people did not believe that he had stolen the book deliberately. Not one witness came against him here, but many were eager to hear him preaching again soon. After that we went to Llanddewi Aberarth, where the owner of the book in question lived. We soon told the people what was in our message, and then they took the news to the village, where the people came together joyfully to see Thomas Harris; but no one was more pleased than Mr. Davies, the owner of the book, who gave his hand affectionately to T. H., confessing in the presence of the crowd these words,—"I never believed, my dear Harris, that you had stolen the book deliberately; and whatever trouble you have had, I can say that it has not been more than has been on us as a family, because of this circumstance." Then Thomas Harris gave a report of the way he found the book in his pocket without knowing how it had come to be there. He admitted also that he was at fault for neglecting to return the book at once himself, instead of trusting another to do that, during which the tears were streaming down the cheeks of Mr. Davies, the owner of the book, out of sympathy.

Then I, W. Evans, stood up, endeavoring to show to the crowd some of the principles of the Saints, and the good character of T. H. while a member with the Independents, and after his coming to the Saints, until the circumstance of the taking of the book; and after that T. H. arose again, and asked if there was anyone there that could say they had seen any unseemly behavior in him while he was preaching in the area? The answer was, that no one had, until the taking of the book. I, W. E., asked the owner of the book, whether he had seen any sign of a drunkard, liar, &c., in T. H.? and I said that I had heard that from a minister who belonged to the Independents. Mr. Davies answered that there was nothing of the sort. Then we went to Aberaeron, and we gave sixpence to a *crier* to go around the town to announce a meeting. Scores of people came together, among which was that *policeman* who had taken me up, and very mockingly; despite that the common people continued to listen politely. We went on in the same way as in Llanddewi; but there was no one there who could say to the face of Thomas Harris that he was guilty of the character mentioned above, despite persuading them to answer; but we had testimonies completely different from that of the *policeman*, and the people of the house where we stayed. When our work was finished, a man came to us, and asked when we would come to preach in his house, which was about three miles from there? We were in Llanybydder Thursday night, when I, T. H., received my place back in the church, and I decided from now on, to the best of my ability, not to leave room for the enemies of truth to revile. May the gracious Lord give me strength, and may this trial continue to be for the benefit of lovers of truth, is the prayer of your unworthy brethren, WILLIAM EVANS,
THOMAS HARRIS.

After Thomas Harris was released from prison, there was a further inquiry before the Council of the Glamorgan Conference, where it was unanimously permitted that he should have his church membership, on the conditions that he go through the environs where he had been preaching when the unpleasant misfortune had taken place, and to make known there, in order to remove the obstruction out of the way of the honest in heart, the truth of all the aforementioned circumstances. At the inquiry additional supportive testimonies of the story which we have published already in the *Prophet* about this matter were given, and they demonstrated even more clearly that T. H. had no intention of stealing this book; and when it is understood that the man referred to in the previous account had come to the house where the book was lost with the express purpose of opposing T. H. as he preached, and that he obstinately argued with him after the meeting,—the same man happened by the next morning, and was the first one to utter a word about the book, to call the attention of the family of the house to it,—that he said he would guarantee that the Saint had stolen it, and then ran to fetch the *policeman* with no one asking that of him, and many other suspicious tricks which came to light with time, it will be understood more fully yet, we say, that the whole thing was one of the wiles of the children of perdition, and that, in order to disgrace and blacken divine truths that they could not gainsay. Again, he who digs a pit for his neighbor will fall into it himself. If there were not one other proof of the divine source of our religion, it would be thought that the union of the children of this world to plan evil, and to persecute the Saints, would be sufficient proof to every sensible man; and the Sectarian and slanderous Editors of our country, prove that they themselves are of the same stripe, by publishing every tale about the Saints, and not only to proclaim the truth of the matter, but barefaced lies, and those often contradicting each other! For example, notice the filthy *Baptist*, and its "scratched out his name," "admitted that he had stolen it," &c., &., when there was not a syllable of truth in them.

MONMOUTH CONFERENCE.

THIS Conference was held in Nantyglo, April 2, 1848. The morning session was begun by singing, and elder T. Pugh prayed. Then Capt. Jones addressed the large crowd that had assembled, by outlining the purpose of the meeting, and the necessity of unity and love in the church of Jesus Christ, and the joy that derived from such things. Then elder W. Phillips offered to preside over the Conference, which was unanimously approved; D. Jones, Penycae, offered to be the scribe, which also was approved. After that Capt. Jones addressed the congregation in English, showing the same duties to the English brethren and sisters. Then the president called on the representatives of the different branches to give an accounting of them, and they were found to be as follows:—

	eld.	prst.	tch.	deac.	bap.	mem.	total	
Nantyglo	6	4	4	2	23	49	65	T. Giles
Penycae	2	4	2	2	12	23	33	D. Jones
Blackwood		1	1		1	16	18	D. Lewis
Tredegar	1	3	2	1	11		27	W. Evans
Cwmcelyn		2	2	1	9	27	32	T. Giles
Abersychan	2	7	5	2	65	82	98	J. Jones
Blaenavon	2	2			2		10	W. Lewis
Victoria	3	5	3	1	50		66	J. James
Total	16	28	19	9	173		349	
Last Conf.	12	25	18	8			209	
Increase	4	3	1	1	173		140	

The representatives reported that all the branches were in good condition, and with signs of great increase, not only in numbers, but also in gifts, love, faithfulness, and unity, and there was hardly any exception throughout the conference.

At half past two o'clock, the Saints' meeting began by singing, and D. Jones, Penycae, prayed. Then the president addressed the meeting briefly and enthusiastically: and he was followed by Capt. Jones, enthusiastically and powerfully on the principles and ordinances of religion.

One was confirmed. Then the Lord's Supper was partaken of. After that eight elders were called, one priest, four teachers, and two deacons.

Then Capt. Jones showed the necessity of the gathering of the Saints to Zion, in Welsh and in English, and he demonstrated clearly that the excellent principle of gathering the Saints together in Zion, contained the Salvation of God for his children; in accordance with the purpose of God through all his previous dispensations, and was speeding along remarkably in this age, despite the opposition from the world and the devil. Also he showed clearly, and to the joy of all the Saints, that poverty will deprive none of this deliverance, if they continue faithful in fulfilling their duties here—their heavenly Father will prepare the way before them—and He who began in them this good work will finish it also before the coming of Christ. We received many other beneficial counsels and teachings from Capt. Jones and the brethren in this wonderful meeting, which would be too long to write now; and we believe, from the signs of dedication and cheerfulness seen on the listeners, that they were like honeycombs to their hearts as well, and they will bear fruit after many days.

In the evening meeting, elders W. Phillips, T. Pugh, W. Davies, Rhymni, preached in Welsh, and Capt. Jones in English: and this wonderful Conference came to a close also after having done much good for the Saints, and eliminating much of the prejudice the malicious tales had created in the hearts of our neighbors against us and our godly religion. The large *Greyhound* Hall was quite full of noble listeners throughout the Conference, despite the many warnings given to believers not to come to listen to us on any account; in spite of that, the honest in heart came to listen to us; and they greatly marvelled because of the false accusations they had heard about us. May the wise and good God break the traditional bonds of our dear fellowmen in haste, so they may become true subjects in the church of Jesus Christ, is my constant prayer.

DAVID JONES, *Scribe*.

N. B.—The above Conference was announced in the *Prophet* as being held on the last Sunday of April. The mistake happened because the president of the Conference misunderstood the time, and prepared for the Conference before the *Prophet* came around, and we did not know of the mistake until it was too late to correct it; and lest so many be disappointed, it was deemed wiser to hold it at the above time. But in case a mistake happen again with respect to the time of any Conference, pay close attention to the *Prophet*, for he will tell the truth, and will advise everyone in good time also, unless some unusual circumstances come up unexpectedly at that time; and as for such things, we shall take care to notify the presidents by letter.

We are delighted to publish the numbers of this Conference to our readers; and we thank Him whose godly work this is for the unusual increase that is happening to it throughout our country. The *false prophets* are very diligent in shouting from their pulpits, &c., that the Saints are perishing here, and fading away, but increasing is what they are doing the more they are persecuted, and growing stronger and increasing in number is what they will do despite everyone and everything that may oppose them, until they bring all the honest in heart from among every party or non-party into the kingdom of God, and save them all in Zion victoriously. May the blessed period come when all the children of Zion will be seen having come out of the great affliction, and having reached the house of their Father to enjoy the wealth of the earth, and the blessings of heaven.—ED.

WHAT IS TO BE DONE WITH THE EDITOR OF THE *STAR OF GOMER ?*

To the Rev. Daniel Jones, Felinfoel.

REV. SIR,—As your reverend brother from Dowlais considers you an experienced minister, and the most competent to say what is best to do with the "SATANISTS," when they come to request their places with the Baptists; I also think that you can give the best answer to the question, "What is to be done with the Editor of the *Star of Gomer ?*

Perhaps you wish to know by now what has happened to him. Oh! it is grievous to tell, he has been excommunicated from the Baptist church in Carmarthen; yes, the Editor of the *Star* has been excommunicated! I do not know for sure the cause of this. Not long ago he was at the zenith, to oppose the Satanists; he opened the *Star* quite readily to the writings of the Rev. W. R. Davies; and what could be his transgression? But that is not the topic;—He has been excommunicated! and what is to be done with him, we wonder? For the sake of his soul, poor thing, he ought to get some religion yet; but which one, is the question. As the religion of the Satanists is the closest one to the Baptists, who knows whether he might obtain a place with those? But the worst thing is that many of the Satanists are Ivorites also; and perhaps they will not accept him—they may kick him out! Why? Was it the Ivorites who kicked the Editor out when he was in their lodge? The Ivorites know; ask them. If the Satanists are not of a forgiving nature, it is not likely that they will accept him, since he persecuted them so often in the *Star*. But what good is it to speak like this? for the Satanists are "very soon" to come to request their place with the Baptists; consequently, what good would it be for the Editor to join with the Satanists, and then be considered unworthy to be received back along with the Satanists? Well, the question is then, What is to be done with the Editor? That is what I wish to know from you. Is there not some sect lower than the Baptists and the Satanists? Let the questions of the Rev. W. R. Davies about the Satanists be, and come to a more important question, namely, "What is to be done with the Editor of the *Star of Gomer* ? A ready reply will please several of the bosom friends of the excommunicant.

They sacked Sam, an accursed thing to do,
From his job in a rather unbecoming manner.

Yours, Rev. Sir, BENJAMIN JONES, *Carmarthen.*

STATE OF THE CHURCHES AND THE BAPTISMS.

MERTHYR.—Around a hundred have been baptized here since the last Conference, which was held at Christmas, which makes the present numbers of this branch over seven hundred faithful and determined Saints, with better prospects than ever for increasing; despite this the Saints are still few, fewer, fewest, dying out, and disappearing, say the false prophets! "A few of the dregs join, and many of the most responsible are leaving them," is the continual chant of Mr. Davies of Dowlais, and his persecuting partners! Yet, it would be a pity to deprive them, poor things, of the only pleasure they have, namely that of persecuting the children of God. The majority of the above have been faithful members with other denominations of the area, and great is their joy, that they have obtained at last the privilege of having membership in the true church of Jesus Christ, and of receiving of the comfort of the Holy Ghost.

DOWLAIS.—Twenty-four have been baptized here since the last Conference; and dozens with them since the time that Mr. R. of Rhymni was there "killing Mormonism," and since the time his foster father said that it had already "become a blight and a curse, and had received the *homestroke*, &c." How can these false prophets show their faces in public now, when their folly and their lies have become so obvious to everyone, and are a topic of wonder to every man who knows what shame is. Yet, among the above there was one who was a full-fledged member with Mr. Davies himself, and had been spotless for close to nine years. Thus Mr. Davies sees, if he believes his own eyes, that Mormonism has not yet received the *homestroke*, nor anything like it. You heads of families, if you want peace in your families, keep such malicious talebearers and persecutors of the Saints out of your houses, or all your endeavors will be in vain, yes, as vain as it would be to carry fire in your bosom without believing that you will burn. This branch is flourishing, despite all the financial obstacles that stood in their way, and they greatly rejoice in the abundant enjoyment of the various gifts of the Holy Ghost, according to the scriptures, and corresponding to their faithfulness.

RHYMNI.—Elder W. Howells, Aberdare, went over to Rhymni one Sunday lately, to preach for the first time since he left preaching with the Baptists, and the result was, during the few hours he was there, that he baptized four under the nose of the head champion of all our persecutors in the his own backyard, and the place where a short time before he "killed Mormonism, and buried it the next day," so he said. But poor Mr. R.; he did not fulfill his promise, to kill it, or else how did the Saints work at least one miracle under his nose, and through that resurrect Mormonism to a better life than ever! Which one will he admit? He proves himself, one way or the other, a very foolish false prophet, and very worthless as well. Despite getting the Rhymni Saints to listen to him preaching a burial sermon of their religion, he failed to cause as much as an inflamation of the eye to any one of them; instead what he did was to strengthen them through all his lying tales. On the other hand, when he went to Aberdare to kill it, for sixpence each from each one who came to hear him, he obliged some of the members of the Baptists, and their listeners, to believe the doctrine of the Saints, and to confess that the morning after his lecture. That is no way to kill Mormonism! But there are scores in these environs who thank him for opening their eyes to perceive the truth of Mormonism! Why has he followed to the brink of outer space all the other meteors that have appeared once before? His professed enemy is on the field, with his banners waving victoriously throughout Wales. But the roar of his cannons has gone silent, except their echoes on the walls of the occasional filthy pigsty. Does he not have another arrow? Is his quiver empty? Or, can he not stir someone else as a *cat's paw*, to burn his paws as he has done, instead of everyone laughing at him? All the better for us, and for the public, the more of his lies he utters, and may he do as he wishes;

for neither he, nor anyone else, can forestall the success of Mormonism any better than by being silent about it. Go ahead and yell, wail, guffaw, lecture, and publish something, whatever it be; but never be silent! It is not known what other *champion* will follow him; for he himself has certainly not killed any part of Mormonism as yet.

SWANSEA.—Eighteen have been baptized since the Conference, and many are receiving the blessed gifts of the Holy Ghost.

LLWYNI.—Nineteen have been baptized, who, despite all the persecution they have suffered, are greatly enjoying the privileges of the church of God.

LLANELLI.—Elder W. Hughes, poor thing, complains that he has baptized only forty-eight since the Conference, but that those, together with the other Saints, are righteous ones, and eager for godly teaching, instead of the traditions of men, and empty husks. Go forward, gentle Saints; there is plenty before you, and hosts yet of honest people who will follow you on this spiritual course towards Zion.

PONT YATES.—Elder H. Williams writes that 35 have been baptized there since the Conference, but that two of them sinned afterwards, bringing disgrace on this godly religion. Again this is grievous; and it is foolishness for their neighbors to scorn the religion because two persons transgressed its rules, while the testimonies and faithfulness of scores of others are the direct opposite to them. Not one who possesses reason will judge them in that manner.

CARMARTHEN.—There is an excellent and numerous hearing in these environs, and a very sizeable call for preachers; and there are good jobs to be had on the new railway there. We hope that some will go soon from here to assist this small sister against the giants of great Babylon. The few preachers who are here are very diligent in their efforts, to the extent of their ability; but they cannot fill more than one place at a time. Four have received their baptism here since the Conference, with an abundant harvest about to ripen. All the Saints are extremely faithful also, and increasing in every goodness.

LLANYBYDDER.—Nine have been baptized here and the vicinity lately, and the whole branch is swiftly identifying itself with the person and the teaching of our faithful brother T. Jeremy. May he and his have more and more of the influences of the Spirit of the truth, is our prayer, despite every "Dark Daniel," and every other persecuting fool.

BRECHFA.—It is only a short time since even the goats bleated along the precipice of the crags, so to speak, in scorn after us when we preached there; but thanks to the God who sent us there, some scores of responsible people of this place, and surrounding areas, have embraced the gospel that we preached there, and God has proved the godly truth to them. God has blessed the labor and diligence of the faithful elder T. Jeremy here also, and his zealous brother D. Jeremy; and we need not exhort the Saints to listen to their counsels, for the Spirit of God directs them to do that. Another 16 have been baptized here lately. Our heart is longing to see the faithful Saints here, and throughout Wales, face-to-face, for paper is not an acceptable medium for us. We shall leave other things undone for a while, so we can satisfy ourselves in this also before long.

TREGARON.—One of the leaders of the Calvinists has come to the Saints lately, from near Tregaron. He has been made an elder now. He preached the gospel zealously to the point that his former brethren practically understood him to be their leader at the time. As soon as they heard his testimony, namely that he knew that the Latter-day Saints were the children of God, &c., they ordered everyone to stop listening to him under severe penalty. In spite of that, some of them were baptized soon, and there is now a flourishing branch there. Elder B. Evans is diligent in those areas, and has baptized some; and T. Harris is there, and has had a better reception and better success than before those evil tricksters bound him off to prison. Gold is only purified in the fire; so it is here.

ABERDARE.—Nineteen have been baptized here since the Conference, and the majority of them since Mr. Roberts from Rhymni was there "killing Mormonism!" This little branch is flourishing and very faithful; and also the new in the faith are receiving solid testimonies, and the gifts of the Holy Ghost in a powerful manner. The pastors have the bellyache because they are losing their flock, and consequently their profit; and the more diligent they are to walk the houses to set the wives against their husbands, by telling their lying tales—the more they curse the Saints from their pulpits, become infuriated, froth at the mouth from rage towards the Saints, all the more of their beguiled ones leave them, and see the "wolves" gnashing their teeth. The faithful elder, W. Howells, has baptized a greater number before being a half-a-year old in the gospel, than all his persecutors baptized in several years, and at a cost to their followers of thousands of pounds.

CARDIFF.—Elder W. Jenkins, and others, are very faithful here, and have succeeded in baptizing 50 since the Conference. All the Saints here are very faithful, and we had great joy in their midst lately. They are enjoying the spiritual gifts in abundance. Several came into the church from the Baptists, among which there was one who had been a deacon for years, and he thanks God for the godly light he has received.

CWMBYCHAN.—The sectarian stewards here, and in Bryn, have turned practically all of the Saints from their work because of their religion; and it is lamentable to think that those who profess bloody and cruel sectarianism are laughing scornfully and boastfully, because they have caused scores of their neighbors, women, and little innocent children, to suffer hunger, without one cause except that their consciences compel them to worship God according to the scriptures, instead of according to the contradictory beliefs of Sectarianism. This is the same inclination in bloody Calvinism in Wales towards the Welsh in this age, as was in its first founder, who was of the taste to burn people at the stake. It is no thanks to these that they cannot burn the Saints of Cwmbychan and Bryn in the same fashion; for the man who oppresses the conscience of his fellowman, and who takes revenge on him in this manner for his religion, I have no doubt, if he but had permission, would pile up the faggots to burn him. Despite it all, the Saints are determined, and some have been baptized. Perhaps we shall yet have a chance to furnish greater detail on this, and to indicate who these oppressors are. For the comfort of the sufferers, we shall say as much as this,—It is your Father who holds the reins of all authority; lift up your heads, and behold the salvation of the Lord on your behalf; behold the fate of the ungodly. The Lord will repay the oppressors an hundredfold, so that your names will be in honor when the remembrance of the oppressors will stink in the nostrils of every humanitarian.

PEMBROKESHIRE.—Elder J. Morris is having success here, and has baptized some lately, in spite of all the persecution.

NORTH.—The state and condition of the churches throughout the North are understood, in the letters of A. Evans, R. Griffiths, &c. With respect to Anglesey, we understand that there is success there because of the labor of R. E.

Many have been baptized in Monmouthshire and Herefordshire lately. It is seen that the increase in the number of Saints is over a hundred each month, and more than three each day, during the past four months. We thank him whose work this is, and we shall strive for even greater success in the days to come. May the gracious God allow it.

*** *Direct letters, prepaid, to* CAPT. JONES, Wellington Street, Merthyr. *No one can expect a response, if there is no stamp on the letter. We are tired at last of paying postage for everyone!*

ANNOUNCEMENT.

TO OUR DISTRIBUTORS.

WE earnestly implore all these our faithful brethren to do all they can to settle all their book accounts by the next Conference, which will be held in Merthyr about the middle of July. The date will yet be noted in time. We have many reasons to give for this sincere urging; namely, that we depend on the assistance of that money to pay our expenses for a while, and to take us to a foreign land far from here, to fulfill the godly and important mission that has been entrusted to us; and whoever of the Saints fails to pay what he owes by that time should remember that he is tying the fetter on our feet to prevent us from fulfilling our duty to God, and to foreign men who lie in darkness. Three-fourths of the money we have paid for printing books for the Saints is now owed to us! And no matter how hard times are now, the payment that each individual owes is so small, that it does not require much effort to pay it, but it is only right to consider the need for it. We hope this short plea will answer the purpose of getting the Saints to free us from this. Also, a book of the size of the TREASURY requires a considerable amount of money to take it through the Press. The third Part of it is off the Press, and the fourth will soon appear. We shall strive to finish it in the fifth, which will be the same size as the two noted. And now, we shall strive to circulate them, to read them, and to pay for them. Not profit, rather your perfection is our aim in all we do.

To our Correspondents.—We beseech the patience of our Correspondents for another issue of the *Prophet*. It is a small one. J. B., T. H., &c., will be answered in the next.

CONTENTS.

MERTHYR TYDFIL:

PUBLISHED AND FOR SALE BY D. JONES, AND ALSO FOR SALE BY THE SAINTS IN GENERAL.

JOHN JONES, PRINTER, RHYDYBONT.

PROPHET OF THE JUBILEE,

OR

STAR OF THE SAINTS.

No. 24.] JUNE, 1848. [PRICE 2*c*.

AZARAIAH SHADRACH A MORMON!

DEAR BROTHER JONES,—

ONE of my chief purposes in writing you this letter is, in order to inform you of one additional proof that I received in one of Azariah Shadrach's columns of the restoration of the church according to the apostolic plan through shadows, which he has foreseen clearly. His method of setting the idea out is, through taking Zerubbabel as a shadow of Christ; with the manner and method of the building of the second temple being a reference to the restoration of the church to its primitive organization. He says that it was in the same manner, and in the same method that the church would be restored to its glorious state in the beginning,—yes, to the same state in which it was established also by the Son of God himself; and to the same state it has to be in before it can ever be the church of God; and to the same state it has to be in before man can have life in it. In a word, it has to be again like it was formerly, or else man cannot be perfected. But thanks to God, it is thus, and has been restored according to the will of God, and in his own good time. That to which I refer is as follows:—

"Zerubbabel was a shadow of Christ, Zech. iv, 9. For

"1. Zerubbabel was chosen and appointed by God to lead Israel from Babylon to Canaan: thus was Christ appointed to lead the Saints back from all their wanderings, to save them from all captivity, and to lead them to heavenly Canaan.

"2. Zerubbabel built the second temple in Jerusalem; his two hands began it, and his two hands finished it: thus did Christ build his church, and he will be certain to complete the entire building, despite working through poor means, with much opposition. The second temple also was a special portrait of the restoration of religion and the church in the thousand years according to the apostolic plan.

"(1.) The first temple was tarnished, and also pulled down by the Babylonians: thus was the apostolic plan of religion tarnished by the Papists.

"(2.) The second temple was built in times of tribulation: thus, in times of tribulation, will the church be restored to the apostolic plan.

"(3.) The second temple was built by those who spent long years in captivity: thus will the church be restored according to the apostolic plan by those who have long been in the captivity of human imaginings, and human traditions.

"(4.) Those who were building the second temple had much rubble to move out of the way: similarly, it will be necessary to move many superstitions and remains of Catholicism, and human imaginings, out of the way, before the church is restored to the plan of the apostolic church.

"(5.) Poor and contemptuous men in the sight of many other men were those who built the second temple: thus will it be with the restoration of religion to the apostolic plan.

"(6.) Many men were very haughty and apathetic concerning the building of the second temple, saying, 'The time has not yet come:' thus are many still concerning the building of the church, and restoring it to the apostolic plan.

"(7.) There was much mocking directed at those who were building the second temple: similarly, there is much mocking directed at those who are restoring the church to the apostolic plan.

"(8.) Although many wished to prevent Israel at that time from building the second temple; yet the work went forward, although it was obstructed for a time.

"(9.) It was not through the foundation or power of men that the second temple went forward; rather it was through the Spirit of the living God: similarly, in the same manner will the church be restored to the apostolic plan. May God hasten the morning when Zion will receive the foremost praise on the earth. And let all people say Amen."

I trust that you will publish the foregoing; and perhaps it will be beneficial to show to lovers of the truth one additional proof of the restoration of the church.

I am, your fellow servant in Christ,

Nantyglo. ABEDNEGO WILLIAMS.

FALSE ACCUSATIONS OF THE BAPTISTS AGAINST THE SAINTS AGAIN!

MR. ED.—The slanderous *Baptist* has been very diligent, for years, as you know, and as Wales knows also, in maligning, persecuting, and publishing everything but the truth about the Saints in many other places; and finally its jealousy failed to leave us alone in Pont Yates, and the environs. In the last issue of the *Baptist*, some "Anthony Fair Play" calls his religious fellowmen "deceitful fiends," &c., without offering to show any of their deceit. What is to be thought of such an unfeeling neighbor? And yet, he accuses the Saints of lies, without offering one proof of that either, which proves that his own truthfulness is not precious to him. He says that "the Saints say that most of the Meinciau church, if not all of it, has come to them."

Now, Mr. "Anthony," or whoever you are, answer who of the Saints said such a thing? Name the person, or the persons, who said that which you accuse the Saints of, so that the same can come under church censure; for we have failed to find out, despite searching, who the liar is in our midst; and you must have known him before you dared to proclaim such a thing to the world; and if you do not tell his name, who will not see that you yourself are the author of that lie? If you desire good for men, there is a better way to reform them than through publishing lies about them through the *Baptist*. Do they say this far and near? How near? If so; then it is all the easier for you to name them, and the more guilty you will be considered if you do not. And yet, if one of the Saints were guilty of saying that; is it fair of you to accuse the thousands who are in the country of lying? There are about eighty of your neighbors, considered as truthful as you (and more truthful from now on), who depend for their lives on the religion you call ("judge of the world," is it?) "deceitful fiends," without proving it so much as once ever. What, and who are you? No wonder you are ashamed to put your proper name by such rubbish, which every honest man would do by the truth.

Another very malicious accusation of this reviler is that the Saints have some "*ingredient*" to affect men who are deceitful. Oh man! declare what is that "*ingredient*," or leave your neighbors alone to worship God according to the scriptures, for shame. Another of his lies is, that only three members of the Meinciau church have come to the Saints. Yes poor thing, more than that have come, and how could you not know that? This assertion of yours must be a blatant lie also. What! can you deny it, when there are people available who are living witnesses for themselves? You boast of your increase now; but on the admission of some of those whom you baptized, those you call "deceitful fiends" and who were convinced of baptism by immersion; and if you doubt this, we have facts to prove it. And say what you wish, there are many about to come from your proven enchantment to the light of the Saints. Time will prove that in spite of you. And as soon as your own heart comes to love the truth, you will be seen begging to become one of them.

But it is useless for me, Mr. Ed., to go into any further detail on the assertions of such a man as "Anthony," for everyone knows who, and what kind of man, he is out here; and his work of maligning his former brethren, and trying to smear their character after they leave the old deceit they professed before coming to the Saints, proves him quite clearly to all of the readers of the *Baptist* as unworthy of the least credence. He labels one of his former brethren a "*Wandering Jew*," because he does what Paul commands, namely "Prove all things; hold fast that which is good." What harm is there in that? That is what every lover of the truth will do, until he has hold of the true religion. The most excellent principle has truth and is condemned by this "Anthony," much like that fox and the "sour grapes." Men who have proved the religion of the sects are the most fit to judge the religion of the Saints; and their departure from the others, and their holding fast to this one, says loudly, that this is the solid religion they were seeking. "Anthony" knew, he said, of the acceptance of this man into their church, that he had a bad principle like this, and yet he denies the "Spirit of prophecy," and communicated with such a man without any opposition! By this he can be judged as not caring what kind of men he sat by at the table of the Lord. His evil principle comes to the light more and more, and his own mouth testifies against him. But he bursts, and his bowels run to the light of day in the following sentence:—"As for the third, he is good for nothing but the *dungheap !*" What! a man who was formed in the pure image of his God—a man who possesses an immortal soul—a man who is a member of society—a man who is a subject of the state, and his neighbor;—yes, that man is "good for nothing but the *dungheap !*" Shame on the man who dared to publish such words before men! Who can believe a word of the man who said such a thing? Praise to the Saints is the abusive language of such an ill-tempered man, says every reasonable man. We shall leave him at that then, to suffer the shame that a man who can declare such false accusations about his neighbors deserves, and that out of jealousy for their religious success.

MR. ED.,—I am pleased to inform you that the truth is gaining ground here rapidly, despite the scorn and false accusations of his opponents, with better expectations than ever. The ears of the people of these environs have been numbed by the malicious tales that are flying on the wings of the breeze through the pulpits and monthly publications of our country. They are one by one souring and becoming disgusted, so that the most reasonable people are quickly coming to understand that they are lies, and loathing them and their inventors. Here we have baptized 74 in less than a year—twenty-one of them since the last Conference; and there are several others who have promised to obey soon. The Saints are remarkably determined and faithful under all the persecution and scorn, and are increasing in godly wisdom, and spiritual gifts, so that it is a heartfelt pleasure to be in their midst; and my constant prayer is, that He who initiated in them this good work will complete it by the day of the coming of our Lord Jesus Christ. Amen. I am your brother in the eternal gospel,

Pont Yates, *May* 26, 1848. HOWELL WILLIAMS.

ANOTHER EXAMPLE OF THE CRUELTY OF THE BAPTISTS, AND OF THE TENDERNESS OF GOD, TOWARDS THE SAINTS.

DEAR BROTHER,—It is a pleasure for me to inform you that there is continuing increase to the numbers of the Saints in this County, and that they are increasing in every spiritual goodness in abundance; and also they are all in great unity and brotherly love.

Persecution is also heating up speedily in some parts of this area, despite your extinguishing the heat of fire and brimstone of that self-agitating Jenkyn Rees from Victoria, and others. Those old lying tales of his, namely that you were swindling the Saints out of their money, &c., &c., have caused an unhealthy savour on his name and memory in the nostrils of every reasonable man, since the time that you were before that large crowd disproving him to his face; and challenging him, and all the people of Monmouthshire and the world, to prove that you were in debt to anyone of a shilling; and the time that you proved that you have never taken any kind of collection of as much as a shilling from all the hundreds of Saints that are in Monmouthshire. It was very good for us that you did that: for many that were hateful enemies to us and cruel persecutors, because they had heard the "godly Minister" and that liar asserting it, have become meek and humanitarian men since you proved it all to be untrue; and the public have ever since changed their behavior towards us completely, and many besides the Baptists know who swindles people's money under the mantle of religion—who takes the *shop books from his members*—and who was that cruel man who insisted on the *shop book of that poor old widow, to take it from her, until she and her little children suffered from want of food because of it !* [See the note at the end of this letter.—ED.] Yes, things are coming to their right order since the truth became evident; and the inventor of the lies, and the shameless abuser, suffers the shame that his villainous works deserve.

I shall note one example to show the tricks of the malicious Baptists in another place, namely Llandovery:—As two of our ministers were preaching there a week ago last Sunday, and hundreds of listeners had gathered, at the start of the sermon some of the crowd began to shout, howl, and bawl almost like wolves, to drown the voice of the preacher; and in the end they pulled the two down from the place where they stood, and trampled them under their feet, and tried to ride them as if they were animals! The preachers had a chance to read their licenses, which gave them the right to protection and defense of the officers of her Majesty to preach, but all was in vain. Two other preachers went there the following Sunday, and received a better hearing than the first that was noted; and the plot had come to the light of day by that time, so that it was understood that the Baptists had hired the rioters to do that. Yes, some of those hired testified that they had received money from the Baptists there to disrupt our worship!! and that the drunkards, and most irreligious of all had been in dread of the oppression and cruelty of these professed *religionists*. The brethren are determined to go there and to declare their message, despite the devil and all his servants until those honest in heart have been offered the gospel of the Son of God. We have overcome similar obstacles and tales of the Reverends and religionists in Llanelli, Breconshire, and two have been baptized there recently, and hopeful signs that the people will soon see the difference between traditions of men of the age and the gospel of Jesus Christ.

It is with very great pleasure that I inform you of the great goodness of our God towards Brother Edward Roberts, Victoria, who was seriously burned in the coal mine. Almost no one believed it possible for him to get better at first; but he became well through the blessing of God. The doctors came to see him, and said that he could not move from his bed before about four months at least, according to their belief; but the power of God was shown greatly upon him, so that he had got up before the end of a month; and he was walking about with me last Tuesday, and he intends going to the meeting next Sunday! The doctors and many others admit that they had not seen a similar healing ever before. This thing caused some of the enemies of the truth to confess the great power of God towards his children and for others to mock, as in former days. But I, and doubtless all the Saints acknowledge the goodness of God with thankfulness of heart for imparting the great blessing to our beloved brother. His name only will have the glory. Amen.

We are able to inform you of several other examples of the power of God in these districts; but I shall forego at this time, lest this letter be too long. All the Saints and officers in Merthyr are in unity and love. The hall was as full of listeners last Sunday night as usual, and nine were received into the Church here in the first Church meeting after your departure, and hosts more are at the door. May the gracious Lord hasten his work to its end, is the constant prayer of your brother in the gospel of Christ.

Merthyr, May 28*th*, 1848. WILLIAM PHILLIPS.

[With reference to the man that was mentioned at the beginning of our brother's letter, I would say that he had verified the old proverb that says "a thief shouts thief first," without doubt. Yes, and we proved to his face through scores of witnesses that he "is the man" that is guilty of the ills that he accused the innocent of. It was judged that there were over a thousand people there, and he himself was also hearing us disproving all his lies about us and our brethren, one by one, and he dared not open his mouth to defend himself and his accusations, although we called him and challenged him to do so; but in vain we called, for he knew that he uttered lies about us in our absence: and thus, we understand that this malicious man has been spreading his invented slime about us along the road he walked, along Carmarthenshire, &c., trying to upset the new in the faith. His tricks in Kidwelly are remembered, and shame for his disgraceful behavior towards those innocent and defenseless women, yes, remember that the day of reckoning is coming ere long. The venom of asps is on the lips of such, says the holy word; and all feel their poison wherever they go. This man has many brothers that are faithful in spreading lies about us through the country, which is praise to us, and proves the jealousy of the *cowards* that are not able to face us to prove their lies. We still stand by our challenge.—ED.]

QUESTIONS, AND THEIR ANSWERS.

MR. ED.,—*What does Paul suggest in* Rom. xvi, 25, *by the words, "The revelation of the mystery which was kept secret since the world began," &c. An early answer will satisfy many besides yours,*—T. H.

We answer that the elimination of the veil that existed between Jews and Gentiles, which made it possible for the latter to have the gospel, is what Paul had reference to, I believe. Paul boasted that he was the apostle to the Gentiles. Gal. i, 11, 12, 16; ii, 7—9; iii, 14, 26—29. Paul was called by Christ through Ananias to be a "chosen vessel unto me to bear my name before the Gentiles."

MR. ED.,—*What do you understand by that phrase in* 1 Cor. iv, 9, *namely, "Apostles last?" Our sectarian neighbors try to prove from this verse that no other apostles were to be in the church after those twelve.*—J. B.

We answer that this verse proves exactly the opposite to us. There are in the phrase but two words, and the latter of the two proves itself to be either an idle word, or else it proves that there are two classes of apostles, namely the earliest ones, and the last ones; and if two classes, why not more? It would be just as fitting for your sectarian neighbors to claim that there will never be any men after them, because they are last men, as to claim that for the apostles. If they have no better basis than that to prove their point, it will never be proved. That is like stating that the days of Paul were the last days, because he says in Heb. i, 2, "*These* last days." At the same time the apostle uses the last word "*these*" as if purposely to prove the opposite: thus he does in the above. For more on this, consult the *Treasury*, under the heading *Apostles*, where it is seen that there were scores of apostles in the church. To deny apostles is to deny apostleship, without which it is impossible to be the church of God.

INVITATION TO GOD.

GOD is calling now,
Oh listen;
He offers great gifts,
Oh listen:
Although disobedient to God,
You have forgiveness through baptism,
And the right to religious privileges,
Oh listen.

God is calling now,
Why do you not come?
He offers great gifts,
Why do you not come?
You will have clarification of the spirit,
Together with his wondrous gifts,
To guide you towards life,
Oh listen.

J. D.

THE BAPTISTS BAPTIZE "SATANISTS AND DEMONS ! !"

WE do not understand the difference between satanists and demons; but perhaps the Baptists understand the difference, for these are the noble names that those devout religionists give to their fellowmen, namely the Saints! These are the respectful names they proclaim from their pulpits for their religious neighbors! These are the names given to a denomination of religious people, through the columns of the publications that they claim teach the age in morality, and guide them to the Christian humility, love, and meekness of the gentle Jesus, "who, when he was reviled, reviled not again." The pious minister—the respected and charitable evangelist—that meek servant of God who preaches the gospel of peace of the Baptists in Dowlais, teaching the children of his God to shout "Satanists and demons" after their neighbors along the streets; yes, after men who were formed in the pure image of God, and who possess immortal souls—loving fathers and mothers, and dear children—who were members of the same "church of God" as they—and who fed him and his family in splendor, &c., from their great need! But after it all, the most suitable names for them now, says he, when they give him no more, rather they embrace the true gospel of Christ, is "Satanists and demons!" And the learned Editors of the *Baptist*, the *Apostolic Witness*, the *Star of Gomer, &c.*, are surely of the same mind as he before they would publish his epistles which label believers thus; for "he that biddeth him God speed is partaker of his evil deeds."

He wrote a lengthy epistle to the *Apostolic Witness*, to prove that "Satanists and demons" are the most appropriate names for his neighbors; and he urges the people of the North to revile them in this manner also! Is this what preaching the gospel is to the Baptists? Well, he is considered a minister of the gospel, and anyone who can believe that "Satanists and demons" are the most appropriate names for men who believe in Christ according to the scriptures, and who worship God in conscience, can believe also something so incredible as this man being a minister of the gentle Jesus, although that is contrary to every fact. Is it possible that the worst of men, while in the flesh, deserve to be characterized as "Satanists and demons?" No, says every man who possesses any reason; and the testimony of every reasonable man about this proves at once that even the respected Ministers, the devout Editors, and those godly and zealous religionists who call the Saints "Satanists and demons," are revilers of the worst kind, whom the scriptures say shall not inherit the kingdom of God. Well, where will these revilers go, poor things? We do not judge anyone; but let their own works testify, by comparing them with the word of God, who is likely to keep company with "Satanists and demons," unless they repent.

But an even greater surprise is the readiness of the *Baptists*, and their great eagerness, to baptize those whom they would call "Satanists and demons!" Yes, they strive in every way, by saying puffed-up words of futility, and the appearance of humility in religious will, to entice back the occasional weak woman who is new in the faith, who had escaped once from their heresies to the way of truth; and at last the *Baptist* screams through its screeching trumpet the victorious news that two women who had been with the Saints have been baptized by the Baptists in Llwyni, namely two *she-Satanists* or *she-demons*, of course! Good gracious! here are the Baptists baptizing "Satanists and demons," namely those whom they themselves call such!

Let the world be amazed! behold two of the Saints turning back to the husks of the revilers, and the revilers suppose that that is a sign that all the Saints will soon turn back to them, and that the victory from their side is sure; when, from the other side, hundreds of the Baptists have come to the church of the Saints—many hundreds in all—with more coming every month, and other hosts of them who believe the gospel the "Satanists" preach, and will soon be "Satanists" just as bad as are their brothers and sisters who went before them; and in spite of it all, the "Satanists" are dying out, and disappearing, say the Baptists, and have received the *homestroke*, and just a few are joining them, and many are leaving them, &c. Well, one can see that it is the Baptists, and not the Saints, who are professing such miracles as these.

Baptizing "Satanists and demons" is another miracle, and a totally new one, we would suppose; but remember that it is the Baptists who are claiming the praise for this miracle also! Our Bible teaches us that the demons are kept bound until the judgment of the great day; but the Baptists say they are not—that that is a lie—that the "Satanists and demons" are free now, and have become flesh—that they have been members with them, deacons, and preachers of the gospel to them for years, and all the time they did not know that it was "Satanists and demons" who were sitting at the table of the Lord with them, who were praying together with them, and who loved them; but now they know they were "Satanists and demons" all along. Good gracious, they say, "perhaps more of us are the same species; and perhaps we ourselves are such." We answer that they will be called such as soon as they obey the gospel of the Son of God, and the Reverends of the Baptists will shout "Satanists and demons" after them unless they turn back to them; and if they do, they will baptize "Satanists" a second time, to be sure. Behold a miracle more incredible than one the Saints ever professed, for the gospel the Saints preach does not claim to save "Satanists and demons;" Oh no, the gospel of the Baptists is the one that does that, they say! Well, even the "Satanists" must give up now,—the Baptists are way ahead of them, for they have the most remarkable gospel ever heard of, I imagine! They can preach until they bring "demons" to believe—"Satanists" to repent,—they baptize "Satanists,"—"demons" receive forgiveness for free with the Baptists! yes, they take "Satanists" and "She-satanists" as brothers and sisters in Christ!—they pray for the "demons" to receive the Holy Ghost!—they partake of bread, and they drink of the cup, together with confessed demons in the holy sacrament! Well, this is making the "table of the Lord a table of demons," is it not? And furthermore, not only do they practice religion together lovingly here, but they pray together to be able to go to the same heaven with Satanists and demons after dying!

Can they deny one word of this? They cannot on their own words; and there is no escape for the Baptists from this severe *dilemma* except by calling back the bad names they gave to the Saints, and admitting that "Satanists and demons" cannot be appropriate names for them. There is no other way possible for escape. It would be a blow to their arrogance to admit this, for that would be to confess themselves as revilers openly and publicly. Let them choose whatever consequence they wish,—it makes no difference to us which one. If they choose the first, then they will go to their imaginary heaven with "Satanists and demons;" but if they admit the latter, that will be only an admission of what every sensible man knows already, namely that they are *revilers*. By your fruits will you be judged always.

Now, devout Baptists; now great Reverends and Editors: what will you do, and which will you choose? You have dug this deep ditch for your innocent fellowmen, but behold you yourselves are in it, and your color is very begrimed! You have built this dreadful gallows for the "Satanists and demons," however, no one but Baptists are seen hanging from it, except for just two small "She-Satanists" or "She-demons," one on either side of Mr. Davies, I suppose, in praise to him for inventing this noble title. Now you are seen in your own appropriate shapes and colors, until Satan himself will be ashamed to claim you, I suppose.

Baptizing "Satanists and demons," is it! Good heavens! who knows how long it will be before hell itself becomes all Baptists! To be sure, it is to the Baptists that the "secret" of salvation of demons has been revealed. Who preaches to the spirits in prison? Do the Baptists baptize for the dead? or are all the Satanists and demons permitted to come to this earth through them? If so, we expect that the depths of the court below will be empty shortly; either all its tenants will have become Baptists, or *vice versa*, who knows which one! But we are sorry to report that the Editor of the *Baptist* is *off-ox* with his mind warped as usual; he is not baptizing "Satanists and demons" with the strength of his arm, I think, rather by what he says; but his plan is to baptize the insane of the *madhouses* first, before beginning on the bottomless *madhouses*. He is not nearly as merciful to the Satanists, poor things, as are his brethren; and his brother from Dowlais, and the other from Felinfoel, hesitate as to whether to the *madhouses*, or to the demons, they will send their missions first. Good gracious, has not this breed of Baptists suddenly become very zealous and fiery. When they fail to get enough men to baptize, they must baptize any that are available, even though they are insane, and "Satanists and demons!" But let us remember the words of Christ, "If they have called the master of the house Beelzebub, how much more shall they call them of his household?"

LETTER OF PRESIDENT BRIGHAM YOUNG.

"*Council Bluffs, January* 23, 1848.

"It is anticipated that brother Orson Pratt, and several other elders, will visit Britain toward the beginning of next summer. George A. Smith will stay here to take care of some related matters, and to direct the emigrants who are yet to come here on their way after us. Orson Hyde will also stay here with him.

"Last December, we held a Conference in the biggest house in these environs; but very soon so many Saints gathered from the surrounding areas, that there was not space for them, and it was deemed wisdom to postpone the Conference for three weeks, when a larger house to contain them could be obtained. Following that, on the 24th of the month, we gathered together again in a log chapel which had been built in the meantime, which had space for over a thousand people to sit comfortably, besides a stand at one end measuring twenty feet by ten. This was built in a number of days, although this weather was the coldest of the winter. I reported in the Conference that the Saints had plowed and sowed as many acres here in the year they have been here in the wilderness, as all the Saints would have done in ten years, had they stayed in Missouri, because of the persecutions; and it is abundantly true that we have already raised as abundant a crop here as was done in a year in Illinois. In this Conference the church was organized according to the plan we hinted at in our general epistle, namely under the leadership of a first presidency and a patriarch, and all the Saints could see the necessity of that under the present circumstances, so that everyone without exception rejoiced in the matter; and thus the hands of the "twelve" can be liberated so they can go and build up the kingdom in all the world. Brigham Young was nominated to be the first president of the church; Heber C. Kimball, and Willard Richards, as counselors to him; which was unanimously approved. Father John Smith was nominated to be patriarch of the whole church, in the same capacity as Joseph Smith, Sen., was, and then Hyrum Smith when he was martyred. The Spirit of the Lord at this time rested in an unusually powerful manner on the whole congregation, insomuch that the Saints' hearts were filled with joy unspeakable. The president said, 'This is one of the happiest days I have seen in my life: this is the fulfillment of the prophecy of brother Heber yesterday: all the teachings have been remarkably genuine and delicious;—I have never heard better. Is this not the bliss of heaven, and the breezes of blessed Zion, encountered here? Who feels hatred, malice, or evil? If you come to the door under the influence of a bad spirit, it would not come in with you—it could not mingle with the Spirit that is in this place; but the minute you enter, your feelings are as cheerful and loving as the seraphs of paradise. I feel the desire in my heart to praise God. Nothing more has been done today than what I knew would be done when Joseph died. We have been driven here from Nauvoo; but it is evident to me that the hand of the Lord is in it, and in all things, and it will be all right. When we see the result of all we pass through, I expect, in this probationary state, I will discover the guiding hand of God in it all, and I will say Amen. We shall make the upper courts ring with all their songs; but we have much to do before then. I do not expect to go beyond the bounds of the distant expanse where there is no opposition—where there is no devil to contend with. I have no fault to find with the providences of God, and I will not waste my time finding fault with the people. The Lord's will is my will all the time; and as he dictates, so I will perform. If He does not guide the ship, we shall all go down in the whirlpool. Joseph told the Twelve the year before he died, 'There is not one key or power to be bestowed on this church, that is necessary to lead it to the heavenly gate, that I have not given you, and that I have not taught you about. You have the perfect pattern, and you can build up the kingdom, and go in at the celestial gate, taking your train with you.'

"We had indeed an excellent time; and on the 16th of January, another meeting was convened by the 'seventies,' which they called a *Jubilee*; but I told them it could not be considered the Jubilee spoken of in the revelations, for all the bands are not broken, and I called it a *Jubilo !* This meeting continued for four days, to organize emigration matters, councils, &c. The hearts of the Saints were comforted through it all and lifted up above all their sufferings, and we rejoiced in the joy and freedom of the gospel of peace, and I pray that they might be kept above all tribulations, and be comforted, and guided to walk in the middle of the paths of righteousness, to the praise and glory of the name of him who called them from darkness to his wondrous light, so they may fill up the remainder of their days in building up the kingdom of Jesus across the earth.

"We have heard from the valley lately. All are healthy and optimistic, having sowed from two to three hundred acres of winter wheat, and there are plenty of provisions in the valley.

"The Saints here are enjoying much better health than ever in Nauvoo. The majority of the brethren are fixing up their wagons, &c., to start along in the Spring towards Salt Lake."—From the *Millennial Star*.

TRAVEL ACCOUNT OF THE MORMON JOURNEY FROM COUNCIL BLUFFS TO CALIFORNIA.

[*Quoted from the letter of Thomas Bullock.*]

"*Council Bluffs*, *January* 4*th*, 1848.

"In a previous letter I made a faint description of the persecutions of the Saints at Nauvoo, the burning of their houses and their possessions, the beatings, and the cruel and needless exile they suffered, &c., how they were fed miraculously with quails, together with their progress on their journey from there to here, &c.; but now I shall begin an account of our journey from here towards the Rocky Mountains. I started, with eight of the twelve apostles, together with one hundred and forty-three other persons, to search out an advantageous spot to be able to worship God according to our conscience, where we could rest from persecution, violence, and the cruelties we suffered for so long because of the word of God and the testimony of Jesus—where we could build houses, and inhabit them, and plant fruit trees, and eat the fruit thereof, with none to hurt or to make afraid. We camped on the bank of the Elk Horn river, until all were ready to begin; then we traveled on the north side of the splendid river called the *Platte*. We crossed several small streams before arriving at the *Loup Fork*, which is the most difficult stream of all to cross, because of the quicksand in it. But by the blessing of the God, we got all through in safety, together with our provisions; then we crossed over a ridge, and we came to the head of *Grand Island*, where on the 30th of April, we could see the first Buffalo: and this was a day long to be remembered, for having seen the first Buffalo hunt. Several of the brethren rode their horses after them. They went in pursuit of one band of about sixty-five for several miles; and from the camp we had a full view of their campaign along the mountain side, until they were enveloped with a cloud of dust raised by the feet of the horses and the Buffalo, and they did not return until they brought back the spoil of eleven bulls, cows, and calves. Our camp looked now like a large butcher's market. The way we preserved the meat was by drying it.

"May the 4th we traveled five wagons abreast in a defensive position, for we had been informed of a large war party of Indians ahead of us. We had a cannon, which we fired several times to frighten the Indians, which had the desired effect, and we went on our way in peace. We held a meeting of gratitude to God for protecting us. Next morning, we saw several thousands of Buffalo, besides many *Antelope*, *Elk*, *&c*. Within a few days afterwards, we saw the face of the land covered with Buffalo for several miles. I think I saw something like one or two hundred thousand of these animals in one day. They were so numerous on the other side of the mountains, that our camp had to wait three times until the droves of them went round us. Several of them turned back and looked at the scene, as if they were amazed at the sight of our camp. We caught several calves alive: but remember that catching one of these calves, and catching one of your domesticated calves, are two different things. They are as swift as swift horses; and despite the ugliness of the gallop of these creatures, they get over the ground with such speed, that they leave the swift rider to admire them in the distance; and if he gets within shooting distance, he should be thankful if they do not cause him to kiss mother earth.

"We arrived at Fort John (Laramie) on June 1st. Here our journey commenced over hills and mountains, along which plenty of timber is available for firewood, which is chiefly *pine;* but in the lower land, the kinds of trees are chiefly *cottonwood.* Afterwards there is before us a journey of five hundred miles, through plains of bushes called *sage*, which grow from six inches to ten feet high, and which do not permit much grass to grow in their midst. About four miles to the east of Independence Rock, there is a lake of *Saleratus*, of which I would advise you to gather one or two hundred pounds' weight for family use, for this is what you will use from now on in place of leaven in your bread; and there is *soda* also in the same lake, which would be very useful to wash clothes. Be sure to remember this.

"The rocks now are bold and high, the roads very sandy, and the *sage* bushes are more plentiful; yet you will be rejoicing that every day brings you nearer home. There is nothing unusual in the South Pass, by which you will know you are in it, except this, namely that the water runs the opposite direction, that is to the west. From this point you will have several heavy days' drive, without seeing much water, except in those places in which you camp overnight. After passing Fort Bridger, you can camp comfortably wherever you have a mind to. The grass out here will sustain your animals practically any time in the year; and when the *muskeet* grass is dry, it answers for corn, hay, and grass for your animals. The mountains between Fort Bridger and the valley are very high, and the road winds through the valleys between them, some of which are very narrow—in some places not more than ten yards wide, and the rocks are steep on either side, sometimes about a mile high. The elevation of the highest mountain ridge we have to cross over on the entire journey is about 7300 feet above sea level. From this ridge you will see the *Twin peaks*, which are covered with eternal snow. The slopes of these two mountains reach to the valley; and when you see them, you will shout out, 'I shall soon be home now.' There is no fear of losing the way between the mountains. After crossing a small creek twenty-one times in about five miles, and between mountains near a mile high, and after coming round a high knoll and making a sudden bend in the road, you come at once in full view of the "Salt Lake," together with a beautiful valley about twenty miles wide, and thirty miles long; and even though there is very little timber to be seen, you will be sure to say, "Thank God, I am home at last." On this spot that I am now talking to you about, our procession arrived on Thursday afternoon, the 23rd of July. The next morning we removed to the place where the city will be built; at noon we consecrated the place to the name of the Lord God of Israel; and before evening four ploughs were tearing up the face of the ground. The next day we had planted five acres of potatoes, and irrigated all the land. Sunday was a day of rest—a day of rejoicing before the Lord, and he poured out his Spirit on us, and peace dwelt in the "valley of the mountains." The first Sabbath that was kept in the valley where a city is to be built unto the Lord, will be preserved in eternal remembrance by those few brethren who first sang there, 'Hosanna to God and to the Lamb.'

"During the space of a month and three days after arriving there, we had planted and sown eighty-four acres of potatoes, Indian corn, beans, buckwheat, turnips, and some garden vegetables. We surveyed the city, and laid out its streets to run from east to west, and from south to north, which will make a block between them containing ten acres; these will then be divided into eight lots of one-and-a-quarter acres, for building a house on each one. The width of the streets is about forty-three yards, with twenty miles of width on each side for sidewalks, to be ornamented with shade trees. Then the houses will be built twenty feet back of that, with flower gardens in the front, &c. One block is reserved for the building of a temple, and two more blocks for the building of public buildings on them. Fountains of pure water run through each square, and it is intended to adorn them with all kinds of trees and flowers, &c. One thing here that will greatly attract the attention of you Englishmen [and the Welsh also], is that you do not have to purchase land here, and there will be no need of clever lawyers to write out deeds, &c., or *stamps*, or *parchments*. At last we have gotten hold of some beautiful land, where we can have their fill of the most fruitful land under the sun, as much as we can take care of, free without money and without value, until it comes to the open market, and then it will cost about a crown an acre. My inheritance is on the second block, near the temple, so you know where you can find me. We also built during the aforementioned time twenty-seven log houses, and a large part of a line of houses around ten acres of land, which will contain a comfortable place for over one hundred and sixty families, until they can build houses on their own inheritances. We also made one hundred and twenty-five bushels of salt. Four barrels of water from the salt lake will make one barrel of the most beautiful salt. The water is so strong that I can swim in it very easily, although I cannot swim at all in fresh water. It is a wonderful place to bathe; and there is a warm stream that boils out of the earth about half a mile to the north of the city, and everyone who has bathed in it, until now, has been healed, whatever his illness. Frequently eight or nine persons are seen in it at the same time. Everyone who has been in it wants to go there again; the temperature of the water is 109 degrees *Fahrenheit*, and it has much sulphur in it. Two miles further to the north, there is a larger and hotter spring, 126 degrees. The water rushes out of a large rock, and I could not, because of the heat, hold my fingers in it while I counted to eleven. There are all together over fifty such springs, varying with respect to the nature of their waters, within an area of three miles in diameter, some of them powerful enough to turn mills or large machines. Like the "pool of Siloam" of old, these fountains heal all the sick, whatever their affliction. The climate is unusually temperate and healthful, in the enjoyment of which, together with the fountains, &c., we can truly say, that we have found a healthful and paradisiacal country. Oh, what a great blessing it is to those who are afflicted with rheumatism, cramps, *scurvy*, and every kind of disease: I believe that every kind will be healed here. In the month of October there were over three thousand souls in the valley! Shout and sound your trumpets, you sons of Zion, far and wide; come ye emigrants, ye poor afflicted children of Zion, from the corners of the earth; come, and worship the Lord God of Israel, that your days and your years will be many and happy, however many he gives you in this beautiful, fruitful, healthful, and peaceful paradise.

"Encourage everyone to bring all kinds of seeds, seedlings, &c., that will be useful, or beautiful, with them.

"Your brother in the gospel of Christ,

"THOMAS BULLOCK."

*** *We earnestly expect that each Distributor will have prepared to settle all the book accounts without fail, by the next Conference, so that our purposes will not be frustrated.*

ANNOUNCEMENTS.

BOOKS FOR SALE.

We have just received nearly one hundred volumes of "Capt. Jones on Mormonism in 1847," from the Binder, bound very nicely, fine, and cheap, for different prices as before. We hope the Saints will strive to own at least one volume of these in every family before it is too late. The volumes for 1846 have already all been sold, with a great call for more, but they are not to be had.

GLAMORGAN CONFERENCE,

Will be held in Merthyr, Sunday, July 16th, and we wish for all the presidents pertaining to it, and as many of the others who are able, to come there to represent their different branches, and the condition of the kingdom in their midst. Also,

A TEA PARTY OF THE MISSIONARY SOCIETY

Will be held the following Monday, the 17th, in the Cymreigyddion Hall, Merthyr, tickets one shilling each, available from the various presidents throughout all the branches. We hope to see a suitable and general effort towards this blessed Society, and let the Saints strive to sell tickets to others, for the call for missionaries is increasing in practically every corner of our country, and our efforts with this Society ought to be increasing proportionately, until our fellowmen throughout the North, and other places, have embraced the truth, so they can sustain their own causes. We hope that our zealous and faithful sisters will not be one whit behind their excellent readiness and faithfulness of last year, which will not be forgotten.

CONTENTS.

MERTHYR TYDFIL:

PUBLISHED AND FOR SALE BY D. JONES, AND ALSO FOR SALE BY THE SAINTS IN GENERAL.

JOHN JONES, PRINTER, RHYDYBONT.

PROPHET OF THE JUBILEE,

OR

STAR OF THE SAINTS.

No. 25.] JULY, 1848. [Price 2*c*.

DESCRIPTION OF CALIFORNIA.

[*Quoted from an account of the American Traveler.*]

"Returning to the area of Sacramento, and the rivers that flow into it, and to the San Francisco bay, we have before us the most scenic, fruitful, and splendid parts of upper California. The most extensive valley in the whole area is the one that the Sacramento flows through. This splendidly beautiful valley stretches nearly four hundred miles from the San Francisco bay, nearly to the foothills of the mountains of California; and its average width is from 60 to 65 miles. The Del Plumas and the American Fork are very wide valleys; and the Tulare valley is 250 miles long, and 35 miles wide. There is a good proportion of trees of various kinds in these valleys, such as the *white oak*, *live oak*, *ash*, *cottwonood*, *cherry*, *&c.*, and along the surrounding hills there are forests of *pine*, *cedar*, *fir*, *pinion*, and *spruce*. The soil and the climate are very suitable for producing the variety of corn, legumes, fruits, &c., that grow in the United States, in addition to many fruits of the hotter climes that grow excellently here.

"Among the corn and the most common grasses here are wheat, rye, oats, clover, and flax, together with a variety of grapes, which grow naturally and abundantly. Sometimes great tracts of land here are covered with several thousand acres of an abundant crop of wild oats, similar to the oats that are produced in the United States, and which grow to the height of two or three feet, and not uncommonly to seven feet. The clover of these valleys is similar to the red clover of our country, and in some parts there is an abundance of it; and its average height is two-and-a-half feet, although it often reaches that much higher than that, and covers the face of the land. Forty bushels an acre is the average yield of wheat, but frequently a very small plot of land will yield sixty or a hundred bushels. This corn ripens within about three months from the time it is sown.

"Indian corn grows excellently. An acre will yield 50 to 60 bushels, with no more trouble than to sow it and reap it. As many potatoes, onions, carrots, &c., are produced as you want, without any trouble. Tobacco is also produced here by some of the inhabitants who have high hopes. I do not think there is soil so fruitful in any other country under the sun, and there is not another country that can produce such a variety of fruit as the Sacramento valley and its environs. The aforementioned fruits grow in most of the lowlands throughout the country, and grapes grow along the banks of nearly every river, the kind that make excellent wines, and good *raisins*.

"The climate is so temperate, that fire is not needed for any purpose, apart from baking food. With a little bit of effort, a variety of garden vegetables can be grown in whatever season of the year you wish, and two crops of corn can be had each year. It is not uncommon to see plants in full bloom in the middle of winter, and all nature is wearing its beautiful garments, especially the lowlands. The traveler, according to his wish, any season of the year, can enjoy perpetual ice and snow, or he can feast his eyes on the fruitfulness and splendor of continual spring, or he can feast his desire on the total enjoyment of the abundant produce of the neverending summer; yes, his eyes, his mind, and his desire will be satisfied here, if any climate, soil, and fruit can satisfy him.

"Practically the only rain to fall here comes down from the beginning of January through March, their winter. For about one third of this time the clouds pour down their rains severely, and the rest of this season is clear, lovely, and temperate."

TESTIMONY OF MORGAN DAVID, FELINFOEL.

Dear Brother,—Behold I am sending you these lines; and if you wish they are at your service:—

I was eighteen years with the Baptists, and I was quite fervent, while my eyes were not open, rather I accepted everything during my time with them, and they offered no proof for anything; but when I took note of the behavior of their preachers, together with their financial principles, my interest began to cool, and I paid greater attention to everything I heard from the pulpits, namely that it was just as necessary to receive the Holy Ghost as it was for Christ to die, and I heard prayers for it, and I prayed for it, and there were special meetings to pray for a more abundant pouring out of it on the churches; but never did I see its effects or feel its influence, and consequently I came to the determination that the Holy Ghost was not to be enjoyed in this age. I supposed that only the word could be obtained, yet I knew that it was a spiritual act to worship God; and in the midst of this confusion I could not enjoy the religion of the Bible. Several times I wanted to relinquish my membership in despair upon seeing everyone like myself. Well, that is the way it was with me while I was a Baptist. But I am grateful to my Heavenly Father that he did not allow me to flounder in the midst of this darkness any longer, rather he sent his servants, the Latter-day Saints, with the eternal gospel in the fulness of its blessings to the neighborhood; and although I took no notice of them at first, I am now thankful to my Heavenly Father for permitting me to take time to listen to them, for despite how much I heard against them, that they were "ready Satanists," &c., yet I saw that what they preached, together with the testimony they gave, was in accordance with the New Testament; but I hesitated with respect to the truthfulness of their promise, namely that I would receive a similar testimony from God through obeying the plan which they had obeyed. I observed carefully the men who were testifying, to determine whether or not they were deceitful. I saw that filthy lucre was not their motivation, rather they paid their own way. Then after I found their doctrine to be completely scriptural, I decided to obey the plan by being baptized; and I am thankful to God, who knows hearts, and who gave me a testimony by giving me the Holy Ghost as they had. I know now that I am a member of the Church of Jesus Christ, because it corresponds to the church that Jesus established on the earth; it has apostles and prophets, together with all the offices and spiritual gifts, to perfect the saints, for the work of the ministry, to build the body of Christ; and I beseech all my former dear brothers and sisters to do the same as I have done. This at present from your humble brother,

MORGAN DAVID.

"DECEIT OF THE MORMONS."

Mr. Ed.,—A lecture on the above topic was delivered by one by the name of Mr. W. Jones, Liverpool, in the Chapel of the Independents, in Rhosllanerchrugog, April 18th, 1848. The points of the lecture were as follows; and if you, or any of your correspondents, wish to review anything concerning the topics, here they are at your service.

"1. Faith of the Mormons:—They believe that God like man has a body, members, parts, &c.,—some little god like this is what they worship. They believe that the animals will come to speak to convince the ungodly and to heal the sick. They believe in dreams, and that this is the rock spoken of by Christ on which the church will be built. They believe that the present state officials are not legal, and that witnesses of the world who are under oath should not be believed, if they have not been inspired.

2. "Leader of the Mormons:—A foolish man, a dreamer, one who looks into his hat for revelation, &c. When he had obtained some followers, he told them to take swords, and work their way, that God had given the land to them, and that the United States would be destroyed in the year 1832.

3. "Book of Mormon:—The Mormons say that this was an ancient manuscript, written by the ancient Indians, and that Joe had translated it through divine power. But the truth is, that S. Spaulding wrote it, a learned and godly man, who did it for amusement. 116 pages of the translation were lost, and Joe could not re-do them.

4. Opinion of the lecturer:—"There is no need for apostles now, for Christ never had more than twelve. Miracles were never intended to convince the world, but to establish the religion. It is appropriate to call the Mormons "Satanists," since it is at night and in the darkness that Satan works, and thus do they practice night-immersion, and their secret work, and no one can know it without joining them."

Next, behold a list of claims of this lying lecturer,—"The Mormons have neither logic nor the Bible. The religion of the Mormons is *all* deceit. *Nothing* of the Mormon religion is of God. But he would take truth from a Mormon if he could find any," &c.

The above lecture was reviewed the following night, April 19th, in Rhosllanerchrugog, to the hearing of scores of people, and that without allowing that any of the above statements are true (but are lying blasphemy, which proves that our enemies have nothing true to say against us), except that God is a spiritual person, that the Book of Mormon is an ancient manuscript, and that 116 pages of the translation were stolen. Miracles were not intended to convince the world, and therefore let not the world ask for a miracle in order to believe ever again! Then if everything the Mormons have is deceit, and he himself is of the same opinion in these things, has he not slipped a bit? My reasons for not reviewing the above topics now are that, 1. They are obvious lies. 2. I have done that in the place where the lecture was delivered. 3. So many such things have been reviewed in a splendid and irrefutable manner, and they have been published by Capt. Jones. 4. I have another lesson, which anyone is fully welcome to review, if he do so with the Bible as the base; namely, 1st, The restoration of the true religion, by calling officials, and ordaining them, and sending them to teach the law, and administer the ordinances. 2nd. That spiritual blessings of the kingdom of God are imparted to those who obey this established law. 3rd. That this is the preparation for the millennium, and the restitution of all things, which God has spoken from the beginning. As I consider the breadth and glory of this work, I do not have time to throw a rock at every dog that barks at us, R. EVANS.

P. S. If any of our Correspondents has time and inclination to defend our religion and our fellow believers against the above slander and shameful false accusations, they can appear in the *Prophet*, lest someone somewhere is so dull as to believe them, which we doubt.—ED.

LETTER OF W. WOODRUFF, ONE OF THE APOSTLES.

Council Bluffs, *April* 25, 1848.

"DEAR BROTHER CAPT. JONES,—It would be an injustice to my own feelings to delay writing to you any further. I have intended time after time to associate with you by means of letters, and give you an accounting of how things are with us, and I desire news of your doings in Wales, together with the state of the divine cause in which the two of us have had the honor of being fellow-workers for God; but until now I have been hindered by the weight of the work that has been entrusted to me and placed on my shoulders to fulfill. But from now on, since I am going to the "Christian" country, as the eastern states, Canada and Nova Scotia are called, I trust that I shall have more time to write to you more often. I spent the last year of my time the same way the others of the "twelve" did,—seven months of it were spent on the journey to California and back here; and indeed, it was a journey filled with marvels.

"The first 500 miles of our journey, to fort Laramie, were on the north side of the Platte river, where only the red nomads of the forest have ever before traveled. We made a new road for that whole distance, and we built several bridges. Along this way we had a great abundance of geese, ducks, *cranes* swans, *deer*, *antelope*, *elk*, and *buffalos*, by the tens of thousands. From there we journeyed through the Black Mountains for about 500 miles. Along these parts the creatures noted were not as numerous as in the aforementioned parts, but we met the occasional bear wandering through the woods for prey, which could be shot easily with a rifle by just being careful: we killed some of them on our journey, but we depended mainly on the buffalo for meat along the way. The meat of a buffalo calf is excellent food. At times we were troubled by a few renegade Indians, who tried to drive away our horses, but we managed to get nearly all of them back by following them to their camp. The leaders of the Indians do not allow anyone to attack us; but from the other side, they behaved in a very neighborly manner toward the Saints, as far as we could see, except for some renegades amongst them.

"On our return back from California, we met 600 wagons loaded with Saints, under the presidency of P. P. Pratt and J. Taylor, on their way towards the Salt Lake in California. The Salt Lake Valley offers the most magnificent, most beautiful, and most paradisiacal scene of any place I have ever witnessed. This valley is surrounded with extremely high mountains, on whose highest points snow remains continually, while the climate in the valley is close to 100 degrees. Rivers of cold and pure water ran down from them past the doors of our tent where we camped, to quench our thirst. Three missionaries arrived here recently, who started from Salt Lake City in the middle of January, and they brought from there an abundance of blessed news, and nothing bad. There were there at that time already 3000 inhabitants, and death and disease were practically unknown in their midst. They had already built a mill for grinding grain, and three sawmills. They had sown at that time 1500 acres of wheat, which looked very promising, and they intend to sow about that much more this season, together with three or four thousand acres of Indian corn, &c. They have built about a thousand dwelling houses. After they have produced an abundance of grain there to sustain the immigrants, emigration will increase there to about five times the annual number. Excellent health is being enjoyed throughout these settlements at present, and there was hardly a death or illness among the Saints here last winter. The Saints who cannot emigrate to California this year intend to remove from here to the other side of the river to settle in the land of the Pottawatamie Indians, until they can make preparations for the remainder of the journey.

"I have watched carefully and eagerly the movement of the gospel ship sailing quickly along over the savage waves of the seas of Wales, with Capt. Jones at the helm, and the Mormon banner nailed to the masthead. And I am happy to say that it is moving forth beyond all expectations, and I have been greatly pleased at seeing the ship under such secure and skillful leadership. Believe me, brother Jones, when I say that my soul is filled with joy at hearing of the powerful work you have done already in spite of the opposition of all kinds you have encountered on the field, and it gives me unbounded joy to hear that thousands are receiving deliverance through your priesthood. The nation of Wales will have cause to rejoice to the endless ages of eternity, that she has at least one son who has a mind sufficiently independent to offer to his compatriots the pure principles of salvation, which were revealed from heaven to save the humble of heart who seek the truth as it is in Jesus, against the judgments and plagues that hang over the ungodly of the earth; and he who is able, willing, and eager to spread and defend the pure principles of the gospel of Jesus Christ, and to offer salvation to his compatriots, despite doing so through seas of obstacles, disadvantages, and oppression, and although he had to suffer the wrath, the rage, and the curses of the blind who do not wish to be benefitted. Be faithful and determined in your calling, for it is certain that the day will come when you will achieve glory, incorruptibility, and eternal life, to rejoice with the thousands of those happy ones who received salvation through you, when all your persecutors and your opponents will sink into the depths of the loathesome pits that they dug for you and the truth, and they will go to oblivion.

"It is true that your mission in Wales is long, yet be patient, for you will lay the foundations for a blessed and majestic work, and take comfort, for you shall not lose your reward. I have thought many times with pleasure about the voyage and the sweet conversations we had on board the ship J. R. Skiddy, from New York to Liverpool. I rejoice that the Lord is with you, and when I hear of the fruit of your labor. But I must end now for this time. My wife and my family wish to be remembered fondly to Capt. Jones, and Mrs. Jones. Be so good as to write me in Boston when you receive this, and give me your news.

"The war between Mexico and the United States has not yet ended, nor is there hope for that soon, rather preparations for battle are being made on every side. It is said that there is a petition before the Senate to have 30,000 more soldiers go there.

"I am, dear brother, yours in the bonds of the N. C.,

"WILFORD WOODRUFF."

A QUESTION, AND ITS ANSWER.

MR. ED.—*What do you understand by the "other beast," in Rev.* xiii, 11—14? *Is it one that is to come after the age of the apostles? If so, will his "great wonders" be visible to the public? When, and how, will his deadly wound be healed? A prompt answer will give satisfaction to several, and will give prominence to the foolishness of those who say that this refers to Joseph Smith, and the Saints, I suppose.* T. JEREMY.

We answer, that the "beast" does not signify an individual person, rather a system, which would contain seven kinds of government, which among them would rule over ten royal kingdoms, as did the first beast (ver. 1). In ver. 2, the strength and cruelty of the chief presidency are signified. The "dragon" is his god, or the god of this world. The power of the "dragon" was to work miracles, through which he persuaded everyone to worship the beast, and through that to worship the devil without their being aware of it themselves. The way that one of his heads received a deadly wound, was through their losing the miraculous power for 1260 years; and the reason for that was because there were no miracles being worked by God through his servants in the meantime, and thus the devil considered his own fake miracles of no use to deceive men. Ver. 7 proves that it was with the saints of the apostolic age that he warred, which proves that it was in those times that the first beast would rise up, and consequently the one under consideration would exist in the last ages, or rather that it was close to the end of the reign of the beast that was revived, or that would be revived, the ruins of the old form to its primitive power through the coming of the second beast; "he exerciseth all the [miraculous] power of the first beast [namely the other beast] before [according to the same plan] him," namely before the first beast, which proves that the second cannot be a new plan, but it is the restoration of the old form that would exist after the apostles. If it is determined which religious and governmental plan persecuted the saints until overcoming them in the primitive times, and which still exists on their ruins, that will answer your first question and your second, and I believe that its name is too well known to us to name it here. But it is seen that it cannot be "Joe Smith," or "Mormonism."

"Its miracles and wonders" will, we believe, be public, numerous, and quite remarkable. They will be so powerful that he will proselyte all those who do not have the gift of "discerning of spirits;" and he has been working in secret for a long time to prepare the whole sectarian world to believe the powerful servants of this last beast, by proselyting the world to believe "that the purpose of miracles was to prove the truth of religion, and the sending of the persons in primitive times," and to teach them through that to ask for miracles and signs from the servants of God, vowing that if they could but see a "small miracle they would believe immediately," regardless of their doctrine; and when the servants of God refuse to satisfy their whims, and instead preach Christ crucified, and deliver their message to the honest in heart, then the beastly *heralds* will come across the world with powers and it will support him who asked our Prince in the wilderness in days of old, to turn that stone into bread, giving great signs to those who seek them, and no doubt they will announce meetings, and they will invite the whole world there to see their miracles at the appointed time, and after getting the observers to promise to believe them, they will fulfill great and incredible things, and then they will hold the sectarians to their offer, and they will be unable to stand against them; for their own theologians will say that the purpose of miracles was to prove that the sending of persons was divine, and they will say at that time, "Here they are; these are servants of God: see their miracles; but as for the lowly Saints, we have never seen one of their miracles." And in this manner there they are in the devil's trap tighter than before, having freed the servants of God from the accusation, by claiming that they do not provide signs and wonders; for it is the false, and not the true, that do so for that purpose, and at the request of the listeners (see Mat. xxiv, 24). Seeing the wonders will deceive the people into believing that the religion of the beast is the divine one, when faith to believe the religion of Christ comes, not by seeing with the eyes, rather by hearing the word of God, as Paul says.

According to his servants it is the devil's fulfillment of this miraculous power, that the "deadly disease will be healed," for this was the life and strength that was in it before; and what could wound devilish or divine religion more than depriving it of its supernatural power? There could be nothing left of the one or the other but a useless skeleton. Every perceptive man who observes the signs of these awful times, will see that that which withholdeth has practically been taken away already, as Paul suggests through the Spirit of prophecy for the last days in 2 Thes. ii, 3—12. It is seen that God will send his servants before the revival of the second beast, not to work miracles, but to deliver their message to the lost world, to teach them what they must do to be saved, namely teaching them in the same commandments and ordinances which the apostles taught to their contemporaries, promising to those who obey, and not to the unbelievers, forgiveness of sins through baptism, and that they will receive "the gift of the Holy Ghost," and that *God*, and not *they*, would confirm their message to the believers, and not to their enemies, through godly signs, which would be *resultant blessings*, and not *preceding signs* to his servants.

All this is evident in the above, and also the devil saw that he could no longer keep the public in the dark by denying miracles, and saying that they were not needed; rather he jumps to the other side of the fence, and he and his servants will immediately be the most zealous proponents of miracles as anyone, in order to blind the people from believing true miracles, namely the gifts of the Holy Ghost, which God will impart to his children, and then the servants of the beast will shout loudly, "Come unto us; we are the ones who work miracles." And they will say at that time, each at the top of his voice, that miracles are needed, taking the form of an angel of light. And on the truthfulness of the above prophecies, and those of our own, we venture to proclaim that the time is not far off when authorities and princes that hold great power in high places in the kingdom of the enemy, will be heard claiming the continuance of their miracles, and the necessity for them in this age as zealously as any of the Saints, and asserting that they have the spiritual gifts, visions, prophets, the gifts of healing, &c., and that they have always been proponents for the doctrine of the continuance of miracles in the church. Some of the giants of sectarianism are already yearning to lead out in this strange revolution to heal the beast's wound by wearing the miraculous jacket in secret, and asking their friends how it would look for them to wear it in public. Then their *hirelings* will shout from their pulpits, "Come unto us; we believe in miracles, &c.; and we have had the priesthood since the days of the apostles." At that time let the Saints lift up their heads, and watch, for the coming days will be dangerous days even for the lovers of the truth, when their ears will be numbed at hearing of the false signs that have been shown here, and their eyes will be weary at seeing the wonders of yonder beast; then it will be understood that the wound of the beast has been healed, and that he has become the chief enemy of "Mormonism."

THE CONDEMNATORY SENTENCE OF JESUS CHRIST.

THE Editor of a French newspaper says it like this:—"By chance there came to our hands the most important, and most interesting *document* for the Christians that has ever been, i. e., the original condemnatory sentence that was pronounced on the Lord Jesus Christ." The following was translated carefully by the editor, who assures that it is a literal translation.

"*The sentence given by Pontius Pilate, the reigning tetrarch over Lower Galilea, proclaims that Jesus of Nazareth must suffer death on the cross.*

"In the seventeenth year of the reign of the Emperor Tiberias Caesar, on the 25th of March, in the holy city of Jerusalem, Annas and Caiaphas are the representative high priests of the people of God. It is Pontius Pilate, the tetrarch of Lower Galilea, who sits on the governing chair of the *Praetory*, and who condemns Jesus of Nazareth to die on the cross, between two thieves—the grand and unanimous testimony of the people says;—

"1. Jesus is treacherous.

"2. He is deceitful.

"3. He is an enemy of the law.

"4. He blasphemes himself as the Son of God.

"5. He blasphemes himself as the King of the Jews.

"6. He went to the temple, and a crowd followed him, carrying palm branches in their hands.

"The head centurion, Quillus Cornelius, is hereby ordered to lead him to the place of execution.

"Any rich person or poor person is forbidden from opposing the death of Jesus."

"The names of the witnesses who described the above sentence are,—"Daniel Robani, Pharisee; 2. Ioannus Rorobable; 3. Raphel Robani; 4. Capet, citizen.

"Let Jesus be taken out through the Struenus gate."

The above was discovered engraved on copper, and placed in a chest of white marble, which was discovered while digging under the ruins of the old city of Abuilla in the kingdom of Naples, in the year 1820, by army officers of the French. Carved on the other side of the copper plate, were the following words:—"Every tribe was presented with a copy of the above condemnation."

NAMES OF THE TWELVE APOSTLES OF THE "DISPENSATION OF THE FULNESS OF TIMES."

AT the request of many of the Saints here and there we publish the names of the aforementioned courageous men, so that we may have an answer for this frequently asked question for everyone at once, and worthy of being recorded on the tables of the hearts of all the lovers of the truth, as they are on our own hearts, are the names of these patriotic, wise, and great men, for the Saints enjoy the rays of light through them from the source above; yet, this is nothing compared to what is yet to emanate from them to those who listen to their godly counsel.

Brigham Young,
Heber C. Kimball,
Willard Richards,
Orson Hyde,
Parley P. Pratt,
John Taylor,
Wilford Woodruff,
George A. Smith,
Amasa Lyman,
E. T. Benson,
Orson Pratt,
Lyman Wight.

WHAT IS TO BE DONE WITH THE PERSECUTORS OF THE SAINTS?

Monmouthshire.

Dear Brother,—Inasmuch as Mr. Rees, and a variety of other ministers in this County, have been on the field so long against Mormonism, telling all manner of stories and lies against it, now their madness has become obvious, until it causes the best men in their midst to come to us, with tears on their cheeks, asking, "What shall we do to be saved?" The answer is, "Repent, and be baptized for the remission of sins, and ye shall receive the gift of the Holy Ghost;" and then they come, and now they rejoice in the promises of their God. We expect to see the persecutors themselves coming with tears on their cheeks, asking, "What shall we do to be saved?" We cannot answer them, for their sins are so many; but we wish you to inform us through the PROPHET what we are to do with them?

We shall delay the matter for now until an answer comes; but I think there will be many tears running down over their cheeks before it comes, if you delay. If there is any way to save them, we wish to know as soon as you can send an answer.

WILLIAM PHILLIPS.

[We must have time to reflect a while, before answering such an important question. Whether the foregoing persecutors have accomplished the high feat of becoming "Satanists and demons," perhaps Mr. Jones, Felinfoel, or Mr. Davies, Dowlais, can answer.—ED.]

LETTER OF D. ROBERTS, LLWYNYGELL.

Dear Brother Jones,—I take this opportunity to inform you of our present success with the work of the Lord. We have baptized three since I wrote to you before, and there are signs for more. We are preaching as forcefully as we can, and frequently have quite an attentive and numerous hearing. The country is as if awakening from its slumber, and is beginning to take notice of the signs of the time, between the preaching of the Saints, and the neighing of the red horse, and the stories of our enemies. Hosts are ready to ask what is the matter, and are beginning to draw near to hear the Saints answer the above question, having failed to satisfactorily answer the question for themselves.

We are greatly desirous of seeing you here this summer, and we hope you do not forget us in the north, in spite of how cold the climate is that we live in at present, but a small fire has been kindled here, and we are keeping the bellows in operation until it becomes a burning flame. Pray for us, so that we will not grow weary, and we do not fail to pray for you, our dear brother. All the Saints kindly greet you in the Lord. Amen. Your humble brother.

D. ROBERTS.

Llwynygell, Blaenau Ffestiniog.

THE TRUE CHURCH OF JESUS CHRIST

Compared to the systems of men.

THE GOD others worship, is not the God for me,
He has no parts, nor body; and cannot hear nor see us:
But I've a God that reigns above;
A God of power, and of love:
And a God of revelation,—Oh, that's the God for me!
Oh, that's the God for me!
Oh, that's the God for me!

Any church without apostles, is not the church for me,
It is like a ship without sails floating on the waves;
But a church led beneath the heaven
By twelve stars around her head,
And a church with a good foundation,—Oh, that is my church! &c., &c.

A church without a prophet, is not the church for me,
It has no head to lead it, it wanders in every direction;

But a church not organized by man,
The one that God himself established,
Namely the church with the "signs,"—Oh, that is my church! &c., &c.

The hope of the Gentiles, is not the hope for me,
Having neither faith nor knowledge, 'tis nothing but black darkness;
But hope will endure while there are an earth and a heaven,
And one who sees beyond the veil,
Such hope is like an anchor,—Oh, that is my hope! &c., &c.

The heaven the sectarians desire, is not the heaven for me,
That one is too obscure, in an empty space somewhere up above;
But heaven here on earth,
The home where I suckled,
A heaven of light, a heaven of knowledge,—Oh, that is my heaven! &c., &c.

Any church not gathered together, is not the church for me,
The Savior would never claim one like that;
But a church that has been called out
From the world and its hateful traditions,
And a church gathered together,—Oh, that is my church, &c., &c.

June 12, 1848. *Trans*. J. D.

SONG OF ENTREATY

Which a sister from Llanybydder composed, the night of the 18th of April, before going to bed.

WELSH people, Welsh people, hear my lament,
And moan and groan,
Because I am heavy hearted,
And lamenting in my tribulations.

I no longer care
Now about the things of this world;
Except to get all my loved ones
To follow Christ despite the obstacles.

My mother and dear husband
Do not believe the gospel,
Which plan Christ, the Son of God,
Ordained before going to heaven.

Oh, my mother! I do wish
For you to come and begin working;
And you my husband, with her,
(It is high time) in the vineyard of Jesus.

There is no promise unless you come,
Nothing but everlasting grief and sadness;
And your part will be the second death,
With those who are imperfect.

I hope to continue faithful,
And be able to go to mount Zion,
To that blessed family
Who have their mind and their love towards Jesus.

I know, that if I continue faithful,
I shall wear the golden crown;
And palm branches shall I have also,
With the Great King of the whole world.

The sects cannot believe
That it is necessary to go to the sea, and cross it,
Over to the place where God promises
To give a place of refuge, if one but goes there,

From the great plagues and the pestilence
That will come because of their sins,
If they do not become faithful,
As did the Ninevites of old.

To the whole neighborhood I declare
That you must get the religion of Jesus,
The one that will bring you signs,
If you but keep the blessed commandments.

Oh, neighbors of Llanybydder,
I testify free from worry
That you will be sure to remember my words,
Without doubt, in the judgment seat.

If I should die before leaving,
Remember to declare this to my nation,
That I now testify to them,
That the day of vengeance is coming upon them,—

A day of weeping, and a day of mourning,
A day of longing will come to earth,
A day that all men will be frightened,
But those who come to the religion of Jesus.

The Saints have the witness,
Though they be in temptations;
Nevertheless they will get to reign
With Christ and King Jesus.

I now bid farewell,
To my dear country, when about to leave,
With every hope of crossing the seas,
According to the commandment of the King of Heaven.

LETTER OF ELDER W. MORGAN.

Merthyr, June 21, 1848.

DEAR BROTHER,—All of us here, and the officers especially, continue in unity and faithfulness in the fulfillment of our duties since you left here, and the Lord is blessing our labor, especially through healing the sick through the ordinances and prayers of faith; I shall note a few of the many instances that have taken place here lately:—One sister was taken sick with a high fever while visiting her relatives in Brecon. Through much effort she was brought to Merthyr in a wagon from which she had to be carried to the house. She sent for the elders of the Church instead of for doctors; and I and one other went to her and administered to her, praying for the Lord to heal her; and the result, thanks to Him who imparts all blessings, was that she received her health immediately, rose from her bed and partook of food in the presence of some unbelieving onlookers. Word spread about the incident throughout the surrounding works until many became angry with the Saints, claiming that her illness was fake and deceitful; others claimed that the sick woman had not gotten better; and some of those who had carried her to the house swore and said that such deceivers were too wicked to be allowed to keep on living. What should be done with men who refuse to believe their own eyes, feelings and ears, do you think?

Another example of the goodness of God happened as follows:—A man by the name of David Davies, a worker in the Penydarren works was covered by a large cave-in of earth to the extent that his co-workers hardly knew where to look for him, and it was a great wonder that he was found alive. After he was freed he was carried out on a *tram* and on horseback to his house, and his co-workers made statements of great sympathy, saying that he would not be back to work for many months if ever. Next day two elders went to him and administered to him and prayed for him, and he arose from his bed immediately and walked with them to Merthyr and to the meeting of the Saints in full health. He went to work the next day and worked as usual; but the opinion of his co-workers had completely changed from thinking that he had received such an injury to claiming now that he had hardly been hurt; except for an occasional exception that was their opinion in spite of everything; and yet they ask for more and more signs to bring them to believe.

The gospel is having general success in these environs. Seven were baptized in Pontypridd lately; and several in Dowlais, Cardiff, Aberdare, &c. I heard also that twelve had been baptized in Hirwaun last week. There are great numbers in Monmouthshire and here, I cannot say how many, who have been baptized in this branch since your departure, with prospects for many more soon. May the gracious Lord permit that it be so is the constant prayer of your brother in Christ,

WILLIAM MORGAN.

TO OUR SUBSCRIBERS.

WE are sorry to inform you that we cannot fulfill the constant and earnest demand there is from several places for the "Old Religion Anew," the "Reply," "Book of Hymns," and the "Reviews," for all that were printed of the above have been distributed; and if our distributors have some on hand, we hope they will not keep them secret, but strive to distribute them since there is such a demand for them. We do not intend to publish a second printing of the above until we have evidence that all the others have been sold, and there will be no better evidence of this than the return of the money to our hand.

Several of the distributors are in heavy debt to us now, and over a hundred pounds of our money is dispersed, while with a little more effort and faithfulness they could have paid for all of them. All the churches of the Saints, throughout England, Scotland, and the world that we know of, except for the Welsh Saints, support the arms and pockets of their publishers, and give the necessary marrow in their bones, by the branches choosing their distributors, and contributing money beforehand to pay for the books they have sent for; and thus the distributors are responsible for them, and they to the office. This is the established rule of the office in Liverpool, and if a distributor does something wrong, that does not all fall on the same person to vex him, but on those who can forestall the wrong by being at his side. But up to now we, as a small operation, have strived to stand under the whole burden ourselves, without one shoulder or plan of assistance, and have contributed the earnings to assist our poor fellow workers on their travels in the midst of a perverse and rebellious generation to preach the gospel of Christ for nothing. While we take pride in our ability to do this, and while we give thanks with all our heart to some of our faithful and dear distributors for their cooperation, not only to sell, but also to pay for the books they have received, yet we are not without cause to worry that some distributors are in our debt for several pounds for years by now, with no hope of reducing it. What is to be done with such is an important question for us, and worthy of the subscribers of such distributors! If they considered how costly it is to publish, no doubt they would strive to pay, unless their intent is to hinder completely this useful tool from spreading divine truths—from defending the children and the religion of God, and from benefitting their fellowmen. We consider that it would be an injustice of the first order for us to use anyone's money for our own personal service without permission, but the wrong would be still worse if it caused obstacles for the work of God. We intend to publish our accounts with our distributors in the *Prophet* after the Conference so the branches can better discern between the faithful and those to whom we refer above, if we cannot succeed some other way. An effective way to get some to apostatize in this age also is by allowing them to carry the "purse," like Judas of old.

The 5th and last Number of the *Treasury* is off the press now, which will also be the last pamphlet we shall publish unless the above *hints* do the trick, except for the *Prophet*. Several hundred of each number of the *Treasury* are still on hand, and we hope that each one who purchased some number of it will strive to purchase them all, or else we shall buy his Number back, if it is clean and tidy. The complete *Treasury* will be available as soon as it can be bound, for different prices according to its binding, from 4*s*. to 5*s*. 6*c*.

ANNOUNCEMENTS.

BOOKS FOR SALE.

We have just received close to a hundred volumes of "Capt. Jones on Mormonism in 1847," from the Binder, and they are extremely well bound, fine and cheap, for various prices as before. We hope that the Saints will strive to possess one volume at least of these in every family before it is too late. The 1846 volumes have all been sold already, with a great call for more, but they are not available.

*** On page 94 of the last Number of the *Prophet*, on the 10th line from the bottom, instead of "twenty *miles* of width," read "twenty *yards* of width."——Page 93, line 23 from the top, instead of "wait *under* times," read, "wait *three* times."

CONTENTS.

MERTHYR TYDFIL:

PUBLISHED AND FOR SALE BY D. JONES, AND ALSO FOR SALE BY THE SAINTS IN GENERAL

JOHN JONES, PRINTER, RHYDYBONT.

PROPHET OF THE JUBILEE,

OR

STAR OF THE SAINTS.

No. 26.] AUGUST, 1848. [Price 2*c*.

TO THE READERS OF THE *PROPHET*.

Dear Readers,—

Since we have completed the task that we undertook a year ago to publish a book mainly for the Saints, but also a book that will be of service to whoever else wishes to understand our principles as we profess them in truth, we avail ourselves of the present opportunity to say a word about it to those who have not yet purchased it for themselves. The book is the "Scriptural Treasury," which contains a compendium of quoted verses, and notes by us, to prove the main points of the religion of the Latter-day Saints.

We have no doubt that this small *Prophet* has many readers who have not yet obeyed the gospel we preach, and possibly many of those are reasonable men, who also admit that a man has the responsibility of striving to come to a better understanding of the principles he professes. Helping our readers to do so was one of our chief aims in composing and publishing the *Scriptural Treasury* in its present format. Although it is organized in a completely different manner from anything we have ever seen; yet, inasmuch as the scriptures of the truth are our rules of discipline, and our religious standard, we trust that a compendium of the views of the inspired writers brought together, and placed face to face in this manner before the eyes of our reader, will be more advantageous for him to be able to understand and defend the principles professed by the Saints, than if he had to search the entire holy volume on every subject, as we did in composing it.

The *Treasury* has required considerable work and research, and many earnest prayers for guidance of the Holy Ghost, so that we would be able to understand properly the ideas and the chronology of the Old and the

New Testament prophecies, about which there are so many different opinions; and not without considering seriously the eternal consequences of teaching the human mind, and penetrating research into its connections backwards and forwards, did we dare to select and gather the scriptures as they are here.

The importance and responsibility of the circle in which we have been placed, together with our love for, and our desire to teach those who have been entrusted to our care, the pure principles of the gospel, together with the understanding that duties will call us out of the country of our birth before long, and deny us the dear association of the Welsh Saints for a while, and consequently the advantages of serving them, are considerations that have motivated us to move forward to break through every obstacle to publish this work.

The remarkable increase that God has already given to this denomination against which so much is being said, besides the more remarkable growth we know that he will yet give it before long, shows that our fears are not unfounded that, after our departure, self-opinionated and self-imposing men will come to the church, trying to entice after them unstable souls, and perhaps the occasional weak and ingenuous Saint, to the old and heretical traditions and the more popular ones of the latest ages. This shows the usefulness of the *Treasury* to forestall them; for it is certain that the Saints' proper understanding of the principles of truth is the best fortress to defend them in those principles.

Dear reader, search, prove, weigh, and seriously ponder, for the truth is valuable to your soul; and if you get more of that with any other party than with the Saints, for the sake of your life go to it at once, and hold fast to it. If you get better truth in any doctrines, than the *Treasury* contains, notify us for the sake of our soul, and we shall run after it; but remember this first, that no one can enjoy sweet virtue, or the blessed society of the Spirit of the truth, or go forward toward perfection, except to the extent that he walks correctly the paths of the truth.

Another motive that prompted us to understake this important work is, we have had, by the grace of God, more opportunities to have personal association with, to listen to, and to extract the honey from the treasures of the inspired servants of the living God, namely the holy apostles and prophets, over the seas, than anyone else we know in Wales, and which have never before been published in the Welsh language; and we could not hide the light we have received through them from our dear compatriots.

Now we shall leave the *Treasury*, and we shall present it to the attention of whoever sees fit to give his time to read it, at the same time hoping that no family of the Saints will be without it, and we pray for the Spirit of truth to bless it to fulfill its mission, that God will be glorified, and thus we shall have the pleasure of hoping that through it, we are serving our nation while thousands of miles away from them. Amen.

*** The *Treasury* can be had complete, as soon as it can be bound, for various prices corresponding to its binding, from 4*s*. to 5*s*. 6*c*.

THE PERSECUTION OF THE SAINTS IN CWMBYCHAN AND BRYN !—TWENTY-NINE SAINTS ARE TURNED FROM THE MINE BECAUSE OF THEIR RELIGION ! !—SECTARIAN STEWARDS ATTEMPT TO STARVE ABOUT FIFTY WIVES AND CHILDREN OF THE SAINTS ! ! !

The following *Petition* of complaint shows the suffering and the oppression that ostensibly religious men can bring on the children of God when they have the power. We know that the Saints have not told all their sufferings in the following. Soon after this execrable deed, the chief Steward was fired from his job by the Company! "And with what measure ye mete, it shall be measured to you again," says Christ. Mr. Bidelph came there as the chief Overseer after him, who, although he is not associated with any denomination, is much more charitable than the others mentioned. Here following is the petition:—

"To John Bidelph, Esq.,

"Inasmuch as we, the undersigned, 29 of us, were turned away from the mine at Cwmbychan and Bryn without just cause, and have as a result been deprived of our livelihoods:—

"And our dear wives, and our innocent children (no fewer than fifty in number), have suffered, and continue to suffer hunger and great poverty;—

"And furthermore, those Stewards who turned us away from the mine have decided to drive us out of this country, they sent the *Bailiff* and the *Policeman* to turn us out of the houses, and to sell our furniture, if the rent money was not brought forward immediately, and through that depriving us and our families immediately, not only of food, but also of refuge or shelter against the fierce storms of February,—and in the land of our birth;—

"The only offense we are accused of, or that anyone can accuse us of being guilty of is, that we dare to worship the God of our fathers according to the dictates of our own consciences, the holy scriptures being the rule of life and conduct. To prove this last statement that is incredible to some, we have in our possession undeniable facts, besides the confession of our persecutors. We have obtained, or all who sought one, and now have in our possession to show to the world, written testimonials, and signed by our employers in the above works for an extended period, that testify that we are 'diligent, honest, sober, and good workers;'—

"And we also have irrefutable witnesses, who testify that the Stewards (apart from a few gentlemanly exceptions) formed, in a council held for that purpose, false accusations against those of us who call ourselves 'Latter-day Saints,' intending to influence their superiors to permit them to turn us out of the work; and among the names of the Saints, they put a few other names, and that to hide their true intent, and those got to go back to the mine right away, while we, and no one else, are shut out; and when work is given to strangers here, we are told time after time by the Stewards, who are either zealous sectarians, or else under their influence,—'If you leave your religion, you will get work, and not without doing that.'

"Inasmuch as the foregoing account is too true, and too easy to prove to anyone who denies it; that we, our dear wives, and our little starving children, are living monuments to this day, and exiles, in a 'free country,' for the sake of conscience, to prove the above as the truth;—

"The oppressive Stewards of the neighboring works are following the examples of the above persecutors, and are turning the Saints from their mines for the same cause,—We earnestly and humbly plead for your kindness in searching into the injustices and the oppression that innocent people are suffering, but with forbearance, and allow us, together with hundreds of others who are in the above mines, who believe, but who do not dare to embrace our dear religion, such freedom and privileges that are allowed to all your other faithful workers; for after much waiting, and humbly beseeching our persecutors, it appears that all our earnest and frequent appeals to them are as ineffective as the sigh of a baby against a rushing whirwind. And we humbly pray, respected Sir, that you will grant us those justices that are assured to us and to all other faithful subjects of her Majesty, for which we pray constantly; that by so doing you will earn for yourself the reputation of father of the oppressed, and defender of freedom; and thus will the earnest prayers of exiled parents, and starving children, ascend on high to the Lord God of all the earth for him to bless you and yours an hundredfold. Amen.

"We humbly beseech you to receive this book from the hand of the bearer, in which you can read the main tenets of our religion, which will enable you to judge for yourself in the face of the accusations against us that are presented to you.

"For the above Society we wish to sign ourselves
Your obedient and humble servants."

Then a list of the names of the sufferers follows.

Let the reader consider who is the God, and what is the kind of religion of these oppressors; and their cruelties and their wicked deeds do not prove which cause motivates them, any more obviously than they prove also the divinity of the religion and the godliness of the sufferers, and the truthfulness of the Son of God, namely, "Ye shall be hated of all men for my name's sake;" also, "A kingdom divided against itself cannot stand," which clearly proves that the Saints are not subjects of the same spiritual kingdom as their cruel oppressors.

Lest anyone doubt that the above is religious persecution, we shall add a few of the many testimonies we have before us. Evan Rees, one of the preachers of the Saints, asked Thomas Jones, Steward, if he could return to the works yet. He answered that the works were too full. Then E. R. asked, "Do you have anything against me as a worker?" The Steward answered, "No, not in the least."

E. R. asked David Hopkin, a higher Steward, "Do you have anything against me as a worker, or anything as a man?" He answered, "Don't bother me; I don't know anything about you; the works are too full." Then E. R. asked him, "Why have you taken scores of strangers in then, when you have turned the Saints out of the works? Tell me what you have against me." D. H. answered, "I have nothing against you," and then he went away angrily.

Once again: Mr. William Williams, Steward, said to William Howell, one of the preachers of the Saints, that he, and practically all the Stewards there, had decided that no one of the Saints will work in those works, as long as they can prevent them from doing so.

A CALL TO A SINNER.

A VOICE from heaven calls out
Strongly on everyone to receive grace,
Through baptismal water to repent,
The end of the world draws nigh.

Before long the time
Will be swallowed up in vast eternity;
Blessed are those who embrace the honor
That is offered by the Saints.

Fear not the frown or scorn of the world,
Come under the yolk, it is high time;
Turn to the Doctor all together,
Without delaying a minute longer.

As Christ was, the Saints will be persecuted,
By men of the world for keeping their honor,
As they walk the path towards Heaven,
By the only path He prepared.

ANTI-MORMON SERMON.

TO THE REV. T. WILLIAMS, EBENEZER, NEAR CARMARTHEN.

REV. SIR,—I had the opportunity to listen to you on Sunday, the second of July last, in your chapel, Ebenezer; and I am pleased to announce that you preached better, in your manner, than I expected you could. Your sermon savored heavily of deep meditation, and was as melodious as if it had been delivered many times mingled with the beautiful sound of the birds in your fields. You had announced this sermon a week previously, and had said that it was through it that you were going to wash your hands of the blood of all your members. The chapel was filled to overflowing, and I had the opportunity to note the most particular things you said. Your text can be seen in Eph. iv, 14,—"That we henceforth be no more children, tossed to and fro, and carried about with every wind of doctrine, by the sleight of men, and cunning craftiness, whereby they lie in wait to deceive." After hearing the text, I understood precisely that you too could through "cunning craftiness, lie in wait to deceive," as well as those the apostle described; because you used words belonging to a church in which there were "some, apostles; and some, prophets; and some, evangelists; and some, pastors and teachers; for the perfecting of the saints, for the work of the ministry, for the edifying of the body of Christ: till we all come in the unity of the faith, and of the knowledge of the Son of God, unto a perfect man, unto the measure of the stature of the fulness of Christ," that the saints be no more carried about (see ver. 11—13). The text would be appropriate for you if there were apostles and prophets in the Baptist church, for the perfecting of the members, for the work of the ministry, and for the edifying of the *body* of Christ, and that until the body becomes "*a perfect man;*" but fie on you, you took a text belonging to a church such as the Mormons have. But since you did not speak of anything relating to the text, it did very well to be the sleight of man, "and cunning craftiness, whereby to deceive" your members into thinking that the text related to the Baptists! At the beginning of your sermon, you said you were not angry with the Mormons, but that you hated Mormonism. You considered that calling the Mormons "Saints" was *blasphemy!* Why so, Mr. Williams? Can the *Baptists* be called "Saints," then? If you say they can, then apostles and prophets, &c., are needed to perfect them; for if Baptists and Independents can be perfected without them, "Saints" can never be perfected without them. You said too that you expected to be believed before the Mormons, because no one has ever been able to bring an accusation of untruthfulness against you in all the time you have been at Ebenezer. Well, if you say that Mormonism is deceit, then all your members should believe you! A fine way to toss "children" to and fro, Mr. Williams! It is not right for you to *judge* for your members, for several of them have been listening to the Saints for themselves, which you have never done. The doctrine of the Saints is not so far from being self-testing, that there is no reason to put trust in persons. How were you believed in at first, Sir, before you established your reputation? Did some urge people not to believe you? You, who are called a servant of God, be just; let others have time to make their reputation known as you did; yes, let them, and do not forbid your members to listen to them, but let them "prove all things, and hold fast that which is good."

Your "craftiness" did not end with your text, but followed you in your sermon. You said that you would judge the Mormons on what is in their books, and that those were still to be seen; but you announced that you would not recite them as they were written, but that you would put a summary of them before your listeners, so that they could judge for themselves. You claimed that the books said that the following things had to be believed before one could be one of the Mormons;—1. That Joseph Smith is a prophet. 2. That the book of *Môr* [*Mormon*, Mr. Williams; is it true that you cannot read properly?] is as divine as the Bible. 3. That Jesus Christ appeared in America, and "preached to the spirits in the prison" of *hell*. 3. That there are two Jerusalems. 4. That the Jews are to be gathered to the Palestinian Jerusalem, and the Mormons to the American Jerusalem. 5. That miracles, associating with angels, visions, strange tongues, exist in the church. 6. That the sick receive health, and the dead are resurrected. 7. That the "signs follow them that believe" (see Mark xvi, 17, 18)! 8. That the earth is to be a place of happiness. 9. That everyone since the time of the apostles, all the famous old revivalists, and our godly fathers, are in the *depths of hell ! !* Those are some of the things which *must* be believed, you said, before one could be a Mormon; and those are the things you saw in the books of the Mormons themselves. In what books did you see the above things in the context you insisted they were in? Did you name where they could be seen in print? It is true that you said you had them in your house, but could the Mormons come there to see them? The truth is, no one has to believe the above things before joining the Mormons; the whole thing is nothing more than an allegation on your part. There is no necessity for anyone to believe more than that he is a sinner, and that he can have remission of his sins through baptism; and that he will receive the Holy Spirit through the laying on of hands, according to the promise of it to "all who are far;" and also to believe that he should keep all the commandments of Jesus Christ till the end. If someone wishes to believe something further after becoming one of the Mormons, he is at liberty to do so. I wish to believe also that Joseph Smith is a prophet, that the "Book of *Môr*" is true—that Jesus Christ appeared to his "other sheep" in America, and that he preached (according to the scriptures) "to the spirits in prison"—that Jerusalem and Zion are places of deliverance to the people of God, from the plagues the scriptures speak of—that the Mormons magnify all the spiritual gifts, as well as that all the "signs shall follow"—that the sick receive health through the laying on of hands and the prayer of faith. But I do not wish to believe that all the believers, from the time of the apostles until now, are in the *depths of hell!* Oh no, Mr. Williams; I have a better belief—all the Saints have a better belief. It is only by you, and in your wicked bosom that such a dreadful belief is harbored. The Saints believe in a just God, who will pay each one according to his deeds, and according to the light he has received. The old fathers have labored diligently according to the knowledge in their possession, and they will be rewarded for their goodness. But as for you, who are kicking against the pricks, and love darkness when light is offered to you,—I do not know what to believe about you. Your condition is bad, and dangerous. You had better slow down, and come to listen to the Saints for yourself, instead of preventing your members from doing so.

But to move on, you remember that you said toward the beginning of your sermon that there was no account of the Mormons having performed so much as one miracle; but before finishing, you said that it was they who would come in the latter days to work "signs and wonders;" and you announced that God allowed Satan to accomplish such things through men, the same as he did to the sorcerers of Egypt, who, you said, performed clear miracles, like Moses! Do you, Mr. Williams, see your confusion? Where was the "craftiness" that is in the text, then? You also remember that you said that Christ's miracles were public miracles, but that the Mormons' miracles are miracles "in the church." Read, if you can, 1 Cor. xii, 28,—"and God hath set some in the *church*, first apostles, secondarily prophets, thirdly teachers, after that *miracles*," &c. If they were outside in the time of Christ, they were inside during the time of Paul. Listen to yourself again:—"If they say that the miracles are 'in the chambers,' believe it not; if they say 'in the desert,' do not believe it either." Did you not perhaps see a mouse when you were studying this piece, which confused you? To mistake the coming of the Son of Man for miracles! [See Mat. xxiv, 26.] You said that miracles are not needed to prove that the New Testament is true: if so, miracles are not needed either to prove that God set "miracles" in his *church*. No, of course not; it can be believed that there are "miracles" in the church as much as "teachers." It is the same verse that says that various things are in it. But you also said that miracles now would be a disgrace on "the miracles of Christ." Why so, Mr. Williams? Would it not be God who would be performing miracles now, as well as then? and would he not receive the glory? If the frequency of miracles makes them powerless, as you claim, then a few can be performed in this age, for none have been since the age of the apostles; they would be quite a new thing. Perhaps you will say in answer, "Let us see some of the Mormons' miracles, then; then I will believe." Multitudes would have believed Christ too, had he come down from the cross, so that they *might see*, that is have proof that he performed miracles. If you and they were to see miracles, you would once again doubt whether God or Satan worked them. If you wish to have proof of God's acts in this age, I say to you, "All things are possible to him that *believeth.*" If you and your sheep want a sign first, then you are "an evil and adulterous generation," and the sign will not be given to you.

I have many things you said written down, but I cannot find space at present to answer them individually. I can refer you to the books the Saints have published, and you will see them answered, if you take off the sectarian spectacles that are on your eyes. They cause frightful misconceptions,—they turn the Book of Mormon into the *Book of Môr,*—the Son of Man "in the chambers," into *miracles* in them; and miracles *in* the church into miracles *outside*. These are the spectacles that saw all the old fathers in the depths of hell, and the Mormon preachers of Carmarthen coming from "the ends of the earth." But one thing you said about the Mormons baptizing more than once, requires particular attention. If it is unscriptural for the Mormons to baptize after the Baptists, it is unscriptural also for the Baptists to baptize after the Mormons, as was done with two women in Llwyni, according to the account given in a recent issue of the *Baptist*. If you say further that the Saints baptize more than once themselves, I say that that is reasonable and scriptural. Your saying that Peter betrayed Christ (which was a great sin), and was not baptized again, does not prove anything; because he wept bitterly, and it is not a usual thing to turn a repentant man out of the church. If Peter had not repented, and thereby had been sent back to the kingdom of darkness, in which kingdom he was at first, how could he have been received back again to the kingdom of light, without being born again of water, in order to have remission of his sins? For every sin between brethren in the church, they are to forgive each other, and ask God's forgiveness too through their Intecessor; and then they will not need to be baptized again. There is "one baptism," or door to the kingdom of God, and one can go through it more than once, if necessary, without causing it to be "*two* baptisms," or two doors. Paul addresses his brethren thus:—"Therefore leaving the *principles* of the doctrine of Christ, let us go on unto perfection; not laying AGAIN the foundations of *repentance* from dead works, and of *faith* toward God, of the doctrine of *baptisms*, and of *laying on of hands*," &c. (Heb. vi, 1, 2.) That, and the following verses, show that one can begin again with religion in the above manner, if the man's sin is not too great, after he has fallen, "to renew *again* in *repentance*," and, of course, to be baptized, &c. What do you think, Mr. Williams, about that? Can the "cunning craftiness to deceive" manage to distort that to mean something else? Try, if you will.

By now, Sir, I am eager to end this letter. Perhaps we shall have the opportunity to write again. But one more thing must be said to you. You know that you gave a very apt sermon to keep your members from giving themselves freely to *prove* the Mormons for themselves. You showed the rebuke anyone would receive who went to hear them, or who gave his house, his garden, or his field to them to preach their views. You pushed down their throats that they should believe you before any of the Mormons, before you knew hardly any of them. If the community belonged to you, the poor Saints would not be allowed to step inside its boundaries. If you governed this kingdom, it would be a good thing for the Mormons that there was such a place as their New Jerusalem, so that they could flee to it. Thank goodness that the Baptist faith is not the established religion, and the Rev. T. Williams, Ebenezer, near Carmarthen, is not the Archbishop of Canterbury. You members of Ebenezer, do you know what you are? I ask in all seriousness, do you know that you are "spirits in prison," and that the Rev. Mr. Williams is preaching to you, and that his intention is to keep you there for a long time? Oh, flee for freedom to the Mormons, "and you shall be truly free." Farewell now, Mr. Williams; God bless you.

Yours, Rev. Sir,
Humbly and lowly,

Carmarthen, *July* 6, 1848. J. DAVIS.

RESTORATION OF THE GOSPEL.

THIS is the new covenant,
Assured by Jesus Christ;
All who refuse, who break it,
Will be remorseful on judgment day;
God was in the old covenant
With his children from early on,
From Jesus came the new one,
And the blessings in it full.

The angel brought the gospel,
And the blessings in his day,
This is the "time and times,"
"And half a time," in their number:
John saw the same angel
Flying in the heaven,
One other came to meet him,
For us lowly ones to partake of the feast.

Several gifts through the same Spirit,
God promised without fail;
To our heavenly Father we give thanks,
That the gifts have been received.
Through the same Spirit are miracles worked,
And prophesying with them,
The tongues and the interpretation,
The church of God is now in force.

The world will hate you,—
This Jesus himself did say;
The opponents will be those,
Who will never taste of virtue.

Gehenna is sufficiently wide,
 They will be punished for their work;
They will harvest the fruit of their life
 In the vast eternity.

ANNUAL CONFERENCE OF WALES,

HELD in the Cymreigyddion Hall, in Merthyr, July 16th and 17th.

Capt. Jones was unanimously elected to preside over the Conference, and he began the morning session at 10 o'clock, through singing and prayer. Then he addressed the congregation appropriately and very effectively on the importance, the consequences, together with the beneficial purposes, of the work that was before us, showing clearly the necessity that each had to be spiritually minded, and to be sanctified in his spirit, before he can enjoy the spiritual benefit that is sought through him.

After that he called on the representation of the branches, which was given as follows:—

Branches.	*Presidents.*	*Eld.*	*Prst.*	*Tch.*	*Deac.*	*Bap.*	*Total.*
Merthyr	W. Phillips	13	17	19	7	153	757
Penydarren	T. Griffiths	2	4	2	2	6	58
Dowlais	A. Clark	7	10	7	2	41	164
Rhymni	W. Davies	4	4	4	1	10	61
Cwmbach	J. Price	4	4	3	2	11	60
Aberdare	J. Davies	5	1	3	3	30	63
Hirwaun	D. Evans	1		1		16	35
Llanfabon	R. Humphreys		1		1	10	15
Cardiff	W. Jenkins	3	4	4	2	68	100
Llwyni	S. Davies	1	5	3	2	31	43
Cwmbychan	T. Pugh	2	2	2	1	3	14
Bryn	ditto		1	1		8	17
Treboeth	J. Mathews	4	2	3	1	20	47
Peele	J. Bowen	2				9	13
Cyfyng	D. Williams	2	4	2	2	14	30
Cwmaman	J. Griffiths	1	4			2	12
Pont Yates	H. Williams	5	6	4	2	50	90
Llanelli	W. Hughes	7	11	8	3	67	166
Carmarthen	B. Jones	4	4	2	2	17	56
Llanybydder	T. Jeremy	1	4	3	1	25	51
Brechfa	D. Jeremy	1	5	3	2	27	56
Swydd Ffynnon	B. Evans	3				4	9
Pontypridd	J. Phillips	1	3			8	18
Dihewyd	E. Morris	1	2	2		2	16
Monmouthshire Conf.	W. Phillips	24	30	18	11	197	404
Herefordshire Conf.	W. Henshaw	9	11	8	4	50	194
Pembrokeshire Conf.	J. Morris	2	4			7	46
Counties of the North	Abel Evans	18	19	9	2	52	152
	Total	127	162	111	53	938	2747

After a few brief and comprehensive observations by the president relative to the remarkable success of the work, and the need there is for the influences of the Spirit of truth to teach the Saints to go forward towards perfection in the proper understanding of, and the practice of sound doctrine, before true love can increase, and that the Saints enjoy great happiness in the Holy Ghost, he called elder A. Evans up, who gave great praise to the Saints who are scattered throughout the North, and said that they were greatly endeavoring to shun evil, and to live in a godly manner, and that they were enjoying the gifts of the Holy Ghost to a great extent, especially the gift of healing. And that the more they are persecuted, the more ingrained they become in the doctrine, and also that they are practically without exception continuing in a unity of the faith, and in brotherly love, and that there are higher hopes there for growth than there ever have been. He said also that there is a great call in many places for more preachers, and he earnestly pleaded for his fellow officers from these parts to come to assist him in the northern reaches of the Welsh vineyard.

Then the following places were established as branches, and the following persons to watch over them;—Pontypridd,—elder John Phillips, president. Swydd Ffynnon,—elder B. Evans, president. Twynyrodyn, near Cardiff,—elder William Thomas, president. Llanfabon,—elder Robert Humphreys, president. Cefnmawr,—elder John Davies, president. Nash Point,—Thomas Llewelyn, president. Peel,—elder John Bowen, president.

Then the president called for whoever had any accusation against any branch president, or conference, to make that known at this time, or if there was any accusation against him, to bring it forward to the light of day, and not to hide anything: and although he called for that many times, no one uttered a word against him, or against any of the others. Then the president asked for a raise of the right hand as a sign of their satisfaction that all the presidents be sustained in their several offices through the faith and prayers of the Saints, which was done unanimously.

The president proposed, and it was seconded, that all of us on behalf of the church in Wales accept, and sustain through our faith and our prayers, President Brigham Young, together with his counselors as the presidency for the church throughout the world,—and president Spencer for the church in Britain. It was proposed by elder W. Phillips that we accept president Jones to preside over all church matters in Wales, which was seconded and approved unanimously. Then the morning meeting was adjourned until the afternoon. The president announced that there was an abundance of food prepared cheaply for the visitors.

Two o'clock, after beginning the meeting as usual by singing and prayer, it was found necessary to dispense with the sacrament this time, because it would be impossible to push through the congregation to distribute the emblems. The president presented details on the main purposes and forms of the temporal deliverance that God provided for his children in the various ages of the world, from the judgments he poured out on the ungodly; and he particularly explained the greatest deliverance in the last days, through the gathering of the Saints together in time from the four corners of the world to Zion. He showed that this was not a work to be done without due consideration, or with haste, rather it was a work that requires and deserves the serious consideration of each one; that there is a need for more wisdom, patience, and determination, to carry it forward than anything that has been done before; and that the chief motto of the Spirit of God, which is working mightily in his Saints to gather, is, with this part as with every other part of the divine work;—"do all things in a seemly and orderly fashion." The president announced that the way of deliverance, after waiting long, was open—that there was an invitation to the exiled children of Zion to gather to their own home, to the country that God has prepared to be a saving Goshen to all the wretched of the earth who obey his commandments. He said that he, together with some other hundreds of the Saints, intended and were preparing to begin as the firstfruits of the other thousands of the race of Gomer who were yet to be delivered before long on mount Zion. He earnestly beseeched all the Saints, and the Officers especially, to be diligent in fulfilling the important stewardship that was entrusted to them of warning their fellowmen of the judgments and the disaster that are to come like a sudden and immediate destruction upon all who refuse this divine mission, and who refuse this deliverance. This lovely meeting was ended with prayer by elder W. Howells.

At six o'clock in the evening, the congregation was addressed by elder W. Hughes from Llanelli. He said that he had gone there a little over a year ago purposely to preach the gospel; and the result was that God enabled him to do so, despite all the rage of the enemy, and his own inability. He had had lectures, false accusations, and all the frowns and scorn, and the obstacles, that the zealous false religion in favor of human tradition, could put in his way; yet he had succeeded in convincing over one hundred and sixty of those dear inhabitants; and they rejoice greatly in their present privileges, and their hopes for the future,—they give thanks that they have come out of darkness to this wondrous light,—and they are striving greatly to live godly lives, and increase in all the knowledge of God,—and they yearn greatly to see the blessed day when they can go to Zion.

Elder W. Henshaw testified in English of his knowledge of the divinity of this great work, the great joy he has received through it in every way, together with seeing his success; and his determination was to do his best for it until the grave.

Elder W. Phillips added his testimony to the same effect. He showed from the scriptures that it was not God's practice in any age to do any work on the earth for which he did not reveal his secret unto his servants the prophets. He showed the absolute necessity there is for apostles and prophets, &c., in the church, before it can be the church of God. He testified that such offices are in the church now, together with the other spiritual gifts, and that to deny those is to deny the religion of Christ, and to say that the above are not needed is to say also in fact that the church of Jesus Christ is not needed, since it is impossible to be the church of God on the earth without having in it such offices and gifts.

Elder H. Williams, declared his joy at seeing such a remarkable growth in this divine cause, and seeing scores of his old contemporaries having embraced it since he was here before, and rejoicing in it; he said also that he, together with his fellow laborers, had had the privilege of being an instrument in God's hand in bringing close to one hundred, from darkness to the light of the gospel, and as children of God, and that they are all striving to conduct themselves in a manner that befits the excellent character they have been given. And he also showed the excellence of the divine plan that has been entrusted to us, inasmuch as imperfect men could not make a perfect plan to perfect themselves, much less to perfect others. Inasmuch as a perfect plan has been entrusted to us, he beseeched his fellow officers of these environs to come to assist him and his brethren here to spread knowledge of that through Carmarthenshire,—that there is there a great call for preaching, but the workers are very few,—that there is there work that several could have,—and that thousands of people who are honest in heart are desirous of having the truth, &c.

Elder W. Evans, Rhymni, said that he had just come back from the North, where he preached for a time, and he reported that the northern Counties are ripe for the harvest, and that there is an earnest call in many places for hearing this divine gospel. He demonstrated that his determination is to do whatever he can, despite every obstacle, to build the kingdom of Emmanuel; and he sincerely exhorted the preachers of the South to come to give a helping hand to their brethren in the North, so the honest in heart can take hold of the truth.

He was followed by the president, who through earnest exhortations persuaded the officers to move towards the North. He reminded them of the "parable of the rusty sickle," which was delivered to the congregation at the previous Conference. He also said, that God, and good men, considered them responsible for the use they made of their talents, &c.

Elder W. Howells, in English, gave many interesting and eloquent counsels on different important matters, together with the above, and he declared his rejoicing for having discovered, after preaching for years with the Baptists, that he had hold of the true church, and the true gospel, and the true gifts of the Holy Ghost, in his great happiness. Then elder A. Clark closed the evening meeting with prayer: the singers sang several sweet anthems during the meeting, to the great enjoyment of the listeners, and praise to the blessed God who is the only one worthy of that.

Monday the 17th, at ten o'clock in the morning, the Hall overflowing with people, elder A. Evans began the meeting, and showed the various duties of the priesthood, together with the manner of calling officers to fill them, the necessity and usefulness for them, and the duties of the members to obey them. He was followed by the president on the same things, and also on the difference between human wisdom and godly wisdom in the calling of persons to fill the various offices, and the difference that is in their manner and their purposes of administering in the human and the godly ordinances. He proved also that it is similar now to what it was in the days of Christ and the apostles, the one age and the other choosing college-trained wise men, and God in the one age and the other "hath chosen the foolish things of the world to confound the wise." He expounded on several things in an instructive manner, too long to note here. Called to the priesthood, elders 15, priests 33, teachers 19, deacons 6, all to be ordained in their various branches.

TEA PARTY OF THE MISSIONARY SOCIETY.

The morning meeting ended by about one o'clock, and at half past two the scene had completely changed, so that the Hall, instead of being overflowing with people, was filled with large tables, and those had been adorned with the finest dishes, and were laden with many delicacies; and not only that, but surrounding them were many of the shining fair sex, and having dressed themselves and the tables in the finest manner possible, and as if they were all eager to excell over each other in cleanliness, cheerfulness, kindness, and everything good and virtuous. After they had all filled their *Teapots*, "each one better than the other," the president asked a blessing on the feast, earnestly praying for the spirit of love and unity to govern every heart and motive. After that they sat at one table after the other in an orderly manner, and ate their fill, with plenty left over, and everyone praised and enjoyed, until close to one-and-a-half thousand partook of that meal until eight o'clock, when the tables were moved, and the scene was changed to a public meeting; and several eloquent and interesting lectures were delivered by several persons; and despite how late this missionary feast continued, we saw no signs of anyone tiring; and during the whole Conference and the feast, we did not hear of one complaint, or reproach, or finding fault with one word or anything of the purposes, or the feast, the method, or the teaching, neither did we see one sign of a sad heart, or a sad face, or a scowling look, rather everyone from the world, and the Saints, especially the merry sisters who served, smiling cheerfully as if they were in their element; and for their incomparable cheerfulness, their efficiency, and their unequaled nobility, they won the unanimous praise, love, and gratitude of every lover of mankind who enjoyed their delicacies.

At the end of the meeting the clerk read the receipts for the past year, which were entirely satisfactory. Many of the beneficial effects of this excellent Society for spreading the gospel throughout the country were made evident, which is strong encouragement to be more energetic in supporting it in the coming year, which, we hope, all will be. The gratitude of the meeting was expressed to our gentle friends of the world for their gentility and their cheerfulness. In short, we say that we have never before seen such love, unity, and orderliness, among such a multitude of people, or any congregations more noble in appearance, or more signs either of the influence of the Spirit of the living God; we could not think of anything that resembled it more than the heaven that the Spirit of prophecy mentions, when the Lord God will make on mount Zion a feast of sumptuous baskets, and of pure clarified wine, when all the children of Zion will gather together, and the veil that covers all the peoples has been done away, when there will be no more pain, or any of the inhabitants saying, "I am ill," or anyone disagreeing, but all singing the songs of Moses and the sweet song of the Lamb, and "everyone's harp in tune like David's harp at the feast." And may that happy time come quickly is our prayer. Amen.

William Davies,
Edward Edwards, Scribes.

ALL THE SAINTS, TAKE NOTE !

On the 25th of July, the Council (with about sixty officers present) decided unanimously;—That, inasmuch as President Jones intends to emigrate from our midst toward Zion in the spring;—That he has printed so many such excellent and useful books and pamphlets, which are, and will be, in great demand and requested, after his departure;—Also that all the branches throughout Wales (with two or three exceptions) do the following:—That every branch contribute, by collection, to be made every week from now until the next Conference, in their church meeting; that the branches choose their distributors by vote, and that each be responsible to the branch for its stewardship to distribute the books, and to give an accounting to them for the money he receives; that he give a public accounting to the branch as to how it is between him and the subscribers, who are in debt, and to encourage them to pay all their debts in full between now and then; that they are to choose their treasurer and their scribe to keep the accounts, and the money that is to be received through the above collections; and that every branch also is to get the full value of the money that is thus collected from books, to be sold to those who request them after that; and thus the branch will have that treasury on hand to be used as they agree, for the benefit of that branch, and not for personal purposes, but according to the agreement of all; and thus all the branches will be enabled to pay their debts easily, and others can get books also.

The council trusts that all the Saints will agree with this, as we are unanimous in accepting it, and propose it for your consideration, and we hope all the presidents will take care to place this plan into operation as soon as possible, and that they will use their influence to explain the necessity and the usefulness of it. For the council,

EDWARD EDWARDS, Scribe.

CONTENTS.

MERTHYR TYDFIL:

PUBLISHED AND FOR SALE BY D. JONES, AND ALSO FOR SALE BY THE SAINTS IN GENERAL

JOHN JONES, PRINTER, RHYDYBONT.

PROPHET OF THE JUBILEE,

OR

STAR OF THE SAINTS.

No. 27.] SEPTEMBER, 1848. [Price 2*c*.

DESCRIPTION OF CALIFORNIA.

[*Quoted from a letter of a recent traveler there, to his friend.*]

"In answer to your last letter to me, I say that it is a pleasure for me to give to you any information about what I saw on my recent journey through California. I traveled past the source of the Platte river, and I crossed the Green river to the south of the windy mountain, and from there through the Rocky Mountains to the valleys of California.

"California has been divided into two parts. One half of it is rich and beautiful valleys, and the other half is mountains and hills. The valleys begin close to the Sea, and stretch for 80 or 100 miles; and some stretch to the big mountain, and others go southward, and they become very broad. The closest valleys to the Pacific Ocean for the most part are from 10 to 50, and sometimes 100 miles in width, and their soil is very fertile; but the rest of the country is not as fruitful, yet it produces grass and plants in abundance. The best land here excells over anything that is on the continent for producing wheat; from 50 to 100 bushels are usually obtained from sowing one bushel. The farmers here grow peas, beans, and every variety of garden vegetables abundantly, and also Indian corn, *melons*, *pumpkins ;* and there is no country in the world more suitable than California for growing grapes.

The few inhabitants here are remarkably healthy, and the climate is remarkably temperate and pleasant; there is hardly any weather here that can be called winter; rather there are two seasons here, namely wet and dry. Hardly any rain falls in the summer, but the rains begin around the beginning of November, and continue off and on until April. The whole plant kingdom appears in its best dresses when the rains begin, increasing through the winter as they do in the spring in our country. December is the planting season, and in April the hills and the meadows are covered with all kinds of beautiful and useful plants and flowers, the sight of which fills the mind of the traveler with wonder, and paradisiacal images; at the end of summer and autumn, all the vegetables and fruits are ripe, and they continue to be excellent food for men and animals until the rains come. All fruits that grow in the hot and temperate climes are to be had here. The chief merchandise that is taken from here at present is, skins, wax, wheat, *furs*, &c. There is here an abundance of streams and rivers running through the valleys to meet all the needs for water. There are many hot and cold springs, *tar* water, salt and bitter waters, for whoever desires them, and they are very medicinal also. A range of mountains and hills rises here and there, stretching to the sea; and a large part of the hills and meadows in April is covered with oats and clover, the latter being the chief natural product of the country. There are here five kinds of clover, three of the red species, and two of the white. The former grows from three to four feet in height, but the latter is shorter. The seed of the red clover is as big as the size of the flax seed, and the inhabitants here live on it, as do the horses.

The main tree in the valleys is oak, which grows for the most part in groves on the banks of the rivers, and it is very useful for furniture, implements, and as fuel, for bearing acorns, and its bark is for marking skins. On the hills grow the biggest and most beautiful trees I have ever seen, and there is a great variety of them. The redwood often reaches over 300 feet in height. I measured one of them about five miles from the sea, and it was more than 59 feet in circumference, and 337 feet in height. There is a great abundance of the trees here that are 200 feet high, without one branch on them; and these trees are most often found in the clefts of the mountains.

The inhabitants settle in the eastern part of California for the most part, and they are very few in number when compared to the size of the country. One farmer owns from 9 to 20 square miles of land. The inhabitants live together in small towns, and often these farmers own from one to ten thousand head of horned cattle, horses, &c.

Slavery is not legal in California; yet the Indians are hardly better off in their conditions in their midst than as if they were slaves. California is a beautiful country, and very easy to live in. Going back and forth to California, I saw 8 large lakes, 6 besides the Salt Lake and the Cutaw. The 6 others lie to the west of the Salt Lake, and large rivers flow into them, although none flows out of them, and one can have all the fish he wants in them. The mountains contain many treasures and ores, and a large variety of salutary and medicinal waters, such as *porter springs*, bitter water, salt, chalk, excellent white clay for making dishes, *slates* for roofs, limestone houses, and in short, nearly everything useful one can think of. There are many excellent "places" available in all these valleys that no one has claimed. A "place" contains from 12 to 18 square miles.

"I am yours affectionately,

"JOHN BARTELSON."

TESTIMONY OF REES PRICE, DOWLAIS.

Mr. Ed.—I beseech your kindness that I might reason and testify a little through your *Prophet* of the truths that I had the privilege of learning recently, and that I might place them before some of my former brethren and the public who are sufficiently free to read the *Prophet.* I was a member with the Baptists for nearly nine years, living in as God-fearing and zealous way as I could, and striving to the best of my ability to obtain the comfort of the Holy Ghost, as the scriptures promise. I had the best advice of the Rev. W. R. Davies, Dowlais, for years. I heard his persecution and false accusations constantly of the "Latter-day Saints" in the meetings, from the pulpits, through the publications, and about the houses and roads, and I searched diligently into them, trying to be as unbiased as I could; I was convinced in the end that they were unfounded and derived from an evil principle, and I understood also that Mr. Davies could not disprove, to my satisfaction, the principles that the Saints professed.

I was not without pleasant feelings at time, and hoped that I was worshipping God satisfactorily while I was with the Baptists; but I was as far removed as all the others of my brethren and sisters from having a *certainty* that we were in the church of God; and when I heard the Saints testifying that if I but obeyed the ordinances of their administration that God would give me through his Holy Spirit this certainty that I desired, I devoted myself to searching the scriptures to determine whether it was still available, or whether it had disappeared and was not necessary, as I had been taught by Mr. Davies and others. While engaged in this careful search, in obedience to the scripture that says, "Prove all things, hold fast that which is good," news of it reached the ears of Mr. Davies, namely that I was inclined toward a judgment and in danger of joining with the Saints; because of this I was publicly disciplined, under the accusation that I had neglected my meeting attendance; but in reality, I say, that I was diligently searching for the truth. When Mr. Roberts came from Rhymni to Dowlais to lecture against the Saints, the meanness of his stories, the illogic of his allegations, his deceit, and his unfairness, convinced me more and more that the religion of the sufferers was better than the religion that caused the attackers to abuse them, to persecute them, and to falsely accuse them as these did. I heard and read the defense of the Saints in the face of it all. I desired that the Baptists excommunicate me, and I accepted baptism from the Saints; and my testimony to all is now that I enjoyed abundant degrees of the influences of the Holy Ghost in the first church service that I went to with the Saints, yes, enough to prove without doubt that the Spirit of God was in this place, that the people of God are the despised, yet blessed ones, and God proved to me many times besides this, through the manifestation of the Spirit according to his promise, that almost all the accusations I heard against these innocent and godly people were false.

My old and beloved friends, reflect and consider this testimony, for it is divine truth; yet, it is truth that stares you in your faces before the strict judgment seat; and this is it—the God of heaven has sent a message of peace unto you, through which he calls you from human traditions to obey his divine commandments. He offers you "the gift of the Holy Ghost," a knowledge of God and eternal life if you obey; you have no promise of these things where you are now. Consider your direction in life, and remember that the tales of your pastors against the Saints are not sufficient reason to cause you to refuse the Saints' message without proving it; for thus have the religious merchants done and will continue to do in every age. Although this appears a hard thing to say at first, yet it is quite true, and you will also have divine proof of that if you obey.

I cannot now describe the difference that is already visible to me between the church of God and the Baptist church, but I know that there is as much difference as between noise and substance, or as there is between talking about a feast and partaking of it.

Also my beloved wife, who was formerly a zealous member with Mr. Davies, Dowlais, has left him and obeyed the order of God; and she also is greatly rejoicing in the privileges of the church of God. We are more content in our family and in every other consideration than ever before, although we are subject to pointing fingers and mocking laughter along the streets, and our old brethren and old our pastor scorn us, treat us like slime, and falsely accuse us publicly. Poor things; let that be between them and the gracious God they kick against.

I desire the Saints of Llwyni to show this our testimony to our relatives there who continue zealous with the traditions of men and profess a form of religion while denying the power of it. Beloved relatives, believe my testimony and obey the commandments of Jesus Christ as we have done; and I assure you, if your hearts are honest, that you will receive the gift of the Holy Ghost yourselves, which even the best of the preachers of the Baptists may not promise you; and the Holy Ghost will show you who are the appointed servants of God, and who are but servants sent by man. Your eternal happiness depends on understanding this difference and behaving differently. Oh, that my old, beloved brethren and sisters were wise and could understand this, and would consider their direction in life! This is the wish of your well-wisher,

REES PRICE.

[This is that man for whom Mr. Davies shows such contempt with his slime through the publications recently, and who denies that the man held any office in his church because he could not write, &c., or was even suitable for that! Yes, this is the man that Mr. Davies said and published that "he had received the Holy Ghost in the pit of his stomach, and he moved under his armpit," &c. All of this is like all his slander, his knowing false accusations, and his slime upon men much more God-fearing and wise than he himself; and he judged him and them by their works. Which testimony of the two is the more reasonable, in fact? The one who has proved both churches, or the other who has never possessed that much honesty!]

WHY AM I AN UNBELIEVER?

To the Editor of the "Prophet."

SIR,—There are various religious denominations in the neighborhood I live in, and in confronting them with the Bible, the rock of proof of the religions of the world, I have not yet been satisfied with any of them. By my saying that there are six different sects, namely the Calvinists, the Independents, the Baptists, the Wesleyans, the Church of England, and the Latter-day Saints, in the area in which I live, and all preaching Christ as the Savior for sinners, myself having refused them all, it is natural to say about myself that I am a stiffnecked and selfish creature. Sir, if that could be said, no doubt there is too much truth in the statement. But if I say that I am stiffnecked in the above point, I am saying that the Bible made me so. I am stiffnecked, not because I do not want to know, but because I was not taught better. Furthermore, it is natural for me to show the inconsistencies, at least as they appear to me to be. We note:—

"If one died for all, then were all dead: and he died for all,"—"That he by the grace of God should taste death for every man," says the Bible.

"He died for some,—the elect," say the Calvinists, the Calvinistic Baptists, the Independents, and some of the vicars of the Church of England.

"The just shall live by faith; but if any man draw back, my soul shall have no pleasure in him,"—"When a righteous man doth turn from his righteousness, and commit iniquity, he shall die in it,"—"Ye are fallen from grace," says the Bible.

"If righteous once, righteous forever: there is no way to fall from grace," say the Calvinists, the Baptists, the Independents, and the Church of England in part; and thus inconsistent; thus also the other two denominations.

"Go ye and teach all nations, baptizing them in the name of the Father, and of the Son, and of the Holy Ghost,"—"Go ye into all the world, and preach the gospel to every creature; he that believeth and is baptized shall be saved," says the Bible.

"We go and baptize all nations, and then we teach them," say the Wesleyans, the Calvinists, the Independents, the Church of England.

"And these signs shall follow them that believe; in my name shall they cast out devils; they shall speak with new tongues," &c., &c., says the Bible.

"They are not to be had now; and they are not needed in this age," say the Wesleyans, the Calvinists, the Baptists, the Independents, the Church of England.

"Yes, they are to be had in this age; and they are to be had now with us; and we correspond exactly to the primitive saints, and assure everyone who hears us, that the miraculous gifts are now with us, as they were earlier with the apostles; and whoever turns to us, and receives his baptism for the remission of sins, together with the laying on of hands of the elders, then he shall be an eyewitness himself of the miracles, as the Bible extends them," say the Latter-day Saints.

Yes, yes, that is the reason I am considered so foolish, namely because I have to differ with you in that matter, as I had to differ with the others in other matters. Thus I do not find anyone who corresponds to the primitive saints. I have conversed with each one of the above denominations about religion, and have asked why they differ from the Bible, some in one thing, and others in another thing; and since they do not have a satisfactory answer at hand, then they generally become angry with me, calling me a stupid fool, or something similar. And thus I am now without religion, since those obscure parts are not clarified.

Now, Sir, I take my message for the first time to ask if you, or some of your kind correspondents will tell me, and others who may be awaiting the same things, namely, Why would *public miracles* not be performed by your various preachers in the South and the North, where they travel, as they were earlier by the apostles? I read now and then in the *Prophet* of miracles being performed, but the witnesses are very sparse, and the deed, perchance, has been performed in some obscure corner. That is not how it was with the primitive saints, Sir. I have been a regular listener to the "Saints" for many years now, and have greatly hoped for the thing I am now inquiring about. And I hope, Sir, that my question will not be scornful in your sight, and also that there is nothing in it that will injure the feelings of any of the Saints, if allowed to appear in the *Prophet*, for I assure you that it is not intended to injure anyone's feelings, but rather to enlighten me, and perhaps others who may be hoping for the same thing.

A FRIEND OF THE BIBLE.

Although our friend's question is a very old question, yes, nearly as old as Jesus Christ, and although we have answered it in many ways, and many times, yet we are glad to see a man letting out his thoughts honestly, and meekly, and we shall answer him once more briefly as follows:—Gentle "Friend," it is not God's way to convince men through their eyes; rather faith comes through hearing, and hearing through the *word* of God, and not through the *miracles* of God. This is not setting the matter aside, but it is penetrating right to its roots, which are obvious when we consider that God is the author of miracles; and then, how unreasonable to seek miracles from men who do not profess to be able to perform the smallest miracle! The testimony of the Saints is a sufficient foundation for the faith of every lover of the truth, to bring him to obey, for he promises him that afterwards, and not before, that he will enjoy that which he requests; and is there not to every promise its conditions? Is it not reasonable for every lawgiver to be able to choose his own conditions? The exceptions by which the public miracles were performed previously do not change the principle, namely that their promised place is *in the church* (1 Cor. xii, 30, 31). Yes, Sir, there are hundreds of blessings being enjoyed by the Saints in Wales, which you and others call miraculous; but who besides the Saints believe them? For more on this, read the *Scriptural Treasury*, under the heading "*Sign-seekers.*"—ED.]

THE GREATEST FREEDOM.

A MAN cannot enjoy perfect freedom until he is ensured the full and free enjoyment of all the elements on which he depends for sustenance. Unless a man has sufficient to satisfy his needs of air, land, water, and fire, he is a slave to the fears of hunger and poverty, which unbearable yoke will be broken sometime.

THE DEATH OF COVETOUSNESS.

LET all fear of poverty and need be removed, and men will cease to hide their riches in the earth, and scatter them on the surface of the waters, in order to have them back an hundredfold, and neither will they give them for usury. That will provide life and movement in all commerce, and the gold and silver will adorn the face of the earth, instead of being buried in its depths. The fears will be destroyed the moment the elements are given freely to man, and bonds of society will be at one with the law of God. "The root of all evil is the love of money." When oppression ceases, so will the love of money. Money opens and closes the rusty doors of prison, and every door from there to the doors of the synagogues, and the doors of the *sanctum sanctorum* (the pulpits), yes, it is money that will open and close practically every room possessed by the human heart. Money is the God of this world, instead of Jehovah and his laws. It is money that makes lawyers, priests, and preachers, as well as thieves, murderers, and prostitutes, and everything that loves and makes lies and deceit.

REMARKABLE HEALING OF A FIRE BURN !

To the Editor of the Prophet.

DEAR BROTHER,—Because there are so many contradictory claims across this country with respect to the misfortune that befell me in the mine, many wish to hear the story from me personally. Well, it is as follows; make whatever use you wish of it, and I shall stand by its truthfulness:—

Three weeks ago, the *damp* in the coal mine ignited, and burned my clothes from me, and my face and my arms severely. There were fourteen yards of fire there. No one was with me at the time. The fire drove me forward from six to seven yards, throwing me against the coal and the stones. In a short time I managed to make my way to the part of the mine where other people were working, who very tenderly put other clothes on me, and covered my face against the breeze, and led me into town. Everyone who saw me in the mine lamented that I was burned very badly, and everyone in the house said the same thing. I heard some along the street saying mockingly, "There's a chance to perform a miracle on Dafydd," &c. They placed me to lie on the straw in the corner, and daubed burn ointment on me, which caused unbearable pains. I kept wanting the elders of the church to come to me, but my family and all those present opposed it cruelly, threatening not to stay with me if the Saints came near me with their oil. I told them that I had to have them, and that I believed that I would get better immediately, according to the promises of Jesus Christ. Within about an hour and a half some of the Saints came there, and despite all the others, they wiped the oil from off me, and they anointed me with consecrated oil. It was necessary to turn the others from the house, and lock the door, in order to have quiet to administer; and while the brethren were praying in the house, the others outside were almost knocking the door down, howling, and making all kinds of jeers and scorn. Immediately when the brethren finished praying, the intensity of the pain ceased, and it no longer burned; and I arose, washed, and put on my clothes, thanking God for this great blessing. Then the door was opened, and the neighbors came into the house, and they impudently claimed to my face that the fire had not come out of my flesh, and that it was all my lies and deceit; and one of the zealous members of the Baptists shouted in my face, deceit, deceit! But I testified to them, like the blind man of old,—where I was once in great pain, as if in the middle of the flame of a fire, I am now healthy and comfortable; and I thought I was the best one able to judge accurately how things were with me.

Soon afterwards someone sent the doctor in to me, who after seeing the burns there had been, and after understanding that I could not use his preparations, went away, and he told some that I would be glad to get help from him before the week was out, which proved him also a false prophet, who could not believe his own eyes! But behold *three* weeks since that, and I haven't needed him yet, nor is there any likelihood of it soon. I had my wife take the straw and the old rags with burn ointment on them out of my sight, which when the neighbors saw her do, rushed out of their houses into the street, howling and screaming like madmen. Some shouted, "Oh, the Saints have cured Dafydd!" and the others even louder screamed, "No they haven't,—it's all deceit," &c. In this manner the neighborhood was stirred up, until we were obliged to lock the door to have peace, although we didn't say a word to anyone to provoke that. As soon as they had dispersed from the door, I went, together with a religious brother who was in the house, to see some of the Saints, and ever since then I have continued without pain. Next morning I went to work as usual. The workers crowded around me, so that I had not peace to work. They were so far from seeing or recognizing the power of God in the matter, that they gnashed their teeth at me in rage, and some of them called me a deceiver, and others said that I had not been burned at all, while the third group claimed that I had not gotten better. But it would be too long for me to explore a hundredth of the unfounded tales that are told about this matter; but this I know, and this I shall testify gratefully to God, that I am a healthy man, and that from God I received this blessing. So many false accusations were brought to the attention of the Steward out of jealousy because of this, that he came to see me in the mine, and after questioning me as to what had happened, he became so angry that he told me that I could not work there any longer! even though I had worked there since my youth; and while I was given over to frivolity, and missing work, before coming to the Saints, I received praise from him, and every kindness from others; but because I have believed the words of Jesus Christ, those which say—"They shall lay hands on the sick, and they shall recover," here I am without a friend, or respect, or a job; but I take comfort in all of this, for this has been the endowment of God's children in every age among the false religionists, and my decision is to stick with the religion that brings me such godly blessings, in spite of all the hatred and wrath of the enemy.

Abercanaid, near Merthyr, July 20, 1848. DAFYDD RICHARDS.

[To the host that have already been given, here is one more clear testimony of the goodness of God to his children— of an answer to the prayer of faith—of the truthfulness of Jesus Christ, and the divine commission of the Latter-day Saints to administer his ordinances; and there is no more evident testimony of that, than the opposition of the spirit of the world, and all its false religionists, to every manifestation of the power of God, just as similar spirits having a form of religion opposed similar happenings in the days of Christ and his apostles. While the Saints thank God for such blessings, others become more angry because of them; and instead of believing and giving the praise to the God who deserves it, if they cannot disprove the happening, they prefer like those before to give the praise to the devil, by claiming that it is through his power that such things are done, which proves their dishonesty; and the purpose of miracles is not to convince the world, but to bless the Saints, and it proves also whose children the one and the other are, by the one and the other wishing to have the glory for their own father.

There are countless scriptural and other testimonies, together with the facts that are to be had, to prove that the devil's way is to try to convince unbelievers, as a general rule, through seeing miracles; while it is seen that the order of God is the exact opposite, namely through preaching Christ crucified, and stirring the faith of the listener to the act of obedience through hearing, and not through seeing.—Ed.]

LETTER OF THOMAS RICHARDS, FROM AMERICA.

Minersville, July 15, 1847.

Dear Brother in the Lord, together with all the Saints,—I send these few lines to you hoping that when they reach you, you will receive them in full health, physical and spiritual, as we now have here. We continue strong in the spirit and have begun the good work of proclaiming the gospel for the last five Sundays, and besides that we are preaching one time during the week as well. There are three here who have obeyed the gospel. Tell Hugh Jones that Dafydd Davies the weaver has believed, but has not yet obeyed. There is plenty of space here to preach, but the people are very slow to come and hear. The old scarecrow has persuaded them that Joseph Smith was a bad man. Also, Bro. Thomas Davies has been in Pottsville lately two Sundays in a row, and a big crowd came to listen, filling the hall and listening attentively. There is here plenty of room to sow the "good seed" in this area, more than we are able to take advantage of; and there is plenty of room for workers also without being in each other's way. I believe that many will come to this field, though there be many obstacles to come against them, as the sectarian ministers and their followers are telling the people not to listen to us, lest they become deceived; and they have tried to discourage us in many ways, but through the strength of God we get strength to stand fast in the face of all attacks, testifying to them without hesitation that this is the kingdom of God.

Brother Daniel Edwards, and his wife, came here a week ago and send their regards to all the Saints.

Two brothers of Mary Evans, Cwmglo, are in this place, and they keep throwing in our faces that it is the height of arrogance to claim that William Hughes received that healing, and they have heard that the whole thing was a lie, and that they have sent a letter to their family there to be able to hear the truth. I beg of you to tell Mary Evans and her brother, William Davies, and have them send the truth back here to their family.

Our brother and sister in the Lord, John and Margaret Edwards, send their regards to Dafydd and John Roberts and their families and to all the Saints. They say that they are pleased to notify you that they have had the privilege of obeying the eternal gospel here even though they had refused it from you when they were there. But the Lord saw fit to give to them a second opportunity by sending his servants after them to this part of the world so that after waiting a long time they could receive the opportunity joyfully, and they have strong testimonies that they are in the kingdom of God. They wish to receive a letter from you since they have not received an answer to the letter which they sent from here; and they hope to have the chance to greet you all after that on mount Zion.

There are eight members in this small branch, and we are rejoicing in the Spirit and wish to have part in the prayers of you, the Saints. This is our request and our wish, for the sake of our Lord Jesus Christ. Amen. I am your brother in the new covenant,

THOMAS RICHARDS.

[It is surprising how quickly the lies of that "*Quick in Water*" travel, those which he published in the *Baptist* about William Hughes. A lie will set the world on fire while the truth is lighting its match, especially when they come against the true religion. We see the necessity of telling the truth and the great responsibility of religious liars.]

COMFORT OF THE SAINTS UNDER PERSECUTION.

IN spite of the knocking from each sect,
There is no need for us to suffer,—our Savior did that;
He bore all contempt, and likewise shall we,
And suffer contentedly, as did he.

He said that thus it should be with us,
Therefore let us strive, let us not give up,
Till we reach Zion, where the Saints will have deliverance,
When our enemies will never again come to do us harm.

A NEW SONG. BY J. P.

HAIL to the day, the day the angel
    Brought the gospel,
The angel that John saw,
Flying in the midst of heaven,
    To proclaim the glad tidings.

To evangelize the entire world
    With the precious and wonderful news;
All the distant nations will have
The news of the Savior of the world,
    Coming to reign.

India, Africa, and great Asia,—
    All countries under the heavens;
Will hear of Calvary,
And the sacrifice that was made on it,
    To save us, the people.

Let us rejoice in the pleasant sound,
    Namely the sound of Jesus's gospel;

Let its banners fly,
And let it resound across the land,
    Till the Saints do reign.

For the time has come, the time
    That the Saints will reign;
And also, the kingdoms of the world
Will all belong to our Lord,—
    With him we shall reign.

Shortly we shall see the Son of Man,
    Coming on a white cloud,
With pomp and heavenly splendor, appropriately,
And with him all the sons of God,—
    And the living will go to meet him.

And then the calf, and the lion's cub,
    Will in lush meadows lie;
No longer harm and destruction will they do,
For the Spirit of God will be on them,
    And they shall experience no pain nor injury.

Blessed will be the Saints, their honor great,
    When the plague shall come;
They shall reign on the earth below,
On them will shine a heavenly dawn,—
    Then they shall see their groom.

Who, who now will not be a Saint?
    Great will be the honor of the family,
Feasting yonder on Zion's mount,
Where no enemy will ever again come near,
    To hurt or to make afraid.

Now will the whole world be restored
    To the state in which it was created;
The lamb and the wolf shall dwell together,
There will be sweet singing throughout the whole world,
    And all will live in bliss.

Oh, let us hasten, let us go to Zion's hill,
    Where in white we shall be dressed,
And also with the laws of the Lord,
And we shall be taught by a heavenly throng,—
    Let us go across the sea, and there.

To the land of California we shall go,
    Where we shall be free,
And there in splendid mansions,
We shall praise the Lamb without any anguish,—
    With splendid temples for the just.

GREETING TO THE SAINTS.

Dear Brothers and Sisters,—Your humble servant is now in the house of our dear and kind president, O. Pratt, in Liverpool, extremely feeble, having impaired his lungs by preaching too much under disadvantages; and the above president, together with others, have counseled that I should not speak in public for some time, which is considered essential before the lungs can get stronger. It is true that nature has her established laws, and that her punishment is according to the transgression of her laws; and thus, we are here and still have faith in the practice of godly ordinances which God has set in his church, in order to receive health, and we are determined to cling to it, by the strength of God, until death. We earnestly petition a share in the prayers of the Saints, for we know before this without doubt that "the effectual fervent prayer of a righteous man availeth much;" and we know just as surely as that, that God blesses his faithful children with needed blessings, according to the day. We do not fear the will of the Lord, whatever it may be, on our part; yet, for the sake of the dear Saints, our wish is to have a long life to serve them, to teach them, and to protect them from wolves, and to lead them all to Zion out of their weary captivity. For this we would desire to live; in doing this we weakened our constitution; and to this end we ask, and hope that all the Saints will ask, that our heavenly Father will restore us.

Our intention is to emigrate to California next January or February (we shall supply details later), and we want everyone to know that, so that if anyone has any transgression or debt against us, they may come forward while we are here. This offer is quite fair, is it not? We publish this challenge, not because we think that anyone will dare to bring the accusation to our face, but so the Saints will be able to close the jaws of the slanderers who try to blacken our character, and do harm to the feelings of our dear brethren, after our departure.

We remind the Saints of that which was published in the previous *Prophet* with respect to the treasury of books; and it is expected that the presidents of all the branches will see to it that that is put into operation. Although we have come from six to seven thousand miles, with our family, and that at our own cost, without asking for a penny from anyone, or taxing or collecting from the Saints in Wales even once, rather leaving each one a free agent to contribute or not; and although we would be proud to return back without asking for a collection, or leaning on anyone: yet, I say, despite all that, we hope that our debtors will consider it fitting and proper for us to have that which is ours, and that we may have that by the next Conference through the above plan.

We have much good news to announce to the Saints through the *Prophet*, from the other side of the ocean, which news we are now unable to publish. We shall only say, that the Lord is prospering the efforts of the saints in California in a wondrous manner, temporally and spiritually. There is endless love and peace throughout them all. An entirely false accusation was the fawning story that flew through the publications of our enemies throughout Wales lately, which said that the Indians had killed some of the Saints, &c. There is not a word of truth in it with respect to the Saints; but it is said that the Indians did kill several Sectarians, in their new settlements in Oregon, and that is all. The Saints will perhaps hear a thousand such tales, and just as baseless. Do not believe their tales, for God watches over his Saints.

Also, we are pleased to announce that there is general success on the preaching of the gospel throughout Wales, and about 150 have been baptized each month, and sometimes more, until this small daughter of Mormon has grown to number three thousand in a short time, and in spite of all her opponents. And not only is she multiplying, but who can ever express the joy, the hope, the godliness, and the goodness, together with the brotherly love that are causing the Saints to grow more in the image of their God? The spiritual gifts are enjoyed here to a greater degree in the churches now than ever before, which is a fact to prove that the Saints are striving to please God. The more they aim to do so, all the greater will be their blessings.

There is no chance to publish here an account of the Manchester Conference, but only to report that there was a more numerous crowd there than we have ever before seen, with excellent talks and counsels, and the Spirit of God cheering every heart through the thousands who were there. It continued for two days. President O. Pratt, one of the twelve apostles, who recently came over from America, was the presiding president there. It was learned that the general increase in Britain, since the last Conference, was far more than seven thousand. But more in the next issue.

Now, dear Saints, be obedient to the godly teaching you receive from your pastors; be earnest in prayer, and devoted in every good work; may the God of peace keep you safe until the day of our Lord Jesus Christ, is the prayer of your obedient servant,

THE EDITOR.

DECAY.

THIS is the cause of nearly every vexation on mankind throughout the world. When God organized the elements, he gave them to our father Adam, or the "ancient of days," to be enjoyed equally by him and all his children, until the end of their generations. His fall is what brought the deterioration in the elements, together with the decay that is characteristic of them; and when their owner comes back, he will remove the curse of decay, and he will restore the laws of God, which will ensure to every one of the inhabitants enough earth, and other elements, for him to enjoy, at least, "his own vine and his own fig tree." There will be no need there for cunning lawyers to make deeds, wills, &c.

HOW TO APPORTION THE FRUITS OF THE EARTHLY ELEMENTS.

LET a Jubilee be called every seventh year, in which all accounts are settled that can be done fairly, and others are forgiven, and all the lawsuits of envy toward one another will cease, and all, as brothers and sisters, will be made eager to do to others as they would have others do to them. At that time we may say in truth that the "Jubilee has come." Neither will there be any work there for lawyers. Whoever wishes to achieve this condition, let him obey the gospel, and let him gather with the Saints to Zion, and he, and all his children after him, will enjoy it.

TO PREVENT THEFTS.

To keep the honest and the faithful from being tempted by that, remove the cause of that, by placing the man in a situation and a condition in which he can have a sufficiency of that which his Father prepared for him in the beginning, which was the free enjoyment of the four elements, without money and without value. Do you wish to have another chance at this? Keep the commandments of your Father, and come to his Zion; there he will give it to you, and there the earth will bring forth her fruit. And there will be no need for lawyers there either.

THE MILLENNIUM.

Before the millennium can come, everyone must have enough land to make a vineyard, in which he can plant a vine and a fig tree, and sit under them, with no one to disturb him, or to make him afraid. This is the kind of *freeholders* those Saints will be who are said to be about to be sold into slavery. There will be no need for lawyers or Sectarians there to free them ever.

ANNOUNCEMENTS.

TO EMIGRANTS.

It is wished for such of the Saints who intend to emigrate with us at the beginning of next year, to send their names to us as soon as they can, together with the names of their children, and their ages. We understand now that a change has taken place in the law that regulates emigration, and that that has caused some increase in the previous prices of transport. The intended amendment is, that the ship would not carry as many, and thus the emigrants would have more space, although the cost is dearer for it. Previously, two children under the age of 14 were counted as one; but now, each one who is more than one year old will be counted as a *passenger*, and it will make a difference of only ten shillings in the price between those who are under, and those who are over, the age of 14. We intend for the *Prophet* to offer more instruction to the emigrants from now on than before. There are some thousands now who are preparing to emigrate from England, and Scotland, toward California, and no doubt some thousands will start at the beginning of next year. "Like doves to their windows," says the prophet.

TO THE DISTRIBUTORS.

SEND all payments at present to "William Morgans, Engineer, Tram Road, to be left at Capt. Jones', Wellington Street, Merthyr Tydfil." All books that are desired can be obtained from him—those bound, or the others. Also, the *Treasury* bound can be obtained as desired, for from 4*s*. to 5*s*.

BOOKS FOR SALE.

WE have just received nearly a hundred volumes of "Capt. Jones on Mormonism in 1847," from the Binder, and they are bound exceptionally well, deluxe, and cheap, for various prices as before. We hope the Saints will endeavor to possess at least one volume of these in every family before it is too late. The volumes for 1846 have all been sold, and a great demand for more, but they cannot be had.

CONTENTS.

MERTHYR TYDFIL:

PUBLISHED AND FOR SALE BY D. JONES, AND ALSO FOR SALE BY THE SAINTS IN GENERAL.

JOHN JONES, PRINTER, RHYDYBONT.

PROPHET OF THE JUBILEE,

OR

STAR OF THE SAINTS.

No. 28.] OCTOBER, 1848. [Price 2c.

THE SECTARIANS BELIEVE IN MIRACLES AT LAST !

We have been informed that in the face of the sign that was, months ago, for a wet winter, that the different Sectarian parties through our country have proclaimed a day of fasting and prayer, to ask the President of the elements, to give them dry weather. It is not the logic or the illogic of this, or their success or their failure with the task, that deserves much of our attention; but what appears to us as very strange, is how the answer to such prayers would not constitute a "miracle!" Would it not be the "supreme rule over the order of nature?" If it would be, that is a miracle according to their own popular interpreation; and if so, why do they not mock and condemn themselves as much as they do the Saints for speaking of miracles? Why do the same people shout so loudly from their pulpits, &c., that the age of miracles has ended, and that there is no need for miracles in this age? How can it be reasonable and scriptural for them to pray for miracles, and for God to work miracles for them; while they say that it is unreasonable and unscriptural for the same God to answer the prayers of their religious neighbors, just as miraculously? If the answer to this prayer is not above the laws of nature, what influence do their prayers through Christ have on the thing? How do they admit the answer to the prayer of Elias for rain as miraculous? Yet, we do not know, nor do we not grasp the logic as to how to believe or comprehend that their God hears and answers their prayers for rain, or drought, or for anything else; while they affirm to us that their God has neither ear to hear their prayers, nor tongue to speak to them, nor arm to do anything for them, nor eyes to pity them. Yes, when they themselves say that their God has neither "body, parts, nor passions! !" How can such nothingness (for reason has no better name for something that is immaterial) hear them or answer them? If we had not better respect for their conscientiousness and their feelings, and pity for them because of their jet-black darkness, we would advise them as Elijah exhorted the prophets of Baal, to shout more loudly, lest their nothingness God be asleep, or away from home, or even worse for him, without a single ear to hear them!

It is enough to cause wonder to any reasonable man, that the devil can blind one human creature, especially a man who has seen a Bible in his age, to believe such an impossibility as the existence of any being "without body, parts, or passions!" And it is no less folly for these miraculous fasters and prayer sayers, to dare to mock their contemporaries ever again for praying for miracles. We hope, for the sake of mankind, that this clan will never again be heard asserting, "that miracles have ceased, or that there is no need for them," &c.; otherwise their own father cannot keep from laughing up his sleeve at their inconsistency. This encourages the Saints to stop being ashamed for professing the miraculous gifts "in the church," for they have friends outside it who profess the same thing. They will come closer before long, and then it will be more popular to profess miracles!

PRESIDENT ORSON PRATT'S GENERAL EPISTLE TO ALL THE SAINTS IN BRITAIN, GREETING,—

DEAR BRETHREN,—

It has seemed good unto the presiding council in the kingdom of God to appoint your humble servant a mission to this part of the earth, the nature of which is expressed in the following letter:—

"Elder Orson Pratt, who belongs to the quorum of the twelve, is hereby delegated to repair to England, to preach the gospel, to publish and print, to superintend the emigration, and to preside over all the conferences, and all affairs of the church of the Latter-day Saints in the British Isles, and adjacent countries; and we call upon all the Saints to listen to, and to obey his counsels in all things; for in so doing they will be blessed. Elder Pratt's family will accompany him, if they choose, and we pray for the Lord to bless them. The duty of elder Pratt is to see that the elders and the Saints comport themselves according to our general epistle that was written December 23rd, 1847.

"Written at Winter Quarters, Omaha nation, North America, the 22nd of April, 1848, and signed in behalf of the above council by

"BRIGHAM YOUNG, *President.*

"WILLARD RICHARDS, *Clerk.*"

In compliance with this appointment, I left the camp of the Saints, which is in Indian territory on the western frontier of the United States, about the middle of May; and through the goodness and mercy of the Almighty, I have, together with my wife, and my three children, safely passed over about one quarter of the circumference of the globe, along canals, in swift steamboats, along large rivers, lakes, railroads, and at length arriving here, where now my field of labor will be for a time.

It is not without feeling profoundly the importance and responsibility of this mission, that I venture to fulfill my duties associated with it. I know from experience that it is not a small matter to be the sentinel over, and to be entrusted as a counselor for more than forty thousand Saints. To impart to the Saints, to individuals, to families, to branches of the church, and to conferences, *the word of life*, requires having a guide other than human wisdom,—nothing less than the inspiration of the Almighty will do. Who, without these necessary qualifications, can give counsel properly—can proportion out the word of truth to so many different people, under so many different capacities and cirumstances, and in the face of so many traditions which have become ingrained so deeply through the influence of the fathers on the children, from which influence even the Saints are not as yet entirely free. The various circumstances that are continually imposing themselves, and as changing as they are, require counsels and instructions adapted to such fluctuations, that the Saints may know in all things how to avoid evil, and to do only those things that will bring them the greatest benefit. Now, who is sufficient for such work as this? Who can give the mind and will of the Holy Spirit with respect to the multiplied and unheard of, yet important and unavoidable circumstances which surround the Saints, unless he has been inspired to understand *future* things, as well as *past* things? Oh! what folly it is for human wisdom to try to be sufficient for all this, independent of the guidance of the Spirit of prophecy! Oh, what vanity it is for human learning only, while denying immediate revelation, to claim competence to guide mankind in all the complicated duties and walks of life!

The present condition of the Saints in America is very different from what it has ever been before. In time gone by, we have gathered together by thousands through the commandment of God, within the vicinity of our enemies and our persecutors, being driven from city to city, building for others to inhabit, and laboring diligently for others to enjoy the fruits of our labor; and all this has taken place so that ancient and modern prophecies might be fulfilled. But now, we have sought out a resting place in a valley of the distant mountains, in the interior of the western continent. There, in the recesses of the "everlasting mountains" we hope to have refuge for a small moment while the indignation of the Almighty is poured upon the nations—there we anticipate to enjoy rest for a season from the fury of our oppressors—there we intend to rear a house unto the God of Jacob, and not be immediately driven from its enjoyments—there we hope to commence the great work of the civilization and redemption of the remnant of Joseph—and, in short, there we hope to serve God with all our hearts, and with all that we possess, and we shall fulfill the purposes of his will in this last dispensation. An extensive, lovely, and rich tract of country, by the providence of God, has been put in the possession of the Saints in the western borders of the State of Iowa. This country is at some distance from all other settlements; there is none on the west, north, or the east; and some forty or fifty miles to the south separate it from the borders of Missouri. This country is called Pottawatomie. It was inhabited by a tribe of Indians by that name until last season, when they were removed by the government, leaving the Saints as sole occupiers of that soil. This part of the country is not yet in market, and when it comes into market, the Saints, being the first settlers, will have a right to it, according to the law of the land, a crown per acre.

There are now about 15,000 Saints living on this land. Their settlements extend some fifty or sixty miles along the east bank of the Missouri river, reaching back from it about 30 miles into the land. The soil is exceedingly rich and fertile—the face of the country is hilly, though not mountainous, and it is far more healthful than the level plains of Illinois and Missouri. The Saints have already opened extensive and splendid farms in every direction; and they will doubtless produce much more grain, and all kinds of provisions, than will be needed by the emigrants who come that way to the valley. From this point, during the months of May and June, many companies will annually leave for the valley of the Salt Lake. These two months are the only time it is safe to cross the Rocky Mountains. The Saints throughout the United States, Canada, British islands, and Europe, are requested to gather up to this place to make preparations to journey over the Rocky Mountains. Three of the twelve, namely Orson Hyde, George A. Smith, and Ezra T. Benson, are remaining here to preside over the Saints in that region. They will give all counsel considered interesting and necessary with respect to all things pertaining to the companies arriving there from the east, and also to the companies who depart from there toward Salt Lake.

Let the conference presidents see that all the Saints are properly instructed in all things in relation to the emigration, in wisdom and in proper order. The gathering of the Saints together to Zion is a very important principle in the doctrine of the Saints. It is founded upon divine revelation, both ancient and modern. Isaiah prophesied repeatedly, and very clearly, that the Lord would gather his sons from afar, and his daughters from the ends of the earth. David in his Psalms has proved this irrefutably, and with very great love. This appears to be a principle that all the ancient prophets enjoyed mentioning and describing. The wonders connected with the gathering engrossed the attention and the love of the Nephite prophets in America also. They enumerated many of the particulars, which appeared clearly in the Book of Mormon. The heavenly revelations given to our martyred prophet, Joseph Smith, while translating the Book of Mormon, show not only the establishment and rise of the church, but also its gathering together from the four corners of the world. In May, 1829, the Lord, referring to those who should receive this gospel, said,—"Behold, I will gather them as a hen gathereth her chickens under her wings, if they will not harden their hearts." In September, 1830, within about five months after the establishment of the church, the Lord said to his servants,—"Ye are called to bring to pass the gathering of mine elect, for mine elect hear my voice and harden not their hearts: wherefore the decree hath gone forth from the Father, that they shall be gathered in unto one place upon the face of this land, to prepare their hearts, and be prepared in all things against the day when tribulation and desolation are sent forth upon the wicked." Many revelations of a similar nature are contained in the book of "Doctrine and Covenants." None of the Saints can be dilatory upon these things, and still enjoy many of the influences of the Holy Ghost. To be negligent about gathering is just as displeasing in the sight of God as it is to be negligent about receiving their baptism for the remission of sins, or any other divine commandment. It is true that the poverty of many of the Saints in this country is great, so that they are unable to emigrate at present because of it; but neither that, nor anything else, should cause them to be indifferent to this glorious principle, but rather it should create in them greater diligence and devotion to make all lawful preparations they can to emigrate. If they do this, they will enjoy the Holy Ghost—the Lord will smile on them, and in due time, he will provide a way for their deliverance. Let the rich remember the poor, and help them from time to time to go home, as they are counseled, and the Lord will bless them also. We counsel all those Saints who have money in lands, houses, goods, commercial or manufacturing establishments, or in any other thing in this country, to immediately set themselves to the task, yet with wisdom and prudence, to make good use of their property, to bring their business to an end, and to collect together all they can of their riches into their own hands, and to go with them to the mountain of the Lord's house—to the valley of the Salt Lake, together with all their valuable goods, and all they possess, and that will be useful, according to the direction of the twelve apostles in their epistle, written the 23rd of December, 1847. Let the elders and the other officers frequently impress upon the minds of the Saints the beneficial and necessary instructions contained in that Epistle. Instruct the wealthy among the Saints not to be covetous, not to set their confidence too much upon their property; but rather, inasmuch as they wish to please God, let them ask a reasonable low price for their property, and ask the Lord to dispose the hearts of some of the children of this world to purchase them from them; and we counsel them not to reject the first offer given to them, if it is a reasonable value for the property, or close to that, for in so doing they may lose greatly, and be unable to deliver themselves before the days of trouble, which are fast hastening upon the nations of this world. Now is the time to be awake and diligent! Now is the day of deliverance! The great and mighty sword is now unsheathed! It hangs swaying over the nations! It will soon fall, and it will devour the mighty and distant nations! And what withholds it now? Surely not the righteousness of the people, for their corruptions, their oppression, and their adverseness cry aloud for judgment. But it is the faith of the Saints—the poor and feeble Saints—that ascends night and day, saying, O Lord, spare us! Cut us not off with the wicked! We are weak! We are poor! We are oppressed! O save us! O deliver us! O bring us to the mountain of thy holiness, and not suffer us to perish in the day of thy wrath, when thou arisest from thy dwelling place to take vengeance on the wicked—to overturn governments—to destroy kingdoms—and to lay waste the nations.

Ye are the salt of the earth. It is for your sakes that the floodgates of destruction are kept closed for a little season. Awake, then, O ye Saints, awake! Set your faces Zionward. Go forth among the nations. Partake not of their sins, neither covet their luxuries; for the day of evil is nigh, yea, at the door. Like the whirlwind it shall rush into the palaces of the great—into the halls of the nobles. Their banqueting shall cease, and their riches shall perish from their hands. Sorrow and trouble shall take hold of them, and anguish of spirit. It shall come from all quarters, like the rushing together of adverse elements—like a raging whirlwind—like the breaking forth of mighty waters. And O, where will be safety then? We answer that it shall be in mount Zion. There only shall the daughter of peace build her palaces, and it will be a calm habitation for her. There only shall be "quiet resting places, and sure dwellings," for the righteous who have escaped from the nations. O ye Saints of the Most High, linger not. Make good your way before it is closed up. Now only is the time that you need not "go out in haste, nor go by flight." Make all preparations before you by him who began this good work in you—by him who calls you out from here—according to your faithfulness and your diligence.

Let the servants of God continue to preach repentance, and baptism for the remission of sins, and do not entangle yourselves in the mysteries of the kingdom, for the world is not worthy of them: they cannot understand them, for they are not understood except by those who have the Spirit of God, and they are not duly appreciated except by the children of the kingdom. Let those of the Saints who wish to understand them go up to the mountain of the Lord, and build a house unto the God of Jacob. There you shall be taught in his ways, and instructed in his paths, to greater perfection. Then your hearts shall rejoice, and your understanding shall be opened; then the glory of the Lord shall shine upon you, and the mysteries of ages past and future shall be revealed to you; and then shall you be properly taught by the Holy Ghost in the right things and in the right time. At that time—in that place, you will teach and understand mysteries. But now shout, and cry aloud to the people in their cities, in their towns, and throughout the land, at every opportunity. Proclaim boldly, and spare not, saying, Repent, and be baptized by divine authority, for the remission of sins, that you may be filled with the Holy Ghost; for behold, the hour of God's judgment is at hand! Except you do this, you shall in no wise escape. Let this be your cry in all places; and if you are faithful, the Holy Ghost will teach you in all things you must do; and the word will be confirmed to the believers in all places by the signs which shall follow; and they shall know of the doctrine, for the Father shall reveal it to them: but the wicked shall not understand, but shall perish in their wickedness.

COUNSELS TO THE EMIGRANTS.

I have been appointed to supervise the emigration of the Saints, and I wish at the commencement to lay down a few clear rules and instructions on this matter, as follows;—

Let it be understood that the time for the Saints to emigrate from Liverpool to New Orleans, will be from the early part of September until March.

Every person or family of the Saints who intend to go, and are able to do so, are requested to send to me their names, written in full and in plainness, and the ages of every man, woman, and child, and every infant, that is going, and also to send one pound in money for each person, both old and young

* * * * * *

The cost of passage on the ship may vary within small limits, from time to time, depending on the circumstances of related things. It will probably never be any less than 2£. 5*s*., or ever more than 5£., for adults. Children who are more than one year old, but under fourteen, will be carried for ten shillings less than the older ones; and infants, under the age of one, will be carried free. The alteration in the fare of children is occasioned by an American law, which went into effect a few weeks ago, and which effects an increase not only of the fare of children, but also of adults. The aforementioned law forbids any ship from carrying the same number of passengers as it carried before; and by that, there will be more space, and more comfort for each one; and also it considers each child over a year old a full passenger, and it requires the same preparation, space, and provisions for it as if it were an adult. For this reason many require the same fare for their passage as for the adults.

In the price of passage, whatever it may be, the following provisions are included for each passenger over one year old, as specified by law,—

Good navy bread, 33 pounds. Rice, 10 pounds. Oatmeal, 10 pounds. Wheat flour, 10 pounds. Peas and beans, 10 pounds. Potatoes, 35 pounds. Vinegar, 1 pint. Fresh water, 60 gallons. Good salted pork, 10 pounds. Also, a good supply of fuel for cooking food, &c.

We inform those Saints who need to purchase tea, coffee, sugar, butter, cheese, more of the things mentioned above, or other things that will be needed for the journey, if they will inquire of us after coming to Liverpool, we can furnish them much cheaper than they can purchase them in any of the shops, for we have the great advantage of purchasing such things from the

Custom House free of duty. You will also need *tin*, cooking utensils, beds, and bedding, &c.

I have also been appointed to receive the tithing of the Saints, and to forward the same to the first Presidency in "Salt Lake City," for the purpose of building in the mountains, a house unto the God of Jacob. The law of tithing was given by revelation several years ago, and it will continue in force upon the Saints throughout their generations. This law requires the contribution of one tenth of the property of the Saints, to carry forward the kingdom and the work of the Almighty on the earth, and after that one tenth of their annual income. In this country there are doubtless many Saints who are too poor to comply with this law, such as poor workers, who depend on their daily labor for their morsel of daily bread. From the hand of such, tithing is not expected; for that would be distressing to them and their families. It would be better for such to receive than to contribute. There are others, not as poor as the class noted, but who can put aside a shilling, or two, or three each week from their earnings, and that for emigrating, &c. Tithing is not required of such. There is another class in much better circumstances, who can contribute their tithing, without distressing themselves and their families, or without confounding their plans to emigrate; of such it is required; and they cannot be justified in the presence of the Judge of hearts by neglecting to pay it. Perhaps some may say, "I am willing to pay, but my property is in such a condition, that I cannot command the tenth of it now." We counsel such to hasten to bring their circumstances to such a condition that they can command, not only the *tenth*, but the *whole* of it. Strive to extricate the whole of it, so that you will be able not only to pay your tithing, but to remove yourself with the balance of your property, to the mountains of America—to the city of the Saints—to the place of the name of the Lord of hosts. In so doing you shall be blessed. And this is the only safe course for you to pursue; this is the will of God, and this is his counsel. Blessed are they who shall comply; they shall flourish like the green herb upon a fertile soil, and they shall not wither away; their children shall grow like willows by streams of water, and they shall be honored among the children of God. But woe unto the covetous, he who loves his property more than he loves to obey the commandments of God; for they shall perish, and their riches will end, and they shall not receive an inheritance among those that are tithed; they shall wither away and become like the dried stubble prepared for the burning, and their names shall not be found among the records of the just.

Let the officers of the church instruct and teach the Saints proper understanding of the law of tithing, that the Saints may not remain in ignorance of that. Tithing money can be sent to me by the *Post-office*, or by any other way judged safe, together with the names of the senders, so they may be properly recorded in the book.

* * * * * *

The Saints in this country are getting remarkably numerous, and thousands are coming into the church constantly; and as the eyes of all are fixed upon them, they must strive to manifest to all, by their good works, that they are actually what they profess to be, namely Saints of God—the children of light.

As I now enter into this great and important field, I hope, by the assistance of God, the prayers of the Saints, and my own faithful exertions, that I may be a benefit to you, and to the cause of God in this country. In the carrying out of all my future responsibilities, I shall strive to have the guidance of the Holy Spirit, and I shall counsel you continually, as I receive from the source. May the God of ancient Israel, who delivered them from the yoke of bondage, and made them a nation unto himself, also look upon his poor, afflicted Saints in Britain, and send them speedy deliverance, and bring them forth soon to his holy mountain, and establish them unto himself a peculiar people, is the constant prayer of your obedient servant,

Liverpool, August 15*th*, 1848. ORSON PRATT.

[We wish to inform the Welsh Saints, that president Pratt has entrusted to our care the preparations for the emigration of the Saints from Wales, and we intend to obtain a shipload of Welsh to go with each other, if there are about three hundred ready by January. I need not mention that it will be much more pleasant and beneficial for them to go with each other, for that will be self-evident to every considerate man for many reasons, especially because of the language. We wish for the presidents of branches from where some intend going next January toward California, to send to us, as soon as convenient for them, the names and ages of everyone who is going—male and female, old and young. We shall inform you again before long when the pound for each one is needed, as part of their cost. This is a custom among all who send emigrants across the sea, and no ship is taken for anyone without that, for the owners of the ship require that as a pledge on the agreement, to assure that the emigrants will come. We are sorry to learn, in some ways, of the new law that has caused an increase in the price of passage; but, on the other hand, it will be more pleasant for the passengers, for in contrast it will provide them with more room and advantages on the ship.

We have great pleasure in announcing to those who will be going, that President Pratt's counselors have allowed your obedient servant to be released, with the first shipload of Saints, from the weary captivity that he has been in for some time—to be able to leave for a short time the "adulterous Babylon," to breathe the fresh air in the valley of the mountains—to have the dear company, and the heavenly teaching, of the sons of Zion, instead of defending the truth from the malicious tales, lying assertions, and poison and slime, of this perverse and stiffnecked generation, or those of them who disregard the counsel of God, and who refuse and oppose this divine message, namely the most glorious one sent from heaven to men in more than fifteen hundred years. They have tormented our souls almost to death, and our constitution has nearly been ruined, under the burden of our effort to convince them, to bring them to the right, and to teach the lovers of truth in the proper way to temporal and eternal happiness. Oh, how delightful to think of the day when we will be released from our captivity, and go ahead, to prepare the way for thousands of Welsh to follow, to the dawning of the Jubilee!]

TO PREVENT RAPE AND ADULTERY.

GIVE everyone a way to support a family (namely freedom of the elements), and punish the rapist and the adulterer by death, and chastity would cease to be a marketable commodity. Men would choose to marry, and keep the first law of their Father, namely, "Be fruitful and multiply, and replenish the earth," instead of suffering death. Thus none of this transgression will be seen in Zion, for that which causes it will not be there, namely the captivity of man from the elements; and so, there will be no need there for lawyers to argue complex laws for or against. That is one contribution of Jubilee, then.

THE MEANS TO HAVE A PERFECT GOVERNMENT, AND TO SUSTAIN IT.

THE government that gives birth to an infant, without being able to endow it with full freedom of the elements, cannot be worthy of that, nor can it make the infant happy, because he is a slave: and that cannot be the government of God, according to the prayer of Jesus Christ, namely, "Thy kingdom come: thy will be done in earth, as it is in heaven." His will is for every man to be redeemed temporally and spiritually, which is enjoyed only through the freedom of the laws of the kingdom of God in Zion.

GIVE THEIR FATHER TO THE ORPHANS, AND HER HUSBAND TO THE WIDOW.

WITH your own two hands open the doors of your prisons, and let the thief return home to comfort the broken heart of his dear wife, and to work to supply the children of his bowels with bread, and then to pay back fourfold: and give him freedom of the elements, then he will never again be called a thief, and he will not be seen within the walls of a prison, but rather, on his own hearth in the midst of his dear children worshipping his God morning and evening.

SIGNS OF THE TIMES.

TO those who are enlightened, it is wisdom to notice the signs of the times, for by so doing they understand the approaching time of their deliverance out of Babylon; but for the Babylonian family, there are no signs that will do to convince them, for their human wisdom gives them sufficient excuse and logic, that all the judgments of God are natural consequences of some easily understood causes. They mock and laugh at the children of the kingdom who acknowledge the hand of their God, and the fulfillment of his prophecies, by the remarkable signs of these tumultuous times. And by so doing are they not fulfilling the prophecy that says,—"The righteous understand, but the wicked go against them worse and worse in their wickedness."

The Spirit of prophecy frequently forewarned the inhabitants of the latter days that God would pour out his judgments on them for their rejection of the gospel of his Son,—that by so doing they would anger Him, until he would release the destroyer in their midst, to stir them up to war against each other,—that he would pour out his plagues upon them in many forms and manners, and on the fruit of the earth because of them. Who can read the troubles of the countries of the world, their wars with each other, their revolutions, and their continual civil wars, without remembering the saying of the scripture that thus it would be in the latter days? When has there ever been such a general commotion which is like a boiling cauldron in the nations now? The Americans and the Mexicans have hardly washed each other's blood from off their hands. Thousands of the red sons of the forests and mountains of Yucatan and Guatemala, and the surrounding area, hunt the inhabitants of those countries like birds into the net, and thirst for their blood. It reminds one of the hideous massacre on the African continent, between Abdel Kader and the French. And still nearer can be heard the neighing of the "red horse." His footsteps are still red from the blood of tens of thousands of our French neighbors. His neighing has caused anguish over nearly the whole continent, until they are in one country after another thirsting for freedom from perpetual captivity, each with his sword eager to pierce the false religious shackles, which have kept the mind of man in the dust almost from the outset. The beast himself has released the reins on his neck, and spurred the pale horse to get him started, who now, say the accounts, has failed to catch him, or to hold himself on his back; but the horse has become a rider, and the rider is being trampled under the feet of the spirit of freedom that started him from his camp. The Pope has lost all his popularity and his influence, and perhaps his crown by now, because he forbade his soldiers to fight against the neighboring countries; and there is a revolution even in Rome threatening to form the papal states into a democracy. The Emperor of Russia, despite the strength of his armies, is afraid of his shadow, and is driving his armies like shooting stars across the world, as if he expected Etna to overflow on top of him from every side at once, fearing the things that hang over his head, and he insists on having seven men from every thousand as a soldier. The small cauldrons of Moldavia and Walachia are boiling over with the blood of men, and the passion of their anger is rising up once again. It is likely that Germany will succeed in getting freedom to worship God in the manner they choose. We hope they do, and everyone else; yes, the Latter-day Saints ought to get this much freedom, instead of being turned from their homes, their lands, and their work places, &c., as they are now by the hundreds by zealous Sectarians, in free and enlightened Wales. The inhabitants of Austria, Prussia, and Bavaria, are as if they spied their advantage to break their iron yoke, as did their neighbors; and their governments are as watchful from the other side to keep them down night and day, for they are not satisfied by administering justice to them. The emperor of Russia keeps four armies of

70,000 soldiers each to keep little Poland under his paw. The revolutionaries in Persia have triumphed over the armies of the government through a bloody slaughter. Several battles have been fought lately in Piedmont, Lombardy, Venice, &c., between the Austrians and the Italians; yes, in short, we ask, Where, rather, is peace? Where are charity and brotherly love, which were the original fruits of Christianity? All these warring nations, or the majority of them anyway, profess to be Christians; and the priests of the one army are just as zealous as the other in praying for the "God of peace" to help them kill the other family of their fellow creatures! And even stranger, the one like the other, in his turn, gives thanks for the victory which the same God gave to them all! Pshaw! No wonder the pagans refuse such bloody Christianity as this is, which floods the world with the blood of men! Is it not high time for all to see that the Christianity this age has is not the right kind, and to leave the bloody one here, and to embrace the gospel of peace, so they may receive the love of truth, and so the people of all the world will love their brothers as Christ loved them. If they were to accept baptism for the remission of sins, and if they were to embrace the religion of the Saints, I am certain that the warring of the world would end in proportion to that, and peace would reign from sea to sea. But is this not a warring age? Are not the hearts of kings failing them from fear? Are not crowns already trampled in the dust, and have not whole systems ceased to exist, as we predicted in the *Prophet* for last January? Let the facts answer for themselves. Who would have foreseen all this without the spirit of prophecy? And yet we have noted but a few of the many warring signs of these troubled days. Look at the accounts of the courts of our own dear country, together with the large cities of England and Scotland; and does one not find in all their chambers poverty, famines, misery, and outrage, which blow up into a violent flame for the day of vengeance, when they can suffer no more. What is portended by all the opposing *factions*, and all the Chartism that is sowing deadly seeds in the veins of the civil systems of our kingdom? If you are not satisfied yet, take a journey to the borders of Ireland, and gaze at them, and read in their faces signs of their times, and then let their pastors and ours shout, "peace, peace," longer, if shame allows them to do so! Awake, ye Saints, from the sleep of the world, and do not drink of their vial, but remember that on mount Zion there is deliverance for you from all the things of the world, though they shout "peace" constantly.

DISEASE OF THE POTATOES.

THE newspapers commonly admit that this disease is worse in nearly all places than before, although it is later in making its appearance in some places. The wise men and the naturalists of the countries have searched all the cells of their imagination for the cause of this disease, together with the best treatment for it. But until now the one and the other are just as useless as are the human imaginations commonly with divine things, or the things that deity has to do with directly, either as plagues, as judgments, as blessings, and are similar to the contradictory explanations of the theologians about the word of God, and the religion of Christ, without his Spirit. Nevertheless, that which he has decided, he will do in his own time and in his own way, and who will impede it?

THE CHOLERA MORBUS.

THIS pestilence has been a destructive scourge across our world for several years now; and it appears from the newspapers of the eastern countries that this broom is coming yet again to sweep hosts of the children of men to the world of the spirits, ready or not. It was increasing in Berlin, according to the news that is before us, and it was killing so frightfully that the average of deaths there was four out of every five. In Constantinople there are fifty or sixty dying every day. In some of the Greek towns a fifth part of the inhabitants were swept away by it. In Egypt, this cholera morbus broke out among the *caravans* of the merchants who came to Cairo with their goods from afar. There were 300,000 people in the fair. This threw everything into such confusion, that the people scattered every which way, lest they be overtaken by it; but despite everything, it killed 2900 of them in three days; and the rest carried it with them wherever they went, spreading it terribly across the country. In one town, 300 died in one day from it. In Alexandria, in about three weeks, it killed 3229 people. It is said to be very destructive in Trebisond and Smyrna. And this awful plague has pushed itself, at last, into Scotland, and to England also. We have not heard that it is in Wales, as yet. Every day some scores are being stricken by it, and over half of them die, in London, Hull, Birmingham, Edinburgh, Glasgow, &c. It finishes its destructive task on some in nine, and twelve, and eighteen hours; it keeps others in excruciating pain for over two days; and it leaves everyone who is able to get better from its grasp, extremely weak and miserable. We have nothing to say, except that this is what has been expected, that this is what was revealed before to the servants of God, and that this is the sum of our warning over several months, now.

This we hope, that as many of the Saints as are able will prepare to escape from Wales before that, to the place where they know that deliverance is to be had, and that those who cannot go now will walk properly and spotlessly before God, and take care to be worthy of their church privileges, so that when this or any other plague comes, God can give them blessings according to their needs, through the ordinances of his Son in his church. O Saints, watch, for the days of trouble draw nigh, in which your persecutors say, "we are finished," and who will stand in the great day of his wrath? He who keeps his commandments correctly, and who plants his feet on mount Zion, blessed will he be forever. You Saints understand the signs of the times, and for that reason lift up your heads the more you see of them, for your deliverance is nigh, says your King.

HAIL TO CALIFORNIA.

[*To be sung by the Welsh on sailing out.*]

When pestilence is harvesting the countries—
Harvesting man like the grass of the field;
When its foul breeze blows
Laying waste the green earth,
California,
Yonder across the distant seas, for me.

When the sharp shining sword
Is bathed in blood;
Yes, blood—the warm blood of men,
In the worst battles ever fought,
California—
Yonder to the Rocky Mountains I shall go.

When the seed of the sower descends
Straight under the soils of the field.
When that sower waits
To reap—but without ever reaping;
California—
The country is for me the Eden of the world.

There the crops are abundant,
There the fruits are sweet;
The end of the winter of Eden's curse;
The beginning of the Lord's blessed summer:
California—
There is the chief paradise of the world.

There the tithing is brought together;
And the great temple is founded;
There it is splendidly sanctified,
With the Lord when the hour comes;
California—
Thou shalt be the new Canaan of the world.

You brethren who have stayed behind,
Hasten to come after us;
Remember, we shall await you
With a longing look;
California—
Sing until you all come there.

Let the dear sailing vessel come,
Let the brethren come aboard;
Farewell to thee, world of the curse,
Thou, breeze, blow away:
California—
Only California henceforth.

STATE OF THE CHURCHES, AND THE BAPTISMS.

WE have great pleasure in hearing through letters we have received from several branches of the church through the South, of the success of the gospel, the unity and the brotherly love that are among the Saints almost without exception. We thank the gracious God who owns this work for the influence of his Holy Spirit and his gifts to his children.

Merthyr,—There is exceptional unity in this council, and in this large branch also. We do not know precisely the number of baptisms during the past month, but we do know that there is a continual increase, with many who are hearing.

Aberdare,—Elder Howells informs us through a letter, that he had baptized 56 by August 23rd, although it has hardly been nine months since he affiliated himself with the church of God! He says that in Aberdare now there is a very flourishing branch, that the old meeting house has become too small, and that they have obtained one that is much larger, and quite comfortable. He says also that all the Saints are in unity and love; and that they have baptized 31 since the Conference, 22 of which he baptized himself; and there are several others who promise to obey soon. They are enjoying the spiritual gifts very fervently there; and, of course, the sectarian wolves are snarling, and gnashing their teeth, when they lose so quickly their subjects who are honest in heart. And perhaps they will seek some "Rev. Roberts from Rhymni," or some other selfish Reverend to drive more of their members to the Saints before long. We hope they will do so, and the sooner the better, we say, if they open the eyes of the people as much as to perceive their own deceit as did Mr. Roberts.

Pont Yates,—Elder H. Williams writes that 13 have been baptized there since the Conference, that unity and love are among the Saints, and that several others have promised to obey soon. There are of his perceptive neighbors, says he, some who are determined to emigrate with the Saints, and who see the excellence of the gathering before they understand the first principles of the gospel. To such, and all of the lovers of the truth who wish to serve God according to the light that is in them, we say, Come all to Zion, and you shall receive temporal deliverance from the destructive judgments of God; and if you cannot agree with the Saints in all things, come; and perchance your understanding will be enlightened, and you will find in them the hearts of brothers, and the comportment of brothers also in all things, this side and the far side of the oceans, for they go to the place where justice dwells.

Elder W. Henshaw writes that the Herefordshire conference is flourishing greatly, and increasing continually in godliness, graciousness, and numbers, and that the power of God is being manifest in their midst.

We were glad to hear by a letter from elder W. Morgans, Merthyr, that elder Thomas Giles, Nantyglo, who had such misfortune in the coal mine lately, breaking several of the small bones in his head, and was injured so badly, that his life was in great danger according to all who know him,—that he, through the power of God, and his blessing on his ordinances, has improved to the extent that he was able to preach zealously and powerfully to a large crowd of people, in the Cymreigyddion Hall, the last Sunday of September. We thank the Lord for his great goodness, and we shall continue to pray faithfully until brother Giles is completely well.

ANNOUNCEMENTS.

MONMOUTHSHIRE CONFERENCE.

THE above Conference will be held in NANTYGLO, on Sunday, November 5th, when the presidents of the different branches will be expected to be there to represent them, and to bring information about conditions and numbers of their different branches.

TO THE BRANCH PRESIDENTS.

WE are confident that the presidents of all the branches throughout Wales will seek to carry out all the counsels of president Pratt in his address in this Issue of the PROPHET in all things; and if anything appears unintelligible with respect to the emigration, ask us by letter, if you are far away, and we shall strive to satisfy the inquirer.

Also, we remind the branch presidents to be alert and faithful in carrying forward the plan that the Glamorgan committee formed for the Saints to obtain books in the future, for the time is approaching very quickly.

MANCHESTER CONFERENCE.—*We had promised to publish a summary of the above conference in this issue; but the length of the Address of President Pratt has shut it out of this number once again. Our readers will have the pleasure and the benefit of reading the talk of President Pratt in Manchester in the next, which is full of honeycombs for them. The increase through baptisms since the previous Conference, is* 8467. *Total,* 17902.

CONTENTS.

MERTHYR TYDFIL:

PUBLISHED AND FOR SALE BY D. JONES, AND ALSO FOR SALE BY THE SAINTS IN GENERAL.

JOHN JONES, PRINTER, RHYDYBONT.

PROPHET OF THE JUBILEE,

OR

STAR OF THE SAINTS.

No. 29.] NOVEMBER, 1848. [PRICE 2*c*.

LECTURE OF APOSTLE O. PRATT AT THE MANCHESTER CONFERENCE.

"O Zion, that bringest good tidings, get thee up into the high mountain; O Jerusalem, that bringest good tidings, lift up thy voice with strength; lift it up, be not afraid; say unto the cities of Judah, Behold your God."—ISAIAH XL, 9.

THE above words, among others, relate to the great events which were to take place just previous to the coming of our Lord, whose coming the following verses mention:—"Behold, the Lord God will come with strong hand, and his arm shall rule for him: behold, his reward is with him, and his work before him. He shall feed his flock like a shepherd: he shall gather the lambs with his arm, and carry them in his bosom, and shall gently lead those that are with young." We shall arrange the different subjects contained in our text under three general heads, or questions.

I. Who were to be those people whom the prophet named "Zion?"

II. What is the nature of the good tidings which Zion shall proclaim?

III. Why is Zion commanded to "get up into the high mountain?"

We do not have time, in a conference such as this, to treat these different topics very extensively; consequently, we shall make mention of only a few particular things that pertain to them.

I. Who were to be those people whom the prophet named "Zion?"—They were to be a people raised up by the Lord himself, just before he "comes with a strong hand" to rule. David says (in Psalm cii), "When the Lord shall build up Zion, he shall *appear* in his glory." The Zion described in these passages could not mean that Zion then existing at Jerusalem, but a Zion that was to be built up in the future. It could not have had reference to the church established under the administration of the ancient apostles; for the Lord did not "*appear* in his glory" to rule with a strong hand in that day. It could not have had reference to any people who have existed for the last seventeen centuries: for, according to their own testimony, the Lord has not spoken during that time, and therefore he has not called any of them Zion. Neither has he built up any city among them called Zion; for if he had, he would have been sure to appear in his glory. But, as a preparatory work for his glorious appearing, both a people and a city called Zion are to be raised up. The people *now* have an existence. The city is yet to be built by them according to the pattern which the Lord shall give by new revelation. The "Latter-day Saints"—the "pure in heart"—have already been acknowledged by the Lord to be "Zion" (Doc. & Cov., page 243). The nations of the earth will not be at a loss to know when the Lord builds Zion; for each dwelling in Zion will have an appendage to it different from what has ever been seen in any of the cities of the nations. Isaiah says, "And the Lord will create upon every dwelling place of mount Zion, and upon her assemblies, a cloud and smoke by day, and the shining of a flaming fire by night." This particular appendage will distinguish the dwelling places of Zion from those of all other cities. We think that this appendage will not be easily counterfeited. It will be a new order of architecture, that will surely puzzle the wise men of Babylon. Gas lights and artificial illuminations will rather get out of fashion in those days, especially in Zion. When the great men of the earth find out that they can neither buy nor steal the *patent* for thus illuminating their cities, they will no doubt feel very anxious to emigrate. In that regard Isaiah says, "And the Gentiles shall come to thy light, and kings to the brightness of thy rising." But some of the kings will get awfully frightened as they draw near the city, and behold a flame of fire over every habitation. They will find out that a city of such splendor is no place for them, and they will haste away as fast as possible. David illustrates this beautifully in the 48th Psalm; he says, "Great is the Lord, and greatly to be praised in the city of our God, in the mountain of his holiness. Beautiful for situation, the joy of the whole earth, is mount Zion, on the sides of the north, the city of the great King. God is known in her palaces for a refuge. For, lo, the kings were assembled, they passed by together. They saw it, and so they marvelled; they were troubled, and hasted away. Fear took hold upon them there, and pain, as of a woman in travail." It seems, then, that God will build up a city before he appears in his glory, that will strike sudden terror to the hearts of kings, as they assemble to see it. They will have something else to think of besides catechisms, creeds, and doctrines of uninspired men. Their imaginary God "without body, parts, or passions," will, for a while, be forgotten, as they look upon the dazzling glory of Zion. Such is the city, and such are the people, whom Isaiah in our text calls Zion, and to whom he addresses his prophetic message.

II. What is the nature of those "*good tidings*" which this people, called Zion, were to bring? The "*everlasting gospel*" no doubt was to form the principal part of this message of "good tidings." God could not raise up a people called Zion, without restoring to the earth the gospel as described by John in his prophecy. That *gospel*, when restored, must produce the same blessings among the children of Zion as were enjoyed in ancient times, namely, visions, dreams, new revelations, healings, and, in fine, all the miraculous gifts promised to believers. Now this, indeed, would be "*good tidings*" to the nations, who for a great many centuries had been destitute of such blessings. The gospel containing such tidings is nothing more nor less than the "everlasting gospel," that is, a gospel that is unchangeably and everlastingly the same, producing in all ages, among all nations, the same fruits, the same blessings, the same miraculous powers and gifts, whenever and wherever it is preached by those sent of God, and received and obeyed in faith. Such a gospel had not been preached by one having authority, on this eastern hemisphere for the last seventeen hundred years, until it was of late restored by an angel from heaven. But it is now preached with power and authority for the last time, and those who receive it are the children of Zion, and they are gathering out by thousands from among the nations, that in the Lord's due time they may build the city of Zion, according to the prophets. This people, then, are the people who are carrying "*good tidings*" to the nations. Never were there better tidings revealed to man than are contained in the present message. O, ye inhabitants of the British isles, rejoice, for Zion hath sent unto you "good tidings" of great joy. She hath sent to you messengers of peace, holding the great seal of authority from her King. If you will hear their voice, and receive their good tidings, you shall become the King's favorites, and assist in building him a beautiful city, and he will come and dwell in your midst, and you shall go in and out of his presence, and his glory shall be upon you and upon your children, and upon your assemblies, and upon every dwelling place of your city, and it shall be called the "*perfection of beauty*," and the great King shall honor it with his presence. Let the poor in the isles rejoice in the tidings, for the day of their deliverance is near at hand; for they shall be gathered to Zion, and flourish in the rich valleys of Ephraim. Let the rich rejoice also, for they shall have the privilege of bringing their gold and their silver with them to beautify the place of the name of the Lord of Hosts—the mount Zion. Let the kings of the earth rejoice, for they shall come to the light of Zion, and shall be taught a perfect system of government; for a perfect law shall go forth of Zion, from which kings and many nations shall learn wisdom. Let all the inhabitants of the earth rejoice, for a feast of fat things is preparing, and all that will come, may come and partake freely. Behold, we publish "*good tidings*" to nations and kingdoms, peoples and tongues, that the preparatory glory of the second coming of our Lord is about to be revealed. Blessed are they who shall take oil in their lamps and gather out from among the nations—from the midst of great Babylon, and go forth to meet the Bridegroom—to the place appointed, and there to build unto him a city and sanctuary, that the place of his feet may be made glorious; for, recollect, the Bridegroom will not come until "*he builds up Zion.*" Blessed are they who shall receive these good tidings, and shall seek with all their hearts to build up Zion, for they shall be filled with the gift and power of the Holy Ghost, and shall perform miracles, signs, and wonders in the name of the Lord God of Israel, and shall receive their inheritance among the mighty ones of Zion. Zion is now sounding her "*good tidings*" in the ears of the present generation.

(To be concluded in the next.)

HEALING OF THE MUTE AND DEAF THROUGH THE POWER OF GOD!

THE prophet Isaiah (chap. xxix) said of the great and strange work that God would do in the last days, that God would use some "SEALED BOOK" as a means of presenting something to an unlearned man, which would denote the beginning of this divine and miraculous revolution, and that God would work miracles so great that "the DEAF WOULD HEAR THE WORDS OF THE BOOK." The following account gives one more example of the fulfillment of this prophecy, and it proves that the *Book of Mormon* is the book referred to, for it was through obedience to the commandments of God, according to that Book, that this deaf man came to hear them. The testimony of the Saints about the miracles of God is opposed, for they happen far away, they say; but we have this circumstance in our midst, the Welsh, at least; and for our part, the man referred to is by our side while we write these lines, and not only does he read, but he also hears the reading of that sealed Book, and he is of age so that he can answer for himself. The Editor of the *Merlin* came to him in person to request this story, and he took him with him to his Office.

"EXTRAORDINARY OCCURENCE.—During the night of Friday week, (the 22nd of September) between the hours of eleven and twelve, a very extraordinary occurrence took place in Newport. A young man named Reuben Brinkworth was, in 1840, at Bermuda, on board the *Terror*, Commodore Franklin, on the northern expedition; and when in the midst of a storm of thunder and lightning, he was suddenly deprived of both hearing and speech; and in this deplorable condition returned to Stroud in England, of which place he was a native. He has since been residing with Mr. Nash, basket maker, Market Street, Newport, who, with several other persons, is attached to the community of people known as "Mormons." Some of those people have been able to communicate their doctrines to Brinkworth, by means of writing, signs, and the finger alphabet. His sad condition, they allege, excited their sympathy for his spiritual as well as temporal welfare; and their doctrines made very considerable impression upon him—perhaps, more especially, because their creed was, that God did perform miracles in the days of old, and that one might be wrought in his favor. On Friday night week, the young man was suddenly seized with a kind of fit, in which he continued some time; and on his recovery, he was called upon, by signs, to believe in the Savior, that the healing power of God might be exercised in his behalf. He was, moreover, earnestly entreated to be baptized; but this was very strongly opposed by a person in the room. The deaf and dumb man, however, signified his acquiescence—he was taken to the *canal* and baptized in the name of our Savior; and immediately on coming up out of the water, he cried out, "Thank the Lord, I can speak and hear again, as well as any of you!" He now speaks fluently and hears distinctly. This happening is attributed to the power of Providence by the friends of the young man, who called at our office with him, and gave us the details. We have heard from another source that this remarkable change in the young man's condition is supposed to have been produced by the action upon him of the *electric fluid* during the thunder storm of Friday night. We shall not take upon ourselves to decide the matter."—*Merlin.*

There has been much shouting after the Saints for miracles, and to give them as much as one sign, such as the deaf coming to hear, or the mute to speak, &c., promising that they would believe the divinity of their message immediately; let the foregoing cause such to know themselves better, although we are not disappointed through their denying the power of God in the matter; for bitter experience has taught us many times before this, that that is what they would do, despite their own eyes and ears; this proves that the purpose of miracles was not, and is not, to convince men to believe the gospel: and why continually ask for them for that purpose, then? The above Editor deserves the character of a free and unbiased man, more than any one of the Sectarian editors of Wales that we know about yet. The Rabbis and the Reverends deserve considerable praise from the idol worshippers, the fruitfulness of their imaginations and their incomparable skill in trying to rob God of the praise for this miracle, choosing instead to give the praise to the *lightning and the thunder.* Strange that they were not so tricky as to deny the thing completely, as they have done with many similar things! Lightning healed him, did it? Well, that was remarkably miraculous lightning, to happen to come and restore the man immediately after being baptized by the Saints! Why did it not come earlier? Why did it not wait longer? Why did it happen to come immediately after he obeyed, for the only time in his life until then, a divine ordinance. The Son of God promises to heal the sick through his ordinances, and we and thousands of others are witnesses of his truthfulness; but the deniers acknowledge this miracle, by affirming that it was the lightning that healed him, the above matter an incomparable miracle; and the more they deny the miracle of it in this way, the more miraculous it appears. Who has ever heard of lightning so beneficial, so obliging and miraculous as that, ever before? But there is one other notable thing relating to that lightning, and even more remarkable, namely that it restored the afflicted so completely, and he did not even see it, he says; and no one else saw lightning, nor heard thunder there, at the time, that we have heard of, or from then until now, that we know of. Let God receive the praise from the Saints, and let them obey his gospel.

A LETTER ON THE SAME MATTER.

DEAR BROTHER JONES,—I take the leisure of writing to you as to how the work of God is succeeding in this place, and how the prayers of the Saints are being answered. There was a young man by the name of Reuben Brinkworth, on board a ship that was called the *Terror*, when on the island of Bermuda, and he was struck deaf and dumb during a storm of thunder and lightning, while five others were killed. He continued in that state until he met the Saints in this town. Brother Nash had occasion to show to him from the scriptures that the God whom the Saints worship is a God of miracles, and that He could have mercy on him as well. The young man, by means of his fingers, asked for the Saints to pray for him. On Friday night, the 22nd of September, the Saints prayed for him according to his wish; and he was led by Brother Nash to the water, where he was baptized in the name of the Lord Jesus Christ, for the remission of sins. As soon as he came up out of the water, he said aloud, "Thank the Lord, I can speak and hear again as well as any of you." The Saints here are rejoicing because the power of God is seen so clearly in their midst. Many in this place previous to that said that they would believe, if the young man came to speak and hear; but the hireling preachers now say they will not believe them, unless they can raise the dead. Many are marvelling about this thing, when they hear the mute speaking so fluently within their hearing. A responsible doctor in the town attributes it all to the exercising of faith, and I cannot fail to agree with him. Some are baptized here each week, and many of those receiving baptism have been several years with other denominations. Last Tuesday night, two ship captains were baptized, and the next night they were heard rejoicing and testifying to their seagoing friends. Five were baptized Friday and two on Saturday. There was a very sizeable assembly here on the Sabbath, and more requested baptism. There is considerable anger shown toward us here; nevertheless, the work of God is going forward. I was glad to hear that you were so well. May God bless you with strength and health to fulfill your office.

Yours in the truth,

Newport, *Oct.* 9, 1848. WILLIAM HENSHAW.

COUNSELS TO THE EMIGRANTS TO CALIFORNIA.

IN response to the frequent and varied questions which we are asked with respect to the preparations and the expense of emigrating, if the inquirers are not satisfied with the following observations, let them ask again.

In the first place, with respect to the preparation for food for the voyage, we say that the state government requires every shipowner to carry on board the ship the various provisions which we mentioned already in our previous observations on this matter in the last issue of the PROPHET; that is, that everything be proportionate with respect to nourishment, for a pound of bread to be apportioned to each emigrant over the age of one each day of the voyage, in addition to 10 pounds of bacon each for the voyage; these supplies will be included in the price of the crossing, that is, the sum which in the last ship was £3 12s 6c for everyone over fourteen years of age. We further observe that the above preparation perhaps may not be sufficient for everyone, and anything else which the emigrants may wish to purchase will be at their discretion, with respect to provisions and abundance. The following list we consider sufficient for each one, in addition to the provisions of the ship; and so each one can determine at his home not only the additional cost he will have to bear for food, but also whether it will be better for those who have such things at home to bring them or to buy them for the following prices in Liverpool:—

PROVISIONS.

	£	s.	c.
10 pounds of hard bread for each one who is over 14 years old, at 3 pence a pound	0	2	6
2 pounds of Rice, at 3 pence a pound	0	0	6
4 pounds of Sugar, at 3 ½ pence a pound	0	1	2
¼ pound of Tea, at 2 pence a pound	0	0	6
2 pounds of Coffee, at 6 pence a pound	0	1	0
4 pounds of Treacle at 2 ½ pence a pound	0	0	10
4 pounds of Raisins, or Currants, at 4 ½ pence a pound	0	1	6
3 pounds of Butter, at 1 s. a pound	0	3	0
3 pounds of Cheese, at 8 pence a pound	0	2	0
	£0	13	0

Take note that this will be in addition to the price of the crossing. It is seen that the above prices are much lower than for such things that are sold in the shops; the reason for that is the advantage which is allowed to the emigrants by purchasing large quantities together from the Custom House, without tax on them, because it is intended to use them at sea. To those who can prepare oat bread, good butter of their own, cheese, *preserves*, *pickles*, or other things they may desire, it will be very good for them to take such things with them from home. The state government sees to it that all provisions that are prepared by the ship are good and tasty; to the head of each family will be weighed out each week that which he needs for the time being, for him and his family, so they can use it how and when they choose themselves. Those who have children under the age of fourteen will probably not need to provide the additional items above for them, since the provisions of the ship will be sufficient, and their cost will be less by that much. It will be up to each one to provide his own provisions also on the way to Liverpool and then until the ship begins the voyage.

NECESSARY CLOTHING.

We do not counsel the Saints to buy very much clothing material here, more than will last them for about two or three years in order to be warm and comfortable; for they will earn more than the difference of prices in the interest they will receive from the money they would spend for them; while from the other side such goods would lie in decay and be useless in comparison. While we warn against extremes on that side, we urge everyone from the other side to prepare, as much as they can, durable, warm and useful clothing; especially let abundant preparations be made for underclothing, dark wool clothes, especially for the children and women; for clear water for washing clothes cannot be obtained on the ocean. Let there be prepared an equal proportion of heavy and light clothing, or summer and winter clothing, such as is prepared for the climate of this country generally. If all the women and their daughters would have a dress of homespun material, or Welsh wool gowns, as are worn in Carmarthenshire, &c., that would be considered valuable by the time they arrive at the end of the journey; if the men could get a suit or two of clothes besides that which they normally have here, that would be sufficient for them to get underway, especially of outer clothes; but as for underclothing, the more you have the better, for one of the main points in the creed of the Saints is cleanliness, comfort and satisfaction. Though we shall experience various climates during the journey, the first part of it will not be too warm to wear winter clothes of this country; and the rest of the clothing, that is, those for the warm weather, we would counsel everyone to get deal chests of the following sizes, if new ones are purchased, that is 3 feet 3 inches long, about 18 or 20 inches wide, and deep, and put their clothes dry and neat in them, so that there will be no need to open them for a long time, especially on the sea, for the breeze and water of the sea will greatly damage clothing. Besides that, the chests of the above sizes will be more convenient than to move the belongings back and forth, and after they are filled with spare clothes, they can be put out of way on the ship, and there will be more space for the passengers. Let all do according to this counsel before leaving town; otherwise they will encounter inconvenience on the way, if all their clothes are in confusion and mixed throughout all their chests. Dress the children warmly and healthily, lest they all start crying from colds or other discomforts. Those who have feather beds may take them along; i.e., as many as wish for their use on the voyage. Notice that all must provide their own beds and bedding on the ship, and every other place and so take care to bring enough blankets and other bedding to be comfortable. The ship provides nothing more than bed boards only, that is, the place on which to put the beds.

NECESSARY DISHES, TOOLS, &C.

The emigrants would be well advised to take with them for the service of their family after arriving home a good proportion of the following things which they will have at hand, that is, plates, knives, forks, spoons, crockery (*china*, if they wish), and the other things which the women deem desirable for their comfort, for we consider their comfort as much, yes, even more than our own, and we hope to see them at the end of their journey having built homes and living in them—having planted vineyards, and enjoying the fulness of their tasty produce with no one to frighten them or oppress them; and as a result, we counsel them to think for themselves about the dishes, &c., on which they will choose to prepare such feasts after arriving home. They can carry them across the sea, in moderation, at no cost—i.e., for their own service; for if the government officials where we land on the other side think that we intend to sell any of such things, they will put a tax on them, which perhaps will make them more expensive than if they were purchased in St. Louis. But for such things for personal use, they rarely tax them there. Since there will be no need for such dishes for normal use on the voyage, it would be best to put them for safekeeping among the spare clothes to keep them from breaking. We do not counsel anyone to take heavy tools, or in fact scarcely any household furniture, except what has been mentioned; and we do not counsel the various craftsmen to take very many of their normal tools with them, for they can probably get new ones, better and cheaper, in St. Louis. As for tin dishes for use on the voyage, they can be obtained in Liverpool best as we get under way.

THE WAY THAT WILL BE TAKEN, THE DISTANCE, AND THE ESTIMATED COST.

We have already been speaking with the captain of the steamboat "Troubadour" about taking the first company of emigrants from Swansea to Liverpool; and that kind gentleman promised to make every provision for the benefit and comfort of the travelers, and to carry them much cheaper than usual. We shall advertise the time later in greater detail; for perhaps the whole company cannot be prepared before the end of January or the beginning of February. After reaching Liverpool, someone else will board the ship which will be prepared by Pres. O. Pratt and will let us know so that we can be there three or four days before sailing, and that is the time that the wisdom and value of that part of the "*Mormon creed*" will be seen, i.e., "everyone mind his own business," lest the *sharpers* and the wolves snatch them and their belongings, while smiling to their faces; but we sincerely hope that the Welsh flock know the voice of their shepherd too well to mistake the howl of a wolf for it. From Liverpool, the normal time for the voyage to New Orleans is from six to seven weeks; the most part of the journey, after leaving the borders of this kingdom, is temperate, and the breezes are lovely, and more often than not there are too few of them. In New Orleans, large steamboats are available during that season of the year to come close to the ship and take the whole procession and their belongings at once, in about five or six days and for about ten shillings each, up the great Mississippi River, for over eleven hundred miles to the great city of St. Louis. There another steamboat will be obtained to take them and their belongings up the Missouri River to Council Bluffs, about eight hundred or nine hundred miles, in about a week for about a pound each. All will need to provide their own food along this part of the journey, besides the prices mentioned; and in short, along the way from the ship to the end of their journey, all will take care of their provisions at their own cost. Yet the uncommon unity and love of the Saints will be very advantageous to them to buy everything required in large quantities; and so, everything that is necessary to buy, especially the *conveyance* along the rivers, will come much less expensive to each one.

After reaching Council Bluffs, you will be outside the western confines of Babylon, among settlements containing thousands of Saints emigrating to Salt Lake City, who make the desert blossom as the rose, and who will prepare themselves there for the rest of the journey; so the Welsh procession will rest in Council Bluffs while preparing wagons and food and buying animals to pull them forward; perhaps this will take several weeks of time before the whole procession is ready to get under way again, besides being more than likely that there will be several thousands of other Saints, besides the Welsh, traveling together from there through the Rocky Mountains. There are in Council Bluffs shops and every kind of necessary skills being carried on by the Saints where wagons and every needed tool can be purchased. In those neighborhoods milk cows cost about 2 pounds each, a yoke of oxen from 5 to 6 pounds; further to the east from here they can be obtained cheaper because the Saints have been buying so many in those areas. We cannot count the cost from Council Bluffs forward to our satisfaction, as well as from there back; but the best estimate we can make is this which follows. If eight persons were to go in together to buy a wagon, one yoke of oxen and four cows, which would carry them and their clothes and their food comfortably, we think that their expense would be not more than £3 10 shillings or £4 each, and the wagon and the animals would belong to them then. Those who have a family of four, five, or six children, will need to get a wagon for themselves; but for families of two or three children, two such families can get together to buy one wagon between them and share the cost. The distance from Council Bluffs to Salt Lake City is considered about one thousand miles, and there is enough game on the journey for sustenance. These few counsels we deem sufficient for this time about the above things, and we wish for all who can see their way open before them to send to us their names, and ages of each one, and the babies also, as soon as possible. We are mindful that these days are the time of gathering and the day of winnowing, that the call is for the children of Zion to come out of Babylon, lest they be made recipients of her plagues; and no doubt each one who neglects the duty to emigrate will sadden the Spirit of God, when God opens his way and provides the circumstances for that. We know of some in this land who began to wither, like the wife of Lot of old, until they became dry trees waiting to be gathered for the fire.

All the latest news from California is very comforting. Apostle W. Woodruff tells us through a recent letter that over 900 wagons loaded with Saints left Council Bluffs toward Salt Lake City during last June and hosts of others are preparing to follow them. Every crop has produced in the valley beyond all expectations; the Saints enjoy generally better health there than in any other place they have been. The medicinal waters which are in the springs there have proven to be a priceless blessing to the sick so far, and what a blessing it would be if we could see all the sick children of God from Wales leaping with joy on the banks of these springs.

The spirit of gathering has taken a strong hold on the Saints in Wales and throughout the world, and we are happy to learn of that. How thoroughly are the words of Isaiah fulfilled when he says, "In that day," not only "shall the deaf hear the words of the book,'' but he clearly says further,—"The meek also shall increase their joy in the Lord, and the poor among men shall *rejoice* in the Holy One of Israel." What greater *rejoicing* could the poor, meek men of Wales desire in this life than to get a way of emigrating to a country where there is and will be abundance for them, and their race after them to all the generations of the earth. Well, such preparation is already awaiting them in Zion, only to go there to enjoy it. And for the comfort of the poor Saints, we state that we have sufficient faith to believe no matter how great their poverty that "He who started them in this good work will finish it," through preparing their way and bringing a means to their hands according to their faithfulness, so that the easiest way for all to arrive home is through fulfilling the role which they are in at the present time. But we do not have sufficient faith to believe that God will allow the poverty of one of His faithful Saints to deprive him of this blessed deliverance. And will they not "rejoice in the Lord" at that time, in spite of the extent of their former poverty? We expect to yet see a nation of meek Welshmen who will strengthen a strong host of brave men from the stock of Gomer dwelling happily and peacefully in the centers of the western continent, and all obedient citizens of heavenly laws. We expect to see the poor in their beautiful carriages along the high roads of the earth, enjoying their fill of its abundance. And before long we shall lend a listening ear to hear the mountains and the hills echoing the sweet songs of rejoicing of the children of Zion; and sometime soon we hope to see kings and queens encouraging this great and wondrous work to be fulfilled. Blessed is he who does it with all his might, because that is the work which continues in praise to his name through his generations, while the work of all the foremost people of the world is like grass, stubble, and clay.

ANOTHER THING THAT MERITS THE ATTENTION OF ALL THE SAINTS !

We would like for the Saints to remember, especially those who intend to go toward Zion, that that is a place "where JUSTICE *dwells*;" and consequently, all children of Zion should be workers of justice, as far as they can, even while in captivity in Babylon. The laws of Zion do not allow any of her children to work injustice with any of the Babylonians; and as far as we can know, we do not allow any who are indebted to anyone of the world, justly, to emigrate without either paying them, satisfying them, or getting their forgiveness, or in some other way working justice toward them. The Saints were warned of this before, and we remind their pure minds again, so they can strive to free themselves from all they can of this tiresome captivity by the time the happy invitation comes to call them home. It is our desire for the benefit and freedom of the Saints, as well as for the glory of Zion, which prompts us to call the attention of the Saints frequently to this important matter. It is true that the wages are low and the time is bad; yet, there was never a time so bad that the principle of justice could not be shown through doing that which can be done; and then if but a penny of the old debt incurred while one of the Babylonians can be paid, that would show a penny's worth of righteousness and so on as much as possible; and then there would be faith to claim the blessing of the just God on every just effort to work justice, and doubtless it will succeed.

NOTICE ALL THE FIRST EMIGRANTS !

According to custom all who transport emigrants over the sea, President Pratt expects each one to send one pound of the money for passage in advance, before he will hire a ship, which will secure for each one passage on the ship for his turn to come there in time by the announced time, through paying the rest of the price of his passage according to that which was mentioned above; and consequently, in order to save expense, loss and cost, we expect that all, or someone for them, will bring the aforementioned pound with them to the NEXT CONFERENCE which is held in Merthyr, which will take place on the LAST SUNDAY OF THIS YEAR; and then, if President Pratt is able to be here on that occasion, as he has promised, he can get them all together; or if he cannot come here, they can be transported to him, and so he can then have a better advantage to hire a ship more cheaply, through getting more time to choose a ship, than if he but takes whatever might be there at the time, and so the crossing will be cheaper for everyone. Notice that a place will not be secured on the ship for anyone except those who follow this arrangement.

DISCOVERY OF A GOLD ORE MINE IN CALIFORNIA !

"FOR BRASS I WILL BRING GOLD."—We are informed by letter, dated San Francisco, June 1, 1848, which is published in the "New York Morning Herald," September 27, of a remarkable discovery of gold ore, in the following words:—"These parts of California are in an unusual uproar (and soon the south will be under the influence of such an uproar), because of the discovery of Placera, or the land of gold, which was found along the banks of the branches of the Sacramento river. Three-fourths of the houses in San Francisco have been left empty; even the lawyers closed their books, and emigrated in haste, with a shovel in one hand and a wooden pan in the other, to get rich by washing out the gold from the gravel of the Sacramento river. Servants refuse the sizeable sum of fifty dollars a month to stay longer in their previous service. Clerking wages have risen to a thousand dollars a year. Carpenters, smiths, and other craftsmen, who worked before for three dollars a day, now refuse ten dollars; very few of such are left in the town, who are night and day making pickaxes, shovels, and tools suitable for searching for gold, and by so doing they earn about twenty dollars a day. One smith is making from ten to fifteen pickaxes a day, which sell for six dollars each. For English shovels, one gets ten dollars each. There is not now in the town one new shovel for sale, or one tin or wooden vessel that would be useful for the above purpose. A boat will be four days in going from here to Sutter's Fort, near the place where the gold is; and the price of passage has risen from four to twelve dollars each. Vessels useful for this task that can be had in New York for five or six pence, now cost here about a pound."

We are happy to inform the Welsh Saints, that it was their Mormon brethren who discovered the aforementioned gold mine. Those on the journey that started from New York, under the leadership of Elder S. Brannan, are the only natives of that country. The gold is found in pieces, from the size of grains, to an ounce in weight, for over a hundred miles of country. One person collects about £20 a day.

THE BLIND MAN AND HIS BOOK.

DEAR BROTHER JONES,—I wish you to put the true story which follows, through the medium of your PROPHET, before the public. Because lying men are trying to put our religion in a bad light, by going about the country, and also to the Works, and selling this pamphlet which is entitled "*The True Mirror*," which book has been reprinted; and those who sell it say that its author is not yet dead ! ! namely Daniel Jones (the Blind), which is a completely unfounded lie. It is a strange thing that men who were fashioned in the image of the truthful God should so succumb to the influences of the father of lies as to claim that he (Daniel Jones) is still alive. If he is alive, he must have taken part in the first resurrection. Where is he, that he may be seen? for that would certainly be a great miracle, so that those who live here near the banks of the Taff can see him, those who knew him so well, and heard him sing ballads in the fairs, and those too who carried him to lie in Llanllwni cemetery. If it is true that (Blind) Daniel Jones is alive now, hundreds of men around Llanybydder and Llanllwni, and the next parishes, would have to believe that miracles are being performed now, or deny that it is Daniel.

Since lies are being spread around the Works, &c., namely that Daniel is alive, that is the reason I am writing this account, and also a little of his story before his death.

He was baptized and received as a member in Llanybydder, on the 7th of July, 1846. He was in the service with us on the Thursday evening and the following

Sunday, and that is all he went to our meetings. Soon afterwards he started persecuting us throughout the community; but he did not succeed in that way in his slander, because they knew him well here. We baptized many in the months following that.

The following October, Capt. D. Jones came this way; he and I went to the community of Brechfa to preach; and as we were returning towards Llanybydder, we met (Blind) Daniel Jones in the mountains, going to Brechfa fair. Capt. D. Jones questioned him about how he had become such a persecutor of the Saints. Daniel did not give one reason in answer, but he indicated clearly enough that he was an enemy of the Saints. Capt. D. Jones told him, that if he persecuted and falsely accused the Saints, the hand of God would be upon him, and his fate would be hotter than that of Cora, Dathan, and Abiram. He told him strongly the danger of persecuting and falsely accusing the Lord's people. Afterwards the facts clearly proved that Capt. Jones told him the truth. He was taken very ill, so that he felt his intestines on fire inside him: he drank a lot of cold water to stop the supposed fire inside him, and also he ran out of the house to wallow in water in order to cool down; but all in vain. He died in this painful condition; although I was not present, I heard about him. I live about three miles from the place where he died. I have been with Mr. James Evans, the *Registrar*, who has *registered* the death of Daniel Jones, and he is willing to give a copy to anyone who wishes, if they pay 2s. 6c. and the postage.

Before finishing I shall give a word of advice to those who accuse us falsely and persecute us. It is this; let them reflect, and consider they are fighting against the good God who sustains them; let them repent for all their sins, and be baptized by the servants of God for the remission of them, and take back their lies as faithfully as they fashioned them. Let the above story about poor Daniel be a warning to all to leave the children of God alone.

May the gracious Lord have mercy on all the honest in heart, by moving away the obstacles so that they may have the great privilege of coming into the Church of Jesus Christ, and sharing in the joy of the Holy Ghost with the Latter-day Saints, is my constant prayer through Jesus Christ. Amen.

Yours in the truth,

Llanybydder, October 24, 1848. THOMAS JEREMY.

[Some of the men who sell the said book admit that it is the sectarians who have paid for them, and presented books to them for nothing, especially the Baptists and the Independents in Llanybydder. Let it be between them and their betrayers as to the accusation, and let it be between them and the great God against whose gospel they are struggling as far as this atrocious work goes. We published a short treatise called "*Haman hanging from his own Gallows*," some time ago, in which can be seen the deceit and lies of this poor blind man; and it is obvious that these pious believers who support such libel and lies, love and make up, publish and spread, the same lies, so as to blind the eyes of their fellowmen lest they perceive the brilliance of the glory of Jesus Christ's gospel. One would think that the father of lies himself would be ashamed to say what the book in question contains; such as, a blind man saying, as is seen on the last page,—"When I went to search in detail (says the blind man) *I perceived clearly* [says a totally blind man ! !] that what the Saints had was trickery." Who would believe anything such a man said, unless he loved lies in his heart of hearts, and hated truth; that is how those who believe this book must be.

Many times rash and arrogant men shout in our face, as the deceased did, daring us to curse him, recalling the example of Elymas of old—yes, sometimes they hold out their hands, and beg us to curse them. Although we do not claim any power to curse anyone, yet we are sure that we worship that God who cuts some down before their time, because of their enmity towards his children, and the faith of his Son Jesus Christ. If that is the case here, let the reader judge, and we will believe what we wish about the matter. It is hoped that the testimony of the respectable man above will be sufficient to send the book in question to the place it deserves, and that the truth will become clearer the more it is investigated.—ED.]

THE EASTERN WELSH CONFERENCE.

THE above Conference was held, in Pontypool, on the 1st day of October. It was begun by singing and prayer, and it was proposed that Eld. W. Henshaw preside. The president announced the purpose of their assembly; and after that he called for bringing forward the matters of the various branches. One branch had been added to the Monmouthshire conference. This Conference contained eight elders, fourteen priests, six teachers, three deacons, and 176 members. Baptized since the previous conference, 34. The total was 202. Brothers Nash, Dallen, and Bowlding were called to be elders, three others to be priests, one as a teacher, and one as a deacon. A sustaining vote was given by the Saints there for the offices of Brigham Young, the twelve apostles, the president of the British Isles, and the president over Wales. A sustaining vote was also given to Wm. Henshaw as the president of the above Conference. Several testified concerning the work of God, and among them was the young man who came so miraculously to speak and hear in Newport, as he came up out of the waters of baptism, after being mute and deaf for years.

WILLIAM HENSHAW, *President.*
URIAH RICKETTS, *Clerk.*

THE GLAMORGAN CONFERENCE

WILL be held in the Cymreigyddion Hall *(White Lion)*, the last day of the Year, and the following day, at which time it is expected that the Presidents of all the Branches will be present to represent their branches, and make sure that all the Distributors under their jurisdiction are ready to close out *completely* all accounts they have for books. This is the last call we can make, and we earnestly implore that it will be *effective*.

N. B.—Visitors are expected to be present at the Conference.

CONTENTS.

☞ We shall give the lacking four pages in the next.

MERTHYR TYDFIL:

PUBLISHED AND FOR SALE BY D. JONES, AND ALSO FOR SALE BY THE SAINTS IN GENERAL.

PRINTED BY J. DAVIS, CARMARTHEN.

PROPHET OF THE JUBILEE,

OR

STAR OF THE SAINTS.

No. 30.] DECEMBER, 1848. [Price 2½c.

LECTURE OF THE APOSTLE O. PRATT AT THE MANCHESTER CONFERENCE.

(Continued from the last Issue.)

III. Why is Zion commanded to "*get up into the high mountain*?" Why did he exclaim so emphatically, "O Zion, that bringest good tidings, get thee up into the high mountain?" Surely he must have seen some cause of an important nature, why Zion should go into a high mountain, or he never would have uttered a commandment to take effect nearly 3000 years in the future. The principal cause why Zion should be required to "get up into a high mountain" is, that they might build a house of God there, in fulfillment of prophecy. Micah (chap. 4) says, "But in the *last days* it shall come to pass that the mountain of the house of the Lord shall be established in the top of the mountains, and it shall be exalted above the hills; and people shall flow unto it. And many nations shall come and say, Come, and let us go up to the mountain of the Lord, and to the house of the God of Jacob; and he will teach us of his ways, and we will walk in his paths: for the law shall go forth of Zion, and the word of the Lord from Jerusalem. And he shall judge among many people, and rebuke strong nations afar off; and they shall beat their swords into plowshares, and their spears into pruninghooks: nation shall not lift up a sword against nation, neither shall they learn war any more. But they shall sit every man under his vine, and under his fig tree; and none shall make them afraid: for the mouth of the Lord of Hosts hath spoken it." All this was to take place in the LAST DAYS. We can see, then, the propriety of Isaiah's calling upon the people of the latter-day Zion to get up "*into the high mountain*." For it is there that the "house of the God of Jacob is to be built." It is from the *mountains* that Zion shall send forth her perfect law to teach the kings of the earth wisdom, and the nations afar off a perfect order of government. It is in the house of God, which shall be in the *mountains*, that "*many nations*" shall be taught in the ways of the Lord, and be instructed to "*walk in his paths*." There must be something connected with the house of God in the mountains which is very peculiar, or it would never excite the attention of many nations. There are many thousands of houses built up at the present day, professing to be the houses of God. Scores of them are to be seen in almost every city in America and Europe; yet there does not appear anything very striking in any of them. There is not one house among the whole of them that has excited the attention of even *one* nation. There is a very good reason for this: for all nations have been entirely destitute of a "*house of God*" for more than seventeen hundred years. Indeed, the house of God was not to be built again until in the LAST DAYS; and, when it was built, it should be built in the *mountains*, and not in several hundred places among the nations. The "house of God" could not be built without new revelation to give the pattern. Without new revelation Zion would not know the precise time to "get up into the high mountain,"—they would not know the precise mountain where God would have his house to be built. The "house of God" never was in any past age, and never can be in any future age, built without express commandments or new revelations being given to the people who built it. When the house of God shall be built in the right time, and in the right place, and according to the right pattern, and by the right people, then it will be acknowledged by the God of Jacob—then his glory shall rest upon it, and his presence shall come into it. Then "he shall sit between the cherubims," and reign in the midst of Zion. Then the wicked shall tremble, and the inhabitants of the earth shall be moved. Then "*many nations*" shall say, Come, let us go up to Zion, for God is there; his house is there; his people are there; his law is there; his glory and power are there; the "perfection of beauty" is there; whatsoever is great, and good, and noble is there! Come then, let us go up, "for he will teach us of his ways, and we will walk in his paths;" and we will no more lift up our swords against nations, but convert them into the peaceful implements of husbandry, and henceforth dwell with the people of God. It is to accomplish this great, this marvellous, this wonderful work, that Zion in the *last days* is commanded to get up "*into the high mountain*." Thousands of her noble sons have already traversed the widely-extended plains of North America, and have ascended the great central range of mountains that form, as it were, the backbone of that continent; and among its deep, retired, and lonely recesses they have "*sought* " out a resting place for the children of Zion. In the spring of 1847, eight of the quorum of the Twelve, in company with 135 others, left Council Bluffs on the Missouri river, as *pioneers*, to explore the great interior of the continent, and find a place suitable for the location of the Saints. We prepared ourselves with astronomical and other scientific instruments of every kind, namely, one *circle of reflection*, two *sextants*, one *quadrant*, two *artificial horizons*, one large *refracting telescope*, several smaller ones, two barometers, several thermometers, besides nautical almanacs, books, *maps*, &c. We also invented a simple machinery, attached to a wagon wheel, by which the whole distance, as well as distances from place to place, were accurately measured. By the aid of these instruments, the latitudes and longitudes of the most prominent places upon our route were obtained, as also their elevations above the sea. Geographical descriptions of the streams, rivers, lakes, plains, deserts, mountains, and vales, will also be found throughout the journals kept by us. Botanical and zoological observations were not forgotten by the scientific among us; and, indeed, the whole journey was rendered intensely interesting to the lovers of nature. New sceneries, sublime beyond description, were constantly exhibiting themselves to our delighted vision. Mineral springs, hot springs, mineral tar springs, caves, and numerous other natural curiosities, were found in abundance which constantly kept our inquisitive friends busy.

In the latter part of July we arrived in the valley, called by us the "*Valley of the Great Salt Lake;* " here we located a site for a city, called by us, the "*Great Salt Lake City*." In this city we reserved a block for the building of a "house unto the God of Jacob"—this we called the "TEMPLE BLOCK." The latitude of the northern boundary of this block, is 40° 45' 44"; its longitude is 111° 26' 34" west of Greenwich. Its altitude above the level of the sea, is 4300 feet. This valley is almost shut up by high ranges of mountains on the east, west, and south, and by the Great Salt Lake on the north. Two of the highest peaks of this range of mountains on the east are elevated about $1\frac{1}{3}$ miles above the level of the valley, and are capped with perpetual snow, which, glistening in the sunbeams, gives to the scenery the picture of eternal winter, wedded in sweet unison with the gentle, mild, varied, and refreshing seasons of the valley beneath. The mountain scenery of this whole region is grand and imposing. The impress of the power of Divinity seems to be *enstamped* in majestic silence on every rugged brow. One would think that SUBLIMITY itself had hewn out an everlasting habitation in these wonderful mountains.

It will be perceived that the site for the city is in the same latitude as the city of New York. And it is highly probable that all the variety of grains and fruit, so abundant in New York, can be raised in the valley. The average temperature during the month of August, in the heat of the day, was about 96° (Fahrenheit's scale), which is about the same as in the same latitude on the eastern coast of that continent. The nights are cool and refreshing. The mountain breezes gentle, generally changing their directions with the sun, so that in twenty-four hours a pure, reviving breeze is experienced from every point of the compass. The winters mild and pleasant; the grass remaining green the year round. Cattle, sheep, horses, mules, &c., graze at all seasons. The cutting and laying up of hay is unnecessary. It will be necessary to irrigate the soil, as there is not much rain that descends into the valley. The showers of rain, and hail, and snow, generally fall upon the mountains, where the vapor is condensed by coming across the snow, and immediately precipitates itself upon surrounding hills and forests, beautifully illustrating the prediction of Isaiah (chap. xxxii.), who prophesies that the calamities of Israel should continue, "until the Spirit be poured upon us from on high, and the wilderness be a fruitful field, and the fruitful field be counted for a forest. Then judgment shall dwell in the wilderness, and righteousness remain in the fruitful field. And the work of righteousness shall be peace; and the effect of righteousness, quietness, and assurance forever. And my people shall dwell in a peaceful habitation, and in sure dwellings, and in quiet resting places: *when it shall hail, coming down on the forest; and the city shall be low in a low place.*" To stand upon the site of our city, and cast our eyes up to the elevated regions above us, and see the showers of *hail* and snow descending upon the dark forests of the mountains, we could exclaim with the ancient prophet, that surely "*the city is* LOW *in a* LOW *place!*"—the mountain storms do not affect her!—the "*hail*" of the high forests does not disturb her "*quiet resting places!*"

If ever a city was *low* in a *low* place, when compared with the mountains in its neighborhood, it is the "Great Salt Lake City." Or if ever a city was *high* in a *high* place, when compared with the general surface of the earth, or with the sea level, it is the Salt Lake City. Well might the ancient prophets speak of Zion going up into the high mountain, and of the house of the God of Jacob being built in the mountains, when it is ascertained that the "TEMPLE BLOCK" is 4300 feet above the level of the ocean. It cannot, for a moment, be supposed that Zion would go up to the top of some mountainpeak, and undertake to build a city and a Temple upon its snowy summit. But the word *mountain*, in those passages, doubtless means some high elevated portions of the earth, and yet not so high as to be rendered sterile by eternal frosts and snows, for this would unfit it for the residence of man. Isaiah (in chap. lxii.) says, "Behold, the Lord hath proclaimed unto the end of the world, Say ye to the daughter of Zion, Behold, thy salvation cometh; behold, his reward is with him, and his work before him. And they shall call them, The holy People, The Redeemed of the Lord: and thou shalt be called, SOUGHT OUT, *A city not forsaken.*" By this passage it seems that the daughter of Zion was not only to "get up into the mountain," but was to locate a city in a place "sought out." From this we learn, also, that the latter-day Zion was not to be built where Zion anciently stood, that is, in Jerusalem, the place of which has been well known for ages; but in the "*high mountain*," in a place unknown, that should be "*sought out*" or searched after; and there they should be called, "*The holy people*,"—"*The redeemed of the Lord*,"—"*A city not forsaken*." This was something, too, that was to take place in connection with the great preparatory work for the coming of the Lord; for it will be seen in the above passage that the "end of the world" was about this time to hear a proclamation concerning his coming, "his reward being with him, and his work before him." "How beautiful upon the MOUNTAINS are the feet of those who are publishing" "good tidings"—that are saying unto Zion, "Behold, thy God reigneth." Let the servants of the Lord cry aloud to the children of Zion scattered abroad, saying, Go ye "up into the high mountain," and build yourselves a city, and the God of Jacob a house; for "he will suddenly come to his Temple," and "reign in *mount Zion*, and in Jerusalem, and before his ancients gloriously."

OBSERVATIONS ON A SERMON ABOUT "THE LATTER-DAY SAINTS AND MIRACULOUS GIFTS."

THE AUTHOR and publisher of the above sermon is the Rev. David Evans, Curate of St. David's Church, Carmarthen; who was brought up in the Carmarthen Presbyterian Academy, and was a minister with the Independents; but after that he was a student in Lampeter College, and now he is an approved priest. The name attached to the sermon is the only reason I consider making comments on it. The great task Capt. Jones has in looking after about three thousand Saints, prevents him from commenting on everything that may be published against our religion; but somehow or other, it happens most often that the books that are published against the Saints, especially Mr. Evans's sermon, have already been answered by him in various books. Now, if our opponents were to be sensible and honest enough to read our books before publishing, they would save a lot of trouble to themselves and us; for they could find their reasons, together with our answers to them, published already. I thought when I gave my sixpence for this ten-page sermon that I was buying an original product, and one worthy of the order of priesthood; but when I saw that the most particular materials of the product had been in the skull of W. R. Davies, Dowlais (Baptist) and a host of other heretics in the eyes of the Pure Church, I was tremendously disappointed.

Having given that much preamble, I come more particularly to note the content of the sermon. The text our preacher chose is seen in Mark xvi, 17, 18, which is, "And these signs shall follow them that believe; in my name shall they cast out devils; they shall speak with new tongues; they shall take up serpents; and if they drink any deadly thing, it shall not hurt them; they shall lay hands on the sick, and they shall recover." Those are the words of Jesus Christ; and heaven and earth must pass before one word of them fails. I wish I could say that about Mr. Evans's sermon: perhaps, maybe, before an uneducated reviewer like myself has passed, and the Bible before me, every syllable of it will have fled from shame. Our friend begins by saying that "many false prophets are rising up, saying of Christ, Behold he is in the wilderness—namely over with the Mormons in the American desert; or behold he is here in the secret rooms with us, and not in the country's churches and chapels;" and later on in his sermon, "he warns the people in the language of Christ, 'Do not go' (to the wilderness, nor to the highways, nor to the secret rooms) 'after them, and do not believe them.'" Where did Mr. Evans learn this? Did he hear that the Saints say that Jesus Christ is now in the American desert, or in some secret rooms in this country? What, Mr. Evans? Did you not hear that the "Princites," (the men who were priests like yourself, and also in the same college as you), say that Christ has come, and that they have him in a chapel in New

Charlinch, near Bridgewater; and this chapel is called by them "Aga Pamona"? (See 'Millennial Star,' May 15,1848.) The Saints do not believe that Christ has come to a wilderness, or a room, or a church, or a chapel, or Aga Pamona either so far, or that he will ever come; but they believe he will come on the clouds of heaven, and that every eye will see him, and that there will then be no argument that he will come to a wilderness or a church, since the matter will be proven with flaming fire, to those "who do not know God, and do not obey the gospel of Jesus Christ." It is not strange that Mr. Evans should have spoken so foolishly, because he is so ignorant of the Saints and their religion that he does not know that they are the same people as the Mormons, and that the followers of Joseph Smith in America are not the same people as the Saints in Wales. For proof of this ignorance, read the first two pages of his sermon. What can be more foolish than seeing a man going to show the deceit of people and their religion, without knowing much of anything about the one or the other? That is like a blind man trying to show who is sightless.

Further, Mr. Evans says of the Saints as follows:—"These men are dissenting from the church of God, as well as from all other religious people of the age, and thus they are some sort of double Nonconformists" (page 4). What church, pray, is "the church of God?" If it is the Church of England, then those of "all other religious people of the age" are the churches of the devil; and the dissent of the Saints from them, as far as that goes, is good; for they are retreating from evil. The truth is this;—if the Saints dissent from the religions of this age, they do not dissent from the religion of Christ and his apostles; but as for the Church of England it has dissented from the Church of Rome, and all other religious believers of the age have dissented from the Church of England. Now, if the Church of Rome was not the Church of God, then God had no church before the existence of the Church of England: consequently, whoever dissents from the Church of England is like the heathen and the publican. Then, if the Saints have withdrawn from the world, they cannot also have withdrawn from the Church of God. I believe in world and church, but not purgatory. Let Mr. Evans decide then, whether it is from the world or the Church that the Saints have withdrawn. Again says our preacher,—"They believe they are particular objects of God's grace and spirit, having received light and wisdom from heaven, that the *world* in general knows nothing of them, and that everyone who does not share their secret is 'innate and without the Spirit.'" This teacher is as earthly as Nicodemus. The "world" of course knows about all his light and wisdom, before it wonders at the Saints' saying; and if he does not receive from heaven, or know much more than the world, he is "innate and without the Spirit." Despite all the colleges that there are in the country, we need one more—one to teach common sense.

On page 6, Mr. Evans comments on the promise in his text, as follows:—"The Lord promises here that he would bear witness to the gospel through miracles; and this promise he fulfilled in the first age of the church." Now, before we can believe that the promise was fulfilled at that time, we need to know to what sort of men it was given; and Jesus Christ gives us this answer—"And these signs shall follow them that *believe*." If we *believe* the gospel as did the men of old, the promise is for us too; and if we do not *believe,* and accept *baptism* as they did, then we cannot be *saved* either. Also, if we *believe* as they did in time past, and without the signs following us, Christ must be lying; or else, if Christ is truthful, then Mr. Evans is lying, because he says they have ended. Perhaps, if we were to look what was the purpose of the "signs to follow" the believers, we would find out if they are needed now or not. We find that casting out devils is one thing; and if devils were some hindrance to Christ's gospel at that time, they are so again, if they possess mankind now, they need to be cast out, of course. Mr. Evans says on this subject on page 18, "The miraculous power is not seen now casting fierce devils out of men's *bodies;* but such cruel and odious devils are cast out of the *souls* of sinners constantly." A man's *soul* is in his body; and if devils are cast out of the soul, they must be cast out of the body: and since "*such cruel and odious* devils" disturb men now, there is as much need as ever for the promise at present. Another thing promised to the believers is "*speaking with new tongues*:" but what could be the purpose of that, I wonder? Mr. Evans can answer first:—"The ability to speak with new tongues is for convincing the *unbeliever*" (see p. 13). Were the tongues the best thing in former times for convincing the unbeliever? If so, why would tongues not be the best thing again? These tongues could not but convince the unbeliever at that time: how is the unbeliever to be convinced in our age? If there is a new way, that is an addition to the scriptures. Now, the scriptures can answer what "speaking with tongues" is; who knows but that the two parties may agree. It is said in I Cor. xiv, 2, as follows—"He that speaketh in an unknown tongue speaketh not unto *men,* but unto *God:* for no man understandeth him; howbeit in the spirit he speaketh mysteries." If it was in unknown languages the apostles were preaching, they were not speaking to "*every creature*," rather to *God*, for the people did not "*understand*" them; and if they did understand them, like those devout men on the day of the Pentecost, they would not believe, any more than they did, because God said, "With other lips will I speak unto this people; and yet for all that will they not hear me" (I Cor. xiv, 21). Perhaps they would not all say that they were "full of new wine," or "becoming mad." A fair trial of the tongues as a means of convincing was had on the Pentecost; but no one there believed until Peter preached after that in the common language (Acts ii, 14—40). The same sort of tongues were spoken on the Pentecost as in Ephesus (Acts xiv, 6); only that men happened to be present in the former place who could understand the languages, and not in the latter. The purpose of the unknown tongues to follow *them that believe,* is to edify the persons who use them (I Cor. xiv, 4), and by interpreting them, to edify the church also (ver. 5). Read the whole Testament, and prove to me that that is not their purpose, and that they are not needed again to edify the believers. If Mr. Evans proves that the apostles preached the gospel in unknown tongues, then I shall prove that no one "understood" them, if they did not "interpret;" or, if some did understand them, that they would not believe them. Our friend is at loggerheads with the scriptures on this subject, anyway, however he may be about the next promise. That promise is, "*They shall take up serpents; and if they drink any deadly thing, it shall not hurt them.*" Now, what could be the purpose of taking up serpents? And would it be when the serpents attacked the believers, or the believers attacked them, that the power to defeat them would be given? If we read (in Acts xxviii, 3—5) about that venomous creature that jumped out of the fire, and stuck to Paul's hand, we find an answer, I should think, to the two previous questions. Again, with regard to drinking poison without sustaining harm; was the purpose of the promise to save the believers from the plots of their enemies, or to show signs to the world? Was it "*if* they drink" in ignorance, mixed with their drinks, or when they drank in obedience to anyone who wished it from them, that our Lord meant? Let the reader judge for himself. If the believers were to grasp serpents, or drink poison, at anyone's bidding, the disciples of Jesus would be more like enchanters than anything else; and if the children of God obeyed the children of the devil, by grasping a serpent or drinking poison for their sake, it would be exactly the same thing as if Jesus Christ had turned the stones to bread for Satan's sake. Now, since the continuance of the promise is most under debate, and not its purpose, we shall hear what reason says. If the purpose of such things was to convince the unbelievers about the gospel, why are they not needed in this age, as there is nothing else for that purpose in the church now, than there was at first? Again, if it is argued that the purpose of the former signs was to plant Christianity, and thus that they are not needed now; why, then, since Christianity is so new in China and other countries, is there not the same need of signs to follow there, in order to plant it, in these days as there was in earlier days? On the other hand, if the purpose of the signs was to benefit and defend the early believers, in the face of the enmity and cunning of the kingdom of darkness, why are they not needed also in this age for the same purpose? The reader can again judge on whose side reason is, and I can go on to something else. The last promise our Lord gave to believers of his gospel is as follows:—"*They shall lay hands on the sick, and they shall recover.*" The rule the believers had to operate by is to be seen in James v, 14—16,—"Is any sick among you? Let him call for the elders of the church; and let them pray over him, anointing him with oil in the name of the Lord: and the prayer of faith shall save the sick, and the Lord shall raise him up [unless it be his time to die, of course]. Confess your faults one to another, and pray one for another, that ye may be *healed.* The *effectual fervent prayer* of a righteous man availeth much." I do not think there is one doctor in the land who will not admit that this was a promise for the benefit of the believers; for it is the benefit of the sick person that he himself has in mind when he gives medication: so too with God, except that his medicine and his rules for the sick person are different from the doctor's. Who thinks that God wanted to give a sign to the world when he was giving health to his children? or that God wished to make believing easier through signs than preaching? Everyone will admit, perhaps, that if one does not believe by *hearing* preaching, one will not believe either by *seeing* the dead resurrected. If it is so, then, signs are not for convincing the unbelievers, but for the benefit of the believers; for the gospel is the most effective and safe instrument for convincing, because by depending on signs, we can be charmed by magicians, &c. If this healing was again something to establish Christianity, why would it not exist in the countries where it is said that Christianity is being established in our age? "How," as Mr. Evans says on page 7, is it "possible to overthrow polytheism and paganism in the world, through preaching the cross, without miracles?" Well, why could he not see that the foreign countries, as well as many unbelievers in this country, need miracles and signs now as much as in former times? But, on the other hand, if the purpose of the signs was to benefit the believers, by healing them, &c., why not again, as the same need exists? Why can "the effectual fervent prayer of a righteous man" not succeed with God in this age, to obtain health, as well as anything else? Can one not receive "whatsoever" one asks in the name of Jesus Christ now? If one can, the signs are following. And if we fail to get health, or something else, let us ask ourselves if there are "transgressions" or a lack of faith which are an obstacle to that; and if there are such things, let us all confess to each other, and pray for each other; for a failure or two is no proof that God does not listen to his children. Let us remember that there were in the early church "many weak and sickly, and many sleeping" (I Cor. xi, 30), because of transgressions; and we should make *allowance* for such things in this age, before we condemn prayer for a failure or two. Also, we should remember Timothy and his frequent weakness, and poor Trophimus, sick at Miletum, without either of them, as far as we know, having transgressed. God's ways are sometimes beyond the understanding of his children; and because of that, let us take him at his word always, believing that he will fulfill everything which is for our good.

Now, Mr. Evans, I have talked a great deal about the signs, and proved that they are promised to the believers of the gospel of Jesus Christ, and also shown my reasons for their continuance. Now we need to know how the Lord worked with his servants, and whether he works with them now? The latter is answered on page 17 of the sermon like this:—"The Lord is again working through and with his gospel;" and he says too, but without any proof, "Now *conversion,* and not *miracles,* is the abiding proof of the divine influences in the church of Christ." What is the worth of an assertion like that? I prefer to believe the assertion in the scriptures, in the last verse of Mark; which is, "And they went forth, and preached everywhere, the Lord *working with them,* and confirming the word with *signs* following." Where is the proof that God has changed his method of working? The absence of the signs in the Church of England, and the country's chapels, is no proof at all; because one first has to prove that they are believers. We shall comment on this later. Mr. Evans, on page 13, brings scriptural proof, in his opinion, that the signs have ended. By doing that, he, like many before him, in his ignorance, is referring to words in the scriptures that prove their continuance. The words are to be seen in I Cor. xiii, 8, and they are as follows:—"Charity never faileth: but whether there be prophecies, they shall fail; whether there be tongues, they shall cease; whether there be knowledge, it shall vanish away." Without reading more than that, it is very reasonable proof; and yet it does not inform us when they were to end. For all that is said to the contrary, they cannot have ended yet. But the thing is, Mr. Evans is safe in Paul's snare: it is strange how many blackbirds this catches. Now, the apostle says more than is in the above verse: the ninth and tenth explain the matter. He says there, "For we know *in part,* and we prophesy *in part.* But when that which is *perfect* is come, then [not before then] that which is *in part* shall be done away." If that which is perfect is not come, then speaking with tongues, prophecy, knowledge, &c., is to be in the church. The church is to enjoy the childish things—to "speak," understand, and think in a childish way, until it becomes "a perfect man, unto the measure of the stature of the fulness of Christ," when it puts away childish things, and instead of looking through a glass darkly, comes to see face to face, and instead of knowing in part, comes to know even as it is known. (I Cor. xiii, 11, 12; Eph. iv, 13.) Now it will be valuable for Mr. Evans to try to prove that that which is *perfect* is come: then he can say that the signs have ended. I shall endeavor to do that for him, like this:—It can mean that that which is *perfect* is come, because the holy scriptures are finished, and we have a sufficient rule to worship by, and nothing more is needed. Mr. Evans probably thinks that a good reason; at least, if he does not think it so, there are plenty who do; for it is not a saying of mine, but of a giant enemy of the Saints. To assist me in this task, I quote Mr. Evans's words on page 14—"If the holy scriptures of the Old and New Testaments are a sufficient rule for our faith and our observance, we fear to fall under God's judgment by claiming a right to some new revelation of his will, as men do these days, 'For I testify unto every man that heareth the words of the prophecy of this book, If any man shall add unto these things, God shall add unto him the plagues that are written in this book,' &c.—Rev. xxii, 18." Now, that is the whole thing locked up, that no one can open except the one who has the key. But let us try, anyway, without any key. What are the "prophetic words of *this book?"* John's Revelation is the only prophetic book of the New Testament; consequently, adding to, or taking away from the Revelation, is what is forbidden. There is a similar prohibition in Prov. xxx, 5, 6, and other places; but the New Testament was added after that. A prohibition to *man* to add does not prevent God from adding. The Revelation is God's word, and not man's word; and because of that, God alone is to add or take away. It was after John was on the island of Patmos, that the scriptures were gathered together, as many as were gathered, because many are missing. (See I Cor. v, 9; Jude 3, 14; Luke i, 1, 2, &c.) What the angel says to John (Rev. xxii, 10), which is, "Seal not the sayings of the prophecy of this book," proves clearly that only the Revelation was meant; because the other books of the two Testaments had been made known to the churches before the angel ever issued the prohibition in question, if it is believed that the Revelation is the last book that was written. On the other hand, if John was not the last, then some have added contrary to the prohibition. But that is probably enough about that. We shall say a word, then, about that which is *perfect.* If a collection of what Paul and others knew and wrote "in part" is what is "perfect," then, according to the same reasoning, many imperfections could constitute perfection ! Everything that Paul and others knew, they knew "in part"; and if a collection in a book of what they wrote makes that which is "perfect," then we should know and prophesy better than they, because we have that which is perfect. Indeed, if the religious people of this age knew in part, they would learn something from God, in order to end the ceaseless arguments; but since they claim to have that which is perfect, God pays them no heed, and so it will be until they learn the lesson that they know nothing. Now, having traced that much, we dare to assert with Jesus Christ that the signs are to follow them that believe, while his gospel is preached; and we say with Paul, that the prophesying and speaking with tongues in part, is to continue until that perfection comes when we shall see face to face.

Our friend Mr. Evans, on page 11, tries to convince us that the signs have ended, by making the following remarks:—"Do we have to believe that there has been no saving faith in the world for more than fifteen hundred years, since no miracles have been performed by the professors of Christ's religion in that interval of time? Has the whole world been condemned for such a long time? Did the active and useful men who labored so much in the name of Jesus in those centuries fall into eternal perdition? Let God not allow us to draw such a frightful conclusion ! And yet, if one must consider the words in the broad meaning in which the Saints take them, this is the *only conclusion* to be drawn from the lack of miraculous faith in the church." Here it is most excellently, at last; for Mr. Evans has proved either that the signs have ended, or else that all the religious people from the days of the apostles have gone to "eternal perdition." But, wait a moment; because "this is the condemnation, that light is come into the world, and men loved darkness rather than light." Is God going to condemn men for refusing the light when they were not offered it? I wonder whether the pagans who have never heard the gospel will go to the wretchedness? Would a merciful God behave in that manner? No, "he that *believeth* not," he says, "is condemned," and not those who had no opportunity for that. All, I should think, are to be judged on their actions, and according to their advantages. I believe that the "active and useful men who labored so much in the name of Jesus in those centuries," have been rewarded by God for every goodness. But the point is, had they obeyed the gospel of Jesus Christ, been "baptized for the remission of sins" by God's appointed servants, and received that Holy Ghost which "calls to mind the things which have passed, and tells things to come," and which is also promised to "all that are afar off" (Acts ii, 39)? And did God through them "confirm his word through the signs which were to follow? If one cannot answer affirmatively, then it is not likely that they received the gospel, which would not come to them "in word only, but in *great assurance* and in the Holy Ghost." The signs together with the fruits of the Spirit, were the marks on Christ's disciples in the beginning; and how can they be known after that time, except by the same marks? Is it by being "without the Spirit," and possessing much human knowledge, that they are to be recognized? Is it because they "forbid speaking with tongues," or "despise prophecy," or else "evangelize differently from the evangelism" of Paul, that one may recognize them? Let it be indicated to me, from the scriptures, that the same marks ought not to be on the believers in this age as in that age. God did not intend to confirm the word of the Catholics, neither those who separated from them, with the "signs," but only his own word; and consequently it is not surprising at all that the signs were not in this country when it was covered by Catholicism, and it is still not surprising, when one sees only branches stemming from Catholicism filling our land. The "mystery of iniquity" which Paul saw beginning to work in his time (2 Thes. ii), is certain to be in full operation in our days, and to have caused a *"falling away"* centuries ago; but such "Wicked" will not be disposed of, until the Lord shall consume him "with the spirit of his mouth, and shall destroy with the brightness of his coming." Everyone who at that time does not *know* God, and has not obeyed the gospel of Jesus Christ, which was restored by an angel from heaven, will be destroyed "with flaming fire." Religions known by the names of men will not do at that time, but a gospel bringing a *knowledge* of God, like the gospel professed by the Latter-day Saints, or the one professed by the apostles. God will provide justice for those who have died without hearing the "eternal gospel," and he will prepare judgment for those who do hear it, and do not believe it. The gifted preachers in recent years were as much servants of God as some men would be servants to the Queen, who thought themselves to be policemen, and doing a great deal of good, when they had never been sent by her. As much authority from God is needed to administer his laws, as is needed from Victoria in order to administer her laws. God does not "call unto him," except through his servants, and they cannot call for him, without receiving a *revelation* of his will. "The active and useful men who labored so much in the name of Jesus in the centuries" past, were servants without *revelation,* and servants also, of course, without authority to administer. Such a one exactly is Mr. Evans, by his own admission; for he can claim no authority except one deriving from Catholicism. If he can, let him prove it. Now, it will be seen that those who died are not lost for not believing what they never heard; and that there is no reason to prove that the "signs" will not follow those who *believe* the same gospel as before.

Further, in order to finish, I shall mix the remains I see of Mr. Evans's reasons in one heap, and I shall shatter them all together. He says on page 17, that "it is not through working miracles that one is reborn:" no, of course, but by being "born of water and of the Spirit." Again, on page 9, he says, "The apostles appealed to the scriptures of the Old Testament for confirmation of the doctrines they preached." So do the Saints appeal to the New Testament, and not to the interpretations and traditions of this dark enlightened age; but who will come out to the field to prove them, face to face? Mr. Evans also says something like this:—"Since miracles are wonders, their daily occurrence would cancel the effect they were intended to have." Well, since none has happened for many thousands of days, perhaps some could be fulfilled at present without cancelling the effect. And since our reverend friend shouts on page 15, "Let the deaf be shown whose ears have been opened through the power of the Saints? Who of them has loosened the tongue-strings of the mute, causing him to speak the praises of God?"—we answer that Mr. Evans can see a person who came to hear and speak—yes, speak the praises of God, after being baptized by the Saints, and that recently, and also in Wales. If anyone wants proof, let him go to Newport, and ask for a man, namely Robert Brinkworth, in the house of Mr. Nash, basket-maker, in Market Street; and let him read what the editor of the newspaper there, the *Merlin,* published in one of the issues for September, 1848. Everyone there admits that he was deaf and dumb, and that he speaks and hears now; but who will say that that was the "finger of God," except those who believe his word. (See further in the PROPHET for November, 1848.) Again, says Mr. Evans, "And if some of them, like Irving, think that they have the gift of the Spirit to speak with tongues that they never learned, let them show what language it is, and what men on earth speak it." Let him come to the church to see, because it is in the church that the commandment is to practice the spiritual gifts; but let him not come there "unbelieving," or "uneducated," otherwise he will say that they are becoming mad, when they utter some language spoken by men. If our friend had a good sign, I believe he would leave the Church immediately, even though he says that no signs exist. Nearly all the religious people of our country are seeking a sign, but no sign will be given them by God; but perhaps the false prophet will have pity on them when he comes, and will draw fire from heaven in their presence, to satisfy them and convince them all of the effectiveness of his religion. (Rev. xiii, 13.) "Wait a little while in faith," for the beast will come upon us before the coming of Jesus Christ.

Now, having been so long, I shall close by saying, If anyone wishes to know that the church of Jesus Christ is on the earth now, and that God has set in it, "first apostles, secondarily prophets, thirdly teachers, after that miracles, then gifts of healings, helps, governments, diversities of tongues," &c. (I Cor. xii, 28)—if anyone wishes to know that, I say, let him do the will of God, "and he shall KNOW of the doctrine."

WHY do you not believe our testimony?
Why do you not prove everything there is?
Why do you not wish to have light,
While it is now as light as day?
Why would you not like to have certainty,
Instead of weak hope and belief?
Why do you not grasp the substance,
Instead of the worthless, fleeing shadow?

Why would you not like to have the gifts—
A gift for all as God sees fit?
Why would you not now believe in miracles,
While He who worked them is alive?
Why would you not like a gift to heal,
And tell of things to come,
And speak in a dialect,
While that which is "in part" persists?

Why do you believe the "form of godliness,"
While wholly denying its "power?"
Why do you always teach,
While you cannot know anything?
Why do you not give full obedience
To the words of the King of heaven,
That you may have real knowledge,
Through revelation, from Him?

Carmarthen. J. DAVIS.

TRUTH VERSUS LIE.

MR. ED.,—I would be pleased if you were to see fit to put these few lines in your useful publication.

On Sunday, the 27th of last August, I had the privilege of hearing two of the preachers of the Saints preach, in the parish of Llansawel, in a place by the name of Pools of the Bristles, at ten o'clock. At two, they and I went to a chapel of the

Independents, called Esgerdawe, where a local minister was present, and one of the scholars of the Ffrwdyfal Academy, the son of a carder of Felingwm, who was preaching in place of the minister. He preached about wisdom, from Proverbs viii, 18; and he spoke of the excellence of the apostolic religion, and the blessedness of those who had it; but he did not show the way to come into possession of it. Before he finished, he addressed the congregation in the following manner:—"My dear listeners, beware of false prophets, those who have come into this chapel this afternoon. They pretend to promise great things to you, but they are nothing more than the worst deceivers; I am quite well acquainted with them." Then, in a frenzy, he gave forth a bit of singing, and he forgot his prayer at the end of the meeting. This caused me to sing as follows:—

Whoever is relentless
In keeping his only soul,
Never let him be so foolish
    As to refuse the laws of God,
By following false prophets—
The ravenous, cruel wolves,
Who are constantly througout the world
    In the clothing of the dear sheep.

CHORUS.

You, the one who is sleeping
In darkness, see the light;
It is now shining
    Brightly in our land.
An angel came from a heavenly country,
With the great eternal gospel,
With its pure spiritual gifts:
    This is quite true.

When in their synagogues
They preach traditions
Established ages ago
    Instead of the precious gospel;
They lead their listeners
To a difficult and twisted path;
From the pure rule of scripture,
    That is clear, they bring them.
        You, the one who is sleeping, &c.

They proclaim the servants of Jesus
As deceivers—false prophets,
And old, pitch-black "Satanists,"
    Coming from utter darkness,
In an attempt to say that gifts
Can be had in such an enlightened age
Of human traditions,
    Now, available as always.
        You, the one who is sleeping, &c.

The children of the sects deny
The divinity of the scriptures,
By alleging that there are no gifts
    To be had now for man;

That there is no need for the Spirit,
Nor his wonderful gifts
That the carnal way of life
    Is far better than any other.
        You, the one who is sleeping, &c.

We now see men
In flesh turning into fiends,
To deny the promises
    Of the Father, the heavenly Lord:
And his gracious son, Jesus,
Who gave promises to us,
And their vows they shall not break
    While there is land and sea.
        You, the one who is sleeping, &c.

The churches are destitute,
Those Jesus did not ordain,
With the dear gifts of the Spirit;
    And thus they go forward,
In fierce anger and strife,
And odious, ugly envy:
They shall lament in their need
    As they meet the fiery deluge.
        You, the one who is sleeping, &c.

Marlais Valley. IOLYN MAI.

RAILWAY FROM COUNCIL BLUFFS TO SALT LAKE CITY !

THE great and iron-like endeavor that is referred to below, is important news for the Saints. Not only will it go past their settlement, but it will greatly facilitate the gathering, by diminishing the costs and shortening the time of the journey. It will also open up an abundant market for the goods, sales, and surplus produce the Saints have in that lush valley, and it will furnish thousands of laborers and craftsmen with ample work. And if it is completed, it will deserve the name, and we hope it will fill the character, of that *"main path"* that the Lord promised to raise for the deliverers of his people. In the space of two or three days, one would be able to reach Salt Lake from Council Bluffs, which journey now takes nearly as many months.

"The railway, according to the plan of Mr. Whitney, is getting more likely to be completed, and every bit of information concerning it is interesting. When a railway to California was first mentioned, the concept was mocked, and the same fate was proclaimed for it as for nearly every other new venture by those who are deprived of understanding to comprehend the possibility of such things. Doubtless there are yet many men who fail to comprehend the possibility of constructing, or the usefulness of having such a railway; but they belong to that class of people who do not believe the possibility of steamships crossing the Atlantic Ocean in ten days, and that fiery vehicles will rush along at 50 or 60 miles per hour. The following is Mr. Whitney's own description of the country where he intends to make his railway:—

"It will start from Council Bluffs, and it will follow exactly the banks of the Platte river; then through South Pass to Green River; then to the south through Muddy Creek to Bear River; from there past Salt Lake to the Cache river, and then north to the southern branch of the Columbia river, and then down with the river to the sea. The length of this railway is about 2,200 miles.

"Description of the county.—From Council Bluffs along the Platte river, the country is mostly flat, and the earth is hard, with practically no great obstacles, such as hills, large rivers, &c.; from the Platte river to the Green river, the country is rather flat, and the earth is mixed with sand; from there to the Bear river, the country is rather mountainous, with ravines here and there 100 feet in width. These run in a such a varied pattern, that they are as advantageous to the railway, as if they were straight. It is likely that it will be necessary to cross the Muddy river about twenty times before reaching the Bear river; but its width is less, and hardly ever over a hundred feet. [Then he gives details about the country from Salt Lake beyond, to the Columbia river.] Snow is sometimes found in this country by the end of November, and it continues at times until the beginning of March. The distance from South Pass to Salt Lake is 250 miles. The whole proposal is now under the attention of a committee, appointed by the U. S. A., which is expected to decide in favor of building the railway." OMEGA.

THE SAINTS' FAREWELL.

Farewell! to everyone now;
We shall sail the great ocean,
In complete longing for God's Zion;
For it is better to go to the land
Given us by our Father;
We have lived captive far too long.
Our freedom has come, after long captivity,
We have been called out of Babel;
At the call, our intention is to go—
To go in spite of the cruel enemy:
Our God, through his great grace,
Will take us safely to his dear Zion.

Farewell! British land,
Our home for a long time,
There is a better home before us now;
Hardship, agony, and violence,
Are perpetually here,
But there is paradise beyond the great sea.
Who is willing to come to Zion?
It is a place of complete deliverance
From the plagues and troubles
Which come to worry mankind;
It is a safe place to live
When storms cover the earth.

Let us also bid farewell
To the Saints for a short while,
Until we see them all at home:
Our farewell is long
To them that deny the truth,
For they are not of the family of Heaven.
Let us go singing across the sea,
Without one fear in our hearts;
God by his kindness shall watch the vessel
As it rides the wave;
And may the Saints throughout this island,
Be also in His care. J. D.

SLAVE TRADE OF THE SECTARIANS !

THE Christian world is full of proofs of the wicked trade that sectarians make of the souls of men, so that we need add nothing. And also they deny the spirit of prophecy among their contemporaries, yet they fulfill one prophecy completely, namely the one in which Peter says—"And through covetousness shall they with feigned words make merchandise of you." But the following shows their covetousness in merchandising the bodies of men, besides their souls, so that on the price of the blood of their black brothers they will be assisted in making the eternal ropes on their souls also tighter and stronger. The *News of the World,* or the *Utica Christian Contributor,* says that the Methodists own 250,000, the Baptists 226,000, and the Presbyterians own 30,000. Add 45,000 from among the variety of other sects, and it is found that the sectarians in the United States claim their right to the bodies of 600,000 of their fellowmen! This is a bloody trade! And yet they all profess to be churches of the gracious God who created everyone free, and yet there is insufficient will or power in their midst to scour from their churches something that is considered by the countries of the world as bad as piracy; but the truth is that the church of Jesus Christ, namely the Latter-day Saints, are completely innocent of making merchandise of the souls and the bodies of black or white men. It is hoped that the bloody sectarians will cleanse their churches of the blood of men, and that they will set their enslaved brothers free by the hundreds, before they again shout that the Saints are being sold as slaves across the ocean. Merchandising friends! facts like the above, and many that could be added, prove that "ye are the men."

LETTER TO THE EDITOR.

MR. ED.,—I beg your kindness to reason and testify with respect to the truth that I came to know after searching for a long time. I was with the Baptists for thirteen years; and during that time I received the best counsels and teachings they possessed. I was conscientious in that which I was taught; but yet I feared at times that I had too little belief to live and die by; nevertheless, I was determined to adhere to it until death if I could not get anything better. But as soon as the Saints came to these areas our teachers, especially Mr. W. R. Davies, began to persecute them and hate them, saying all manner of evil against them. Mr. Davies said one time in our house that his desire was to do the same with their elders as was done to Joseph Smith, that is to kill them. That, together with many other things prompted me to look into their principles; and after having the honor of associating with the Saints, I saw that they were not the way Mr. Davies and others had described them. I saw also that their doctrine was harmonious with the doctrine in the scriptures; and when I heard their testimony, I decided immediately that it was true. I gave obedience to it and gained a sure knowledge about the truth of their message. I am thankful to God for this great privilege, and for the valuable testimony which my Heavenly Father gave to me through his spirit. And now I testify that the message of the Saints is true, and that God, the knower of hearts, gives witness now as in former times through giving the Spirit to those who receive baptism by the servants of God. I also know that the spiritual gifts are in the Church of Jesus Christ of Latter-day Saints as the scriptures mention them; and I know these things through the Spirit of God bearing witness to my spirit. Oh, that I could express the happiness that continues in my heart for the great honor of having part with the children of God; for I know that they are the children of God in spite of what is said against them. I greatly wish to see my old brethren leave their empty shells and turn to inquire for the true belief of Jesus Christ and to get hold of substance instead of feeding on sound the way they have been doing. I would like to see everyone obey the message of the Latter-day Saints; for I know that there is as much difference between it and the belief of the Baptists as there is between light and darkness, or between sound and substance. Now, I close, hoping that thousands will yet be seen obeying the gospel; that is my prayer and my wish for Christ's sake. Amen.

Dowlais. JOB ROWLAND.

SONG IN PERSECUTION.

TUNE—"Gadlys."

O SING another song, my soul, leave thy lamenting;
A complete deliverance from the land of mourning will come to thee;
Bravely keep thy faith up, and thou shalt have Jesus neath thy burdens.

Some of the songs of Zion, sing in thy weary captivity;
Though thy terrible enemies are against thee, thou hast one to save thee,
Namely the true and complete heir of God; put all thy trust in him.

See the land of thy inheritance, through the difficult and vast distances,
The bright and wide lands, where the end of thy journey shall be,
Where all availing joy comes through, with no barriers to its mansions;

Where thy King reigns, in incomparable majesty,
Where every brother dwells without fear, under his blessed fig tree,
And all in joy with no pain or hurt, through love pure and eternal;

Where all the harps will be, felicitous happiness, in full sail,
And a numberless host of Saints, brave and well in their playing;
All the soldiers of Jesus, strong and weak, will there receive their crowns.

NATHAN DDU FROM HYWEL.

MONMOUTHSHIRE CONFERENCE.

THE above Conference was held in the Greyhound Hall, Nantyglo, on the 5th of last November. The morning meeting was opened by William Phillips, president of the conference, by singing and prayer. It was proposed by brother Phillips, and seconded by brother D. Jones, that Capt. D. Jones preside at the conference, which was unanimously approved. Then the president addressed the congregation briefly on the occasion, while the meeting was in progress, namely about enlarging the boundaries of the kingdom of our Lord, &c.—also a sincere exhortation for unity and cooperation for this purpose. Then it was proposed by the president that brothers D. Jones and Wm. Davies be clerks; then the president called for a representation of the branches, which took place as follows:—

Branches.	*Presidents.*	*Eld.*	*Prst.*	*Tch.*	*Dea.*	*Bap.*	*Total*
Nantyglo	Thomas Giles	6	5	6	2	35	97
Penycae	David Jones	3	3	2	2	33	60
Blackwood	Evan Evans	1	4	0	1	11	36
Tredegar	William Evans	2	2	2	0	4	28
Blaina	Thomas Parry	1	1	2	0	5	27
Abersychan	John Jones	4	6	2	2	27	88
Blaenafon	William Lewis	2	0	0	1	3	13
Victoria	James James	4	3	3	1	21	87
Abercarn	William Parker	1	3	1	1	23	27
Bedwas	Evan Jones	0	1	0	0	5	8
Total		24	28	18	10	167	471

The above presidents gave their testimony unanimously that unity and love were common among the Saints in the branches, together with the likelihood of great success in the gospel from that time on. Then the president brought the cases of the various presidents before the Saints, by asking if there were any accusations against them. Failing to get any, the president proposed to sustain the various presidents through their faith and prayers, beginning with the president of the conference, which was approved unanimously; the same for all the presidents in the same manner. Then it was decided to organize the following branches together with their presidents:—Cwmteleri, Ed. Protheroe; Bedwas, Evan Jones; Rosau, Penycae, William Rees; Brynmawr, Abednego Jones; Garnddiffaith and the Varteg, John Jones. Then the meeting was closed with a prayer by brother Wm. Davies, Rhymni.

At half past two o'clock, the Saints came together, and the meeting was begun with singing and a prayer by brother Wm. Henshaw. After this, the president addressed the Saints, in a lively manner, about government and order of the kingdom of God, and about the fruits of the Holy Ghost, &c. Then four brothers and one sister were confirmed, by elders William Phillips, William Howells, and Wm. Henshaw. After this the president showed in a clear manner, the duties of the Saints at the table of the Lord, &c.; but because of the shortness of time, the ordinance was passed over without partaking of it, and the president went on by calling the following officers:—*Elders* David Watkins, Victoria; Evan Jones, Bedwas; William Jones and Charles Watts, Abersychan; John James, Blackwood; John Rees, Nantyglo; and Griffith Davies, Penycae. *Priests*—Charles Probert, Victoria; William Davies, Abercarn; and Thomas Harries, Nantyglo. *Teachers*—John Davies and David Jones, Victoria; Edward Rees, Bedwas; John Master, Blackwood; John Harries, Penycae; and James Williams, Nantyglo. All of these were approved unanimously. Then it was proposed by the president, that all the Saints in this conference acknowledge, and support by faith and prayers, the presidency in Zion, and also Orson Pratt in Britain, and all his counselors, &c., which was all approved with one voice. After this the president went on, showing the temporal salvation of the Saints, by the collection for the Valley of the Salt Lake, &c. Then the meeting was closed with a prayer by the president, having received particular contentment in the gathering.

At half past six o'clock, the evening meeting was opened by singing and a prayer by brother John Jones, Aberysychan. After an anthem sung by the choir, the president addressed the crowd briefly, allowing time for other officers to do likewise. The first that was called was Wm. Howells (in English), who showed the excellence of the Salt Lake Valley and the land of Canaan, or Palestine, with a sincere wish that he would have the privilege of meeting with all the Saints there. Next, Wm. Evans, Rhymni, brought the first principles of the gospel before the congregation in a clear and forthright manner, together with his wish for them to accept them. William Henshaw after that, in English, set out the excellence and glory of the dispensation of the last days, which was superior to all the ones before it, with his testimony that the angel that John saw (in Rev. xiv, 6), flying in the midst of heaven, had the everlasting gospel, together with his message, "Fear God, and give glory to him, for the hour of his judgment is come;" and he showed also the way that each one could escape this judgment. Then the president arose, and he showed that God was the only worker of miracles; in connection with that he brought forth the case of brother Brinkworth from Newport, who was present. The president called him to come forward and answer for himself. He stood up, and testified boldly that it was through obedience to the gospel that he had received the blessing. "I was," he said, "mute and deaf for years; but when I obeyed the ordinance of baptism for the remission of sins, in the name of Jesus Christ, the God of miracles saw fit to loosen my tongue and open my eyes, so that I can now hear and speak as you can. My testimony is true, and to God be the glory. Amen."

Thanks were given to the man of the house for his kindness, together with others who were responsible for the hall, and also the warmest love to the cheerful crowd of listeners. Then the meeting was closed by a prayer by brother W. Phillips.

WHO WILL GO ?

ALL supporters of dear Jesus,
Who will go?
To show the power of God,
Will will do it?
Namely, that his virtuous arm
Works powerfully today;
Praise God forevermore,
Who will do it?

Today he invites,
Who will go?
By offering a heavenly gift,
Who will go?
No one may preach,
And that to please Jesus,
Without being authorized by him;
Who will do it?

And with this message,
Who will go?
Over the regions of the round earth,
Who will go?
To preach for a witness,
Giving knowledge to all,
That they may be delivered,
Who will do it?

There is a host of mankind,
Who will go?
Who have not come to know God,
Who will go?
God himself is willing
To give his signs,
To all men who obey him,
Who will do it?

There is but a poor existence,
Who will go?
Without much gold to be had,
Who will go?
Their bread and water are sure,
To all of the true worshippers,
As the scriptures say,
Who will do it?

The "reverends" of the world,
Who will go?
Will be against those in wrath,
Who will go?

The wise will mock them,
As their blind forefathers did
To Christ and his apostles;
Who will do it?

NOAH.

SORROW AND BLISS.

THE families of the earth will grieve,
When the Son of Man comes;
And because they do not believe him,
They will experience a tiresome vengeance.

But, listen! blessed are those
Who believe in precious Jesus;
When the others are tormented,
They will be taken on high.

ENLARGEMENT OF OUR MONTHLY PUBLICATION !

IT is intended that our monthly publication for next year will contain 24 pages, twelve-fold, for the same price as before, namely *Two Pence* per Issue; and we depend on the zeal and devotion of our subscribers and our distributors to compensate us in this, through their efforts to spread its circulation; and their previous faithfulness encourages us to believe that our expectations will not be in vain. The remarkable growth and success of this divine work that our publication endeavors to support, requires an enlargement of its size; and the continual growth and appetite of its subscribers, cry aloud and continually for the same thing; and not only that, but the time and circumstances of these wondrous days and their consequences overload our columns to overflow their banks as they pertain to the Saints, all of which loudly prompts the expansion of our publication for the attention of our compatriots. We are pleased to be able to say that the testimonies we have of the good the PROPHET has done, are already more than enough to fill one issue of its columns: and the following is the testimony of one familiar to us when he read the PROPHET:—

A small one is the "Star of the Saints,"—yes, and short,
To cause exceptional privilege;
A large jewel, her size should be
Appropriately seven times as large.

ZION'S TRUMPET !

IT has been decided to publish our periodical under this name from now on, and we hope that changing its name will not pose any difficulty for our subscribers, how much they many have loved the previous name. Changing the name does not change the voice or the flavor; and we are confident that our TRUMPET will trumpet forth better and louder news for ZION and her success, far and near, than the PROPHET has done, and that it was able to do in its day. We consider the name appropriate for the work that it will do, for its chief purpose will be to proclaim the remarkable news and the interesting counsels that proceed from that godly source in Zion, so that all her children scattered throughout Wales can drink from her streams, to quench their thirst through the wilderness of Babylon homeward; and we hope that as the weary traveler thirsts for the water of the cool fountain on the way, that the Saints, and all the subscribers, will every new moon long for the voice of the TRUMPET to sound forth the happenings of Zion in their ears, and its guidance for their footsteps temporally and spiritually. We earnestly beseech every distributor to spread the leaflets that were printed for the purpose of keeping the accounts of the subscribers, and to strive to fill them with the names of the regular subscribers for the year; and we expect the president of each branch to inform us in the next Conference, what number of the ZION'S TRUMPET he can sell: do not forget to do this. The leaflet contains instructions for that purpose. We notify our subscribers that Elder John Davis will be the Editor and Printer of the TRUMPET in our absence: send to him all correspondence and payments, to this house, as you did to us before; and we are confident of having the privilege of greeting our subscribers through it often, although from afar.

THE GLAMORGAN CONFERENCE.

WILL be held in the Cymreigyddion Hall (*White Lion),* on the last Sunday of the year, and the following Monday, when we are confident that we shall see all the presidents punctually and ready to represent their branches; and since this will be the last conference that we shall have with our dear brethren for a time, we would be pleased to see here all of the Saints who can attend, *especially the Emigrants,* since we have many things to tell them which are of importance to them. We also expect the visit of President Spencer at that time, who is visiting the conferences to collect the tithing for the building of the temple to the name of the Lord of hosts in the Salt Lake Valley; and we hope that those who can, will be prepared to do so at that time. We have not received a definite promise that President Orson Pratt will be coming.

TO OUR DISTRIBUTORS.

DEAR FELLOW-WORKERS,—You know by now that this is the last call we can give to you for the debts of the PROPHET, and the other publications you have received, because we intend to emigrate to Zion at the beginning of the year, which testifies for us of our need to have all our debts settled before beginning—besides the fact that the end of every volume is the period that every publisher expects to settle all his accounts. We are confident that all distributors will prepare to do this by the next Conference.

TO OUR SUBSCRIBERS, &c.

OUR subscribers will see the reason why this Issue is two-and-a-half pence; for the title page, the foreword, and the table of contents are given in addition, besides the fact that this number and the previous one are in finer print than the others.

Our correspondents will be answered as soon as possible in the TRUMPET.

CONTENTS.

MERTHYR TYDFIL:

PUBLISHED AND FOR SALE BY D. JONES, AND ALSO FOR SALE BY THE SAINTS IN GENERAL.

PRINTED BY J. DAVIS, CARMARTHEN.

INDEX

INDEX

1846w refers to the 1846 Wrappers.

I

N

O

Q

R

S

W

Y

Z